Marxism and Historical Practice
VOLUME I

Historical Materialism Book Series

The Historical Materialism Book Series is a major publishing initiative of the radical left. The capitalist crisis of the twenty-first century has been met by a resurgence of interest in critical Marxist theory. At the same time, the publishing institutions committed to Marxism have contracted markedly since the high point of the 1970s. The Historical Materialism Book Series is dedicated to addressing this situation by making available important works of Marxist theory. The aim of the series is to publish important theoretical contributions as the basis for vigorous intellectual debate and exchange on the left.

The peer-reviewed series publishes original monographs, translated texts, and reprints of classics across the bounds of academic disciplinary agendas and across the divisions of the left. The series is particularly concerned to encourage the internationalization of Marxist debate and aims to translate significant studies from beyond the English-speaking world.

For a full list of titles in the Historical Materialism Book Series
available in paperback from Haymarket Books, visit:
https://www.haymarketbooks.org/series_collections/1-historical-materialism

Marxism and Historical Practice

*Interpretive Essays on Class
Formation and Class Struggle*

VOLUME I

Bryan D. Palmer

Haymarket Books
Chicago, IL

First published in 2015 by Brill Academic Publishers, The Netherlands
© 2015 Koninklijke Brill NV, Leiden, The Netherlands

Published in paperback in 2017 by
Haymarket Books
P.O. Box 180165
Chicago, IL 60618
773-583-7884
www.haymarketbooks.org

ISBN: 978-1-60846-688-7

Trade distribution:
In the US, Consortium Book Sales, www.cbsd.com
In Canada, Publishers Group Canada, www.pgcbooks.ca
In the UK, Turnaround Publisher Services, www.turnaround-uk.com
In all other countries, Ingram Publisher Services International,
intlsales@perseusbooks.com

Cover design by Jamie Kerry of Belle Étoile Studios and Ragina Johnson.

This book was published with the generous support of Lannan Foundation
and the Wallace Action Fund.

Printed in Canada by union labor.

10 9 8 7 6 5 4 3 2 1

Library of Congress Cataloging-in-Publication data is available.

To the hummingbirds of Sangster Lake:
'From each according to their abilities, to each according to their needs.'

∵

Contents

Acknowledgements

Permission to republish material that first appeared elsewhere is gratefully acknowledged. I am indebted to the scholarly journals *Labour/Le Travail*, formerly known as *Labour/Le Travailleur*, *Histoire Sociale/Social History*, *The Review of Radical Political Economics*, *Osgoode Hall Law Journal*, *International Review of Social History*, *Online Journal of the Canadian Historical Association*, *Left History*, *Historical Materialism*, *American Communist History*; to the left-wing publications *Against the Current* and *Monthly Review*; and to the publishers McGill-Queen's University Press, Oxford University Press, Verso, Academic Press, Merlin Press, Escuela Nacional de Antopolígia e Historia, Jaca Books, and Manchester University Press. In the order in which they appear in the present volume of *Marxism and Historical Practice*, specific permissions to reprint are as follows:

Palmer, Bryan D. 1978, 'Discordant Music: Charivaris and Whitecapping in Nineteenth-Century North America', *Labour/Le Travailleur*, 3, 5–68.

——— 2008, 'Popular Radicalism and the Theatrics of Rebellion: The Hybrid Discourse of Dissent in Upper Canada', in *Transatlantic Subjects: Ideas, Institutions, and Social Experiences in Post-Revolutionary British North America*, edited by Nancy Christie, Kingston and Montreal: McGill-Queen's University Press, 403–39.

——— 1979, 'In Street and Field and Hall: The Culture of Hamilton Workingmen, 1860–1914', adapted from *A Culture in Conflict: Skilled Workers and Industrial Capitalism in Hamilton, 1860–1914*, Kingston and Montreal: McGill-Queen's University Press, 35–70.

——— 1981, 'The Bonds of Unity: The Knights of Labor in Ontario, 1880–1900', *Histoire Sociale/Social History*, 28, 369–412, co-authored by Gregory S. Kealey.

——— 1975, 'Class, Conception, and Conflict: The Thrust for Efficiency, Managerial Views of Labor, and Working-Class Rebellion, 1903–1922', *The Review of Radical Political Economics*, 7, 31–49.

——— 2008, 'Wildcat Workers in the 1960s: The Unruly Face of Class Struggle', in *Labouring Canada: Class, Race, and Gender in Canadian Working-Class History*, edited by Bryan D. Palmer and Joan Sangster, Toronto: Oxford University Press, 373–94.

——— 1988, 'Reformism and the Fight Against the Right: British Columbia's *Solidarity*', in *Reshaping the US Left: Popular Struggles in the 1980s*, edited by Mike Davis and Michael Sprinker, London: Verso, 1988, 229–54.

——— 1984, 'Social Formation and Class Formation in Nineteenth-Century North America', in *Proletarianization and Family History*, edited by David Levine, New York: Academic Press, 229–308.

———— 2012, '"Cracking the Stone": The Long History of Capitalist Crisis and Toronto's Dispossessed', *Labour/Le Travail*, 69, 9–62, co-authored by Gaetan Heroux.

———— 2003, 'What's Law Got To Do With It? Historical Considerations on Class Struggle, Boundaries of Constraint, and Capitalist Authority', *Osgoode Hall Law Journal*, 41, 466–90.

Introduction

I am not sure what makes some people historians. But I have concluded that there are those predisposed to think historically and inclined to take an interest in the past. It is, often, a matter of environment and the stimulations of family and surroundings. Readings are encouraged and things old are layered in meanings, invested with intrinsic value rather than calculated in terms of market considerations.[1]

With others this attraction to history can seem almost *sui generis*. Brought up in a house without books, by parents whose educations were either truncated by dropping out of high school or being streamed into practical, gendered employment and living in what could have been considered a suburban retreat from any traditions that connected the present and its antecedents, my privileging of the historical was not so much learned as it was resourced, held as a kind of antidote against what I came instinctually to regard as a barren, philistine upbringing. So I suppose I was *always* a historian, at least in terms of basic inclinations.

But what *kind* of historian one becomes is what really matters. This has less to do with instincts and much more to do with industry. Yet there is also more than a bit of the accidental in this production of orientation. This labour of becoming is inevitably about time, place and happenings of various kinds, of influences in part serendipitous. The context in which sensibilities are forged, paths started down and tendencies taken up is always, in some ways, fortuitous. And then possibilities harden into outcomes.[2] The consequences of consequences lead us to where we end up, a process in which we have made our personal histories, but never exactly and only as we might have chosen – if choice was ever a simple, clear-cut option. It is all reminiscent of a passage from William Morris's *A Dream of John Ball* (1888):

> [M]en fight and lose the battle, and the thing that they fought for comes about in spite of their defeat, and when it comes turns out not to be what they meant, and other men have to fight for what they meant under another name.[3]

---

1 Stedman Jones 2001.
2 See the exchange on 'deciding to be a historian' between Michael Merrill and E.P. Thompson in Abelove et al., 1983, p. 13.
3 Quoted in E.P. Thompson 1976a, p. 722.

What is crucial in this Morris quote is not just the chance outcome that results from a series of decisions and actions, but the importance of conflict, of a clash of thought, a struggle of positions.

Or so it has been with me. My childhood interest in history came of a certain age in the 1960s, although I was still too young to consider becoming a historian. Then, after largely missing the turmoil of 1968 – I was barely 17 at the time and lived in a medium-sized Canadian city not galvanised by youthful rebellion – I was drawn to the radicalism of the New Left, and from there into a variety of causes and a course of reading. My apprenticeship in Marxist history commenced in the late 1960s and intensified in the 1970s, originating in non-academic encounters with theories and texts as well as mobilisations and movements. All of this unfolded as I dropped out of university in Canada after only one year, and lived for a time in the heady atmosphere of New York City. There I tested the waters of dissidence, as what had once been the headline-catching Students for a Democratic Society imploded. Crashing lecture halls at the New School (where I was not officially enrolled and was eventually asked politely to leave by Robert L. Heilbroner, whose chapter on Marx in *The Worldly Philosophers* from 1953 I considered scandalous), immersed in late-night study and affinity groups, arguing with all manner of leftists in a radical educational experiment known as Alternate U (where Murray Bookchin and Revolutionary Youth Movement II leaders debated the nature and meaning of the Russian Revolution and American slavery), struggling unsuccessfully to read Hegel and spending a part of every day either working in or frequenting bookstores, was more of an education than I would later receive in any formal university setting. There were leaflets to prepare, protests to organise and demonstrations to attend. But there was always time to pore over books. I first read historians such as Moshe Lewin, W.E.B. Du Bois, E.P. Thompson, C.L.R. James and Eugene Genovese, not to mention Marx, Engels, Lenin, Mao, Stalin, Gramsci, Luxemburg and Trotsky, as well as writers like Kate Millett, Shulamith Firestone and Malcolm X, in the intellectually and politically intoxicating atmosphere of the aftermath of May '68. Inebriated discussions often broke out in dug-out cellar bars of the East Village, now almost all gone, such as the Frog Pond; to this day I remember fiercely contested clashes in which anarchism, Maoism and Trotskyism were argued through, often with allusions to historical events. My 'classrooms' had no formally credentialed professors and involved no grades; positions seldom involved 'sucking up' to any credentialed authority.

When, after an exhilarating year of this, I decided to return to my hometown of London, Ontario, and complete the undergraduate degree I had abandoned with my departure for New York, sitting in staid lectures, prodding through the syllabus and writing term papers seemed rather anti-climactic. Fast-tracking myself through it all, I paused to participate in a summer student works project on the labour history of London, then struck out for the State University of New York at Binghamton, enrolling in a master's and then a PhD program. I was soon part of a loose network of graduate students affiliated with the history department or the Braudel Center, amongst whom Art Hirsch, Peter Friedlander and Phil McMichael were my best friends. We were all Marxists then![4]

That Marxism, however, was worn in scholarly settings with a genuine humility. I know that I was no wallflower in graduate seminars, and the baptism of fire that I had received in movement discussions where forceful argument was valued rather than questioned made me partial to polemic, always striving for strong stands. But I was nonetheless reluctant to decisively declare myself a Marxist. I felt I had a lot to learn and needed to earn the right to proclaim myself a Marxist historian. It was not until sometime in the early 1980s that I began to associate myself publicly in published work with Marxism. At that point, after roughly 15 years of growing familiarity with Marxism, I was apparently willing to acknowledge that my apprenticeship had come to its close and could actually name myself politically.

Far easier was considering oneself a working-class or labour historian. The vocation of studying the history of class formation and detailing the nature of class struggle was, in fact, embedded in the guild that I had joined by virtue of embarking on graduate studies. And with the large numbers of nascent working-class historians who had flocked to seminars run by professors like David Montgomery, Herbert G. Gutman and my supervisor Melvyn Dubofsky, it was easy to situate yourself in the mid-1970s within a cohort for whom study of workers defined a significant slice of the entirety of the past, that illusory totality we then aspired to explore and explicate. As social historians of labour, those of us doing working-class history considered ourselves to be moving from a privileged part of social history into the history of society.[5]

The essays that appear in these two volumes are a reflection of the parallel processes of becoming a Marxist *and* becoming a working-class historian. In my case, these makings were reciprocal endeavours. They were not bifurcated into the theoretical and the empirical but were always linked, as the process of conceptualisation wrestled with the discoveries of the archives or the exploration of bodies of evidence that could be gleaned from newspapers, government reports or statistical series. If my area of inquiry focussed on the tensions gen-

---

4 For a brief autobiographical statement, see B. Palmer 2005.
5 Hobsbawm 1971a.

erated around capitalist class formation, this is not to say that I necessarily considered labour to be a subject studied always in the same way and regarded from the same vantage point. To be sure, my approach was, I think, always that of the historical materialist, but how and in what ways historical materialism addressed class formation and class struggle necessarily exhibited subtle shifts over time. Again, this is precisely because the theoretical informed the empir- ical – not only in terms of what was researched and why, but how evidence was examined, what questions were asked of it and why it was interpreted in specific ways. Conceptual priorities, while exhibiting basic continuities, also experienced change according to the intellectual and political climate of the moment. *Marxism and Historical Practice*, then, is about doing history in ways informed by Marxism. This project has always been about making histories in 'circumstances directly encountered, given and transmitted from the past'.[6] All of the writing republished here was very much influenced by the particular context in which each piece was written. Discrete circumstances of political economy, social struggle, the politics of power and its exercise and the nature and possibilities of dissent all had their impact.

So too did the shifting contours of historiography, especially the changing accent placed on aspects of class formation in writing on the past. It is for this reason that these volumes are arranged thematically, bringing together articles, contributions to edited collections, components of particular books that I now offer as free-standing chapters and review essays – all of which are aligned in specific sections that might bring together writing concentrated within a few years or spread over as much as three decades of time. The themes explored in particular sections of these volumes, as well as the volumes themselves, convey both common concerns and divergences in perspective and orientation. In specific short introductions to the designated parts of each volume, all of which contain from two to four essays, I locate briefly the impetus behind particular writings.

If it is imperative to recognise the extent to which all of the writing in these two volumes emerged at the interface of Marxism or historical materialism as a particular animating theoretical framework and the place of class within both history and historiography, event and analysis, it should also be noted that the two volumes each privilege a particular side of this duality. Volume I draws together interpretive essays on class formation and class struggle; the com- ponents of various sections address particularities of working-class experience in Canada and United States in the nineteenth and twentieth centuries. That

---

6   Marx 1968, p. 97.

volume accents the historical practice of Marxism. Volume II, in contrast, is composed of essays that are meant to highlight Marxism's insights as they can be brought to bear on how history is written, presented visually and embodied in the lives and writings of specific movements and individuals. While the focus is once more on Canada and the United States, the reach of particular interventions and appreciations in Volume II extends also to Europe and the United Kingdom.

The developing world is, admittedly, an understated presence in these volumes. Such original research as I have done has been conducted overwhelmingly in English-language sources. This is, I acknowledge freely and with a large sense of limitation, inhibiting. That said, I have been the beneficiary of translations of theoretical work and rich historical studies, and in both *Descent into Discourse: The Reification of Language and the Writing of Social History* (1990) and *Cultures of Darkness: Night Travels in the Histories of Transgression* (2000), my concerns in theory and in historical interpretation have been anything but narrow. Both works, as well as other writings on historiography such as *E.P. Thompson: Objections and Oppositions* (1994), have appeared in Korean, Greek, Portuguese and Spanish editions, with articles translated into Chinese, Italian and other languages. Nothing has pleased me more than exchanges across borders, languages and cultures with historical materialists engaged in the critical scrutiny of the past and active involvement in the present, all of us drawn to the different ways in which analysis and activity animated by Marxism can bridge divides and build new ways of seeing human possibility realised.

A proper accounting of the debts incurred over the course of more than three decades of historical writing is not possible. The colleagues, friends, students and comrades who have shared with me a sensibility of the politics of our times, from the late 1960s to the present, are too numerous to mention, and the risk of leaving unacknowledged a particular individual of importance too great, for me to attempt anything approximating adequate acknowledgements. I have also benefitted enormously from the institutional support of the universities with which I have been affiliated in Canada – Queen's, McGill, Simon Fraser and Trent – all of which provided hospitable climates for writing and reflection. The journal *Labour/Le Travail*, in which the lead article in the first issue of 1976 was one of my earlier publications, has been a mainstay of my intellectual life for the better part of four decades, 30 years of which I have spent as either book review editor or editor, often working closely with Gregory S. Kealey, whose initiative was responsible for bringing *LLT* into being. Since 2000 I have the Canada Research Chairs program to thank for supporting my research, which has been located within the Canadian Studies Department at Trent University. Two women in my life, my daughter Beth and my partner Joan, each in their different ways, are the stars that light my dark nights and the suns that bring new meanings and hopes every morning.

This collection of essays owes a great deal to two of the mainstays of the *Historical Materialism* project, Peter Thomas and Sebastian Budgen. The latter, with his indefatigable attentiveness to email lists, latched on to a seemingly inconsequential response to an obscure posting seeking suggestions of what might be read on class formation in the United States of the nineteenth century. Forwarding me an email in which it was suggested that my 1983 essay 'Social Formation and Class Formation in North America, 1800–1900' remained a good guide to a particular way of approaching the problem, Sebastian wrote, economically, 'Perhaps time for a collection of your essays'. What resulted was anything but economical, and I must thank Sean Carleton and Julia Smith, two doctoral candidates at Trent University's Frost Centre for Canadian Studies and Indigenous Studies, for their laborious efforts in reformatting a disparate collection of writings for re-publication. I benefitted greatly from the help and diligent editorial advice of an extremely able trio of Historical Materialism Book Series mainstays: David Broder, Danny Hayward and Sarah Grey. The essays that follow were improved by their interventions, although I alone bear responsibility for their contents. I am indebted to Martin Schoots-McAlpine for preparing the index.

These volumes of essays constitute something of an imperfect and faint representation of how I have tried to depict the legacies of working-class struggle and the rich reservoir of Marxist understandings that I consider timeless in its relevance. T.S. Eliot's 'The Hollow Men' (1925) seems an appropriate note leading in to what follows:

> Between the idea
>   And the reality
>   Between the motion
>   And the act
>   Falls the shadow.[7]

As a shadow crossing the chasm separating theory and practice, mobilisation and historical activity, the essays collected here struggle, inevitably somewhat incompletely, to link Marxism and historical practice, a conception of the past with an appreciation of the necessity of changing our present and realising a better future. They can, at this point, fall where they may.

---

7 Eliot 1971, p. 58.

PART 1

Class Struggle before the Consolidation of Class

∴

Introduction to Part 1

At first glance the essays in this section seem remarkably different. One is a broad treatment of rowdy behaviours over the course of a century, examined from a vast geographic expanse that now constitutes Canada and the United States. Another examines the nature of radicalism in the single decade of the 1830s, focussing on a specific region in Upper Canada that broadly fits with today's Ontario. To further complicate matters, these specific writings were published thirty years apart.

The first, a study of rituals of shaming known as charivari or rough music and whitecapping, explores an aspect of popular culture that, at the time of publication in 1978, was little known and written about in Canada. To be sure, Natalie Zemon Davis, E.P. Thompson, and Alfred Young had been research-ing the ways in which rough music figured in the histories of early modern France, eighteenth-century England, and revolutionary America.[1] However, next to nothing had been written in scholarly circles on the topic in Canada before I delivered a paper on the subject to a conference audience at the Cana-dian Historical Association and published the piece in what was then a newly-established annual review, *Labour/Le Travailleur*. I opted for a broad overview, rather than the kinds of detailed microhistories that have subsequently been published on rough music.[2] Canvassing newspapers, folklore accounts, legal records, gazettes and whatever else came to hand in an era pre-dating Google searches, I amassed sufficient information to generalise about the horn blow-ing, pot banging, hooting and jeering assemblies of discordant men, women, and youths who gathered, at various venues, to show their displeasure to those who violated behavioural norms dictated by collective sensibilities about right and wrong, rather than individual understandings of what it was prudent to do.

'Discordant Music' quickly became something of a touchstone of how working-class history in Canada, from around the late 1970s, was changing. For in its implicit suggestion that the history of the working class encompassed much more than trade union organising and the politics of respectable, parlia-mentary reform, this article broke out of certain constraints that had limited understandings of class to the respectable faces of a particular kind of institu-tional labour history. There were those for whom my discussion of rough music

---

1   See, for instance, Davis 1975, pp. 97–123; Thompson 1972b; and Young 1984.
2   Greenhill 2010. Greer 1990 discusses the shift to political charivaris in Lower Canada in the 1830s.

and whitecapping was representative of what was wrong with the developing field; they were adamant that the piece should never have been published in a journal of labour studies. To be sure, there was much that was ugly and lacking in progressive sensibilities in the 'direct action' tradition of rough justice that I explored. Charivari parties and whitecappers were not always guided by a sense of the collective that we would want to embrace or reproduce today.

Yet I caught glimpses of plebeian and popular refusals to be unreflectively structured into the hegemonic grip of acquisitive individualism. These rituals, especially the charivari, with its longer and more complex history, could also be read as scores in which the nature of class complexities played out over time. There is no doubt, for instance, that as the nineteenth century wore on, rough music sounded out the changing configuration of class forces, its notes indicative of widening social cleavages. The utilisation of charivaris and whitecapping to shame scabs was a concrete case of cultural forms associated with the regulation of private life, transposed onto the public arena, and drawn upon to sustain class struggles. For all the messiness and complicated meanings that were involved in understanding charivaris and whitecappings, their history seemed to me to be a necessary part of appreciating how classes were made and remade in the cauldron of industrial-capitalist transformation. This reconfigured not only the productive process and its relations, but also the cultural aspects of everyday life through which working men and women, at least in part, expressed themselves. These rituals of shaming were thus articulations, however muffled and melodramatic, of what Herbert Gutman, drawing on anthropologists such as Sidney Mintz, insisted was a process of culture being used as a resource within the arena of society where relations of power were constantly exercised. Cultural forms like charivaris and whitecapping illuminated, through time, how power was routinely confirmed and denied, undermined and reinforced, changed or preserved. Just how this was done, and which parts of culture might be drawn upon in what ways and by whom, was therefore a part of how we might, in particular contexts, appreciate the nature of class forces and gain insights into the shifting character of the class struggle.[3]

How can this study of charivaris and whitecapping in nineteenth-century North America possibly relate to a discussion of popular radicalism and the theatrical performativity of rebellion in Upper Canada's 1830s? The second essay in this section addresses the discourse of oppositional politics at the moment that dissent threatened to erupt in armed struggle. Written at the height of the influence of discourse analysis and the postmodern linguistic turn that

---

3   Gutman 1976b, pp. 16–17.

captivated so many social historians in the 1980s and 1990s, this exploration of Upper Canadian representation and rhetoric was undertaken to establish that it was indeed possible to study language and image in ways congruent with historical materialism, something that I had suggested in *Descent into Discourse: The Reification of Language and the Writing of Social History* (1990). It was also important to intervene in the historiographic impasse characteristic of the study of the rebellions in Upper and Lower Canada in the 1830s. For this period, especially in seemingly Loyalist Upper Canada, had been in the grip of an unimaginative and empiricist historiography for some time.[4] To be sure, the rebellion was easily put down, and this allowed conventional wisdom's writing to represent it as little more than a tragicomedy of error, an ill-fated uprising destined to fail. Although some accounts grudgingly acknowledge that the politics of 1830s dissent helped pave the road to responsible, representative forms of government, the trajectory of much of the (conservative) literature silences voices of complaint which, if they are heard at all, are routinely caricatured. Yet this opposition grew increasingly outraged and widespread over the course of the 1830s, and cries of resistance railed against the inequalities and undemocratic nature of governing, colonial power. I thus challenge the conventional, conservative historiography, suggesting that the subterranean currents of popular radicalism ran deeper and with more conviction than has been assumed, and that a Tory elite necessarily mobilised terror to suppress the challenge of political critique and revolt. But I also strive to explain why it was that the rebellion failed, and that class grievances foundered on the shoals of class formations that were incompletely developed. Compromised by the powerful reach of patriarchy and paternalism into the social relations of subordination, a process that inhibited the capacity of the popular classes to resist, the consciousness and organisation of class forces in Upper Canada in the 1830s were insufficiently developed to effectively displace the social order of oligarchy and privilege.

In both a study of rough music and an analysis of the representation of radicalism in the 1830s, what I was grappling with, over thirty years of research, was how class struggle unfolded. In the phrasing of E.P. Thompson, this happened within a particular field-of-force, through the pull of contradictory impulses that often revealed social tensions of a class nature in an era before class had properly crystallised. Class struggles, so integral to class formations that were emerging on a foundation of productive relations, however inadequately they

---

4 Suggestions of alternative readings of this era can be gleaned of late in Bonthius 2003; and Schrauwers 2010 and Schrauwers 2011.

defined class, bore the imprint of a confusing swirl of developments: patrician and plebeian social strata both interacted with one another and grew increasingly apart; law, in an epoch attempting to consolidate a hegemonic acquisitive individualism, struggled to displace older moral economies and a face-to-face regime of collective, ethical regulation; class distinctions blurred as ideologies and practices of patriarchy and paternalism struggled to retain their grip on a social fabric fraying at the edges, tearing into the substance of changing relations of power and subordination. In the shifting meanings of customary practices like the charivari, which can be discerned in the discoveries of how the ritual's reception and meanings changed over the course of a century, the nature of class consolidations are revealed. Patrician-plebeian bonds loosen and fade into the antiquated relations of a world that is increasingly perceived as lost. Appreciations of how, at a moment of intensified struggle, radical criticism of oligarchy's ossified forms of rule faltered on an inability to break out of age-old constraints expose the precariousness of rebellious initiative in which class is invariably caught in the contradictions of its own incomplete development. The two essays that follow thus represent forays into a history of class struggle that predated the formal arrival of later nineteenth-century class formations – into a history that Thompson designated, in his eighteenth-century studies, with the ambiguity of a question mark, 'class struggle without class?'[5]

---

5   Thompson 1976b.

CHAPTER 1

Discordant Music: Charivaris and Whitecapping in Nineteenth-Century North America*

That monster custom, who all sense doth eat,
Of habits devil, is angel yet in this,
That to the use of actions fair and good
He likewise gives a frock or livery,
That aptly is put on.
> *Hamlet*, III, 4.

•••

Friend, hast thou hear'd a Strong
   North Eastern roar,
Or the harsh discord of Charivari,
   or Cat's wild scream ere them to
   love agree?
> *Quebec Gazette*, 12 January 1786

••
•

1

On a Saturday night in late March 1890, at approximately ten o'clock, William Misner, alias William Black, popularly known among the lumbermen with whom he worked as 'Yankee Bill', was killed near Holmesdale, Ontario. Misner was originally from Toledo, Ohio, and was survived by his wife and family, still living in the United States. He was known to the lumbering community, nestled along Lake Huron on the St. Clair branch of the Michigan Central Railroad, as a charitable man, although one prone to excessive drink. Perhaps he

---

* 'Discordant Music: Charivaris and Whitecapping in Nineteenth-Century North America', *Labour/Le Travailleur*, 3 (1978), 5–68.

had been too charitable. When a fellow worker, named McFadden, had fallen on bad times, Misner had aided the family. As McFadden went on the proverbial tramp, searching for the work that was seldom to be found, Misner and Mrs. McFadden, a woman of 'poor reputation', struck up an 'undue intimacy'. For two years McFadden lived apart from his wife, but when he reappeared in the cold, winter months of 1890 he apparently sought a return to the *status quo*; a brief separation, to the husband's mind, provided scant justification for the deterioration of a relationship sanctioned by God and law. Mrs. McFadden saw things differently. Quarrels, bitter and violent, ensued, and the woman eventually moved in with Mr. Misner, living in his shanty, cooking meals for 'Yankee Bill' and his hired men. This, however, was a transgression that the community could hardly sanction. Taking another man's wife, a valuable commodity on the timber frontier, was a serious breach of unwritten law. A group of woodsmen from nearby Weidman and Glenrae, led by Alexander Stewart, Frank Hall, Abe Charlton, Archie Thompson, Aaron Mitchell, and a man named Kelly, decided to charivari[1] Misner and thrash him for his imprudence. McFadden, however, proved a reluctant participant. Only with the inducement of a couple of drinks was he drawn to the ranks of the charivari party. The group consolidated, they headed for Misner's shack, looking forward to the prospects of a fight. It was more like a massacre. As a number of men howled, shouted, and fired their guns in the air outside of Misner's shanty, others climbed on the roof, tearing boards off of the structure, demanding two dollars to appease their anger. Misner offered a brief moment of opposition, and then wisely agreed to the lumbermen's terms. As he prepared to pay up, Aaron Mitchell burst through the locked shanty door. Seeing Misner reach for his gun, he unloaded both barrels of a shotgun into the woodsman's body. Two hours later Misner was dead. Mrs. McFadden was not heard from while, oddly enough, her husband was held for trial after an inquest at Petrolia, although all agreed that he had played no role in the actual shooting, and only a minor part in the affray at the shack. Justice, apparently blind to the social indiscretion that had precipitated the act of violence, proved no more perceptive in its tragic aftermath.[2]

This vignette could serve as an introduction to a number of themes of importance in the social history of nineteenth-century North America: the social impact of transiency; the fragility of the plebeian family; or the under-

---

1 Charivari is another word for rough music, a cacophonous mock serenade, typically performed by a group of people in derision of an unpopular person or in celebration of a marriage.

2 *Globe* (Toronto), 25 March 1890.

current of brutality associated with lower-class life. Here, Mr. Misner's death, a consequence of a particularly violent confrontation, prefaces a wider discussion of ritualised methods of enforcing community standards and morality. Charivaris and whitecapping, two prominent forms of extra-legal authority in North America that have received little scholarly attention, reveal important dimensions of the nineteenth-century past.

The following examination of these two mechanisms of enforcing popular standards rests upon evidence drawn from a number of Canadian and American regions and communities. Statistically, the data encompass 197 references to charivaris, and 141 references to the practice of whitecapping. Chronologically, the period involved is the nineteenth century, although there are excursions both before and after those hundred years, 'cultural phenomena being no devotee of the time categories of the historian's card index boxes'.[3] These references are drawn from newspapers, travellers' accounts, literary works, contemporary journals and magazines, reminiscences, dictionaries of popular speech and 'Americanisms', and current scholarly works (largely within the disciplines of history, anthropology, linguistics, and folklore) which have touched on the ritualistic enforcement of appropriate behaviour, either directly or in passing.[4]

So as not to inflate this body of sources, it is necessary to note that some of the references are of a very general nature, while others refer to detailed accounts of an actual charivari or case of whitecapping. Moreover, one source may have yielded a number of references. Thus, Susanna Moodie's chapter on the charivari in *Roughing it in the Bush* contains a general discussion of the ritual set within the context of five references to specific cases: Madeleine Noble's unpublished dissertation focusing on the White Caps of Harrison and Crawford counties, Indiana, contains an appendix listing 80 cases of whitecapping in the years 1873–93.[5] But these are rare finds, and much of the material, like the opening account of the Holmesdale charivari, is culled from sources depicting an individual, local event.

Finally, it needs to be stressed that this evidence defies quantification. There is simply nothing to be gained by counting how many cases of whitecapping were directed against this or that form of misbehaviour; nor would reliable trends be established if one counted the number of charivaris in particular years, relating the ritual to seasonal or economic cycles. It is possible to speak,

---

3   Colls 1977, p. 13.

4   See J.H. Hexter, 'The Burden of Proof', *Times Literary Supplement*, 24 October 1975, for a comment on the problems associated with this kind of 'source mining'.

5   Moodie 1962, pp. 144–9; Noble 1973, pp. 177–90.

in the most general of terms, of the kinds of behaviour that precipitated the charivari or whitecapping, but beyond that few patterns emerge. Nor could they, for the data base is itself fragmentary and problematical, dependent upon what was reported, and what was found through research undertaken by a single individual, aided by his colleagues. In short, what was missed may have been as important as what was found, and what went unrecorded may well have been as significant as that which found its way into the record of the past, where the atypical and the particularly violent were likely to draw attention.[6]

Bearing in mind these preliminary caveats, this essay attempts a number of tasks. First, a brief discussion of the charivari in its European setting introduces the essential background to the North American phenomenon. Second, the charivari, as practised in a number of North American regions and communities, is investigated. Third, the process of whitecapping, prominent across North America in the years 1888–1905, at approximately the same time that the charivari was falling out of use, is dealt with. Finally, the problems of interpretation and analysis are raised.

2

Perhaps one of the most persistent cultural forms known to scholars of popular customs and traditions was the charivari. As a ritualised mechanism of community control, with roots penetrating back to the medieval epoch, the charivari was known throughout the Atlantic world.[7] Although it could be directed against virtually any social offender, the custom was most often used to expose to the collective wrath of the community adulterous relationships, cuckolded husbands, wife and husband beaters, unwed mothers, and partners in so-called unnatural marriage. Many variants were possible, and the phenomenon had a rural as well as an urban presence, but the essential form was generally cut from a similar cloth. The demonstration was most often initiated under the cover of darkness, a party gathering at the house of the offender to

---

6 Lacking a strong folkloric tradition, North American scholars cannot draw on the kinds of detailed works available to the French and English, including van Gennep's studies and surviving prefecture's lists of charivaris in specific regions. Van Gennep 1943, and 1946, have proved invaluable. See Gauvard et Gokalp 1974, p. 694. An article drawing on prefecture lists is Bonnain-Moerdyk et Moerdyk 1977. See for the English case, Alford 1959.

7 See Bassinet 1833; Mellinkoff 1973.

beat pans and drums, shoot muskets, and blow the ubiquitous horn, which butchers often rented out for the occasion. Sometimes the guilty party was seized, perhaps to be roughly seated on a donkey, facing backwards, and then paraded through the streets, passers-by loudly informed of his or her transgression. The charivari party was often led by youths, on other occasions by women. In seventeenth-century Lyon and eighteenth-century Paris we know that journeymen and artisans were particularly active, as were rural tradesmen in eighteenth- and nineteenth-century England. As a constant check on misbehaviour, the charivari served an important purpose in many communities and in many different cultural contexts. Its disappearance, usually dated around 1850 at the latest, has been interpreted as an indicator of the potent rise of the nuclear family, which no longer required the collective surveillance of neighbours and townsfolk to assure its stability and continuity.[8] But let us examine some specific national and regional variations, beginning with England and France, where the literature is most developed, and concluding with some comments on a number of other European nation states.

The English charivari was practised under a multitude of names: rough music, known in East Anglia as tinning, tin panning, or kettling,[9] skimmington, skimmerton, skimmety riding, or wooseting, recreated in literature by Thomas Hardy, and in art by Hogarth's print, 'Hudibras Encounters the Skimmington';[10] riding the stang, apparently most popular in the northern counties and in Scotland;[11] Devon's stag hunt;[12] the occupational variation, the butcher's serenade, artfully employed by London's Clare Market men;[13] or, the American term, shivaree, common among Cornish miners.[14] E. P. Thompson has recently described

---

8   As an introduction to the charivari see Shorter 1975, pp. 46, 64, 217–28; Pinon 1969, pp. 393–405.

9   Chambers 1864, p. 510; Grose 1785, p. 291; Evans 1970, p. 937; Huggett 1972, p. 64; Cope 1883, p. 75; Porter 1969, pp. 8–10; and 1974, pp. 27–8; Hole 1940, p. 23; Wright 1905, pp. 156–7.

10 Evans 1970, p. 1009; Cope 1883, p. 83; Hardy 1920, pp. 335–43; Hole 1940, p. 23; Roberts 1856, pp. 534–7; Cunningham 1930, pp. 287–90; Wright 1905, p. 475; Hazlitt 1905, pp. 551–2; *Notes and Queries*, 15 March 1873; 31 May 1873; 5 June 1869; 26 June 1869.

11 Wright 1914, pp. 276–7; Gutch 1912, pp. 130–3; Henderson 1967, pp. 29–30; *Notes and Queries*, 25 March 1876; 25 November 1882.

12 Hole 1940, p. 23; Brown 1952, pp. 104–9.

13 Chambers 1864, p. 360; Walsh 1898, p. 156. The Butcher's Serenade is depicted in Hogarth's 'The Industrious 'Prentice Out of His Time and Married To His Master's Daughter', the sixth print in the *Industry & Idleness* series.

14 Rowse 1947, pp. 8–9, where Rowse questions whether the 'shivaree' was an old Cornish custom, or whether it was brought to the region by miners returned from America.

the particular forms, and there is no need to recreate his argument here.[15] But Violet Alford's early note on the stages of the English charivari bears repeating, for virtually all of these variations on an essential theme follow a classic pattern: 'Rough music is the beginning of popular justice, the overture on pots and pans, whistles and bells outside the house of a culprit; the second and more deadly stage is the *Ride on a donkey*, a ladder or a pole ... The third stage is a *public play*, a re-enactment of the censured conduct, with a mock-judgement and sentence'.[16]

Two cases of English charivaris waged against wife-beaters indicate the general contours of the practice.[17] The first instance, recorded in 1860, documented the use of the custom in the Surrey and Sussex region during the 1840s. It was suppressed by the police, who grew irritated with forms of rough music because it frequently rendered the roads impassable. Offending wife-beaters were first warned of the community's wrath, chaff from the threshing-floor strewn on their doorsteps in the dead of night. If the offence continued, the man was subjected to rough music. Under the cover of darkness a procession formed, headed by two men with huge cow horns, followed by an individual with a large old fish kettle around his neck, representing the trumpeters and big drum of a serious parade. Then came the orator, leading 'a motley assembly with hand-bells, gongs, cow-horns, whistles, tin kettles, rattles, bones, frying-pans, everything, in short from which more and rougher music than ordinary could be extracted'. At a given signal, the group halted, and the orator began to recite:

> There is a man in this place
> Has beat his wife!! (*forte*. A pause)
> Has beat his wife!! (*fortissimo*.)
> It is a very great shame and disgrace
> To all who live in this place,
> It is indeed upon my life!!

A bonfire was then lit, and the charivari party danced around it, as if in a frenzy. The noise was heard as far away as two miles. The orator closed with a speech

---

15   Thompson's discussion replaces Alford as the definitive treatment. Rich in detail and subtle in analysis, it is a pathbreaking effort. Thompson 1972b. Note, too, the brief comments in Stone 1977, pp. 145, 374–5, 504.

16   Alford 1959, pp. 505–6.

17   Thompson has outlined the English charivari's increasing concern with wife-beating in the nineteenth century in Thompson 1972b, especially p. 297.

recommending better conduct, and the practitioners of rough music departed, encouraged by the offender's neighbours, who provided beer for 'the band'.[18]

Another case, this time from Hedon, in the East Riding of Yorkshire, outlines the events of 18–20 February 1889. Jack Nelson had cruelly beaten his wife. An effigy of Nelson was carried by two men through the village, accompanied by a large crowd, wielding the traditional instruments of rough music. The procession eventually came to a halt in front of Nelson's door, and the clatter of pans and horns quickly ceased, the crowd breaking out in voices loud and harsh:

Here we cum, wiv a ran a dan dan;
It's neather fo' mah cause nor tha cause
    that Ah ride this stang
Bud-it is fo' Jack Nelson, that Roman-nooased man.
Cum all you good people that live i' this raw,
Ah'd he' ya tk wahnin, for this is oor law;
If onny o' you husbans your gud wives do bang
Let em cum to uz, an we'll ride em the stang.
He beat her, he bang'd her, he bang'd her indeed;
He bang'd her afooar sha ivver stood need.
He bang'd her wi neather stick, steean, iron nor stower,
But he up wiv a three-legged stool an knockt her backwards over.
    Upstairs aback o' bed
    Sike a racket there they led.
    Doon stairs, aback o' door
    He buncht her whahl he meead her sweear.
Noo if this good man dizzant mend his manners,
The skin of his hide sal gan ti the tanner's;
An if the tanner dizzant tan it well,
He sal ride upon a gate spell;
An if the spell sud happen to crack,
He sal ride upon the devil's back;
An if the devil sud happen ti run,
We'll shut him wiv a wahld-goose gun;
An if the gun sud, happen ti miss fire,
Ah'll bid y good neet, for Ah's ommast tired.

---

18   *Notes and Queries*, 15 December 1860. See also Thompson 1972b, p. 297; Shorter 1975, pp. 224–5.

Upon the conclusion of this serenade, the clamour of rough music was again initiated. Amidst cheering and loud noise, the effigy was carried around the village for three successive nights. The ceremony was terminated on the third evening, when Nelson's likeness was finally burned on the village green.[19]

In France, and indeed on the continent in general, wife-beaters were seldom subjected to the charivari. But the practice was nevertheless quite common, often initiated by the young, resentful of old men who married young women, supposedly robbing youth of its rightful access to the marriageable females of the community. Payment was often demanded to appease those who saw themselves wronged by such acts of ostensibly unnatural marriage:

> Fork up, old pal
> The dough that you owe
> We're the boys of the block
> And we want a good show
>
> We're wild as they come
> And off on a spree
> So out with the cash
> Or charivari![20]

Once their palms were greased with coin of the realm, the young men often retired to the nearest tavern, and left the married couple to their wedding-night pleasures. Occasionally, however, the charivari was actually used to punish those who had deprived the local young of potential spouses, and no amount of cash could deflect the final reckoning.[21] In certain cases, widows or widowers remarrying would be charivaried out of a public concern for the dead spouse, a concern often grounded on religious sentiment.[22] Regardless of its motivation, the charivari was a popular custom frequently resorted to by the rural and urban masses. Jeffrey Kaplow, noting that the victim *par excellence* was a journeyman who married his master's widow, contends that among the Parisian labouring poor of the nineteenth century, the charivari was 'perhaps their favourite amusement ...'[23]

---

19   Gutch 1912, pp. 132–3. On other folk-rhymes directed against wife-beaters see Northall 1892, pp. 253–7, all of which were recited in the midst of subjecting an offender to 'riding the stang'.
20   Van Gennep 1943, p. 626, quoted and translated in Shorter 1975, p. 221.
21   Caston 1971, p. 106.
22   Fortier-Beaulieu 1940b, pp. 67–9; and 1940a, pp. 1–16.
23   Kaplow 1972, p. 108. See also Weber 1976, p. 400.

Marital mismatches, while a prominent cause of French charivaris, were rivalled by a series of sexual offences. Married men who impregnated single women, cuckolded husbands, unwed mothers, and those engaged in adulterous relationships were all subjected to the charivari, censured for the threat they posed to community social order.[24] In the period preceding *Carnavals au bois*, for instance, the charivari was used by young villagers to publicly sanction married persons involved in illicit liaisons. The first stage in the charivari was the carnage, or horning, initiated in February as village youths serenaded each guilty party with all kinds of unlikely musical instruments. Then followed the public unmasking, the formal Carnival procession bearing effigies of the two victims. After the singing of specially composed songs, broadcasting the event for a period of three or four days, came the final judgement: a mock trial in which judges, lawyers, and attendants were present in costume. The whole affair was terminated with the symbolic execution of the offenders, their effigies burned or hung in the public square.[25]

Finally, the French situation reveals graphically the potential of the charivari as a political force, turned against constituted authority. Indeed, in a fine article discussing youth groups and charivaris in sixteenth-century France, Natalie Zemon Davis notes that at this early date the ritual could be moved to explicitly political purpose, a mechanism whereby petty proprietors, artisans, and merchants marshalled the urban poor to voice their critique of king and state.[26] Closer to the modern period, charivaris assumed importance in the years of revolutionary upsurge of the 1790s, and in the turbulent political climate of 1824–48.[27] And yet, even in this context, charivaris are perhaps best seen as a pre-political form of class action, admittedly set firmly against the wall of nineteenth-century authority, but lacking in conscious, political direction. A case in point, perhaps, is provided by the Limoges prostitutes. In 1857 they faced persistent harassment and incarceration in a local hospital. Escaping from the institution, the women resisted efforts to curb their business activities by organising charivaris that drew the enthusiastic support of the local barracks.[28]

24   Saintyves 1935, pp. 7–36; Shorter 1975, pp. 219–20; Weber 1976, 400–1.

25   Daunay 1966, pp. 1–19.

26   Davis 1975, pp. 97–123.

27   Weber, 1976, p. 403; Bonnain-Moerdyk et Moerdyk 1977, pp. 381–98; Bercé 1976, pp. 40–4.

28   Weber 1976, p. 404. On similar uprisings by prostitutes in England in the 1860s and 1880s see Cluer 1974, an account of prostitutes besieging a workhouse, seeking shelter, 'beating tin kettles and blowing tin whistles'; and House of Commons Select Committee 1882, p. 340. A later account, in which prostitutes again use rough music against efforts to suppress their activities, is found in Robinson 1913, p. 148. I am indebted to Judith

This was, to be sure, a political undertaking, and one revealing important social tensions, but it implies no condescension to place it in the category of primitive rebellion.[29]

Outside of France and England, the charivari was also a force of considerable stature, although we know far less about its use. In Germany, the custom was generally known as *Katzenmusiken*, but the *polterabends*, the traditional bombardment of the newly-weds' door with old crockery, pots, pans, and assorted other missiles seems to have been a form of the charivari.[30] Dutch wife-beaters were subjected to treatment remarkably similar to the rough music of the English:

> In the Akr-Thal and on the neighbouring Eifel, the country people still keep up a kind of self-instituted police, called *Thierjagen* (Beastchasing). It revives each time that a husband beats his wife and woe to him that is found guilty. With kettles, fireshovels, and tongs, boys and women assemble under the venerable village lime-tree ... the mob hurries towards the culprit's house, before whose door soon resounds a music whose echoes a lifetime does not shake off.[31]

The Andalusian *cencerrada*, forcefully depicted in Pitt-Rivers' classic discussion of *el vito* in the village of Alcalá, resembles variations of the charivari common in France and England.[32] Strawboy activities at Irish weddings, where horn-blowing, gun shooting, shouting and masks were commonplace, remind one of the charivari,[33] as does the Welsh practice of the *ceffyl pren*, or wooden horse.[34] In Italy, the charivari was known as *scampanata*.[35]

R. Walkowitz, whose continuing studies of prostitution and the Contagious Diseases Acts promise much, for bringing these sources to my attention.

29   See Hobsbawm 1971.

30   Ripley and Dana 1864, pp. 722–3; Schele de Vere 1872, p. 589; Phillips 1860, pp. 26–92; Meuli 1953, pp. 231–4. On the *polter-abends* see Mayhew 1864, p. 457. Compare Mayhew with the account of a similar custom, directed at ill-assorted marriages, outlined in Wagner 1894, p. 107. Another practice, in which the wedded couple was showered with shoes, was apparently common in England, and was revived in Canada. See 'An Old Custom Revived', *Ottawa Citizen*, 6 June 1871.

31   *Notes and Queries*, 8 September 1860.

32   Pitt-Rivers 1954, pp. 169–77.

33   Súilleabháin 1963, pp. 204–8; St. Clair 1971, p. 15.

34   Williams 1955, pp. 54–5.

35   Ripley and Dana 1864, pp. 722–3.

The charivari, then, was hardly an isolated phenomenon. Bound by neither region nor nation, it was a universally practised custom, an essential component of the 'invisible cultures' and 'limited identities' of the plebeian world.[36] It belonged, as Claude Lévi-Strauss has noted, 'to the European popular tradition'. But Lévi-Strauss errs when he argues that attempts 'to generalize the institution do not seem very convincing'.[37] For the charivari has a North American presence, as well as a European one. Those migrating to the New World brought much of their culture with them: traditions, values, language, and specific forms of ritualised behaviour. Woven into the very fabric of this culture was the charivari, and it would not easily be displaced.

3

Conventional wisdom has it that the charivari was brought to North America by the French, that it was originally prominent in the settlements of Lower Canada, Louisiana, and Alabama, and that it was gradually adopted in English-speaking areas, where the derivative term shivaree was used to denote the custom.[38] And, indeed, the first recorded instances of North American charivaris that have come to my attention occurred in Lower Canada. A Quebec charivari of 28 June 1683 illustrates a common pattern. François Vezier dit Laverdure died 7 June 1683, leaving his wife a widow at 25 years of age. Three weeks later his mourning spouse took a new husband, Claude Bourget, aged 30. Twenty-one days of widowhood seemed an unreasonably short time for the people of Quebec, and they turned out to charivari the couple. Disorder reigned for more than a week, and the Church authority eventually intervened. Monseigneur François de Laval, first Bishop of Quebec, issued a Mandement, 3 July 1683:

> Having been informed that in consequence of a marriage celebrated in this city of Quebec, six days ago, a great number of persons of either sex

---

36 Note the discussions in Careless 1969, pp. 1–10; Stock 1973, pp. 29–33.

37 Lévi-Strauss 1969, p. 300.

38 On the French origins of the term see Fielding 1942, pp. 50–1; Moodie 1962, p. 145; *The Charivari; or Canadian Poetics: A Tale After the Manner of Beppo* 1824, p. 49 [This source has recently been republished in the 'Early Canadian Poetry Series', authorship attributed to George Longmore, edited and introduced by Mary Lu Macdonald. See Longmore 1977. See also, Klinck 1976, pp. 140–41, 145, 147]; Farmer 1889; Walsh 1898, pp. 209–13; and 1893, p. 149; Clapin n.d.; *American Notes & Queries*, 27 October 1888; 15 June 1889. Hereafter *A.N. & Q.*

have gathered together every night under the name of Charivari and ... as there is nothing more prejudicial to religion, to good customs, to the public good and to the peace of all families, We for these reasons and to bring a remedy appropriate to such a great evil ... very expressly prohibit and forbid all the faithful of either sex in our diocese, from finding themselves hereafter in any of the said assemblages, qualified by the name Charivari, the fathers and mothers from sending their children or allowing them to go, the masters from sending their servants or permitting them to go voluntarily – this on pain of Excommunication.

In suppressing these riotous gatherings, the Church relied upon 'the Secular Arm'.[39] This early tumultuous charivari, then, posed problems of order and disorder that church and state would contend with throughout the eighteenth and nineteenth centuries.[40]

During the nineteenth century the French influence in North American charivaris continued to be felt. In Upper Canada, for instance, the ritual was generally considered to be a French institution.[41] In the town of York in 1802 the marriage of Augustin Boiton de Fougères, a French Royalist who had come to Canada with de Puisaye, to Eugenia Willcocks gave rise to a charivari:

the young beaux of the Town remindfull of the happy occasion and the French Custom of Shivierieing the Parties a number of them in disguise assembled and made a great noise about the old Esquires House, till, the Esquire, his Son and Doct. Baldwin came in a great passion with their

---

39   AA.VV. 1887, pp. 114–5. See Massicotte 1926a, reprinted in Roy 1930, pp. 447–8; and Riddell 1931, pp. 522–4. There seems to be some confusion dating this event, the quoted source placing it in the year 1682, and Riddell dating it 1684. I have followed Massicotte's note. On charivaris in New France see Séguin 1968, pp. 70–5. The practice was common in the 1670s. See Jaenen 1976b, p. 140. See, for a later period, Long 1922, pp. 46–7.

40   Church resistance is documented in Wallot 1971, pp. 81, 89; Jaenen 1976b, p. 140. Charivaris were outlawed in a number of North American communities, either by local by-laws or police regulations. See McNab 1865; Kingsford 1878, p. 151; Joseph 1889, pp. 401, 423. In Kingston, Ontario, the first city by-law, passed in 1846, was aimed at the suppression of charivaris. See City of Kingston 1907, p. xxx. My thanks to Patricia Malcolmson for making this source available to me. On the reaction of the Montreal and Hamilton police to charivaris see Robert 1977; Hamilton Board of Police 1842, p. 50. My thanks to John Weaver for directing me to this source. See also Johnson 1977, p. 233.

41   Gourlay 1822, pp. 254–5; Guillet 1933, pp. 308–9; Canniff 1869, p. 631; Howell and Howell 1969, p. 11. See also MacTaggart 1829, pp. 41–2.

Guns and threatened to Shoot if the disguised Party did not disperse, and some run of, one frenchman was taken, the guard that was in the Town, was sent for, the Constables call'd, and the noisey Party soon ware all gone about 10 o'clock, all was quiet and we went to bed ...

For three more nights the young men kept up the 'shivieree', dressed as Indians, demanding liquor from local residents and innkeepers, 'cutting capers til 2 OClock in the morning'. The affair ended, finally, as 'the Esquire threatened vengeance on the perpetrators'.[42] In regions with a sprinkling of French Canadians, the charivari was always present. Ottawa and Peterborough were well known for the practice, and the Smith's Falls and Gatineau regions also witnessed the custom on a number of occasions. Well into the 1870s the ritual remained intact.[43]

Lower Canada, too, was familiar with the charivari. Bishop Pleissis, in 1807, noted with horror that the *habitants* of Laprairie had staged an unprecedented 'affreux et horrible charivari ... soit pour la durée, soit pour les injuries, obscénités, imprétés, de toute espère ... les travestissements, mascarades, profanations des cérémonies, ornements et chants funèbras de l' Eglise'.[44] Montreal was the scene of a veritable epidemic of charivaris in the early 1820s, eliciting this response in the *Règles et Règlements de Police*:

Quiconque étant déguisé ou non sera trouvé dans aucune partie de la ville ou des fauxbourgs de jour ou de nuit, criant, *Charivari*, ou fesant avec des pots, chaudières, cornes ou autrement, un bruit capable de troubler le repos public, ou qui s'arrêtera de la même manière devant aucune maison, en fesant un tel bruit, encourra une amende de cinq livres courant pour chaque contravention.[45]

These affairs, as John Bigsby noted, were 'intended to reach delinquents not amenable to the common process of law – offenders against propriety and the public sense of honour'. The form was remarkably consistent:

---

42   Ely Playter's Diary, in Firth 1962, pp. 247–8.

43   *American Notes & Queries*, 27 October 1888; *Smith's Falls News*, 23 July 1875; 6 August 1875; *Globe* (Toronto), 2 May 1877; *Pembroke Observer*, cited in *Smith's Falls News*, 4 May 1877.

44   Wallot 1971, p. 81, n. 128.

45   Cited in Robert 1977, p. 197. Longmore's poem *The Charivari*, was developed in the context of this outbreak. Note the discussion of horning in Séguin 1970, pp. 127–39.

First came a strange figure, masked, with a cocked hat and sword – he was very likely the grotesque beadle we see in French churches; then came strutting a little humpbacked creature in brown, red, and yellow, with beak and tail, to represent the Gallic cock. Fifteen or sixteen people followed in the garb of Indians, some wearing cows' horns on their heads. Then came two men in white sheets, bearing a paper coffin of great size, lighted from within, and having skulls, cross-bones, and initials painted in black on its sides. This was surrounded by men blowing horns, beating pot-lids, poker and tongs, whirling watchmen's rattles, whistling, and so on. To these succeeded a number of Chinese lanterns, borne aloft on high poles and mixed with blazing torches – small flags, black and white – more rough music. Close after came more torches, clatter and fantastic disguises – the whole surrounded and accompanied by a large rabble rout, who kept up an irregular fire of yells, which now and then massed and swelled into a body of sound audible over all the neighbourhood.[46]

Edward Allen Talbot documented the case of a Montreal charivari, in the winter of 1821, where the object of ridicule was a widow of considerable fortune, recently married to a young gentleman. After a pitched battle, involving the local constabulary, a crowd of 500 managed to extort £50 from the couple, presenting it to the Female Benevolent Society.[47]

Similarly, in New Orleans in March 1804, Madame Don Andres Almonaster was 'sherri-varried', an immense crowd 'mobbing' her house. Thousands of people gathered, ludicrously disguised, to give the old woman and her unpopular new husband the Creole version of rough music. Effigies of the woman's present and late husbands were paraded about the house, the latter in a coffin, the widow impersonated by a living person sitting near it. Civil authority, it seemed, was 'laid aside'. After three days, the crowd was eventually appeased with the sum of $3,000, the money apparently given to the orphans of the city.[48] Common throughout the *Cajun* districts of the American South, the charivari supposedly gained acceptance out of 'an indisposition to allow ladies *two chances* for husbands, in a society where so few single ladies [found]

---

46   Bigsby 1850, pp. 34–7.

47   Talbot 1824, pp. 299–304. For a remarkable early discussion of Canadian charivaris, largely in early nineteenth-century Lower Canada, see Massicotte 1926b, pp. 712–25.

48   Watson 1843, p. 229. See also, Davis and McDavid 1949, p. 251. This incident is also dramatized in Stephens 1929, pp. 143–66.

even one husband! a result, it is to be presumed, of the concubinage system so prevalent [there]'.[49]

But we must not mistake the French presence for the whole of the story, writing the North American charivari off as a custom borrowed from the French, as Susanna Moodie seemed to do.[50] Indeed, this conception of the American shivaree as a mere derivative form was attacked early on by Edward Eggleston, whose nineteenth-century novel lauded, 'That serenade! Such a medley of discordant sounds, such a clatter and clanger, such a rattle of horse-fiddle, such a bellowing of dumb bell, such a snorting of tin horns, such a ringing of tin pans, such a grinding of skillet-lids'.[51] And a closer look will indicate that the North American charivari thrived outside of the reach of French culture. Alice T. Chase argued that the charivari was common, in the 1860s, in most rural hamlets from Pennsylvania west to Kansas and Nebraska, being particularly prominent in Ohio, Indiana, and Illinois. She identified the ritual as coming to America with the Pennsylvania Dutch.[52] Among New Englanders the practice was well established, known as the serenade.[53] In Nebraska in the 1870s 'belling the bridal couple', giving them a 'warming', was a frequent occurrence.[54] 'It was understood', within the Tennessee mining community, 'that every bride and groom had to be shivareed'.[55] The *sanserassa*, a serenade of tin pans, horns, kettles, and drums, was actively practised by the Spanish population of St. Augustine, Florida, where the ritual was common in the 1820s.[56] Scandinavian settlements apparently incorporated the practice into their language and their culture.[57] Even in early Upper Canada, or post-Confederation Ontario, where the French influence was operative, numerous cities, towns, villages, and rural communities sufficiently removed from the shadow of French culture, utilised the charivari, repeatedly directing it against those who flaunted community

49   On the practice of the charivari in Louisiana and Alabama see *A.N. & Q.*, 20 October 1888; Atwood 1964, pp. 68–70; Hoffpauir 1969, pp. 3–19; Hall 1835, pp. 121–4. An excellent discussion is found in the different editions of Cable 1883, pp. 54–5; and 1890, pp. 220–1. The quote is from Watson 1843, p. 229.

50   Moodie 1962, p. 145.

51   Eggleston 1872, pp. 293–9.

52   Alice T. Chase, 'The "Shivaree"', *A.N. & Q.*, 29 September 1888, also in Walsh 1898, pp. 209–13.

53   Hanley 1933, pp. 24–6.

54   *Lincoln Nebraska Daily State Journal*, 22 November 1874; 1 January 1878, quoted in Meredith 1933, pp. 22–4.

55   Thurman 1969, pp. 86–94.

56   *A.N. & Q.*, 20 October 1888.

57   Flaten 1900, pp. 115–26; Stefanson 1903, pp. 354–62; Flom 1926, pp. 541–8.

standards.[58] Across North America, then, the custom had a vital presence, known, according to local and regional taste, as serenade, shivaree, charivari, tin panning, belling, horning, bull banding, skimmelton, or calathump.[59]

Skimetons, or skimmeltons, were apparently common in the Hudson Valley region of New York State, with no newly-married couple exempt.[60] An early letter, dated 3 April 1822, described these escapades in some detail, documenting three skimetons in February and March. When the Reverend Robert Forest married Mr. Edmund Lamb to Mrs. Eliza Munger on 14 February 1822, they were greeted with a Skimeton: 'one man mounted up on a white horse haveing a home made pung slay behind him with an intoxicated man on it and was furnished with something like eight or ten Cow Bells ...'. Another marriage, again involving a widow, was addressed by 'one man armed with one goose Quill and went squacking into the house and salluted the wedding guest and returned without any further interruption'. But the real discord was saved for the marriage of Mr. Peter Tripp and Mrs. Abby Lyon of Kortwright, Delaware County, 14 March 1822:

> about sun set the Skimetonians assemblyed together with their insterments of music wich had been preparing for about three Days before – the number of them was between thirty and forty wich choosed their Captain and was formed in a line two a breast the first section was armed with a fifte and drum second section with horse fiddles third section with sea shells and tin horns forth sec with Cow Bells fifth sec with Goose Quills sixth section with Pans seventh sec with guns and two men behind one blowing a rams horn and three or four Goose Quills into it and the other crowing like a rooster whos voice echoed thru the village decently. During this music there was a dish of gun powder feathers and Brimstone set onfire at door step wich made no small smells and there was stones against and in the house wich broke out 24 or 25 lites and damaged the sashes the people in the house being much interrupted was for nowing who they was one going out with a lantern it was dashed out of his hands and he was thrown into the mud and his hat was took by someone and was cut in pieces that was worth six dollars. during this there was others come out and one of them got a fighting with one of the skimeton boys

---

58   See the discussion of the charivari in Palmer 1977, pp. 184–92.

59   Kurath 1949, p. 78, and fig. 1874; Wood 1971, p. 39; *Time* (Canadian edition), 25 July 1949; Avis et al. 1967, pp. 141, 656, 689.

60   *A.N. & Q.*, 13 October 1888.

and got whipt by this time there was 16 or 18 warrants got out this stopped their music the next mornig they took all they could finad and was a week or more before they got them all.

The account concluded with the note that the charivari had been 'carried on in the way of a riot ...'.[61]

The shivaree, common in the American mid-west, as well as in certain eastern states, such as Maine, also often resulted in riotous gatherings.[62] When Hi Hatch, or 'Laughing Hatch', a bachelor of fifty, married an Illinois woman in Des Moines, Iowa, in the winter of 1869, 'the city turned out to serenade him'. For three nights the clamour and din continued, the section of the city where Hatch lived turned into 'Pandemonium'; the mayor ordered the marshal to preserve order, but without effect. Finally, the city calmed down, the crowd's energy apparently dissipated. Hatch and his bride had not even been in the city, having secretly departed for Indianola, 13 miles away. The tumult was raised outside a darkened and empty house.[63]

But the objects of the shivaree were seldom as farsighted, or as fortunate, as Hatch. In the second quarter of the nineteenth century, Robert Carlton described a ' "shiver-ree" of John Glenville, of Guzzleton, as 300 locals gathered to do special dishonour to 'd---d 'ristocraticul and powerful grand big-bug doins'. With the aid of two corn baskets full of cowbells tied to saplings, a score and a half of frying pans beat with mush sticks, 32 Dutch oven and skillet lids clashed as cymbals, 53 horse shoes played as triangles, 10 large wash-tubs and seven small barrels drummed with fists and corn-cobs, 195 quills, prepared and blown as clarinets, 43 tin whistles and baby-trumpets, used vigorously until they cracked, two small and one large military drum with six fifes, scalp and war cries, and all manner of yells, screams, shrieks, and hisses, the party descended upon the newly-wedded couple's house. When the group's demands for wine were met with silence, anger was aroused. A fifty-pound pig was promptly hoisted through the bedroom window and into the honeymoon chamber, and the proceedings quickly degenerated into riot. Southerners, the organisers of the shivaree, were soon opposed by a Northern contingent, and amidst cries of 'Knock 'em down! – drag the big-bug yankees through the creek', the fight was on. The shivaree could highlight sectional, as well as social, tensions.[64]

---

61   Winner 1964, pp. 134–6.
62   On shivarees in Maine see *A.N. & Q.*, 20 October 1888; 3 November 1888.
63   *A.N. & Q.*, 3 November 1888.
64   Carlton 1843, pp. 228–34.

As should by now be apparent, the shivaree in the United States was commonly directed against the newly-wedded couple. From Orlando, Florida to Ann Arbor, Michigan, peals of shivaree would often greet the nineteenth-century bride and groom. The ritual survived well into the twentieth century, with actual cases being recorded in central Indiana, Grant County in the 1890s; in Ithaca, New York in 1891; in Jackson County Missouri in 1892; in northern New York and northern Ohio in 1896; in Broome County, New York in 1900; in north-west Arkansas in 1902; in Kentucky and Nebraska in 1905–6; and in Aroostook County, Maine in 1909.[65] The list is virtually endless, popularised in literature and reminiscences.[66] Nor was the situation all that different in Ontario or the west, where the shivaree was an established institution, also directed against the recently married, particularly those unions that appeared to be mismatched.[67] But despite its rather mundane purpose, often mere enjoyment at the expense of the newly married couple, the charivari could pose acutely the problem of social order and disorder.

In nineteenth-century Upper Canada, for instance, the charivari emerged as a force undermining social authority, resolutely opposed by magistrate and police. Ely Playter's diary tells of a 'sheriverie' in the town of York in 1804, occasioned by the marriage of a Miss Fisk. Playter and a friend heard the clamour of rough music and, as they 'could not be easey without being with them', went in disguise to the house. There, 'the old man shot at [them] 3 times & then came with his sword'. After 'some fun', the men dispersed. The next evening, however, they were back, confronted by the Magistrates who were attempting to stop the noise and punish the leaders. By the end of the week, 'several people were bound over to Court by the Magistrates for being in the Shivarie ...'.[68] Another York charivari, in August 1828, also drew the ire of constituted authority, condemned as a practice that would 'disgrace even the walks of savage life'.[69]

---

65   Wentworth 1944, pp. 550–1; Mathews 1951b, pp. 1523, 1885. See also Lynd 1956, pp. 245–6.

66   Herrick 1949, pp. 25–6; Stuart 1938, pp. 268–9; Stuart 1941. A fascinating dramatic rendition notable for its feminist perspective is O'Dea 1922, pp. 27–52.

67   Riddell 1931, pp. 522–4; Edward O'Brien Journals, Public Archives of Canada, Journal #4, 12–28 November 1828; Mr. and Mrs. James Dixon, Marburg, 'The Chivaree', in *Tweedsmuir Histories: South Norfolk District*, Public Archives of Ontario, MS-8, Reel 69; Wintemberg 1918, pp. 137–8; Scherck 1905, pp. 224–5; Haight 1885, p. 74. On shivarees in the Canadian West see Morgan 1965, pp. 45–6; McClung 1910, p. 350; Onslow 1962, p. 248; *Eye Opener* (Calgary), 25 February 1905, cited in Avis et al. 1967, p. 689.

68   Cited in Firth 1962, p. 250.

69   *Canadian Freeman*, 21 August 1828.

Three charivaris took place in Kingston, Upper Canada, in the mid-1830s, all directed against remarriage, forcing the hand of the local authorities, one leading to two arrests, another necessitating the calling into operation of the Summary Punishment Act, the third culminating in the creation of a special force of constables, 40 strong, to enforce the peace.[70] The latter event, led by one Henry Smith, Jr., illustrates well the deliberate, planned nature of some of these undertakings, revealing the importance, perhaps, of local groups consolidated around a popular figure. Smith was a barrister with a long history of involvement in shady legal entanglements, a man who had himself been in court on charges of assault, perjury, and riot. Indeed, in July 1835, he had led two popular assaults on the house of a black resident of the town, James Anderson, and on the dwelling of a local master shoemaker, John Murray. In the first case Smith led a group of rowdies in pulling down partitions upon the negro inmates of the domicile, attacking a woman named Mary Johnson as an 'improper character', forcing her and her children to take refuge in the yard. Commanding in a military fashion, Smith, who had experience as a Captain in the Kingston Volunteer Fire Company, directed his followers with shouts of, 'Make ready, present, fire'! His other leading role in a crowd's action involved a group of journeymen shoemakers, angered by their employer's 'curtailment of their wages'. They gathered at Murray's house and daubed its front with 'human ordure'. After this 'outrage', Smith and the shoemakers assembled outside of Murray's door to smash windows and scream insults. When Dr Barker, the editor of a local paper, the *British Whig*, printed accounts of the crowd actions, he was threatened by an anonymous letter, signed 'Pugnator', promising him a thrashing if he continued to slander Smith's name in the pages of his newspaper. The front of the *Whig* office, too, was smeared with excrement. Smith, it would seem, was a man of some stature in early nineteenth-century Kingston. A patrician being, who would become, in the early 1840s, the city's Chief Marshall, who would occupy a prominent place in Kingston's political structure, and who was the son of the Kingston Penitentiary's infamous warden, Henry Smith, Sr., Mr Smith, Jr., could obviously gather the forces of the plebeian world to his cause, a testimony, perhaps, to his intimate contact with local youth groups and gangs.[71] It could well have been men like Smith who provoked this response from the Hamilton Board of Police, 22 March 1842:

---

70   *British Whig*, 18 March 1834; 11 March 1837; 31 July 1835. A Kingston charivari of 1877, complete with costumes and effigy is noted in Massicotte 1926b, p. 717.

71   Smith's chequered career in the 1830s is well documented in local newspapers. The crowd actions are briefly described in *British Whig*, 7 July 1835. On his later political activity see Swainson 1974, pp. 161–79.

> Whereas the custom of meeting together at night by ill disposed persons disguised by dress, paint, and for the purposes of indulging in what is commonly called a chevari, has been a source of great annoyance to all the peaceable inhabitants of this Town, and whereas such assemblages endanger the peace of the Town, the safety of property and person and are highly disgraceful to all concerned in them ... it is ordered that all persons convicted of being a party to any such proceedings shall be fined ...[72]

Nor were the consequences of the charivari conducive to the maintenance of stability and order. In fact, in both Canada and the United States, fatalities and serious maimings were often the result, as we have seen. Under the headlines, 'Married and Murdered' and 'One More Charivari Victim', the *Globe*, discussing the fatal beating meted out to an Ottawa man in 1881, noted that: 'In many previous cases participants in the *charivari* have lost their lives or innocent persons have been laid low by misdirected blows, but in this case the bridegroom was the victim'.[73] If actual death did not result, order could be dealt a severe blow by the sheer violence of the affray. In a charivari near Lucan in the 1870s, for instance, Will Donnelly, the club-footed, second oldest boy of the famous Irish clan, used the event as an excuse to vent his frustrations against the Thompsons, a family that resented their daughter, Maggie, being courted by a Donnelly. When Maggie's brother and his new bride returned to their home, Will and his friends broke every pane of glass in the house, smashed the walls with sticks and stones, used the chimney for target practice, demolished a rail fence, and started a bonfire that almost burned down the house.[74] The charivari, as Mrs. Moodie's neighbour put it, was 'not always a joke'.[75]

Perhaps the one charivari that most explicitly raised the question of public order occurred in Montreal, in late May and early June, 1823.[76] Directed against

---

72   Hamilton Board of Police 1842, p. 50.

73   *Globe* (Toronto), 12 August 1881. Other charivaris, ending in death or serious injury, are recorded in *Sarnia Observer and Western Advertiser*, 23 November 1853; 9 June 1865; *Globe* (Toronto), 3 September 1867; 17 December 1867; 26 August 1868; 2 May 1877; 4 November 1881; *Sarnia Observer and Lambton County Advertiser*, 27 December 1867; *Perth Courier*, 27 December 1867; *Ottawa Citizen*, 1 June 1871; *Smith Fall's News*, 4 May 1877; *Hamilton Spectator*, 30 January 1880; 1 November 1881; 29 October 1881; *Windsor Evening Record*, 13 January 1896; 14 January 1896; *A.N. & Q.*, 14 December 1889; 27 October 1888.

74   Robin 1976, p. 100.

75   Moodie 1962, p. 146. See also *Hamilton Spectator*, 24 February 1883; *Globe* (Toronto), 19 August 1869, for cases of police intervention.

76   As an introduction to this event see Longmore 1977, pp. 3–10; Robert 1977, p. 196.

the remarriage of an old widower named Holt, the 'charivary' had been kept up for 'ten or fourteen days', to the 'incessant annoyance of one or two respectable families'. The 'disguised rabble' made the usual demands for money, to be used to aid 'charitable and useful institutions', and assailed the house with a 'persevering uproar'. Eventually the objects of the harangue tired of the proceedings and informed the Magistrates, who 'most properly issued a Proclamation for "suppressing the RIOT and bringing the offenders to justice"'. This action was taken 30 May 1823. On Monday, 2 June 1823, another proclamation was found placarded in various places throughout the city:

NOTICE
The Charivary will meet this evening at half
past eight o'clock on the Hay Market.
By order of
Capt. Rock

Drawing upon the anonymous traditions of extra-legal authority common throughout the Irish countryside, where Captain Rock was feared as 'the commander of one of the most cruel and blood-thirsty banditti', the organisers of the charivari galvanised their followers to action. They were described by the Magistrates as 'persons of various characters and dispositions from other countries', 'émigrés'.[77]

Meeting on the Hay Market they proceeded to Holt's house. Several shots were fired into the crowd and a servant of one of the parties defending the house, John Swails, was killed; many others were seriously injured. Irritated by such defiance, the charivari party dispersed, vowing its revenge. The next evening a body of 'several hundred persons' descended upon the house of their opponent. Before the Magistrates and militia could arrive, 'a scene of outrage and plunder took place as would reflect disgrace on the most savage and barbarous inhabitants of the woods':

> Every door in the house was burst open and every window, with its blinds and other ornaments, was shattered into a thousand pieces, not a stick of furniture was allowed to remain together ... and all that the eye could see or the hand could reach was in a moment involved in one general confusion and ruin. Neither fireplace, mantlepiece, nor stair

---

77   On Captain Rock see the reprints from the Irish newspapers in *Montreal Gazette*, 28 June 1823; Broeker 1970, pp. 7, 193.

railing escaped their desolating hands, and even the very partitions and walls of the house were battered and crumbled in some places to rubbish. In short, no ruin could be more complete than that which has visited the inanimate dwelling of the object of revenge, who, fortunately for him, made a timeous escape with his family, to another country, we believe.

'Well-disposed' citizens reacted with vigour, establishing a City Watch that, in conjunction with the Constables, paraded the city nightly to preserve 'public order'. By mid-week, the city was once more governed by calm and respectable elements; the threat to order had been stifled. But Captain Rock made his presence felt even in the midst of defeat. Placards were posted on public walls denouncing several individuals, and threatening letters were sent to members of the watch. In late August the event remained imprinted on the consciousness of constituted authority, when Judge Reid commented that:

> ... it is greatly to the discredit of the laws, and of good order, that such tumult and violence should happen among us – it is impossible to foresee the outrages that may be committed by a mob, or where it will stop, when put in motion – the assembling of it for a *Charivari* may also be used as a pretence by evil disposed persons, to effect purposes of a very different nature, or more dangerous to the public security, and it is therefore to be hoped, that by the vigilance and exertion of those charged with the administration and execution of the laws, such disturbances will be oppressed, and never permitted to recur in any shape, nor under any pretence.

Charivaris directed against domestic impropriety, particularly remarriage, could thus raise issues that went well beyond popular distaste for 'unnatural marriage'.[78]

In other cases, too, the charivari extended beyond the purely domestic concerns that so often defined its purpose. Indeed, the custom often reflected essential social tensions. Mrs. Moodie documented the case of Tom Smith, 'a runaway nigger from the States', charivaried for his pretentious, and successful, bid to have an Irish woman marry him. Dragged from his bed, ridden on a rail, and beaten, the African American died under the hands of the charivari

---

78   The above account draws on *Montreal Gazette*, 7 June 1823; 14 June 1823; 6 September 1823; *Canadian Courant and Montreal Advertiser*, 4 June 1823; 7 June 1823; 30 August 1823; *Quebec Gazette*, 16 June 1823.

party.[79] Perhaps a similar motivation lay behind the charivari described in the *Cincinnati Commercial*, where 'a party of disguised Ku-Klux visited the house of a citizen in that locality while a wedding was in progress, and took possession of the premises. They fired off pistols and danced over the floor, and the fright occasioned to the daughter of this citizen caused her to go into spasms, succeeded by insanity'. In Franklin, Virginia, in 1867, a Northern clergyman was treated to 'tin-horn serenades' for starting a school for former slave children.[80] Anti-semitism, too, could fuel the fires of the charivari crowd, as 'the execution of the Belleville Jew', in effigy in April 1837, testified:

> Last Friday night some wicked boys
> Thought they would something do:
> So they turned out, and wheel'd about,
> And hung the Belleville Jew.
> ...
>
> Jew Benjie then to get revenge
> Did raise a cry and hue
> Of Maw-worn snarling hypocrite,
> Oh! Saintly Belleville Jew.
>
> The Mayor's clerk by way of lark
> Some say did lead the crew
> While others say without delay
> 'TWAS PORK, AND DONT KNOW WHO.
>
> Let's stop to pause a double cause
> To show this guessing true,
> For Pork's the meat Jews must not eat
> No doubt it killed the Jew.
>
> But oh! my eyes! 'tis all surmise –
> The rope that hangman drew,
> That brought to shameful sacrifice
> The slandering Belleville Jew.

---

79   Moodie 1962, p. 147.
80   Quoted in *Ottawa Citizen*, 18 January 1872; Gutman 1973b, p. 577.

The neck and brains were hung in chains,
And would have swung till two,
Had not a smith with pole forthwith
Pulled down the Belleville Jew.

George Benjamin, founder of the Belleville *Weekly Intelligencer* in 1834, was
the object of this ritualised derision, the crowd contending that his 'Belleville
Smut-machine / Spoke nothing that was true'.[81]

More explicitly, the charivari was often used to show open disapproval
for certain forms of behaviour, particularly those judged immoral or illicit.[82]
Thus, in 1867, John Cummings, James Cummings, John Lewis, Hiram Anderson, Jacob Palmer, and John Palmer led a riotous charivari directed against a
widow, Rachel Mugg, whose daughter had recently been married. According to
local authorities, 'Mrs. Mugg's mode of managing her household affairs did not
come up to the social standard of moral ethics observed in the romantically
situated village of Millgrove'.[83] A Bowmanville, Ontario, lawyer, Mr Loscombe,
faced the rough music of his neighbours in 1868, when a crowd gathered at his
office to tar-and-feather him, punishment for his unlawful bestowing of affec-
tions upon a servant girl. A constable eventually had to escort Loscombe home,
but the crowd captured the lawyer, handled him roughly, and threw him over
a fence. After an announcement that the man's wife was ill, the crowd dis-
continued the disturbance. The next morning Loscombe escaped the city, but
the group assembled anyway, burning effigies in front of his house.[84] At Sand
Point, Ontario, a small hamlet in the Perth-Ottawa region, a labourer named
Fitzpatrick had been caught in some 'disorderly act' during the progress of a
charivari. The following day he was straddled over a rail, 'and rode through the
village to his heart's content'. Obviously not reformed, Fitzpatrick was next dis-
covered in the act of stealing a coat. No rail being handy, an old pump was procured, and the labourer was daubed with black car-grease and carried through
town by his tormentors. The administrators of 'Sand Point law' – among them
'Nigger' Ross, 'Two-Fingered Jack', 'White Bear', 'Nigger' Lew, and 'Corny Toes' –
retired to the nearest tavern.[85] An Ancaster, Upper Canada, lawyer, accused

81   *British Whig*, 27 April 1837; Herity 1931, p. 400. Benjamin was not even Jewish and the attack
       was likely motivated by political animosity. See Swainson 1968, pp. 77–9.
82   An early eighteenth-century reference is Diary of Simeon Perkins 1976, Liverpool, Nova
       Scotia, 9 October, reprinted in Clark 1942, p. 160.
83   *Hamilton Times*, 7 August 1867.
84   *Globe* (Toronto), 9 July 1868.
85   *Perth Courier*, 6 December 1872.

of living adulterously with a woman who had deserted her husband due to ill treatment, a New York City woman thought to be a murderess, and a free-love advocate, cohabiting with his mistress in Utica, New York, in 1860, faced similar forms of rough justice. The process of community control of sexual standards was sufficiently entrenched to draw comment in a fictional account of life in an early twentieth-century Newfoundland fishing village.[86] Prostitutes, too, were likely candidates for the charivari, bearing the brunt of a vicious form of popular justice in the Quebec timberlands and American west well into the twentieth century.[87]

A jealous eye towards property, or resentment of those who attempted to establish themselves as superior elements in a community of equals, also elicited the charivari. The daughter of an innkeeper in the village of Moore, located near Sarnia, Ontario, was charivaried before her marriage, because the local youths thought that she was unworthy of her chosen partner.[88] Edward Littlejohn, aged 74, was charivaried in 1881 by a group of young men who hoped to drive him off of his Highland Creek, Scarborough Township property so that they could secure access to the land.[89] In Hamilton, in 1894, Old Man John Christie was subjected to the jeers and clamour of rough music when he married 'pretty Widow Andrews'. Leading the assembly was Christie's daughter, determined to keep her father from entering his old, Catherine Street home. Devoid of any daughterly sentimentality, the woman claimed the house as her own, vowing that her mother had left it to her, and that if her father entered it he would exit in a coffin.[90] When Jennie and Emily Groombridge attempted to exclude certain youths from a party they were having in Weidman, Ontario, in 1884, their soiree was rudely disrupted by a gang of young men bearing arms, blowing holes in the wall of the house, proclaiming that they would allow 'no private parties' in their district. Later, after the conviction of four members of the charivari party, Mrs Groombridge was jostled on a train by

---

86   Phelan 1976, pp. 17–23; *Sarnia Observer and Lambton Advertiser*, 21 May 1857; *Utica Morning Herald*, 19 March 1860. My thanks to Mary P. Ryan, currently engaged in a fascinating study of women in Utica in the mid-nineteenth century, for this latter reference. Although no ritualistic forms are involved see also, Horwood 1966, a novel constructed around the central passage, 'Even within earshot of the last trump the force of habit remains strong' (p. 90).

87   Note the discussions in Goulet 1961a, translated as Goulet 1961b, esp. pp. 33, 89, 93, 168–9; 171–4, 314–15, 331–2; Hart 1910, pp. 326–7; *Sarnia Observer*, 24 April 1885.

88   *Sarnia Observer*, 24 April 1885.

89   *Globe* (Toronto), 15 December 1881.

90   *Hamilton Spectator*, 14 August 1894.

one of the leaders of the men, resulting in further fines. Social pretensions drew immediate reaction in the timberlands of western Ontario.[91] Finally, the hostility with which a 'ruffian mob' greeted a Saltfleet marriage in 1868, the husband 'revoltingly maltreated', and the bride 'taken out *en dishabille*, and conveyed some distance in the piercing cold on an ox sleigh, meanwhile being taunted on the felicities of her bridal tour', suggests a strong sense of resentment.[92]

Occasionally, the charivari could be directed, not at domestic impropriety, sexual misbehaviour, or social pretension, but at constituted authority itself, a brazen display of popular contempt for law and order. This appeared to be the case in a series of noisy parades in St. John's, Lower Canada, in August 1841. As the local police seemed incapable of quelling the disturbances, they asked for deployment of troops to the town to aid the civil power in suppressing disorder. Upon official investigation the Magistrates were informed that:

> ... the disturbance, in the first instance, had only amounted to the putting in practice an illegal, but long established custom throughout Canada, called a 'chri-vri' – a boyish frolic liable to be treated by the police as a common nuisance or actionable under the more serious charge to extort money ... The indiscreet conduct of the Magistrate who appeared to have worked himself up into a state of nervous excitement led some idle persons of the Village to direct their petty annoyances against him with too good success.

A small patrol eventually suppressed the charivari, but not before constituted authority had exposed itself 'and Her Majesty's troops to the amusements and derision of the mischievous persons who sought to annoy [it]'.[93]

In Lower Canada, during the Patriot agitations leading up to the events of 1837–8, charivaris were organised to show popular disapproval for the repressive measures of the state.[94] The shoe appeared on the other foot, however, in Upper Canada, where the reform agitations drew a crowd to the office of the Belleville *Plain Dealer*, which had recently appeared with an inverted

---

91   *Sarnia Observer*, 31 October 1884; 7 November 1884.

92   *Hamilton Times*, 13 January 1868.

93   Public Archives of Canada, RG8 C 316, Cathcart et al., to the Magistrates, St. John's, Lower Canada, 27 August 1841; 24 August 1841; 25 August 1841, 219–23. On the charivari in the Maritimes in the twentieth century, where it was often known as saluting, see Morrison 1974, pp. 285–97; Buckler 1952; Avis et al. 1967, p. 656.

94   See Massicotte 1926b, pp. 720–22; Séguin 1968, pp. 73–4.

British coat-of-arms on its masthead. Manhandling the staff, upsetting the paper's type, the crowd eventually seized Mr Hart, the manager, and trailed him through the snow and slush.[95] In 1857 St. Thomas, Upper Canada, residents used a 'procession through the town of sleighs, ... with a band playing enlivening airs' to voice their contempt for a judge who had imprisoned a defendant's counsel in the midst of his trial.[96] Perhaps one of the most striking uses of the charivari to show popular disapproval, in the political realm, occurred in the Placentia, Newfoundland election of 1869, where the ritual was employed to express the inhabitants' hostility to Confederation. Ambrose Shea, the island's delegate to the Quebec conferences, paid a visit to Placentia, where he was greeted by locals carrying pots of hot pitch and bags of feathers, angered at 'de shkeemer's' effort to 'sell his country'. In addition, a crowd of 50 'sounded melancholy insult to the candidate through ... large conchs which the fishermen get upon their "bull tow" trains in summer, and another band of about thirty, ... blew reproaches and derision through cow horns'. Insulted and disgusted by the display, Shea could not even land on the shore.[97]

But this use of the charivari must have been rare. When directed to explicitly political purpose, the charivari was most often a mechanism of popular endorsement, waged to celebrate some notable event, or to support a popular candidate. The Callithumpians, for instance, were a group of Baltimore 'rowdies', patterning themselves after the 'Ancient and Honourable Artillery Company' of Boston, who ushered in the fourth of July with grotesque attire and the clamour of tin pans, kettles, bells, and rattles.[98] In New York City the Callathumpians were prominent in the 1830s, when an American storyteller first witnessed them:

> I was in New York, New Years, and all at once I heard the darndest racket you'd ever wish to hear. There was more than ten thousand *fellers* with *whistles, penny trumpets, tin pails, shovels, tongs, spiders, gridirons, warming pans*, and all such kind of implements. Why, they made more noise than a concert of *cats*, or a meeting house full of niggers.[99]

---

95 Belden & Co. 1878, p. iii; Gardner 1923, pp. 84–9; Riddell 1922, p. 139; Guillet 1968, p. 166.

96 *Sarnia Observer and Lambton County Advertiser*, 12 February 1857.

97 Collins 1883, pp. 311–12. My thanks to James Hiller for providing me with this reference.

98 Farmer 1889; Bartlett 1877, p. 93. The Callithumpians were also active in the American west, as late as the 1880s. See Mathews 1951a, p. 248, citing cases from Glendale, Montana (1879) and Reinbeck, Iowa (1881).

99 Hill 1836, p. 9.

In old Ontario the term Kallithumpian Klan, or 'Terribles', often referred to the grotesquely attired processions organised to celebrate the Queen's Birthday or Dominion Day. The term callithumpian band, an American variation of the charivari, seemed appropriately fitted to these parades, always marked by 'the sound of discordant "music"', and outrageous disguise.[100]

> First came the general, bearded like a pard, and equipped in a cocked hat of gigantic dimensions. Then came an individual of 'exceedingly suspicious appearance', as the Police Reports say, looking very much like the Pictoral Representations we have seen of the Prince of Evil; then came a large crowd of grotesque characters, where the irrepressible negro was largely represented; a number of individuals half Irish half nigger in appearance, going through a number of salatory exercises upon a platform, which was placed on wheels for their accommodation ... Among the rest we omitted to mention a fearful looking monster something between a gigantic frog and rhinoceros, that rode among the rest.[101]

Aside from these kinds of festive parades, the charivari was sometimes used to endorse a specific politician, as in 1848 when John Van Buren was tin panned in Albany, New York.[102] Certainly one of the last recorded cases of this use of the charivari occurred in 1910, after Harry Middleton Hyatt's father was elected to the Quincy, Illinois, City Council. A progressive reformer, the elder Hyatt had fought 'the City Hall Gang' for years in his newspaper column. Upon his victory, 'the old time charivari bunch' turned out to pay their respects, pounding on drums stamped R.A.R., initials proclaiming them the 'Ragged Assed Rounders'.[103]

Where the charivari was turned most emphatically to purposes of a political or social nature was when it was used by working men and women to register their discontent. The custom had a long history of this type in the Brit-

100 On the American use of the term and its relationship to the charivari see *New York Times*, 25 May 1904; Schele de Vere 1872, p. 589; Craigie and Hurlbert 1938, p. 393; Clapin 1897a, p. 769; Mathews 1951a, p. 248; *Atlantic Monthly*, March 1865; *Harper's Magazine*, July 1886.

101 *Hamilton Spectator*, 26 May 1868. See also, *Hamilton Spectator*, 3 June 1870; 26 May 1867; 15 May 1868; *Hamilton Evening Journal*, 21 June 1870; *Ottawa Citizen*, 29 June 1868; *Sarnia Observer and Lambton Advertiser*, 9 July 1869.

102 *Albany Weekly*, 5 August 1848, cited in Mathews 1951b, p. 1885. See also, Buchanan 1857. Robert Storey originally brought this source to my attention.

103 Hyatt 1965, pp. 468–9.

ish Isles.[104] When the English government attempted the enclosure of lands and forests in the western districts in the years 1628–31, popular resentment flared in the anonymous personage of Lady Skimmington.[105] In 1696 journeymen hatters battled their masters over the lowering of rates. They chose to make an example of a journeyman who had remained at work, and stirring up the apprentices to seize upon him, tied 'him in a wheelbarrow, and in a tumultuous and riotous manner' drove him 'through all the considerable places in London and Southwark'.[106] The Welsh practice of the *ceffyl pren*, a disorderly procession mocking those who had broken with the popular sentiments of the community, parading the offender, in effigy, on a wooden pole or ladder, assumed a prominent place in the Rebecca Riots of the late 1830s.[107]

In the United States the charivari, or similar forms of ritualistic derision, could also be turned to working-class purpose. As early as 1675 a group of Boston ship carpenters had forcefully ejected another worker from their presence, claiming he had not served his full seven years' apprenticeship. John Roberts and eight other defendants admitted having carried John Langworth, 'upon a pole and by violence', from the north end of Boston to the town dock. A constable eventually rescued the carpenter, and the men were fined five shillings each, payable to the government and the victim. But they justified their action on the grounds that 'hee was an interloper and had never served his time to the trade of a ship carpenter and now came to work in theire yard and they understood such things were ususall in England'.[108] In Gilded-Age Trenton, New Jersey, potters often burned effigies in the midst of strikes, as did Chicago workers in 1894, when confronted with the spectre of imported black 'scabs'.[109] A Pittsburgh court prevented three women from 'tin-horning' strikebreakers in the midst of a coal miners' strike in 1884. After the Civil War, a Fall River cotton manufacturer greeted the arrival of some Lancashire operatives with the boast to his overseer that they now had 'a lot of greenhorns'. But his supervisor was more perceptive, spotting potential trouble with the remark, 'Yes, but you'll find they have brought their horns with them'.[110]

104   See Thompson 1972b, pp. 304–8, for a brief introduction.
105   See Allan 1952–3, pp. 76–85.
106   Webb 1920, p. 28.
107   Williams 1955, pp. 54–6.
108   Morris 1965, p. 147.
109   Gutman 1973a, p. 141; Tuttle 1969, pp. 87–9; Cayton and Mitchell 1939, pp. 228–20; Harris and Spero 1968, p. 265.
110   Gutman 1973b, p. 577. Note the prominence of noise, enriched by the clamour drawn from

In Canada, the use of the charivari in this manner remains obscure. Strikers, of course, often utilised mock processions to denigrate opposing forces. In the aftermath of the riotous clash on the London street railways in 1899, workers paraded with a coffin labelled 'For a Small-man', a reference to T.C. Small-man, resident director of the Street Railway Company. Trailing the casket were a number of moulders and cabinetmakers, dressed in mourning clothes. Un-skilled labourers at the Chaudière Lumber Mills, engaged in an 1891 battle with their employers, mocked the militia, summoned to preserve order, with a charivari in Hull, Quebec, twenty of their number blackening their faces. Dressed as 'Terribles', the men paraded with sticks on their shoulders 'and went through military movements in a laughable manner'. Frederick Philip Grove's enticing fictional account of the process of industrial-capitalist development chronicles workers' utilisation of ritualised effigy burnings, an expression of their discontent with the gross inequalities of the emerging order. When the object of their derision, Sibyl Carter, estranged wife of a mill official, flaunted herself in their presence, a crowd of hands gathered outside of her door: 'In the utter dark hundreds of shapes had sprung up out of nowhere. Their voices, accentuated by whistlings, serenaded the temporary inmates of the house with bawdy songs'. Ms Carter, an archetype of the 'new woman', eventually faced the charivari party personally, as she sought escape from the town. '[A] crowd of women resembling those of a witches' sabbath', confronted her with jeers of, 'Run, if you want to catch that train. Run, you bitch, run'. The fur coat, silk dress, and elaborate petticoat that stood as visible reminders of her class were torn from her body, and 'she ran naked, save for her corset', to the train and the policemen guarding it.[111]

The most explicit use of the charivari in this manner, however, occurred in the midst of a weavers' strike in Hamilton, Ontario, in the spring of 1890.[112] On two occasions the striking weavers, blowing fish-horns, shouting and acting, according to the local newspaper, like a procession of 'Grit schoolboys', attempt-ed to intimidate women who refused to join their cause. Mrs Trope, one of the victims, testified before the local courts,

---

pots and pans, in the strike processions led by Mother Jones in the late nineteenth century. See Parton 1972. See also, the discussion in Perrot 1974, pp. 562–7.

111   Palmer 1976a, p. 122; *Ottawa Evening Journal*, 17 September 1891 (my thanks to Russell Hann for directing me to this reference); Grove 1967, pp. 155–62. The Chaudière conflict is discussed in detail, although this incident is ignored, in McKenna 1972, pp. 186–211. See also, Ferns and Ostry 1976, p. 79.

112   The strike is discussed in Palmer 1977, pp. 190–2.

... that she had worked at the mill for eight years. The mill had been shut down for five weeks because of the weavers' strike. She did not attend any meetings of the strikers and at the request of Manager Snow she went to work last Monday. When she was on her way home that evening she went along Ferrie Street. At the corner of John and Ferrie street she was followed by a crowd of men and women. The defendants Maxwell and Irwin had fish-horns and were blowing them. She estimated the crowd at a couple of hundred, many of them being weavers. Mrs. Trope turned down Catharine Street and was followed by the crowd. She stopped to let the people pass and Mrs. Wright struck her. She tried to strike back and Mr. Carlisle pushed her into the road, and she fell down, injuring her hip.

Another woman, Mrs Anne Hale, was subjected to similar treatment, charging Moses Furlong, Richard Callan, Henry Dean, and Ann Burke with disorderly conduct. The proceedings ended in $5.00 fines for the 'charivaring weavers'.[113]

Perhaps this kind of legal suppression took its toll. The charivari certainly continued into the twentieth century, but only the carcass remained; it became a pleasant sport for villagers and small-town North American youth.[114] Sinclair Lewis described Cyrus N. Bogart, Main Street America's foremost practitioner of the charivari, and one couple's response to him:

Cyrus N. Bogart, son of the righteous widow who lived across the alley, was at this time a boy of fourteen or fifteen. Carol had already seen quite enough of Cy Bogart. On her first evening in Gopher Prairie Cy had appeared at the head of a 'charivari', banging immensely upon a discarded automobile fender. His companions were yelping in imitation of coyotes. Kennicott had felt rather complimented; he had gone out and distributed a dollar. But Cy was a capitalist in charivaris. He returned with an entirely new group, and this time there were three automobile fenders and a carnival rattle. When Kennicott again interrupted his shaving, Cy piped, 'Naw, you got to give us two dollars', and he got it. A week later Cy rigged a tic-tac to a window of the living room and the tattoo out of the darkness frightened Carol into screaming. Since then, in four months, she had beheld Cy hanging a cat, stealing melons, throwing tomatoes at the Kennicott house, and making ski-tracks across the lawn, and had heard him explaining the mysteries of generation, with great audibility

---

113   *Hamilton Spectator*, 4, 5, 9, 10 June 1890.
114   See Wentworth 1944, pp. 550–1.

and dismaying knowledge. He was, in fact, a museum specimen of what a small town, a well-disciplined public school, a tradition of hearty humour, and a pious mother could produce from the material of a courageous and ingenious mind.[115]

With Cyrus N. Bogart at the head of the charivari party, and with the automobile fender present as an instrument of rough music, we are seeing the emasculation of a tradition. It is impossible to date the decline of the ritual; indeed, numerous colleagues have witnessed forms of the charivari in Canadian villages and towns as late as 1963.[116] But the research index cards can tell us something. By the mid-1890s the custom is increasingly rare, and the last nineteenth-century Canadian charivari I have located in the newspapers occurred in 1896, near Brantford, Ontario, on Christmas Eve. Like so many similar affairs, it ended in death, a young farmer succumbing to the shot-gun blast that was meant as a warning.[117] In Adams County, Illinois, the charivari had disappeared in the immediate pre-World War I years.[118] And yet, despite the unmistakable demise of the custom, its function was to be fulfilled by another ritualised method of enforcing community standards and appropriate behaviour. In the years 1888–1905, whitecapping, a distinctively American phenomenon, took up where the charivari had left off.

---

115   Lewis 1961, pp. 103–4.
116   George Rawlyk, A.R.M. Lower, Donald Swainson, and Peter Goheen all had some personal knowledge of the ritual. My grandmother remembered it practised near Hawkesbury, Ontario. A student tells me that it is still common in Listowel, Ontario. John Weaver witnessed a charivari in Madoc, Ontario, north of Belleville in 1963, the groom being tied to a rocking chair and driven around the town in the back of a flat-bed truck. Neil Rosenberg, Director of the Memorial University of Newfoundland Folklore and Language Archive, tells me that the practice is known in Newfoundland, but that the ceremony does not have a standard time. Lawrence Stone, relying on a colleague's recollections, contends that the charivari was still practised in Oregon in the twentieth century. See Stone 1977, p. 504n. As late as 1958 Edmonton passed a law prohibiting charivaris. See *Edmonton Journal*, 30 October 1958.
117   *Windsor Evening Record*, 13, 14 January 1896. Craig Heron has recently informed me that charivaris in St. Catharines, Ontario and Lacrosse, Wisconsin were documented in the *Hamilton Spectator*, 11 August, 9 June 1904. The St. Catharines event, in which the victim drove off his tormentors with the spray from a garden hose, hints at a changed twentieth century context which makes the violent clashes of the previous century a thing of the past. But note, too, the violent charivari at Bishop's Mills (near Brockville) described in *Hamilton Spectator*, 15 November 1906.
118   Hyatt 1965, p. 468.

4

John S. Farmer, author of *Americanisms – Old and New*, described the White Caps as, 'A mysterious organization in Indiana, who take it upon themselves to administer justice to offenders independent of the law. They go out at night disguised, and seizing their victim, gag him and bind him to a tree while they administer a terrible whipping. Who they are is not known, or if known no one dares to make a complaint against them. They are particularly severe', concluded Farmer, 'against wife beaters'.[119] Other popular dictionaries offered similar definitions of the White Caps, stressing their efforts to regulate public morals, and to administer justice to offenders independent of the law.[120] One source concluded that, 'The whole White Cap movement was borrowed from English outlawry'.[121]

These kinds of assessments, often based on the scantiest of evidence, tell us very little. In some cases they may even lead us into further confusion. For the White Caps owed little to any English predecessor, developing, rather, as a peculiarly North American form of rough justice, one strand in the long history of vigilante activity and popular tribunal that stretched from the tar and feather feats of Cornet Joyce, *jun.*, leader of Boston's revolutionary crowd,[122] through the Carolina regulators,[123] and into the nineteenth-century associations emerging in San Francisco and Montana to curb the activities of criminals and highwaymen.[124] Lynch-law, and the more individualised acts of cowhiding, rawhiding, and horsewhipping, sustained themselves as part of the same long tradition of American popular justice.[125] These forms, reaching well into the twen-

---

119   Farmer 1889, p. 557.

120   Clapin 1897b, p. 6910.

121   AA.VV. 1911, p. xx.

122   See Cutler 1969, pp. 46–72; Longley 1933, pp. 112–14; Hersey 1937–42, pp. 429–73; Brown 1973, pp. 103–12; Young 1973; Bridenbaugh 1955, pp. 121–2. Tarring and feathering, of course, did borrow heavily from the English experience, as many of these sources indicate, and continued well into the nineteenth and twentieth centuries. For the use of tarring and feathering in early Upper Canada see Phelan 1976, pp. 17–23. Cases of the use of tar and feathers in late nineteenth-century Milan, Monroe County, Michigan, and St. Thomas, Ontario, are outlined in *Ottawa Citizen*, 11 May 1871; *Globe* (Toronto), 11 November 1886. For popular punishment of sexual offenders in Puritan New England see Calhoun 1917–19, pp. 129–52.

123   See Brown 1963; Adams 1972, pp. 345–52; Whittenburg 1977, pp. 215–38.

124   Williams 1969; Bancroft 1887; Dimsdale 1953. A fascinating account is Royce 1886, pp. 271–376. See also, Turner 1920, p. 212; Hill 1932, pp. 303–6; Barde 1861.

125   The standard treatment is Cutler 1969. See also, *Ottawa Citizen*, 3 February 1872; 3, 4 August

tieth century, were often used against radical dissidents, as the history of the
Industrial Workers of the World and the 1919 Winnipeg General Strike reveal,[126]
or against oppressed groups, but they could also be employed by those significantly removed from the bastions of social and economic power, for their
own purposes. Thus, nineteenth-century workers often threatened, and practised, tarring and feathering, utilising the ritual against strikebreakers; in the
depression decade of the 1930s tarring and gravelling was one popular punishment inflicted on landlords who attempted to exploit hard times, evicting
tenants of long residence, drawing out the last penny of rents that, to the suffering victims, seemed highly extortionate.[127] For the student of North American
legal and social history, then, the popular tribunal is a realm of vital importance.[128]

   Whitecapping drew much of its vigour from this essential continuity in the
North American tradition of vigilante activity. But it buttressed this strength,
tapping other sources of attachment and commitment. It may, in certain parts
of North America, have drawn on the White Cross Movement, a religious
crusade of the 1880s raging against prostitution, drink, and lewdness, for moral
tone and rigour.[129] The regalia of the White Caps, most commonly masks,
hoods, and robes, likely borrowed heavily from the experience of the Ku Klux
Klan, and must have attracted many to the ranks of the movement.[130] More
important, perhaps, were the elaborate passwords, rituals, and secret oaths that
bound members to a fraternity of associates; in many cases the forms were
taken directly from organisations like the Knights of Labor or the Masons.[131]
The Bald Knobbers, a Missouri group remarkably similar to the White Caps,
cemented their membership with the following oath, solemnly repeated by
men gathered in groups of thirteen, their hands clasped together:

   1871; 22 February 1872; 27 May 1871; 1 June 1871; 3 May 1871; *Perth Courier*, 18 December 1868;
   3 April 1868; *Globe* (Toronto), 2 September 1868; *Hastings Chronicle* (Belleville), 23 April
   1862; Caughey 1960, esp. p. 98.

126 Dubofsky 1969; McCormack 1977, p. 161.

127 *Hamilton Spectator*, 3 April 1882; McKenna 1972, p. 204; Broadfoot 1973, pp. 338–48. John L.
   Lewis supporters tarred and feathered an insurgent miner in Indiana in 1930. See Dubofsky
   and Van Tine 1977, p. 165.

128 Note the comment in Watts-Dunton 1902, p. 659. The best brief, accessible introduction
   to whitecapping is Graham and Gurr 1969, pp. 70–1, 806.

129 DeCosta 1887; Hopkins 1883.

130 Crozier 1899, p. 31; Pelham 1891, p. 2; Haswell 1923–4, pp. 30–1; Noble 1973, pp. 71–2;
   AA.VV. 1889, pp. 670–1; AA.VV. 1911, pp. xx; Graham 1967, pp. 3–8.

131 Crozier 1899, pp. 8, 12–13.

Do you in the presence of God and these witnesses, solemnly swear that you will never reveal any of the secrets of this order nor communicate any part of it to any person or persons in the known world, unless you are satisfied by a strict test, or in some legal way, that they are lawfully entitled to receive them, that you will conform and abide by the rules and regulations of this order, and obey all orders of your superior officers, or any brother officer under whose jurisdiction you may be at the time attached; nor will you propose for membership or sanction the admission of anyone whom you have reason to believe is not worthy of being a member, nor will you oppose the admission of anyone solely on a personal matter. You shall report all theft that is made known to you, and not leave any unreported on account of his being blood relation of yours; nor will you willfully report anyone through personal enmity. You shall recognize and answer all signs made by lawful brothers and render them such assistance as they may be in need of, so far as you are able or the interest of your family will permit; nor will you willfully wrong or defraud a brother, or permit it if in your power to prevent it. Should you willfully and knowingly violate this oath in any way, you subject yourself to the jurisdiction of twelve members of this order, even if their decision should be to hang you by the neck until you are dead, dead, dead. So help me God.[132]

There was much, then, beyond the purpose of regulating economic and moral behaviour, that bound nineteenth-century men to such organisations.

Aside from these attractions, and the extent to which all forms of whitecapping utilised extra-legal forms of authority to regulate behaviour, the history of whitecapping was an intensely local affair. Indeed, one early commentator noted the importance of the terrain in southern Indiana in facilitating the growth of the White Caps: the hilly, forested land serving as a haven for those who sought to impose their own brand of rough justice, keeping their distance from the law.[133] Bald knobbing, the Missouri variant of whitecapping, drew its name from the 'balds' and 'knobs' of the mountains in the south western corner of the state, the home of the masked regulators of Taney, Christian, Stone, and Douglas counties.[134] Madeleine Noble has argued that this regional

---

132 *Daily Republican* (Springfield, Missouri), 29 December 1888, cited in Morris 1939, pp. 56–8. See also, Tuck 1910, pp. 7–8.

133 Henry Clay Duncan, 'White Caps in Southern Indiana', paper presented before the Monroe County Historical Society 1900, pp. 4–6, cited in Noble 1973, p. 65.

134 Tuck 1910, pp. 7–8.

context even affected the direction which whitecapping took: in the midwest and border states, the phenomenon was directed against moral improprieties, while the south and far west witnessed the dominance of whitecapping directed against economic ills.[135] She has a point, for this certainly seems to be the case, but the dichotomy is drawn a little too rigidly, and the Canadian material complicates the issue further. But what emerges, in spite of local differences, is the way in which whitecapping was used as an American form of rough music. Was Nettie Pelham's play *The White Caps*, of 1891, depicting the whitecapper with 'a small tin horn at side', symbolic of some essential, but forgotten, link in the chain of Anglo-American popular culture?[136]

Consider Indiana, the home of whitecapping, where the movement had precursors in the mid-1850s and attained prominence in the mid-to-late 1880s, gaining a place in the popular literature of the times though Booth Tarkington's first novel.[137] Of the 80 instances of whitecapping or White Cap warnings, uncovered by Noble in Crawford and Harrison counties in the years 1873–93, most were directed against those who neglected their family, engaged in wife- or child-beating, exhibited a marked laziness, or stepped outside of the boundaries of appropriate sexual behaviour. Sally Tipton was whipped in July 1884 for giving birth to a child out of wedlock. She claimed to have seen Cornelius Grable in the White Cap party, the man she had previously named in a paternity suit. Mrs. Lucinda Lynch and her daughter Mary were whipped for 'lewdness' in June 1887. On 13 December 1888, the *Wooster Republican* warned those citizens who 'continually practice adultery' to desist or suffer a visit from the White Caps. Dan Bowen and Mrs. Conrad Baker were whitecapped in November 1887, their conduct being 'more than respectable people could stand'. When H.T. Taylor and Nancy Hilson were found in bed together in 1892, they were treated to a switching. Aaron Bitner, John Hilderbrand, and Fielding Berry were all whitecapped in October 1887, drawing the ire of the White Caps for their ill treatment of wives, daughters, stepchildren, and neighbouring youths.[138]

---

135 Noble 1973, p. 6.
136 Pelham 1891, p. 2; Thompson 1972b, p. 308.
137 Background on the Indiana White Caps is found in *New York Times*, 12 October 1887; Henry Clay Duncan, 'White Caps in Southern Indiana', paper presented before the Monroe County Historical Society 1900, p. 9, cited in Noble 1973, p. 65; *Journal of the Indiana State Senate*, 38th session of the General Assembly, 4 January 1855, quoted in Noble 1973, p. 65. See Tarkington 1899; Woodress 1967, pp. 111–12, 119–20; Woodress 1955, p. 82; Phillips 1908, p. 68; Nicholson 1915, pp. 43–5, for the impact on literature.
138 Noble 1973, pp. 10, 72–6, 165, and especially the list on pp. 177–90.

This kind of community regulation of sexual behaviour and family standards reminds one of forms of the English charivari, and the uses to which they were put in the nineteenth century.[139] If the White Caps lacked the traditional mock processions and instruments of rough music characteristic of the English charivari, they replaced them with appropriate ritual, depositing a bundle of hickory switches on the doorstep of the offender, containing a threatening letter. Should the warning not be heeded, a whipping followed. And public shame, so crucial in all European forms of the charivari, was also central in the history of whitecapping.[140] From Indiana, whitecapping spread quickly to Ohio, and by 1889 had attained a foothold across North America.[141] Its victims were often men like Adam Berkes, of Sardinia, Brown County, Ohio, dragged from his bed on 17 November 1888, to face the rough justice of thirty to fifty horsemen who whipped him for his immoral conduct.[142] Were it not for the horses, which denote a measure of affluence, the scene might have been taken from a rural corner of early nineteenth-century Bavaria.[143]

Whitecapping moved most forcefully against immoral activities in Sevier County, Tennessee. Originally convened to rid the county of lewd, adulterous persons who had successfully avoided punishment in the courts, the Tennessee White Caps whipped six women, driving them out of Emert's Cove, a place notorious for harbouring prostitutes. They later whitecapped a man who was living with a woman who was not his wife. The influence of the association soon spread, and the order controlled local politics and jury selection, assuring the vigilantes immunity from legal prosecution. This entrenched power drew strong opposition, and another grouping, supposedly allied with local prostitutes, calling itself the Blue Bells, engaged in open warfare with the White Caps. Degenerating into a 'lawless rabble', the White Caps soon succumbed to legal suppression, and by 1896 they were no longer active.[144] A similar fate befell the Missouri Bald Knobbers. Led by Nathaniel N. Kinney, a Union Army Captain in the Civil War, the Bald Knobbers of the Ozark Mountains of Missouri

---

139   Thompson 1972b, pp. 285–312.

140   On the importance of ritual and public shame see Noble 1973, pp. 70–1; Crozier 1899, pp. 10–11.

141   On the emergence of whitecapping in Ohio see John M. Gresham & Company 1889, p. 35; *Ohio State Journal*, 26, 29 November 1888; 1, 3, 5, 10, 12, 21 December 1888.

142   AA.VV. 1889, pp. 670–1.

143   Shorter 1975, p. 226.

144   Crozier 1899, pp. 7, 10–11, 17–19, 20–31. An opposition group, the Black Caps, apparently also formed in Indiana. See AA.VV. 1889, p. 441.

were formed in 1885 to oppose 'lawlessness and disregard of social proprieties'. Targets of Bald Knobber justice were thieves, drunkards, whiskey sellers, gamblers, and prostitutes. Wrongdoers were given a switching, and whiskey barrels and beer kegs were often smashed. But the order soon deteriorated, taken over, according to the standard histories, by 'rougher elements'. As these social types exercised increasing influence, the Bald Knobbers became little more than a vehicle of personal vendetta. Kinney was eventually assassinated, and a local militia formed to rid the region of its masked night-riders. On 10 May 1889, after more than four years of existence, the Bald Knobbers succumbed, and three of their members were executed for murder.[145]

These highly organised forms of whitecapping, prominent in the midwest and border states, were supplemented by activities in the south and far west, where the ritual was directed against economic ills, often complicated by the issue of race.[146] Mississippi's White Caps, active in the years 1902–6, directed their anger against black tenant farmers, scapegoats in the battle between small dirt farmers and the mercantile elite that controlled credit and dictated land policy.[147] In North Texas, too, blacks were frequent targets of White Cap gangs.[148] Perhaps the most interesting case of whitecapping emerged in New Mexico, in the mid-to-late 1880s, led by Juan José Herrera, a migrant from Colorado or Utah. Dominated by small squatters of Mexican-American descent, *Las Gorras Blanca* fought large cattle ranchers and landowners who began fencing the best pasturing and watering lands. As they burned fences, cut barbed wire, and terrorised the cattle men, the New Mexico White Caps proclaimed their platform: 'To Protect the lives and Property of Our People. Lawyers and judges be fair and just as we are or suffer the consequences'.[149]

This kind of structured movement remained rare in Canada, although whitecapping was frequently practised, often in an organised fashion. White Cap gangs battled other youth groups and police in turn-of-the-century Hamilton,

---

145   See Tuck 1910, pp. 7–8; McConkey 1887; Haswell 1923–4, pp. 27–35; Morris 1939; *New York Times*, 28 April 1887; 24, 25 August 1887. On the role of Civil War veterans in the Indiana White Caps see Noble 1973, pp. 68–70.

146   In Indiana White Caps occasionally directed their attacks against blacks that had defied their authority. See AA.VV. 1889, p. 441; Noble 1973, pp. 177–90; Mathews 1951b, p. 1865.

147   Holmes 1969, pp. 165–85; *New York Evening Post*, 21 December 1904.

148   Noble 1973, pp. 156–8; Evans 1960, pp. 320–1. See also Woodward 1966, p. 87; Cutler 1969, p. 154.

149   Graham 1967, pp. 3–8; Larson 1975, pp. 171–85; Schlesinger 1971, pp. 87–143. An early instance of fence-cutting is described in *Pembroke Observer and Upper Ottawa Advertiser*, 30 January 1885.

Ontario.[150] But the most impressive documentation comes from Georgetown, Ontario where the White Caps were led by E. Copeland, 'an American desperado, who carried on the same business in the United States, and defies the officers of the law to arrest him'. Like their counterparts in Indiana, Georgetown's White Caps drew on the nineteenth-century community's distaste for wife-beaters.[151] Their first victim was a Mr Crowe, notorious for his acts of cruelty to his wife. In mid-February 1889 Crowe was sent a warning. On a Saturday evening, in early March, a dozen armed men attacked Crowe's house, seized the wife-beater, stripped him naked, switched him, and rolled him in the snow. Crowe left town shortly after. From this beginning, the White Caps broadened their activity, sending threatening letters and bundles of hickory switches to a number of persons known for their laziness or social indiscretions. But the Georgetown group took particular delight in tormenting the Salvation Army, penning obscene and threatening letters to the Captain of the religious band and his female officers. Their anger seemed to have been directed against the Salvation Army's tendency to 'run on the boys', probably a resentment of the religious body's attacks on irreligious behaviour. Then, too, a letter warned the Captain 'to be careful what he says about the Catholics, as we would White-Cap him quick'. Tensions finally erupted in an attack on the Salvation Army's barracks: shutters were torn off the building, windows broken, and a meeting loudly disrupted. Three leaders – Copeland, Jack Hume, and Fred Board – were eventually incarcerated, the movement broken. But for days the White Caps had defied the police, pelting them with stones, avoiding arrest, stalking the streets with impunity, accosting innocent women. Like the charivari, white-capping could reveal vividly the fragile basis of social order in the nineteenth-century community.[152]

These forms of whitecapping, from the highly structured bands of Indiana, Tennessee, Missouri, and New Mexico, to the less cohesive groupings of the southern states and Georgetown, Ontario, were but the most visible peak of the movement. They have survived historical oblivion because they are entrenched in local folklore, because their presence spanned a number of weeks, at least, if not a number of years. But it is entirely likely that the phenomenon of whitecapping was most prominent as a spontaneous, sporadic effort to enforce

150 *Hamilton Spectator*, 2 May 1900; 19 June 1900.
151 Note the comments on wife-beating in *Hastings Chronicle*, 30 July 1862; *Perth Courier*, 27 October 1871; *Palladium of Labor* (Hamilton), 17 October 1885.
152 This account draws on sketches in the *Globe* (Toronto), 8, 23, 30 March 1889; 1 April 1889. These sources also document the emergence of White Cap bands in other, nearby towns.

standards and traditional rights. Like the charivari it would be used on the spur of the moment, when local outrage exploded at one final transgression.

This was likely the case in Battle Creek, Michigan, December 1888, when White Caps left notices at several saloons, demanding sober and righteous behaviour.[153] An 'outrage' in 1896, perpetrated by the 'Wingham Whitecaps', also conforms to this pattern. On 10 March a crowd of 60, faces blackened, had marched through the streets of the Ontario town, broken into a house, and dragged J.G. Field from his bed. As Field's son was held silent by a loaded revolver, oaths were administered to the whitecappers. Field was then horse-whipped and left in the snow, where he eventually died of exposure. The leading figures in the crowd action were sentenced to two and three years in the penitentiary. Local feeling nonetheless rallied behind the convicted whitecappers, there being 'a certain amount of sympathy with those implicated' in the vigilante activity: '... a partial investigation of Field's past life has been made and many horrible stories of cruelty and immorality are being reported on apparently good authority ... circumstances in connection with the case should have been investigated some years ago ...'.[154]

In Berlin, Ontario, two Germans received three-year prison sentences for their role in whitecapping a Mrs Koehler. On 20 May 1896, Mrs Koehler, who had recently subjected a stepchild to considerable abuse, was aroused from sleep by cries that a neighbour was ill. As she opened her door she was seized by four men. Then followed the ritualistic enactment of rough justice: her bed-clothes were violently torn from her body; she was ridden on a rail for a certain distance; and, finally, 'tarred and feathered'.[155] When the White Cap idea struck New Rochelle, Westchester County, New York, in late 1888, it emerged in the form of two men with white caps and masks warning young men and women not to stay out late 'or they would be made the objects of discipline'.[156]

White Cap actions against wife-beating, probably the most often punished transgression against social propriety, were also likely to be spontaneous affairs. This seems to have been the case in 1901, when whitecappers in Trenton, New Jersey, threatened a wife-beater.[157] In Lambton, Ontario, near London, four or five neighbours whitecapped William Lawson in 1889. On the night of 26 November they rushed up to him, grabbed him, and accused him of mis-

---

153   *Battle Creek Journal*, 12 December 1888, cited in Mathews 1951b, p. 1865.

154   See *Windsor Evening Record*, 26 March 1896; 14 May 1894; 4 April 1896; 7 April 1896.

155   *Napanee Star*, 29 May 1896; *Hamilton Spectator*, 10 June 1896.

156   *New York Times*, 18 December 1888.

157   *Hamilton Spectator*, 11 January 1901.

treating his wife. They then took him to the pump where, according to Lawson, they 'half-drowned' him. When Lawson refused to beg his wife's forgiveness, the men forced a large pole between his legs and danced him about the yard. They concluded this version of rough justice by parading the offender up and down the town's streets.[158] One rare occasion when women took a prominent part in whitecapping occurred near Tavistock, Ontario, in 1889. A man of independent means, Richard Semmler, and his wife had annoyed their neighbours with frequent rows for many months. On 13 March 1889 a crowd gathered outside of the Semmler home, and secured a confession from the wife-beater. The largely female assembly, aided by Jacob Schaeffer (a cousin of Mrs Semmler and reeve of South Easthope) and Conrad Eichenauer (formerly a constable in South Easthope) then removed Mrs Semmler from the house, dragged her belongings and all of the furniture from the building, and loaded it on sleighs. Before proceeding to the wife's father's home, they threatened both Mrs and Mr Semmler with dire punishment if they should ever attempt a reconciliation. Divorce and separation, in the era of whitecapping, could be a popular as well as legal undertaking.[159]

Finally, to conclude, we must note one more way in which whitecapping functioned in nineteenth-century North America. In both its highly structured, organised forms, and in its more spontaneous instances, whitecapping could be turned to a distinctly working-class purpose, as a threatening tactic employed to enrich the process of class struggle. This was most obvious in the case of *Las Gorras Blancas*, the New Mexico squatters who battled the rich for the right of access to traditional grazing lands. The link between this White Cap group and the working-class movement was explicit, the association attempting to establish itself as a *bona fide* assembly of the Knights of Labor. Efforts in this direction failed, however, and the group moved towards another labour-reform body. When Charlie Siringo, the cowboy detective infamous for his activities in the Coeur D'Alene strike of 1894, infiltrated the White Caps in the early 1890s, he found them to be an adjunct of the Populist Party. Nor did the New Mexico White Caps' involvement in working-class activity end there. During the building of the Sante Fe Railroad, whitecappers stopped sectionmen hauling ties, burned the squared timber used in constructing new railway tracks, and proclaimed that the railroad was setting wage rates below an acceptable standard. A blunt note was posted on railroad buildings:

158 *Globe* (Toronto), 8, 9 April 1890.
159 *Globe* (Toronto), 19 March 1889.

All section foremen and operators are advised to leave at once or they will not be able to do so.

Signed,
White Caps[160]

This kind of threat, relying on the fear inspired by the White Cap name, may well have been common in nineteenth-century labour struggles. Herbert Gutman notes what may have been an early use of this form, during a lockout of 1873–4 at the Cambria Iron Works, Pennsylvania. The general manager of the works, Daniel J. Morrell, was sent threatening 'Ku Klux letters' by the miners warning him to 'prepare for death'.[161] In Hamilton, Ontario, during an iron moulders' strike in 1892, a non-union moulder, Clendenning, was prosecuted by a constable for carrying firearms. Clendenning attempted to justify possession of the weapon, arguing that whenever he went out he was followed by union men. He noted that another strikebreaker, a French Canadian named Fleury, had received a threatening letter, headed by a skull and cross-bones, a whip, and a club:

> Scabs, beware! We have formed an association to go and club the life out of scoundrels if you don't cleare this town before Wednesday night. Ye will a lashing such as white man never got before what you are looking for badly.

The communication bore the sinister signature, 'WHITE CAPS'. Clendenning was bound to hold the peace for six months, or forfeit $50. But the strikebreaker's fear was hardly pacified by the judge's restraining order. 'If the union men get their way', he complained, 'I won't be here for six months'.[162]

Whitecapping, then, like the charivari, was a ritualised form of enforcing community standards, appropriate behaviour, and traditional rights. As part of a long tradition of extra-legal authority, it drew on a rich and complex heritage. As a force directed against immoral, illicit, or unjustifiable behaviour, it shared an essential place, along with North American forms of rough music, in the history of popular culture. But what are we to make of these two ritualised manifestations of rough justice?

---

160   See Graham 1967, pp. 3–8; Larson 1975, pp. 171–85; Siringo 1912, pp. 120–2.
161   Gutman 1976b, p. 335.
162   *Hamilton Spectator*, 11 April 1892.

5

Faces blackened or masked, voices drowned out by the clamour of a perpetual din, figures obscured by the shadows of the night or the dim light of the moon, the ubiquitous anonymity imposed on the charivari party or the White Cap gang by the threat of prosecution – this is not a process that lends itself easily to identification. And yet the first interpretive question begging of an answer is a most elementary one. Who practised these two forms of rough justice? In confronting this analytical query some important conclusions can be reached regarding the place and importance of charivaris and whitecapping in nineteenth-century North America.

In the case of the charivari the question as to who participated is a complex one, although a pattern does seem to emerge from the data. The ritual was apparently practised by all social groupings and classes in the first half of the nineteenth century, each stratum subjecting its own members to the discordant sounds of rough music. Hudson Valley skimetons, for instance, were utilised by rich and poor alike.[163] While the weight of the evidence indicates clearly that the plebeian world was the more appropriate setting for the charivari, upper-class figures could also be drawn to the customary wedding night celebrations. The involvement of the well-to-do, perhaps, testifies to the social acceptability of the practice; a complex web of legitimation seemed to encase both the participants and the victims. But this legitimation had its limits. Even in the opening decades of the century, plebeian crowds gathered to charivari their social betters seldom, if ever, received endorsement. The custom was not meant to cross class lines, unless it was the rich who were obviously in the lead.

It was in this context that the ritual thrived in early nineteenth-century North America. Even when opposed, it was recognised as an established institution. A case from the Newcastle District of Upper Canada, in 1814, illustrates the point. David Greene, a labourer, told a Justice of the Peace that on the night of 8 September 1814 he 'was taken out of bed at Elijah Burks Inn in Hamilton about eleven or twelve oclock at night and was carried some times on a rail and some times on horse back'. Beaten during the ride, Greene was eventually 'tied in the woods with his ribs broken and other wise much bruised'. Ten or twelve men had perpetrated this act, although the records do not indicate why. A month later these men faced the majesty of the law, but were held over on £100 bonds until January 1815. The case was once more postponed because the defendants were on militia duty. On 11 April 1815, the issue was finally settled, a number

---

163   *A.N. & Q.*, 13 October 1888.

of men were convicted of riot and assault and fined £5. The fine, although a substantial amount, indicated how gingerly early courts trod on custom, even where violence was involved. Other convictions for riot and assault often drew fines of £10, and in the late nineteenth century similar transgressions were severely dealt with, imprisonment for two or three years being common. But more revealing than the court's handling of the case was the response of the local people. Harry Thompson, a soldier assigned to guard the lakeshore in the midst of wartime hostilities, was awakened by the incident: there was 'a great noise' followed by cries of 'spare my life'. He followed the group for four miles. Obviously armed, he did nothing. Five others witnessed the event, and they too failed to intervene. The *Canadian Freeman* [of York] noted in 1828 that the charivari 'has been carried on latterly in this town to a very great extent without interruption', and then proceeded to chastise the Magistrates for their failure to suppress such gatherings.[164] As late as 1837, a Kingston editor could defend charivaris, arguing that the magisterial authority had no place interfering in such popularly sanctioned assemblies:

> Charivari parties may be unlawful, and much mischief may at times be committed by them, but the custom is an ancient one and cannot easily be suppressed. It is the only way in which the public can shew their distaste of incongrous or ill-assorted marriages. The interference of the magistrates on this occasion we fear is injudicious, since if we know anything of the spirit of the young gentlemen of Kingston, the more they endeavour to preserve the fair lady from annoyance, the more they will subject her to insult.[165]

Kingston, Upper Canada, was perhaps a good locale for a defence of the ritual, for in few cities was the patrician influence so pronounced. Carl Fechter, friend of the Canadian poet Charles Sangster, described three 'notable' charivaris of the 1840s, led by men of property, standing, and respectability. In 1846 some young, but obviously established, Kingstonians had founded the 'physiogno-scosphochraphy society'. Upon the marriage of one of their number, John Metcalfe, proprietor of the Duke of York Inn, on 20 July 1846, they turned out in a charivari parade. Heading the assemblage was a large carriage drawn by six

164   Newscastle District Minutes of Quarter Sessions, Public Archives of Ontario, RG 22, Series 7, Case File Envelope 9; *Canadian Freeman*, 21 August 1828. My thanks to Dale Chisamore for the first reference.

165   *British Whig*, 11 March 1837.

horses, carrying the ubiquitous band. Thirty horsemen followed, splendidly attired. Completing the entourage was the main body, on foot, bearing torches, flags, and banners. After serenading the couple for an hour, the society was entertained with cake and wine, and £5 'was placed in the leader's hands for the purpose of buying bread for the necessitous poor'. Costing $1500, the celebration was hardly the work of the lower orders, but some of the 'boys' still managed to offend local authorities, landing themselves in jail. Two years later, on the night of 11 September 1848, the order again turned out, to charivari Jeremiah Meagher. The first night was spent in consuming a small barrel of whiskey and two kegs of beer. Next evening the display was more awesome, judged the best showing of the 'terribles' in the city's history:

> First of all came three marshals on horseback, with torches, clearing the road. Then followed a band of sixty horsemen, all dressed fantastically, the outer files bearing torches. Next was a carriage drawn by six horses, the effigy of the culprit exalted on high and held up by eight pall bearers dressed becomingly. Two other carriages followed in order, the first bearing 'the minister of war', of the society, and his eminence the secretary Santillanum Femando, together with other officials; and the other bore the public executioner and his satellites, all dressed in red.

The last of these three 'notable events' occurred when Captain R. Gaskin took his second wife. Marking the charivari procession as an extraordinary exhibition was the representation of the *Britain*, the Captain's favourite vessel, mounted on wheels, fully rigged, over twenty feet long, and manned by Neptune and his helpers.[166] Even if the charivari was not exclusively a patrician affair, as it most certainly was in these cases, a plebeian following could be led by an upper-class element, Kingston's Henry Smith, Jr., of the 1830s being a prime example.[167]

Nevertheless, it is difficult to regard these gala Kingston processions, or the patrician leadership of the plebeian charivari party, as anything but aberrations. Patrician acquiescence, and even occasional participation, undoubtedly legitimised the ritual in plebeian eyes, but it was a fragile foundation of support.

---

166   Carl Fechter, 'Charivaring in Kingston: Some Notable Events and Who Participated in Them', *Kingston Daily Whig*, Supplement, Special Issue, December 1886. My thanks to Donald Swainson for pointing me in the direction of this source. On Fechter see Gundy 1964, pp. 11–18, who mistakenly identifies Fechter as Sangster, and *Whig*, 18 January 1887.

167   Smith, the patrician leader of the plebeian crowd, perhaps had a counterpart in Peter Aylen, leader of the Shiners in the Ottawa Valley in the 1830s. See Cross 1973, pp. 1–25.

While European charivaris of the sixteenth and seventeenth centuries may
have been instigated by patrician elements, willingly sanctioned by constituted
authority, recognised as 'according to custom' and 'in some sort necessairie',
there is little indication that North American forms of rough music were ever
given the formal blessings of the socially superior.[168] The threat to public order,
as we have seen, was always too potent:

> The crowd around were of a motley sort,
> All shout, and bustle, – wantonness – vulgarity –,
> Some vicious as the hirelings of a court.
> (Nor speak of these things with mark'd disparity) –
> And some, in frolic, made it a resort,
> For such a crowd in Canada's a rarity,
> Not as in England – where your mob's a measure
> For people to declare their 'Freedom's' pleasure.[169]

As the Montreal magistrates well knew, as early as 1823, charivaris had to be
suppressed, like all 'riots, bruits, troubles ou réunions tumultueses'.[170]

This understanding gradually permeated the consciousness of patrician elements. From the mid-century on, one must look long and hard to find an upper-
class element involved in some variant of rough music. And as patrician forces
departed, the complex legitimation encasing the custom melted into the background: charivaris were more vigorously suppressed; victims began to respond
to the insulting taunts of the crowd with hostility rather than good humour;
and violent confrontations often developed. As the charivari became exclusively an affair of the lower orders, then, the ritual came to be associated with
the barbarism and savagery of the masses. What had once been defended was
to be harshly condemned. It is this process of the proletarianisation of a cultural form that marks the charivari as a ritual of particular concern to those
interested in an autonomous, working-class culture, and explains the fear and
loathing with which bourgeois elements perceived that development.

Contemporary sources commenting directly on the class makeup of the
charivari party are strikingly explicit in rooting the custom in the plebeian
world. Arlo Bates, for instance, argued that the shivaree was common in his
boyhood days in East Machias, Washington County, Maine, 'although it was

---

168   See, especially, Capp 1977, pp. 132–3; Davis 1975, pp. 97–123; Thompson 1974, pp. 382–405.
169   *The Charivari* 1824, p. 37.
170   Robert 1977, p. 197.

confined to the rougher elements of the town'.[171] Another commentator, also
addressing the use of the shivaree in Maine, claimed that it was 'reserved
for the rougher elements'.[172] A Saltfleet, Ontario, the charivari was described
as a 'ruffian mob', while in Tweedsmuir, Upper Canada, the 'charivaree' was
'something to be prevented at all costs, gotten up by the rowdies and toughs and
heavy drinkers with the sole idea of making life a burden for their respectable
neighbours'.[173]

The very location of the charivari often conveys some message as to the composition of the group gathered to subject someone to the clamour of pot, pan,
horn, and musket. When twenty to thirty men and boys of Guelph, Ontario,
assembled at a round house near Sleeman's brewery to charivari a man named
Foster, they likely betrayed their occupational place in the nineteenth-century
city.[174] Striking workers who gathered outside of workplaces to subject 'scabs' to
the screech of the fish-horn left no doubt as to the social standing of the members of their particular 'tin pan bands'. Finally, the Callithumpians of New York,
Baltimore, and the American west, or the Kallithumpian Klan or 'Terribles', of
old Ontario, grotesquely attired, revelling in the rude or the risqué, were most
likely not of the upper crust. The North American rich, at this late date, had
likely repressed such traditional forms of revelry; they kept a tighter lid on their
emotions, expressing their political involvement in more socially acceptable
forms.

With the custom linked explicitly to the lower orders, and as any form of
legitimation, however mild, collapsed, the charivari drew attack from many
quarters. 'Such pastimes as we refer to will not exact any portion of "young
Canada"', argued the *Globe* in 1867. 'Those inclined in such a direction had
better take warning, and turn their attention to more becoming, more respectable and somewhat more civilized amusements'.[175] The terrain of the rough,
unpolished multitude, the shivaree was, in Alice T. Chase's words, 'a survival of
semi-barbaric times; the curious point to note is how nearly this barbarous custom touches our advanced civilization of the present day'.[176] And barbarity, of
course, was not of the genteel, bourgeois world. Neither, apparently, were the
practitioners of rough music, who instead were denigrated, condemned, and

171   *A.N. & Q.*, 20 October 1888.
172   *A.N. & Q.*, 3 November 1888.
173   *Hamilton Spectator*, 13 January 1868; Mr. and Mrs. James Dixon, Marburg, 'The Chivaree',
      in *Tweedsmuir Histories: South Norfolk District*, Public Archives of Ontario, MS-8, Reel 69.
174   *Sarnia Observer and Lambton Advertiser*, 27 December 1867.
175   *Globe* (Toronto), 17 December 1867.
176   *A.N. & Q.*, 29 September 1888.

persistently held up to the ridicule of the defenders of public virtue: '... lunatics assaulting a man's house after dark and making the night hideous with their howls'; '... a collection of wild, ignorant, howling savages, whatever may be the particular colour of their skins or the depth and variety of their gutturals'; '... the abolition of horning would be very cheaply purchased by the sacrifice of a horner in every community in which the disgusting practice survives'.[177]

By the late nineteenth century, the charivari had shed its patrician elements; its very vulgarity, often culminating in violence that posed a serious threat to order and stability, repelled any bourgeois support it had once attracted. And victims who had once accepted the authority of the ritual now challenged its power, precipitating the violent encounters often chronicled in local newspapers. This process occurred over the course of the nineteenth century; the timing varied from location to location, altered by the unique situations prevailing in innumerable North American communities, but the end result was likely to be the same. The large urban centres were apparently the first to succumb, followed by the smaller cities, towns, and villages, trailed by the frontier regions, the outposts of North American civilization. Where bourgeois consciousness matured earliest, the charivari was first attacked; where such consciousness was developing weakly it tended to survive longest. It was in this context that the ritual came to be monopolised by the lower orders. Although certain working-class trades, organised and enamoured of their skilled status, understandably attracted to more respectable, rational forms of protest, may have shied away from the custom as it drew increasing hostility, other members of the plebeian community retained their allegiance: immigrants new to America's shores; agricultural labourers; the urban armies of the unskilled; decimated crafts like shoemaking, weaving, and blacksmithing; small farmers; rural tradesmen; timber workers, socially, culturally, and geographically on the margins of society; miners in isolated communities; and the underclass of town and country. It was men, women, and youths drawn from these groupings that breathed life into the charivari in late nineteenth-century North America, despite a relentless attack, and in the face of concerted opposition.

The practice of whitecapping proves similarly elusive, defying a precise analysis of those involved in the organised and spontaneous manifestations of the movement. Many histories of whitecapping, including Madelein Noble's recent assessment, argue that the White Caps drew upon respectable elements of the community, prominent citizens organising and leading the crusade against

---

177   *Globe* (Toronto), 9 July 1868; 2 May 1877; *A.N. & Q.*, 14 December 1889.

immorality, lewdness, vice, and general social impropriety.[178] And, yet, many
of these same sources attribute the decline of whitecapping, especially its legal
suppression, to the degeneration of the movement, its take-over by rougher
elements, and the increasingly insignificant role of men of position.[179] The
transition from patrician to plebeian control, however, is never satisfactorily
explained. Moreover, there is more than a hint that historians have been blind
to the not inconsequential role that the lower orders played in the beginnings
of the local movements of whitecapping. A.H. Haswell, in an effort to establish
the positive contributions of the Missouri Bald Knobbers, noted that the organisation had been given a bad name by those who 'seized upon [it] ... after it had
done its work, and after its founders had almost to a man withdrawn from it'. A
page later, however, Haswell, who was a manager of lead and zinc mines in eastern Christian county (a centre of Bald Knobbing), claimed that 'every man on
his pay rolls had been active in the movement from first to last'.[180] In Hamilton,
Ontario, the leaders of the White Cap gang were Robert and George Ollman,
the Macklin Street brickmakers.[181] When the Georgetown White Cap leader,
Jack Hume, was arrested, his bail was paid by Bob Ingalls, 'a shop-mate'.[182] In
Mississippi, the White Caps were a plebeian grouping, small dirt farmers resisting the encroachments on their land and livelihood by a mercantile elite.
While they attributed their declining economic fortunes to a familiar scape-
goat, the southern black, their racism did not totally blind them to the realities
of their situation. How else explain the presence of a *black* among the White
Cap gang attempting to drive an African American sharecropper off his land
in 1903?[183] And where White Cap letters were directed against working-class
enemies, the class essence of the situation allows no misinterpretation. Finally,
the working-class foundation of New Mexico whitecapping, where squatters
battled the Western counterparts of 'the interests', needs no further elaboration. Whitecapping, like the charivari, was never a process totally dominated
by men of property and standing. Both forms of enforcing community standards and appropriate behaviour were the terrain of the *menu peuple*.

178   Noble 1973, pp. 5, 67–8, 83–6; *New York Times*, 28 April 1887.
179   Haswell 1923–4, p. 27; Tuck 1910, pp. 8–9. Noble argues that the White Caps of Indiana
      declined because of an accommodation to the transformation of society and economy
      that occurred in the 1890s, marking a shift away from the resistance characteristic of the
      1880s. The argument is far from persuasive. See Noble 1973, p. 148.
180   Haswell 1923–4, pp. 27–8.
181   *Hamilton Spectator*, 19 June 1900; City of Hamilton 1902.
182   *Globe* (Toronto), 1 April 1889.
183   Holmes 1969, esp. p. 171.

If, in fact, working people did figure centrally and persistently in the charivaris and white cap raids of the nineteenth century, does an historical examination of these ritualised forms of popular activity tell us anything about working-class culture, a process that has received such scant attention in North American scholarly circles?[184] To be sure, the question is not generally posed in this manner, either by historians who have studied the charivari, or by social scientists commenting on such traditional, ritualistic behaviour. Natalie Zemon Davis, for instance, considers charivaris in early modern France in the context of a general discussion of youth groups and the social nature of play and mock ceremony. A concern with modernisation dominates Edward Shorter's treatment of rough music. And Claude Lévi-Strauss, whose brief comments on the charivari in *The Raw and the Cooked* impose a structuralist straightjacket on the custom, linking it to the way in which primitive peoples greet an eclipse of the moon, seems unduly fixated on the form of the charivari, paying scant attention to questions of its meaning, in social or cultural terms.[185] But these interpretations are not overly helpful in the context of nineteenth-century North America, where charivaris and youth groups seem only peripherally related (and largely unstudied), where nation states appeared to be born modern, and where any effort to link popular culture to the activities of primitive peoples must be highly strained. We have, in short, few benchmarks to guide us in our analysis of charivaris and whitecapping. Some general observations, however, can be made.

The historical study of whitecapping and charivaris in nineteenth-century North America reaffirms Raymond Williams's forceful depiction of culture as a complex blend of residual and emergent strains. In this analysis, working-class culture is seen as a coalescence of old and new forces, strands in the culture hearkening back to a world seemingly lost, other forms arising that recognise the essential changes that have altered the context of daily life. It is this fundamental unity of residual and emergent, past and present, that delineates much of the history of charivaris and whitecapping in North America. Charivaris, and their persistent use throughout the nineteenth century, thus lend force to an interpretation of culture stressing continuity in the midst of change. None of our history, it appears, is ever quite dead.[186] The use of the

---

184   Here, the work of Herbert G. Gutman, conveniently assembled in *Work, Culture, and Society in Industrializing America* (Gutman 1976b), stands out as a forceful exception. Note, too, the strikingly innovative discussion in Sider 1976, pp. 102–25.

185   Davis 1975, pp. 97–123; Shorter 1975, pp. 218–27; Lévi-Strauss 1969, pp. 288–9, 338.

186   See Williams 1973, esp. pp. 9–12; Thompson 1972a, pp. 402–4.

ritual against strikebreakers, for instance, illustrates well the way in which a residual cultural form could be adapted to new purpose, bridging the gap between past and present. Whitecapping, too, drew on cultural continuities: the long tradition of violent enforcement of morality characteristic of American vigilante groups; the southern heritage of resistance to black emancipation. ('The people of the "White Cap" belt [of Indiana]', claimed the *Chicago Record*, 'came originally from the South').[187] But it also could be turned to new purpose, continuing in the footsteps of the charivari, moving forcefully against social impropriety, or adapting to the economic needs of the working-class community.

For those who would probe the process of working-class culture this adaptive capacity of the class virtually leaps out at one from the pages of histories of numerous communities.[188] An understanding of this process of cultural formation, in which residual and emergent *together* loom large, does much to negate efforts to 'disentangle' the strands of working-class culture, neatly categorising the progressive and retrogressive fibres of the cloth of working-class life.[189] In fact, working-class culture was cut from a whole cloth, a finely-textured quilt of the traditional and the modern, residual and emergent, progressive and reactionary. Isolating fragments, detaching them from their intimate relationship with other segments of the fabric, only serves analytically to dissect the process: one is left, not with a culture, but with discreet, disembowelled sections of what once was a living unity.[190]

It is this very unity that moves the historian to confront the complexity of the working-class experience, for within this coherence one glimpses moments of brutality and banality, undercurrents of savagery and racism, as well as instances of principled stands against the increasing impersonality of an age caught in the midst of transformation.[191] If the picture is not always pretty, it is, nevertheless, enlightening. These awkward collisions of evidence, however, pose interpretive problems of considerable dimension.

---

187   *Chicago Record*, 13 April 1894, cited in Mathews 1951b, p. 1865.

188   I have attempted a larger discussion of this phenomenon in Palmer 1977. For other important statements see Neary 1973, pp. 105–36; Walkowitz 1978; Kealey 1976b, pp. 13–34.

189   Despite its attractions, a recent work exemplifies the pitfalls of this kind of approach. See Dawley and Faler 1976, pp. 466–80.

190   Here one is reminded of Thompson's statements on class as historical process. See, in particular, Thompson 1963, pp. 9–11; 1965, pp. 311–62; E.P. Thompson, 'A Nice Place to Visit', *New York Review of Books*, 6 February 1975.

191   See, for an insightful comment, Chevalier 1973, pp. 416–17.

One could, of course, condemn the ritualistic enforcement of community standards, drawing attention to the savagery with which the plebeian constituency guarded its conception of right and wrong. The 1817 *Quebec Gazette* did just that, making its contribution to the stream of abuse heaped on the charivari:

> The days of barbarism seem to be returning to us. Can it be creditable to a country for its youth and others, to put it in the power of historians and travellers to say of it, that the peace of society is disturbed night after night by the most dissonant noises suitable only to barbarians? Can it be reputable to our youth and others, to have it said of them, that instead of cultivating their minds, and seeking rational amusements they delight only in uncouth discordance? ... The *Charivari* has been wisely long suspended here; it were better no more heard of, being a custom more honoured in the breach than in the observance.[192]

Over 150 years later, Margaret Atwood, pouring over Susanna Moodie's journals, revealed her revulsion at the proceedings of a charivari party with the exclamation, 'Stop this. Become human'.[193]

Another approach would be to denigrate the importance of ritualised cultural forms, like the charivari and whitecapping, contending that they represented little more than frolic diversions, aimed at easing the pain of life in the nineteenth-century world. And, indeed, the charivari was often just that, as one early authority testified:

> 'Tis pleasant to get rid of some curs'd care
> Of aching malady or blustering people,
> Life hath enough of ill for each man's share,
> And fortune's ladder gainless as a steeple
> With no ascent to 't but a broken stair;
> Few are there born, who do not oftener reap ill,
> Than gather good, for life we know at best
> Is care – and we, its riddle and its jest.[194]

Or, in the rendition of one French-Canadian folksong:

---

192   *Quebec Gazette*, 9 October 1817.
193   Atwood 1970, p. 37.
194   *The Charivari* 1824, p. 7.

Si cette petite fete
    Vous fait plaisir (bis)
Vous êtes, messieurs, les maitres
    D'y revenir (bis)
Et je permets qu' on fasse ici
    Charivari! Charivari! Charivari!
Sans un peu de jalousie
    L'Amour s'endort (bis)
Un peu de cette folie
    Le rend plus fort (bis)
Bacchus et l'amour font ici
    Charivari! Charivari! Charivari![195]

But mere condemnation or deprecation, obviously, misses the point. And that point is the response of constituted authority, which seldom failed to regard charivaris and whitecapping in their proper light, as threats to social order and stability:

> Such assemblies of people, are calculated to cover the most nefarious designs – The many, probably from ignorance, lend their aid, but the few may have in view the indulgence of private malice, revenge, and the darkest passions of the human heart. The very circumstances of being capable of perversion to the most dangerous purposes, ought to enhance every good subject with a determination, not merely to give a negative reprobation to the practice, but to furnish positive aid in suppression thereof, hereafter, for ever.[196]

The author of this attack, 'A Friend to Tranquility and Good Order', saw the charivari for what it was, the threatening order of custom counterposed to the rule of law. The sight, to some eyes, was not a pleasant one.

The rule of law, as a number of recent works have suggested, is a complex and subtle force. Much more than a mere expression of class interest, the law fulfils its hegemonic function, perpetuating class rule, precisely because it addresses vital concerns of the masses at the same time that it serves as the indispensable foundation and guarantor of social stability. The rule of law, in short, secures a society resting upon harmonious social relations, a respectable

---

195   Massicotte 1926b, p. 725.
196   *Montreal Gazette*, 14 June 1823.

working population and, by implication, the natural authority of men of wealth and standing, while at the same time displaying an independence from crass manipulation, convincing the lower orders that the potential for justice can be achieved under its majesty.[197]

But in nineteenth-century North America there were obscure corners of everyday life where the rule of law could or would not intervene, where, by the law's very concerns – in which property always figured centrally – it had little place.[198] Domestic discord, appropriate marital unions, and immoral behaviour were hardly the concern of the law, except in exaggerated cases of gross cruelty or sexual 'deviance', as in infanticide, incest, or rape. But these extremes suggest the point. The mundane wife-beater, or the old widower coming to life in the midst of his apparently unnatural marriage, remained outside the rule of law. So, too, was the employer who refused the just demands of 'manly' workers, or the strikebreaker imported to break the resistance of working-class forces. Yet, in the plebeian world, such behaviour seemed a serious transgression, a violation of time-honoured conceptions of appropriate behaviour.

In the absence of any recourse to law, the lower orders turned instinctively to custom, posing the discipline of the community against the perceived deficiencies of legal authority. As a force within the plebeian world, custom was obeyed because it was 'intimately intertwined with a vast living network of interrelations, arranged in a meticulous manner'.[199] It posed an order, an authority, that was, in contradiction to the law, spontaneous, traditional, personal, commonly known, corporate, and relatively unchanging.[200] William Graham Sumner, an essentially nineteenth-century being, knew this process well. 'The masses', he wrote, 'are the real bearers of the mores of the society. They carry tradition. The folkways are their ways'. Sumner also perceptively rooted the order of custom in specific realms: 'The mores cover the great field of common life where there are no laws or police regulations. They cover an immense and undefined domain, and they break the way in new domains, not yet controlled at all'. And within this context, the authority of custom assumed a particular strength when buttressed by ritual, '... acts which are ... repeated mechanically ... connected with words, gestures, symbols, ... music, verse, or other rhythmical points'.[201] This, of course, is what much of the history of charivaris and whitecapping is all about.

---

197   See the stimulating discussions in Thompson 1975, pp. 258–69; Hay 1975, pp. 17–64. Another perspective is outlined in Genovese 1974, pp. 25–48.

198   In the words of Jeremy Bentham: 'Property and law are born together and die together'.

199   Radin 1953, p. 233.

200   The best brief treatment of this subject, to my mind, is Diamond 1974, pp. 255–80.

201   Sumner 1906, pp. 45–7, 56–61.

But Sumner did more than simply catalogue the attributes of the folk-ways. He recoiled at their threatening potential. For when the masses turned to custom, they did so as they saw fit, 'being controlled by their notions and tastes previously acquired'. They may accept standards of character and action from the classes, warned Sumner, 'but whatever they take up they assimilate and make it a part of their own mores which they then transmit by tradition, defend in its integrity, and refuse to discard again'.[202]

Defending and enforcing popular standards and appropriate behaviour, then, posed the order of custom against the rule of law.[203] In the process an autonomous culture reared its head, an implicit challenge to the hegemony of the bourgeoisie. Built on the residual, it could move toward an emergent purpose. Charivari and White Cap gangs thus posed a threat to constituted authority. 'Such assemblies of people', our friend to tranquillity and good order maintained, 'are calculated to cover the most nefarious designs'. 'The mob is a demon, fierce and ungovernable', declared the general orders for the guidance of Canadian troops sent to aid the civil power.[204] Condemning one particularly violent charivari, a magistrate warned:

> ... it is scarcely to be credited that such a tumultuous concourse of persons would have dared to assemble at different days and times, and to proceed to such violence, in the heart of a populous town, where order and authority existed – it would lend to a belief that we had no laws for enforcing order and tranquility, or for protecting life and property, or if such laws did exist that the execution of them was an object of listless indifference.[205]

The threat of custom to the rule of law could not have been more eloquently stated.

William Graham Sumner, a cantankerous sociologist with a deeply-entrenched distrust of history, closed his discussion of folkways, first published in 1906, on an odd note:

---

202 Sumner 1906, pp. 46–7.
203 For particular reference to this process and the English charivari see Thompson 1972b, p. 310.
204 *Extracts From General Orders for the Guidance of Troops in Affording Aid to the Civil Power* 1868, n.p.
205 *Montreal Gazette*, 6 September 1832.

> The modern historians turn with some disdain away from the wars, in-
> trigues, and royal marriages which the old-fashioned historians con-
> sidered their chief interest, and many of them have undertaken to write
> the history of the 'people'. Evidently they have perceived that what is
> wanted is a history of the mores. If they can get that they can extract from
> history what is the most universal and permanent in its interest.[206]

But Sumner's assessment was overly optimistic. Historians have yet to write
their history of 'the mores', have yet to even appreciate the significance of
the subject. If they had, we would know more about obscure practices like
charivaris and whitecapping; we would be more informed about general processes of ritual and rebellion; we would have a more finely-developed sense of
the relationship between custom and law.[207] Given this, historians could perhaps begin to explore the process by which the cultures of the working-class
and plebeian worlds clashed with constituted authority: in border, seaside, and
river-towns, where smuggling was a way of life; in the settlement of petty scores,
where the rule of law was forsaken for the more immediate satisfaction of barn
burning, fence destruction, or animal maiming; in urban crowds, purposively
directing their anger against perceived threats and recalcitrant employers; in
the backwoods and obscure valleys in the shadows of North American civilization, where law always played second fiddle to brute force.

Environments like these spawned men like Peter Aylen, leader of the Irish
raftsmen in the Ottawa Valley in the 1830s. Admittedly an atypical element,
closer to the status of the privileged than he was to the harsh realities of
working-class life, Aylen probably stood for much that the lower orders could
identify with. 'The laws', a contemporary once said of Aylen, 'are like cobwebs to
him'.[208] They were of the same insubstantial material to charivaris and whitecapping. And in knowing more about these two forms of enforcing popular
standards our understanding of nineteenth-century society and culture, order
and disorder, cannot help but be richer and fuller.

---

206 Sumner 1906, p. 638.

207 Note Dechêne 1971, pp. 143–83, for a discussion of the mediating influence of custom on
contractual, or legal, relations. An extreme statement, but one worthy of attention, is
Foucault 1975, pp. 192–3, 198.

208 Cross 1971, p. 182.

Popular Radicalism and the Theatrics of Rebellion: The Hybrid Discourse of Dissent in Upper Canada in the 1830s*

I could repeat a thousand stories,
  About the Radicals and Tories,
The Banks, the Merchants and Mechanicks,
  The Church Reserves and Ceaseless Panicks
That all of you must know as well,
  Or better far, than I can tell.
But what's the use of telling o'er
  A string of news you've heard before.[1]

∴

The current historiography of Upper Canada is curiously unconcerned with what was once a major preoccupation: the importance of the Rebellion of 1837–8 and the nature of the radicalism associated with the politics of dissent that emerged in the 1830s and culminated in a rare, if ineffective, uprising.[2] Whereas older writings exhibited obvious partisanship, there is no denying that the scholarship on Upper Canada in the 1830s, prior to the 1990s, was insistent on staking out interpretive ground, focusing on the meaning and significance of the radical edge of the age.[3] Undoubtedly, the liberal,[4] conserva-

---

* 'Popular Radicalism and the Theatrics of Rebellion: The Hybrid Discourse of Dissent in Upper Canada', in *Transatlantic Subjects: Ideas, Institutions, and Social Experiences in Post-Revolutionary British North America*, edited by Nancy Christie (Kingston and Montreal: McGill-Queen's University Press, 2008), 403–39.

1 'New Year's Address', *St. Catharines Journal*, 3 January 1839.
2 Consider, for instance, the unfortunately neglected Guillet 1938, and the still extremely useful Clark 1959, pp. 255–508.
3 Landon 1974, pp. 154–70.
4 Categorisations of liberal historiography are by necessity rather elastic. Especially significant are contrasting assessments of the leading figure of the Upper Canadian Rebellion, William

tive,[5] or Marxist[6] writings on the 1830s have not aged particularly well. There were serious shortcomings within all schools of thought. But what is striking in reading the major relevant studies of the last decade is how far they are outside of older readings of Upper Canada in the 1830s. Like much historical writing in our time, there is a tendency to sidestep engagement with conventional preoccupations. In the resulting displacement, claims made on behalf of the sophistications of newer approaches – be they theoretical or analytic – are often oddly complacent in their lack of attention to past scholarship, perhaps even to aspects of the past itself that bear on their concerns and arguments.[7]

My approach in this chapter is to resituate the politics of Upper Canadian dissent in the 1830s at a particular interface. The popular radicalism of the 1830s[8] was a hybrid of transplanted practices, thoughts, assumptions, and sensibilities. In the material circumstances of a new and emerging society, these translated into an ensemble of arguments about rights that were simultaneously British and American. A hybrid discourse of dissent was rooted in readings of Enlightenment thought and Age of Revolution ideology that were not so much articulated in political tracts as they were performed in a theatrics of discontent. This both animated the highly politicised atmosphere of everyday life and gave new meanings to elections, tavern debates, and even domestic relations. I draw not so much on concerns with constitutional issues, the diversity

---

Lyon Mackenzie. Nevertheless, a long line of liberal commentary on the rebellion draws its interpretive meaning from considerations of the importance of the event, the justification of grievance, and the role of the uprising in consolidating a new, and improved, social order. I consider the following to be representative: Lindsey 1862; Dent 1885, and 1881; Landon 1960, and 1931, pp. 83–98; Wait 1976.

5   The conservatism of older works such as Read 1896 and Lizars and Lizars 1897 continued into the late twentieth century with Frederick H. Armstrong's defence of oligarchy. See Scadding 1966 (ed. Armstrong), especially p. xx for a conservative statement defending oligarchy; Armstrong 1989, pp. 513–36; and for a distilled statement of animosity to William Lyon Mackenzie, Armstrong 1971, pp. 21–35. While the more middle-of-the-road scholarship tended to blur lines of differentiation between liberal and conservative accounts, the historiographic trend was toward a more subtle conservatism. See Dunham 1927; Craig 1963; Read 1982; Read and Stagg 1985. This latter group of writings might well be appreciated as crossover scholarship bridging interpretation and sustaining a liberal/conservative historiography.

6   See, as rare examples, Ryerson 1937, and 1968; Fairley 1946, and 1960; Vance 1965, pp. 29–42; Bonthius 2003, pp. 9–44.

7   Consider, for instance, how little informed by an older body of writing on the rebellion are some current texts: Greer and Radforth 1992; Morgan 1996; McNairn 2000.

8   For one recent account which takes this popular politics of radicalism seriously and scrutinises it usefully through an examination of petitions and other mobilisations, see Wilton 2000.

of constituencies of reform and localised elite governance, or the substantive scrutiny of key tenants of various ideologies, be they liberal or conservative. Rather, I try to place the meanings of popular radicalism more on the surface of everyday life in the period, as they were lived, articulated in language that was often extreme, and put on display through symbols that could be expected to garner sympathy and support in particular quarters. The meaning of all of this was not unambiguously settled, and that has confused many interpretive forays into this period. A fresh look at the rituals, rhetoric, and refusals of the era, especially in the representational realm of political theatre, will perhaps take us back to some old scholarly concerns at the same time as it follows more contemporary routes of analysis.[9] If I return to what an older scholarship often accented, the *oppositions* that ran through the politics of the period, I also acknowledge certain shared, and influential, reciprocities. These can be explored usefully through the lens of representation that figures so forcefully within a range of contemporary academic preoccupations.

Joseph Gould, the Black Rod, and Compact Rule

Let me begin with Joseph Gould, whose father had migrated from the United States to take up farming in the Uxbridge area, approximately 70 kilometres from present day Toronto, then known as York. Gould joined the ranks of political dissidents in the late 1820s and 1830s. He was a moderate reformer driven to insurrection in 1837 by a combination of Tory obstinacy, Sir Francis Bond Head's patronising paternalism, the cajoling of Reform leader and eventual advocate of Rebellion, William Lyon Mackenzie, and charges of cowardice from the ranks of those pushing for armed resistance.

Gould's life was summarised in 1887 by W.H. Higgins. Like countless accounts of the settlement of Upper Canada, Higgins's assessment of Gould stressed how this young colonial subject fought for the rough egalitarianism of the popular classes. This penchant for politics seemed intrinsic to life one step removed from the agricultural frontier. When Gould came to York in 1830 he was bewildered by the inhabitants, who were 'all politicians', spending their

---

9 Consider, for instance the direction of Epstein 1994; Thompson 1994, pp. 94–140; and Brewer 1976, which differ from the accent on ideology evident in studies of Upper Canada such as Errington 1987; Mills 1988. That the historiography of the Upper Canadian Rebellion, *the* central event in the 1830s, needs an injection of ideas and creative thinking is evident in the presentation in Greer 1995, pp. 1–18.

time 'talking politics and walking the streets'. The backwoods farmer was at first taken aback by the contentiousness of this agitated political scene: 'excitement ran so high that quarrels between neighbours were of frequent occurrence'. Knowing 'little or nothing of the constitution of the country', Gould read the newspapers and soon gravitated to Mackenzie and the Reformers. His prose was peppered with the discourse of dissent: he railed against 'despotic tyranny' and a 'grasping oligarchy', protesting 'the open corruption and bribery everywhere prevailing'. He lost political patience with the coterie of governors, dubbed by Mackenzie 'the Family Compact'. In Gould's words this ruling elite was composed of 'superannuated old military officers, or tenth-rate Poor Law Commissioners who knew nothing about the principles of popular government, and had no sympathy with the people over whom they were sent to rule'. Against the Lieutenant-Governor, Francis Bond Head, he nurtured particular resentment, as much directed against the haughty demeanour of the British figurehead as against his policies.[10]

Indeed, Gould's sense of political grievance was nothing if not intensified by the ritualised articulation of political inequality visible in the structured pomp and ceremony of what he came to see as the imagery of despotism:

> First to be seen was the Lieutenant Governor, a mere figurehead, surrounded by six placemen, called Executive Councilors, who held the Governor as a mere puppet in their hands to do their will. These were appointed by the Crown during pleasure, and were not responsible to any other body. They received large pay and salaries for their services, and had sinecures that made them quite independent of the popular will. Their duty was to advise the Governor on all matters pertaining to the Government, and to recommend candidates to office. Below them sat an assembly – mostly of old men – some lame, some halt, some nearly blind, some quite deaf. These men had a chairman, or speaker, to preside over them – mounted on a high chair, called a throne, with a table in front of him. A clerk sat at the high table to record the proceedings, and before him on the table was laid the mace, representing a brass crown, and at the other end of the room stood a little black-haired, black-eyed man in black coat and black knee-britches, and black silk stockings and pumps. The duty of the latter was to carry the brass crown before the speaker when he left the chair, and to summon the chamber below when required by the Governor. On these latter occasions he carried a little black rod in his hand to rap at the door

---

10   Higgins 1887, especially pp. 54–9, 100–3.

of the Chamber and this was called the 'Black Rod'. The men composing this chamber were called the Legislative Council. They were appointed by the Crown for life and were not responsible to any man or set of men for anything they should do ... They had the power of supervision over all legislation.[11]

Gould was eventually pressured to take up arms against this intolerable state of political affairs and for his troubles was arrested and, ironically, incarcerated in the Legislative Council chambers. After a month's confinement, he was paraded before five figures of august Family Compact authority, Messrs Jamieson, Jones, Gurnett, Sullivan, and Robinson. When asked what he did for a living, Gould answered that he had a saw mill and a small farm. 'What more do you want that you should rebel?' thundered an obviously irate Jamieson. 'I want my political rights', responded Gould with coolness. 'Why you have got them now – quite enough for so young a man as you', replied the patriarchal Jamieson. Gould shot back with a list of grievances, drawn from the well of Reform resentment. Having had enough of this, Jamieson turned on his heels and huffed: 'You are a dangerous fellow and you ought to be hung for believing and spreading your damned treason'.[12]

John Prince and the Reciprocities of Terror: The Subterranean Terrain of Popular Radicalism

Gould did not go to the gallows. He even managed to narrowly escape transportation to Van Dieman's Land.[13] That the Black Rod did not come down on him with its full force is part of the overlapping social constructions of a liberal/conservative historiography that emphasises the lenience of the Upper Canadian authorities in the suppression of the rebellion (which is seen, on the one hand, as the folly of a 'lunatic fringe' or, on the other, as 'reasonably' handled by constituted authority).[14] But what Jamieson wanted was occasionally enacted by his counterparts in the suppression of the uprising.

John Prince, for instance, ordered the summary execution of five prisoners captured in the December 1837 Patriot invasion of Windsor. Prince's extra-legal executions were done in ways that were consciously meant to enhance the

---

11   Higgins 1887, pp. 55–6.
12   Higgins 1887, p. 109.
13   Wait 1843.
14   Jackman 1958, p. 90.

impact of what Fred Landon, one of the most sensitive of the early radical-liberal historians of the Upper Canadian rebellion, once referred to as a 'veritable reign of terror'.[15] Carried out by Prince's quarter master, Charles Anderson, the killings were staged with bloodthirsty glee, at widely separated points, for the benefit of the greatest number of onlookers. This was done in the face of officer demands to deal with the prisoners according to the rule of law, and the refusal of a First Nations man involved in the capture of the Patriots to participate in the butchery. 'No we are Christians', said the Native, 'we will not murder them – we will deliver them unto our officers to be treated as they think proper'. When Prince was entreated 'not to let a white man murder what an Indian has spared', this humanitarian, if racist, plea, fell on deaf ears. 'Damn the rascal, shoot him', was Prince's curt condemnation.[16]

Tory judges had long counselled the use of 'terrible examples' to prove that 'justice does array herself in terrors when it is deemed necessary'.[17] The period 1837–9 was one such moment when justice could be seen to be dripping in blood. 'Where there was one patriot last fall there are now ten', wrote a correspondent to *Mackenzie's Gazette* in August 1838, explaining this as a 'consequence of the abominable conduct of the government agents and volunteers, who have plundered, pillaged, ravished, and committed all sorts of excesses throughout the winter'.[18] The climate was conditioned by a flood of correspondence from across the colony, warning of dire consequences if the authorities did not act to suppress the drift towards revolt. John Black, a recently arrived British emigrant, wrote in a panic to Francis Bond Head from Chippewa in November 1838, pleading to be granted a hearing with the Queen and demanding that his safety be guaranteed, for 'the enemy is powerful'. Begging Bond Head to 'send a speedy dispatch to England', Black warned, 'Let the Empire awake. Let it not run itself for a few Treacherous speculators ... all is Speculation, Craft, Policy, Perjury, and Trachery. I cannot trust even you. All being bribery'. Black's admonitions to trust the information that he could provide perhaps faltered on his request to be paid £20 for information relating to rebellious doings in his locale, but other reports were no less fearful. From Brockville came the claim that the loyal supporters of the Crown were 'surrounded by a great number of disaffected persons who would at once join the standard of rebellion were it raised in the Province'. An Ingersoll correspondent nar-

---

15   Landon 1941, p. 166.
16   Douglas 1980, pp. xxvi–xxvii, 28–31.
17   Beattie 1977.
18   Quoted in Clark 1959, p. 404.

rowed his complaint to identify only a singular threat: 'A Yankee rascal of the name of N.P. Hoague ... has threatened that if any rising took place that the whole of Ingersoll's buildings and property should be burned; this fellow is a wagon-maker – has no stake in the country, but is a perfect firebrand'. Oaths of allegiance were refused in Belleville, where dangerous societies were forming, harbouring rebellious sympathies. In Delaware, Scots farmers were rumoured to have been lured towards the Rebel camp by claims that the Government was about to introduce tithes to pay for the Church of England. The era was often depicted as one of 'party spleen and commotions', as a Perth writer bluntly reported: a 'Revolutionary party are organising themselves to disturb the peace of this province'.[19] Jeremiah Smith and Joseph Walker wrote to Sir Francis Bond Head on the goings on in the nursery of radicalism, Lloydtown, immediately after the suppression of the Mackenzie uprising: a marauding band of 20 rebels brutalised loyalists in the street and, in defiance of all deference, pulled off 'their hats twirling them in the air and hurraing for Mackenzie stating that they were to be at the same nefarious business again'. Begging His Excellency 'to devise a plan in this sad emergency to better our wretched and defenceless condition', Smith and Walker pleaded for the suppression of 'these wretched Men ... prowling about with feelings malignant and revengeful'.[20]

For all the claims of a liberal/conservative historiography that the authorities reacted with lenience and moderation to the movement of organised sedition, there was a counter-revolutionary terror in play. One exile from Lockport, New York, claimed that thousands had fled Upper Canada in the aftermath of the Rebellion, 'driven from their farms, their shops, their professions, their families, and their homes by the lawless violence of an excited and unprincipled soldiery'.[21] Even allowing for exaggeration, it is apparent that a terror was unleashed in the late 1830s and very early 1840s that was the last gasp of an old order forced to respond to the demands of dissidence with violence. In April 1839 came a Tory plea for restraint, occasioned by fear that loyalist shootings on American steamers on the St. Lawrence and other acts of retribution

---

19   Provincial Secretary's Correspondence, Public Archives of Canada (PAC), RG 5 C1, John Black to F.B. Head, Chippewa, 18 Nov. 1838, Vol. 8, #1085; Jas Morris et al., to J. Joseph, Brockville, 1 Dec. 1837, Vol. 9, #1142; John Haycock to J. Joseph, Ingersoll, 11 Dec. 1837, Vol. 9, #1172; C. Murray to J. Joseph, Belleville, 12 Dec. 1837, Vol. 9, #1178; Wilson Mills to A.B. Hawke, Delaware, 31 Oct. 1838, Vol. 13, #1665; Joseph Dailey to F.B. Head, Picton, 2 Aug. 1837, Vol. 7, #820; G.H. Read to Head, Perth, 6 Nov. 1837, Vol. 8, #1077.

20   Sanderson 1957, pp. 52–3.

21   Civil Secretary's Correspondence, Upper Canada Sundries, PAC, RG 5 A1, Petition of John Van Orman to S.G. Arthur, Lockeport, New York, 22 Mar. 1838, Vol. 189, pp. 105267–8.

were having an adverse effect on calming a discontented populace: 'I should point out to your Excellency the painful anxiety which I am constantly exposed to from an unnatural state of things which compels this Government to be as much on its guard against the acts of its ultra friends as those of its enemies, and to apprehend almost as much mischief from the loyal as from the disaffected inhabitants of the country'.[22]

This, and copious other evidence, nevertheless distracts us from seeing and hearing the activities and resonances of popular radicalism. For the thunder of Tory terror was the loud clap of only one hand in the reciprocities of a political culture that, by the late 1830s, had come to be ordered by irreconcilable antagonisms. The terror of oligarchic officialdom had long been opposed by a counter-terror of those ground down by oppression and slights large and small. Dr John Newburn of Stamford had his barn burned in June 1839. Newburn was a backer of the Family Compact who had made statements about rebel cowardice. Threatened with a tar and feathering, confronted by a musket-touting blacksmith who informed him impolitely that bullets were a cure for the Queen's Evil, Newburn was warned by a radical innkeeper on the eve of the rebellion that he and his family were targeted to be butchered. He rode out the storm, but later saw one of his outbuildings go up in flames. As he turned to the courts to secure redress, the loyalist gentleman was denounced throughout the district and, according to Newburn, 'The Magistrate, who had dared to perform his duty, was styled, *in the language of the People*, A Tyrant and Oppressor'.[23]

Newburn's complaint, worded as it was in hostility to The People and their politics of dissent, echoed across the colony. In 1840 two men from Norwich wrote to the Lieutenant Governor to report that a man had come into their workplace to tell them that they and 'all British subjects are to be murdered. He said they are bound by oath (as soon as the first stroke to be struck) to turn out at Night, and surround each house and set Fire to it, and burn all men, women, and children – we thought we would let your Excellency know for we can't rest easy in our beds – surely there ought to be a force stationed here for it is a bad place'.[24] There were similar reports from Newmarket, and in the London

---

22   Provincial Secretary's Correspondence, PAC, RG 5 C1, George Arthur to His Excelency, H.S. Fox, Government House, Toronto, 24 Apr. 1839, Vol. 16, #1992.

23   Provincial Secretary's Correspondence, PAC, RG 5 C1, Dr John Newburn to Harrison, Stamford, 8 June 1839, Vol. 18, #2168; P. Delatre to J.B. Harrison, Drummondville, 11 Apr. 1840, Vol. 26, #700.

24   Provincial Secretary's Correspondence, PAC, RG 5 C1, Francis Davis and Joseph Ayan to George Arthur, Norwich, 21 Apr. 1840, Vol. 27, #887. Norwich had been described, in 1837,

District spies claimed that Hunters from Detroit had been dispatched to torch the government buildings in Toronto and elsewhere, to destroy Colonel Prince and his property, and to execute Sir Allan MacNab.[25] In Kingston a militia colonel found his dog shot and a note left on his gate: 'God damn Colonel Hill and all his crew shall die so God help me, if I have the strength to kill the old bugger let the curse of God await him. He had better have stayed home'. The Chief Magistrate of the same locale was promised 'death and destruction' if he dared pass judgement on Patriot invaders and captured Rebels.[26]

As rumours spread that the insurrectionists had taken Toronto, long buried resentments surfaced in condemnations of local Tory figureheads. A postmaster-coroner unleashed a political tirade of grievance and retribution: 'You d------d Tory your Dye is Cast your doom is sealed Your person and property is Consigned to a Conflagration and I shall rejoice to see it. You may escape one week and the longest two weeks and then you will come as a supplicant to me, and what judgment will I meet out to you; then we will have the Laws of Liberty established here, we will not be ruled by Tryanny and oppression any longer'.[27] A Toronto official was the recipient of a threatening, anonymous letter, typical of 1838 or 1839: 'you damned crab your officiousness last winter against the cause of liberty shall meet its just reward ... death shall be your work nothing can save you I think I see the case quiver your limbs shall give'.[28] From upstate New York, letters were posted to the 'chief magistrate of Kingston upper canady', promising revenge if any Patriot invaders were banished or put to death: 'I can rais in a fornit a army of 10,000 affective men that neather fears death nor hell they are redy and willing when they are calde upon if you put them or cos them to be put to death nothing but death shall hinder you & your executors from sharing the same fate'.[29]

With subterranean streams of rebelliousness unblocked in the Upper Canada of the 1830s, the world seemed, to some, turned upside down. Those

---

as 'a regular nest of Radicals'. J.P. Askin to J. Joseph, London, 12 Nov. 1837, Vol. 8, #1088. See also Read 1982, which contains much on Norwich.

25   Provincial Secretary's Correspondence, PAC, RG 5 C1, Statement of Artemus W. Cushman, London District, 1 July 1840, Vol. 32, #1378, p. 14792.

26   Provincial Secretary's Correspondence, PAC, RG 5 C1, J. Hill to J. Macaulay, Kingston, 15 June 1839, Vol. 14, #1795.

27   Civil Secretary's Correspondence, Upper Canada Sundries, PAC, RG 5 A1, John Davis to C. Hagerman, St John's. 19 Jan. 1838, Vol. 85, pp. 103263–4.

28   Civil Secretary's Correspondence, Upper Canada Sundries, PAC, RG 5 A1, Anonymous Letter sent to George Munroe, Toronto, no date [1838–9?].

29   Quoted in *Bathurst Courier and Ottawa Gazette*, 14 December 1838.

who had for so long dispensed fear found themselves on the receiving end. In Sandwich the following paid announcement was printed:

> Having received certain threatening letters against my life and Property, I hereby give notice that from this day, on every evening at sundown, I shall cause 12 spring guns with wires and strings complete and each loaded with 30 buck shot, to be set about my house and farm buildings, also 2 man traps. All persons are hereby warned not to come within the grounds on which my premises are built between *sun rise and sun-set*.[30]

It was signed John Prince.

Notices such as these appeared as Tory mobs assailed post-rebellion bands of reformers gathered at 'Durham Meetings', the defeated 'Liberals' ironically emboldened by a representative of Empire (Lord Durham, known as 'Radical Jack'), sent to the colony to address the shaken foundations of order:[31]

> O the 'Family Compact' is made of a set
> Of most ignorant ninnies, who office do get,
> By lying and cheating, for with poison they fill
> All our Governors' ears: but my hearties, keep still;
>   For Durham is coming
>   To give them a drumming
> That he surely shall do with a hearty good will.
>
> Then the two hundred couples of brothers and cousins,
> Will all to the right about turn them by dozens,
> And the John O'Groats Bishop and rattlesnake tail
> Of the 'Compact' uprooted will be by the gale,
>   Which swiftly is coming
>   To give them a drumming
> And the plans of Lord Durham shall ever prevail.[32]

At one such example of 'Lynch Law at Cobourg', the clash of forces resulted in torn flags, torched podium scaffolding, and head wounds, a Reform newspaper

30   *Western Herald*, 6 June 1839.
31   Provincial Secretary's Correspondence, PAC, RG 5 C1, Adam Meyers to J. Macaulay, River Trent, 7 June 1839, Vol. 18, #2165. On Durham see Cooper 1959, and on the Durham meetings in Upper Canada, Wilton 2000, pp. 194–200.
32   *Upper Canada Herald*, 23 July 1839.

declaring: 'This is Tory government and Canadian freedom ... Such conduct will rouse the spirit of the people by making them know and feel that they are very slaves and deserve to be so if they do not maintain their rights in the face of every opposition'.[33] Prior to the public clash of forces, a Reformer's livestock had been cruelly 'altered' in the dead of night. The cattle maiming involved a Durham Bull.[34]

The *Niagara Chronicle* fanned the flames of discontent by reporting on Radical political charivaris and nightly effigy burnings in Buffalo, where the protections of Republican indifference to such transgressions gave free rein to Patriot anti-Toryism:

> The 'Sovereigns' of Buffalo had a glorious carnival of three days duration Last week – they had a regular auto-de-fe of effigies. On the first night Captain Drew was brought to the stake under the 'Liberty Pole'. Sir Allan Napier MacNab was the victim the second night, and on the third, Sir George Arthur, Chief Justice Robinson, and some other bloody Britisher, whose name we have not learned, suffered martyrdom. All the cracked fifes, fiddles, and bugles in the modern Gomorrah were screeching Hail Columbia and the Rogues March – the latter was played in character. Tar and feathers are now at a premium in the City of Sympathy, as no more of these exhibitions can take place without a fresh supply ... A great deal of readable enough English has recently been expended in the discussion of the question: Is There to be War?[35]

As late as 1841, political meetings in support of the government were challenged and disrupted. In Ingersoll, a blacksmith designated a 'traitor' threatened riot against supporters of the state, and faced down a Justice of the Peace with the statement that he lacked the strength to arrest him, adding for good measure, 'there are too many Jack knives among us'.[36] This, then, was a theatre of popular politics animated by clear enough popular understandings of antagonisms, one that rocked the old, paternalist order of Upper Canadian governance to its very foundations.

---

33 *Upper Canada Herald*, 16 July 1839.
34 *St Catharines Journal*, 11 July 1839.
35 Reprinted in *Bathurst Courier and Ottawa Gazette*, 1 Feb. 1839.
36 Provincial Secretary's Correspondence, PAC, RG 5 C1, P. Graham to S.B. Harrison, Woodstock, 9 Feb. 1841, Vol. 51, #3044.

Thomas Talbot: Patriarchal Paternalism and the Demise of Old Authority

One measure of this was the socio-political transformation of a bastion of older, localised, compact rule: the Talbot District, centred in St. Thomas.[37] Compact authority, as a longstanding historiography has made abundantly clear, was loosely consolidated on an interlocking grid of compacts, many of which were only tangentially structured into the official York-Kingston axis of Family Compact governance.[38] South-western Ontario's Thomas Talbot was perhaps the leading example of a crusty, militarily-designated patriarchal authority, the personification of what Graeme Patterson has called a 'courtier compact'. In 1817 the settlers in the St. Thomas area convened to honour their leader and benefactor with the proverbial address to paternal authority:

> Sir, Having assembled to commemorate the institution of this highly favored Settlement we beg leave to present you with the tribute of that high respect, which we collectively express, but which we individually feel. From the earliest Commencement of this happy patriarchy, we date all the blessings we now enjoy: And regarding you as its founder, its patron, and its friend, we most respectfully beg leave to associate your name with our infant institution. To your first arrival at Port Talbot, we refer as the auspicious hour which gave birth to the happiness and independence we all enjoy, and this day commemorate. In grateful remembrance of your unexampled hospitality, and disinterested zeal in our behalf, and contemplating with interested feelings under your friendly patronage and patriarchal care, we have unanimously appointed the 21st of May for the Talbot Anniversary. And this public expression of the happiness among ourselves, and of our gratitude to you, we transmit through our children to our latest posterity.[39]

A pristine statement of paternalism's successes and compact governance's victorious incarceration of its subjects into the categories and identifications of its own making, this homage identified the social, economic, and political

---

37   See Ermatinger 1994; Coyne 1909; Hamil 1955.

38   For a sense of the historiography of Compact rule and the diffusion of Tory factionalism see Saunders 1975, pp. 122–39; Aitken 1975, pp. 153–70; Cook 1975, pp. 338–60; Wise 1993, pp. 91–114 and 169–84; Patterson 1989, pp. 485–512; Nelles 1966, pp. 99–114; Armstrong 1962, pp. 161–81. For the best discussion see Patterson 1970.

39   Ermatinger 1994, pp. 110, 117–18, with quote on pp. 352–3; Davin 1877, p. 113.

glue that held a nascent social order together. It demonstrated how patriarchy proved a powerful rationale for elite rule, providing a gender-based diffusion of the metaphor of family authority into the realm of civil society.

By 1832, however, the paternalist capacity to bond together elements of the social formation was weakening. In the Talbot District of St. Thomas-London and their rural environs, the Father's power was shaken. Talbot was forced to issue his own address, prefaced by a revealing acknowledgement:

> Notice: Having seen the proceedings of different Meetings held in the Talbot Settlement on the subject of imagined grievances, and of finding that it is now necessary to ascertain the real sentiments of the inhabitants, so as to at once put down the fever (by a few only) manifested, to encourage disaffection to the British Government, I give this notice, recommending a general meeting of my Settlers on St. George's Day, the 23rd of April, next, the King's Arms at St. Thomas, at noon, when I shall attend.
>
> Thomas Talbot
> Father of the Talbot Settlement[40]

Talbot, jocularly known as Thomas Tough, and represented as a 'jolly plethoric rubicund aristocratic steward' whose 'Despotic Self' was excused by his 'kind and benevolent heart' and his zealous protection of his settlement from 'Yankee organizations' offensive to the local 'Ripstavers and Gallbursters', sensed his paternalist power and patriarchal authority waning in the 1830s. It was under assault from political reformers and land-hungry Scots quick to refuse the mantle of deference he demanded.[41] John Howison described the Talbot settlers as a 'lawless, unprincipled rabble consisting of the refuse of mankind, recently emancipated from the subordination that exists in an advanced state of society ... a democracy of the most revolting kind ... addressed by the titles, sir, master, or gentleman'.[42] This kind of identification occurred only in the later 1820s and took on new force in the 1830s. Indeed, as late as 1824, Mackenzie noted in the Colonial Advocate that he had seen Talbot, enjoyed his company,

---

40   Hamil 1955, p. 188.
41   See, especially, 'Historical Sketches of the Stewardship of Thomas Tough', *St. Thomas Journal*, 13 December 1832, reprinted in Coyne 1909, Part 2, pp. 146–7; Hamil 1955, pp. 188–210.
42   Howison 1821, pp. 172–6.

and hoped his 'children, for so he may call all the settlers in Middlesex, will teach their little ones to revere him as Peter Patriae, founder of his country'.[43]

When Talbot appeared before his charges at St. Thomas in 1832, however, he needed to shore up his sagging political authority with more than the reverence the young feel for the old. British flags flew in abundance, banners of scarlet were emblazoned with crowns and the words, 'Sir John Colborne and the Constitution', 300 footmen, accompanied by fife and drum, bellowed out 'Rule Britannia', and Talbot was escorted to the assembly by 200 horsemen, with a bugler at their head. Mounting the podium at the King's Arms Hotel, Talbot regaled the crowd, pausing for good effect to take some snuff. He decried the presence in his settlement of what he referred to as a few 'black sheep', and then went straight to the heart of the matter of sedition:

> it was not until recently that these intruders openly declared themselves. It was not until they formed a damned cold water society here, at which they met night after night in secret enclave to concoct measures for the subversion of our institutions, that I was aware of the prevalence of such principles. This well organized band first commenced the study of their tactics at Ealahide where they have the greatest strength and where they had the advantage of the military skill of a Yankee deserter for a drill seargeant, aided by a tall stripling, the son of a former UE Loyalist, whom they transformed into a flagstaff ... They next tried their strength in Yarmouth, where aided by a few Hickory Quakers they succeeded in organizing a committee of vigilance whose duty I suppose was to sound the conch shell of sedition in every valley and on every hill, where aided by certain characters who making a cloak of religion to cover their seditious purposes and who secretly lent them the light of their countenances they prospered to the present time.[44]

From other quarters, too, came denunciations of 'peddlers and strolers', and attributions of dissent to 'runaway negroes and people who have neither habitation nor property in the country'. At the end of the Talbot meeting, it was claimed that only one man hurrahed for Mackenzie, described as a 'stout looking Tennessee Negro'. Merchants, likely Americans, who harboured reformist sympathies, were assailed as grasping Jews, and Colonel Talbot was quick to point the finger of faction at 'Ryersonian strolling priests'. Clearly any counter

43   *Colonial Advocate*, 2 September 1984.
44   Hamil 1955, p. 188.

to paternalist authority – temperance society or dissident religion (both of which smacked too much of a feminised challenge to the rough masculinity of the frontier), economic alternative or race (which ran headlong into the culture and content of conventional power) – was grist for Talbot's theatrical pronouncements from the platform of the King's Arms.[45] For his part, the curmudgeonly Colonel thought he had done rather well, writing complacently to Sir John Colborne: 'I had a splendid turnout on St. George's Day, when the rebels were all silent and quiet, and I gave my children some wholesome advice. The disaffected are but few, considering all the noise that has been made'.[46]

The Theatre of Denigration

What we are seeing here is a beleaguered, albeit complexly differentiated, patriarchal paternalist authority, challenged by a diverse set of economic, political, and cultural transformations. All were associated with the consolidation of a market society and the consequent heterogeneity of a population no longer capable of being subsumed under the rule of older compacts. Upper Canada's governance had since its beginning been defined by paternalists of whom Talbot was arguably one of the more obstinate and extreme. This paternalist rule, supported as much by an elaborate theatre of political governance as by any narrowly conceived Constitutionalist practice, meant that the relations of subordination could be lived in particular locales far distant from the Black Rod of the York Executive Council. It is not surprising, then, that the politics of dissent in Upper Canada unfolded less within the formal structures of institutional politics than in a confrontational theatre and counter-theatre in which rhetoric and symbolic representation figured forcefully. This was a public sphere as

---

45 Patterson 1970, pp. 94–102. Race was used by both advocates of Compact rule and their opponent reformers. Thus a riotous procession of anti-Reform Orange elements assailed Liberal voters in London in 1836. Heading the noisy parade was 'a Negro with a national standard ... shouting five pounds for any Liberal heads'. As Tories in London mounted campaigns of intimidation directed at outlying Middlesex County Radical meetings of 1837, they marshalled support of the Wilberforce community of Ohio blacks who had settled in the area. The response of the Reform press was to chastise the composition of these Tory political crowds as composed of 'squalid Orangemen and NEGROES!' or to deride the local Compact's inability to galvanise the 'Niggers' of Wilberforce. See Landon 1974, p. 166; Landon 1960, pp. 41–2; Read 1982, pp. 71, 73.

46 Landon 1960, p. 63.

much of performance, however, as it was of logical debate and articulate speech and it easily slipped into postures of extremism, in which both language and imagery, as well as physical engagement, could veer towards the violent.

Consider, for instance, the Tory-Orange denunciation of the Reform candidacy of Mathew Howard in the Johnstown District in eastern Ontario in 1830. Said to be supported by Methodists and social levellers, one of Howard's meetings drew this sarcastic response from the conservative press:

> a great noise was heard at the doors of the Committee, when lo in walked Mathew Mushroom Howard, Esquire, carrying a Millstone round his neck and supported on the right and the left by the most reverend fathers William Hallock and James Cameron his tail and other habillments upheld by an innumerable host of 'Saddle Boys'. Cameron introduced Howard: Gentlemen, slaves, Mr. M.M. Mulberry Mushroom Howard is a Miller, a grist Miller, a Farmer, a Trader, a straw hat Maker, a pumpkin pie maker, an onion sauce stewer and ... a mighty clever man and what more do you want for the good of the country.[47]

There is in this account a denigration of the popular classes, a virtual repudiation of the rights of producers, broadly defined, to partake of political action. The message of Howard is ridiculed in its egalitarianism, and the appeal to the rights of all citizens is scoffed at in the duality, 'Gentlemen, slaves'. The usual linking of dissident religion, race, and plebeian status is evident as an entrenched Tory paternalism in the 1830s finds the Reform challenge difficult to take seriously. After a Howard victory, however, the response of reaction accelerated to an uglier physical intervention. In an 1833 electoral gathering outside of what is now Athens in Leeds County, reformers placed one David Fairbairn in the Chair, only to find that this action of constituting authority in the hands of a mere painter drew the ire of assembled Tory Orangemen. A mob dragged the mechanic from the podium, and in a craft equivalent of tarring and feathering, varnished him in red paint, also taking the time to pull Howard and other well-known Reformers away from the meeting to dump them in the snow. Leeds elections would be punctuated with tumultuous riots for the next three years.[48]

---

47 Quoted in Patterson 1970, p. 220.
48 *Cobourg Star*, 20 March 1833; Civil Secretary's Correspondence, Upper Canada Sundries, PAC, RG 5 A1, George Crawford et al., to J. Joseph, Brockville, 20 June 1937, Vol. 176, p. 97247. For a broader discussion note Akenson 1984.

The Enigma of Class in the 1830s

This introduces into the realm of power – bounded by compact rule, oligarchy, paternalism, and patriarchy – the element of class.[49] It is a shadowy presence in the Upper Canada of the 1830s, for the social formation in this period of nascent capitalist development is by no means demarcated clearly by obvious material polarisations. Yet what is striking is the extent to which aspects of the theatre of popular politics are infused with trade and craft symbolism and a rhetoric of occupation. The link between labour and politics was recognised intuitively by an antagonistic paternalism, just as it was lived out by those producers of town and country who had assimilated a populistic grasp of the labour theory of value. At a Radical London District gathering in 1837, the *Liberal* claimed that the 1,000-strong throng was the largest political assembly in the history of Middlesex township, adding its description of those who came together: 'It is true there were none of the Squirearchy there, none of the Office-holders, none of the half-pay, half-witted Aristocrats, but the cultivators and OWNERS of the land were there, the WORKINGMEN were there – the people and intelligence of the country were there'.[50] Paternalism, with its accent on the master side of the master/man relation, choked audibly on the kind of producer ideology that was beginning to be voiced in the 1830s:[51]

---

49   What follows draws on an argument first elaborated in Palmer 1983b, pp. 45–59.

50   Quoted in Read 1982, p. 72.

51   An empiricist mainstream in Canadian historiography has steadfastly refused to see nascent class formation in the Upper Canada of the 1830s as significant, but historians of trade unions, labour law, and class conflict have identified the decade as one of beginnings, however hesitant and complicated. See, among a number of sources that could be cited, Tucker 1991, pp. 15–54; Palmer 1980, pp. 7–32; Palmer 1987a, pp. 61–84. One recent treatment of political culture in the period acknowledges that most historians of Upper Canada have tended to see class eclipsed as an explanatory variable with respect to political commitments by such indices of identity as religion and nationality, at the same time that it suggests the salience of differentiations that turned on the material structures of early class formation. See Wilton 2000, especially p. 229. This resonates with interpretations of early timber work and canal labour in the 1830s, where the accent is placed both on the development of class distinctions and their mediation by power and paternalism. Consider, for instance, Cross 1973, pp. 1–26; Pentland 1981. There is also not enough treatment of the 1830s, for example, in the essays in Craven 1995. The 1840s and 1850s would see increasing class agitation, the former decade associated with canal labour upheavals, the latter with what the contemporary press dubbed 'an insurrection of labour', the centrepiece of which was a rash of strikes by craftsmen in 1853–4. See Bleasdale 1981, pp. 9–40; Way 1993; and the excellent unpublished account in Appleton 1974. Evidence of

Ye merry mechanics, come join in my song,
And let the brisk chorus go bounding along:
Tho some may be poor and some rich may be,
Yet all should contented be and happy and free.

Ye tailors of ancient and noble renown,
Who clothe all the people in country and town,
Remember that Adam, your father and head,
Though lord of the world was a tailor by trade.

Ye Masons who work with stone, mortar and brick,
And lay the foundation in deep, solid, and thick,
Though hard be your labour, yet lasting your fame,
Both Egypt and China your wonders proclaim.

Ye smiths who forge tools for all trades here below,
You have nothing to fear while you smite and you blow.
All things may you conquer, so happy your lot,
If you're careful to strike while the iron is hot.

Then follow stanzas on stevedores, cabinetmakers, hatters, carders and spin-
ners, coopers, printers, coachmakers, and shipbuilders.[52] The constituency of
popular radicalism, as the list of those 885 individuals confined on charges of
insurrection and treason in the aftermath of the rebellion indicated, was the
broad array of producers.[53] In those regions, such as the Home District, where
capitalist development was more advanced, the shock troops of rebellion were
most definitely the dispossessed proletarians of town and country. Fully three
hundred of the roughly four hundred arrested were labourers.[54]

---

working-class activism in the 1830s, 1840s, and 1850s is also presented in the appendices on
strikes and riots in Palmer 1983b, pp. 299–320 (data was dropped from the second edition
of this book for consideration of space).

52   Palmer 1983b, pp. 31–3; Forsey 1982, pp. 9–13. The verse appears in a newspaper that
opposed the Reformist cause, although such doggerel was also appearing in more radical
circles, where the 'producer ideology' was gaining credence. *Brockville Gazette*, 30 August
1830; 7 December 1830. I am grateful to Sean Cadigan for first providing me with the
reference.

53   See Lindsey 1862, Vol. 2, Appendix I, pp. 373–400.

54   See Johnson 1975 and 1973, pp. 95–127.

By 1836, Orange figurehead and aspiring Tory political wire-puller, Ogle Gowan could write to Charles Jones of the Reform threat in language that merged perceived dangers in the political arena with the discourse of class: 'The radicals here in Bastard and Crosby are getting up a union! ... How superlatively absurd are the Radicals when their craft is likely to be endangered'.[55] Tories such as Christopher Hagerman and John Beverley Robinson understood well the necessity to placate the mechanics in the emerging political crisis, although in the case of Robinson he deplored the resulting intrusions of class into the techniques of governance. 'Everybody knows everything', he wrote in despair to Sir John Colborne, 'and all the shoemakers and tailors in town are discussing ... the "Cabinet pudding"'.[56] After the routing of the Reform cause in the 1836 election, Bond Head was quick to compare the newly constituted Tory assembly with that of its predecessors. His language was as unmistakably condescending as was his penchant for class dichotomisations. Convinced that the people of Upper Canada 'detest democracy, ... revere their Constitutional Charter, and are consequently staunch in their allegiance to the King', Bond Head revelled in the 1836 election that returned to rightful authority men of a certain station: 'In place of blacksmiths and carpenters reeling from daily labour with no farther knowledge than that which appertained to their calling, and with obstinacy and perverseness proportionate to their ignorance and vulgarity, we have for the most part GENTLEMEN of an intelligence, information, and talent, capable of discussing the measures which they are called upon to deliberate and decide'.[57] Three years later, a trio of carpenters said to possess 'no property, principles, or influence', would erect a mock gallows on the banks of the Humber River, hanging effigies of John Beverly Robinson, Christopher Hagerman, and Bond Head, suspending signs from their dangling bodies: 'I will condemn right or wrong; we must have a rebellion; and I will prosecute unto death'.[58] To the west, in St. Catharines, there were reportedly Chartist meetings called. With the fusing of Upper Canadian political unions, Lower Canadian Sons of Liberty, and British working-class radicalism, English textile

---

55   Quoted in Patterson 1970, p. 278.

56   Civil Secretary's Correspondence, Upper Canada Sundries, PAC, RG 5 A1, Macaulay to Arthur Monohan, Kingston, 11 June 1836, Vol. 167, pp. 91314–16: 'Hagerman has made all right here with the Mechanics and is sure of his election'. For context see Palmer 1980, pp. 7–32. Robinson is quoted in McNairn 2000, p. 197.

57   Read and Stagg 1985, p. 10; Head 1839; Dunham 1927, pp. 164–76; Dent 1885, pp. 329–43; Landon 1974, p. 166. Bond Head quote from Palmer 1983b, p. 51.

58   Civil Secretary's Correspondence, Upper Canada Sundries, PAC, RG 5 A1, Thomas Fisher to the Lieutenant-Governor, no date [1839], Vol. 210, pp. 121052–54.

workers sided with the struggle for 'Canadian liberty' and the London-based
Workingmen's Association offered an Address to the Central and Permanent Committee of the Patriots of the County of Montreal. Beleaguered Tories
pounced on the class character of political mobilisation. 'Canadian Chartists',
declared the *Cobourg Star*, were a 'contemptible collection of chiefly liberated
traitors, notorious rebels, and men without either character, property or education'.[59]

Small wonder that an anonymous 'Observer' concluded, in 1842, that the
politics of an incipient class experience lay at the root of Upper Canada's recent
unsettledness. He thought the province was 'infested with a vile crew of incendiaries', declaring that, 'The very chips of democracy are those Mechanicks that
pour in upon us from the States – Even at home they are discontented; and
ever thriving for mastery and from their envious hearts and evil dispositions
they are driven about, from place, to place, and like Cain become wanderers
and vagabonds on the face of the Earth, with their hands against every one and
every ones hands against them except the members of their own felon community'. Convinced that upon their arrival in Canada, such miscreants enlisted
'in the Corps of the rebellious', and that they sustained 'the faction of which
Mackenzie, Ryerson, and Bidwell are the heads' with their discord and disaffection, 'Observer' suggested that mechanics and labourers from the British
Isles be encouraged to immigrate to Canada. Their numbers, he suggested,
would 'reduce the wages at once', thereby materially undercutting the 'hate-
ful presence', 'upsetting impudence', and 'envious malignity' of a pernicious
class. Driving such irksome mechanics either out of the province or into economic submission would nip the germ of 'future rebellion' in the bud, laying a
foundation on which the constitution and laws protective of life and property
could survive. 'Intense and unremitting perseverance' was required to thwart
the 'felon cheats slanderers and Democrats of the States', who were infinitely
worse than 'the Wolves and Bears of the Wilderness', but 'the industry of Old
England, of Canada, and the human race demand it'. 'Observer' called on the
nascent Upper Canadian state to wage a class war of retaliation against the mas-
terless men of the emerging capitalist labour market, a 'proletarian imaginary'
that some clearly both loathed and feared deeply.[60]

59   *Cobourg Star*, 3 July 1839; 10 July 1839; 11 September 1839; Lipton 1968, pp. 12–13; Ryerson
     1937, pp. 72–3, 132–6; Ryerson 1968, pp. 64–5; 'The Permanent and Central Committee of
     the County of Montreal to the Workingmen's Association of London', *Montreal Gazette*, 20
     January 1838.
60   Civil Secretary's Correspondence, Upper Canada Sundries, PAC, RG 5 A1, An Observer to
     McMahon, York, February 1842, Vol. 257, pp. 140295–8. Sir John Colborne noted as early as

This is not, of course, to argue that Upper Canada in the 1830s was a fully-formed class society, with a mature process of class formation and the institutions, perspectives, and struggles of a workers' movement close at hand. That would not come for 40 or 50 years, and then only incompletely. It is to argue that we have something, to borrow E.P. Thompson's metaphor, of a field of force, in which the theatre of politics moves within the oscillations of class formations clearly in motion and a class society obviously in the making. Pulled to one magnet pole or another of these class formations, sometimes suspended in a highly unstable, even erratic state, the actors within the theatre of politics in the 1830s are not dressed in the unmistakable fashion of class, nor do they speak lines easily scripted with the accent of a mature working class. But neither is the period devoid of the demarcations of nascent class formation.[61]

In the words of William Lyon Mackenzie's Toronto paper, *The Constitution*, 'Labour is the true source of all wealth', and good governance was premised on this maxim:

> What is bad government, thou slave
> Whom robbers represent
> What is bad government thou knave
> Who lov'st bad government
> It is the deadly will that takes
> What labour ought to keep
> It is the deadly Power that makes
> Bread dear and labour cheap.[62]

For Mackenzie to make even this kind of elementary stand for the producing classes, linking political reform to the cause of labour, broadly defined, was sufficient to draw the wrath of constituted authority. Power's resentments were most effectively voiced in the verse of vernacular denunciation:

> Sermon or song for a boodle he spins ya
> Pulpit or dungill, its all the same to Mackenzie
>
> Speer ye who holds the Reformers in prate
> Yelpin like curs at the Kirk and the State

1832 that Mackenzie drew on the support of 'Mechanics who lived some time in the States before they settled in the Province'. See Clark 1959, p. 415.

61   Thompson 1978a, pp. 133–65.

62   Kilbourn 1977, p. 147; 'What Is Bad Government?', *The Constitution*, 9 November 1836.

Crazed with religio-politico frenzy
Sheep-stealin, maggot-eye seein Mackenzie

Who day a think on a mission was sent
The breedin of Johnny's bulldogs to prevent
Because they made havoc on Janathan's hens see
Who but the white liver't mawkin Mackenzie
Midden-bred, filthy-jakes scourin Mackenzie

Ken ya know who truly hae need o Reform
Who but the unlicket cubs of the storm
Got on mischance by the father of sin see
Ryerson, Radcliffe, an roarin' Mackenzie
O what an orthodox trio, Mackenzie
Methdoy Yankees and Pagan Mackenzie[63]

This kind of diatribe, so easily aimed at the contentious Mackenzie, slipped over into the generalised theatre and counter-theatre of politics in the 1830s. From Bytown came this 1836 'Recipe to Make an Ultra Radical':

Take the herbs of Hyprocisy and the root of pride each of them two hands full. Two ounces of Ambition and Vain Glory, bruise them in mortar of faction and boil them in a quart of dissembling tears. Set them over the fire of sedition, till you perceive the scum of Falsehood arise on the top, then strain in the rough cloth of Rebellion, put it in the bottle of envy, then stop it down with the cork of Malice, let it stand and settle and make it into pills ... called Conspiracy. Take two over night and three the next morning and then you will know how to cozen and cheat, and curse the church, pull down bishops, behead kings, let knaves rule over the nation, and cut the throats of all honest men.[64]

Mackenzie, of course, gave as good as he got:

Ye false Canadians! Tories! Pensioners! Placemen! Profligates! Orange-men! Churchmen! Spies! Informers! Brokers! Gamblers! Parasites and knaves of every description, let me congratulate you! Never was a vaga-

---

63   Quoted in Palmer 1983b, p. 50.
64   *Bytown Gazette*, 9 June 1836.

bond race more prosperous. Never did successful villainy rejoice in brighter visions of the future than you may indulge. Ye may plunder and rob with impunity – your feet is on the people's necks, they are transformed into tame, crouching slaves, ready to be trampled on.

Ever willing to personalise his attack, Mackenzie named the McNabs, Robinsons, Gowans, Hagermans, Boultons, Princes, Strachans, Merrits and other Compact figures as 'refuse and scum of God's creation ... besoms of heaven's wealth against poor sinners, let loose from below ... to curse a portion of mankind ... mocking the idle hopes of those who believe that you would do ought for a suffering and ruined population'.[65]

The Hybrid Discourse of Dissent

To work towards a conclusion, it is useful to pause to provide an analytic note. The popular radicalism of Upper Canada in the 1830s was a hybrid, one in which the crossings of a transplanted, transatlantic world were evident in a plebeian attachment to the rough egalitarianism of a nascent capitalist order that was still governed by an *ancien régime*. Precisely because that old order was itself transplanted, it lacked a measure of longstanding legitimacy, and the winds of change blew through it with gusto in the 1830s. But the hybridity of this contested terrain was not only the complex amalgam of British, American, and Canadian that took root in the soil of productive and cultural life in the new world of muddy York and in the clearings and the bush described by Susanna Moodie.[66] To understand the popular politics and power relations of the 1830s, it is necessary to treat the meaning of patriarchy, paternalism, and class in this new world order seriously. It is only through this treatment that the failures of the rebellion of 1837 can be reformulated.

First, patriarchy. This was the unquestioned, often unarticulated foundation of the social and cultural assumptions of the age. It linked domestic life and political rule, spilling over necessarily into the economic realm, it being no accident that the metaphorical term of derision, aimed directly at power, was that of the Family Compact. Patriarchy was the foundation of Upper Canada's social formation in the pre-1840 years, its institutionalisation a pervasive pres-

---

65   *The Constitution*, 12 July 1837.

66   Raible 1992; Moodie 1913, especially pp. 245–50. Still worth consideration is the presentation in Johnson 1973, pp. 65–127.

ence in all spheres of activity, and one that dominated the relations of private life, in which an unquestioned subordination of women and children to male authority prevailed. The family as the basic unit of social life was headed by a ruling patriarch, whose powers of governance were widely understood to be far-reaching. Women and children were, of course, never totally powerless, but the boundaries within which they could operate were always understood to be limited by male prerogative. In the sphere of popular politics, patriarchy was significant precisely because Upper Canadian society established the family as the model early on, not only for the private realm, but also for public life: civil society was merely an extension of the domestic relations of governance and subordination.[67]

Thus in Upper Canada, patriarchy was an unmistakable and powerful political reality. Tory figureheads were referred to explicitly by reformers as white-haired patriarchs. Patriarchy was also assumed by the ruling authority itself, as when Talbot referred to himself as the Father of His Settlement, or when Jamieson chastised Gould, commenting that he had quite enough political rights for a man of his young years. The dominance of the father in the family became the rationale for the absolute dominance of father-like figures in the various communities that linked Colonel John Prince's western outpost of the Windsor region to eastern Ontario's Bytown gentry. Mackenzie's actual *naming* of elite rule as *the* Family Compact was never merely metaphorical: the connections of family were, of course, embedded in powerful posts, dispensed through patronage, but more to the point, authority itself was conceived as familial, justified as an ideology *and* practiced as a set of entitlements that existed (in the eyes of the powerful) prior to any responsibilities or obligations. The generalised symbolism of this congealing of governance as a political phenomenon associated with compact practices, and authority as familial, was so widespread in Upper Canada in the 1830s as to be universally understood. It was this familiarity that both prompted Mackenzie to label oligarchy as a Family Compact and insured that this designation of power would immediately and widely resonate in the political theatre of the era.[68]

Second, paternalism. This was intricately related to patriarchy, yet distinct from it. Paternalism was the set of practices through which patriarchal and

---

67   My accent on patriarchy and its *political* significance is thus different from the current
      concern with gender regulation. See Morgan 1996; Cour, Morgan, and Valverde 1992,
      pp. 163–91. For other useful statements see McKenna 1994; Errington 1995; Potter 1989,
      pp. 3–24.

68   I am here adapting something of the argument in Patterson 1989, but reading it somewhat
      against its analytic grain.

class authority was lived and experienced, from both above and below, and there were varieties of paternalism, as scholars as different as Graeme Patterson and Sean Cadigan have shown.[69] They turn on the reciprocities and mediations of the superior and the subordinate, the texture of everyday life in which the dominated submitted to the power of ruling authority because of governance's acknowledgement that its right to rule was balanced by its need to provide, and not only materially, but in a host of other ways as well. Paternalism was thus never a one-way street but a constantly negotiated exchange relation. If it was backed up with an immense coercive capacity, it was also held in place by the powerful subordinating apparatus of moral, religious, economic, and political identifications that bound layers of society into a seemingly common kinship.

Opposition to Mackenzie, for instance, was early voiced in a language challenging his right to consider himself worthy of patriarchal, or paternal respect. In 1830 the *Brockville Gazette* assailed the York agitator for mistreatment of his son, his mother, and his journeymen printers. Claiming that Mackenzie had beaten his son John with 'Turkish barbarity', these 'unnatural cruelties' forcing 'the poor youth ... to fly from thee', the paper asked derisively, 'What thinkst thou of the parental character'? When Mackenzie's mother supposedly protested, the reformer ostensibly ridiculed 'thy mother before thy servant [made] a laughing stock of her'. Mackenzie's 'filial character' was thus also found wanting. And to close the paternal circle, the editor's relations with his workmen were queried: 'Hast thou never played the tyrant among thy workmen? Never exacted untimely hours of attendance? Didst thou never subject men, of inferior capacity and conduct for low wages? and didst thou never defraud them of even these wages'? Mackenzie simply did not measure up to a standard of manliness, his accuser closing 'with disgust at these glances at thy domestic character, as a parent, a son, and a master'. He who could not rule his family and his business dealings with proper decorum was, necessarily, unfit to rule society.[70]

In the transplanted world of Upper Canada, there is an abundant evidence of cracks in the wall of this paternalism, but there are equally clear-cut indications that constant arm-twisting in the paternal arena consolidated elite governance and secured the hegemony of compact rule. As cracks in the paternalist wall widened, the fissures that appeared in the 1830s channelled most prominently out of the diversification of economic life and the making of a market society. One measure of this process of change was the incomplete, but certainly

---

69   Patterson 1970; Cadigan 1991, pp. 319–47; Cadigan 1987.
70   *Brockville Gazette*, 18 September 1830, quoted in Cadigan 1987, p. 341.

discernible, socio-economic differentiation that would reconfigure the body of paternalist and patriarchal power. Once robust mechanisms of hegemony, lived out in patriarchal and paternalist practices, inevitably carried less and less of their majesties and terrors. Both the challenges to and counter-thrusts of the authorities were nowhere more clearly played out than in the theatre of popular politics, reliant as it was on the rhetoric and representation of patriarchy and paternalism. With the rise of radical dissent throughout the 1830s, repeated blows were struck against the old order of status and subordination.

In all of this the language and identification of paternalism was under siege, surfacing in Bond Head's charges to the electors in 1836. Paternalism thus continued to structure the tone and meaning of loyalist resolutions, evident in this statement passed in St. Catharines in 1838 by American residents:

> That the Leaders of the Revolutionary Party have endeavored to excite the sympathy and secure the support of the Inhabitants of the United States, to their desperate enterprise, by comparing the situation in this province to that under the older colonies which sought a separation from the British Empire, and have pretended to draw a parallel, which this meeting is enabled to declare fallacious, as well from a knowledge of the political circumstances of the two countries, derived, in the one case, from the page of history, and in the other from a conviction that the British Government entertains toward us feelings the most mild and paternal.

The fusion of patriarchal and paternal authority also surfaced in pardon proclamations of the same year, where the responsibilities of lesser patriarchs were hierarchically ordered, with due obeisance demanded to God, Sovereign, Country, and Family:

> Let me take this affecting and impressive occasion to entreat you for the future to remember your duty to your Sovereign, your wives, and to your children, to all of whom you have been restored, by the Mercy of the Government you assisted in attempting to overthrow. To your Queen; you not only owe obedience and submission on all lawful occasions, but also your strength in arms and your lives if necessary, in defence of her Crown. To your wives, you owe manly protection, attachment to your homes and firesides, peaceable and respectable demeanor and, for their sake, if for no other, you should be foremost with all of your power to save your Country from the miseries of war in which your conduct so nearly involved it. To your children you owe a religious moral and loyal education. The man who teaches your child insubordination and Treason

is more your enemy than he who attempts to take your life and property. The Almighty has left the maintenance and comfort of your children dependent upon your bodily exertions; upon your immortal interests he has cast the responsibility of training their tender minds in the path of religion, and loyalty and obedience.[71]

How could such a powerful concoction of hegemonic responsibilities be challenged?

It is when class, the third element, is brought into the equation that some explanatory possibilities emerge with respect to the politics of the 1830s. The discourse of popular radicalism was a hybrid, in part, because class lacked the elementary clarity that a more developed capitalist formation would have provided. The ambiguities and even contradictions of this period in Canadian history dictated that class alignments were in the making, rather than in any sense made or over-made, as they would be in future moments of class upheaval and challenge, from 1886, through 1919 and 1946, to the present.[72] This insured that they were posed ambivalently. The popular radicalism of Upper Canada *was* class ordered, but it often took on the symbols, the rhetoric, the defiant posturing of struggles other than those of class, such as Irish and American republicanism, or religion or race. This left class buried beneath other demands: to overthrow the entrenched age-old rule of monarchs, a demand that, once unleashed, led to calls for democracy and the marshalling of plebeian forces that threatened an assault on the longstanding edifice of elitist class power.

Within the rhetoric of Reform journalism in 1836 and at the monster rallies of Radical Reformers in 1837, for instance, there was reference to erecting huge liberty poles. The American eagle figured prominently on banners, and the slogans 'Liberty or Death', 'Daniel O'Connell', 'Bidwell, and the Glorious Minority', and '1837, Victoria and a good beginning' were carried proudly. Pikes, muskets, swords, trumpets, and cannon were often depicted on placards and flags. Loaves of bread smothered in butter were hoisted on sticks, or made the object of target practice, a Radical statement on what many regarded as Bond Head's insulting 'homely phrase' that 'to dispute with me, and live on bad terms with the Mother Country, you will ... only quarrel with your bread and butter'.[73] There was reference to Revolution:

---

71   Civil Secretary's Correspondence, Upper Canada Sundries, PAC, RG 5 A1, Vol. 251, pp. 136654–7.

72   For a broad overview see Palmer 2003, pp. 465–90.

73   See, for instance, *The Constitution*, 27 July 1837; 17 August 1836; 7 September 1836; 2 August 1837; 9 August 1837; Ryerson 1968, p. 120; Jackman 1958, pp. 90, 107.

Take this piece of advice from an ignorant elf
Let each ipso facto reform one himself
And then my dear Roger, you'll see in conclusion,
A glorious, a grand, a great, Revolution.

A young boy paraded with a sign of a girl over which was pencilled the phrase:

Of Monarchs tender, Monarchs tough,
We thank our stars we've had enough.[74]

This, then, was a conflicted socio-political environment, in which the emerging tensions of class formation were evident, even if they were not moved by a pristine class consciousness and the presence of mature, formal working-class institutions. This has led the most sophisticated conservative historian of the era to conclude that 'Considerations of economic interest, as is so often the case in the Canadas, seemed to be outweighing ideological commitment. Considerations of "class" seemed to be outweighing those of "nation".'[75]

This kind of perspective takes us in new directions of understanding with respect to the failure of the Rebellion of 1837–8. The enigma of class in the turbulence of the 1830s is little discussed in accounts of the rebellious uprising and what it meant and why it failed. Too much has been made in past historical writings of the ineptness of Mackenzie as a leader, of the military confusions of the eleventh hour that debilitated rebel ranks. An older conservative historiography constructed the rebellion of 1837–8 as a tragicomedy of fated failure, depicting the popular radicalism of the age as a non-entity: Loyalism, rather than rebellion, was the hallmark of nineteenth-century Canada. This view was later countered by a radical liberal/Marxist historiography, but this writing never really swept aside the condescending view of the challenge posed in the 1830s. A conservative presentation of Mackenzie and the insurrection as one of those historical 'deviants' easily marginalised in the linear march of Progress and Nationhood has been too easily assimilated in contemporary historical writing, which generally pays inadequate attention to Upper Canada as the site of a spirited, if limited, opposition to inequality, oppression, and exploitation.

---

74   *The Constitution*, 2 August 1837.
75   Patterson 1970, p. 120.

Patriarchal Power and the Failure of Popular Radicalism in the 1830s

In explaining the failure of the Upper Canadian Rebellion, and in understanding the popular radicalism that helped to shape it, the analytic possibilities are indeed more interesting and expansive than conventional wisdoms would suggest. I would like to bring into relief the pervasive continuity of patriarchal authority and the ways in which it obscured already blurred class lines within the Reform ranks. At exactly the same moment that the Family Compact was being assailed by Mackenzie and others, patriarchy survived and remained unchallenged in the domestic and socio-economic realm. This is evident in a reading of the newspapers of the decade, which are full of notices of runaway wives and, less commonly, absconding apprentices. Such 'advertised' escapes warned that no one should treat with these dependants economically and that in the future patriarchal and paternalist masters would not be responsible for the debts and actions of their charges. These announcements of absconding wives and young workers appeared under the same illustration that often graced notices of runaway slaves in the southern states of America; rewards were sometimes offered for the return of these subjects, albeit modest ones, ranging from a penny to a few pence. Francis Collins of the *Canadian Freeman*, in jail for his political ideas at the time 'his' apprentice left his employment, offered a curt reminder that Radicals, too, were capable of insisting that patriarchal authority should be recognised: 'As this boy has always received good treatment, and has thus basely taken advantage of my confinement under a political persecution, to abscond, it is hoped that no person will harbor or employ him'. Patriarchy thus lived in the social, economic, and domestic realms, as it was being subjected to increasingly harsh condemnation in the political sphere.[76]

It remains questionable, then, how resolute the Radicals were in their opposition to patriarchy and paternalism, as distinct from their antagonism to how these forms were practised by an odious oligarchy. A warning to 'Runaways, Horsethieves, and all other long legged, long nosed, long eared, long mouthed, and long winded inmates of the Devil's Kitchen' from Cobourg's Tom Tough, indicated the class limitations bred in the bone of acceptance of patriarchal authority. Advocating a colony-wide society of tradesmen to keep an eye on apprentices about to take to the roadways, Tough snorted:

---

76   For a discussion of runaway wives see Errington 1995, pp. 44–8. For the Collins statement, see *Gore Gazette*, 24 May 1829. Cadigan has an extensive discussion of runaway apprentices and paternalism in Cadigan 1987, chapter 6.

You Scoundrels: We have been tormented long enough with you, and so long as you are allowed to escape from the hands of justice with impunity, so long as we are aware we shall be cursed with your prowling, marauding, swindling and thieving practices. More than one hundred of you have made your escape from this and the two adjoining towns within a very few weeks, and if it was not that you are constantly replaced with a more hungry set, we would say amen to it all.[77]

Patriarchal and paternalist assumptions about class and gendered power underlie such statements and explain Mackenzie's oscillating relations with his printers. They toasted him and vice versa in the 1830s, only to find themselves locked in a nasty strike within a few years. This complexity, rather than any blunt depiction of Mackenzie as simply a grasping, exploitative capitalist deserving of nothing but radical condemnation, is what marks the age.[78]

And it is this complexity that situates the promise and the tragedy of insurrection in the 1830s, marking the decade as a fulcrum on which socio-economic transformation and the making of modern capitalist society, with its freedoms and its constraints, perched precariously. The popular radicalism of the period was, in Fredric Jameson's words, something of a 'political unconscious', an articulation of an alternative that spoke to new and largely uncharted depths of change, in which the very substance of the relationships of rule were poised as if staring into an abyss.[79] The boundaries of political possibility were being redrawn, not only in the tangible relations of land and labour, but in the materialised subjectivity of mind and style as well.

---

77   *Cobourg Star*, 13 February 1833.
78   It is obviously entirely the point of this paper that the contradiction in Mackenzie espousing a populist labour theory of wealth, even lauding 'his' printers organising their own union, and then, at the point of class conflict, lashing out at the journeymen for their 'interested' spirit and 'arbitrary means', was not an individual 'failing'. Rather it was a determined, structured relation centred in the paternalism of the 1830s workplace. Thus, the argument in Armstrong 1967, pp. 187–96, misstates the complexity of the interpretive issues. See, also, Conner 1923, pp. 555–7. The writing on Mackenzie is of course voluminous, but Gates 1959, pp. 185–208 and Donnelly 1987, pp. 61–73 continue to inform on such matters.
79   Jameson 1981.

Popular Radicalism and the End of the Old Order: Crisis and the Scar of Patriarchy

This was no secret at the time. It did not take John Beverly Robinson long to conclude that in the aftermath of the rebellion, oligarchic authority now rested on a fragile and increasingly unstable foundation. He bemoaned the fact that the scruples and first principles of his beloved gentrified order seemed to have vanished in the conduct of public affairs. The old values and loyalties, indeed the British connection to Empire and its stabilities of governance, seemed to count for less and less among what remained of the Compact layer of patriarchal rulers. If Robinson would indeed oppose the drift of the times, he often privately despaired about the seeming inevitability of the displacement of a way of life, a style of paternal rule that demanded what could no longer be secured: acquiescence and unquestioning loyalty. In the face of Lord Durham's report, which he judged 'highly injurious' to 'the state of public feeling in Upper Canada', he worried about the fate of 'men of judgment and right feeling'. The theatrical politicisation of life in Upper Canada, culminating in the drama of reform and reaction in the 1830s, helped write *finis* to Robinson's undisputed right to rule. The convictions, honour, and loyalties that Robinson and others of his class held in such esteem, and that were so intimately related to patriarchy and paternalism, seemed to have shattered under the pressures of material change, the challenge of dissent, and the transition from Reform to Rebellion. Even as the Mackenzies and the Goulds were defeated, the powerful symbolism of the Black Rod imploded in the mid-to-late 1830s. The right to compact rule was, with the Rebellion of 1837–8, no longer tenable in the long term; it could not be reproduced cavalierly. A way of political being, constituted in a particular kind of economy and lived in the vice grip of patriarchal expanse *and* limitation, ended forever in the 1830s. The John Beverley Robinsons of Upper Canada knew it.[80]

Allan Napier MacNab, staunch Tory defender of King & Country in 1837, provides an ironic comment on this passing of the *ancien régime*. McNab, like Robinson, valued loyalty and honour greatly. Awarded a Knighthood in recognition of his gallant defence of Her Majesty's colonial interests, MacNab appeared to have reached, in the aftermath of 1837–8, the paternal pinnacle of influence and reverence. When his militia men paid him homage, presenting MacNab with a sword valued at 100 guineas, the old commander responded

---

80   Bode 1984; Robinson's letters, scattered throughout Sanderson 1957, Vol. 2; Robinson 1957, pp. 119–28.

politely with patriarchal gratitude: 'While living I shall cherish this Gift, among
the richest prizes of my life – and dying, shall bequeath it, as the most venerated
heir loom which a father could transmit to his Children'. But behind the public
façade of familial grace lay the private recognition of the new realities, put into
popular doggerel by Charley Corncobb, 'poet laureate of reform':

> Toryism's sun is set
> Tis down, tis gone forever
> Some say that it will start up yet,
> But will it? Nonsense, never.

As MacNab was feted by the Upper Canadian Assembly, he scrawled on the
back of its printed testimonial the terse comment, 'Not worth a fart'.[81]

The ways in which that harsh judgement was tolerated by those who saw
patriarchal authority undermined to the point of inevitable defeat, has not
really registered with historians. Yet these wounds were deep, and they cut
across lines of class in ways that complicate the politics of alternatives in Upper
Canada in the 1830s. There is perhaps no more dramatic an indication of this
than Robert Baldwin. Moderate and judicious in his politics, he recoiled from
much of the popular theatre of antagonism to authority, just as he rebelled
against the arbitrariness of oligarchy and compact rule. His was, ironically, one
of the voices that would be heard loudest in the emergence of modern political
institutions and the evolving governance procedures of civil society. Baldwin's
name would be linked unmistakably with Responsible Government and the
respectable reform of political life that flowed out of the defeat of the rebellion,
ordered in a reasoned constitutionalist direction. Yet Baldwin also lived within
the bounds of disintegrating patriarchy, albeit of an extreme, personalised sort.
By 1851 he had come to question where all the agitation of the 1830s had led.
He complained bitterly of the 'reckless disregard of first principles' that he
judged to be running rampant in the seismic political shifts of his time. He was
apprehensive about 'widespread social disorganization with all of its fearful
consequences'. 'If the sober mind of the country is not prepared to protect our
institutions', he reflected, there was little hope for the future. As he made his
exit from the political stage, a Reformer from the district of Sharon, represented
in the legislature by Baldwin, wrote to the chastened Radical, William Lyon
Mackenzie, offering a prescription for success in the changed political times of
the 1850s: 'The watchword is to be no lawyers, more farmers and machinists'.

---

81   Beer 1984, pp. 146–7; Charley Corncob quoted in Palmer 1983b, p. 58.

It would not quite work out that way – barristers would remain commonplace in politics – but that the matter could be articulated in such a counter-posed language of class spoke to the accelerating pace of socio-economic change.[82]

Baldwin stood astride the class divisions of the epoch, and their uncertain outcome troubled him greatly. One critical institution – patriarchy – was obviously centrally placed in Baldwin's focus. It cut deeply into the political and social relations of Upper Canada, and while it affected women, the young, and those incarcerated in the dependencies of class most adversely, it registered elsewhere as well. Baldwin was predeceased by his wife, who was also his cousin, and throughout the last years of his life he carried a written memorandum in his waistcoat pocket. It stated that should he be carried away suddenly, he was not to be buried before an incision was made into the cavity of his abdomen. It was Robert 'Responsible Government' Baldwin's last wish that he should go to his grave, his God, and eternity bearing the same surgical wound as his wife, the scar of a Caesarian section.[83]

The power of patriarchy left its mark, then, on the bodies of those who lived within its defining authority, in the terror of loyalist repression as well as in the theatrics of dissent. It scarred the politics of popular radicalism, which never quite shed its indebtedness to the politics of a civil authority rooted in understandings of familial duty. In the hybrid, transplanted world of Upper Canadian politics in the 1830s this meant that the aspirations of those who so often staged a counter-theatre of insurrection and rebellion were destined in the short run to be thwarted. But in the longer unfolding of Canadian political culture, the blows against patriarchy and paternalism, first struck on the ambiguous anvil of class, did indeed sound the death knell of the *ancien régime*. Popular radicalism made history in the 1830s, if not in ways that it either entirely understood or proved able to articulate with political precision.[84]

---

82 On the persistence of lawyers in politics see Swainson 1968. For a statement that overemphasises continuity among the personnel of governance, to the detriment of an appreciation of what had altered with the passing of the *ancient regime*, see Johnson 1989.

83 The above paragraphs on Baldwin draw on Cross and Fraser 1983, pp. 164–83; Cross and Fraser 1985.

84 Marx 1968, p. 97.

PART 2

*Workers's Cultures, Struggles,
and Mobilisations in the Age of
Capitalist Consolidation, 1860–1920*

∵

Introduction to Part 2

The three essays reprinted in this section represent discrete aspects of a larger focus on the consolidation of class in Canada and the United States in the late nineteenth and early twentieth centuries. All developed, in one way or another, out of research associated with the writing of my dissertation, a study of skilled workers in a Canadian city associated with the rise of heavy industry and the Second Industrial Revolution. This was later published as *A Culture in Conflict: Skilled Workers and Industrial Capitalism in Hamilton, Ontario, 1860–1914* (1979), and became associated with what was often labelled a culturalist turn in the so-called new Canadian working-class history of the 1970s. But this ostensible culturalism was more a figment of certain imaginations, and compared to later developments in historiography was far more integrated with socio-economic developments than was often acknowledged. In as much as culture was of interest in this writing, it was never far removed from the structured determinations of political economy or the changing nature of class struggle.

'In Street and Field and Hall', subtitled for clarity in this volume 'The Culture of Hamilton Workingmen, 1860–1914', shows how central the associations, institutions, and leisure activities of the industrial city were to the texture of workers' everyday lives. Addressing this milieu, seemingly apart from the workplace and politics, but indeed connected to them, was central to new research into Canadian labour history in the 1970s. But this overview, which appeared as chapter two in *A Culture in Conflict*, had been prefaced by a Marxist analysis and periodisation of capitalist development, and it would be followed by detailed explorations of specific kinds of class struggles, from which the cultural forms detailed and interpreted in this republished statement were seldom separable.

This focus on class struggle, and the necessity of situating it within particular kinds of capitalism, was the impetus behind my interest in managerial initiatives such as Taylorism, evident in the discussion of shop floor rebelliousness that erupted in the opening decades of the twentieth century, and that proved especially significant in the years of World War I and its immediate aftermath. In the mid-1970s few books were as influential as Harry Braverman's *Labor and Monopoly Capital: The Degradation of Work in the Twentieth Century* (1974). David Montgomery expanded upon Braverman's general discussion of Fredrick Winslow Taylor's influence with his strikingly rich research forays into the ways that workers' knowledge of the production process subverted managerial efforts to subordinate labour to the interests of efficient production.[1] My article 'Class, Conception, and Conflict' emerged at the interface of Braverman's and Montgomery's concerns, and was in fact my first academic publication in article form. It appeared in the *Review of Radical Political Economics* in 1975, an important interdisciplinary forum for discussing the hierarchies of capitalist production and the nature of working-class resistance. Having grown out of a graduate student essay, it is to my great surprise that it is still referenced and discussed in certain circles.

The middle essay in this trio of 1970s and early 1980s publications constitutes a distillation of my work with Gregory S. Kealey, our collaboration aiming to create a different kind of working-class history. Our independent studies of class formation in Hamilton and Toronto over the course of the late nineteenth century brought us together around overlapping interests in the enigmatic Noble and Holy Order of the Knights of Labor, or what was known in the 1880s as the Great Upheaval. We chronicled this history in a 1983 study, *Dreaming of What Might Be: The Knights of Labor in Ontario, 1880–1900*. The Knights redefined and stretched the bonds of unity among all manner of workers and, as our essay shows, were simultaneously a trade union, a political movement of mass mobilisation, a cultural undertaking, and an alternative religion.

If there was a moment in which the *making* of the Canadian working class might have been argued to be taking place, the Knights of Labor and the 1880s is not a bad place to look. Workers' cultures, struggles, and mobilisations in the 1860–1920 years thus revealed a world ordered far more by class and its discontents than had been evident in the class struggles without class that preceded them in the 1800–1850 period. They also figure forcefully in setting the stage on which future, twentieth-century mobilisations of the working class would take place, and which mainstream labour historians had long associated with the first stirrings of a Canadian working class.

---

1   Montgomery 1974; Montgomery 1979.

CHAPTER 3

In Street and Field and Hall:
The Culture of Hamilton Workingmen, 1860–1914[*]

The workingmen once held in dis-esteem – looked upon as unhonored and unhonorable – as a serf, a thrall, fit only for merest drudgery – now comes to be recognized in his true claims. Labor being so fundamental and necessary, all ingenuous, noble minds feel that the workingman is worthy of double respect. He is worthy because he is a man – and because he promotes that which is fundamental to the advancement of society. Nor can anyone doubt the importance of self-culture to that class. It may be that the workingman is undistinguished – obscured by his position and must always remain so. That all men are to be distinguished – and great, no one can reasonably imagine, and yet wherever you find human nature, that which makes a man, you find elements of greatness. The workingman has intellect, judgement, conscience; is capable of affection, sympathy, love, can exercise fancy, imagination, perceive the grand, the beautiful, as well as the statesman, the philosopher or student; what he wants is inward culture – development – and he will be prepared to put forth outward influence of the highest character ... Men and especially workingmen are so absorbed in small details that they sometimes grow unstable; are like children who turn from one thing to another. What they want is something broad, permanent, something established, fixed, that alone is found only by culture.

The Workingman's Advocate, 2 June 1866

∴

Thomas Briggs, a Grand Trunk rail worker, died in early April 1904. As the funeral procession wound its way through city streets, it reflected social ties

* 'In Street and Field and Hall: The Culture of Hamilton Workingmen, 1860–1914', adapted from *A Culture in Conflict: Skilled Workers and Industrial Capitalism in Hamilton, 1860–1914* (Kingston and Montreal: McGill-Queen's University Press, 1979), 35–70.

that had been of importance during the mechanic's lifetime. Numerous friends and relatives gathered to pay their last respects, but it was perhaps a closer, final, proximity to Briggs that tells us something of the loyalties that dominated his life in Hamilton. For carrying him to his grave were two members of the Ancient Order of Foresters, two members of the Sons of England, and two of his former workmates at the Grand Trunk yards.[1]

The response to the death of Thomas Canary in 1885 typifies the skilled workers' reaction to the loss of a fellow craftsman. As an active member of Hamilton's Cigar Makers' International Union, a delegate to the 1885 Cincinnati convention, and prominent in the Emerald Beneficial Association, Canary's funeral was attended by scores of the city's workers. Eulogised by his union as an 'earnest, intelligent, and foremost worker in our struggles', Canary was the recipient of a solemn tribute: after his burial the Cigar Makers would drape their charter in mourning for a period of 30 days, a mark of respect for a man of substance and worth.[2]

These men were not atypical, and in Hamilton, as well as in other Canadian communities, the funeral procession was one of many persistent continuities in the culture of the skilled workingman.[3] It was a moment of appreciation of the accomplishments of ordinary men, as well as a chance to celebrate the ties that had meant so much over the course of a lifetime. Funerals, in fact, were often regarded as the touchstone of solidarity. 'Men who fail to show respect to the dead', argued the *Palladium of Labor* in 1884, 'seldom or ever respect anything outside of their own precious selves'.[4] Fire companies,[5] baseball teams,[6] fraternal lodges and friendly societies,[7] and reform clubs[8] all

---

1   *Hamilton Spectator*, 7 April 1904.

2   *Palladium of Labor*, 5 December 1885; *Cigar Makers' Official Journal*, October 1885.

3   Note the vivid accounts of funeral processions in London and Ottawa in *Ontario Workman*, 11 December 1873; 24 April 1873.

4   *Palladium of Labor*, 15 November 1884.

5   On funerals of Hamilton fire company officials and members, many of whom were skilled workingmen, see *Hamilton Times*, 20 April 1863; *Hamilton Spectator*, 18 November 1865; 19 November 1865; 25 March 1867; 29 April 1872.

6   James Shuttleworth, a shoemaker and co-founder of the Maple Leaf Base Ball Club, was followed to his grave by his working-class teammates. See *Hamilton Spectator*, 27 August 1869.

7   See *Hamilton Spectator*, 15 October 1873; 26 May 1882; 19 February 1883; 11 October 1890; 29 June 1906; *Typographical Journal*, November 1911.

8   A deceased Hamilton glass worker, Ephraim McHenry, received a resolution of condolence from his union and from his American currency reform club, the National League. See *Labor Union*, 27 January 1883.

mourned the loss of working-class brethren. Among the membership of craft unions or assemblies of the Knights of Labor attendance at a funeral was a matter of principle and pride, a collective as opposed to individual choice; 'in a body' was the usual manner in which they paid their last respects.[9] The funeral procession, then, hints at the strength of the associational life of the Victorian workman, a key component of his social and cultural existence. In the sheer size of the mourning procession, or the unanimity of the trade union attendance, we are reminded of the tenacious bond of solidarity cementing the working-class community.[10]

So prominent, indeed, was working-class attendance at funerals that the event came to occupy a place within the language of the trades. An 'Old Timer' reminisced:

> I would tell what I know about team shoe making. The men are a jolly set and have their own little rackets. A team is composed of a laster, healer, burnisher, and finisher. The best thing is to get a steady team, for unless you have that luck you are never sure of a full weeks work. Shoemakers have more 'uncles' and 'aunts' than any other mechanic. If in the summer the day be fine, some one of team gets the 'flem', and the others cannot work without him, so they are obliged to stop, and as a rule, they get the 'hines'. He may turn up next day. Ask him where he was? 'To be sure, to a funeral'. His 'wife' died. I knew one man to bury a wife every other week. The funniest thing is that all the wives died to order, always Sunday so they

---

9   Printers were perhaps the strongest supporters. See *Hamilton Spectator*, 28 November 1861; 29 September 1891; 8 June 1893; 28 August 1895; 26 October 1895; 12 February 1898; *Typographical Journal*, November 1911. Funerals of cigar makers, glass workers, moulders, and rail workers are noted in *Hamilton Spectator*, 26 May 1882; 19 February 1883; 11 October 1890; *Palladium of Labor*, 24 October 1885; *Iron Molders' International Journal*, May 1882; July 1882; United Green Glass Workers' Association of the United States and Canada 1893, p. 147. For Knights of Labor funerals see *Palladium of Labor*, 8 May 1886; 15 May 1886; *Hamilton Spectator*, 25 June 1887; 7 September 1887. On funeral policy in the Knights of St. Crispin, see Knights of St. Crispin, London Lodge, No. 242, 1872, p. 23.

10 On the general importance of working-class funerals see Kealey 1976b, pp. 23–4; Roberts 1976, pp. 132–3; Kealey 1973a, pp. 137–58. Cf. *Iron Molders' International Journal*, 4 April 1904; *Canadian Labor Reformer*, 19 June 1886; *The Craftsmen*, 20 November 1886; 5 March 1887; 'Memorial Service of the Knights of Labor', Powderly Papers, Catholic University, Washington, D.C. Particular instances of importance are recorded for Hamilton moulders, carpenters, and nail makers in *Hamilton Spectator*, 26 March 1880; 1 October 1890; *Palladium of Labor*, 23 February 1884; 7 February 1885.

can take Monday to attend the funeral. What work the laster gets out for the week the other four will get paid for, and it happens that the other men will get paid for work not finished. The boys call that 'dead horse', after him the team must pay for it, so it is in their interest to keep him until he finishes the work. The Dutch shoemakers call it 'swine' and it is now left for the French to give it a name. Tell all who desire to become shoemakers to see that the team are steady men; but look out for 'dead horse', 'swine', and 'funerals', and you may succeed.[11]

This 'Old Timer's' account of resistance to work discipline in the shoe industry suggests another context in which to view the customary attendance of funerals. Relief from the drudgery of work may well have prompted the exodus from the workplace accompanying the burial of a fellow worker. An iron moulder, 'J.C.', outlined the consequence of this alternative, the deterioration of the long-standing practice of funeral attendance among foundry workers:

> In former years it was customary for the shop's crew, and even the entire union to take a day for attendance, not altogether because of their grief or affection for the brother, but because of the custom that had been established in years gone by, and often I regret to say because the members desired to take in a ball game or other athletic event or visit a neighbouring town. It was frequently happened that not one-fourth of the men have attended the funeral services, and one instance came under my notice where, out of 173 molders working in six shops, but eleven were present, the others spending their time in other ways.

In the midst of this kind of inattention to tradition, some craftsmen undoubtedly advocated the abandonment of the obligation of funeral attendance. This was 'J.C.'s solution, and he must have had his followers.[12] Historians with an acute urge to pigeonhole, and a finely honed sociological bent, will perhaps perceive a modernist-traditionalist divide separating 'J.C.' and the 'Old Timer'. It is a neat categorisation, and one that will appeal to those who crave order and precision, but working-class culture knew few such tidy distinctions. The old and the new, the residual and the emergent – to use Raymond Williams's terms – were much more likely to exist symbiotically, and in late nineteenth-century Hamilton, at least, it is the continuities in the cultural lives of working-

---

11   *John Swinton's Paper*, 1 February 1885.

12   *Iron Molders' International Journal*, June 1904. Cf. *Hamilton Gazette*, 8 July 1852.

men that are striking.[13] The tradition of funeral attendance, for instance, lived on, albeit in a less rigorous form. When David Ross, a printer once prominent in the Hamilton Trades and Labor Council, died in Toronto in the winter of 1898, his body was returned to Hamilton, and members of the city's International Typographical Union attended the funeral in large numbers. Non-residency had done little to stifle their sense of obligation, and Ross's funeral spoke of the persistence of an established tradition.[14]

Other attachments also survived and proved important. The culture of the nineteenth-century skilled workingman embraced a rich associational life, institutionalised in the friendly society, the mechanics' institute, sporting fraternities, fire companies, and workingmen's clubs. Complementing these formal relationships were the less structured but equally tangible ties of neighbourhood, workplace, or kin, manifesting themselves in the intimacy of the shared pail of beer, or the belligerence of the charivari party. Lingering at the edge of this culture, and illuminating its contours, stood events of importance to the community of the skilled: Confederation, marked by celebration and trade procession; self-proclaimed workingmen's holidays, later legitimised by government proclamation, and declared Labour Day; or less momentous happenings, such as the coming of a circus, or the visit of a minstrel troupe. But by the early twentieth century entire realms of this culture would be emasculated, if not destroyed. The mechanics' institute, poisoned by the condescension and contemptuous patronage of the city's elite, had withered and died, while professionalisation siphoned off much of the cultural essence of the baseball teams and fire companies. Yet the passing of institutions or the sublimation of once specifically working-class activities hardly signified the obliteration of a culture. Much lived on, transplanted to other formal settings, craft unions being particularly fertile ground; and other cultural forms and traditions continued to thrive in their own right.

---

13   One recent attempt to categorise working-class cultural types is Dawley and Faler 1976, pp. 466–80. The Dawley-Faler argument, positing traditionalist, modernist, loyalist, and rebel dichotomies, fractures the complexity and subtlety of continuities in the working-class cultural experience. It draws upon Faler 1974, pp. 367–94. For a more sophisticated conception of working-class culture, resting on the basic premise that cultural forms are a complex fusion of residual (old) and emergent (new) forms see Williams 1973, pp. 3–16; 1977, especially pp. 11–20, 75–144. Williams's concepts have been fruitfully employed in Kealey 1976a, p. 33; Fink 1975, pp. 56–73. For another critique of the Dawley-Faler article see Walkowitz 1975, pp. 13–18.

14   *Hamilton Spectator*, 12 February 1898.

Cultural continuities, then, testify to the basic resiliency of working people in the face of the industrial-capitalist transformation of the nineteenth century.[15] It was perhaps this fundamental continuity which lent coherence and stability to the working-class community, mediating the disruptive impact of massive population turnover, pervasive upward and downward social mobility, and the chaotic upheavals associated with the transition from handicraft production to modern industry – all prominent in the years 1860–1914. And, finally, this essential cultural continuity may be seen as the background of coherence against which new forms of working-class protest evolved, forms that in Hamilton assumed importance in the struggle for the nine-hour day, the rise of the Knights of Labor, and the emergence of an aggressive craft unionism in the pre-World War I years. For culture is nothing if it is not *used*: a process that constantly brings into relief the specific social relationships of a given society, relationships that often reflect basic antagonisms under industrial capitalism.[16] What is too often seen as trivial and commonplace in the cultural arena may be, as Henri Lefebvre points out, an important source of creativity and inspiration, perhaps even a sustaining force underlying the process of resistance:

> As a compendium of seemingly unimportant activities and of products and exhibits other than natural, everyday life is more than something that eludes natural, divine and human myths. Could it represent a lower sphere of meaning, a place where creative energy is stored in readiness for new creations? ... It is not a chasm, a barrier or a buffer but a field and a half-way house, a halting place and a spring-board, a moment made on moments (desires, labours, pleasures – products and achievements – passivity and creativity – means and ends, etc.), the dialectical interaction that is the inevitable starting point for the realization of the possible.[17]

It was, perhaps, in just this kind of way that culture operated in past times in Hamilton's community of skilled workers. Despite the irksome fact that working-class involvement in friendly society and fire-engine hall, mechanics' institute and baseball team, is shrouded in obscurity, a ubiquitous anonymity

---

15   Herbert Gutman's work remains the most extended discussion of this phenomenon. See his essays in Gutman 1976b; and especially his discussion of the family in 1976a. For an attack on Gutman's orientation see Fox-Genovese and Genovese 1976, pp. 205–21. More confusing is the attack in Katz, Doucet, and Stern 1978, p. 700.

16   See Palmer 1976b, pp. 5–32. Important theoretical statements on culture are found in Stock 1973, pp. 30–1; Mintz 1975, pp. 477–94; Bauman 1968, pp. 161–73; and Geertz 1973, pp. 3–30.

17   Lefebvre 1971, p. 14.

being imposed on historical knowledge by the lack of surviving sources, it is possible, and even probable, that the associational life of skilled workers cultivated a sense of solidarity that strengthened the ability of the skilled to resist the encroachments of industrial-capitalist disciplines and development. And it is undeniable that within a shared cultural context there were age-old customs and traditions – the charivari, to name but one – that could be turned to the purposes of protest. Historians who by-pass this culture, denigrating its importance, miss a complex component of nineteenth- and early twentieth-century life.[18]

Clearly one of the most visible corners of associational life in Hamilton in the years 1860–1914 was the fraternal lodge. Friendly societies attracted the city's residents with striking regularity: Orangemen met to celebrate the Battle of the Boyne, or reminisce over dinner on Guy Fawkes Day; Masons often found themselves attracted to festivals honouring the traditions of their ancient craft; and the Foresters, Emerald Beneficial Association, Sons of England, Workmen, Odd Fellows, St. George's Society, and Knights of Pythias all sank deep roots in Hamilton's soil.

These voluntary associations can be viewed in different ways. Some have suggested that they were primarily bases of community power, led by men of property and standing.[19] Others have looked in another direction, focusing instead on the involvement of many working-class elements.[20] Both perceptions touch on important truths. On the one hand, merchants, professionals, clerks, and propertied men did indeed exert disproportionate amounts of influence in many friendly society circles, although it is important to realise that this hegemony was uneven, varying from society to society as well as within different lodges of the same organisation. On the other hand, skilled workingmen certainly, and even some labourers, were common in all of the societies, and in many their role was far from subservient.

There was much to draw the skilled worker into the halls of the fraternal order. We have already noted the important contribution of the friendly societies in time of death. Beyond this the very language of the fraternal order was often borrowed from the crafts, appealing to a sense of dignity and pride of workmanship well understood by the mechanic.[21] For the wandering emig-

---

18   This, I fear, is a major flaw in Katz 1975b, especially p. 6. It appears to survive in Katz's more recent work. See Katz, Doucet, and Stern 1978, p. 700.

19   Katz 1975b, pp. 183–5; Glazer 1972, pp. 151–68.

20   Kealey 1976b, pp. 13–34; Palmer 1976a, pp. 106–24; Harrison 1973, pp. 107–38.

21   Grand Lodge of Ancient Free and Accepted Masons of Canada 1866, pp. 10–11.

rant, on a 'tramp' of unnatural severity, the comforts of shared sympathies and impressions must have drawn many a Scot to the St. Andrew's Society, a number of Englishmen to the St. George's Society, and more than a few Irish to the St. Patrick's Society or the Orange Lodge.[22] The elaborate ritual and solemnity of the secret oath undoubtedly cultivated a sense of fraternity cherished by the men of the trades and, in the case of an old Crispin or a dedicated Knight of Labor, thoroughly familiar.[23] And, as a means of transcending the tight bounds of economic insecurity, many nineteenth-century workingmen might well have been attracted to the charitable impulse, so important in the germination of the voluntary society.[24]

All of this, and more, pushed the skilled worker towards friendly society halls, an environment in which cooperation, fraternity, and equality thrived. The motto of the Ancient Order of United Workmen, for instance, proclaimed adherence to mutual aid: 'The one needs the assistance of the other'.[25] Among the Odd Fellows an old axiom – 'In union there is strength' – achieved a place of prominence. 'A single individual', proclaimed the *Correct Guide in all Matters Relating to Oddfellowship*, 'if he labor with a will, may accomplish much in the field of fraternity, but a host, united in solid phalanx in the service of Benevolence, may revolutionize the world'.[26] Class distinctions were to have no place within their order: 'we aim to abolish all considerations of wealth or poverty in our fraternity; to make all feel that as Odd Fellows, at least, they are not only brethren, but equals'.[27] Small wonder, then, that the Odd Fellows aimed their sights directly at a working-class constituency: 'It is probably the most adapted to working men, who from changes in locations of trade, and

22   See St. Andrew's Benevolent Society of Hamilton, Ontario 1882, p. 5; Hamilton St. George's Benevolent Society 1844, n.p.; St. Andrew's Benevolent Society of Hamilton 1860, p. 3; 'Cornelius Donovan', *Cathedral Magazine*, reprinted in *Papers and Records of the Wentworth Historical Society*, 1924; Orange Association of British America 1892, p. 4.

23   See Palmer 1976a, pp. 111–12; Kealey 1976b, pp. 16–17; 1973a, pp. 137–58; Smith n.d., pp. cxxi–cxxii; Morgan n.d., pp. 1–9; *Palladium of Labor*, 13 October 1883. Possibly the most explicit working-class endorsement of secrecy and ritual is found in the *Labour Standard*, 16 November 1878. For a discussion of the importance and place of ritual in the Knights of Labor see chapter 6 in Palmer 1979a.

24   See King 1891, pp. 10–13; *Hamilton Times*, 16 January 1866. Note also the role of the Hamilton societies in providing aid for the unemployed cotton operatives in Lancashire amidst the disruption of the American Civil War. See *Hamilton Times*, 2 October 1862; 4 November 1862; 13 November 1862.

25   Ancient Order of United Workmen n.d., p. 29.

26   Ridgely 1867, pp. 44–5.

27   Gosh 1869, p. 1.

other causes, are daily becoming more migratory in their habits, and who are also emigrating in great numbers from our shores to our colonies and distant lands'.[28] This was an attractive package to the workingman of the Victorian city.

Few indeed were the Hamilton men prominent in trade affairs who had no connection with a fraternal lodge or benevolent association. John Pryke, president of the Hamilton Nine Hour League, and a staunch Crispin, was an active member of the Orange Lodge.[29] A machinist, William Derby, Grand Master Workman of the Hamilton District Assembly of the Knights of Labor, and an early pillar of the Trades and Labor Council, was a leading official of the Young Men's Protestant Benevolent Association.[30] A prominent activist in the organisational drive of the pre-World War I years, Harry Obermeyer, was enrolled in a number of societies.[31] Among printers the penchant for involvement seemed particularly acute. Cornelius Donovan, a typographer serving as president of the Hamilton Trades Assembly in 1872, assisted in the founding of the St. Patrick's Society.[32] Two printers – A.T. Freed and David Hastings – stood out as dedicated members of the Acacia Lodge of the Ancient, Free, and Accepted Masons, documenting its early history.[33] Probably the most ardent supporter of the friendly society, however, was William J. Vale. Vale, whose experience in the working-class movement included participation in the Toronto printers' strike of 1872, a term as Grand Master Workman of the Hamilton Knights in 1883, scurrilous indictment as a member of the Order's notorious 'Home Club'

---

28   Independent Order of Oddfellows, Manchester Unity Friendly Society 1879, p. 3. Cf. *Ontario Workman*, 24 April 1873.

29   *Hamilton Spectator*, 1 December 1872.

30   *Labor Advocate*, 30 January 1891.

31   *Labor News*, 19 January 1912.

32   'Cornelius Donovan', *Cathedral Magazine*, reprinted in *Papers and Records of the Wentworth Historical Society*, 1924. Cf. *Hamilton Herald*, 6 January 1895.

33   Freed, a staunch Tory and eventual editor of the *Hamilton Spectator*, was the Hamilton representative on the Royal Commission on the Relations of Labor and Capital, and came under attack by organised labour for his views. See Kealey 1973b, pp. ix–xxvii. For his central place in Hamilton Conservative Party politics see Freed to MacDonald, 6 September 1884, Sir John A. MacDonald Papers, MG 26 A, vol. 318, pp. 144008–14, Public Archives of Canada; Freed to MacDonald, 23 October 1888, vol. 465, pp. 231552–3; Freed to MacDonald, 11 June 1889, vol. 63, pp. 25728–31; MacDonald to Freed, 10 December 1889, vol. 527, p. 343; Freed to MacDonald, 1890, vol. 332, pp. 150046–50. On Freed's prominence in Masonic circles see Freed to MacDonald, 25 June 1886, Sir John A. Macdonald Papers, MG 26 A, vol. 427, pp. 208867–8, Public Archives of Canada; Hastings 1905, p. 16. On Hastings see *Hamilton Spectator*, 5 September 1896; *Typographical Journal*, 1 September 1896.

in 1886, long affiliation with the International Typographical Union No. 129, and leadership of the Trades and Labor Council in the late 1880s and early 1890s, also found time to patronise the Foresters, Odd Fellows, and St. George's Society. He viewed the fraternal order as the practical embodiment of the principles of the cooperative movement; his intimate connection with and understanding of Hamilton societies won him a position as insurance inspector in 1892.[34] Vale's associate in the printers' union, the workingman's alderman William C. McAndrew, was the recipient of a 'past preceptor's jewel', an honour attained by few Orangemen.[35] Men like these prompted the working-class press to keep abreast of fraternal society activities, allocating columns to the progress of the secret orders. 'A large number of union men are members of the Woodmen of the World', noted the *Industrial Banner* in 1907.[36]

The most convincing evidence of the skilled worker's presence in the friendly society, of course, would be complete membership listings, which could then be used to formulate a conception of the occupational structure of specific lodges.[37] Such data is extremely rare. Only two such compilations exist for Hamilton societies in the years 1860–1914 and these, unfortunately, are from

---

34   *Hamilton Spectator*, 9 May 1892; *Labor Advocate*, 8 January 1891; 6 February 1891; *Ye little Home booke of ye revelles of Sanct George* ... (Hamilton: Times, 1893), n.p., notes Vale's role in a St. George's Society carnival.

35   *Hamilton Spectator*, 19 February 1895.

36   Cf. *Industrial Banner*, April 1907; *Palladium of Labor*, 1 September 1883; 13 October 1883; 15 December 1883; 7 June 1884; 19 July 1884; 9 August 1884; 31 October 1885; *Labor Union*, 14 July 1883; *Bobcaygeon Independent*, 5 June 1896; *The Lance*, 26 November 1910; *Labor Advocate*, 27 February 1891; 12 June 1891; *Labor News*, 19 January 1912; *Hamilton Spectator*, 21 July 1904.

37   Many problems are posed by occupational classification. See Katz 1972, pp. 63–88; 1975b, pp. 343–8; Smith 1975, pp. 134–46. Despite these warnings, however, it is not clear that quantitative methods can overcome problems in the original data; it is entirely possible that sophisticated technological methods may simply mask fundamental ambivalences. Given these shortcomings, socioeconomic rankings are probably not needed. There is no problem for instance in differentiating the merchant tailor of the 1880s from the working tailor, or the contractor from the carpenter, and most of Katz's classifications are of real importance in the earlier years of industrial-capitalist development, when lines between master and journeyman were blurred. There is very little to be mistaken in the cases of moulders, boilermakers, blacksmiths, machinists, or labourers. They were, in fact, what they said they were. True, many would understate their occupational classification, but a knowledge of the inhabitants of a city, in which men of wealth and substance generally stand out, is the safest means of guarding against this problem. Katz, Doucet, and Stern have, however, made considerable progress in their efforts to distinguish master craftsmen from journeymen. See Katz, Doucet, and Stern, 1982.

a body – the Ancient, Free, and Accepted Masons – which, along with the
St. George's and St. Andrew's Societies, had a particularly weak working-class
constituency, one factor, no doubt, contributing to the survival of these lists.[38]
Between 1855 and 1905, 709 Hamiltonians joined the Acacia Lodge of the
Ancient, Free, and Accepted Masons; of these, the occupations of 489 could
be determined.[39] Within this latter group a clear majority of 282 belonged to a
social stratum distinctly removed from the world of the skilled workingman, led
by merchants (14), manufacturers (five), and proprietors (29), and supported by
a vast body of clerks (45), accountants (23), and salesmen-travellers (30), and a
retinue of doctors, bartenders, managers, insurance agents, architects, brokers,
bank tellers, teachers, and barristers.[40] The skilled worker, however, was not
without a voice in Acadia Lodge: approximately thirty six percent of this identified sample, or 176 members, belonged to the skilled trades, among them 21
machinists and 19 carpenters.[41] Rounding out these figures were 31 members

38   See for instance St. George's Benevolent Society of Hamilton, *Collections of Programs, Invit-
      ations, Announcements, Etc.*, Hamilton Collection, Hamilton Public Library, on the prom-
      inence of non-working-class elements. St. George's Society officers were listed in *Hamilton
      Times*, 15 January 1862, 16 January 1866; *Hamilton Spectator*, 17 January 1865. Checking the
      occupations of these officials in the city directories revealed few workingmen. A similar
      procedure was followed in the case of the Masonic Lodges, whose officials were listed in
      Hamilton Times, 25 June 1861; 29 December 1863; 15 February 1866. Cf. listings of officials
      of both societies in *City of Hamilton Directory, 1895*, pp. 325–9; *Vernon's City of Hamilton
      Directory, 1911*, pp. 767–74. Most lodges or chapters were dominated by merchants and
      proprietors, with the exception of St. John's Lodge, A.F. & A.M., in which a jeweller, boiler-
      maker, fitter, watchmaker, and carpenter held positions of prominence.
39   The listing is in Hastings 1905, pp. 39–54. Occupations were determined by checking
      names in city directories. Some of the Masons simply did not appear in the directories,
      while others, often those with common names (William Brown, Charles Frank, Richard
      McKay, etc.), could not be identified because of multiple listings.
40   Some of this group may well have had some ties to the working-class community for it
      included professional firemen, foremen-superintendents, and grocers. I also considered
      any craftsmen prefacing his trade with merchant or proprietor in this group.
41   The others: seven each of engineers, printers, hatters, blacksmiths, and butchers; six tail-
      ors; five bricklayers and five bakers; four from each of the trades of harness-making/
      saddliery, watchmaking, cabinetmaking, fitting, moulding, shoemaking, tinsmithing; four
      from each of the railway occupations of engineer, brakesman, and conductor; three
      upholsterers, three dyers, and three electricians; two each of jewellers, tanners, stonecut-
      ters, plumbers, cigar-makers; and a single furrier, finisher, street railway conductor, cutter
      plasterer, foundry-man, ironworker, stove-mounter, bookbinder, mason, hammer-smith,
      ornamental japaner, painter, carver, slater, glass engraver, boilermaker, picture framer,
      lino-type operator, and locksmith.

from the ranks of the unskilled and service occupations: labourers, mariners, sorters, checkers, watchmen, and teamsters. In the Barton Lodge the story was almost identical. There, of the 159 identified members, 269 joined in the years 1845–1911, and 36 percent, again, belonged to the skilled trades.[42]

In the absence of comparable data from other societies, we can only speculate as to the extent of the involvement of the skilled worker. There are, however, indications that many fraternal bodies housed significant numbers of craftsmen and other working-class elements. James Hennigan, president of the Hamilton branch of the Emerald Beneficial Association and an advocate of the cause of the Knights of Labor, wrote to Terence V. Powderly requesting him to speak at a gathering of his association, which apparently contained large numbers of Powderly's followers.[43] When William Vale was asked 'What kind of membership constitutes these societies?', he replied bluntly: 'Working classes – nine-tenths of them'.[44] Listings of friendly society officials, common in the daily press and in city directories, are also useful as barometers of working-class involvement. A few examples suffice. The Ancient Order of United Workmen, often confused with the Knights of Labor in the parlance of the 1880s, boasted a tinsmith, a conductor, and a printer among its officials in 1881, two brief years after its founding in the city.[45] A glance at the 1901–10 minute book of Lodge No. 49 of the Hamilton Workmen depicts an organisation overwhelmingly working class in composition, in which picnics, lectures, banquets, and sporting rivalry figured prominently.[46] The hegemony of the skilled manifested

---

42   See MacDonald 1945, pp. 234–9. Skilled workers included seven engineers, six moulders, five cutters and five carpenters, three cabinet makers, blacksmiths, machinists, and tailors, two painters, plasterers, telegraphers and tinsmiths, and one from each of the following: iron melter, engine driver, iron worker, core-maker, lithographer, jeweller, brakesman, boat builder, electrician, shoemaker, brick maker, broom maker, conductor, tobacco roller, and stonecutter.

43   Jas. Henigan to Powderly, 26 January 1884, Powderly Papers, Catholic University, Washington, D.C.

44   Royal Commission on the Relations of Labor and Capital in Canada 1889, p. 813.

45   Officers were cited in *Hamilton Spectator*, 25 December 1880; 24 December 1881. Occupations were culled from the 1880–1 and 1881–2 city directories. The Workmen had a membership of 79 in 1880. See *Hamilton Spectator*, 20 March 1880. On the confusion prevailing throughout the 1880s regarding the Knights and the Workmen see *Canadian Workmen*, June 1886.

46   Ancient Order of United Workmen, Lodge No. 49, *Minute Book*, Hamilton Collection, Hamilton Public Library, especially pp. 25, 181, 211, 231, 238, 244, 277, 286, 290, 293. Membership stood at 357 in 1904 (p. 86). Cf. *City of Hamilton Directory, 1895*, pp. 325–9; *Vernon's*

itself blatantly in the Commercial Lodge of the International Order of Odd Fellows in 1863. Daniel Black, a saloon-keeper patronised by many early unionists, shared the leadership of the lodge with his brother William, a machinist at the Great Western shops, John Williams, another machinist, and William J. McAllister, a printer.[47] Officers of the Lodge Britannia No. 8 of the Sons of England in 1883, similarly, included two labourers, a printer, painter, fitter, porter, machinist, butcher, and carpenter.[48]

The organisation with the most substantial following of skilled workingmen, however, was undoubtedly the Orange Lodge. Between the years 1863 and 1878 the officials of various Orange Lodges included representatives from virtually every Hamilton craft, the machinists being especially visible. And, if there was a threat to the hegemony of the skilled, it was posed from below rather than from above, common labourers being the single most prominent occupational category in positions of responsibility.[49] By 1895 the situation was much the same, the officers of the city's Orange Order including two machinists, two cabinetmakers, and a bricklayer, carpenter, moulder, and packer.[50] In 1911 the officials themselves had changed, but the trades persisted; among Hamilton's leading Orangemen printers, moulders, machinists, iron workers, labourers, and carpenters were to be found.[51]

What are we to make of this presence and involvement? It is a thorny question, and one that defies any simplistic answer. Workingmen sought many things in the halls of friendly societies: a measure of security against sickness and death; association with their peers or, perhaps for some, the chance to cultivate ties with their betters; simple recreation away from the confines of family and work, often realised in a game of carpet ball or quoits, or an excursion on

---

Directory, 1911, pp. 767–74, for more listings of officials of the AOUW, many of whom were skilled workingmen.

47 Officials cited in *Hamilton Times*, 28 September 1863, and occupations checked in city directories. On Black see *Hamilton Times*, 16 August 1875.

48 Officials cited in *Palladium of Labor*, 22 December 1883, and occupations checked in city directories.

49 Officials were listed in *Hamilton Times*, 6 November 1863; 6 November 1866; 19 February 1867; 18 February 1868; *Hamilton Spectator*, 19 February 1868; 15 December 1869; 13 December 1872; 12 December 1877; *City of Hamilton Directory, 1874*, pp. 12–13. I was able to identify 63 of these officials occupationally: 39 were skilled workers; 15 belonged to unskilled categories; and 9 were non-working-class elements (salesmen, proprietors, clerks, and grocers).

50 *City of Hamilton Directory, 1895*, pp. 325–9.

51 *Vernon's Hamilton Directory, 1911*, pp. 767–74.

the steamboats of Burlington Bay; an affirmation of their status as respectable members of the community, dispensers of charity and good works, and not just, as in occasional times of great need, recipients. The lessons they learned would be equally varied: the benefits and attractions of equality, fraternity, and cooperation, on the one hand, all deeply embedded within the consciousness of the emerging labour movement; or, on the other hand, deference, accommodation, and an exclusionary contempt for those less attuned to the practices of sober thrift and appropriate propriety.[52]

William J. Vale, in a paper delivered before the Hamilton Trades and Labor Council, stressed the positive contribution of the benevolent society in the evolution of working-class consciousness. Such organisations had, he maintained, done much to further the cooperative impulse, providing a mechanism of collective protection for the lower orders. His views were vehemently opposed by John A. Flett, a Hamilton carpenter later to emerge as a central figure in the rise of the American Federation of Labor in Canada. Flett considered these associations 'merely poultices on the cancer' of the social system, and concluded that '[if] there were no benevolent societies there would be a revolution among the workingmen of the country. The sooner the country comes down to actual want, as a matter of fact, the sooner we'll have change'.[53] Both men caught something of the truth, and if we seek a hard and fast explanation – a sociological model – behind the popularity of the fraternal order in working-class life, we will only stifle the diversity of human motivation and complexity of consequence surrounding the skilled workingman's participation in lodge and chapter.

In one realm of fraternal order activity, however, there was no mistaking the potentiality of divided loyalties that could foster antagonism between two distinct working-class groups. Orange and Green were badges worn by many nineteenth-century workingmen. If Toronto can be taken as a standard, then conflict between Irish Protestants and Irish Catholic workers was common

---

52   On the problems associated with interpreting friendly society involvement see the recent discussion in Foster 1974, especially pp. 216–18.

53   *Labor Advocate*, 6 February 1891. For evidence of the validity of Vale's argument see *Hamilton Spectator*, 23 July 1883, where the AOUW supports striking telegraphers. Note the widespread friendly society endorsement of street railway strikers documented in Palmer 1976a, pp. 106–24. It was not uncommon for Orange Lodge Bands to participate in processions of craft unions or parades of the Knights of Labor. See *Hamilton Spectator*, 4 August 1884; *Industrial Banner*, January 1899; September 1899; *Labor Standard*, 16 December 1877; 4 October 1879; 5 June 1880, for other instances of friendly society ties to the working-class movement. On Flett see Babcock 1974.

and violent.[54] The Jubilee Riots of 1875, for example, stand as one of the most virulent sectarian clashes in the history of Canada.[55]

Yet, in Hamilton, at least, Orange and Green rarely met in violent confrontation. Scattered references to individualised combat do, of course, exist. George Douglas, a boot and shoemaker, was viciously beaten by his neighbour, John Halloran, who while wielding the iron bar he used so effectively upon his opponent's head, was heard to scream, 'I'll take your life! I'll take your life you b----y Protestant'! He did not succeed, but it was not for want of trying.[56] In the fall of 1860 many local Orangemen were outraged when the visit of the Prince of Wales and the Duke of Newcastle was marred by the appearance of 'the Romish Bishop, in full canonicals', and the St. Patrick's Society, bearing aloft '*a green flag and green badges*'.[57] Likewise the flooding of the city by the Toronto 'Prentice Boys in 1887, celebrating the Relief of Derry, gave rise to a brawl, Hamilton's Green contingent apparently having been not at all pleased with the invasion of their turf.[58]

The only serious affair occurred on the night of 6 August 1878, and it was overblown by the local press. Orange-Green relations in the city were apparently at a low point, for there were rumours circulating that the Emerald Beneficial Association was planning to burn an effigy of King William III in retaliation for some insulting acts perpetrated by the Orange Young Britons. The timing of the outburst was conditioned by a visit of some Toronto friends to the King Street rooms of the Emerald Association. After escorting their confrères to the steamer bound for Toronto the Catholic body returned to their rooms, only to be confronted with a large number of men and young boys. A row appeared imminent, and when the Emerald Association's band dispersed, the True Blue Fife and Drum Band appeared, three hundred to four hundred bringing up the rear. After a brief flurry of yelling, singing, and marching around the Gore, the

54   A general introduction to Orangeism, of limited utility, is Senior 1972a. In treating the Order as an adjunct of the Tory Party, and in stressing the leadership of propertied elements, Senior misses much of the importance of the Orange Lodges, including their community context. See Senior 1972b, pp. 136–53. On Toronto conflict see Kealey 1976b, pp. 13–24. For a comment on Orange violence see Cross 1971, pp. 177–90.

55   Gavin 1959, pp. 93–107; *The National*, 30 September 1875; 7 October 1875.

56   *Hamilton Gazette*, 17 January 1853. Cf. *Hamilton Gazette*, 19 January 1852; 26 January 1852; 25 July 1853; 4 August 1853; 7 November 1853, on Hamilton's Orange Lodge in the 1850s and its efforts to consolidate local autonomy.

57   *The Orange Herald and Protestant Intelligencer*, 27 September 1860. Note the general discussion in Conway 1977.

58   *Hamilton Spectator*, 16 August 1887.

procession headed towards James Street, during which time it was interrupted by cries of 'Fight! Fight'! Almost immediately two carters, Dan Collins and Tom Brick, found themselves surrounded by a sea of unfriendly Protestant faces. It was not long before Collins and Brick, armed only with their whips, and the stones thrown at them by their adversaries, were engaged in a battle with the crowd. One must give them their due; they fought admirably. Police eventually extricated them from the street war, and they drove off in the direction of Corktown.

The crowd, 'yelling and maddened', was not so easily put off, and it headed for Brick's house, which was 'reached in a few minutes'. Windows were soon being smashed as the crowd stoned the Brick residence, driving Mrs. Brick, an infant clutched to her breast, to shelter in a neighbour's house. Two or three policemen eventually arrived, but even then 'it was sometime before quietness could be restored. The whole region was in a ferment, women and children running hither and thither and the mob hooting, yelling, swearing and conducting themselves generally in a most outrageous style'. After an abortive attempt to continue the fun at Collins's residence, the crowd finally dispersed, but not before they saw Collins and Brick drive down from the Mountain, denouncing the 'Orange body, whom they blamed for all the trouble'. Brick had not even been in his house during the melee.[59]

Some of the actors met in court the next day, and the testimony, as in most courtroom theatre, was both revealing and humorous.[60] Dan Collins swore that 'there was 600 or 700 there, but I didn't have time to count them; the tune the band played didn't annoy me a bit; you can bet your life I didn't make any remarks, thinking it better to keep my mouth shut'. Michael Begley, a Great Western Railway policeman charged by Brick and Collins with assault, insisted that Collins called him an 'Orange s-- of b----', but denied that he had said that he had 'stood enough of the d----d Papist row', and that he 'wasn't going to have any Montreal here'. Brick seemed undaunted by the whole affair, informing the court that he did not recall 'how often I have been before the Police Magistrate for acts of violence; I guess I have been up twenty times'. The Irishman then assured those gathered to witness the proceedings that 'if there hadn't been 600 or 700 they wouldn't have tackled us'.[61] Brick apparently had not learned an elementary lesson in court etiquette, for his belligerence cost him $10 and

59   The above account is based on the detailed and graphic account, 'Orange and Green: Disgraceful Rowdyism in the City Last Night', *Hamilton Spectator*, 7 August 1878.

60   See the path-breaking overview in Hay 1975, pp. 17–64.

61   *Hamilton Spectator*, 8 August 1878. For a representative case of Brick's clashes with the local police see *Hamilton Times*, 4 November 1863.

costs; the other cases were dismissed. Both Collins and Brick, however, would resurface in the 1880s as members of the Knights of Labor, the latter serving as a workingman's alderman for many years.

This, of course, was a major battle, but a war waged against two carters should not be overdrawn. And there may have been something more to this skirmish than Orange-Green antagonism. Many a man must have had a score to settle with the likes of Dan Collins and Tom Brick. Nevertheless, the event stands out as the most prominent case of aggravated sectarian assault in the city in the years 1860–1914.[62] As such, Hamilton's experience pales in comparison with the upheavals common in Toronto, New York, or Belfast. Part of the reason for this lack of conflict was undoubtedly the strength of the Protestant community. Like London, Ontario, Hamilton was most emphatically a Protestant city, and this hegemony may have gone unquestioned.[63] Equally important, however, was the strength of the working-class movement, and the solidarity it conditioned; Hamilton's Orange and Green workers apparently knew how to keep divided loyalties in perspective, and their allegiance to their class may have mediated many hostilities.

Richard Trevellick said as much in a letter to Terence V. Powderly, comparing the Hamilton Knights of Labor with the Toronto assemblies. In Toronto, Trevellick maintained, the Order was a failure: 'The large assembly of shoemakers as a class are Orangemen and Ladies and if they are not Orangemen they are self-conceited flunkeys and not fit for Heaven'. Hamilton, however, had many trustworthy workers, and meetings were well attended and properly run: 'our house is doing well', Trevellick assured the Grand Master Workman.[64] Workers such as 'Unity', 'Anti-Bigot', and 'Pinkerton' urged upon Hamilton mechanics the politics of class unity, rather than division, and with the realisation that Orange-Green antagonism was 'the bloody shirt' waved in the face of the working-class movement, the cause of unity won important victories.[65] Sec-

---

62   It is interesting to note that the affair occurred in 1878, a time of severe recession. It is thus worthy of comparison with David Montgomery's analysis of ethnic and cultural conflict in Philadelphia in another period of economic downturn. See Montgomery 1972, pp. 411–46.

63   See my discussion of London, where Orange-Green conflict was virtually non-existent, in Palmer 1976a, pp. 106–24. On the Protestant ethnic structure of Hamilton see Katz 1975b, p. 41.

64   Trevellick to Powderly, 8 December 1883, Powderly Papers, Catholic University, Washington, D.C. Trevellick's comments were coloured by a disappointing speaking engagement in Toronto, where he may have been influenced by D.J. O'Donoghue.

65   *Palladium of Labor*, 27 March 1886; 27 November 1886; 18 July 1885; 15 August 1885; *Hamilton Times*, 24 October 1863.

tarian conflict would impinge only peripherally on Hamilton's workingmen in the years 1860–1914, and virtually never after 1887.

Rivalling the friendly society as a centre of the skilled worker's associational life, and less ambiguous both in terms of its class composition and its impact, was the fire company.[66] The history of the Hamilton companies commences in 1833, following a devastating conflagration in 1832. They remained peripheral to community life until the early 1850s, when the growing awareness of the importance of manufacturing to the city's welfare prompted an expansion in the number of companies as well as an increase in the number of volunteer firemen. By 1857 the force stood at eight companies, with a combined membership of 518 officers and men. A series of disputes and disbandings weakened the brigade. By 1867 membership had dropped to 220, with only a hook and ladder company, one hose company, and three engine companies. By the mid-1860s manufacturers and merchants had reacted to this decline, questioning the competency and efficiency of the volunteer corps, advocating the establishment of a professional fire service. It only required a major loss to prompt them to action. With the burning of the D. McInnes and Company warehouses on 1 August 1879 they received their stimulus, and a professional, standing fire department was created, supplemented by volunteers.[67]

For over twenty years, however, the fire companies were created, led, and staffed by Hamilton workmen.

> On the brakes of the old machine
> They worked from day to day,
> Putting out the raging fire,
> Although they got no pay.

A successful craftsman, like the carriage-maker John Amor, who would establish a lucrative agricultural implements works in the city in the 1860s, often

---

66   On fire companies see Laurie 1974, pp. 337–66; 1973, pp. 71–88; Schwartz 1974, pp. 159–78; Neilly 1959; Doctorow 1975.

67   This overview is based on Fireman's Benefit Fund 1920; Campbell 1966, pp. 148–51; Jehan n.d., p. 3; *Sutherland's City of Hamilton Directory, 1862–1863*, pp. 21–2; as well as the many references in *Hamilton Spectator* and *Hamilton Times*. The companies of the 1860s were the Hook and Ladder Company, the Neptune Hose Company, Phoenix Engine Company No. 1, Cataract Engine Company No. 2, and Rescue Engineer Company No. 3. The Great Western Railway also had its own brigade, organised by the mechanics in 1862, composed of a hose company, a steam engine company, and two hand engine companies, with a total membership of 300 in 1867.

played a prominent role, but the majority of firemen were skilled workers of small means.[68] In the Hook and Ladder Company, embracing a membership of 30, the key officers were M.W. Attwood, a watchmaker; A. Green, a brush manufacturer; P. Colvin, a carter; and H.E. Eliot, a tailor. A salesman, an engineer, a compositor, and a shoemaker served as officials in the 40-member Hose Company, while the Rescue Company, with 45 members, was led by a scale maker, a machinist, and a brush maker. John Amor and his brother William, a fruit dealer, seemed to control the No. 1 Company, but they were aided by a hatter and a foundry helper.[69] Nothing had changed by 1867.[70] The composition of the Great Western Brigade in 1867 states the case clearly: the hose company was led by a millwright and two labourers; the No. 1 engine company's officers were a painter, a machinist, a boilermaker, and a fitter; the officials of No. 2 Company included a foreman, an upholsterer, a clerk, a carpenter, and a cabinetmaker; while the steam engine company was presided over by four fitters and a turner.[71] Of the 93 fire company officials classified occupationally in the years 1860–72, 65 were from the skilled trades, 11 came from unskilled occupations, with the remaining 17 falling into a category composed of clerks, foremen, manufacturers, contractors, and merchants.[72]

Like the friendly society, the engine house had much to offer. Some were attracted by the opportunity to serve the community in a time of crisis, for the nineteenth century knew few fears worse than that of fire. Others were undoubtedly drawn to the rich texture of engine-house life, with oyster sup-

---

68   On Amor see Campbell 1966, p. 151; *Hamilton Spectator*, 18 September 1871; 13 March 1893. The verse is from William Haley, 'More Remarks from Old Timer', *Hamilton Spectator*, 17 November 1906. Cf. Wingfield 1873, pp. 190–1.

69   Officials were listed in *Hutchinson's Directory, 1862–1863*, pp. 21–2, and their occupations obtained from the same source.

70   *Sutherland's Directory, 1867–1868*, pp. 21–2. Of the 25 officials, only eight were not skilled workers, and these included two foremen.

71   *Sutherland's Directory, 1867–1868*, pp. 21–2.

72   Officials were listed in *Hamilton Times*, 14 February 1863; 12 February 1864; 17 February 1864; 13 February 1866; 15 February 1866; 26 February 1866; 14 February 1867; 15 February 1867; *Hamilton Spectator*, 10 February 1860; 9 February 1864; 18 November 1865; 3 March 1868; 9 February 1872; 10 February 1872. Occupations were then traced in directories and, among the skilled, included seven carpenters; six blacksmiths; four each of machinists, hatters, tailors, and shoemakers; three printers and three engineers; two painters, bakers, tinsmiths, watchmakers, boilermakers, moulders, scale makers, and masons; and one of each of the following: bookbinder, piler, plasterer, whip maker, cooper, collarmaker, brush maker, jeweller, harness maker, fitter, engineer, coppersmith, gunsmith, and turner.

pers and alcoholic refreshments served by many companies, or the festive gatherings that marked the end of a successful year.[73] Fierce rivalries, bred of neighbourhood jealousies and reinforced by the maintenance of separate companies for each ward, must also have attracted some, for there was no company which did not count it as the highest accomplishment to arrive first at the scene of a fire. So ingrained was the competitive impulse that firemen sacrificed their wages, dropping their tools at the shout of 'Fire!' or ringing of the bell. On one unfortunate occasion, in their haste to arrive first, the Hose Reel Company trampled a young boy underfoot on their dash to a fire.[74] For others the lure of a uniform – consisting of cap and belt, red shirt, light blue coat, white staff and the badge of the office – displayed in the handsome torch-lit procession of a summer evening, or in the spring parades celebrating the Queen's Birthday, must have been irresistible. Also for many, the fire company reinforced other realms of associational life, bringing together patrons of similar causes, Orangeism and temperance being only two of many examples.[75]

Richard Butler, reminiscing on the 'History of Hamilton Fire Department', recalled many an evening spent in the engine house, polishing the equipment and passing the time with other volunteers. His memoir tells us much about the texture of life in a mid-century fire company. At the time of his service in the Cataract Company No. 2, he described the brigade in 1854 as:

> a department of four engine companies, a hose company and a hook and ladder company, comprising an active membership of about three hundred, mostly all young men who did not own a dollar's worth of property in the city, and gave their services without fee or reward for the benefit of their home town. Day or night, when the fire alarm bell called,

73   *Hamilton Times*, 26 December 1863. Cf. *Hamilton Times*, 18 July 1863; 29 July 1863; 10 March 1864; 29 November 1866; 12 January 1867; 1 June 1867; *Hamilton Spectator*, 15 September 1863; 10 March 1864; 1 June 1867; 14 July 1867. On the importance of fires in nineteenth-century cities see Weaver and de Lottinville 1978; Cowherd 1884, pp. 287–8.

74   Campbell 1966, pp. 149–50; *Hamilton Times*, 2 March 1866; 12 February 1867; 8 June 1867. On violence among competing brigades cf. Laurie 1973, pp. 71–88; and Neilly 1959.

75   Campbell 1966, p. 149; *Hamilton Times*, 16 February 1866; 1 May 1866; 25 May 1869; *Hamilton Spectator*, 8 August 1868; 25 May 1869; 21 August 1875. A prize broom, symbolic of the superiority of a company, was presented to the most efficient company, and was an honoured possession. Superiority was determined by periodic match contests. On fireman's parades and dinners in London and Hamilton see *Canadian Illustrated News*, July–December 1872, p. 274; July–December 1874, p. 120.

the boys answered promptly, leaving their work in daytime, at a loss to themselves, for their employers as a general thing charged up the lost time they were absent from the workshop; and at night they would turn out in a cold winter storm, half dressed, buttoning up their clothes as they raced to the engine house. It was the pride of every fireman to pull on the drag rope, and if possible, get to the fire before the other company and have the first stream on the burning building.

Butler also noted the distinctive social character of each company. 'The boys of No. 3', he remembered, 'were a convivial set, and often indulged in crackers and cheese and beer, especially after a fire'. Business meetings were often the scene of hotly contested debates over the beer bill accumulated since the last meeting, a thorn in the side of Charley Smith, captain of No. 3, and a teetotaller who worried 'to think his Company had such an appetite for beer'. No. 4 Company was composed solely of young Orangemen, 'a wild lot of boys' occupying an engine house on James Street North at the Railroad Bridge. Butler's own company, No. 2, had started out as a temperance venture, but found it difficult to adhere to the cause; the heat of the flames cultivated a thirst that water could not quench. And apparently No. 2 was sufficiently devoid of competent leadership to give rise to this early indictment:

> It is a reflection upon the character of our town that as miserable a piece of machinery is, called Engine No. 2, no better person can be found to manage it than that buffoon, Bill Morin, who at the late fire appeared as Captain of it in some kind of grotesque coat, said to have been taken from a Yankee deserter, and afterwards trimmed with shilling-a-yard red flannel. When he could amuse himself no longer with throwing water on some burning rubbish, he commenced trying experiments with his double and twisted thousand dollar Jim Burke engine at some persons who were placed on the roof of Sam Kerr's store, to prevent it taking fire. How can it be expected that fire companies can be efficient with such men to conduct them.

The author concluded his harangue with the observation that in many companies 'there was not much attention given to fire fighting'.[76]

---

76   The Butler recollections are from Fireman's Benefit Fund 1920, n.p. Butler was a printer, and his place in the Hamilton fire brigade is outlined in *Hamilton Spectator*, 18 December 1879. On Charles Smith see *Hamilton Times*, 4 January 1866.

Such disorder was not likely to continue in the aftermath of the economic expansion of the 1850s and 1860s. Nor were employers prone to accept the infringements on labour discipline posed by the volunteer brigades. As capitalists increasingly sought to rationalise and standardise fire fighting procedures they turned to the panacea of a municipal fire department.[77] Butler remembered the shift in character of the No. 2 Company as businessmen joined its ranks, and men of the type of Bill Morin got the shunt.[78] During the late 1860s clashes between the volunteer companies and the City Council became increasingly common as fire fighting methods, inefficiency, and the personnel of the brigade's leadership came under attack. By the early 1870s it was clear that professionalism had won the day, and local officials saw a trained, standing force, paid by the municipality, as the solution to the many problems posed by the workingmen's volunteer companies.[79] It was a process opposed by many a 'Hoseman', but it was destined to run its course, and by 1879 the volunteer brigade had been replaced by a permanent, paid force, headed by a professional fire chief.[80]

Even after the demise of the fire companies, however, old ties retained some force. Firemen's celebrations and reunions continued to draw many skilled workingmen well into the 1880s, and as late as 1908 the *Industrial Banner* paid tribute to Larry Clark, a London fire chief who had been a charter member of Hamilton's Federal Labor Union and an outspoken advocate of workers' organisation.[81] As thinly disguised workingmen's clubs, the fire companies would be replaced by other associations of workingmen throughout the 1870s, 1880s, and 1890s. Discontinuity would be compensated by a fundamental functional continuity.

Closely approximating the experience of the fire companies was the rise and fall of the Hamilton and Gore Mechanics' Institute, founded in 1839 and disbanded 25 April 1882, its library sold in small lots to appease its many creditors. Originally convened in an engine house, the Mechanics' Institute

---

77   On this process see Hennock 1973, pp. 118–20; Schwartz 1974, pp. 159–78.

78   Fireman's Benefit Fund 1920, n.p.; Campbell 1966, pp. 149–50. Cf. 'Saturday Musings', *Hamilton Spectator*, 19 December 1908.

79   *Hamilton Times*, 11 July 1864; 30 July 1867; *Hamilton Spectator*, 3 August 1860; 11 August 1865; 19 March 1868; 18 December 1872.

80   *Hamilton Spectator*, 1 March 1878; Fireman's Benefit Fund 1920, n.p. On opposition to professionalisation see the letters by 'Hoseman' and 'Mechanic' in *Hamilton Spectator*, 1 May 1862; 29 November 1879.

81   On Clark see *Industrial Banner*, September 1908. On an outing of firemen and workers to Brantford see *Palladium of Labor*, 23 May 1885.

grew in size and importance, its purpose of 'diffusing scientific and literary knowledge, by a library of reference and circulation; by the formation of a museum of specimens in zoology, geology, or other subjects of nature, science, or manufactures; by lectures, by philosophical apparatus; by conversations; and by any other method the committee may judge necessary', apparently exercising considerable appeal. By 1852 the institute had erected a building composed of a library, reading room, and public hall. Ranked as one of the foremost associations of its kind in the Dominion, Hamilton's Mechanics' Institute would serve as a centre of community life until its collapse in the early 1880s.[82]

Like many realms of working-class associational life, the mechanics' institute has been the focus of much recent scholarly work. The tendency is to view the institute as a vehicle through which the crusading, rational middle classes successfully controlled both programme and clientele, utilising the halls of the mechanics' institute to inculcate a submissive respect for authority and an appropriate attitude towards work, offering courses and lectures designed to attract clerks and accountants, rather than working men and women. Foster Vernon, in an unpublished study of the development of adult education in Ontario, states the case baldly: 'they were essentially a middle class organization run by people with middle class values which they constantly sought to impose on members of the lower class who came to the institutes searching for help with their learning problems'.[83]

In fact, however, such a generalisation distorts as much as it clarifies. For mechanics' institutes cannot be divorced from their local context, in which the strength of the working-class movement would contribute to the vibrancy of the working-class presence in these early buildings of adult education. Nor must we mistake the hegemony of propertied elements, so common in many institutes, for an acquiescent working-class constituency. Merchants, manufacturers, and clerks could often control local institutes, while workingmen utilised the services and facilities for their own purposes, often expressing distinct dissatisfaction with the policies and practices of the directors. It is necessary to recognise both the dreary demise that so many institutes suffered, stifled by

---

82   See the overview of the Hamilton and Gore Mechanics' Institute's history in *Hamilton Spectator*, 28 May 1881; Vernon 1969, pp. 242–5.

83   Vernon 1969, p. 520. Similar perspectives can be found in Wilson 1973, pp. 43–54; Graff 1976, pp. 58–82, especially n. 16; and the more subtle treatment in Keane 1975, pp. 255–74. For the best study of education reform in Hamilton, illuminating the case of the hegemony of non-working-class elements, see Davey 1975.

the efforts of men who knew all too well what was best for other men, and the submerged involvement and struggle of workingmen, who learned much in the process.[84]

Hamilton's Mechanics' Institute was directed by men far removed from working-class life. There is no mistaking this basic continuity of control. Prominent in the history of the Hamilton Institute were men like Dr William Craigie, a wealthy surgeon; Archibald Macallum, a principal active in educational reform; Thomas McIlwraith and C.W. Meakins, local businessmen and promoters. Sir Allan MacNab, a 'pillar of the community' and prominent in early railroad construction and speculation, was the Mechanics' Institute's Honourary Patron. There was little of working-class leadership here, albeit for the aberrant upholsterer or isolated painter who occasionally occupied a position of responsibility.[85]

Such blatant control was not without an effect. In 1861 the membership stood at 396, and Adam Brown, president of the local institute, and Archibald Macallum concluded their report on the Hamilton and Gore Mechanics' Institute with a sorry refrain: 'The profound object ... is the improvement of our artizans and working classes ... but there is reason to fear this design has in many instances been lost sight of ... as other classes of the community other than operatives constitute not infrequently the majority of subscribers and attendants'.[86] After 1861 the directors frequently complained of the apathy of their constituents, and the membership declined year after year.[87]

In the absence of membership listings we can only speculate as to the degree of working-class involvement in the Hamilton Institute, or the extent of the mechanics' utilisation of the facilities. It must have been significantly greater,

---

84   See the excellent discussion in Royle 1971, pp. 305–21. Cf. Palmer 1976a, pp. 112–13; and
      Keane 1975, pp. 263, 267.

85   Directors and officials were listed in *Hamilton Times*, 27 February 1863; 2 March 1863;
      Hamilton Spectator, 2 March 1863; 8 January 1863; 1 March 1869; *Hamilton Gazette*, 27
      February 1852; Hamilton and Gore Mechanics' Institute 1867, pp. 3–4. Occupations were
      culled from city directories. On the class character of the directors see *Hamilton Spectator*,
      28 May 1881; AA.VV. 1864, p. 77. On individual directors (Craigie, Macallum, McIlwraith,
      Meakins, and McNab) see Davey 1975, p. 30; AA.VV. 1863, p. 236; Smith 1903; Katz 1975b,
      pp. 176–208; *Hamilton Spectator*, 9 August 1862.

86   AA.VV. 1861, pp. 105–7.

87   *Hamilton Times*, 1 March 1862; 7 February 1863; 25 February 1865; *Hamilton Spectator*, 1
      March 1869; 28 May 1881; 27 July 1881; 10 August 1881; Hamilton and Gore Mechanics' Insti-
      tute, *Minute Book, Proceedings of the Management Committee, 1839–1851*, 7th anniversary
      meeting, February 1846, Hamilton Collection, Hamilton Public Library.

however, than working-class activity in the Mutual Improvement Association or the Mercantile Library Association, bodies catering to merchants, manufacturers, and clerks.[88] There are indications that many more mechanics used the facilities of the local hall than actually joined the Mechanics' Institute,[89] and the books prominent in the library must have drawn more than one worker into the reading room to thumb the well-worn pages of *Les Miserables*, or study the arguments of classical political economy.[90] The Great Western Railway, for instance, subsidised the local hall, on the condition that 50 of its mechanics receive reductions in their membership fees. It withdrew its support in 1866 after its employees built their own reading room to accommodate their needs.[91] Undoubtedly the most common form of working-class patronisation of the Mechanics' Institute, however, was attendance at the many festivals, reunions, readings, lectures, minstrel troupe performances, and evening classes so prominent in the late nineteenth century. As a community centre, Hamilton's Mechanics' Hall knew no rival.[92]

If the extent of working-class participation in the affairs of the institute is veiled in ambiguity, working-class opposition to the directors often seethed below the surface of seemingly tranquil relationships. The *Hamilton Times* hinted at the manipulation of key positions that characterised the election

88   See *Hamilton Times*, 12 December 1862; 20 January 1863; 12 February 1863; 20 February 1863; 18 April 1863; 2 May 1863; 25 September 1863; *Hamilton Spectator*, 25 February 1860; 9 December 1863; Hamilton Mutual Improvement Social and Literary Society, *Declaration of Incorporation*, 15 February 1876, Hamilton Collection, Hamilton Public Library; Hamilton Association for the Advancement of Literature, *Members Book, 1857–1911*, Hamilton Collection, Hamilton Public Library; Hamilton Mercantile Library Association and General News Room 1845, pp. 5–6, 18–19.

89   Hamilton and Gore Mechanics' Institute, *Minute Book, Proceedings of the Management Committee, 1839–1851*, annual report, 1850, Hamilton Collection, Hamilton Public Library.

90   *Les Miserables*, which the library possessed, was one of the most popular books in Victorian Hamilton. See *Hamilton Times*, 11 October 1862. Lists of books held by the institute are recorded in *Hamilton Times*, 19 February 1864; *Hamilton Spectator*, 14 December 1868; 13 October 1869; 21 December 1872; Hamilton and Gore Mechanics' Institute 1867, p. 26.

91   *Hamilton Times*, 20 January 1866.

92   *Hamilton Spectator*, 24 January 1860; 7 March 1862; 3 March 1863; 18 April 1864; 17 February 1865; 8 March 1865; 7 November 1878; 7 November 1879; *Hamilton Times*, 9 January 1858; 17 February 1859; 24 May 1859; 28 May 1861; 25 June 1861; 20 February 1862; 3 September 1862; 18 March 1863; 5 November 1863; 10 March 1864; 24 March 1864; 26 September 1864; 5 November 1864; 23 November 1864; 14 February 1866; 25 May 1866; 3 September 1867; Hamilton Mechanics' Institute 1865, especially pp. 4, 9. Cf. the positive assessments of the institute in *Hamilton Spectator*, 6 December 1871; and *Hamilton Times*, 11 May 1864.

of officials.[93] 'A Mechanic' complained of the poor workmanship so common in repairs to the local hall, and implicitly raised the questions of graft and corruption, positing profiteering by the directors on contracts undertaken by the Mechanics' Institute.[94]

Often the critics touched on more substantial issues. A series of letters to the *Hamilton Spectator* in February 1860 complained of the degeneration of the institute, and the deterioration of the library. 'W' protested the board's policy of 'objecting to this paper or that periodical because it happens to advocate views or express opinions which do not coincide with their own'. A similar theme was reiterated by 'an incorporated member', who disliked the prejudices and narrow vision so often exhibited by the Board of Directors.[95] In the aftermath of the withdrawal of the Great Western Railway's $200 yearly grant, occasioned by the exodus of the GWR mechanics to their own reading room (itself an act of protest), one workingman was scathing in his indictment of the directors, whom he feared would utilise the financial loss to cover their own blunders. 'Men of ease, who lack enterprise', he wrote, 'should not be permitted thus to sacrifice the best interests of the society; if they have not time and are unwilling to meet manfully the difficulties of their position, let them at least make room for others who both can and will'. He also criticised the directors' willingness to sacrifice the library at the first sign of economic stringency, while they took pains to maintain the newsroom, used by mercantile and professional men who were able to spend their time away from their homes. The library served the interests of more humble men, who borrowed books to read in the privacy of their dwellings, in brief hours of leisure enjoyed after a day's labours.[96] Less than a month later, on the eve of an election of the Board of Directors, 'Watchman' argued in a similar fashion, calling for evening classes and library improvements.[97] But such a mundane purpose gained few adherents among those at the helm, and the institute stumbled along, apparently blind to the needs and desires of common labouring men and women. When it eventually foundered in 1882, the *Spectator* correctly concluded that 'the people had lost confidence in the management of the library'.[98]

---

93   *Hamilton Times*, 27 February 1863.
94   *Hamilton Times*, 24 June 1862.
95   *Hamilton Spectator*, 20 February 1860; 21 February 1860; 24 February 1860.
96   *Hamilton Times*, 29 January 1866.
97   *Hamilton Times*, 23 February 1866. Nineteen years later 'Watchman' was still penning letters to the press, this time condemning wage-payment practices. See *Palladium of Labor*, 2 May 1885.
98   *Hamilton Spectator*, 31 March 1883, quoted in Vernon 1969, p. 245.

Oddly enough, the working-class response to the fall of the local institution is perhaps the most substantial indication of the importance of the hall in the lives of the city's workingmen. Few causes were more dear to the Victorian workman than that of self-improvement, cultivated in the reading room, and nourished by the holdings of an accessible library. When the means to this end were threatened, Hamilton's mechanics reacted with vigour. In October 1881 a petition supporting the Mechanics' Institute was signed by 865 persons, a total far in excess of the registered membership.[99] After the institute's collapse, 'Humanitas' condemned the city for the lack of a library which it had once possessed 'before some of [its] citizens became too wealthy to care for the comforts of their less fortunate brethren'.[100]

Throughout the 1880s Hamilton workingmen threw their support behind the free library movement, and it was largely because of their efforts that the cause was won. With the establishment of a Free Library Board in 1889, of which Fred Walters, a long-time member of the International Iron Molders' Union No. 26 and a delegate to the Central Labor Union, was a member, Hamilton's workingmen had finally rid themselves of the unpleasant taste of class distinction and manipulation that the Mechanics' Institute's Board of Directors had left in their mouths for so many years.[101] With that achievement gained, and their library secure, they had won a victory dear to their hearts.

Completing this structured realm of associational life so ardently patronised by Hamilton's skilled workingmen was the baseball club. Baseball remains an unexplored component of the working-class experience. Craft unions were seldom without a team, and across North America weekend and after-work games among printers, cigar makers, moulders, butchers, and other craftsmen attracted workmates, friends, and families to local fields, where the tensions of life dissipated with the excitement of a close match, the clowning of a par-

---

99   *Hamilton Spectator*, 31 October 1881.

100 *Palladium of Labor*, 23 August 1884.

101 On the struggle for a free library, led by the organised section of Hamilton's working class, see *Hamilton Spectator*, 31 March 1883, 2 May 1885; 7 May 1885; 10 June 1887; 16 February 1889; 26 February 1889; 15 April 1889; *Palladium of Labor*, 1 September 1883; 25 April 1885; 2 May 1885; 13 November 1886; 4 December 1886; H.B. Witton to Macdonald, 23 March 1889, Macdonald Papers, vol. 471, pp. 234404–7, Public Archives of Canada; A.T. Freed to Macdonald, 11 June 1889, vol. 63, pp. 25728–31, Public Archives of Canada; *Minute Book of the Trades and Labor Council, 1888–1896*, pp. 7, 9, 20, 121, Hamilton Trades and Labor Council; *Labor Union*, 27 January 1883. Hamilton's Knights of Labor DA 61 established a reading room and library in 1886. See Ontario Bureau of Industries 1888, pt. iv, p. 46; 1889, pt. iv, p. 18.

ticular player, or the refreshment of a beer, a keg of which was usually within easy reach.[102] Unlike sports that would find a ready place within university curriculums, and unlike those games attracting clerks and professional men (football, cricket, rowing, for example), baseball was a distinctively working-class activity.[103] The emergence of professional teams in the late 1870s and 1880s would siphon off some of this early enthusiasm, but the adherence of the working-class community to active participation on the fields and diamonds of the city was startlingly resilient. To Hamilton's mechanic ballplayers, sport was to be something more than a spectacle.[104]

One early account in the *Hamilton Evening Journal* conveys something of the importance of baseball in the lives of ordinary men: 'The east end of the city presents a lively appearance every evening. All the avenues in the vicinity of the commons, as well as the commons themselves, are occupied by baseball clubs ... There is also a club from the workshop of McPherson & Co., who are well up in the game and no doubt will, ere long, compete favourably with any

---

102   On the importance of baseball see *Cigar Makers' Official Journal*, September 1884; December 1902; 15 August 1907; *Labor Leaf*, 17 February 1886; *Craftsman*, 12 March 1887; 11 June 1887; *Typographical Journal*, 15 August 1901; 15 January 1902; March 1906; September 1911; October 1912; *Iron Molders' International Journal*, March 1906; *Labor Standard*, 5 June 1880; *Workingman's Advocate*, 3 August 1867; 3 June 1871; 10 June 1871; 18 May 1872; Laurie 1973, p. 88.

103   See the path-breaking essay on the dominance of 'the middle class' in the historical evolution of sport in Ontario and Quebec: Wise 1974, pp. 93–118. Wise considers curling, lacrosse, rowing, and football, but unfortunately neglects baseball, which could have altered his argument. On the particularly working-class nature of baseball see Howe 1976, pp. 181–2. Contradicting Wise's thesis is the case of the Hamilton Mechanic's Curling Club, in *Hamilton Spectator*, 12 February 1873. Buttressing his position is the case of the Leander Rowing Club, which 'decided to admit *no mechanic* to membership, nor allow such to take part in any of their competition matches'; see *Hamilton Spectator*, 23 September 1879. The Hamilton Football Club was composed entirely of young clerks. Officers and members were listed in *Hamilton Spectator*, 4 November 1869, and their occupations checked in city directories. A similar situation prevailed in the Hamilton Cricket Team, where clerks and young professionals dominated the membership. See *Hamilton Times*, 1 August 1864. The first case of university football players being hired to protect strikebreakers is recorded in *The Typographical Journal*, May 1906. Note the illustration and discussion of the GWR employees' Queen's Birthday celebration in 1863, where sport figured prominently, in *Canadian Illustrated News*, 30 May 1863.

104   On professionalisation see Cosentino 1975, pp. 75–81. The development of professional teams in Hamilton is outlined in *Hamilton Spectator*, 3 March 1887; 4 May 1889; Johnson 1958, p. 258.

"professional" club in the city ... It is understood that the shoemakers intend playing a match with the Hat-Factory Club in a few weeks, and no doubt it will be well contested".[105] Hamilton's working-class enthusiasts thus played baseball first and foremost as members of a club, employees of a specific shop or factory, or practitioners of a particular craft.

The clubs, apparently the most disciplined of the groupings, were prominent in the 1860s and 1870s, although the Young Mechanics Ball Club was active in the early 1880s. They were presided over by a serious group of officials who practised diligently, and bred a strong bond of personal loyalties and friendships, reinforced at annual suppers held in prominent city hotels. Organised by two brothers, William and James Shuttleworth, a clerk and a shoemaker, the Maple Leaf Club dominated the early scene. Those officials and players whose occupations could be determined included five clerks, three shoemakers, two turners and two labourers, and one of each of the following: coach manufacturer, broom manufacturer, saloon keeper, hatter, painter, hammer man, foreman, butcher, machinist, marble cutter, brakeman, carriage maker, boiler maker, tinsmith, horse collar maker, teamster, watchmaker, cigar maker, cabinetmaker, grocer, book binder, plasterer, tobacco worker, carpenter, sailor, and wool sorter.[106] Other clubs – the Star, Independent, Eagle, Mechanics, Rising Union, Ontario, Social, and Dundas Mechanics – were even more firmly in the grip of the skilled worker, as their names often suggested. The 1868 roster of the Star Club, for instance, included three moulders, a turner, a tobacco worker, a cigar maker, a labourer, and two men whose occupations could not be determined. On the Independent's 1867 team were three boot and shoe makers, a moulder, a tinsmith, and four others whose occupations could not be ascertained. Among the Young Mechanics of 1881 were a trunk-maker and two shoemakers.[107]

Games between various shops and factories complemented the activities of the clubs. Wanzer's, MacPherson's, Copp's foundry, Reid's furniture works, and

105 *Hamilton Evening Journal*, 14 July 1870.

106 Officials, players, and information on the Maple Leaf Club are found in *Hamilton Spectator*, 4 July 1863; 27 August 1863; 11 September 1863; *Hamilton Times*, 4 April 1863; 17 April 1863; 30 July 1864; 5 April 1865; 6 May 1865; 7 July 1866; 23 February 1867; 24 February 1867. A brief history of the club, founded in 1854, appeared in *Hamilton Spectator*, 2 December 1865. Occupations were found in city directories.

107 Lists of players for each of these clubs were found in *Hamilton Spectator*, 26 August 1868; 26 July 1869; 24 May 1881; *Hamilton Times*, 25 April 1866; 31 May 1867; 20 July 1867; 30 September 1867. Occupations were checked in city directories. Note also the case of the Hop Bitters Club in *Labor Union*, 17 March 1883.

other local businesses all fielded teams, and judging from the scores of some
of the contests (73–54 and 58–35) these were raucous affairs, punctuated with
much merriment.[108]

But the most persistent participants were craft unionists. The printers exemplify the case. In the fall of 1871 the Hamilton printers initiated an attachment
to baseball that would continue for over forty years. 'The Great Typographical
Base Ball Match' was the billing attracting many to the Maple Leaf grounds to
watch the nines of the *Spectator* and the *Times* compete, with Bauer's brewery having transported large quantities of ice and beer to the park 'to quench
the thirst of the large crowd anticipated'. After the game the printers retired to
a local pub where they enjoyed a hearty meal and abundant refreshment. By
1884 the city's typos had established a baseball club, and games between married men and bachelors, as well as contests involving printers from other towns,
were commonplace throughout the 1880s and 1890s. In September 1911, in what
may well have been a commemoration of their 1871 match, the local union held
a stag picnic, at which the major attraction was a baseball game, interrupted
by bouts of drinking. A month later the printers challenged the cigar makers in
the traditional Labour Day ball game.[109]

Small wonder, then, that baseball was Hamilton's 'favourite game' and the
city known as 'the baseball centre' of Canada.[110] Despite disenchantment with
the deterioration of old practices, and the growing commercialisation of the
game,[111] skilled workers owed a strong allegiance to a sport many of them had
known intimately in their youth; attendance at strictly amateur games often
exceeded 1,000 persons.[112] The Knights of Labor knew the drawing power of
a good game and attracted city workingmen to rallies and demonstrations
with the promise of a baseball match.[113] Even within the professional teams an

---

108   *Hamilton Spectator*, 22 July 1869; 30 July 1869; 31 July 1869; 10 May 1870; 23 May 1870;
15 September 1871; 30 August 1875; *Hamilton Times*, 18 August 1866; *Palladium of Labor*,
27 June 1885; 18 July 1885.

109   On the Hamilton printers' penchant for baseball see *Hamilton Spectator*, 1 September 1871;
2 September 1871; 4 September 1871; 22 July 1881; 15 August 1881; 31 August 1885; 11 August
1890; *Palladium of Labor*, 9 April 1884; 11 September 1886; *Typographical Journal*, July 1911;
September 1911. The printers were also drawn to other sporting activities, establishing a
fishing club and a bowling league.

110   *Hamilton Spectator*, 5 August 1884; *Palladium of Labor*, 3 May 1884.

111   For condemnations of professionalism and the gambling and commercialism following in
its wake see *Palladium of Labor*, 26 July 1884; 1 August 1885; 12 April 1886.

112   For a working-class defence of the game see *Palladium of Labor*, 1 May 1886; 19 June 1886.

113   *Hamilton Spectator*, 4 August 1883; 5 August 1884.

awareness of their origins must have stirred, for in December 1884 a Cooperative team was formed; members of the Clippers had grown disgusted with their management's practices and sought just compensation for their labours on the diamond.[114] While 'Old Sports Pabulum' could mourn the passing of the 'regalia, long ovations, rabid fans, and west end vs. east end rivalry' characteristic of ball games in an earlier period, the sport nevertheless remained embedded within working-class culture.[115] Assuring its continuity was the union picnic, where a baseball game was almost a matter of course. 'Picnics as a rule', noted the *Hamilton Spectator*, commenting on a past gathering of the Bricklayers' and Masons' Union, 'now have little interest manifested in them unless there is a baseball match'.[116] The demise of the mechanics' baseball club, and the transferral of its function to the union picnic, thus leads us out of the structured, institutionalised realm of associational life and into a more eclectic, but equally pervasive domain.

At the centre of this more diffused culture stood the craft union, its disciplined apparatus organising events of importance and meaning to its membership. In the late nineteenth and early twentieth centuries spring, summer, and early autumn months were a time of picnics and outings and among certain crafts, such as the printers, these undertakings had a long history.[117] Winter nights were often warmed by festive gatherings of craftsmen commemorating the founding of their union, paying their respects to a workmate moved out of the shop by promotion or old age, or simply enjoying a hearty meal. Also conspicuous were dances and balls attended by members of the fraternity and their wives.[118] Parades, in which the workers often appeared in uniform, proudly dis-

---

114   *Hamilton Spectator*, 5 December 1884. The Primroses, a semi-professional team, tendered a benefit for an unemployed comrade. See *Hamilton Spectator*, 3 March 1885.

115   *Palladium of Labor*, 17 April 1886. In the spring of 1889 the employees of John MacPherson and Company met to organise a baseball club, the Hamilton Shoemakers. A leading participant in the formation of this team was William Berry, an activist in the Knights of Labor. See *Hamilton Spectator*, 9 April 1889; 6 June 1904.

116   *Hamilton Spectator*, 29 August 1881.

117   The printers' picnic, known as wayzgoose, is especially noteworthy. See the engaging discussion in Anglo-American's 'The Wayzgoose and Other Printer's Customs', *Typographical Journal*, 15 June 1899; 'Red-Ink' 1890, pp. 19–20. For the general importance of picnics to the crafts see *Typographical Journal*, 1 August 1899; *American Workman*, 5 July 1869; *The Craftsman*, 3 September 1887; *Iron Molders' International Journal*, May 1881; *John Swinton's Paper*, 12 September 1886; *Labor Standard*, 14 September 1878; *Palladium of Labor*, 6 September 1884.

118   On balls, suppers, festivals, and smokers see *Typographical Journal*, 15 February 1902; *The*

playing their wares, and always 'in full number', were common occurrences, marking the celebration of a major event or prefacing the sports, speeches, and frolicking of 'labour's holiday', later to be officially proclaimed Labour Day.[119] In Hamilton these events constituted an important aspect of the skilled worker's everyday experiences.

Picnics were perhaps the most numerous. After the traditional skirmish in late April and early May over wage increases and job conditions, Hamilton's crafts settled into a summer of labour, pleasantly interrupted by trips to the Oaklands, Dundurn Park, or the Crystal Palace Grounds. A weekend in mid-August 1886, for instance, saw countless small picnics, as well as gatherings of the Bricklayers's, Masons's, and Labourers's unions, an outing by the employees of D. Moore and Company and the Burns and Robinson manufacturing company, an excursion to Niagara Falls by 700 Grand Trunk workers, and trips and picnics by the workers of the Ontario Cotton Mills and two assemblies of the Knights of Labor.[120] Throughout the years 1860–1914 virtually every Hamilton craft held regular summer picnics and outings. These excursions were complemented by gatherings of workers of specific shops and factories and assemblies of the Knights of Labor. Occasionally the city's skilled mechanics formed committees to organise grand workingmen's picnics encompassing all of the crafts, as well as the unskilled. These were gala events, drawing anywhere from three to five thousand people, whose presence was often taken as an indication of the strength of labour's cause.[121]

Like picnics, banquets, dances, balls, and festivals were exceedingly common. A plumbers' gathering in the winter of 1874, a year of severe economic downturn, must have done much to lift the spirits of men exposed to the pinch of hard times.

Craftsmen, 29 January 1887; 25 June 1887; 25 February 1888; *Industrial Banner*, May 1902; *Labor Standard*, 2 September 1877; *Labor Advocate*, 2 January 1891; 16 January 1891; *Labor Union*, 17 March 1883.

119   See the accounts of parades in *Typographical Journal*, October 1908; *The Carpenter*, 15 August 1889; *Labor Leaf*, 7 October 1885; *Iron Molders' International Journal*, May 1881; June 1881; *Ontario Workman*, 18 April 1872; 2 September 1872; *Industrial Banner*, September 1903; September 1905; *Palladium of Labor*, 18 August 1883; 6 September 1884; 22 August 1885; Palmer 1976a, p. 117; and Gutman 1973b, pp. 531–88.

120   *Hamilton Spectator*, 16 August 1886.

121   See *The Craftsman*, 28 August 1886; *Palladium of Labor*, 5 September 1885; 12 September 1885; 28 August 1886; *Hamilton Spectator*, 4 September 1869; 6 September 1869; 7 September 1869; 10 September 1881; 30 August 1886.

> Come, all ye mechanics, for no dreadful panics
> Will meet you with grim spectre-faces.

A local newspaper noted 'the hilarity manifested by members of the craft', and judged the gathering a success, 'tending greatly to promote feeling and sociability in all branches of the trade'.[122] Pride in their work and recognition of their place in the community were also common themes and consequences of these craft gatherings.

> Come, each son of labour, and do us the favour
> Of tasting the good things provided.
> A truce to your moiling! for hard daily toiling
> Gives Rank that must ne' er be derided

John Hargreaves, foreman of the locomotive works of the Great Western Railway, toasted the mechanic at an 1860 festival: 'The mechanic was a progressive being and he would, bye-and-bye, take the lead; he was strong and his object should be to endeavor to elevate himself in the highest scale of mental culture'. Another speaker noted the fraternal relations predominating: 'Here they behaved themselves like men, and no coldness was visible among them; they all appeared like brothers; and if the aristocracy can have their assemblies, and enjoy themselves, he could not see why the mechanics should not have their reunions also'.[123]

Moulders, cigar makers, glass workers, stove mounters, brush makers, printers, carpenters, engineers, masons, and skilled workers associated with various assemblies of the Knights of Labor apparently agreed, for they appeared only too willing to organise a ball or socialise over dinner.[124] Typical of these festive occasions was the celebration of International Typographical Union No. 129,

---

122 *Hamilton Spectator*, 17 December 1874.

123 *Hamilton Spectator*, 23 January 1860. The verse in the above paragraph is from 'A Call to the Soiree' in Cowherd 1884, p. 266.

124 On these gatherings see *The Carpenter*, March 1904; *Labor Union*, 27 January 1883; 17 March 1883; *Labor News*, 12 April 1912; *Palladium of Labor*, 20 October 1883; 10 November 1883; 10 December 1883; 12 January 1884; 19 January 1884; 2 February 1884; 19 April 1884; 28 March 1885; 11 April 1885; 9 May 1885; 1 August 1885; 3 October 1885; *Hamilton Times*, 19 January 1858; 15 November 1865; 22 November 1866; *Hamilton Spectator*, 23 January 1860; 10 February 1860; 1 January 1864; 12 December 1867; 16 January 1869; 21 January 1869; 17 February 1872; 1 January 1878; 8 July 1881; 7 January 1882; 11 December 1883; 19 February 1887; 6 December 1890; 27 December 1890; 28 October 1893.

commemorating its sixtieth anniversary with a 'Feast of Oratory and Good Eatin' at the Strand Cafe in March 1914. Old hands reminisced about 'washing rollers' and 'bucking wood', common chores in their early days as apprentices. Extolling 'the art preservative of all arts' were two charter members of the Hamilton Typographical Society, A.T. Freed and Reese Evans. Talk eventually turned to an early conflict:

> The reminiscence of the first strike in Hamilton told by Mr. Butler was interesting; how there were no railways running between Hamilton and Toronto then; but Mr. Smiley who owned the daily that refused to yield, went to Toronto and brought the 'rats' by boat, only to be captured by the big Tom Cat of the 'Vigilance Committee'. The men won after being out ten days. They asked for a raise from 9 to 10 dollars a week.

For the printers, at least, the commemorative supper was one means of preserving a rich heritage.[125]

The most striking assertion of the craft unionist's presence, however, was the trade procession.[126] One of the earliest and certainly one of most impressive instances of the forceful presence of the Canadian Victorian workman was his avid enthusiasm for the union of the Canadas, and skilled craftsmen presented a united front in Hamilton's Confederation parade. Many skilled mechanics would have marched in the ranks of the Fire Brigade on 25 May 1867, under the banner 'Success to Confederation'.[127] In late June preparations began in earnest. The Crispins, butchers, and tailors, in concert with the St. George's Society and the Kalithumpian Klan – a motley crew of pranksters that must have included some skilled tradesmen and young apprentices – pledged their support for the scheduled events of 1 July 1867.[128] On the 'Cel-

---

125   See *Labor News*, 20 March 1914; *Typographical Journal*, April 1914. On the organisation of the printers' union see *Hamilton Gazette*, 2 August 1852; Lloyd Atkinson and Eugene Forsey, 'The Labour Movement in Hamilton', typescript, Canadian Labour Congress Collection, MG 28 I 103, vol. 249, p. 1, Public Archives of Canada.

126   As a brief introduction to this phenomenon, as yet unstudied in any systematic fashion, see 'Labour History: Notes and Articles', Eugene Forsey Papers, MG 30 D 84, vol. 12, Public Archives of Canada, especially the quotations from *Halifax Weekly Citizen*, 22 June 1867, and *Montreal Witness*, n.d. Cf. Katz 1975b, pp. 3–4, 316; *Canadian Labor Reformer*, 18 September 1886; *Hamilton Spectator*, 25 May 1860; 26 May 1860.

127   *Hamilton Times*, 25 May 1867.

128   *Hamilton Times*, 25 June 1867; 26 June 1867; 28 June 1867; 29 June 1867; *Hamilton Spectator*, 1 July 1867.

ebration Day' the trades turned out in force, the *Hamilton Spectator* describing the unionists, preceded by the fire companies, splendidly attired in colourful uniforms:

> Then came the butchers who made an excellent show. The ox which had been profusely ornamented with red and blue rosettes and artificial flowers (furnished by Mrs. Ridder), was in a wagon from which he surveyed the admiring spectators with a mild and placid gaze. Round him clustered the sturdy butchers, all of them well mounted and exceedingly 'old countrified' ... The Iron Moulders were not a showy looking, but an exceedingly respectable set of men, and they marched well and preserved good order. The Shoemakers with King Crispin and his champion and sundry other worthies grotesquely habited were a decided attraction. The King was dressed in robes of pink, with a crown of gold upon his head, while the champion looked decidedly like a warrior of olden time. The Bakers, next, made a good display. In fact, they attracted more observation perhaps, than any other body. The process of breadmaking, etc., was carried on during the progress of the procession.

It was a proud moment for Hamilton's workingmen.[129]

The labour parade resurfaced in the 1880s, amidst the general festivities surrounding the celebration of 'labour's holiday', the prelude to the officially sanctioned Labour Day of later years. In a procession honouring the birthdate of Uriah Stephens, founder of the Knights of Labor, Hamilton's crafts assumed a place of prominence. At the head of the throng of 2,000, embracing skilled and unskilled, marched 'the flag bearers, blending in one breeze the Union Jack, the Stars and Stripes and the flag of our own Dominion, emblematic of the international fraternity of labour'. Then marched the Molders, the Carpenters and Joiners, the Shoemakers Assembly of the Knights of Labor, the Art Assembly, composed of Woodworkers, the women of the shoe factories, riding in union hacks, the Telegraphers, currently embroiled in a bitter struggle with their employers, the Tailors Assembly of the Knights of Labor, the Amalgamated Association of Iron and Steel Workers, and the Ontario Rolling Mill men, complete with a decorated wagon. The Bricklayers and Masons came next, 'present[ing] a solid front on holiday, as they [did] on every other occasion, the secret of their organized success. They wore the apron, symbolic emblem of their craft'. Completing the procession were the Glassworkers, the Hatters,

---

129   *Hamilton Spectator*, 2 July 1867.

Local Assembly 2225 of mixed callings, largest in the city, Vulcan Assembly, the Brushmakers, the Brickmakers, and the Harnessmakers. The printers were represented by the staff of the *Palladium of Labor*, borne in Dan Collins's wagon, proclaiming 'the press as the defense of Labor and the medium of intellectual elevation of the masses', distributing a sheet entitled 'The elevation of Labor is the advancement of the State'. It was a stirring spectacle, involving over three thousand working men and women. 'Union is strength', concluded the *Hamilton Spectator*. 'This old adage was never more forcibly illustrated in Hamilton than yesterday afternoon, when the monster procession of the city's artisans filed its way through the street ... the present occasion will long be recollected, marking as it does a memorable epoch in the history of trades unionism'.[130]

Parades celebrating 'labour's holiday' and 'labour's carnival' continued to draw the city's workingmen in the 1880s and 1890s. With the institutionalisation of Labour Day in 1894, their energies were directed to similar ends. But if Hamilton failed to launch a procession in honour of its mechanics, the city's unionists often travelled to neighbouring towns – Buffalo and Brantford to name two – to march with others who shared their sympathies. Festive celebrations, these parades often prefaced a gigantic picnic or a well-attended baseball game.[131] However, with the early years of the twentieth century, Labour Day suffered a serious emasculation, and the older practices often seemed regrettably remote. The tradition lived in the customary baseball game or the union picnic, but the autonomous class activity of a self-proclaimed holiday had been shattered by government proclamation. Many of Hamilton's craft workers mourned the passing of the Labour Day parade, a visible reminder of previous carnivals and festivals.[132]

---

130 *Palladium of Labor*, 11 August 1883; *Hamilton Spectator*, 31 July 1883; 4 August 1883.

131 On the parades in honour of 'labour's holiday' and, later, Labour Day, see *Palladium of Labor*, 19 July 1884; 9 August 1884; *Hamilton Spectator*, 19 July 1884; 9 August 1884; 29 August 1894; 5 August 1895; 8 August 1895; 31 August 1895; 3 September 1895; 7 August 1896; 7 September 1897; 4 September 1900; 5 September 1904; *Labor Advocate*, 25 September 1891; *Cigar Makers' Official Journal*, August 1894; *Minute Book, Trades and Labor Council, 1888–1896*, pp. 55–6; 315–19; 390–5, Hamilton Trades and Labor Council.

132 On the early vigour of Labour Day parades and the workingmen's recognition of their importance see *Hamilton Spectator*, 4 September 1900; 21 August 1903; 6 September 1904; Trades and Labor Council of Hamilton 1897. Representative of Labour Day's degeneration is Supplement to the Labor News 1914. See *Labor News*, 30 August 1912 for regret at this deterioration.

These were not insignificant minor events, inconsequential in the grand context of class conflict or the progressive expansion of the labour movement. Baseball games, mechanics' festivals, union balls, commemorative suppers, picnics, and parades formed a vital part of the stuff of everyday life, important in their own right, and too long ignored by labour historians lusting after the episodic or the explicitly political. They were part of a culture that bred and conditioned solidarity, a prerequisite to any struggle attempting to better the lives of working men and women. Their continuous presence in the years 1860–1914, despite shifts in their locale and importance, lent strength to the working-class community, contributing to a coherence and stability that had important ramifications in other realms.

Baseball clubs and weekend games cultivated, for instance, fraternal relations that were welcomed by men active in the working-class movement.[133] Moreover, sport could illuminate class inequalities, and generate opposition to the fundamental wrongs of the social order. 'Why does the law allow a millionaire to play golf on Sunday', queried the *Industrial Banner*, 'and arrest a mechanic for playing baseball'?[134] Games were often a subtle means of popularising labour's cause, as with the Cigar Makers' Union, utilising the baseball diamond to advertise the merits of the Blue Label, or to raise money for striking comrades.[135] As in the case of London, Ontario, where iron moulders were locked in a protracted conflict with the McClary Stove and Range Works in 1906, baseball leagues, firmly controlled by union men, often stood staunchly behind skilled workers in their battles with employers:

> Last year the McClary base-ball team won the pennant after an exciting contest. The question that now arises, is whether the other clubs, who are largely composed of union men, will feel disposed to play with a club who are largely acting as an advertisement of the McClary firm. Union men throughout the city, while they have no antagonism to the McClary team, say they don't propose to patronize a league that advertises said firm ... It is a well known fact that the patronage of the City League comes largely from union men and in the past the iron molders have taken a great interest in the game, in fact take away union support for the league and it would not pay rent for the park.[136]

---

133   *Palladium of Labor*, 12 July 1884.

134   *Industrial Banner*, October 1901.

135   *Cigar Makers' Official Journal*, September 1884; December 1902; 15 August 1907.

136   *Industrial Banner*, April 1906.

'Old Sports Pabulum' could even link the cause of the shorter-hours movement to the interests of baseball, predicting greater attendance at games if the eight-hour day was won.[137]

The importance of festivals, dinners, and workingmen's balls should be even more clear. In the formative years of Hamilton's working-class movement, the Iron Molders' Union utilised a ball to attract moulders to their ranks, as well as to cultivate ties with other organised crafts.[138] Throughout the 1860s the GWR mechanics periodically met over a glass of beer at Dan Black's Fountain Saloon, which attained a reputation as the favourite haunt of 'the Western boys'. In later years Black's Club House would be a focal point in the emergence of the Nine Hour League.[139] Balls and suppers, as well as picnics, were often used by Hamilton crafts to raise funds for other unionists who were suffering the anxiety of unemployment or the plight of a prolonged strike.[140] A union ball could be the scene of a stark reminder of class relationships, as in 1883, when the moulders offered thanks to their employers for a recent wage reduction with a printed programme entitled 'To Our Generous Employers'.[141] Even a supper presided over by an employer, a situation geared to foster deference, could give rise to dissent. Four hundred Ontario Rolling Mills workers booed and hissed a speaker at such a function when he insisted on extolling the achievements of the Tory government.[142] But the most forceful impact of such gatherings was the 'cementing together [of] the bonds of unity', a consequence of great importance in future years of arduous struggle.[143]

---

137   *Palladium of Labor*, 10 April 1886.

138   *Hamilton Spectator*, 24 December 1863.

139   *Hamilton Times*, 12 January 1867; *Hamilton Spectator*, 4 September 1869; 6 September 1869; 7 September 1869. Lloyd Atkinson and Eugene Forsey, 'The Labour Movement in Hamilton', typescript, Canadian Labour Congress Collection, MG 28 I 103, vol. 249, p. 5 and n. 27, Public Archives of Canada, note the importance of Dan Black's in early union organisation. Note also 'Amalgamated Society of Carpenters & Joiners, Canada, 1871–1924, Statistical Notes', and 'Amalgamated Society of Engineers, Canada, 1853–1920, Statistical Notes', Eugene Forsey Papers, MG 30 D 84, vol. 11, Public Archives of Canada, on the Fountain Saloon and Dan Black's Club House as meeting places of early unions. On Black's Club House and the nine-hour movement see chapter 5 of Palmer 1979a.

140   *Palladium of Labor*, 14 February 1884; 30 May 1885; 6 June 1885; 13 June 1885; 28 August 1886; *Cigar Makers' Official Journal*, 10 February 1878.

141   *Palladium of Labor*, 14 December 1883.

142   *Labor Advocate*, 2 January 1891.

143   *Ontario Workman*, 27 March 1873, commenting on a gathering of Hamilton moulders at Victoria Hall, honouring a visit of their International's president.

Picnics, of course, were a major means of attracting workers to craft bodies, or solidifying ranks in times of crisis.[144] The *Palladium of Labor* championed their role, congratulating the carpenters and joiners on a picnic's success:

> Such outings do far more good than is generally supposed – they bring together members of a craft and make strangers into fast friends, and any person of common discernment can see the benefit of common mechanics knowing each other. It is of the greatest benefit to them to do so, either in fair weather when clouds are gathering, or when they burst. For that reason we hope that tradesmen will never fail to have their annual outings in the summer season and social gatherings in winter, as it all tends to make them more united and competent to fight the monster (Capital) when occasion requires.[145]

One of the most vehement turn-of-the-century industrial conflicts, the 1905–6 McClary moulders' strike mentioned earlier, was precipitated when men defied their foreman by attending a Saturday afternoon picnic, held by their union. The moulders were consequently fired, their places taken by non-unionists, and a struggle that was to last well over two years initiated. As late as the summer of 1909 no union men worked in the London shop, and its products were boycotted by Canadian unionists.[146]

Workingmen's parades, aside from their significance as moments of exhilaration and craft pride, also possess an inner history of importance. Two brief months after their participation in the Confederation procession, Hamilton's shoemakers would play an important role in the creation of an Ontario-wide boot and shoemakers organisation.[147] And behind the parades and processions celebrating 'labour's festivals', in an age when an officially sanctioned Labour Day was scarcely considered a possibility, lay a history of toil and trouble that no government proclamation could appease. 'That parliament has made Labor Day a national holiday', thundered the Hamilton engineer Edward Williams, 'is a tardy recognition of those noble beings who in the past, through vitupera-

---

144 On Hamilton see *Palladium of Labor*, 30 May 1885; 6 June 1885; 13 June 1885; 5 September 1885; 12 September 1885; *The Carpenter*, September 1883; *Labor Union*, 14 July 1883.

145 *Palladium of Labor*, 15 August 1885.

146 *Industrial Banner*, September 1905; October 1905; November 1905; January 1906; and especially August 1909.

147 *Hamilton Spectator*, 24 August 1867; *Hamilton Times*, 21 September 1867. Cf. Kealey 1973a, pp. 137–58.

tion and calumny, suffered persecution for defending the rights and liberties of men, and who claimed that the Trades Union was destined to develop the highest type of manhood in the march of civilization, and as feudalism followed barbarism, so education and enlightenment would tend slowly but successfully to bring about the freedom of thought and action which asserts the equality of rights before the law'.[148]

This, then, was a collectivist culture, institutionalised in mechanics' institute, friendly society, fire company, and baseball club. It was buttressed by the social activities of craft unions, as well as informal networks of associations bred of neighbourhood, tavern, and workplace. Enmeshed in an obscurity that inhibits precise analysis, either in terms of its meaning or its class composition, the nuances of this cultural activity suggest that skilled workingmen were important figures. And once again it is the continuities in this realm of associational life, set against a background of economic change and transformation, that are significant.

Artisans and apprentices, for instance, have historically been prominent in ritualised forms of mock ceremony, aimed at undercutting the solemnity of constituted authority, building an arena of legitimised dissent that struck sharply at the rigid inequality of social relationships.[149] It would have been surprising if some of Hamilton's craftsmen, or their younger apprentices, had not been present at a ribald outing of 1863, described as a strictly private picnic. Members of 'the worshipful company of chislers' met at the Railroad wharf and sailed to the beach. After a game of baseball, a mock trial was conducted upon constitutional principles; the county attorney, judge, special high sheriff, and police magistrate coming in for particular derision. This was a gathering at which little was sacred, and few prominent local officials escaped its ridicule.[150]

More conspicuous was the Kalithumpian Klan, a New England political variant of the age-old ritual of charivari. The Klan, and its presence in Hamilton, suggests strongly the process of cultural diffusion. It paraded city streets on notable days of celebration, such as the Queen's birthday: 'First came the General,

---

148 Williams 1897, pp. 3–5. Cf. *Trades Union Advocate*, 20 July 1882; 29 July 1882.

149 This is a central theme in Malcolmson 1973, a source with obvious relevance to our earlier discussion of sport, picnics, parades, and festive balls and suppers. It is also forcefully presented in Davis 1975, pp. 97–123 and 152–88. Cf. Thale 1972, pp. 65–8; Young 1973; Bamford 1905, vol. I, pp. 126, 140; Wright 1867; Thompson 1974, pp. 382–405.

150 *Hamilton Times*, 3 July 1863. Note the case of the Hellfriar's Club in London, Ontario, a similar body active in the period, composed of soldiers, cabinetmakers, and printers. See Miller 1949, pp. 169–74.

bearded like a bard, and equipped in a cocked hat of gigantic dimensions. Then came an individual of "exceedingly suspicious appearance", and as the Police Report says, looking very much like the pictoral representations we have seen of the Prince of Evil; then came a large crowd of all kinds of grotesque characters ... going through a number of salutory exercises upon a platform, which was placed on wheels for their accommodation'.[151] Always led by their Generalissimo, 'a ferocious looking military official', their shouts barely audible over the din of a perpetual 'discordant music', the Klan marched in a manner that hinted at its class composition. It was not likely to be a meeting ground for men of property and standing.[152]

Both the Company of Young Chislers and the Kalithumpians had lapsed by the mid-1870s; their social and cultural role, however, was perhaps assumed by the rise of the workingmen's clubs. First appearing in the city in the 1870s, the clubs may well have come into being in the context of the decline of the volunteer fire companies, which had served as workingmen's clubs throughout the 1860s. Hamilton's workingmen had praised the British club movement as early as 1864, but little apparently came of this endorsement.[153] The first Hamilton clubs, other than the sporting associations of the 1860s, probably had their roots in the desire for conviviality and good fun. This was most likely the case in the club of 'Jims', all over six feet tall, who met regularly in rooms over the Market Square. Each member was known as Jim, with a prefacing sobriquet suggestive of his appearance, character, nationality, or line of work (such as Pretty Jim, Dumpy Jim, Railroad Jim, Dutch Jim, or Slim Jim). Their rooms had been 'neatly fitted up and supplied with books and papers'. Only those capable of giving and receiving a good joke were allowed to join.[154] From this innocent beginning the clubs mushroomed.

They were of various persuasions, but in many clubs activities were reputed to centre around drinking, gambling, and the subtle art of seduction, young sewing girls and domestics being particularly attractive prey. All of these acts

151 *Hamilton Spectator*, 26 May 1868.

152 *Hamilton Times*, 26 June 1867; 29 June 1867; 15 May 1868; 26 May 1868. The Kalithumpians often met in friendly society halls or engine houses. The last recorded instance of a gathering was in June 1870. See *Hamilton Spectator*, 3 June 1870; *Hamilton Evening Journal*, 21 June 1870. For a wider discussion of the Kalithumpian Klan, as well as an introduction to charivaris and white-capping, both to be dealt with below, see Palmer 1978, pp. 5–63.

153 *The Workingman's Journal*, 18 June 1864, supported the club movement in England. On Victorian workingmen's clubs see Jones 1974, especially p. 44; Taylor 1971; Shipley 1972.

154 *Hamilton Spectator*, 22 January 1876.

aroused the ire of both local and working-class newspapers.[155] Other clubs, more respectable in nature, including the Maple Leaf Social Club (a probable outgrowth of the early baseball club), the Workingmen's Club Room, and the Patience Athletic Club, drew their strength from workingmen with a social or sporting bent.[156] Yet even these more acceptable bodies generated opposition. The Patience Athletic Club, whose leaders included a wagon-maker, a shoemaker and a mason, was routed by the police early one Sunday morning, three of its patrons charged with vagrancy. The charge collapsed, however, 'as they work [ed] every day and [paid] their way'. In its stead, the police substituted charges of keeping a common gaming-house, and the men were eventually convicted. Regarding their arrest as just one more case of police subservience to wealth and position, the *Palladium of Labor* stressed that many of Hamilton's prominent citizens belonged to clubs, including the chief of police, yet these men went unmolested; it was the workingman who was subjected to abuse. Taking a stiff jab at the constables involved in the arrests, the paper concluded: 'Ignorant, crawling, syncophants clothed in authority are dangerous animals to run at large ... It is no wonder that the wealthy tyrannize over those in the (what is called) lower walks of life when such parasites are to be found amongst them'.[157]

The police quite possibly did an excellent job in their repressive assault, for there are no indications that the Patience Athletic Club survived into the 1890s. But they may also have been overly zealous in their work. Replacing the numerous small clubs of the 1880s, organised around athletic and social activities, were the turn-of-the-century East and West End Workingmen's Clubs. In their halls workingmen also fraternised, but the activities were more structured, more explicitly political in orientation. It was there, for instance, that Hamilton's workingmen debated the questions of overtime work, wages on

---

155   *Hamilton Spectator*, 19 November 1878; 20 October 1884; *Palladium of Labor*, 10 December 1883; 12 June 1886.

156   See *Palladium of Labor*, 3 November 1883; 10 November 1883; 6 December 1884; 28 March 1885; and the fictionalised accounts of 'Our Social Club', an association of working-class intellectuals debating aspects of popular political economy in *Palladium of Labor*, 8 September 1883; 15 September 1883; 22 September 1883; 29 September 1883; 13 October 1883. Cf. *Hamilton Spectator*, 19 March 1885, on a tradesmen's club meeting in a local tavern; and the case of the Burlington Quoiting Club, whose officers included a tinsmith, a painter, and a cabinetmaker, listed in the *City of Hamilton Directory, 1872–1873*.

157   *Palladium of Labor*, 18 October 1884; *Hamilton Spectator*, 14 October 1884; 16 October 1884; 20 October 1884. Officers of the club were listed in *Palladium of Labor*, 28 March 1885, and their occupations checked in city directories.

civic projects, shorter hours, and the effects of offering manufacturers tax exemptions and bonuses to locate in the city. There too they heard papers on socialism and the relations of labour and capital. In 1904, in the midst of a strike at the International Harvester Company, the Workingmen's Club would serve as the headquarters of the embattled machinists.[158] By 1910 the Workingmen's Clubs were no longer in existence; they had been replaced by the May Day Committee and the Marx Club.[159]

The continuities in club life – from the informal Company of Young Chislers of the 1860s to the early twentieth-century Marx Club – hint at an important process of adaptation. While the 1860s and early 1870s, when club life centred on the jocular, were years of an emerging working-class movement, the later decades of the nineteenth century saw the development of class polarisation and an accelerating pace of industrial conflict. In this context it is quite possible that workingmen once drawn to the company of pranksters transferred their loyalties to informal groups more dedicated to the protection of working-class interests. Their sons were even more likely to do the same. We have already noted one early instance of this, the Typographical Society's 'Vigilance Committee', led by Tom Cat, surfacing in an early strike. From the 1880s to the early years of the twentieth century, workingmen's clubs would assume an increasingly political role, opposing certain tenets of the emerging capitalist order. Club life in the years 1860–1914 brings into relief the importance of cultural continuities as a force sustaining working-class protest. A similar process, illustrating the adaptation of traditional cultural mechanisms and activities to explicitly working-class purposes, was also at work in the arena of the enforcement of community morality, where charivaris and whitecapping were features of Hamilton social life.

There is incontestable evidence that in 16 separate instances, between the years 1865 and 1895, various parts of Hamilton and its environs were noisily awakened by the clamour of rough music. This must be only the tip of an iceberg, long since melted into back woodlots and dark alleys. Many of these occurrences were rural affairs, but King and John streets, to name but two major

---

158   On the East and West End clubs see *Hamilton Spectator*, 4 November 1897; 11 November 1897; 23 December 1897; 14 January 1898; 3 February 1898; 17 November 1898; 20 January 1899; 15 February 1899; 17 March 1899; 7 June 1904. The only case found of a club similar to those of the 1880s existing in the 1890s was that of an association of young boys, ages 13–17, who worked during the day. See *Hamilton Spectator*, 28 March 1893.

159   *Minute Book, Hamilton Trades and Labor Council, 1910–1914*, pp. 51–2, Hamilton Collection, Hamilton Public Library; *Cotton's Weekly*, 4 March 1909; 22 June 1911.

city thoroughfares, were not spared the hoots and cries, the thumping of tin pans, and the unmistakable bellow of the fish horn, characteristic traits of the charivari party.[160] Hamilton must have been well acquainted with such acts, for Isaac Buchanan entitled his 1858 election appeal to the city's workingmen, *Hamilton Charivari: An Election Fly Sheet*.[161]

In Hamilton, charivaris were usually mounted against those managing their households in a manner frowned upon by the community, or raised in mocking hostility to old men who took younger women into their matrimonial bed. A village widow whose 'mode of managing her household affairs did not come up to the social standard of moral ethics', a newly married couple that had offended the neighbours' sensibilities, and an old widower who took a woman 30 years his junior as his wife, were typical targets of the charivari party in the Hamilton region.[162]

The nineties saw the passing of the charivari. In 1890, 300 youths assembled at the corner of Catharine and Hunter streets, charivaried Charles John Williams and his bride, Miss Elizabeth Reid, who was 'considerably his junior in years'. Yelling, blowing fish horns, and singing parodies of 'Annie Roonie', the crowd was eventually dispersed by the police, but not before they had physically assaulted the old shopkeeper.[163] One of the last charivaris known to take place in Hamilton occurred in 1894. 'Old Man Christie' had married 'pretty Widow Andrews', and insisted on his new wife's right to join him at his long-time residence, formerly occupied by himself, his late wife, and their daughter. The young woman was not amused, claiming that the house had always been the property of her mother, and that it had been left to her. She mobilised a threatening charivari party to shame her newly-wedded father.[164] As Mr Christie learned to his displeasure, and as Susanna Moodie had been told dec-

---

160 Data on Hamilton and district charivaris were culled from the local press, where accounts ranged from brief passages in the police and court dockets to extraordinarily detailed descriptive articles on specific events. See *Hamilton Times*, 7 August 1867; 13 January 1868; 16 July 1875; *Hamilton Spectator*, 9 September 1879; 30 January 1880; 1 November 1881; 29 October 1881; 24 February 1883; 17 March 1884; 16 June 1885; 15 May 1886; 4 June 1890; 5 June 1890; 9 June 1890; 19 July 1890; 24 February 1892; 14 August 1894.

161 See Buchanan 1857, in the National Library, Ottawa. I am grateful to Robert Storey for making this source available to me. It is possible that the circular drew its name from the British periodical, *Punch, or the London Charivari*, which in turn borrowed from the earlier French satirical journal of the 1830s.

162 *Hamilton Times*, 7 August 1867; 13 January 1868; *Hamilton Spectator*, 1 November 1881.

163 *Hamilton Spectator*, 10 July 1980.

164 *Hamilton Spectator*, 14 August 1894.

ades before, charivaris were 'the custom of the country' and they were not 'so easy to put down'. They were also 'not always a joke'.[165]

Blackened faces, voices obscured by the perpetual din, and shadows illuminated by moonlight do not lend themselves easily to identification, and the threat of legal action, always present in this period, pushes the participants of the charivari further out of view. We would be hard pressed to place Hamilton workingmen at the scene of any of these boisterous gatherings, although what we know of the practitioners of rough music in other settings suggests strongly that apprentices, mechanics, and craftsmen contributed to the proceedings. It would be strange indeed if a crowd of '300 young men, girls, and boys' gathered on Hamilton's street corners on a Sunday afternoon contained no workers. Finally, the harassed victims, generally from the lower orders or petty shopkeepers, suggest that the charivari was utilised by the labouring poor. The rich, after all, were likely to keep their houses in better order, at least visibly, and would at this late date shy away from any form of public exhibition. Fortunately, there is more than a suggestion that the charivari was employed by working men and women.

On 29 April 1890, 150 weavers, threatened with a wage reduction of 25 percent, struck the Ontario Cotton Mills. Half of the strikers were women, and their earnings were already depressed, the majority making only $1 or $1.25 a day. For over a month the strike continued, the firm obstinate, the weavers determined.[166] Some women, among them a Mrs Trope, returned to work. The first week of June saw the weavers respond violently to these cases of strike-breaking: among their tactics, a charivari, waged against Mrs Trope and another woman, Anne Hale, on two separate occasions. Charged with assault and intimidation, 'the charivaring weavers' were sent up for trial. Mrs Trope, suffering from 'nervous prostration', charged Elizabeth Wright, Mary H. Kingsley, and William Carlyle with assault and, in another case, had George Maxwell, Robert Irwin, and Carlyle brought before the bench to answer a charge of intimidation. Similarly, Mrs Hale accused Moses Furlong, Richard Callan, Henry Dean, and Anne Burke of intimidation. Mrs Trope testified

> that she had worked at the mill for eight years. The mill had been shut down for five weeks because of the weavers strike. She did not attend any meetings of the strikers and at the request of Manager Snow she

165 Moodie 1962, pp. 145–6.

166 *Hamilton Spectator*, 29 April 1890; 3 June 1890; *Minute Book of the Trades and Labor Council, 1888–1896*, pp. 99, 102–4, Hamilton Trades and Labor Council.

went to work last Monday. When on her way home that evening she went along Ferrie Street ... followed by a crowd of men and women. The defendants Maxwell and Irwin had fish-horns and were blowing them. She estimated the crowd at a couple of hundred, many of them weavers. Mrs. Trope turned down Catharine Street and was followed by the crowd. She stopped to let the people pass and Mrs. Wright struck her. She tried to strike back and Mr. Carlisle pushed her into the road, and she fell down, injuring her hip. Trope found his wife surrounded by the crowd, and took her home.[167]

With Mrs Hale's charges it was 'the same old case of fish-horn blowing, shouting, and general disturbance', the crowd bearing a likeness to a 'procession of Grit schoolboys'. The rough-musicking strikers found the court unsympathetic to their use of the customary shaming ritual, and they drew fines ranging from $2.00 to $5.00.[168]

Charivaris, as traditional forms of community control, proved resilient in Hamilton, apparently falling into disuse only with the coming of the twentieth century. Yet even here the process of cultural continuity was evident, for another cultural phenomenon, that of whitecapping, followed quickly on the heels of the decline of rough music. Whitecapping was probably a fusion of a number of nineteenth-century experiences. It may well have drawn its intense appreciation of moral purity from Ellice Hopkin's White Cross Movement, a religious crusade of the 1880s that raged against prostitution, lewdness, and manifestations of so-called social impurity.[169] It certainly borrowed heavily from the tradition of Southern vigilantism, the white caps and masks of the Ku Klux Klan often being the badge of the White Cap. In the South, at least, racism may also have been a potent force in the history of whitecapping, black sharecroppers and contract labourers being prominent targets of abuse.[170] Whitecappers may also have drawn upon the rituals, oaths, and secret ceremonies of the friendly societies or Knights of Labor to bind members to the purposes and promises of the association.[171] This kind of cultural coales-

---

167 *Hamilton Spectator*, 10 June 1890; 4 June 1890; 5 June 1890.
168 *Hamilton Spectator*, 9 June 1980.
169 DeCosta 1887; Hopkins 1883.
170 See Holmes 1969, pp. 165–85. On the Georgia White Caps, and the lynching of two blacks who 'had run away from contract labor after having got into debt', see *Hamilton Spectator*, 1 March 1901. On the regalia of the White Caps see Pelham 1891, p. 2; Crozier 1899, p. 31.
171 See Crozier 1899, pp. 12–13; Graham 1967, pp. 3–8; Siringo 1912, pp. 120–2.

cence bred strong attachments, and the White Caps had a significant presence in many communities in Canada and the United States.

Hamilton's White Caps may have had their beginnings in the mid-1880s, with the rise of the White Cross Army, a movement dedicated to the protection of maidenly virtue and wifely chastity. The *Palladium of Labor* saw the preservation of such attributes as important, but cautioned that the real problem was the low wage structure and consequent poverty that was characteristic of women's work: 'If the white cross army would strike at the root of the evil and protect women from wrong and degradation they should seek to secure her industrial position, to abolish the evils of starvation pay and long hours'.[172] Throughout the 1890s and early years of the twentieth century, Hamilton's White Caps remained an obscure grouping. Their presence, however, was established by a number of street confrontations and assaults, as 'Whitecap gangs' battled local police constables and youths.[173] Robert and George Ollman, two brick makers, apparently headed the Hamilton White Caps.[174] As in other communities, the city's White Caps were known for their willingness to defy constituted authority and their readiness to by-pass proper channels in the enforcement of popular standards. Forces like these could be harnessed by the working-class movement in times of crisis.

The winter and spring months of 1892 were just such a moment of crisis for Hamilton's iron moulders. In a fierce contest precipitated by their employers, the Iron Molders' International Union was being tested in a strike which, if lost, would spell their extermination as an organised craft. The founders, led by the Gurney and Copp brothers, had imported non unionists to man their foundries, but the moulders had resisted, hanging on with grim determination.[175] One non-unionist, William Clendenning, was prosecuted by a local constable for carrying a loaded revolver. He claimed it was a necessary precaution, taken after he noticed that whenever he stepped out of his room he was followed by gangs of unionists. Moreover, along with another strikebreaker called Fleury, Clendenning had been the recipient of a chilling, threatening letter, written in pencil and headed with a skull-and-cross-bones, a whip, and a club: 'Scabs, beware! We have formed an association to go and club the

---

172   *Palladium of Labor*, 21 June 1884.

173   On the Hamilton White Caps' defiance of authority see *Hamilton Spectator*, 2 May 1900; 19 June 1900.

174   The Ollman brothers were cited in *Hamilton Spectator*, 19 June 1900, and their occupations culled from city directories.

175   On the importance of the strike, which is discussed in more detail in chap. 3 of Palmer 1979a, see Kealey 1976a, pp. 45–6 and n. 80.

life out of scoundrels if you don't cleare this town before Wednesday night, Ye will a lashing such as white man never got before what you are looking for badly'. The note bore a sinister signature, 'WHITE CAPS'. Given a suspended sentence for his crime, Clendenning was told that it was not necessary for him to carry a revolver, for the non-union men were afforded every possible protection. Bound over for six months by the court, the 'scab' moulder expressed his pessimism: 'If the union men get their way I won't be here for six months'.[176]

Both the charivari and whitecapping thus illustrate a process of cultural continuity and adaptation. Traditional mechanisms of community control had been converted into tools of working-class protest. Other realms of working-class culture also highlight this process of continuity and adaptation. The workingmen's clubs, for instance, in their evolution from the jocular associations of the 1860s and 1870s to the organised forums of radicalism in the 1898–1914 years, exemplify an important trend. Even such superficially mundane activities as baseball games, picnics, and suppers could bring into relief the class interests of Hamilton workingmen. Finally, the institutional sphere of associational life, centred in the friendly society, mechanics' institute, fire company, and craft union, provided a stability and coherence to working-class life that, over time, fostered an important solidarity. It was in this context that events like the nine-hour movement of 1872, the Knights of Labor parades of the 1880s, or the Hamilton street railway strike of 1906 would draw universal support.

This, then, was a rich and vibrant culture; its subtle interconnections speak of an important continuity. Conscious of the transformation of economic life over the course of the nineteenth century, historians have perhaps emphasised change too much, ignoring the cultural continuities in working-class life.[177] And these continuities were not without meaning, for they could soften the blows of industrial-capitalist development, ease the strain of the many disciplines seemingly engulfing the Victorian mechanic. In certain circumstances, too, cultural continuities could be adapted to new purposes, confronting directly the harsh realities of the new order. But even this was not enough. The impingements of capitalist society were often too oppressive, the strains of

---

176   *Hamilton Spectator*, 11 April 1892. For other anonymous, threatening letters see chaps. 5 and 7 in Palmer 1979a, and *London Free Press*, 1 November 1898; *Globe*, 1 January 1881 (my thanks to Gregory S. Kealey for bringing the latter source to my attention).

177   One attempt to transcend this tendency to ignore continuities in working-class life is Gutman 1973b, pp. 531–88. A brief but illuminating discussion of cultural continuity is found in Thompson 1972a, p. 404.

everyday life too exhausting, the toll in human terms too great. It was in this kind of context that 'Vincent' could write to the *Labor Union*, an organ of the Hamilton Knights of Labor:

> Culture ... is a grand thing for the workingman ... There is often a vast difference, however, between theory and practice; between the ideal and the real. The ideal workingman never has any stomach or nerves; is never hungry, or tired, or cross, or discontented, and has no more passion nor temper in him than a yellow sunflower in an idiot's buttonhole. His wife is a sort of faded wallflower who never disagrees with him; his boys are goody-goody little cherubs, and the girls, bless their little hearts, they are just like primroses, and they always hold their mouths just so, and they keep their handkerchiefs ready so they can burst into tears when any of the great ladies condescend to speak kindly to them or offer them charity. Suffice it to say that workingmen and such families are phantoms and not realities; they don't exist in nature, they only exist in the imagination of certain fine people, such as those who honour the home of poverty occasionally with an official visit in state dress, when they want to collect missionary money for the poor heathen. The real workingman is a different article than this. He is not a phantom, he is a *fact* and I hope some of those fine people who are making a living out of him now, and honoring him with a little of it back sometimes by way of charity, will find him a stubborn fact before they get through with him. His wife too is a reallty, probably has a temper of her own and surely has feelings. His children are not too well clothed, and have democratic tendencies which are very hard to control. The real workingman always has a stomach, which is necessary. After his day's work he is hungry and tired; sometimes he is discontented, especially Saturday night if he can't get any money. Sometimes he has nerves, which are not necessary. He has to work ten hours a day; sometimes he walks a mile or two before and after work, and saws wood when he comes home. In that case he has not much energy left for culture and education, especially if the children have the whooping cough, and his wife is worn out working. As far as culture is concerned, mental labor, if severe, is worse than bodily labor, as it leaves the mind so exhausted as to be incapable of further effort after the day's work is done. So you can see in case of severe labor, either bodily or mental for small wages a man's whole existence is necessarily a sacrifice for the mean's of sustaining mere animal life. All culture or improvement of mind is out of the question. Life becomes a barrier, and hopeless slavery, the only release from which is death and the only result of which is to prepare a few more

lives for a fate possibly similar. The above picture is not overdrawn, it is true to life. I am a workingman myself, and I see such cases everyday; I can put my finger on a dozen of them. The object of a labor union is to remove the cause and the necessity for such cases, and to make it possible for a man to live by his labor independently as a man ought to live.

Bitterly resentful, 'Vincent' at least had not lost hope, and his solution to the problems besetting the workingman lay in organisation.[178]

Hamilton's skilled workers lived their culture in street and field and hall. But as 'Vincent' so passionately argued, this was not enough. They had other realities to contend with, many of them far from pleasant. The workplace in which they spent so much of their lives was also the arena of a culture vigorously enforced by Hamilton's craft unions, a culture that sought to defend and extend the boundaries of workers' control.

---

178   *Labor Union*, 10 February 1883.

CHAPTER 4

The Bonds of Unity: The Knights of Labor in Ontario, 1880–1900*

Gregory S. Kealey and Bryan D. Palmer

There has historically been no moment in the experience of North American labour that weighed so heavily on the collective mind of the working-class movement in the years 1900–30 as that of the Knights of Labor upsurge of the 1880s. Until the resurgence of labour in the 1930s, revealed most dramatically in the rise of the Congress of Industrial Organizations, workers recalled this past and drew upon its many and varied inspirations. Thus, when John L. Lewis consciously strove to create an image of himself as part of a long line of 'tough people', 'fighters', and class militants, he recalled (or fabricated) the story of his father's early involvement in the Iowa Knights of Labor: when Tom Lewis helped lead a bitter 1882 strike he found himself blacklisted from employment and exiled from town.[1] Clinton S. Golden, labour intellectual and founder of the United Steel Workers of America, first drank from the fountain of labour solidarity with 'Big John' Powderly, brother of the Order's central figure, Terence V. Powderly. 'Big John', for whom Clint worked as a helper at the tender age of twelve, preached the gospel of the Noble and Holy Order long after the Knights had succumbed to employer resistance, the economic crisis of the 1890s, and internal divisions and trade-union opposition. But even in the face of the Knights' ultimate defeat, Powderly's brother remained true to the cause of an all-embracing organisation of American workers. He imparted his enthusiasm to his young helper, and Golden recalled of the Knights that:

> Their ritualism, the secrecy with which their meetings were conducted, the signs and symbols that gave notice to their members as to when and where meetings were to be held, fired my interest and imagination and in my own mind I resolved that henceforth my lot was cast with that of the wage earners. I began to see class lines and distinctions. I discovered that

---

* 'The Bonds of Unity: The Knights of Labor in Ontario, 1880–1900', *Histoire Sociale/Social History*, 28 (November 1981), 369–412, co-authored by Gregory S. Kealey.
1 See Alinsky 1970, p. 15, and Dubofsky and Van Tine 1976, pp. 9–11.

there were people in America besides those who lived their lives upon farms that were largely self-sufficient. People who worked long hours for low wages in hazardous employment, lived in miserable tenements and hovels, whose very life depended on having a job, earning money but rarely more than enough to provide for the bare necessities of life.[2]

John Peebles, a jeweller and watchmaker in Hamilton in the 1880s, and later mayor of that city in the difficult years of 1930–3, remembered his early attachment to the Order, commenting in 1946:

> I became a member of the Knights of Labor about sixty years ago, when I was quite a young chap. I thought its programme would revolutionize the world, not only because of its programme which included co-operation and State ownership of all public utilities ... and the purification of Politics and of all law and State Administration which also included the full belief in the honesty and sincerity of all members of the order. In short it was a crusade for purity in life generally.[3]

Gordon Bishop, active in the organisation of steel workers in eastern Ontario, buttressed the assessments of Golden and Peebles, arguing that the ritualistic passwords and secrets of the Order insured large attendance at ordinary meetings, and riveted workers to a cause. Members of the Knights of Labor, he recalled, 'did not forget their obligation easily'.[4]

These individual statements were supplemented by a more general remembrance of the place and significance of the Knights of Labor. 'Never since the palmiest days of the Knights of Labor', declared Toronto's *Citizen and Country* in the midst of the craft union boom of 1898–1904, 'have trade unions taken such a firm hold of the toilers as today'.[5] As these turn-of-the-century organisational gains were consolidated, however, some workers could still tar the American Federation of Labor (AFL) with a brush dipped into the resentments of the 1880s and 1890s. In 1903 a Western Federation of Miners member from Slocan, British Columbia wrote to the *Miners' Magazine*: 'Now there are thousands of old-line

---

2 Brooks 1978, pp. 17–18.
3 Hamilton Public Library, Hamilton Collection, 'Recollections of John Peebles, mayor of Hamilton, 1930–1933', 7 February 1946.
4 Gordon Bishop, 'Recollections of the Amalgamated', unpublished typescript, Gananoque, in possession of authors.
5 *Citizen and Country* (Toronto), 7 February 1946.

K of L's in the WFM and the unsavoury acts of the AFL officials have not been altogether forgotten'.[6] Twenty years later many radicals and socialists regarded this new, and increasingly conservative, international craft unionism with even more antagonism. When the One Big Union in Canada sought a glorious past to contrast with the dismal realities of American Federation of Labor-Trades and Labor Congress trade unionism in the 1920s, it was the fires of the Knights of Labor that it chose to rekindle. 'One of the great land-marks in the history of class struggle', the Knights were regarded as 'a mass organization grouped in Geographical units' that prefigured the industrial unionism of the One Big Union. The Order, claimed these dissident workers, had been the very same 'one big union' that they were trying to build and sustain.[7] For their part, as David J. Bercuson has noted, the AFL pure and simple unionists linked the OBU with the Knights of Labor, the American Railway Union of Eugene Debs, and the American Labor Union. It was the latest 'subtle and pernicious plea again resorted to for the purpose of severing the wage earners from their orderly and practical course of action'.[8] By 1929, the radical challenge of the post-war reconstruction years had been at least partially undermined, and in this context of 'normalcy' the AFL met in Toronto in October. With southern textile workers urging the organisation of their mill towns, observers at the convention reported 'a pitch of enthusiasm not seen in labour gatherings since the spring tide of the Knights of Labor'.[9]

For these reasons among many others, Norman J. Ware, perhaps the most perceptive student of the Knights of Labor, saw the Order as just that 'sort of One Big Union of which Karl Marx would have approved, if – and this is a large "if" – it could have been transformed into a political organization under social-ist leadership'. Given this kind of orientation, which rests on the argument that the Knights of Labor 'more fully represented the wage-earners as a whole than any general labour organization either before or after its peak year, 1886',[10] it is odd indeed that Gerald Grob's intellectual history of the Knights of Labor has gained such widespread acceptance, achieving something of an interpretive hegemony. Grob's focus is on the Knights' political activity, and he places them unambiguously in a late nineteenth-century utopian reform stream character-ised by 'a lack of mature class consciousness'. Within this meandering current

6   Dubofsky 1974, p. 383.
7   University of Toronto, Kenny Papers, *The Knights of Labor, the American Federation of Labor and the One Big Union*, One Big Union Leaflet No. 2 (Winnipeg, n.d. [c. 1920]).
8   Bercuson 1978, p. 120.
9   Bernstein 1960, p. 34.
10   Ware 1968, p. 258.

we find a confused swirl of politicians and professional reformers, inept leaders, and archaic thought, all drifting towards the *petit bourgeois* dream of reestablishing the relationships of an earlier era, 'based on the dominance of the small producer'. Only in the rare eddy does an actual worker rear his or her head, or a specific class-action flow off into some small tributary: but they are all diverted, or sucked under by the visionaries and utopians who chart the course of the ultimate direction of the river.[11] It would not do to dismiss totally the Grob analysis, for there was much muddled thinking within the Order, and political activity was a realm highly charged with charlatanism; many less than admirable figures played out their roles, and not a few dealings and events were dirtied with the sordid business of self-interest or party serving.

But the Ware interpretation will also not stand the test of close scrutiny, for as Leon Fink has argued, it tends to distance the Knights too readily from electoral politics and established institutions.[12] Collapsing the Knights' so-called struggle for democracy into a 'popular movement' without necessary and organic connections to the politics of late nineteenth-century America, Ware comes perilously close to anticipating Grob by associating the Order with a broad-based reformism 'engrafted upon the movement by the farmers or the radical fringe of socialists and communists of one stripe or another'. Ware is at least sensitive to the appeal and potential of such a reform thrust, while Grob is clearly antagonistic and sceptical. But if Ware thus sees the Order as a working-class movement, he regards its class content as resting outside the sphere of political engagement, traditionally defined, directed by forces peripheral rather than central to the movement's history and experience. In the Ware framework, then, the Knights rush, leaderless, and without coherence, into the political fray in the highly charged atmosphere of 1886–7, then abdicate totally in 1890–4, as the Order's national leadership suffers paralysis and the agrarian or 'western' section takes over, highlighting the populist content of the Knights' world-view. Again, it is not that this depiction of the Order lacks value, but that it neglects important realities and compresses too much into a rather small package.

The Knights of Labor were not this kind of small package, in either the Grob or Ware sense, and we propose to interpret the experience differently. By examining the structural situation of the Order, where and when it organised in Ontario, and how many (in rough terms) it drew to its ranks, we believe that we

---

11   Grob 1961, especially pp. 34–59, 79–80.

12   Fink 1979; 1977. The Ware argument is stated most concisely in Ware 1964b, pp. xi–xiii, 350–70.

can establish the class character and importance of the Knights of Labor. We shall argue that the Noble and Holy Order of the Knights of Labor represented a dramatic shift away from past practices within the history of Ontario workers. Although the Knights built very much on the accumulated experience of the working class, they channelled that experience in new directions. In the terms of Raymond Williams they took a whole series of residual aspects of class experience, constructing upon them a structural and intellectual apparatus that was the beginning of emergent purpose. In short, the Knights of Labor in Ontario created, for the first time, what Lawrence Goodwyn has called a cultural movement of alternative, opposition, and potential. In the breadth of their vision, the scope of their organisation, and the unique refusal to collapse the cause of workers into this reform or that amelioration or restrict entry to the movement to this stratum or that group, the Knights of Labor hinted at the potential and possibility that are at the foundation of the making of a class.

Politically, the Order's efforts in the federal, provincial and municipal fields testified to the movement's willingness and ability to transcend the economistic concerns of the workplace. At the same time, the Order's important place in the class struggles and confrontations of the last two decades of the nineteenth century points to problems inherent in viewing the Knights of Labor from the perspective of its leaders' anti-strike rhetoric. To be sure, both in the political sphere and at the workplace, the Knights found themselves caught in many ambiguities and contradictions. Among the most important were their political relationship to the established Grit and Tory parties, and their capacity to defend the interests of their membership in the face of fierce employer resistance and a post-1886 trade-union opposition.

Some, but not all, of these difficulties were of the Order's own making. As an early expression of the social, cultural and political emergence of a class, the Knights of Labor understandably groped for answers more than they marched forcefully towards solutions. The Order was itself inhibited by the context of late nineteenth-century Ontario which, aside from its own peculiar 'regional' divisions, stood poised between an economy of competitive capitalism, but recently arrived, and the monopoly capitalism which stood literally around the corner with the Laurier boom years of the twentieth century. The Knights, in many ways, straddled each epoch, looking simultaneously forward and backward, longing for the rights they knew to be justly theirs, attacking the monopolists they saw controlling the business, politics and culture of their society.[13]

---

13 Previous Canadian work on the Knights of Labor in Ontario includes Chan 1949; Kennedy 1956; Forsey 1971, pp. 245–59; Ostry 1961, pp. 141–61; Watt 1959, pp. 1–26. Cf., given the above,

Beyond this general interpretive thrust, two final points need to be made, for they are as much a part of our purpose as any attempt to shift analysis of the Knights of Labor in new directions. First, we have attempted to work through the history of the Knights of Labor in ways which convey as adequately as is possible the human forces behind the doctrines, practices and campaigns of the 1880s and 1890s. In this abbreviated statement, which is a severe compression of a larger, book-length manuscript, something of this orientation may well be lost, but we are nevertheless in agreement with one principled member of the Order, whose reminiscences are prefaced by this general statement:

> When there is so much warmth in the making of labor's history it is strange that there has been so little in the writing of it. As a rule, it has been written by dry-as-dust economists who treat it as if it were the record of the advance of an economic doctrine. As well write the history of the religious movement as if it were the record of the advance of theological doctrine. Labor doctrines have never advanced except as they have been lived and loved by individuals.[14]

Second, we want to insist that the experience of the Knights of Labor be considered, not as some minor episode in labour history, but as an integral part of the late nineteenth-century Canadian past, in all its complexities. The rise of the Order was intimately related to the economic and political developments of the period. It was an implicit component of that 'manufacturing condition' that came into prominence in the late nineteenth century, but that is so often written about with only a cursory view of the labouring class.[15] That historians of politics and business have been willing and able to do this is perhaps understandable, but it does not make for a history that might comprehend totality and interrelationships. It is odd, for instance, that much of the political history of these years can be written with only a fleeting glance at the working-class constituency which was so consistently courted by John A. Macdonald, Edward Blake, and others. Even a source as unimpeachable as the *Journal of Commerce* noted in 1888 that 'the future of the artizan fills the whole horizon of politics,

---

Landon 1937b, pp. 1–7. While all this work provides valuable empirical detail it has been dated by the availability of new sources and lacks a firm grounding in local contexts. Interpretatively, it presents us with few benchmarks in understanding the Knights of Labor. We have drawn upon Williams 1973, pp. 1–16; Goodwyn 1976.

14   Buchanan 1970, p. vii.

15   Nelles 1974, pp. 48–107.

and no other class is considered at all'.[16] The Royal Commission on the Relations of Labor and Capital in Canada (1889) was likely the impetus behind such a caustic comment, and revealed how seriously the established political structure regarded the pressing question of labour.[17]

One cannot, then, divorce the experience of the Ontario Knights of Labor from all that has been considered as central to the history of Canada in these years.[18] Comprehension of the late nineteenth-century milieu demands a knowledge of the Order, and this in turn sheds new light on the history of economic, social and political life. We start our journey towards this understanding with a brief discussion of the economic and social context of late nineteenth-century Ontario. We then close with particular attention to the structural features of the Knights of Labor, the movement culture created and generated by the Knights, and the political and social confrontations at the polls and in the workplace.

1   Economic Background: Labour and Industrial Capitalism to 1890

The nineteenth century was the crucible from which Canada would emerge as a capitalist economy and society. Regardless of whether one looks towards a tradition of dissenting scholarship that begins with Myers, consolidates around Pentland and Ryerson, and continues with much recent work, or in the direction of an economic history erected upon aggregate data and estimates of real manufacturing output, it is indisputable that the latter half of the nineteenth century saw momentous change. This involved the creation of a sophisticated transportation network, the articulation of a strategy of industrial development that pinned the hopes of Canada's rising capitalists on political consolidation, tariff protections and settlement, and the evolution of a diversified manufacturing sector.[19] All this, to be sure, developed in the context of a social order wracked by major depressions and frequent recessionary downturns. Nevertheless, as early as the 1860s the transforming power of capital had become visible in the rise of the factory, the increasing use of steam power, and the

---

16   *Journal of Commerce* (Toronto), 7 September 1888, cited in Bliss 1974, p. 120.

17   See Kealey 1973b, especially pp. ix–xxvii; Harvey 1978.

18   R.J.K., 'The Dynamic Year of 1886', *One Big Union Monthly*, 23 September 1927, courtesy Allen Seager, is one good example of this.

19   Myers 1972; Pentland 1959, pp. 450–61; 1960; Ryerson 1968; Bertram 1964, pp. 93–146; Palmer 1979a, pp. 3–31; Kealey 1980, pp. 1–34.

mechanisation of important industries such as tailoring and boot and shoe production. For the *People's Journal* these were the hallmarks of momentous change, factors which had 'set agoing an industrial revolution'.[20]

Between 1870 and 1890 the industrial sector tasted the fruits, both bitter and sweet, of this great transformation: establishments capitalised at $50,000 and over increased by about 50 percent; employment in manufacturing rose by 76 percent and output in constant dollar terms climbed by 138 percent; railway mileage went from 3,000 in 1873 to over 16,000 in 1896; manufacturing's place, in terms of value added, rose from 19 percent of the Gross National Product in 1870 to 23.5 percent in 1890; the rate of real manufacturing output climbed from 4.4 percent in the decade 1870–80 to 4.8 percent in the 1880–90 period, slipping to 3.2 percent in the 1890s. The 1880s became an extremely significant moment in the historical rate of growth, surpassed only by the boom years 1900–10 and 1926–9. Indeed, it is the growth of manufacturing facilities in many industries during the cresting fortunes of the National Policy that is most striking. Between 1880 and 1890, for instance, the value of cotton cloth output rose by 125 percent, but even this dramatic increase understated the gains of the decade's first five years: the number of mills, spindles, looms, and capital investment tripled in that short period.[21] Such developments took place, moreover, within the context of a general decline of prices which, using Michell's index, plummeted from roughly 100 in 1873 to a low of about 75 in 1886.[22]

Ontario stood at the very centre of this process of capitalist development. Aggregate data begins to tell the story. Capital invested more than doubled in each decade between 1870 and 1890, while the number of hands employed increased 90 percent over the twenty-year period. These aggregate data can give us an imprecise measure of the character of social and productive relations, the setting within which the Knights of Labor operated, and one which they must have influenced (Table 4.1).

---

20   *People's Journal* (Hamilton), 1 April 1871, cited in Langdon 1975, p. 3; Board of Arts and Manufactures for Upper Canada 1867, p. 220.
21   Bertram 1964, pp. 93–146; Bland 1974, pp. 8–39; Acheson 1972, p. 144; Warrian 1971, p. 11.
22   Bertram 1964, p. 133. On the importance of this period of price deflation in the United States see Vatter 1975, and on the twentieth century, Braverman 1974a.

TABLE 4.1   *Aggregate Ontario data, 1871–1911*

Year	Capital invested ($)	Hands employed	Yearly wages ($)
1871	37,874,010	87,281	21,415,710
1881	80,950,847	118,308	30,604,031
1891	175,972,021	166,326	49,733,359
1901	214,972,275	151,081	44,656,032
1911	595,394,608	216,362	95,674,743

Year	Value raw material ($)	Value product ($)	Value added ($)
1871	65,114,804	114,706,799	49,591,995
1881	91,164,156	157,889,870	66,825,714
1891	128,142,371	231,781,926	111,639,555
1901	138,230,400	241,533,486	103,303,086
1911	297,580,125	579,810,225	282,230,100

Source: Canada, *Census*, 1871–1891. Note that the 1901 and 1911 figures are unadjusted in light of the changing criterion employed by the census in enumerating manufacturing establishments. All firms were considered for 1871–91, while only those firms employing five or more hands were considered in 1901 and 1911. The capital invested figures for 1901 and 1911 are computed by adding together the figures for fixed and working capital. There had been no distinction between these realms in the earlier period.

Table 4.2 illuminates trends within the aggregate data for the years 1871–1911. However crude and unrefined the categories, they reveal important shifts and developments. If, for instance, we take capital invested as a percentage of value added, we note a steady increase over the years 1871–1901, with the decadal rate of that increase dropping precipitously in the opening years of the twentieth century. Wages, however, exhibit a different trend, and as a percentage of value added were relatively stable until they fell dramatically in the 1901–11 years. When we take capital invested and wages as a percentage of the total product value other trends emerge: capital as a percentage of product value rises steadily over the entire period, while wages as a percentage of value added decline only in those years of most pronounced economic growth, the 1880s and 1900s.

TABLE 4.2   *Trends within the aggregate Ontario data, 1871–1911*

Year	Capital as % of value added	Wages as % of value added	Capital as % of product value	Wages as % of product value	Per capita yearly wages ($)	Capital invested yearly per worker ($)	Yearly national growth rates in manufacturing output (%)
1871	76	43	33	18	245	433	} 4.4
1881	121	45	51	19	257	684	} 4.8
1891	157	44	73	18	284	1,057	} 2.4
1901	208	43	89	18	295	1,422	} 6.0
1911	210	33	102	16	441	2,751	

Source: Our calculation from census data. Same reservations as in source note to Table 4.1. Yearly national growth rates in manufacturing output are taken from Bertram 1964, pp. 93–146.

Such rough calculations gesture toward essential processes in the sphere of social and productive relations. First, we note that wages declined as a percentage of product value precisely in those years, 1881–91 and 1901–11, that the growth rates in national manufacturing output soared. This suggests a growing intensification of labour; that these periods, then, saw increasing organisation among Ontario workers – first in the Knights of Labor, and second in the craft unions during the upheaval of 1898–1904 – should cause no surprise. But to study the character of exploitation we must probe the relationship of wages to value added, considering the capital input. This leads us to our second speculative hypothesis: it would appear that the social cost of labour was relatively high throughout the late nineteenth century, years which pre-dated Taylorism, broadly conceived. It is not until the turn of the century that wages as a percentage of value added plunged, even in the face of soaring per capita yearly wages (largely a consequence of inflation, for real wages declined).[23] These turn-of-the-century years also witness a virtual doubling of the capital invested yearly per worker, and leave behind the more modest decadal increases in this relationship characteristic of the 1871–1901 years. And yet, even given this mammoth dose of capital in the years associated with the beginnings of Canada's century, capital as a percentage of value added makes only a marginal, clearly insignificant, gain. Thus, although both the 1880s and 1900s are years of economic growth and increasing intensification of labour, it is not until the 1901–11

23   See, for instance, Copp 1974; Piva 1979; Millar 1980.

years that one sees the actual rationalisation of productive relations, a shift in the character of exploitation, and the probable heightening of the degradation of labour. Before that the social costs of labour remained relatively high.[24] What gains in output that did occur late in the century were probably more a consequence of capital input than of extraction of surplus from the hide of labour, although these spheres are ultimately impossible to separate analytically.

If this was indeed the trend then it becomes important to ask what forces kept the social cost of labour relatively high in this period. The lack of a managerial strategy at the workplace, 'scientifically' conceived, was no doubt one aspect, as was the technological foundation of production, weak in the 1880s compared to the post-1900 years. However, the mass character of the Knights of Labor, as a movement aimed at uniting all workers, probably played a considerable role in resisting capital's quest to increase output and reduce labour costs through wage reductions or increasing the pace of work. Looking at the yearly per capita wage figures confirms this picture. While yearly wages rose only $12 in the 1870s and only $8 throughout the 1890s, the increase for the 1881–91 years was at least two-and-a-half times as great, or $30. Even granting all the ambiguities in this admittedly speculative and tentative argument, much of the data points towards the high social cost of labour in the late nineteenth century; labour seemed relatively better off in these years, in terms of its capacity to extract a larger portion of its product, than it would in later times, when capitalistic appropriation was undoubtedly more refined and effective. The social relations of production, in which worker stood counterposed to employer and in which the nature and extent of organisation was of vital importance, must have contributed to this outcome.

There is no mistaking the tremendous expansion in the manufacturing sector. An analysis of county data shows impressive quantitative gains in workers employed in manufacturing between 1871 and 1891. This growth displayed tangible regional patterns: the dominance of Toronto-Hamilton, the underdeveloped but nevertheless significant economic activity along the St. Lawrence and Ottawa Rivers, and the manufacturing importance of various small towns. More than fifty percent of the manufacturing of the 1880s was located in small Canadian communities, where the population never climbed above 10,000.[25] The regional economy of Ontario, then, was a far from homogenous entity, even as late as the 1880s. The closing years of the century were something

---

24   Ferland 1980.
25   Acheson 1972, p. 162; see maps on 'Manufacturing Employment by County', in Dean 1969.

of a struggle for industrial hegemony, in which the small manufacturing unit servicing a local market gave way to the larger productive concern, often contributing towards the decline of the small town and a shift in the location of industry to the population centre of a larger city. Thus the value added in all manufacturing activity in York County (Toronto) rose from 27.44 percent in 1870 to 32 percent in 1890. Toronto and Hamilton each accounted for 20 percent of industrial employment in southern Ontario in 1881, although they contained only 6.5 percent of the region's population. But even given this increasing specialisation, localisation and gross expansion in the manufacturing sector the 1880s were still a decade of contrasts: handicraft forms of production still co-existed with thoroughly mechanised processes; the large factory still occupied minority status given the number of small shops.[26]

How did this process of advancing but uneven development stamp itself upon the character of specific Ontario locales, where the Knights of Labor would come to prominence in the later years of the nineteenth century? As we have already seen, the industrial cities of Toronto and Hamilton led the way. (We have commented briefly on the experience of these major centres in other works).[27] Beyond the boundaries of these reasonably well-studied industrial cities lies a virtual no man's land, where our knowledge of economic activity is severely restricted. Yet it is clear that in countless Ontario communities capitalist development touched the lives of many workers and employers. Linked closely to this process was the importance of railways, which served as a connecting link to integrate the developing home market. This revolution in transportation was perhaps the key element in the shifting location and expansion of manufacturing in these years from 1870–90.[28]

Most of the railways built in southern Ontario after 1881 radiated out from Toronto, further contributing to that city's metropolitan dominance. Of great significance was the increasing importance of the old established lines in western Ontario – the Grand Trunk, Great Western and Canada Southern – which received great stimulus as the Canadian Pacific and Grand Trunk battled for control of the country's rail lines. In this struggle for dominance local traffic was actively sought, mileage was expanded, and efforts were made to capture a greater share of the American through-traffic. Centres such as St. Thomas and Stratford became links in a chain of economic development, and

---

26   Spelt 1972, pp. 101–86; Chambers and Bertram 1966, pp. 225–55; Bland 1974, pp. 8–39. See the important statement in Samuel 1977, pp. 6–72.

27   On Hamilton see Palmer 1979a, pp. 3–31, and on Toronto Kealey 190, pp. 1–34.

28   Note Lenin 1964, p. 551.

their wage-earning class was often tied directly to the shops that served the railways or the rail systems themselves. St. Thomas, for instance, grew rapidly in the 1870s, being transformed from a modest pre-industrial service town to a dynamic railway centre linked to the major Ontario metropolitan markets. Major shops of the American-owned Canada Southern Railway located there, employing about seven hundred men by the mid-1880s, and the Great Western established a repair shop in the city. By 1885 the New York Central had also commenced similar operations. Because of this rapid growth the city's class boundaries were rigid and geographically specific.[29]

The railways, through declining freight rates and economies of scale, helped to concentrate economic activity in a number of diversified manufacturing centres, whose growth took place at the expense of the smaller towns where factories were insufficiently developed to capitalise on transport costs compared to their larger, better situated rivals. London was just such a place. Its strength seemed to reside disproportionately in the food-processing sector, with concentrations of capital in bakeries, breweries, and tobacco related works. But this city also gained prominence as a marketing and distributing centre for the dairy belt of western Ontario's Middlesex, Oxford, Elgin, Lambton, Perth and Huron counties. In the textile sphere, the city's garment industry grew on the basis of its proximity to the Niagara Peninsula's cotton mills. Finally, in the wood-processing sector, concerns like the London Furniture Company employed 50 men, while in metal fabricating the city's McClary Manufacturing Company, Ontario Car Works, and E. Leonard & Sons produced stoves, engines and other goods. These latter firms employed between 80 and 450 hands throughout the decade of the 1880s.[30]

Other western Ontario towns also exhibited indications of the importance of industrial activity. Brantford's economic place in late nineteenth-century Ontario was dominated by the Harris, Wisner, and Cockshutt agricultural implements companies, and a hosiery factory. Harris & Son, taken together with the Massey works of Toronto (with which it would merge in 1891), accounted for 60 percent of all agricultural implements sales in the Dominion by the mid-1880s. Guelph, Galt, Berlin, Hespeler and even Collingwood to the north all housed similar, if much smaller, manufacturing concerns, producing for local, even regional, markets. In Guelph a hosiery factory employing over 100 workers, the Raymond Sewing Machine Company, the Guelph Sewing Machine Company, and the Crowe Iron Works dominated the industrial landscape.

29   G.P. de T. Glazebrook 1964, II, pp. 91–118; Clark 1976.
30   Trumper 1937; Scott 1930, pp. 56–65; Grimwood 1934, p. 3.

Further to the north and to the east industrial production was less well established, particularly in the area of secondary manufacturing. By the 1880s the Ottawa-Hull and Muskoka regions had established hegemony over the production of wood products, and a number of mills engaged in the preparation of sawn lumber, shingles, and matches. The dominance of lumber was even more pronounced in the Ottawa Valley, where the five largest producers in Canada had congregated by 1874. Over 2,500 men were employed in the production of lumber in 1891 in the city of Ottawa alone, and the industry found market outlets in both Britain and the United States.

East of Toronto, along the St. Lawrence River and Lake Ontario, small-scale processing industries and metal-fabricating plants attempted to capture a share of a largely local market. In the larger regional towns, however, there was room for some consolidation. Gananoque, Brockville, Cobourg, Belleville, Smiths Falls, Oshawa and Kingston all had the ubiquitous foundries, machine shops, and agricultural implements works of the period. G.M. Cossitt & Brothers and Frost & Wood Company established significant agricultural factories in Smiths Falls, the latter company employing over 150 skilled hands, producing goods valued at $150,000 destined for the farms of Canada, Australia and South Africa. Kingston's large engine works employed over 350 workers in the early 1880s, and a cotton mill with approximately two hundred hands opened in 1882. In the southern section of Ontario County, Oshawa-Cedardale was dominated by the Joseph Hall Works. Concentrating on the production of threshing machines, mowers and ploughs for the Canadian market, the plant employed 250 men as early as 1867. By the 1880s other important shops had long-established histories: the McLaughlin carriage works, Masson's seed-drill plant, A.S. Whiting Agricultural Implements, Oshawa Stove Company, W.E. Dingle's Fanning Mills and Seeders and the Robson & Lauchland Tanneries.[31]

But the most dramatic expression of industrial growth in eastern Ontario was Cornwall's cotton mills. Here was one city where the National Policy tariff of 30–5 percent was never challenged. In 1876 Cornwall's Canada Company cotton mills were the largest in the nation, the value of the plant hovering near the half-million dollar mark, the annual product valued at $400,000. Approximately three hundred and fifty workers (100 males and 250 females) toiled over 20,000 spindles to earn yearly wages of $75,000. Five years later, protected by the newly-revised tariff and stimulated by the return to prosperity,

31   Johnson 1973, pp. 250–2; 1903, pp. 455–65; information on Smiths Falls courtesy Peter de Lottinville.

Cornwall's three cotton mills – one was a relatively small firm – employed 133 men, 277 women, 186 boys and 190 girls. Their yearly wages totalled $179,900 and $456,000 worth of material was used to produce cotton goods and cloth valued at $833,000. By the time another half-decade had passed, Cornwall's two major textile producers – the Canada Company and the Stormont – had made impressive expansionary strides.[32]

Across the province, then, in spite of the increasing dominance of Toronto and Hamilton, of underdevelopment, uneven growth, and reliance upon primary production of the old timber staple in some areas, capitalist production was a force to reckon with by the 1880s. It transformed social and productive relations in the large cities as well as in the tiny rural hamlets. In this changed context class came to the fore as a clearly perceived reality; a culture premised upon this historic relationship of antagonism emerged more forcefully than it had in the past, and old distinctions appeared to fade in the face of a common experience and a recognition of the unity of life and work within a generalised system of appropriation. Railroads began the process of integrating a large regional unit, and linked the province to national if not international markets. Town and country increasingly found themselves enmeshed in a setting in which their pronounced differences began to pale before significant similarities. Social costs were many and varied: the growing impersonalisation of the wage relationship; the sooty environment of iron-and-steel-dominated Hamilton; the stark landscape of the mill town. Workers, of course, did not passively accept such developments, which had necessarily been part of a protracted process, and years well before the 1880s witnessed the first stirrings of Ontario's working-class movement. In that decade, however, came the essential changes, as class arrived on the scene, forcefully and unambiguously, for the first time. This class, which had been more than 50 years in the making and had at its back a culture of ambiguity and diversity, became unmistakably entwined with the rise of the Knights of Labor. As a body the Order took the ambivalence of the past cultural context of working-class life and forged it into a movement culture of opposition. In the expanding economic context of the 1880s, Ontario workers made strides towards unifying their labouring lives as productive men and women, and their everyday lives as citizens, family members, neighbours and advocates of change. A whole series of cultural expressions thus linked up with a class content, and the fragmented and sectional concerns

---

32   Select Committee on the Causes of the Present Depression of the Manufacturing, Mining, Commercial, Shipping, Lumber and Fishing Interests 1876, pp. 142–8; Kealey 1973b, pp. 179–92; Chambers and Bertram 1966, pp. 242–55.

of the past gave way to a broader demand that encompassed fundamental challenges to the established order of capitalist society. In whatever area one wants
to consider – economic, social, political, cultural – the Noble and Holy Order
of the Knights of Labor voiced the need to go beyond the social relations of
production as then constituted. An alternative hegemony was finally on the
agenda, finally in the process of formation. The significance of the 1880s, as
this moment of reaching out, was further confirmed by the gains in organisation among workers not necessarily affiliated with the Knights. But this growth,
however significant, paled in comparison, quantitatively and qualitatively, to
the upsurge of the Knights of Labor.

2   **Warp, Woof and Web: The Structural Context of the Knights of
        Labor in Ontario**

'To write the history of the Knights of Labor is an impossibility', warned Terence V. Powderly. 'Its history was the history of the day in which it moved and
did its work'. The much-maligned leader of the Order was aware that 'some
young men fresh from college have tried to write the history of the organization',
but they had failed: 'They applied logic and scientific research; they divided the
emotions, the passions, and feelings of the members into groups, they dissec-
ted and vivisected the groups; they used logarithms, algebraic formulas, and
everything known to the young ambitious graduate of a university'. Given this,
Powderly felt that it was not advisable to take 'the historian too seriously; at
best he but weaves the warp of fancy into the woof of fact and gives us the
web called history'. Powderly's words of warning are worth remembering. Yet,
in spite of our recognition of the importance of his sceptical assessment of
a history premised on impersonal data and mere quantities, we nevertheless
commence with plenty of numbers. They, too, were part of the day in which
the Noble and Holy Order moved and did its work.[33]
     Organisationally, the Knights drew workers into their ranks through a relat-
ively simple procedure and institutional apparatus. Individual members joined
local assemblies, either in mixed (diverse occupational affiliations) or trade
assemblies (adhering more rigidly to specific craft categories). Normally those
who were part of a particular trade assembly followed a designated skilled
calling, but occasionally the trade assembly was merely an organisation of all
workers employed in the same plant, shop or factory. For a local assembly to be

---

33   Powderly 1940, pp. 3–4, 102.

organised formally a minimum of ten members was required, and once established local assemblies were known to swell in membership to over a thousand. If a geographical region or trade contained five or more assemblies a district assembly could be formed. District assemblies were of two types: the national trade district, representing the interests of all assemblies of a specific craft, such as the window glass workers or the telegraph operatives; or the mixed district assembly, in which diverse interests of many mixed and trade assemblies were represented. In Canada it was this latter mixed district assembly that was pre-eminent, and in Ontario the various district assemblies were always mixed in form and representative of specific geographical and territorial units. Local assemblies were allowed one delegate in the district assembly for each hundred members they had enrolled, and one for each additional hundred or fraction thereof. Presiding over all these bodies were a series of leading elected officials: the master workman of the local assembly; the district master workman; and many lesser figures. Each district elected delegates to the annual convention of the Order, the general assembly, and at this gathering, in turn, were elected the national officers and the general executive board. The Order, then, was a highly centralised body, with a well defined hierarchy and structure; yet it was also egalitarian, and the local assemblies had a large measure of autonomy, with their own courts to prosecute those who transgressed the discipline and regulations of knighthood.

How many of these local assemblies were there, where were they, and what type of assembly prevailed in specific places?[34] Although strongest in Ontario's rapidly expanding industrial cities like Toronto and Hamilton, the Knights also penetrated the province's towns, villages and tiny hamlets. In its approximately thirty year lifespan (1875–1907), the Order organised locals in 82 towns from Amherstburg in the west to Cornwall in the east, and from Port Colborne in

---

34   All organisational data throughout are based on our own calculations. We should note, however, a debt of gratitude to two pieces of pioneering research on the Knights which were of inestimable value to us. Eugene Forsey's massive compilation of materials on organised labour in Canada before 1902 includes plenty on the Knights and a helpful attempt at a locale-by-locale reconstruction. See Forsey 1982. Garlock 1973a and 1974 have been of considerable help. For a description of the data bank, see Garlock 1973b, pp. 149–60. Our corrections to the data bank will be incorporated into the computer file at Ann Arbor. These corrections are based on the labour and local press of Ontario, on the Ontario Bureau of Industry, *Annual Reports*, on various trade-union minutes and proceedings, and on the extensive Ontario correspondence scattered throughout the Powderly Papers, recently indexed at the Public Archives of Canada (hereafter PAC) by Russell Hann. The population data are from the 1881 and 1891 censuses.

the south to Sudbury in the north. These 82 towns contained a total of at least 249 local assemblies (LAS), which in turn formed 10 district assemblies (DAS). Toronto, Hamilton and Ottawa led the way with 58, 30 and 12 local assemblies respectively, but the Knights were also active in eight communities of less than 1,000 people, and there were 31 local assemblies in places with populations of under 3,000. Ontario's five largest cities in the 1880s (Toronto, Hamilton, Ottawa, London and Kingston) contained 46 percent of all Knights of Labor assemblies, but it was the range and dispersal of the Order that was perhaps most significant: of the 47 Ontario towns with a population of at least 3,000 in the 1880s, fully 38, or 81 percent, witnessed the formation of a local assembly.

In Ontario there was an almost even division between trade and mixed locals, but if we consider the size of the town where the assembly was located a discernible pattern emerges. Mixed assemblies were far more popular in smaller places, while trade assemblies were most often found in the cities. As always there were exceptions to this general pattern. St. Thomas and London, for example, although large and important Knights' centres, possessed almost no trade assemblies. On the whole, however, the large manufacturing cities contained sufficient numbers of skilled workers to form trade assemblies, while in the smaller towns the mixed local assembly proved a more flexible organising device. Since many of these less populous centres were not large enough to support sufficiently numerous groups of tradesmen to give rise to craft unions, the mixed assembly fit their needs well. Thus in towns under 5,000 the mixed assembly was dominant with 58 percent of all local assemblies, while trade assemblies and locals of unknown character each provided 21 percent of all local assemblies. Cities with a population in excess of 30,000, however, were the more likely home of the trade assembly; 57 percent of all local assemblies were of this type and 30 percent were mixed, with 13 percent of unknown character.

How many members were drawn into the ranks of the Knights of Labor? This is a difficult question. In the United States, the Knights were said to have enrolled, at their peak, between 700,000 and 1,000,000 members, but this is a static count taken in the spring months of 1886. The data is questionable and tends to underestimate the membership. Moreover, the central problem is the timing of influx into the Order, for the Knights peaked at different moments in different regions. Thus, Jonathan Garlock has estimated that if one looks beyond peak membership the American Order may well have enrolled over three million workers in its assemblies over the course of its history. We are plagued with problems of comparable, if not greater, magnitude in the case of Ontario, for membership data after 1885 are shaky at best, and official estimates seldom reliable. As in the United States, the Ontario Knights did not peak until 1886, a year which saw the founding of 99 local assemblies, and even then the dating of the upsurge varied from region to region within Ontario. Thus, across south-central Ontario the Knights of Labor climbed to their highest membership point in 1886 and then deteriorated, rapidly in some places, more slowly in others. Towns close to the American border (Brockville and Hamilton, for instance) experienced the Order's impact earliest. But in the northwest, in the timber country of the Muskoka region, the Order achieved prominence later, as it did in some eastern Ontario towns like Kingston, where the Knights had 1,500 supporters in 1887. In Ottawa the Order's successes came, not in the 1880s, but in 1891. All this is further complicated by the fact that even *within* industrial cities like Toronto and Hamilton, which followed the classic pattern of cresting in 1886, there were some working-class sectors – letter carriers, longshoremen and labourers – who joined the ranks of the Knights after the Order was in obvious retreat. Thus, any attempt to address the numerical significance of the Order will founder if it is reduced to a count of peak membership at any given point.

We can, nevertheless, start with peak official membership at single points in time for some specific locales. Toronto DA 125's 41 local assemblies had 5,000 members in 1886, while Hamilton DA 61's 2,200 workers were organised in thirty local assemblies. District Assembly 6, of Ottawa, had 2,000 affiliated in 1892. The London-St. Thomas DA 138 reported a membership of 4,435 in 1886–7, enrolled in 36 LAS and extending out of the two major cities into western Ontario towns like Aylmer, Ingersoll, Listowell and Wyoming. St. Catharines DA 207 encompassed some two thousand advocates in 22 local assemblies. Other district assembly peaks were Windsor DA 174's 616, Belleville DA 235's 1548, Uxbridge DA 236's 523, and Berlin DA 241's 348. Perhaps more striking still are some of the individual town reports: Brockville's Franklin LA 2311 with 430 members in November 1883; Gananoque's seven- or eight-hundred members in 1887; Gravenhurst LA 10669's 300 lumber workers in June 1888; the 500 cotton workers in Merritton's Maple Leaf LA 5933 in 1886; Petrolia's Reliable LA 4570 with 500 members in 1886; LA 16722's 200 workers at the Frost and Woods agricultural implements works in Smiths Falls in August 1887; and the 500 workers of Woodstock's Unity and Concord LA's 3151 and 4922 in 1886. If we recall our earlier discussion of the localised nature of manufacturing activity in various Ontario cities and towns, in fact, we see that the Knights were strong wherever particular industrial activity predominated: among Cornwall's cotton workers, Hamilton's iron and steel workers, or St. Thomas's railway workers the Order had many advocates.

Available data do not allow us to make any firm calculations on the percentage of the workforce organised by the Order, nor would the official membership figures necessarily reveal the true impact: the tendency is always to under-represent the strength, and the volatility of the rank and file further compounds this problem of undercounting. Thus in five selected Toronto local assemblies the membership fluctuated greatly between the date of their initial report and 1 July 1885. In these assemblies 96 members were enrolled on the books at the time of the first membership report to Philadelphia. Between 1882 and 1885 these assemblies added 666 members but they also deleted 573, and so on 1 July 1885 they reported a total membership of only 189. Their peak strength, then, would hardly address the question of the masses of workers who passed through specific assembly halls. The case is made strongly in the instance of Toronto's LA 2305, which reported a mere 29 members in July 1885, swelled to 550 in the following months, and then fell back to 45 within a year. To appreciate fully the numerical significance of the Order we need to understand, not a static cross-sectional profile, but a process and flow, determined, in part, by the movement's vitality and particular events, developments in the economic realm, and social relations. But the figures do not readily allow this, and we are forced to consider the Knights in the context of peak membership figures that defy all this, a problem further exacerbated by the problems of reliance on census data that correspond only to decadal points and that mask local situations in larger county calculations.

We can begin with the larger picture. If we take the total peak memberships (at specific points in time with no account taken of volatility) across the province and add them together we see that over the course of their history the Knights organised a minimum of 21,800 members. (A figure double this might not overstate the numbers actually enrolled). This represented 18.4 percent of the hands employed in manufacturing in 1881 and 13.1 percent of those so employed in 1891. If we add to these figures the percentages of workers who were enrolled in trade unions but not members of the Knights of Labor (and we have no accurate statistics on this phenomenon, although it is estimated that in the United States approximately one-half of the Knights' members were trade unionists) it is apparent that at a very minimum the 1880s saw twenty to twenty-five percent of the total non-agricultural workforce drawn to the ranks of organised labour. This, we need remember, is a higher percentage than any period prior to the post-World War II upsurge, and it is only with the increasing unionisation of the public sector in recent decades that we have seen the figure climb to 35 percent and over. For much of the early twentieth century, especially prior to World War I, no more than 10 percent of the workforce was organised.[35]

---

35   Smucker 1980, p. 209; Pentland 1968, pp. 70–1.

TABLE 4.3   *Knights of Labor membership as percentage of hands employed, 1881 and 1891*

City or county	1881	1891
Essex (Windsor)	30.0	22.2
London	29.3	22.5
Elgin East (St. Thomas)	80.0	58.6
Hamilton	33.8	22.8
Toronto	39.3	20.4
Brockville	44.9	31.9
Kingston	101.8	56.0
Cornwall	32.3	14.8
Lanark South (Perth, Smiths Falls, Carleton Place)	21.1	18.1
Ottawa	–	31.7
Lincoln, Niagara and Welland (St. Catharines, Welland, Merritton, Thorold)	–	50.5
Perth North (Stratford, Listowell)	36.0	30.5

Source: Canada, *Census*, 1881 and 1891; Knights of Labor, General Assembly, *Proceedings*; Ontario Bureau of Industry, *Annual Reports*. Percentages can exceed 100 because peak memberships could include those drawn from outside the census area, and calculations of hands employed might understate actual figures, both for a centralized locale and at a given historical date. Table 4.3 should thus only be taken, as commentary below indicates, as gesturing towards significant trends.

These aggregate data, of course, distort the facts dramatically, for they include all workers with no regard for region, sex, or age. Some, but not all of this distortion can be eliminated by looking at particular places, presented in Table 4.3. The limitations of the census impose themselves here, for in attempting to focus on the percentage of the total workforce organised we are handcuffed to the 1881 and 1891 figures: the former are problematic because the Knights were not even on the scene at that early date, while the latter are equally flawed because the Order was, by that time, in the throes of decline. Moreover, such data are often available only on a county basis. Locales like St. Thomas get buried in the total county employment figures. Nevertheless, the figures are an indication of the impressive numbers of workers drawn to the Order, and in places like St. Thomas, Kingston, and the Lincoln, Niagara and Welland region there is no doubt that the Knights of Labor organised an absolute majority of the people employed in manufacturing.

The census, moreover, did not report on the hands employed in such small

TABLE 4.4   *Knights of labor membership as percentage of workforce (estimated at between twenty and forty percent of 1881 population)*

Town	20% of 1881 population	40% of 1881 population
Chatam	25.4	12.7
Woodstock	46.5	23.2
Petrolia	72.0	36.0
Merritton	139.0	69.5
St. Catharines	51.8	25.9
Guelph	17.6	8.8
Hespeler	71.4	35.7
Oshawa	52.0	26.0
Gananoque	87.0	43.5
Smiths Falls	47.9	23.9

Source: Canada, *Census*, 1881 and 1891; Knights of Labor, General Assembly, *Proceedings*; Ontario Bureau of Industry, *Annual Reports*. Note the qualification about percentages exceeding 100 in Table 4.3 above.

towns as Merritton, Chatham or Gananoque. Yet we know from many sources that the Order was actively engaged in such places. To attempt a crude estimate of the percentage of the workforce organised we have taken our figures on membership and compared them to a rough calculation of the number of hands employed. This latter figure was obtained by taking the total population for 1881. In no case would the workforce have been more than 40 percent of the population, and it is unlikely that it would have even reached 20 percent in these years, but we have taken these poles as our gauge. (Note that if we took 20 percent of the populations of Toronto, Hamilton and Kingston for 1881, we would expect workforces of 17,283, 7,192 and 2,818, respectively. The census recorded 1881 workforces of 12,708, 6,493 and 1,473, so in no case have we underrepresented the workforce. Our method, then, largely understates the impact of the Order. Since the small towns considered here did not expand greatly in the 1880s, using the 1881 population figures does not pose a great problem). Table 4.4 reveals how thoroughly the Order penetrated these small Ontario manufacturing towns, organising an extremely high percentage of the workforce.

What all this means, we would argue, is that the Knights of Labor represented the most important moment in the history of Ontario labour until the coming of the Congress of Industrial Organizations in the late 1930s. More workers were drawn to the cause of the Order in more Ontario communities and in greater numbers than one would, at first, consider credible. Across the province between 10 and 80 percent of all workers in particular cities, and we stress once more that these are minimum estimates, became Knights of Labor. That structural context was a large part of the warp, woof and web of the history of the 1880s. We have, against Powderly's advice, divided this out from the passions, emotions and feelings of the membership, and it is now time to turn to another aspect of the history of the Order. For if the Knights of Labor represented a quantitative breakthrough for Ontario's workers, they also represented a crucial qualitative shift in the orientation of the working class. The Order took the raw material of a class culture – ambiguous, fragmented and unfocused – and moulded it into a movement culture of opposition and alternative.

3   Spreading the Light: The Emergence of a Movement Culture

There is no such historical phenomenon as an alternative hegemony attained. At the moment that it is realised, an alternative hegemony passes into hegemony and assumes its place as arbitrator of social, economic, political and cultural values, expressed through the control of state power, the majesty of the law and a wide range of formal institutions and informal sanctions. A subordinate class can thus only reach towards an alternative hegemony but it cannot 'dominate the ethos of a society'.[36] Alternative hegemonies can, historically, pass into new hegemonic cultures, although this necessarily involves fundamental socioeconomic transformation and the dissolution of old ways of life. The revolutions of 1789 and 1917 were just such epoch-shaking moments of transition, although it is questionable if North America has ever witnessed upheavals of such magnitude. Certainly Canada has not.

In the Ontario of the 1880s, however, there was an alternative hegemony in formation. It did not win the day, although it raised a series of challenges and oppositions that remain with us yet. If its lifespan was indeed short, the issues it addressed seem timeless. We refer to this creative moment as a movement culture, a recognition that the Knights of Labor built upon a culture of class experience that had little direction and unity to consolidate a class effort that sought to transform the very nature of the society in which workers found themselves.

---

36   Thompson 1978b, p. 74.

The movement culture was formed in the process of daily life, both on and off the job, and it was tempered in the political and workplace struggles that we will examine shortly. It began with the worker's initiation into the Knights of Labor assembly, where a whole series of symbolic and ritualistic practices rooted the member in the movement, reinforcing traditions of collectivity and solidarity in an age of hostile, individualistic pieties. Each new initiate vowed to defend the interest and reputation of all true members of the order, be they employed or unemployed, fortunate or distressed, and was instructed that 'Labor is noble and holy. To defend it from degradation, to divest it of the evils to body, mind, and estate, which ignorance and greed have imposed; to rescue the toiler from the grasp of the selfish is a work worthy of the noblest and best of our race'. Upon admission to the Order, the recently christened Knight was informed that 'open and public associations have failed, after a struggle of centuries, to protect or advance the interest of labor', and that the Knights of Labor merely imitated 'the example of capital', endeavouring 'to secure the just rewards of our toil'. 'In all of the multifarious branches of trade', the convert was told, 'capital has its combinations, and whether intended or not, it crushes the manly hopes of labor and tramples poor humanity in the dust'. To counteract this distressing tendency of the modern age, the Order asserted: 'We mean to uphold the dignity of labor, to affirm the nobility of all who earn their bread by the sweat of their brow'. In these ritualised incantations, which resounded in local assembly halls across south-central Canada, lay much of the promise and potential of the Knights of Labor.[37]

That promise and potential reared its head in many cultural events: in the many picnics, parades, demonstrations, dances, hops and balls that the Knights organised across the province in the heady days of the upheaval of the 1880s. These occasions were no doubt moments of recreation, diversions which moved people away from the everyday concerns of the next day's work, the next week's groceries and the next month's rent – the range of insecurities the next year could bring. But they were also exhilarating reminders of self-worth and class strength. They were prominent in Toronto and Hamilton, as we would expect, but places like London, Woodstock, Ingersoll, Chatham, Thorold, Gananoque and Belleville were also the sites of such cultural activities, and the Order was capable of drawing anywhere from one to five thousand people to these 'monster' gatherings. After an 1887 Gananoque Knights of Labor picnic,

37   Cook 1886; Catholic University of America, Washington, D.C., Powderly Papers (hereafter PP), 'The Great Seal of Knighthood' and 'Secret Circular: Explanation of the Signs and Symbols of the Order'; Wright 1887, pp. 142–3; Powderly 1940, pp. 434–5.

the local newspaper commented: 'Probably no gathering anywhere near the size ever took place here, where there was such good order ... They have shown that they are a power in the community, able to command respect'.[38]

In all this, from the pounding footsteps of workers marching by the thousands in Toronto, Hamilton or Ottawa, through a day of sports and frolicking in Ingersoll, Belleville or Kingston, to a mammoth picnic and long-winded speeches on an island in the St. Lawrence near Gananoque, we catch mere glimpses of a self-generating culture of collectivity, mutuality and solidarity. An understanding of class place and pride stood at the core of this culture, as well as individual longing for a better world. Forging a multitude of diverse, often contradictory, ideals into a collective assertion was the movement itself. As a strikingly creative effort, the Knights of Labor was the very embodiment of human striving that evolved out of residual components of a class culture. As a movement, the Order nudged men and women associated with it towards a new, or emergent, purpose. The cause of labour reform was advanced as men and women worked to create a culture of 'democratic promise'. The difficulty we ourselves experience in comprehending their vision and their striving is a measure of significant failures – theirs *and* ours.[39]

But in the 1880s that failure was not a settled fact, embedded in the historical record in indisputable concreteness; the sharp clarity of defeat was not yet there for all to see. Thousands of Ontario workers took Richard Trevellick's words to heart when he promised that the Knights of Labor would 'make Labor respectable by having men and women respect themselves, and while courteous and kind, refuse to bow and cringe to others because they possess wealth and social position'. Certainly Thomas J. O'Neill, of Napanee's Courage Assembly (LA 9216), regarded such proclamations with appropriate seriousness, writing to Powderly that 'this section of the country is sadly in need of organization, but fear of the money kings [The Rathbuns] keep the working class in slavery'.

Railroad men, organised in Headlight Assembly (LA 4069) of St. Thomas, acted upon Trevellick's words in 1885. They conducted their own statistical survey of their town of 11,000 with the intention of using 'all lawful means of obtaining their rights, also to educate those of our members who heretofore have permitted others to do their thinking, thereby allowing themselves to be used as mere machines in the hands of unscrupulous men'. The *Labor Union* proclaimed its mission in mid-January 1883: 'To Spread the Light; to expose the

---

38   *Gananoque Reporter*, 25 August 1887.
39   Note the comments in Hann 1976, p. 57; Goodwyn 1976, pp. 540–3.

inequalities of distribution by which the few are enriched at the expense of the
many. To call things by their right names, and to point out to workingmen how
these inequities could be redressed and the workingman secure the full reward
of his toil'. Employers found much to dislike in the words of Trevellick, O'Neill,
LA 4069 and the *Labor Union*. Their actions throughout the 1880s spoke loudly
of their fears and antagonisms. They regarded the increasing consciousness
of class, and threat of active opposition, as a dangerous development. By 1891
the business community was convinced that 'the spirit of trades unionism is
strangling honest endeavour, and the hard-working, fearless thorough artisan
of ten years ago is degenerating into the shiftless, lazy, half-hearted fellow who,
with unconscious irony, styles himself a knight of labor'. The culture had, as
well as advocates, staunch opponents.[40]

It was in the midst of a virtual war between these contending forces (in
which battles were both practical and intellectual) that the labour reform cause
gained hard-won adherents. And it was in this context that the 'educational'
thrust so prominent in the Order's own priorities consolidated. Local assemblies became, in the parlance of the 1880s, 'schools of instruction' in which
the lessons learned turned on the principles of labour reform, reaching a mass
audience in literally hundreds of reading rooms, Knights of Labor libraries, and
assembly halls. In the words of Trevellick, it was in the 'schoolroom' of the local
assembly where members first learned 'their duties and their rights'.[41]

Providing much of the text of instruction was a handful of committed publishers and editors. Often themselves practical printers, these men struggled
through the 1880s and 1890s, working into the early mornings to put out their
weekly journals, devoted, as in the case of the *Palladium of Labor*, 'to the
Interests of the Workingmen and Workingwomen'. Always on the brink of
financial ruin, such newspapers kept afloat during these years only by the
extraordinary effort and personal perseverance of dedicated Knights of Labor
and occasional support from long-established trade unions. Smothered by their
dependence on advertising revenue, limited by their subscribers's inability to
contribute financially, with circulation often hovering around the 1,000 mark,
seldom over 5,000, these papers occupied an unenviable position in the often

---

40   *Palladium of Labor* (Hamilton), 5 September 1885; PP, O'Neill to Powderly, 13 January 1885;
      Headlight Assembly No. 4069 1885, p. 3; *Journal of Commerce*, 13 March 1891, as cited in
      Bliss 1974, p. 78; *Labor Union* (Hamilton), 13 January 1883.
41   Ontario Bureau of Industry 1888, Part IV, p. 18; *Palladium of Labor*, 21 February 1885; *St.
      Thomas Times*, 21 April 1886; *Journal of United Labor* (Philadelphia), March 1883, quoted
      in Fink 1977, p. 399.

gloomy world of the nineteenth-century press. Small wonder that the men who kept them going were often ill-tempered, and indiscriminately combative, as with Hamilton's William H. Rowe or St. Thomas's George Wrigley, or constantly manoeuvring to attain economic ends, like the notorious but resourceful A.W. Wright. But whatever their personal idiosyncrasies these men attempted to move the class beyond economism, striving 'to take a broader and more comprehensive view of the entire subject of Labor Reform than is embodied in mere unionism, and to grasp and apply those great underlying principles of equity and justice between men which alone can permanently and satisfactorily solve the issues between Labor and Capital'. This was an important component of what Frank Watt has referred to as the 'freely germinating' radicalism of the 1880s, a phenomenon spawned by the presence of the Knights of Labor.[42]

This radicalism was popularised by a group of brainworkers and local advocates: men like Toronto's Phillips Thompson, as well as more obscure, but highly talented and committed local figures. Among these were Joseph Marks of London, who began as a Knight, organised the Industrial Brotherhood in the 1890s, and edited the *Industrial Banner* well into the twentieth century; Galt's J.L. Blain, a lecturer who described himself to Powderly as a well-educated 'rat from the sinking ship of aristocracy'; a Hamilton coppersmith, George Collis, who boomed the Order under the nickname 'Sandy the Tinker', travelling to Oshawa, London and other southern Ontario towns; poets like the carpenter Thomas Towers and Listowell's blind and deaf Walter A. Ratcliffe; or anonymous supporters – St. Thomas's 'Knight of the Brush' and 'True Reformer'; Brantford's 'Drawbar'; or 'Pete Rolea' from the oil-producing community of western Ontario. Individuals like these helped the Order to establish itself in countless communities, and made the cause of reform a popular and lasting one. 'Lignum Vitae' reported to the *Journal of United Labor* on the progress of Guelph LAS 2980 and 4703: 'The masses are beginning to believe us when we tell them this endless toil for a miserable existence was never intended by an all wise creator. I wish I had only more time that I could go out to these people and invite them into an Order whose object is the complete emancipation of all mankind, and lift from off their necks the yoke of subjection, and often tyranny of a few'. From virtually every corner of the province anonymous correspondents informed labour newspapers of the local state of reform agitation.[43]

---

42   G. West Wrigely, 'Socialism in Canada', *International Socialist Review*, 1 May 1901; Watt 1959.
43   *Journal of United Labor*, 25 March 1886.

This agitation contributed much to the attainment of class cohesion, strengthening the bonds of unity. The old sectarian quarrels between Orange and Green were, for the most part, left behind; the Order itself assumed the place and role of a religion of reform, labour sermons being preached in local assembly halls; the Irish, once despised by all respectable workers, were at the centre of the Knights of Labor activity. Education became, not the responsibility of the schools, the press and the élite, but the duty of all. 'L.C.S.' of Gananoque argued that the Knights were 'engaged in solving the greatest problem of the age', urging all wage labourers to drink at the fountain of labour reform, rather than from the cesspool of the 'capitalistic press', which consistently suppressed facts, failed to consider just causes, and aligned itself with 'upper anarchy', money and monopoly. 'Educate yourself and you will be in a position to enlighten others', he wrote. That accomplished, working people had only to 'obey the laws of knighthood, be loyal to self and manhood, defend the interest of the Order, and labor for the new era until it dawns upon the toilers of our country, until the weary men and women chained by the wage-system can see justice enthroned, and this, the land of the free'. As Albert V. Cross reported to Powderly from Hamilton's LA 2481 in 1887:

> When we entered the Order we were taught that in the home of labor there would be no distinctions of Country, Creed & Color because all were of the Earth and with equal rights to Earth, when we understood this great truth that all men are brothers we rejoiced, and we solomly resolved that we would do all in our power to strengthen the bonds of unity between the workers of the world.[44]

Perhaps the most significant aspect of this strengthening of the bonds of unity was the Order's role in overcoming past deficiencies of workers' organisations. Nowhere was this more visible than in the Knights of Labor effort to draw *all* workers into one large movement. Across the province skilled and unskilled workers, craftsmen, factory operatives and labourers, united in local assemblies to oppose a common enemy and to cultivate common ties. Unlike virtually every previous chapter in the history of Ontario workers' rebellion, the Knights of Labor stamped these pages of the 1880s with concern for those whose status in the working-class community ill-suited them to wear the badge of respectability, a consensual cultural norm that the Order recast to express class ant-

---

44   PP, Cross to Powderly and G.E.B., 9 June 1887; *Gananoque Reporter*, 3 December 1887.

agonisms. Premised on the fundamental rejection of exclusion (tarnished only by the Order's stand on the Chinese), the Knights of Labor, most often led by skilled workers, offered their ideals and their strengths as a force protecting and speaking for all of those 'below' them. As Leon Fink has argued in the case of the United States, masses of workers who had never experienced the fruits of full citizenship joined the skilled leadership sector of the Order, forging an alliance of the 'privileged' working class and a younger thoroughly proletarianised group, composed of male and female factory operatives and unskilled labourers.[45]

Indeed, the introduction of women into the mass struggles of the 1880s shattered decades of complacency and effected a fundamental shift in attitude. To be sure, the Knights acted out of chivalrous intent, and did not abandon age-old conceptions of hearth and home, domesticity and place. But they could turn all this to new purpose, and strike out at forces which they felt to be undermining all that was good and proper in such traditional practices. Thus, at a London speech by the popular and well-travelled Knight, Richard Trevellick, members of the Order raised 'their hands to heaven and pledged themselves that wherever women were employed, they would demand equal pay for equal work without regard to sex whatsoever'. It is difficult to see in such action only a retrogressive glance over one's shoulder to a pre-industrial arcadia: the language is unmistakably that of an industrial society, and the problem has yet to be resolved. Finally, the Knights did not stop and settle comfortably in this economistic niche, but attacked those who would define women's rights in some circumscribed way. In Knights of Labor centres like Belleville, Brantford, London, Stratford, St. Thomas, Thorold, Hamilton and Toronto, 'the ladies' joined the Order in assemblies named 'Advance' and 'Hope'. They attended musical and literary entertainments as 'Goddesses of Liberty', to be sure, but they also struggled for wages and rights, speaking their minds in the cause of large reform. With the passing of the Knights of Labor such women's lips were sealed for a time, but the possibility of change that they had addressed in the 1880s could not be written out of the past.[46]

It is this notion of possibility, this movement towards alternative hegemony, that is central to an understanding of the Knights of Labor in the 1880s. To rescue that moment, and to realise that its insights and social practice were achievements of considerable stature is part of our purpose in presenting this

---

45   See, especially, Fink 1977.

46   *Brantford Expositor*, 16 July 1886; *London Advertiser*, 29–30 October 1886; Levine 1978; 1979a.

analysis of the Knights of Labor. With the vision of a more humane social order always before it, the culture forged by the Knights of Labor is worth knowing today. In the words of Phillips Thompson, member of Toronto's Victor Hugo LA 7814, that culture taught men and women to 'dream of what might be'. By doing their part in 'spreading the light', Thompson argued, labour reformers were bringing close to realisation the 'beautiful ideal of universal democracy and co-operation'. Far from a utopian fantasy, the promise of a better society was merely 'a faint presentation of what might be – what cannot be at present solely because of the blindness, ignorance, and want of union among work-ingmen – but what I trust yet will be when the scales of error, of misleading education and of temporary self-interest have fallen from their eyes – so they can see the light'.[47] To explore both the strengths and weaknesses of this reform crusade we now turn to the political and workplace struggles in which the Knights of Labor both thrived and foundered.

4   The Knights in Politics

The Knights articulated this new 'movement culture' in the realm of Ontario politics. On all levels, municipal, provincial and federal, the Order expressed the class interests of Ontario workers in new ways. This unprecedented upsurge of labour involvement menaced both old-line parties' control over their re-spective electorates. In Ontario this represented a significant danger to Mac-donald and the Tory party, while Blake regarded it as the key to potential polit-ical success, especially given Oliver Mowat's record in Ontario.[48]

The role of the Order in the politics of the 1880s may come as a considerable surprise, given that the Knights of Labor have been given scant consideration in mainstream accounts of the elections and policies of Victorian Canada. Yet it was no secret to the political partisans of the day. Not only in Toronto and Hamilton but throughout the south-western Ontario manufacturing belt, and even penetrating into eastern Ontario, the Knights created a political move-ment that demanded attention. Macdonald, assessing the political climate in the summer of 1886, worried that the Conservative party was 'not in a flourish-ing state'. The 'rocks ahead' which threatened the Tory 'ship' were 'Riel, Home Rule, the Knights of Labor and the Scott Act'.[49] The Knights thus merited 'the

---

47   *Palladium of Labor*, 26 December 1885.
48   On Mowat and Labour see Evans 1967, especially ch. 3.
49   Sir John A. Macdonald to Sir Charles Tupper, 21 June 1886, in Pope 1921, p. 382.

old chieftain's' close attention and two of the three other threatening reefs were movements intimately tied to the Order and its ideals, namely the Irish question and temperance.[50]

From the moment of their entrance into Canada the Knights actively engaged in politics. December 1882 saw the first stirrings of these activities when in Hamilton labour helped elect two aldermen.[51] Meanwhile, in Toronto the Labour Council played a prominent role in defeating a candidate identified as particularly anti-labour.[52] Those initial successes propelled labour reformers in both cities into independent campaigns in the 1883 provincial election. In Hamilton locomotive engineer and prominent Knight Ed Williams, an English immigrant and the epitome of the respectable working man, ran and won a solid 23.4 percent of the vote in a three-way race.[53] The campaign results were more mixed in Toronto, where partisan politics had complicated the nominating process. Painter John Carter, a labour leader of the 1870s and a member of Toronto's Excelsior LA 2305 ran in Toronto West and won 48 percent of the vote for what was an incipient independent labour mobilisation. His candidacy, however, had gained the unstated support of the Reform (or Liberal/Grit) Party, which ran no candidate against him. In Toronto East, carpenter Samuel R. Heakes faced nominees from both old-line parties, Reform/Liberal/Grit and Conservative/Tory, and finished a distant third with only 7 percent of the vote.[54]

Despite the relative success of these campaigns, partisan recriminations followed and were to re-emerge in subsequent campaigns. In both Toronto and Hamilton disgruntled Tory workingmen accused the Grits of double-dealing.[55] In Hamilton these charges died down, however, and labour reformers created the Hamilton Labor Political Association to continue the thrust for an independent working-class party. In subsequent municipal elections in 1883 and 1884, the Association, under the leadership of Knights' activist Robert Coulter, enjoyed some success in electing members of the Order as aldermen. The best

50 On the Knights and the Irish see Foner 1978, pp. 6–55; on Home Rule see Kealey 1980, ch. 14.

51 PP, George Havens to Powderly, 4 January 1883.

52 Kealey 1980, ch. 11.

53 *Labor Union*, 3 February 1883; 10 February 1883; 3 March 1883; PP, Gibson to Powderly, 7 February 1883; PP, Powderly to Gibson, 9 February 1883.

54 *Trade Union Advocate* (Toronto), 11 January 1883; 18 January 1883; 25 January 1883; 1 February 1883; 8 February 1883; 15 February 1883; PAC, Toronto Trades and Labor Council, Minutes, 19 January, 2 February 1883; *Globe* (Toronto), 5 February 1883; 8 February 1883.

55 PP, D.B. Skelly to Powderly, 15 December 1884; PAC, Macdonald Papers, Small to Macdonald, 10 April 1883.

known of these figures was Irish carter Thomas Brick who provided Hamilton workers with a colourful and bombastic leader.[56]

In Toronto Excelsior LA 2305's leadership core of old labour reformers – led by Daniel J. O'Donoghue with the able support of Charles March and Alfred Jury – consolidated the position of the Knights of Labor, first in the newly-created Trades and Labor Congress of Canada (which first met in 1883) and subsequently in the Toronto Trades and Labor Council (TTLC). Once entrenched there they proceeded to make good use of both bodies as effective lobbying agencies, especially against the federal Tory government.[57] Their success in attracting political attention was evident with T.V. Powderly's 1884 Toronto visit. The stage at his major address was graced by the presence of Grit provincial leader, Edward Blake; former Speaker of the House of Commons and influential newspaper editor, Timothy Anglin; Toronto Tory Mayor Boswell; and numerous Conservative aldermen.[58] In the ensuing 1884 municipal election, Toronto workers threw a considerable scare into the Tory machine although it held the mayoralty by a slim margin.[59] In 1885, however, this hold was broken with the sweeping victory of W.H. Howland, who enjoyed the united support of the Toronto reform community, including the extremely active support of both the Knights of Labor and the TTLC.[60] His victory led to considerable soul searching on the part of the Tories both in the provincial capital of Toronto and in federal political circles in Ottawa. The results of this re-evaluation manifested themselves in a remarkable labour settlement at the *Mail* newspaper, where the imposition of an iron-clad agreement barring employment of union members had caused disaffection among Tory workingmen,[61] and later in the equally striking creation of the Royal Commission on the Relations of Labor and Capital.[62]

---

56   *Palladium of Labor*, 25 August 1883; 28 September 1883; 13 October 1883; 20 October 1883; 24 November 1883; 12 January 1884; 31 May 1884; 5 December 1884; 8 May 1885; 15 May 1885; 4 July 1885; 28 November 1885; 5 December 1885.

57   Kealey 1980, ch. 11.

58   *Globe*, 14 October 1884.

59   PAC, Macdonald Papers, Boultbee to Macdonald, 12 September 1884; 29 December 1884; 30 December 1884; Macpherson to Macdonald, 27 December 1884.

60   PAC, Toronto Trades and Labor Council, Minutes, 4 December 1885; 14 December 1885; 18 December 1885; 29 December 1885; *News* (Toronto), 4 January 1886; *Palladium of Labor*, 5 December 1885; PP, O'Donoghue to Powderly, 7 January 1886.

61   PAC, Macdonald Papers, Piper to Macdonald, 2 February 1886; 3 February 1886; *Toronto World*, 13 March 1886; 16 March 1886; Kealey 1980, chs. 6, 11; PP, O'Donoghue to Powderly, 29 March 1886.

62   Kealey 1973b, pp. ix–xxvii; Harvey 1978.

These quite considerable concessions to the political strength of the working-class movement did not prevent it from contesting the December 1886 Ontario provincial election and the February 1887 federal election. In December seven labour candidates took the field. One could be described as Lib-Lab, two as Tory-Labour and the other four were independents who faced candidates from the other two parties. St. Thomas brakeman and leading Knight Andy Ingram won West Elgin,[63] while a Lib-Lab candidate, William Garson, succeeded in Lincoln.[64] In Lambton A.W. Wright, running as a Conservative-Labour candidate, caused considerable controversy when many of the Knights repudiated him. Not surprisingly he did not run strongly.[65] In London, however, cabinet maker and Knight Samuel Peddle, campaigning with temperance support, gave Tory Opposition Leader W.R. Meredith a considerable scare before going down to a narrow defeat. In the previous election Meredith had gained his seat by acclamation.[66]

Toronto witnessed a confused race owing to the extraordinary gerrymandering of Oliver Mowat. Toronto had gained a third seat in a redistribution, but the three MPPs were to be elected at large for a city-wide riding, *and* each voter would be allowed to vote for only two candidates. The logic of this tactic was, of course, to ensure that at least one Grit would be returned from Tory Toronto. The strategy eventually paid off, but the race saw two Tory, one Grit, and two Labour candidates. Knights of Labor organiser Charles March finished fourth overall, while his running mate, Order member, temperance advocate, and evangelical Christian, John Roney, finished fifth. Statistical calculations in this anomalous electoral situation are complex but March did win over 4,000 votes and Roney some 3,400. (Tory E.F. Clarke, an Orange printer, topped the poll with 7,000).[67]

---

63 *St. Thomas Daily Times*, February–December 1886; *Canada Labor Courier* (St. Thomas), 29 July 1886; 30 December 1886. See also McKenna 1978.

64 PP, William Garson to Powderly, 21 March 1884; 22 October 1885.

65 *London Advertiser*, 21 December 1886; *Sarnia Observer*, 10 September 1886; 7 January 1887; *Canadian Labor Reformer* (Toronto), 18 December 1886; *Toronto World*, 2 December 1886; *Globe*, 8 December 1886; *News*, 22 December 1886.

66 *London Advertiser*, 24 November 1886; 7 December 1886; 9 December 1886; 10 December 1886; 11 December 1886; 16 December 1886; 17 December 1886; 18 December 1886; 29 December 1886; 30 December 1886; 7 January 1887; 11 January 1887; *Palladium of Labor*, 27 November 1886; 11 December 1886; *Canada Labor Courier*, 30 December 1886; PP, Hewit to Powderly, 13 December 1886.

67 Kealey 1980, ch. 12.

In Hamilton, complications also arose when the Tories nominated a leading moulder, John Burns, as their candidate and then called on Labour to endorse him. The Labour convention refused, however, roundly condemning Burns and the Tories. Instead they nominated Grand Trunk machinist and Knight Hamilton Racey. In the bitter three-way race that followed Racey finished third with 17.2 percent of the poll, a total which fell short of Ed Williams's 1883 vote.[68] This result did not prevent Hamilton workers from trying again in the federal election in which moulder Fred Walters ran as a Lib-Lab candidate in the two-seat constituency. He out polled his Liberal running mate, but nevertheless trailed the two victorious Tories, although his 48.8 percent was a respectable showing.[69]

In Toronto E.E. Sheppard, the controversial editor of the *News*, campaigned in West Toronto for labour, while in East Toronto Knights' leader Alfred Jury ran. Neither was opposed by a Liberal although Sheppard's previous ties were Tory, if anything. Sheppard won 47 percent and Jury 35 percent, but expectations of victory had been so high that this was viewed as a significant set back.[70] Fierce factional fighting ensued which pitted D.J. O'Donoghue and his *Labor Record* against A.W. Wright and the *Canadian Labor Reformer*. The charges back and forth only confirmed for many the growing fear that independent labour politics was a diversion from the Knights' major tasks.[71]

Workers had entered politics with considerable scepticism and their failure to make a quick and decisive breakthrough led to much discouragement, especially since it appeared that their leaders were still intriguing in partisan politics. Nevertheless throughout the late 1880s municipal politics continued to gain much attention from the Order and victories were recorded which ranged from Brantford and Chatham to Brockville and Ottawa.[72] In Cornwall, for example, the Knights helped defeat a municipal railroad bonus in the 1888 city election and two years later were reported to have elected nine of 13 aldermen and the

68   PP, Freed to Powderly, 2 December 1886; *Palladium of Labor*, 4 December 1886; 7 December 1886; 11 December 1886; 18 December 1886; *Hamilton Spectator*, 4 December 1886; 7 December 1886; 8 December 1886; 14 December 1886; 22 December 1886.

69   *Hamilton Spectator*, 13 January 1887; 24 February 1887.

70   Kealey 1980, ch. 12.

71   Kealey 1980, chs. 12–13.

72   *Courier* (Brantford), 4 January 1886; 15 April 1886; 28 December 1886; *Branford Expositer*, 16 April 1886; 20 August 1886; 24 September 1886; 17 December 1886; 31 December 1886; *Canada Labor Courier*, 30 December 1886; 13 January 1887; *Brockville Recorder*, 1887–8; *Ottawa Citizen*, 1890–1.

mayor and reeve.[73] The Order also became particularly prominent in lobbying activities in Ottawa after the creation of a Canadian Knights of Labor Legislative Committee.[74]

The Knights, then, made significant political efforts and enjoyed some success, but they certainly did not overcome all the tensions in the working-class world. Partisan politics had established a deep hold on Canadian workers and the battle to create an independent working-class party was sharp and difficult. Yet on the local level, tangible gains were made – early closing, union wages and jobs in corporation work, just assessment rates, more responsible public transit. Nevertheless the Knights had never regarded the political arena as their major battlefield. It was only one campaign in a war on many fronts. This war was perhaps sharpest at the workplace.

5   The People's Strike

Much of the previous literature on the Knights of Labor has focused on their dislike of strikes. Frequent citation of major Knights' leaders such as T.V. Powderly and lengthy consideration of splits within the Order, such as the expulsion of the general executive board member T.B. Barry in 1888, lead to the image of an organisation committed to class cooperation through arbitration. Like most long-propounded views, these arguments contain a kernel of truth, but they also disguise much that is central to an understanding of the Knights of Labor. In Ontario the Knights either led or were involved in almost all the major strikes of the 1880s and early 1890s. This should not surprise us since, as we have already argued, the Order should not be viewed as one contending force within the working-class world, but rather as the embodiment of that class in these years. Thus in the period of the Order's growth in Ontario from 1882 to 1886, the Knights of Labor came to represent a solid working-class presence united behind its eclectic but critical aims.

In the Order's earliest years in Canada it grew owing to its willingness to organise the larger class forces on behalf of localised trade or industrial struggles. Thus in Toronto the Knights emerged from the coalition of forces knit

---

73   *Brockville Recorder*, 4 January 1888; *Cornwall Freeholder*, 3 January 1890, 10 January 1890, 7 February 1890. These newspaper discussions are somewhat confusing as various candidates denied formal connections with the Order. Yet in the aftermath the *Cornwall Freeholder*, 7 February 1890, argued that one loser 'had arranged against him the workingmen, which is no mean factor in election contests in Cornwall these days'.

74   Kealey 1980, ch. 12.

together by experienced trade-union militants to support the striking female boot and shoe operatives in the spring of 1882.[75] This was apparent again in the following summer when DA 45 (Brotherhood of Telegraphers) engaged in a continent-wide strike against the monopolistic telegraph companies. Although DA 45 had done little preparatory work within the Order before this epic struggle, as a bitter Powderly would argue again and again, it did appear to have established sufficient local contacts so that organised labour, and especially the Knights, rallied to its cause.[76] In Hamilton and Toronto, for example, support came from union contributions to the strike fund, benefit concerts, lectures and theatricals.[77] Meanwhile the first wave of massive Labour Day demonstrations organised by the Knights, but involving all organised workers and many outside of the formal labour movement, took place in Toronto, Hamilton and Oshawa.[78] In each case, support for the telegraphers played a prominent role in the speeches and provided a compelling symbol for the necessity of working-class solidarity. The ultimate failure of the telegraphers' strike and its bitter aftermath, which saw DA 45 withdraw from the Knights of Labor, appear to have been less important than the solidarity expressed in its course. As the *Palladium of Labor* declared: 'The telegraphers' strike is over. The People's Strike is now in order'.[79]

'The People's Strike' took many forms in the following few years. At its most dramatic it involved mass strikes which crippled whole industries or communities. Examples of struggles of this magnitude included the two Toronto Street Railway strikes of the spring and summer of 1886, a Chatham town-wide strike of December 1886, the cotton strikes in Merritton (1886 and 1889) and Cornwall (1887, 1888 and 1889), and the massive lumber strikes in Gravenhurst in 1888 and in Ottawa-Hull in 1891.[80] Each of these struggles rocked their communities with previously unmatched levels of class conflict and involved workers previously untouched by trade union organisation. Yet the Knights of Labor also led or took part in conflicts far less riveting. In the early 1880s this often meant coming to the support of striking operatives or craftsmen, as with Toronto female shoe operatives in 1882 and their Hamilton sisters in

---

75   Kealey 1980, chs. 3 and 10.

76   Kealey 1980, ch. 10; Palmer 1979a, ch. 6; and Forsey 1971.

77   Kealey 1980, ch. 10; Palmer 1979a, ch. 6.

78   *Iron Molders Journal* (Cincinnati) (hereafter *IMJ*), 31 August 1883; *Palladium of Labor*, 18 August 1883.

79   *Palladium of Labor*, 25 August 1883.

80   For Toronto see Kealey 1980, ch. 10; for Chatham see *Canada Labor Courier*, 30 December 1886, 13 January 1887; for cotton and lumber see below.

1884, or Toronto printers in 1884.[81] In these cases and in countless others, the Order proved its mettle by practising what it preached and aiding all workers' struggles. It was this type of activity which initially helped to break down entrenched conservative craft suspicions of the Order. Then, as craft unionists and craft unions flooded into the Order in 1885–6, the Order continued to fight their battles. These struggles, often involving issues of worker's control, represent the second major type of Knights strike activity.

It would be impossible to chronicle all these strikes here. Toronto Knights alone, for example, fought 19 strikes between 1883 and 1889, and this number does not include the large number of work stoppages which they actively supported or in which some Knights were involved. Let us turn instead first to a perusal of strike activity among one important group of craft workers, the moulders, and then turn to an analysis of a few of the mass strikes.

Moulders had their own international craft union which dated from the late 1850s in Ontario. The Iron Molders International Union (IMIU) had very strong locals in Hamilton (No. 26) and Toronto (No. 28) and after 1887 had an Ontario-wide district organisation.[82] The relationship between the IMIU and the Knights cannot be plotted with mathematical certainty but in Brantford (Standard LA 3811), Hamilton (Library LA 1864), Kingston (Frontenac LA 10539) and Oshawa (Tylers LA 4279), there existed trade assemblies identified as moulders. In addition, however, we know from scattered sources that Toronto (Maple Leaf LA 2622), Brockville (Franklin LA 2311), Smiths Falls (LA 6772), Lindsay (LA 5402) and Oshawa (Aetna LA 2355 and LA 4428) local assemblies all contained moulders and other metal workers as well. Finally we have considerable reason to suspect that Cobourg (LA 2598), Toronto (LAS 5254 and 5650), Woodstock (LAS 3151 and 4992), Galt (LA 6112) and Peterborough (LA 6952) might also have had moulder Knight of Labor members.[83] The lines between the craft unions and the Knights were never drawn as sharply in reality as they have been by historians subsequently.

Organised throughout Ontario in stove foundries and in the agricultural implements industry, the moulders played a significant role in one of Ontario's most successful industries. This prominence and their skill, which resisted mechanical innovation throughout this period, gave them a high degree of

---

81   Kealey 1980, ch. 10; Palmer 1979a, ch. 6.

82   For background on the Iron Moulders see Williams 1964; Palmer 1979a, *passim.*; and Kealey 1980, ch. 5. The following is also based on the *IMJ* and the International's convention proceedings.

83   Organisational data are drawn from Garlock data bank; Forsey 1982; and Kealey and Palmer 1982, ch. 1.

workplace control which they fought vigorously to maintain.[84] These issues led
to at least 25 strikes between 1880 and 1893.[85] The major strikes in 1887, 1890
and 1892 in Toronto and Hamilton have already received historical attention,[86]
but much smaller Ontario centres such as Brockville, Oshawa and London
also saw frequent struggles in their foundries throughout the 1880s. These
smaller centres demonstrate well the interrelationship of IMIU members and
Knights.

Brockville, a railroad and manufacturing centre on the St. Lawrence in eastern Ontario, illustrates these themes. The James Smart Manufacturing Co.
(est. 1854) dominated the local economy of the 1880s and by 1890 employed
200 workers in the production of stoves and lawn mowers.[87] The IMIU first
organised in Brockville in 1868 or 1869 and had a spasmodic existence there
throughout the 1870s, which included work stoppages in 1875, 1879, 1880 and
1881 – the last three of which appear to have resulted in union victories.[88]
The last two struggles took place after Robert Gill replaced James Smart as the
manager of the works and tried to break the union by demanding the workers
abandon it. After this failed, there was a single year of peace at the foundry,
a hiatus in which the Knights strongly established themselves in Brockville.
In August 1882, Ogdensburg Knights' leader Archer Baker organised Franklin
LA 2311, which grew rapidly. By the following summer the assembly numbered
in the hundreds and contained many of the most prominent of the moulders'
leaders in town, including Samuel Miller, a former IMIU international convention delegate and a perennial member of the moulders's local executive.[89] The
year of peace ended in June 1883 when Gill refused the moulders' demand
for a wage increase. The ensuing 11-week strike was eventually lost but the
polarisation of the community continued to increase. During the strike, Brockville's working class demonstrated its solidarity when the corpse of 28-year-old
moulder William Hutcheson, murdered by a scab in a strike in Troy, New York,
was returned to his native town for burial.[90] The delegation of Troy Knights

---

84   Montgomery 1979, ch. 1 and *passim.*; Kealey 1980, ch. 5; Palmer 1979a, ch. 3; Roberts 1978,
      ch. 3.

85   Strike data are drawn from *IMJ*; Iron Molder International Union (hereafter IMIU), *Pro-
      ceedings*, 1860–1895; and Ontario Bureau of Industry, *Annual Reports*.

86   Kealey 1980, ch. 5; Palmer 1979a, ch. 3.

87   Chisamore et al. 1975, ch. 4.

88   Chisamore et al. 1975, ch. 5; *IMJ*, 1868–92; IMIU, *Proceedings*.

89   Chisamore et al. 1975, ch. 5.

90   Walkowitz 1978, pp. 211, 213, 239–40; and a review of Walkowitz by Bryan Palmer (Palmer
      1979b, pp. 261–7).

and moulders which accompanied the body joined with the Brockville Knights in commemorating his death with 'one of the largest funerals' ever seen in Brockville.[91] Building on this solidarity, the Knights grew rapidly that summer, enrolling over one hundred members in one week shortly after Hutcheson's funeral. The town also had a telegraphers' LA 2335 with about forty members which struck solidly and with 'manifest public sympathy' during the continent-wide strike.[92] In the early fall Franklin Assembly held a picnic which attracted five to eight hundred and by November the assembly reported a membership of 430.[93]

The stage was set for the next bitter conflict between Gill and his moulders which began in January 1884. Seven months later in late July the moulders returned to work, their union crushed and their vestiges of craft control destroyed, at least for the moment. This time the Gills ignored community sentiment and engaged in active union-smashing. They recruited scabs from Connecticut, housed them in the foundry, and ignored the public discontent which labelled company managers 'the enemies of Brockville'. When forced to defend his position, Gill explained simply:

> The question at issue is simply one of 'control'. It is a fact, however humiliating the acknowledgement, that during the past three years of the company's existence, the business has been practically controlled by the Moulder's Union. If the conditions are such that 'control' cannot be gained by the proprietors, then Brockville will lose the industry which we are trying to carry on.[94]

In Brockville the owners won back their control over production, but only after a long history of struggle in which the Knights helped to provide the opposition. The intimacy of Knights and moulders in Brockville was evident in the latter stages of the 1884 strike when Franklin Assembly selected the moulders' leader Sam Miller as its general assembly delegate and when John S. McClelland of the general executive board arrived in Brockville to investigate the strike. McClelland's visit resulted in a $500 grant from the Order's assistance fund.[95]

Oshawa, west of Brockville on Lake Ontario, witnessed an analogous set of struggles in the 1880s and a very similar organic relationship between IMIU

---

91   *Brockville Recorder*, 12 June 1883; 13 June 1883; 14 June 1883.
92   *Brockville Recorder*, 25 July 1883.
93   *Brockville Recorder*, 17 November 1883.
94   *Brockville Recorder*, 5 March 1884; 6 March 1884; 10 March 1884.
95   Knights of Labor, General Assembly 1884, p. 652.

Local No. 136 and the Knights. The IMIU which dated from 1866 was joined in Oshawa by the Knights on 12 August 1882 when Aetna LA 2355 was organised by a Buffalo Knight.[96] This large assembly with nearly 300 members in 1883 was entrenched in the local iron and agricultural implements industry. Cooperating closely with the IMIU, the Oshawa Knights hosted nearly two thousand workers at their August 1883 labour demonstration. IMIU Local 136 marched in a uniform of 'gray shirts, black hats and black neckties' and the organisation was joined by brother moulders from Toronto (Nos. 28 and 140) and Cobourg (No. 189) and over 1,500 Knights of Labor. Local 136 provided the 'main feature of our procession', 'the moulding, melting, and casting of iron in the line of march', reported LA 2355 and IMIU No. 36 Recording Secretary Joseph Brockman. The commemorative coins that they struck during the procession were distributed to participants in the working-class demonstraation.[97] Two months later the labourers at the Malleable Iron Works, members of Aetna LA 2355, struck against a wage reduction. The moulders, walking out in support of the labourers and facing a similar wage cut, were warned that if they did not return, the shop would 'be permanently closed against them'. Six weeks into the strike the Oshawa Stove Works and the Masson Agricultural Implements Works locked out their moulders to create a solid employer block against the workers. Even then it was only after the Oshawa moulders' sister unions in Hamilton (No. 26) and Toronto (No. 28) accepted 10 percent wage cuts in December without striking, that Oshawa No. 136 felt compelled to concede defeat. Earlier in December the labourers had returned to their work on the advice of the LA 2355 executive, which argued that 'it would have broke Jay Gould with his seventy-three millions of stolen money to have kept labourers and immigrants away from here'.[98]

By the next fall, however, the union had reasserted itself and another of its leaders (and a charter member of LA 2355), Lewis Allchin, wrote Powderly seeking his support for a profit-sharing plan at the Oshawa Stove Works. He also mentioned that they had 'affected every Reform obtained in the shop, one for instance, piece workers used to work almost all noonhour, and not later than last spring, we managed to institute a rigid observance of noonhour, we also limited the wages to $2.50 per day'.[99] The new success of the moulders

96   PP, James R. Brown to Powderly, 29 September 1882; Johnson 1973.
97   *Palladium of Labor*, 18 August 1883; 25 August 1883; *IMJ*, 31 August 1883; Stunden 1974, pp. 1–2.
98   *Palladium of Labor*, 20 October 1883; 8 December 1883; 15 December 1883; 22 December 1883; *IMJ*, 31 August 1890.
99   PP, Lewis Allchin to Powderly, 20 October 1984; 25 October 1984.

probably made another struggle almost inevitable and it came two years later in late January 1886 when the Malleable Iron Works again tried to force the union out of its foundry. This time the issue was simply the question of a closed shop. John Cowan, the manager of the works, insisted on continuing to employ two non-union moulders; IMIU No. 36 and Tylers LA 4279 (Moulders) refused to work with the non-union men. After a bitter two month strike in the depths of a severe winter which witnessed alleged incendiarism, a 'surprise party' (perhaps a charivari), a widespread sending to Coventry of the non-union moulders, and considerable public support for the men, the company finally caved in and recognised the closed shop. The concession came at the end of March when the union and LA 4279 began to call for a total boycott of the foundry's goods.[100]

Similar events involving moulders and Knights occurred in Lindsay in 1886,[101] in Kingston in 1887,[102] in London in 1882 and 1886,[103] and in Ayr, Galt and Smiths Falls later in the decade.[104] Success varied dramatically, but in all these cases the principles of the Knights, of craft control, and of labour reform were carried on. Lewis Allchin, Oshawa moulder-Knight and the author of 'Sketches of our Organization' (a serialised history of the IMIU from its founding to 1890 published in the *Iron Molders Journal*), summed up the close intertwining of these themes: 'The object, in brief, is the *complete emancipation of labor*, and the inauguration of a higher and nobler industrial system than this of the present, under which one human being is dependent upon another for the means of living'. Denying at the outset later historians' views of the Knights, he emphasised: 'We cannot turn back if we would; we cannot return to a primitive system of working, however much we might desire it'. Trusts and syndicates, he viewed as 'an inevitable phase' of 'an excessive and pernicious competitive system', but they would not 'be the *finale* of the whole question'. They 'contained within themselves the germs of their own dissolution', since 'selfishness and greed were but foundations of sand to build upon'. The future he would not predict, but he hazarded one final conclusion:

---

100 *News*, 23 February 1886; 6 March 1886; 9 March 1886; 15 March 1886; *IMJ*, 30 September 1890.

101 *Labor Record* (Toronto), 14 May 1886; Trent University Archives, Gainey Collection, I.M.I.U. Local 191, Minutes, 1886.

102 *British Daily Whig* (Kingston), 13 May 1887; 14 May 1887; 16 May 1887; 18 May 1887; 19 May 1887; 23 May 1887; *Gananoque Reporter*, 21 May 1887; and Ontario Bureau of Industry 1887, p. 42.

103 IMIU, *Proceedings*, 1882 and 1886; *IMJ*, 31 May 1890.

104 IMIU, *Proceedings*, 1890 and 1895; *IMJ*, August 1889.

That no system which does not recognize the right of labor to a first and just share of its products, which refuses each and every toiler a voice in the business transactions of the enterprise, that does not establish a just and relative measure or standard of value for all services rendered, labor performed, products manufactured, and commodities exchanged, will ever be a just or permanent one.[105]

Here, quite clearly, we can see that the values and ideas of the late nineteenth-century working class world were shared by its articulate leadership, be they Knights or craft unionists, and, as was so often the case, the membership overlapped. For our chosen group of skilled workers, the moulders, this unity demonstrated itself most clearly in the streets of London in the late summer of 1886 when the IMIU held its seventeenth convention. The city's first labour demonstration 'of 4000 unionists in line' was held to honour the assembled moulders and was witnessed by crowds estimated at between eight and ten thousand.[106] Addressed by Captain Richard Trevellick, the Knights' chief itinerant lecturer, the convention also considered at length a motion to amalgamate the IMIU with the Knights of Labor. After a full day of debate the resolution was soundly defeated but it did win support from militant moulders' strongholds such as Albany and Troy, in New York. In registering his opposition, the IMIU president made clear his support 'for always remaining on the most friendly terms with the Knights of Labor, and rendering them all the assistance that our organization can possibly give them in all legitimate undertakings in the interest of labour'.[107] This solidarity began to disintegrate the following year during the vicious war between the Founders Association and the moulders in the Bridge and Beach strike.[108]

The solidarity so evident in the London streets in July 1886 had also spread far beyond the moulders and their other skilled worker brethren. The Knights also successfully organised the unskilled – women factory workers, male operatives, and large numbers of labourers both in Ontario's cities and towns, and in the province's resource hinterland. These workers, organised for the first time under the banners of the Knights of Labor, also engaged in militant struggles in the 1880s and early 1890s. Strikes to gain either the right to organise or to win modest economic advances occurred in these sectors, differentiating them from the struggles of the skilled workers for shopfloor control. Ranging in size

---

105   *IMJ*, 31 January 1891.
106   Palmer 1976a, pp. 106–24; *IMJ*, 31 October 1890; 31 July 1886.
107   IMIU, *Proceedings*, 1886; *IMJ*, 31 October 1890.
108   IMIU, *Proceedings*, 1888; Oestreicher 1979, ch. 7.

from minor affairs to massive, almost general, strikes which polarised single industry communities, these class conflicts were most prominent in the mill towns of eastern and western Ontario.

Cotton mill struggles hit Merritton in 1886 and 1889 and Cornwall in three successive years, 1887, 1888 and 1889. The Merritton mill, which remained well organised as late as 1892, witnessed numerous work stoppages led by the Knights in 1886.[109] Three years later a week-long strike over a wage reduction won a compromise settlement.[110] None of these represented major victories for workers, but in an industry known for its exploitation and anti-unionism, Maple Leaf LA 5933's 500 workers were more successful than most. Their achievement may well have been one of the factors that led Canadian Coloured Cottons to shut down the plant after the merger of 1892.[111]

Cornwall's cotton workers joined the Knights of Labor in 1886 in LAS 6582 and 6583. The first test of the Order came in the summer of 1887 when 18 dyers demanded that their hours be reduced from ten to nine. Although the Order provided $400 in financial assistance to its striking members, they still lost the strike.[112] In February 1888, wage reductions at both the Canada and Stormont mills precipitated strikes involving from 1,300 to 1,500 employees. After a few weeks the workers returned with a compromise settlement. The wages were still cut but by an estimated 10 percent instead of the alleged twenty to twenty-three percent originally imposed. This settlement held at the Stormont mill, but the Canada mill was struck again when workers accused the company of not living up to the agreement. After another month these workers again returned.[113] One year later in the spring of 1889 the Stormont mill workers struck once again. After five weeks the 600 operatives returned when the company agreed to honour the weavers' demands.[114]

The lumber industry, another long stalwart against trade unionism, also experienced two major strikes led by the Knights of Labor. Gravenhurst LA 10669 was organised in 1887 under the leadership of Uxbridge DA 236 after a short lumber strike in which the hours of work in the mills on Muskoka Bay had

---

109   Ontario Bureau of Industry, *Annual Report*, 1886; 1889; 1890.

110   Ontario Bureau of Industry, *Annual Report*, 1886; 1889; 1890.

111   De Lottinville 1979.

112   Ontario Bureau of Industry, *Annual Report*, 1887; *Brockville Recorder*, 12 July 1887.

113   Ontario Bureau of Industry, *Annual Report*, 1888; *Cornwall Standard*, 28 January 1888; 2 February 1888; *Montreal Gazette*, 14 February 1888. Our thanks to Peter de Lottinville for these newspaper references. See also *Gananoque Reporter*, 4 February 1888; 11 February 1888; 18 February 1888.

114   Ontario Bureau of Industry, *Annual Report*, 1889; *Gananoque Reporter*, 16 March 1889.

been reduced from 11 to ten and a half, with a promise that in 1888 they would be further shortened to ten. In 1888, however, a province-wide agreement was signed by the Muskoka, Georgian Bay and Ottawa River lumber barons. It prevented a further reduction of hours under pain of forfeiting a bond. The angry workers of LA 10669 consulted the DA 236 leadership, which counselled caution and urged the assembly to strengthen its ranks. By June, 300 of the 375 workers had joined the Order, which then appointed a committee to meet with the mill owners. This resulted in a blanket refusal from the employers and the workers again sought aid from DA 236. Although reluctant, the district assembly had no choice but to sanction a strike, which began on 3 July 1888. A few mills acceded but the majority held out. Aylesworth of the Knights' general executive board responded to an emergency call from DA 236, but his efforts were unsuccessful and by September the men had returned to work with no gains.[115]

In the Chaudère region of the Ottawa-Hull area, another lumber workers' strike erupted in September 1891.[116] As in Muskoka, the Ottawa Valley was ruled by a closely-knit group of entrepreneurs who had made fortunes and consolidated power on profits from sawn lumber and lumber by-products. Nine firms were involved in the 1891 strike and they were headed by a distinguished group of Canadian capitalists, notably J.R. Booth, E.H. Bronson and E.B. Eddy. While they prospered, their mill hands eked out a marginal existence on wages of \$7.00 to \$9.50 for a 60-hour week. The Knights' success in the Ottawa Valley came late and it was only in the fall of 1890 that they had gained a foothold in the mills with the creation of Chaudère LA 2966.

As three years earlier in Gravenhurst, a particularly harsh winter created the situation which would lead to that autumn's huge mill strike. Already late returning to work because of the weather, the workers were informed of a 50-cents-a-week wage cut. In return for the reduction, the owners offered the ten-hour day but soon violated their own concession. With the working day again extended to 11 and 12 hours, the workers sought the aid of the Knights of Labor in May. When informed that the Order would not sanction a strike until they had been in the organisation for at least six months, the workers remained

---

115   This draws on: PP, R.R. Elliot to Powderly, 12 July 1888; 19 July 1888; William Hogan to Powderly, 21 September 1888; 5 November 1888; Archy Sloan to Powderly, 3 September 1888; Powderly to William Sloan, 10 September 1888. *Journal of United Labor*, 12 July 1888. See also PP, D.J. O'Donoghue to Powderly, 9 August 1888; *Globe*, 25 July 1888; 10 August 1888.

116   The following draws on: McKenna 1972, pp. 186–211; Forsey 1982, ch. 7; Gillis 1975, especially pp. 72–81; Ontario Bureau of Industry, *Annual Report*, 1892; and *Ottawa Citizen*, September–October 1891 and *Ottawa Journal* September–October 1891.

on the job. By autumn, however, their tempers had worn thin and on Saturday, 12 September 1891, the outside workers at Perley and Pattee demanded that their wages be reinstated to the 1890 rate. Denied this on Saturday, the workers met on the Sunday and agreed to repeat their demand the next day. Again rebuffed, they proceeded to march from mill to mill pulling all the workers out. Over 2,400 workers left their jobs and the Knights quickly took over the strike leadership. The mill workers were subsequently enrolled in Chaudèire LA 2966 and Hull's Canadienne LA 2676.

Over the next few weeks some of the smaller mills conceded to the workers' demands for the previous year's rate and a ten-hour day, but the larger mills stood firm. As community support for the workers stiffened, massive meetings of three to ten thousand people were held. Meanwhile incidents of violence occurred, the militia was mobilised, and workers responded with a charivari and the creation of their own security force. Over $1,500 was raised by the Order and an extensive relief system was established. By the end of September, however, strike leaders urged their followers to seek employment elsewhere and by early October the relief system began to break down. By 12 October, the workers were back with their 1890 wage, but with the same long hours of work. Two hundred of Bronson's workers promptly struck again on 14 October, when they claimed he had reneged on his agreement. By the end of the month, however, work was back to normal. Although not an unmitigated success, the Order had won a limited victory and the mill men stayed with the Knights. The next year Ottawa DA 6 was created with an impressive 2,000 workers, largely from the lumber industry. These workers finally won the ten-hour day in 1895.

Turbulence, strikes and class conflict thus played an important role in the history of the Knights of Labor in Ontario. The oft-invoked image of an organisation interested in avoiding strikes at all cost and the implicit projection of a class-cooperative, if not collaborationist, body begins to dissipate under more careful scrutiny.

6   Conclusion

The 1880s were a critical decade in Canadian history – a decade which witnessed the fulfillment of the National Policy industrial strategy with a rapid expansion in Canadian manufacturing, especially in textiles. Yet these years also saw the breakdown of the previous consensus on industrial development, as Canadian workers, especially in the country's industrial heartland, began to raise their voices in an unfamiliar, concerted fashion to join the growing debate about the nation's future. Ontario's mainly British and Canadian workers, many with previous trade union and industrial experience, provided leadership to the emerging working-class movement which found its most articulate expression in the Knights of Labor. The challenge which this movement mounted in all realms of Ontario society – the cultural, intellectual and political as well as the economic – engendered in turn a class response from employers and from the state. Capital engaged in a virulent, open warfare with their labour, targetting worker-Knights, especially in the period of economic decline after 1886. In the 1890s, employers began as well to turn to the ever-increasing concentration and centralisation of capital and later to the modern management devices of a rampant Taylorism in their battle with labour. Meanwhile the state and political parties responded in a more conciliatory fashion. Mowat and, to a lesser degree, Macdonald interceded to provide workers with many of the protections they demanded – factory acts, bureaux of labour statistics, arbitration measures, suffrage extension, employers' liability acts, and improved mechanics' lien acts. The political parties proved even more flexible and managed through patronage and promises to contain much of the oppositional sentiment which flared up in the 1880s. Thus the Canadian political system functioned effectively to mediate the fiery class conflict of the 1880s.

In the following decade, with the exception of eastern Ontario, the Knights were moribund. Their precipitous decline was halted by a slight resurgence in the late 1890s, but by 1902 – when the craft-union dominated Trades and Labor Congress of Canada delivered a final *coup de grace*, in effect banishing the Knights of Labor from the official national House of Labour – a chapter in the history of Canadian workers had largely come to a close. Yet as we suggested earlier, the heritage of the Order lived on. Its major contributions to working-class memory centred on its oppositional success as a movement, which for the first time provided *all* workers with an organisational vehicle, that could, for the moment at least, overcome the splintering forces that so often divided the working class.

CHAPTER 5

Class, Conception, and Conflict: The Thrust for Efficiency, Managerial Views of Labour, and the Working Class Rebellion, 1903–22[*]

Introduction

Perhaps no subject has received such intense treatment within recent years as the development and impact of hierarchical work arrangements and the fragmentation of the labour process. These intricately related phenomena have rightly been recognised as fundamental aspects of the capitalistic organisation of production. Stephen Marglin's explication of the origins and function of the specialised gradation of the division of labour within the English Industrial Revolution,[1] Katherine Stone's study of the development of job structures in the steel industry,[2] Harry Braverman's chronicle of the degradation of work in the twentieth century[3] and Michael Davis's discussion of one militant union's response to the disciplines of a 'rationalised' labour process,[4] all reflect the growing interest in and awareness of the significance of the capitalistic organisation of work. Over time, this rationalisation of labour has assumed an increasingly oppressive tone. In Raya Dunayevska's words, it has been 'the hierarchic structure of control over social labour' that has revealed itself as 'the despotic plan inherent in capitalist production'.[5]

Yet within this basic problematic – hierarchy and the work process – the literature remains far from satisfactory. Marglin, in emphasising the preeminent role of consciousness in the evolution of the division of labour and the

---

[*] 'Class, Conception, and Conflict: The Thrust for Efficiency, Managerial Views of Labor, and Working-Class Rebellion, 1903–1922', *The Review of Radical Political Economics*, 7 (Summer 1975), 31–49.

[1] Marglin 1971. An abridged version of the argument appeared in the *Review of Radical Political Economics* (Marglin 1974, pp. 60–112), and a sequel appeared in the Spring 1975 issue of the same journal (Marglin 1975, pp. 20–37).

[2] Stone 1974, pp. 113–73 (also published, in slightly different form, in *Radical America* [Stone 1973, pp. 19–66]).

[3] Braverman 1974a. Cf. Braverman 1974b, pp. 1–134.

[4] Davis 1975, pp. 69–95.

[5] Dunayevska 1958, p. 92.

factory system, has taken Marx's argument in *Capital* and stood it forcefully upon its head. As Marx repeatedly stressed, it was not human volition, but the structural dictates of a production geared to the development of domestic and international markets, that catapulted the disintegrating social strata of pre-capitalist society into the epoch of industrial capitalism.[6] Katherine Stone, in her attempt to argue that Gilded Age steel barons fought a relentless battle against skilled craftsmen and their union, the Amalgamated Association of Iron, Steel, and Tin Workers, in order to secure unchallenged control of the labour process, stands on much firmer ground than Marglin; she, of course, is dealing with a later period of capitalist development, one in which class form-ation and consciousness of class interests had attained some foothold within the social order.[7] Yet Stone underestimates the extent to which the skill dilu-tion so energetically encouraged by Andrew Carnegie and his managers flowed directly from the process of technological advance and innovation. As much as the steel magnates desired to break the back of the craft unions, this end would have been accomplished even without their active encouragement; the inner logic of mechanised steel-making was itself capable of destroying craft distinctions within the industry.[8] Braverman's book, *Labor and Monopoly Cap-ital*, remains a most authoritative source on the labour process within capit-alist society, yet it errs in its treatment of technical change. In dichotomising technological innovation, techniques of administering the social organisation of work and managerial utilisation of personnel and welfare schemes, Braver-man arbitrarily separates vital and complex relationships that formed part of a basic unity.[9] Moreover, Braverman inhibits his analysis by refusing to consider the working-class response to this unity: just as Baran and Sweezy, in *Mono-poly Capital*, neglected to consider the labour process, Braverman has focused on the labour process without acknowledging the working-class reaction to the emergence and consolidation of that process. Accordingly, he is limited in his understanding of the extent to which working-class opposition 'defeated' Taylorism and pushed capital to employ more subtle means of control in its

---

6 I have developed this argument more completely and forcefully in a forthcoming article, 'Hierarchy and the Work Process: An Assessment of the Marglin Thesis'.

7 That capital considered the smashing of powerful craft bodies to be a priority throughout the 1880s is argued, in a most compelling fashion, throughout Robert Ozanne's treatment of labour-management relations at International Harvester. See Ozanne 1967, *passim*.

8 Thus, I take David Brody's argument in Brody 1960, chapters i–ii, to be a more convincing comment on the origins of job structures in the steel industry. For a theoretical statement on technical change which has influenced my perspective see Levine 1974.

9 Cf. Levine 1974, *passim*.

quest for authority.[10] And, finally, Mike Davis's analysis of the Industrial Workers of the World (IWW or Wobblies) response to 'scientific management' takes much too eclectic a view of Taylorism, considering virtually any attempt to 'rationalise' the productive process as an outgrowth of Taylor's conception of 'scientific management'. Like so many recent histories of the Wobblies, Davis's tends to romanticise the ideology and practice of the IWW, a tact William Preston has argued can only obscure the history of the organisation and the lessons to be learned from its demise. Given these shortcomings in recent treatments of hierarchy and fragmentation, we can legitimately ask, as did Preston in another context, 'Shall this be all?'[11]

This chapter concerns itself with the 'thrust for efficiency', rather than a study of more esoteric managerial systems, for it is our belief that left scholarship – most notably Braverman and Stone – has focused too explicitly upon Taylorism, without appreciating the extent to which it was a movement limited in applicability and impact. While Taylor's works – *Shop Management* and *The Principles of Scientific Management* – were widely read, and while it is possible to maintain that Taylor's conception of 'scientific management' was the cutting edge of the efficiency movement, there is little to indicate that Taylorism was adopted by large numbers of industrial concerns. It was simply too rigorous a system of total management to be implemented in most establishments. Permitting no piecemeal adoption, Taylorism was thwarted wherever an 'idiosyncratic' employer demanded close contact with the productive processes he owned and desired to control, wherever skilled craftsmen perpetuated some degree of craft autonomy and, more importantly, wherever production itself, because of working conditions or the logic of mechanised apparatus, demanded excruciating physical labour followed by bouts of paced leisure. Thus, 'scientific management' secured a foothold only in certain small-scale precision production industries – gun smithing, typewriter production, button manufacturing – of the industrial north-eastern states. Elsewhere it is difficult to determine the extent to which Taylorism, or, as Taylor himself preferred to call

---

10   This point has been stressed repeatedly, in numerous papers delivered to conferences and seminar groups, by David Montgomery. It should form an essential theme within his forthcoming study, tentatively entitled *The Rise and Fall of the House of Labor, 1880–1920*. Cf. Aitken 1960, *passim*, for one account of the vehemence with which workers greeted Taylorism.

11   Preston's review essay, focusing on some recent accounts of the Industrial Workers of the World, remains one of the best cogent presentations of the tasks facing historians dealing with the Wobblies. See Preston 1971, pp. 435–71.

his system, scientific management, was a basic component of the social organisation of production; in many instances it was certainly nothing more than an
intellectual curiosity.[12]

It is also imperative, at the outset of this essay, to clarify the meaning of
'efficiency'. A great deal has recently been made of what 'efficient' production
entails. The current left orthodoxy argues that efficiency (by which is meant
more output for less input) is not predicated upon hierarchical work arrangements, the rationalisation of the division of labour, or, indeed, any form of the
social administration of work characteristic of capitalist production. This, it
seems to me, is patent nonsense; but, more importantly, it is a non-issue. The
question of technical superiority, as Marx long ago recognised and as David
Levine has recently reiterated, has no relevance outside of the context of capital's expansion. Thus, if a new technique (be it an invention or an innovation
in the organisation of the work process) increases the expansion of capital and
contributes towards the processes of expansion, it is, according to the needs
of capital, and the social system it defines, superior. This superiority is of a
dual nature. On the one hand, it is quantitative, raising output and increasing productivity *absolutely* (here no question as to increased inputs, i.e. labour,
bears on the problem). On the other hand, this expansion creates a qualitative
transformation, elevating capital's status as a hegemonic force within the social
order.

Thus, what I refer to as a 'thrust for efficiency' embraced an eclectic collection of managerial reforms and innovations, the underlying feature of which
was the attempt to implement a thoroughgoing rationalisation of the productive process. This 'thrust for efficiency' was hence part and parcel of the process Marx referred to as 'the intensification of labour'.[13] Did this intensification
give rise to more efficient production? Some of the reforms and innovations
did, undoubtedly, produce a more sophisticated refinement of the division of
labour, and such developments could increase output, contributing towards
the expansion of capital. Other efficiency measures, often vociferously proclaimed to be 'the million dollar savers', were nothing if not farcical; they made
no contribution to capital's expansion.

The critical feature within this development, however, *was not* its impact
upon productivity. Rather, the critical component of 'efficiency's' character,

---

12   Calvert 1967, pp. 278–9, argues that 'Scientific management provided a role for the elite
     engineer; significantly, it did not take over American Industry (as a movement) as the
     engineers planned'.

13   Marx 1967, Volume I, pp. 409–17.

as a social movement, was that it gained momentum within a social context in which capital had already gained the upper hand. 'Efficiency' functioned, regardless of its relationship to productivity, which was problematic and highly variegated, to perpetuate the hegemony of capital. In spite of the fact that few employers could agree as to what comprised 'efficient' production, and in spite of the fact that fewer still agreed upon a common managerial technique or system, the 'thrust for efficiency', as a pervasive attempt to 'rationalise' production, contributed towards the subjection of labour. As Marx noted:

> All means for the development of production transform themselves into means of domination over and exploitation of the producers; ... they estrange him from the intellectual potentialities of the labour process in the same proportion as science is incorporated in it as an independent power, they distort the conditions under which he works, subject him during the labour process to a despotism the more hateful for its meanness; they transform his life-time into working time, and drag his wife and child beneath the wheels of the Juggernaut of capital.[14]

In this context it is not the fragmentation of the labour process or the institutionalisation of hierarchy which lies at the root of the inequities of the class structure, but the logic of capitalist development itself, which, as a self-determining process, posits capital and labour in contradistinction to one another.[15]

Within this context, this chapter structures itself around a discussion of three distinct, but interrelated, phenomena. Firstly, we focus on the origins and development of the 'thrust for efficiency' in an effort to comment on its complexity, importance and essential characteristics. Secondly, we relate this drive to rationalise production to a transformation in the realm of ideas, the changing manner in which men and women viewed labour. This is critical for it should be obvious that capitalism, as a totality, demands the diffusion of attitudes and perceptions conforming to the structural dictates of production if it is to perpetuate itself and maintain its continuity as a social order. Thus, this second aspect of our study, the emergence of a managerial view of labour, stands as a specific case study of the dialectical relationship between structure and thought. We make, however, no mechanistic assumptions as to the causal link between 'base' and 'superstructure'; indeed, these terms are specific-

---

14   Marx 1934, p. 708, cited in Dunayevska 1958, p. 124.
15   This is, once again, developed more fully in my assessment of the Marglin thesis.

ally rejected as distorting a complex and intricate historical process in which thought and structure flow into and out of one another. Finally, we argue briefly that the working class response to 'efficiency' and its implementation was characterised by a persistent militancy which has been understated by previous studies. It was this very rebelliousness, on the part of American labour, that contributed to the demise of the crude Taylorism of the pre-World War I years, and the rise of more sophisticated modes of managerial repression in the postwar years and the 1920s. We are dealing, then, in a very real sense, with three critical categories of analysis. Class, because the 'thrust for efficiency', as an active agent within the processes of skill dilution, rationalisation of the division of labour and intensification of work, played a vital role in the creation of the homogeneous, mobile labour force that capitalism depends upon. Conception, for we focus upon the transformation in the realm of ideas that flowed out of and exerted influence upon this drive to 'rationalise' production. And conflict, for we attempt to show the social upheaval paralleling these developments.

The Thrust for Efficiency

Recent works tend to date the beginnings of sustained economic growth within the American economy from the 1830s.[16] With the widening of markets, the expansion of transportation facilities and the rigid, disciplined output of the emerging factory, per capita productivity soared in the years after 1840. Growth seemed endemic. Yet this expansion was, despite its rapidity, largely of a quantitative nature, building on the gains and consolidations of the past, rather than remaking the economic and social relations of the societal structure. While the factory represented a development of considerable import, it was hampered by its infancy. It was not, as it would be in future decades, dominated by attempts to rationalise every movement within the productive process. Few manufacturers possessed the consciousness of a market society, and attempts to utilise science to secure hegemony over the processes of work were rare. Indeed, Marx's three cardinal facts of capitalist production – concentration, the division of labour, and the creation of a world market – remained conspicuously absent.[17] As late as the 1880s the economy continued to be fettered with out-

---

16   Taylor 1965, pp. 1–22; North 1966, pp. 15–17; Pessen 1969, pp. 93–153; Rostow 1965, pp. 36–58. Bruchey 1965, pp. 76–91; and Taylor 1964, pp. 427–44, both find significant indicators of economic growth prior to the 1830s, but their findings are highly tentative.

17   Marx 1967, Volume III, p. 266.

moded business practices and archaic forms of productive relations.[18] While technological innovation and industrial expansion accelerated, the management of the work process retained many of the trappings of an earlier era; the development of a mature industrial capitalism was accordingly inhibited.

If industrial capitalism were to proceed at the quickened pace required to assure its continuity, changes were clearly on the agenda. Capitalists became cognisant of two major impediments to the rising output they so ardently desired. The first encumbrance was the capitalists' inability to systematically organise their productive, distributive and accounting functions. Largely a matter of bookkeeping and cost accountancy, these deficiencies were well on their way to being resolved by the turn of the century. In the vanguard of this movement for the systematisation of the capitalistic tabulation of expenses, stocks, overhead and accumulated capital, and the twin realms of productivity and profitability, was the engineer, a social type rooted in the precision of figures and the desirability of regularity. By defining himself as subservient to capital, consciously aware of its interests and protective of them, the engineer achieved a position of prominence in what was an emerging managerial movement; his critical importance came to be articulated in the pages of the *Engineering Magazine* and the *Transactions of the American Society of Mechanical Engineers*. As systematic management continued to elicit favourable responses and concrete gains, the presence of the manager became institutionalised in innumerable small and 'middling' size productive concerns, as well as in many larger factories and shops. In many cases, the distinction between manager and capitalist blurred, as partnerships formed and managers became owners of specific establishments.[19]

Yet, despite this systematic reform of certain fundamental capitalist functions, much still plagued the capitalist in his quest for authority and control of the work process he ardently desired to 'rationalise'. The most formidable task was that of solidifying hegemony over the work process, particularly where

---

18   Gutman 1973b, p. 563; Chandler 1959, pp. 1–31.

19   I will not delve too deeply into the origins and function of systemic management. Those wishing a more thorough treatment of the subject should consult the following: J. Slater Lewis, 'Works Management for Maximum Production', *Engineering Magazine*, October 1899; J. Slater Lewis, 'Works Management for Maximum Production', *Engineering Magazine*, May 1900; Metcalfe 1886, p. 441; Church 1900, pp. 391–8; Towne 1886, p. 425; Taylor 1895, pp. 856–903; Litterer 1963, pp. 369–91; 1961, pp. 461–76; Jenks 1960, pp. 421–47; Day and Melay 1962, pp. 127–52. On the social and historical roots of the engineer see Burlingame 1938, pp. 400–20. See Calvert 1967, *passim*, on the links between managers and ownership.

it involved a measure of skill and craftsmanship. Some employers turned to paternalistic policies in the hopes of securing a docile, stable producing class. Although this tactic would remain embedded within labour-management relations until the onslaught of the Great Depression, the economic downturn of 1893 and the eruption at Pullman dealt this strategy a severe and early blow.[20] As late as the initial years of the Progressive Era, reaching in North America from roughly 1900–20, capital still lacked decisive control over the basic processes of work. Systematic management, for all its contributions to capitalistic bookkeeping, offered little in the way of solutions to this irksome dilemma.

With the onslaught of Progressivism in the first two decades of the twentieth century, a movement in which capital attempted to institutionalise reform in the interests of its preservation and continuity, rationality and science were given an unprecedented impetus. Within this context 'efficiency', as a specific ideal, was paraded as the solution to all of industrial capitalism's problems: slum housing and construction, municipal government, social services and welfare, labour legislation and workers' compensation. Yet nowhere did this 'thrust for efficiency' attain such prominence as in the evolution of scientific management into a newer, more forceful, 'Science of Management'. This development had a major impact on the relationships of work within American industrial establishments and was to prove invaluable to the capitalist in his quest for undisputed control over the processes of work.[21]

Although there was a noticeable thread of continuity linking the systematic managers and the efficiency engineers of the Progressive Era, a group which came to the fore in the first decade of the twentieth century represented something of a new breed. With science and natural law as their guidelines and a precise grasp of the logic of time dominating their method, these men and women transformed older conceptions of efficiency and managerial function. They were, in a very real sense, the prophets of a new age: Frederick Winslow Taylor, the father of 'scientific management', whose writings and practices offered all interested parties a comprehensive critique of previous management technique and sought to standardise all tasks; Frank and William Gilbreth, whose time-and-motion studies refined certain skilled trades such

20   On the persistence of welfare and paternalistic modes see Brody 1960, pp. 147–79; 1968, pp. 147–78. On Pullman and the depression of 1893 see Lindsay 1924, *passim*, Hoffman 1956, pp. 137–64.

21   See Haber 1964, *passim*; Callahan 1962, *passim*; and the literature cited in Galambos 1970, pp. 282–4. Contemporary sources which emphasised this thrust for efficiency include: Jones 1924, pp. 1–8, 237–93; Brandeis 1911, pp. 35–43; Emerson 1911, pp. 17–25; Tolman 1909, *passim*; *New York Times*, 11 March 1911; *New York Call*, 24 August 1911.

as brick laying; Carl Barth, who introduced the exactitude of the slide rule to the shop floor; C.B. Thompson, a Harvard professor, whose many speeches and articles popularised the tenets of the new creed of efficiency. The movement suffered from no lack of advocates. Neither was it devoid of a certain theoretical clarity.

Participants within the managerial movement were not, however, blessed with unity and singleness of purpose or method. In this they differed little from innumerable other movements which rose and fell during the years 1900–20. Men and women of considerable arrogance and ego, the individuals within the managerial school often disagreed violently over the means by which labour could be 'efficiently utilised' or 'scientifically managed'. The Gilbreths and Taylor, for instance, continually clashed over the significance of motion studies, and Harrington Emerson, patron saint of the 'Efficiency Society', was often ruthlessly attacked by the more doctrinaire followers of Taylor.[22]

One of the most cohesive groupings came to be a collection of individuals who coalesced around the writings of F.W. Taylor. Henry Gantt, Sanford E. Thompson, James Dodge and Morris Cooke became the locus of a group of avid disciples; together they formed the Society for the Promotion of Scientific Management. After Taylor's death in 1915, they would unite within the ranks of the Taylor Society, an organisation whose character assumed more and more the traits of a sect as time went on.[23]

Persons associated with the 'thrust for efficiency' gravitated to Taylor for obvious reasons: of those associated with managerial innovation, Taylor's contribution, on the theoretical plane at least, had been the greatest. With his logic of time and armed with a stopwatch, Taylor redefined the age-old conception of the division of labour and elevated it to new heights. Through him management, once systematic, took on the trappings of a 'science'. In enacting what he perceived to be a social physics of work, whereby each and every task was plotted and standardised, Taylor far surpassed the regulatory, observe-and-record approach of his predecessors. Through their theory, if not in their practices, Taylor and his accomplices left their imprint on an epoch of capitalist production.[24]

---

22 The diversity of the movement and the resulting conflict is adequately dealt with in Nadworny 1957, pp. 23–42; Nadworny 1955, pp. 14–33; Hoxie 1966, pp. 140–68; and Thompson 1915, pp. 262–307.

23 On the Taylor Society see R.T. Kent, 'The Taylor Society Twenty Years Ago', *Bulletin of the Taylor Society*, February 1932; Nadworny 1953, pp. 244–7; Haber 1964, pp. 31–50.

24 Taylor's impact, as I have suggested earlier, is highly problematic, the critical issue involving a determination of the extent to which Taylor's system of scientific management was

As the 'thrust for efficiency' reached fruition in the Progressive Era, certain dates emerged as benchmarks in the history of managerial theory and practice. In 1903, at a meeting of the American Society of Mechanical Engineers convened at Saratoga, New York, Taylor read his paper 'Shop Management', outlining his basic approaches to the refinements of the labour process needed to ensure 'efficient' production. One authority accordingly spoke of 1903 as the date properly marking 'the beginning of the present movement to establish industrial management as a profession subject to scientific laws'.[25] The coverage which 'efficiency' received in the popular press as early as 1911 attested to the widespread interest in the subject, and by 1922 virtually every individual in a position of authority lavishly praised the managerial innovators.[26] Dissenting voices, originally amplified by the leadership of organised labour, appeared to fade quickly, and society warmly embraced the panacea of 'efficiency'. The managers had achieved a notable victory.[27]

In the midst of this achievement the managerial movement for industrial reorganisation remained factional and sectarian. The Taylors, Emersons and Gilbreths of the movement seemed incapable of resolving their differences, and capital, as a class, seemed even less sure of its endorsement of specific managerial systems; 'efficiency' was everyman's panacea, but its implementation ran an extremely uneven course. Yet within the parameters of dissent, which seemed on a superficial level to dominate the relationships and theory of the 'new science', there existed certain common ground upon which all could and did tread with little difficulty. The resultant managerial synthesis increasingly rested upon specialisation, standardisation and the simplification

---

capable of being implemented. Those who stress Taylor's contribution almost without exception deal only with his theoretical contribution. See Braverman 1974a, chs. 4–6; Bell 1970, pp. 5–9; Friedmann 1955, pp. 37–66; Davies 1959, pp. 4–7; Urwick 1958, pp. 5–8; and Wood 1941, *passim*.

25 Lewis 1914, pp. 233–4; Shaw 1914, p. 217; Thompson 1914b, pp. 12, 23. Drury tabulated the number of periodical articles related to efficiency published between 1907 and 1912 as follows: 1907 (8), 1908 (5), 1909 (7), 1910 (15 – 6 in December alone), 1911 (59), and 1912 (38). See Drury 1922, p. 41.

26 McKelvey 1952, pp. 64–78; Brandeis 1919, pp. 127–30; Nadworny 1955, pp. 122–54; Samuel Gompers, 'Labor and Research', *American Federationist*, December 1920; Samuel Gompers, 'Industry and the Engineer', *American Federationist*, December 1920; Samuel Gompers, 'Organized Labor and Industrial Engineers', *American Federationist*, January 1921; Herbert Hoover, 'A Plea for Industrial Co-operation', *American Federationist*, January 1921.

27 See Taylor 1911, p. 570; *The Nation*, 11 May 1911; *New York Times*, 29 March 1911; 30 March 1911; 2 April 1911; *The Outlook*, 13 May 1911; 11 September 1911.

of the job. Moreover, the determining factors in both a fair day's work and a fair day's wage were held to be quantifiable and dependent upon certain laws, naturally derived and indisputable. Despite their sectarian squabbles, the 'efficiency engineers' and their masters, the capitalist class, embraced a common perception of the working class. Regarding labour as simply one input in the productive process, the managerial-capitalist visualisation of labour diverged diametrically from older, entrenched views of the work process and its practitioners.

The Managerial View of Labour

The closing decades of the nineteenth century witnessed unprecedented changes in the social and economic realms of American life. From 1865–1900 the country was transformed; out of the ruralism and handicraft production of the past – broken only by the occasional textile mill or mercantile centre – emerged a United States which, by 1890, led the world in industrial output. Yet at the same time these were also years of mobility and fluidity, years of vital clashes and intense conflict. American society was, in one author's word, distended. Lines of class, status and community power remained blurred and diffuse. If workers engaged in a ubiquitous quest for 'power', other social strata were equally adamant in their struggle to impose 'order'.[28]

By 1918 this discord remained prominent, but the question of who controlled the essential foundations of the social order had all but been settled. The industrial-financial elite, a class well advanced in the process of its making, had secured hegemony, not only in the economic sphere, but in the political and social arenas as well.[29] It is the purpose of this section to argue that one aspect contributing towards the attainment of this hegemony was the shift in the manner in which society viewed labour, a shift arising out of and exerting an impact upon the creed of efficiency.

The perception of labour characteristic of nineteenth-century America was rooted in past traditions and cultural affinities. It rested firmly on what could be called a populistic worldview. Labour, that most ubiquitous of human activities, bore none of the stigma originally attached to 'fallen man'. On the contrary, work was regarded as the bastion of the social order and was glorified, per-

---

28   Gutman 1968, pp. 263–87; 1970, pp. 31–54; Wiebe 1967, pp. 11–75. For a slightly different view see Dubofsky 1975, *passim*; Cumbler 1974, pp. 395–415.

29   Weinstein 1968, p. 3; Gutman 1968, p. 282.

sistently portrayed in the most glowing of terms. To labour by the sweat of one's brow was, admittedly, man's lot, but a noble lot it was. Farmer, shop-keeper, labourer, artisan, small manufacturer – all viewed their social contri-bution in terms of the goods and services they created with their own skills, talents and resources. Monopoly was emphatically eschewed, while individu-alised production was exhorted. No slur was so great as that of being para-sitical, a critique aimed at the degenerate, the speculative, the misfit and the lawyer. While certain strata of the working population were the butt of nat-ivist and racist slurs, this was no anti-labour tirade, but rather an attack on characteristics attributed to particular racial and ethnic groups. The popu-listic view of labour could never sanction a social system which produced the class differentiation that gave rise to a concept of 'the swinish multi-tude'. This was both un-Christian and un-American. It was also to be un-efficient.[30]

Perhaps nothing, outside of massive working-class upsurge, was so distaste-ful to the rising capitalist as the contention that labour, and labour alone, was productive. Such a perspective had a tangible impact in the factory, shop or mill: it encouraged the continuation of, and lent credence to, an artisan mode of consciousness from which emanated a belief in certain inalienable rights of labour, the most significant of which was the autonomy of the skilled craftsman.[31] This remnant of a pre-capitalist productive consciousness was an impediment to the realisation of the employer's control of the work process.[32] Many capitalists thus came to see the erosion of this populistic conception of labour as a priority within their struggle for hegemony. With the failure of Social Darwinism to fundamentally alter working people's perception of their self-worth, an alternative view of labour emerged and gained widespread accept-ance among capitalists and their hirelings.[33]

Articulated most forcefully by the proponents of efficiency, the new percep-tion of labour was a radical departure from older, populistic notions. Although the managerial view evolved over the first two decades of the twentieth cen-

---

30 My views on the populistic view of labour prevalent in the nineteenth century are drawn from a number of sources, the following of which are, perhaps, the most forceful: Neufeld 1969, pp. 5–43; Montgomery 1967, especially pp. 90–134, 230–60; Gutman 1970, pp. 31–54; 1968a, pp. 263–87; 1968b, pp. 137–74; Pollack 1967, pp. 404–66; 1966, *passim*.

31 On artisan consciousness see Laurie 1974, pp. 337–66; Gray 1973, pp. 428–52.

32 This is the basic theme pervading Stone's analysis of the origins of job structures in the steel industry. See Stone 1974, *passim*.

33 Social Darwinism gained no foothold within the 'producing classes'. See Fine 1967, *passim*; Boller 1969, *passim*.

tury, it developed within two distinct periods. From 1903–15, the managerial perception was voiced in its crudest and least sophisticated form, and came to be subsumed under four distinct, but interrelated, headings: (1) an acceptance of the inherent laziness of man; (2) a perception of labour as bestial and/or machinic; (3) an endorsement of the economistic nature of the needs and aspirations of working people; and (4) a rejection of unionisation and collective bargaining, indeed of all concerted working-class action or behaviour. Given the violent opposition with which labour – both organised and unorganised – greeted capital's attempts to implement efficiency measures, coupled with the dictates of a wartime economy, these views underwent some revisions in the years 1916–22. Essentially, capital and its managers were forced to abandon the more ruthless and authoritarian aspects of their platform and substitute the more tantalising carrot for the unrelenting stick.

Acquiescing to a conservative analysis of men and human nature, the men and women whose writings propagandised efficiency and its standards seemed as one in denouncing man as inherently lazy. Taylor noted the seriousness of the 'natural laziness of man' and considered it a fact that there were many places 'in the United States where the men [were] so lazy and demoralized that no sufficient inducement [could] be offered to make them do a full day's work'.[34] Harrington Emerson, in an implicit condemnation, presented the most scathing attack on man's laziness when he recounted an anecdote from his experiences on the railway: 'A railroad track foreman and gang were recently seem burying under some ashes and dirt a thirty-foot steel rail. It was less trouble to bury it than to pick it up and place it where it could be saved'. To a man whose approach to efficiency was fetishistic, disgust at such behaviour did not require articulation. It was understood.[35]

The problem was not, however, solely relegated to the realm of the physical. Human nature was seen to be at the root of man's inability to transcend laziness and the product of that human nature, civilisation, reflected that deficiency. Men were, as a rule, 'obviously not of an ambitious, intellectual type'. Forrest Cardullo stated that 'the first and most prolific source of inefficiency is mental laziness'. Men were prone 'to complain and ... anything new, especially if it involved a change of habit, [would] be the butt of complaint'. Static in their approach to life, overly cautious and incapable of deferring gratification, working people, in the eyes of the capitalist-manager alliance, denied themselves

---

34   Taylor 1947, p. 32; 1914c, p. 655.
35   Emerson 1912, p. 67. Cf., Edwards 1912, p. 355.

the potentiality of dramatic self-advancement.[36] Locked into a conservative framework, from which they viewed man's failings as innate, the advocates of efficiency remained convinced that the paths of progress were illuminated by an elite of which they were the most conscious expression.[37]

Given the managerial understanding of man's limitations, discipline – an earlier prerequisite in the development of the factory – was relegated to a position of prominence within the emerging orthodoxy. Described by one author as 'an autocrat by birth, training and experience', Taylor's tactic in dealing with workers was summed up in an early statement: 'First, Holding a plum for them to climb after; and Second; Cracking the whip over them with an occasional touch of the lash'.[38] Henry Gantt and Harrington Emerson, allied with different and opposing factions of the efficiency drive, both regarded discipline as the cornerstone upon which the implementation of their theories of labour-management relations rested. In a system where 'obedience to directions and mastery of the standard method' was the foundation upon which success was built, the role of the foreman, as shop disciplinarian, took on increased importance.[39] If the usual means of discipline (lowering wages, layoffs, fines, demerit points, etc.) did not inculcate in the worker the proper respect for authority, then 'four or five foremen (sic) [should] stand over a worker and by a species of industrial "third degree" compel obedience'. Robert Hoxie correctly concluded that, in practice, the 'new science' of management was little more than a 'reversion to industrial autocracy'.[40]

Closely related to the assumptions concerning man's nature and the consequent need for discipline was the prevailing notion that labour, and the social stratum that lived by its toil, was animalistic or bestial. Taylor and his associates never tired of comparing men to beasts of burden and equated a 'first class man' with the more competent variants of a specific species. A 'first class man' was one who, like a dog, 'does just like he's told to do, and no backtalk'. In his work at Bethlehem Steel, Taylor began by taking 'a proper human animal, just as we would take a proper horse, to study'. Attempting to raise output in the

---

36   Drury 1922, p. 241; Cardullo 1914, pp. 67, 77–8; Taylor 1914b, p. 674; Taylor 1914a, p. 262; U.S. Congress 1916, p. 774.

37   See Drury 1922, p. 7, on the characteristic conservatism of the managerial school.

38   Thompson 1914a, pp. 315–27, cited in Nadworny 1955, p. 78; Taylor 1869, p. 7, cited in Kakar 1970, p. 65.

39   Henry Gantt, 'The Compensation of Labor', *The Engineering Magazine*, March 1905; Emerson 1912, chapter 4; The System Company, p. 85; Thompson 1914c, p. 404; Kolker 1948, p. 88.

40   Hoxie 1966, p. 112. Cf., Taylor 1947, pp. 191–9; U.S. Congress 1911, p. 27; Meyers 1914, p. 147; and Copley 1923, Volume I, p. 183.

handling of pig iron, Taylor chose 'Schmidt', 'a man more or less of the type of the ox, heavy both mentally and physically'. 'Schmidt' apparently fulfilled Taylor's expectations, for he raised production from 12.5 tons per day to 47 tons per day. The increased wage which he ultimately received, and which the managers made so much of, did him little good. After such a day's labour 'Schmidt', exhausted, was fit only for the beer hall, and drank his remuneration away. The man who had previously had the energy to run home after a day's work to till his garden plot became, under Taylor's guiding hand, a virtual pub dweller.[41]

At times the new managers revised their perception of labour's bestiality and substituted the analogy of the machine for the analogy of the ox, the horse or the cow. Frank Tannenbaum described a Slovak woman pointed out to him by management as 'one of the best workers we have':

> She stood bending slightly forward, her dull eyes straining down, her elbows jerking back and forth, her hands jumping in nervous haste to keep up with the gang. These hands made one single precise motion each second, 3600 in one hour, and all exactly the same. The hands were swift, precise, intelligent. The face was stolid, vague and vacant.

The superintendent explained the woman's utility:

> It took a long time to pound the idea into her head but when this grade of woman once absorbs an idea she holds it. *She is a sure machine.* For much of our work *this woman is the kind we want.* Her mind is on the table.

The managerial perception of labour was not, it appears, so much conditioned by the innate characteristics of the workforce, as it was structured by the desires and needs of a social group dedicated to production at any cost.[42]

A third precept of the emerging managerial view was the economistic analysis of working-class needs and aspirations. Wages were seen as *the* fundamental issue: provide the worker an adequate return for his/her labour and, regardless of the nature and conditions of work or the structure of society, the class would remain content. C.B. Thompson wrote that 'in spite of the preval-

---

41   The 'Schmidt' incident is chronicled in: U.S. Congress 1916, I, p. 777; Taylor 1947, pp. 46, 137; Copley 1923, Volume II, pp. 56–67; Kakar 1970, pp. 141–5; Carlton 1914, p. 725, editorial footnote.

42   Tannenbaum 1921, pp. 59–60 [my emphasis]. Cf. Dodge 1914, p. 231; Aufhauser 1973, pp. 811–24; Gramsci 1971, pp. 279–318.

ence of the talk about sanitation, safety, welfare, esprit de corps, etc., the most vital point of contact between managers and the men is the pay envelope'. It was an accepted dictum that 'the workman works for money and appeals through other motives must be subordinated'.[43]

The manifestations of this economistic perception of wage labour emerge most clearly in Taylor's description of his conversation with 'Schmidt', the Pennsylvania Dutchman who succeeded in loading 47 tons of pig iron every day for three years. The content of work relationships under a 'rationalised' labour process leaps vividly to the forefront in this insightful passage:

> Schmidt, are you a high-priced man?
>
> Vell, I don't know vat you mean.
>
> Oh yes you do. What I want to know is whether you are a high-priced man or not.
>
> Vell, I don't know vat you mean.
>
> Oh come now, you answer my questions. What I want to find out is whether you are a high-priced man or one of these cheap fellows here. What I want to find out is whether you want to earn $1.85 a day or whether you want to earn $1.15, just the same as all these cheap fellows are getting.
>
> Did I vant $1.85 a day? Vas dot a high-priced man? Vell, yes, I vas a high-priced man.
>
> Oh, you're aggravating me. Of course you want $1.85 a day – everyone wants it! You know perfectly well that that has very little to do with your being a high-priced man. For goodness' sake answer my questions, and don't waste any more of my time. Now come over here. You see that pile of pig iron?
>
> Yes.
>
> You see that car?
>
> Yes.
>
> Well, if you are a high-priced man, you will load that pig iron on that car tomorrow for $1.85. Now do wake up and answer my question. Tell me whether you are a high-priced man or not.
>
> Vell, did I got $1.85 for loading dot pig iron on dot car tomorrow?
>
> Yes of course you do, and you get $1.85 for loading a pile like that every day right through the year. That is what a high-priced man does, and you know it just as well as I do.

---

43   Thompson 1913, p. 631; Thompson 1914d, pp. 684–705; Franklin 1915, p. 6.

Vell, dot's right. I could load dot pig iron on the car tomorrow for $1.85, and I get it every day, don't I.

Certainly you do – certainly you do.

Vell, den, I vas a high-priced man.

Now, hold on, hold on. You know just as well as I do that a high-priced man has to do exactly as he's told to do from morning until night. You have seen this man here before, haven't you?

No, I never saw him.

Well, if you are a high-priced man, you will do exactly as this man tells you tomorrow, from morning till night. When he tells you to pick up a pig and walk, you pick it up and you walk, and when he tells you to sit down and rest, you sit down. You do that right through the day. And what's more; no back talk.

Taylor concluded that this may seem to be 'rough talk', but he justified the tone and content of his conversation with 'Schmidt' because with 'a man of the mentally sluggish type of Schmidt it is appropriate and not unkind, since it is effective in fixing his attention on the high wages which he wants and away from what, if it were called to his attention, he would probably consider impossibly hard work'.[44] Men's actions on the job, it was commonly agreed, were seldom governed by abstract principles or conceptions of rights centred on just and humane treatment; under the sway of a capitalistic labour market the cash nexus reigned supreme. 'Schmidt', intentionally chosen from a group of 75 hand-picked men, proved the case.

Despite the managerial conviction that the dollar ruled the lives of working people, it was generally agreed upon that wage increases beyond a certain point instigated a process of diminishing returns for management:

> ... when workmen of this caliber are given a carefully measured task which calls for a big day's work on their part, and that when in return for this extra effort they are paid wages up to 60 percent beyond the wages usually paid, that this increase in wages tends to make them not only more thrifty but better men in every way; that they live rather better, become more sober, and work more steadily. When, on the other hand, they receive more than a 60 percent increase in wages, many of them will work irregularly and tend to become more or less shiftless, extravagant and dissipated.

---

44   Taylor 1947, pp. 44–6.

When Taylor concluded that 'it does not do for most men to get too rich too fast' he excluded the owners of Bethlehem Steel who, through the implementation of efficiency measures, increased output from three hundred to five hundred percent, cut costs 60 percent and saved, strictly on the level of labour expenditure, $126,000 over a two-year period.[45]

These beliefs in the laziness of man, the bestial nature of labour and the supremacy of the wage rate within work relationships, culminated in the managerial rejection of unionisation and collective bargaining. To those schooled in the 'thrust for efficiency', unions personified evil. Legitimising man's natural laziness and inefficiency, unions sanctioned 'systematic soldiering', the conscious restriction of output workmen apparently thought crucial to 'their best interests'. Setting a work pace geared to the lowest common denominator, unions robbed workingmen of incentive and buttressed the inherent lack of ambition common to all working people. The union was obviously 'a hindrance to the prosperity' of both the employer and the employee. Efficiency experts jealously guarded their right to determine what lay in the best interests of the working class. Workers could not embrace two loyalties: their choice either lay with capital and productivity, or with the union and, if the managers had their way, unemployment.[46]

In two letters to close friends Taylor made explicit his views on working-class solidarity, mutuality and union affiliation. To James Dodge he wrote:

> I am very much interested in your statement that shop committees should be selected by the workmen of your Chicago-Link Belt Company to discuss the rates, etc. I think you are making a great mistake in doing this. I do not believe that there is the slightest dissatisfaction among your men, and having these shop committees would only have the effect of stimulating your men in the direction of trades unionism.

And again to Dr. Lyman Abbot in 1912:

> I look upon it as of the greatest importance that the working people should come to see that their hope for a better future lies in increasing their productivity, whether it be by labor saving machinery, by increased

---

45   Taylor 1947, p. 74. Cf. Farnham 1919, pp. 124–5.
46   Taylor 1947, pp. 32, 187; McKelvey 1952, pp. 12–21; Drury 1922, pp. 211–16; School 1911, p. 24; Copley 1923, I, pp. 160–1; 1923, II, pp. 403–16; 'Taking Ambition Out of the Working Man', *Century Magazine*, July 1911.

efficiency, or any other device, rather than quarrelling with their employers over the wages they are to receive, while at the same time doing nothing to increase productivity.

As a man who rejected all 'collectivist schemes', Frederick Taylor would have had 'men look within themselves for their progress' rather than ally with 'the most bitter, unscrupulous and ignorant representatives of American trade unionism'.[47]

The managerial distaste of unionisation and collective bargaining was voiced most vehemently in testimony before the Commission on Industrial Relations in 1916. Carl Barth, an associate of Taylor, demanded that union officials must 'come to me to go to school for two or three years' before he would consider talking to them. 'They [must] be educated to the ideas we are trying to work out, so as to come in and argue on the question'. As they were presently constituted, however, Barth considered the trade unions 'a set of biased fools' who would merely waste his time. On the question of collective bargaining Barth was most explicit:

> Thompson: Then you have not taken into consideration the question of collective bargaining?
> Barth: No; not very seriously because I do not shake hands with the devil.

Considering the whole investigation something of a joke, Barth departed with the observation that the Commission was functioning as if it were a circus. Efficiency, to its practitioners, appeared above reproach.[48]

With Taylor's death in 1915, and in the face of intense attack by organised and unorganised labour, the development of the managerial view underwent a marked reorientation.[49] The essence of the 'thrust for efficiency' remained

---

47   Copley 1923, II, pp. 423, 428, 430; Thompson 1914a in Nadworny 1955, p. 78.
48   U.S. Congress 1916, I, pp. 887–8, 895, 899.
49   This shift is discussed tangentially in Derber 1966, pp. 259–88; and 1967, pp. 3–29. On labour's early estrangement from efficiency see Aitken 1960, *passim*; James Duncan, 'Efficiency – Real, Unreal and Brutal', *American Federationist*, May 1911; John Golden, 'Scientific Management in the Textile Industry', *American Federationist*, August 1911; Samuel Gompers, 'The "Miracles" of Efficiency', *American Federationist*, April 1911; Samuel Gompers, 'Machinery to Perfect the Human Machine', *American Federationist*, February 1911; Paul W. Hanna, 'The Flaw in Efficiency', *Machinists Monthly Journal*, September 1911; Hoxie 1966, *passim*; Nadworny 1955, pp. 23–9; 53–71; McKelvey 1952, pp. 12–26; Commons 1911, pp. 463–72.

stable and unaltered. The priorities were still increased production for profit and hegemony over the process of work. Yet within this imperative arose a consciousness of the importance and utility of paternalistic policies in securing from labour both stability and productivity. Although efficiency schemes and new concepts of welfare and/or personnel management often clashed in practice, they were universally applauded as contributing toward the same end.[50]

Within this context efficiency engineers came to endorse collective bargaining, unionisation, increased leisure, recreational activities and psychological counselling. The most prominent advocate of this new tendency was Bob Valentine, an industrial counsellor from Boston. Emphasising the need for constitutional democratic relations within the plant, Valentine, the first managerial authority to break with the orthodoxy of Taylor, was greeted with strong opposition from the rearguard of the efficiency movement. The enthusiasm which his revisions generated within the upper echelons of organised labour, however, caused the efficiency advocates to sit up and take notice. Valentine eventually convinced Morris Cooke of the sagacity of his views and by 1920 the Taylor Society had contributed to an issue of the *Annals* of the American Academy of Political and Social Science, co-authored by Sam Gompers, in which cooperation was heralded as the key to efficiency.[51]

Efficiency advocates even took up the task of attacking the lack of creativity characterising work in mass-production industries. Human relationships once callously ignored, or explained away by the dollar, seemed to emerge as legitimate realms of study in the post-1915 years. In 1916 Robert Wolf, manager of the Burgess Sulphite Company, pointed to the necessity of harnessing the creativity of the working class:

> The opportunity for self-expression ... is something that the workman is entitled to, and we employers who feel that management is to become a true science must begin to think less of the science of material things and more of the science of human relationships ... It is beginning to

50   Nelson and Campbell 1972, pp. 1–16; Drury 1922, pp. 7–28; Luke Grant, 'Cooperative Plan of Philadelphia Rapid Transit Company', unpublished manuscript, U.S. Commission on Industrial Relations Papers, Department of Labor Files, cited in Adams 1966, p. 188; Korman 1967, pp. 77–84; Brissenden 1922, pp. 29–33 et *passim*; Brody 1960, pp. 187–8.

51   Valentine 1916, pp. 586–8; Valentine and Tead 1917, pp. 241–58; 'Valentine – An Industrial Counselor', *Live and Labor*, January 1971; McKelvey 1952, pp. 21–5; Nadworny 1955, pp. 122–41; Cooke, Gompers, and Miller 1920, *passim*.

be understood that when we deny to vast numbers of individuals the opportunity to do creative work we are violating a great universal law.[52]

With the outbreak of war, necessitating increased and stabilised production, the cooperative spirit of the 'new management' was given further stimulation. Amid the exigencies of wartime the government and the War Industries Board granted organised-labour leaders and the efficiency experts (two sides of the productivity coin) concession after concession. As policy and practice increasingly forced the dissident groups together, their mutual suspicions lessened and both labour's leadership and the capitalist-managerial alliance rallied to the call for 'responsible' contributions to the war effort.[53]

With organised labour's post-war desire to retain an image of respectability, and the concomitant concern with productivity, this trend could not help but continue. The 'new science of management' quickly adapted to the changing climate; as managerial techniques became more sophisticated the efficiency drive of the 1920s became increasingly alien (in form if not in content) from the older, unpolished sentiments of a Frederick Winslow Taylor. No longer could an efficiency engineer proclaim that he didn't 'care a hoot what became of the workman after he left the factory at night, so long as he was able to show up the next morning in fit condition for a hard day's toil'. To Taylor, welfare schemes and benevolent or paternal modes of management had been objects of ridicule; to the manager of 1922 they were the most useful of tools.[54]

Both scholars, viewing this development with the benefit of hindsight, and contemporaries, witnessing the unfolding of this process before their eyes, have tended to regard the divergence of management's early and later views of labour as indicative of a major change in thinking which had noticeable repercussions in the evolution of class relations. That the transformation had an impact is undeniable. Nevertheless, it would be foolhardy to perceive an abrupt break in the essence of the managerial perception of labour. The adoption of paternalistic or welfare-orientated policies was simply a better, more efficient means of attaining a similar goal: greater per capita output.[55]

If it is a truism that the carrot is more functional than the stick, it is also true that the managerial innovators learned after 19 long years of trial and error. As the budding friendship of the efficiency spokesmen and the upper

52   *Bulletin of the Taylor Society*, October 1916, cited in McKelvey 1952, p. 25.

53   Alford 1918, pp. 97–100; Kaufman 1972, pp. 17–44; Kaplan 1956, pp. 354–5; Haber 1964, pp. 117–33; Jones 1925, pp. 7–8; Drury 1922, pp. 17–18; Brody 1960, pp. 180–98.

54   Frank B. Copley, 'Frederick Winslow Taylor: Revolutionist', *The Outlook*, September 1915.

55   One of the most cogent presentations of this view is found in Bendix 1956, pp. 274–86.

echelons of organised labour consolidated, Taylor may well have turned in his grave. Capitalism, ever more perceptive than mere individuals, breathed a sigh of relief, for the 'new management' was an effective vehicle in maintaining the structural continuity of the social order. By 1922 efficiency had admittedly 'acquired a character and flavor ... somewhat different from that of former years ... Less rigid it [had] become more adaptable, more comprehensive, *more useful*'.[56]

Working-Class Rebellion, 1903–22

The major impact of the thrust for efficiency lay in the contribution of this tendency to the attainment of bourgeois hegemony. Called into being by the structural imperatives of a developing industrial capitalism which required a refinement of the division of labour, efficiency fulfilled another, more specific function. In relegating the labouring man and the capitalist to their respective positions within the hierarchy of production, the new managers buried the populistic conception of labour and took a long and forceful stride in the direction of lessening working-class autonomy on the shop floor. In short, they secured for the bourgeoisie a measure of control over the processes of production which it had previously lacked.

As the industrial capitalist rose the craftsman fell, and the story of efficiency is also the story of the elimination of skill, the immiseration, in the most profound sense, of the working class. This decline of the skilled worker was held by many to be an important causal factor in the increase of industrial unrest.[57] The relationship between efficiency, the dilution of skill and class conflict did not go unnoticed. Louis Duchez claimed that scientific management was acting as a catalyst in the development of class struggle in the United States. P.J. Conlin, International Vice-President of the Machinists, attributed the rise of syndicalism, sabotage and passive resistance to the thrust for efficiency. 'We [did] not hear of any of these things', he testified, 'until we heard of scientific management and new methods of production'.[58]

Historical interpretations of the working-class response to the thrust for efficiency posit an initial period of resistance and rebellion from 1911–15, a transitional period from 1915–19 in which the foundations of a managerial-labour

---

56   Drury 1922, p. 28 [my emphasis].

57   See sources cited in number 49. Also, Fitch 1921, pp. 371–88; 1969, *passim*; Williams 1921, pp. 293–318.

58   Duchez 1911, pp. 628–31; U.S. Congress 1916, I, p. 874; Montgomery 1971, pp. 509–29.

alliance were constructed, followed by uninterrupted harmony in the years after 1919. By 1920 the working class, according to standard sources, had made its peace with the proponents of a more efficient work process.[59]

Such an analysis, resting upon the articulations of an elite group of 'pure and simple' trade unionists (whose most vocal elements remained Gompers, Frey and the officials of the American Federation of Labor (AFL) as well as the leadership of the more backward-looking craft unions – most noticeably those in the building trades), tends to ignore large segments of the labour movement as well as the rank and file and the unorganised workers. Unions guided by socialistic or syndicalist world views receive scant attention and the persistent disillusionment of the ordinary working man with premium systems, piece work, bonus plans and the rigours of standardised production is studiously avoided in the traditional analysis. Close scrutiny suggests that the prevailing conventional wisdom – in which labour's relationship to scientific management and the thrust for efficiency is regarded as harmonious by 1919 – demands critical reevaluation and, in all likelihood, substantial revision.

Labour's early estrangement from the practice and principles of the efficiency movement is an established fact that generates little controversy. Taylor's statement that there had never been a strike in an establishment ruled by scientific management was, for instance, fanciful; but even if it had been true, the intensity with which labour, through its press, attacked Taylorism was indicative of organised labour's distrust of the drive for more efficient forms of production.[60] As early as 1903 the International Association of Machinists had gone on record opposing 'work by the piece, premium, merit, task or contract system'. The vehemence with which the skilled moulders protested Taylorism's introduction at the Watertown Arsenal is well documented. That the moulders resented the incursions made upon what they felt to be their domain as skilled workers was voiced most explicitly by Joseph Cooney who stressed the mechanics' disgust at 'being put under the clock'. And, at the infamous textile strike in Paterson, New Jersey, long regarded as a simple economistic labour-capital conflict, aggravated by the irksome presence of the IWW, workers assaulted many planks of the efficiency programme: piece work, bonus plans, premium payments and the arbitrary discipline of the foremen.[61]

---

59   McKelvey 1952, p. 12, *passim*; Nadworny 1955, *passim*; Dale 1954, pp. 359–72.

60   McKelvey 1952, pp. 12–26; Nadworny 1955, pp. 5–101; Haber 1964, pp. 18–30; Hoxie 1966, *passim*; Hoxie 1916, pp. 833–54; Frey n.d., pp. 400–11; U.S. Congress 1916, I, pp. 940–55, 985–90; and the sources cited in number 49.

61   *Machinists Monthly Journal*, October 1905, cited in Nadworny 1955, p. 25; Aitken 1960, p. 151, et *passim*; Adams 1966, pp. 77–9; Davis 1975, *passim*.

   Perhaps no other conflict epitomised the working-class response to efficiency so cogently as the Illinois Central and Harriman lines Railroad Carmen's
Strike. Initiated in September of 1911, sustaining itself until 28 June 1915 and
involving between 28,000 and 35,000 workers, the strike is an important and
neglected chapter in the history of American labour.[62] Many saw the conflict
arising from the carmen's desire to unite their numerous and isolated craft bodies into a single federated body, and indeed management stated that this was
the critical issue involved in the struggle.[63] In reality, the railwaymen's urge to
federate stemmed from a number of basic causes, not the least of which was
the erosion of the carmen's craft autonomy and skilled status occasioned by
the implementation of efficiency measures. Despite capital's denial that scientific management had been introduced, the carmen were conscious of the
transformation of their trade wrought by piece work, premium plans and bonus
systems, speed-up and time and motion studies. In 1908 blacksmiths, boilermakers and sheet metal workers had struck numerous lines (ranging from the
Missouri Pacific and St. Louis to the Canadian Pacific Railroad) upon the introduction of piece work. The conflict of 1911–15 represented the continuity of the
craft workers' discontent.[64] Thomas J. Short, Secretary Treasurer of the Federation of Railwaymen on the Chicago and Eastern Illinois Railroads assured
A.O. Wharton that the workers had organised to 'prevent the introduction of
piece work, bonus systems, physical examination and unfair efficiency systems'.
In Paducah, Kentucky, J.S. McCreery noticed that 'beginning with the change in
management of the Illinois Central, the attitude of the officials of the Company
toward our organization seemed altogether different from the old management. They began to introduce piece work ... Another thing to my knowledge
was the introduction of the speed-up system'.[65]
   Few strikes in the history of American labour have been marred by the violence and degree of personal suffering which dominated the carmen's dispute:
gunplay was regularly resorted to; a number of black strike-breakers were killed

---

62   On the Carmen's strike see Montgomery 1974, *passim*; Foster 1939, pp. 48–51, 146–8; Person
     1918, *passim*.; U.S. Congress 1916, X, pp. 9697–10048; Adams 1966, pp. 127–45; Gibbons 1914,
     pp. 72–8; 'War! War! War!', *Blacksmith's Journal*, XVI, October 1914; Comerford, 'Organized
     Labor Demands to Be Heard', *Railway Carmen's Journal*, July 1913; 'Twelve Months of Train
     Wrecks', *Literary Digest*, 28 December 1912.

63   Foster 1939, pp. 146–8.

64   U.S. Congress 1916, X, pp. 9756, 9761–2, 9768–72, 9787, 9791, 9880, 9911; Montgomery
     1974, *passim*; Adams 1966, pp. 129, 143; *Machinists Monthly Journal*, August 1911; *Railway
     Carmen's Journal*, Feburary 1913; May 1913; *American Engineer*, May 1913.

65   U.S. Congress 1916, X, pp. 9787, 9816, 9818.

in the South and Southwest; 533 strikers were jailed; 91 percent of the men were forced to move out of their dwellings to cheaper accommodations; 50 percent of the strikers were reduced to living off charity; and 16 workers committed suicide as a direct consequence of the conflict.[66]

While the strikers were far from passive, it must be noted that much of this violence was precipitated by the company, which regarded the working-class rejection of efficiency measures as an encroachment upon managerial prerogatives. Denigrating the skilled craftsmen who manned the shops, two company officials, Graham and Kruttschmitt, voiced the opinion that the strike was 'simply a demand that they [the carmen] be put in control of the company's shopwork; that they should be given the power to dictate whether any shopwork could be done or not; and if so, the conditions under which it should be done'.[67] Nothing was so repulsive to the efficiency-conscious manager as workers' control of the productive process and it was this issue which the shopmen implicitly raised. The railroad workers' ability to launch a struggle of such acuteness, over the duration of four years, suffering intense personal losses all the while, revealed the depth of their hatred for capital's recent drive to 'rationalise' production.

If the carmen's strike exemplified the pre-war response to efficiency, the war years – supposedly an era of transition in which both labour and management mellowed towards one another – represented no real break in the continuity of working-class rebellion. Despite the pervasiveness of the 'no strike during wartime pledge', Alexander Bing found that 'more strikes did occur at this time than during any previous period of similar length in the United States'. Although many of these clashes were simply attempts to secure higher wages under optimum conditions for labour (a constricted labour market coupled with the dictates of wartime production), a significant number of strikes were rooted in grievances emanating from the application of various efficiency measures. Following the massive walkouts of the textile workers in Massachusetts and Rhode Island in May of 1918, 1,800 weavers struck the American Woolen Company for the abolition of the premium system. Wartime workers initiated a concerted offensive against piece work and bonus systems, and where strikes were deemed inappropriate, disgruntled workers resorted to 'soldiering' and absenteeism to curtail production. At the very time when AFL leaders and Taylor's dedicated following were 'consumating their

---

66   U.S. Congress 1916, X, pp. 9937–44; Adams 1966, p. 142; *Railway Carmen's Journal,* April 1913; *Machinists Monthly Journal,* January 1923.

67   U.S. Congress 1916, X, pp. 9895, 9907–8. Cf. Adams 1966, p. 143.

celebrated reconciliation', workers' opposition forced the National War Labor Board to abolish incentive pay and bonus systems in a number of prominent firms.[68]

In the needle trades, which by the early years of the Great Depression would witness efficiency's ultimate triumph, the war years were distinguished by persistent calls for the worker to control the nature and conditions of work. Approaching efficiency and the problems it posed somewhat differently than more orthodox unionists, the socialist immigrants in the clothing industry criticised the inefficiency of the new managers. They rejected piece work and struck hard at the harsh, and often unwarranted, discipline of the foremen. The preamble of the Amalgamated Clothing Workers of America, adopted in May of 1918, reflected the militancy of the garment workers: 'The industrial and inter-industrial organization, built upon the solid rock of clear knowledge and class consciousness, will put the organized working class in actual control of the system of production, and the working class will then be ready to take possession of it'. By calling for *actual control* the 'new unionism' left no ambiguity as to its lack of respect for managerial authority.[69]

The 'new unionist' tactic of rejecting the pretensions of a 'scientific' management represented a consciousness that only the working class, because of its skill and experience in production, could restructure work relationships along lines of efficiency. This critique appeared to gain momentum in the post-war years as Joseph Schlossberg addressed the Amalgamated Clothing Workers to 'establish order in the industry in the place of the chaos created when the employers had their own way'.[70] Clinton S. Golden, noting the 'sorry mess of things' created by the efficiency experts, called attention to:

> The tremendous difficulty of our Russian comrades in successfully administering the machinery of production, distribution and exchange after they had seized it in the interests of the workers; then being compelled to rely to a large extent on the technicians, managers and experts of the old regime; the awful sabotage practiced by this class causes the student of social and industrial changes to marvel at the fact that the Russian work-

---

68   Bing 1921, pp. 156, 138, 205, 209–10, 242. Cf. Montgomery 1974, *passim*.

69   On the triumph of efficiency in the needle trades in the 1930s and the subsequent debasement of a craft see Hardy 1935, pp. 189–95; Seidman 1942, pp. 76, 103–4, 118. The quote from the preamble of the ACWA is from Budish and Doule 1966, p. 307, cf. pp. 37, 136, 202, 275, 263, 336–9.

70   Schlossberg is quoted in Clark 1920, p. 59, cited in Montgomery 1974, p. 529.

ers are still in the saddle. Surely their experiences should furnish us with an object lesson on the difficulties to be surmounted before the workers of this country can hope for anything like industrial freedom.

To Golden the managerial elite was both inefficient and, more to the point, a class enemy: the AFL's strategy of allying with experts to increase production was seen to be fraught with pitfalls. Golden preferred to have workers organise themselves 'to gain control of management of the industry which is *theirs* by every right'.[71]

With the advent of Henry Ford's mass-production techniques in the auto industry, much of Taylor's method was translated from the machine-shop to the auto plant, the rubber works and the electrical industry.[72] In the first few years of the 1920s, rationalisation became the guiding premise of an emerging school of productive technique and efficiency. Needless to say, this development wrought havoc with working people's lives. One German observer described American factory hands as 'bound to the conveyor the way the galley slaves were bound to the vessel'.[73] The transition from the old to the new management at the White Motor Company of Cleveland from 1920–3 was documented by Wyndham Mortimer: while 'production rose over one hundred percent ... earnings increased about twelve percent'. With the arrival of strange men, premium plans and that most abhorrent of apparati, the stop watch, old ideas and allegiances to a paternalistic employer vanished and the 'men came closer together as workers'.[74] Even in the doldrums of the 1920s, with organised labour rendered relatively impotent in the face of the open shop of the employers, sporadic outbursts of reaction against efficiency measures came to the forefront. Clayton Fountain, a young auto worker at the Briggs Mack Avenue plant in 1929, chronicled the workers' dissatisfaction with piece work and their subsequent reaction, a 'quickie' sit-down strike which won concessions from their boss.[75]

The argument that labour opposed the integration of efficiency measures into the work process could be extended to the sit-downs of the 1930s,[76] the

---

71   Clinton S. Golden, 'The Workers and Problems of Management', *Machinists Monthly Journal*, 34, April 1922.

72   Links between Fordism and Taylorism are made explicit in Sward 1972, pp. 33–5.

73   Adamic 1931, pp. 401–2; 1938, p. 408; Bimba 1927, pp. 221–5.

74   Mortimer 1971, pp. 48–9.

75   Fountain 1949, pp. 28–9; Brecher 1972, pp. 234–6.

76   A careful reading of the extant sources dealing with the sit-downs reveals that a major preoccupation of the discontent culminating in plant takeovers was the speed of the line,

wildcat struggles of the early World War II years,[77] and indeed to the labour militancy of the late 1960s and early 1970s which erupted so startlingly at Lordstown, Ohio and other centres of American industry.[78] Sociologically, numerous articles document the development of a work ethos which opposes, with considerable ingenuity and sophistication, the symbolic and tangible aspects of managerial authority.[79] Although such studies reveal much about the persistence of labour's opposition to the tenets of efficiency, a discussion of such matters transcends the immediate concerns of this paper.

The essence of efficiency had always been the expansion of capitalistic production and the rationalisation of the organisation of work; from this inevitably flowed the by-product of bourgeois hegemony. In the post-war years the drive for efficient and rational production became more subtle and, in many ways, more effective. And yet efficiency, despite its adoption of more sophisticated techniques of repression, never altered its conceptual framework, in which labour was perceived as one of many inputs in the productive process. Given the basic continuity of the managerial view of labour it is worth considering the possibility that labour's response, originally one of intense and undeniable opposition, was also characterised by continuity.

Conclusions

In conclusion we can see that the years 1903–22 witnessed a significant transformation in the dominant view of labour. As industrial capitalism matured

---

piece work complaints and the rigours of shop discipline – all measures of efficiency rooted in the developments of the Progressive Era. See Kraus 1947, pp. 8–9; Adamic 1931, p. 402; Adamic 1938, pp. 362, 402; McKenney 1939, p. 134; Fine 1969, p. 321. Brecher correctly concluded that 'Workers had used the sitdown to establish a direct counterpower to management – freedom to set the pace of work, to tell the foreman where to get off, to share the work equitably, to determine their share of the profit, and the like' (Brecher 1972, p. 213).

77   The wildcat traditions of the early 1940s directly countered attempts by management or capital to secure greater wartime output. See Brecher 1972, pp. 221–31; Morris 1949, pp. 399–417; Kerr 1949, pp. 43–76.

78   On the 'new mood of working class militancy', often a direct response to the rationalisation of the work process, see Brecher 1972, pp. 264–93; Aronowitz 1973, pp. 1–133; Serrin 1973, pp. 219–42; Judson Gooding, 'Blue Collar Blues on the Assembly Line', *Fortune*, July 1970; Emma Rothschild, 'GM in More Trouble', *New York Review of Books*, 23 March 1972; Barbara Garson, 'Luddites in Lordstown', *Harper's Magazine*, June 1972.

79   Roy 1969, pp. 359–79; and Roy's earlier articled cited therein.

it required rationalisation: first, over its internal distributive and bookkeeping functions; and secondly, over the nature and conditions of work. While the systematic managers of the 1890s resolved the first deficiency, the 'scientific managers' of the early twentieth century, proponents of a vigorous efficiency, went a long way towards securing, for capital, control over the processes of work. Under the imperatives of the need for hegemony within work relationships, the social regard with which the 'producing classes' had been held in the late nineteenth century was undermined. Such developments readily lent themselves to the rise of the industrial capitalist as a preeminent social and economic force.

Continuously assaulting the working class's perception of its self-worth, the efficiency experts played a large part in undermining the populist view of labour which had been so widespread in the Gilded Age. John Stevenson, a Professor at New York University in 1914, expressed the tendency to see labour as merely another appendage of capital, intrinsically worthless, dangerous without a well-defined master: 'Unskilled labour is merely animated machinery for rough work and adds very little to the final produce ... One E.H. Harriman is of more lasting service to the nation than would be 1,000,000 of unskilled labourers, without Harriman they would be a menace'.[80]

With labour so denigrated, and mechanisation eroding skill levels at a quickening pace, capital and its managers launched a concerted attack upon the autonomy of the skilled craftsman and rigidified the structure of discipline dominating work relationships. The transformation from a populistic to a managerial view of labour thus mirrored two social processes: the dilution of the craftsman's skill; and the employer's attainment of a more pervasive control over the work process. Workers, particularly in skilled trades, where remnants of an earlier artisan mode of work remained, responded to these changes with a vengeance. Granting the complexity of the labour-management-capital relationship, it is nevertheless clear that many workers resented the solidification of managerial authority which inevitably accompanied the rationalisation of the work process.

While this paper has sacrificed precision – we have admittedly made no attempt to assess conditions within specific industries, nor have we paid sufficient attention to divisions within the working class and the consequent differential response to efficiency[81] – in order to develop an overview, it is suggestive

---

80   Stevenson 1914, pp. 459–70, cited in Adams 1966, p. 167.
81   Katherine Stone (Stone 1974, *passim*) and David Montgomery's unpublished work remain indicators of the potential that might be realised by more specific studies. Brief comment

of two hypotheses deserving of further research. First, there is the extent to which the thrust for efficiency contributed to the attainment of what could be termed bourgeois hegemony. Such a perspective necessarily undermines the corporate liberalist interpretation and explanation of the subordinate position of labour and the preeminent status of capital in the modern epoch.[82] Second, our brief glimpse of the working-class response to efficiency questions the validity of traditional conceptions of the labour-efficiency relationship. What Irving Bernstein has referred to as 'a friendship ... blossoming into a love affair' probably never existed; it was certainly never consummated.[83]

---

on the ethnic response to efficiency include: John Golden, 'Scientific Management in the Textile Industry', *American Federationist*, August 1911; Korman 1967, pp. 77–84; and Leiserson 1921, pp. 66–76; 169–233.

82   The corporate liberal argument is presented in Weinstein 1968, *passim*; Radosh 1969, *passim*; and Radosh 1966, pp. 66–88. Philip Foner's rebuttal of the Radosh article remains the only critique of the corporatist model, and it is necessarily restricted in scope. The Weinstein-Radosh thesis thus awaits a comprehensive critique.

83   Bernstein 1960, p. 102.

PART 3

Class Struggle in the Aftermath of the Post-War Settlement

∴

Introduction to Part 3

The nature of class struggle in Canada and the United States changed dramatically in the late 1940s. As a plethora of studies, often conflicting in their assessment of meaning, have established, what workers struggled to achieve shifted in the aftermath of the Second World War. Although the nature of this change contained subtle differences, not only regionally but between different industrial sectors, a general reordering of the lives of workers took place because of a legal recognition of collective bargaining rights and the rise of the welfare state. Both of these achievements owed much, if not everything, to the class struggles of the past, for the kinds of concessions that were made in the late 1940s and beyond would not have been implemented were it not for the pressures exerted by trade unions and other social movements that demanded the expansion of civil rights.

In any case, the arrival of what scholars have come to call the post-war settlement institutionalised what is now designated industrial pluralism or industrial legality. Trade unions were now recognized legal bodies, unlike the illegal conspiracies in constraint of trade that they had often been regarded as in the nineteenth century. Organised workers won rights and entitlements that extended beyond anything imagined by earlier beleaguered members of craft unions, Knights of Labor local assemblies, or red-card carrying Industrial Workers of the World. What seemed unfathomable to workers of the 1930s was often, by the late 1950s, taken for granted.

With this great victory, achieving working-class rights to union recognition and the entitlement to bargain wage rates, job conditions, and other terms of employment, which had long been seen as the sole prerogative of the boss, came certain constraints. For what the state granted, it could, of course, take away; what the system of industrial legality sanctified necessarily demanded adherence to certain practices.

The contract, so sought after for decades, was not just a legal recognition of rights. It was also an obligation to adhere to specific responsibilities; demands that unions and their members follow through on this pact with a certain kind of devil were enforceable by courts, jails, and the armed might of the state. Before the post-war settlement, workers were guided by the maxim that their collective strength dictated what they might do. Even if their power paled in comparison to that of employers, who could call on agencies of state authority to act in their interest, workers might well, especially in times of economic prosperity, twist the arm of capital in ways that secured tangible gains for labour. Often their actions flowed from a sense that they could 'strike now, grieve later', a recognition that if there was something wrong it was possible to mobilise workers' antagonism in job actions that were meant to elicit the employer's immediate response, so as to avoid costly bottlenecks in the production process. Quickie strikes, spontaneous walkouts, even sit-downs, were expressions of workers' power and extended the reach of a galvanising solidarity that addressed immediate grievance with at least the possibility of immediate gratification. As signed collective agreements came to dominate the understanding of what was possible in the aftermath of the post-war settlement, workers were held to the responsibility of fulfilling their productive commitment, and a curb was placed on when and how workers might take forceful job action. The courts were there to enforce this, and police, federal troops, and National Guardsmen were often brought in to patrol picket lines, seeing to it that judicially-ordered injunctions were obeyed, as well as arresting strikers who violated legal norms.

Early signed agreements between workers and their employers might, as late as the 1920s and 1930s, constitute a few handwritten leaves of paper, but by the 1960s trade unions relied more and more on teams of legal experts to negotiate contracts that could run into hundreds of pages. Whereas union advocates and shop stewards had once been forced to meet face to face with rank-and-file members and collect their individual dues, under the regime of industrial legality workers' monthly union payments were deducted from their paycheques by employers, who deposited the entire workforce's dues payments into union bank accounts. The consequence of these developments was a growing separation of leaders and led, an inevitable bureaucratisation of union officialdoms, and a consequent dampening of militancy. Striking during the life of the contract was illegal, and subject to fines that might drain union treasuries and result in imprisonment of those increasingly rare labour movement leaders who refused to keep their unruly ranks in line. Instead of mobilising workers' anger and resentment, unions were often called upon to keep the temper of class conflict in check, to police the hotheads who might foment discord and throw up a spontaneous picket line in defiance of the industrial order sanctioned by the collective agreement.

All of this took place, moreover, at the same time that trade-union officialdoms waged an internal war against communist and other dissident forces inside the workers' movement. The Cold War that pitted the two superpowers – the United States as the leader of the Free World colossus and the Soviet Union as the advancing edge of a threatening communism – against one another in a relentless struggle for global dominance, was also fought out in the unions. Members of the Communist Party were eventually, by the mid-1950s, largely vanquished, and certainly subdued, in what amounted to an orgy of labour movement red-baiting.

Workers remained, of course, antagonists of their capitalist employers and the state that so often served the powerful interests of the corporations; unions continued to be locked into struggles with their longstanding adversaries. Collective agreements were still the site of contested negotiations, and as they often broke down, the strike was anything but obsolete. But there is no denying that with the post-war settlement organised labour was contained within the industrial relations system, in which unions, employers, and the state were all expected to play particular roles, monitored by codes, courts, councils, and a variety of coercive forces, all of which were now part of a project of containing the tumultuous class relations of advanced capitalism.[1]

By the mid-1960s the post-war settlement was wearing thin. A new generation of workers, unaffiliated with the red-baiting Cold War struggles of the 1950s and unschooled in the pragmatism of accommodation, was increasingly disaffected. These young workers had grown into their jobs in a context of relative economic affluence; they had known nothing like the Great Depression, and, not having experienced the rough-and-tumble class struggles that won collective bargaining rights over the course of the late 1930s and throughout the 1940s, they regarded the hard-won victories of a past era as routine entitlements. Like its counterpart in the universities, this youthful demographic cohort in the unions posed a rebellious challenge to constituted authority. It bent its knee to no boss, regardless of whether such a figure was ensconced in the corporation, the union, or the state. No doubt aided and advised by older militants,[2] these youthful working-class rebels may not have had a cause, but by the mid-1960s they were sufficiently fed up with the bureaucratic 'establishment' to express themselves in collective protests that defied distant trade-union leaderships, seemingly complacent layers of the state apparatus that monitored the institutions of labour-capital regulation, and recalcitrant employers, whose resistance to rising wages and a crescendo of apparently endless proletarian demand caused them to dig their heels into the proverbial 'bottom line'. The result, in Canada, was the 1965–6 'wildcat wave', an unprecedented explosion of strikes that took place outside the boundaries of collective agreements. As the post-war settlement appeared to unravel amidst the violence of picket lines that were not officially sanctioned by unions, young militants in the labour movement challenged the social order in factories and mines, on postal beats and in

---

1   For the US, three studies published in the 1980s remain indispensable: Harris 1982; Tomlins 1985; and Goldfield 1987. My own most explicit statement for Canada remains Palmer 2005, with another view expressed in MacDowell 2001.

2   See McInnis 2012.

teamster-driven trucks, doing something like what their counterparts in universities did in classrooms and teach-ins. Whereas the one group marched the streets outside of United States embassies, expressing its opposition to the war in Vietnam, the other battled police and shouted down trade-union presidents in the streets adjacent to sprawling industrial plants like Hamilton's Steel Company of Canada. My study of this labour upheaval, 'Wildcat Workers in the 1960s: The Unruly Face of Class Struggle', was written for a larger and more broad-ranging account entitled *Canada's 1960s: The Ironies of Identity in a Rebellious Era*, published in 2009.

Less than twenty years later, after such 1960s protests, little was left of the post-war settlement in Canada. As Leo Panitch and Donald Swartz have shown, in a widely read, oft-republished, and rightly influential study, now titled *The Assault on Trade Union Freedoms*,[3] the 'good times' that had fuelled the engines of both production and the relative class harmony associated with the flush years of the post-war settlement lasted barely a quarter of a century.

The wildcat strikes of the mid-1960s were an opening shot in the war that would ensue as this always fragile class harmony started to break down. In 1965–6 the battleground was around wage demands seen by capital and the state to be fuelling inflation, which seemed to be soaring in a dangerous upward spiral. But during the wildcat wave almost any other demand might trigger illegal job actions as well, including some that many in corporate boardrooms, newspaper editorial offices, judicial bodies, and state agencies thought outrageous.

By 1975, the gloves came off as the state stepped in to hammer workers into compliance with a programme of wage-and-price controls that placed a hard cap on workers' take-home pay while it loosely tried to exercise moral suasion in restraint of prices. The end of seeming post-war affluence, which always contained significant poverty, inequality, and economic imbalances, had arrived by the early-to-mid 1970s. Like most states in the advanced capitalist economies of the west, Canada and its provinces were feeling the pinch of tough times by 1973: resource revenues were flagging and the economy was obviously battling the perplexing threat posed by a flat lining of production (stagnation) and the upward creep of all of the costs of doing business (inflation). As Panitch and Swartz show, governments, more and more influenced by the rightward trajectory of ideological trends, and the emerging hegemony of what was crystallising as a neo-liberal attack on trade-union and welfare-state entitlements, addressed a growing fiscal crisis by implementing restraint. This meant cutting

---

3   Panitch and Swartz 1986, 1988, 1993.

back on the social expenditure associated with universal programmes whose purpose was to provide the vulnerable with a series of social safety nets, and suppressing trade-union freedoms, thereby erecting barriers to the wage push that many in corporate and government circles regarded as the decisive force behind surging inflation. The result was a virtual outlawing of strikes in the public sector. Almost all work associated with the state was declared an essential service exempt from the 'rules' of collective bargaining. Canada's post-war settlement, first assailed by wildcat strikers in 1965–6, was now being dismantled from above, as the state attacked and employers in the private sector took their cues from initiatives that proclaimed the need for 'downsizing' and 'cut backs'. Class war was revived, waged relentlessly from above.

Nowhere was this clearer than in Canada's west/left coast province, British Columbia (BC). The province had long abandoned the mainstream players in an electoral politics of Canadian federalism, in which Liberals and Conservatives contend for power. Instead, in BC the provincial parties were more clearly aligned with politics judged to the left or to the right of the centre. In 1983, a newly elected Social Credit government held the reins of power, and its political orientation was decidedly rightward leaning. Social Credit took its cues from the Chicago School of Milton Friedman, its local think tank being the free marketeering ideologues of the Fraser Institute. The first 1980s budget introduced by the Socreds took decisive aim at trade unions, welfare state provisioning, and all manner of so-called 'special interest groups' that needed, in the eyes of a right wing on a roll, to be curbed and brought to heel. The result was a massive mobilisation of resistance, known as the Solidarity Coalition and Operation Solidarity.

I was personally affiliated with this movement that sought to turn back the budget measures proposed by the Socreds and the provincial premier, Bill Bennett. I served as a delegate from the New Westminister Solidarity Coalition; a contributor to the newspaper of the movement, *Solidarity Times*; a figure often interviewed by mainstream radio, TV and press; a participant in rallies and demonstrations; and someone on strike for a time at Simon Fraser University, where I taught in the History Department. Months of protest, in which large and militant demonstrations were commonplace, culminated in public-sector strikes that threatened to break into a full-scale General Strike. How this was derailed is the story of my essay 'Reformism and the Fight Against the Right: British Columbia's *Solidarity*', a distillation of a larger argument that appeared in a short book I published in 1987, *Solidarity: The Rise and Fall of an Opposition in British Columbia*.

The events in British Columbia in 1983 were a tragic defeat, and impressed upon me, like no other historical event I had lived through, the necessity for

Marxists, whatever their field of expertise, to lay bare, in unvarnished, truthful ways, both our understandings of the world and our desire to see it changed. Doing this necessarily means exposing those forces – however much they may appear to be aligned with the project of progressive politics – that hold us back, and which too often condemn us to a sad denouement. Telling this kind of Marxist truth is never easy, and it seldom wins you much in the way of conventional reward. But it is, in my view, fundamental to what I value in the endeavour of Marxism and historical practice.

CHAPTER 6

Wildcat Workers in the 1960s: The Unruly Face of Class Struggle[*]

> The wildcat strike might be regarded as the trade union equivalent of the students' sit-in.
>
> ED FINN, 'The New Militancy of Canadian Labour', *Canadian Dimension*, November–December, 1965

⁖

Workers and their unions appeared relatively secure as they entered the 1960s. With the apparent attainment of collective bargaining rights secured at the end of the 1940s, an historic breakthrough appeared to have been realised in what was championed as a new era of 'industrial pluralism'. The Cold War vanquishing of the communists in the labour movement seemed to secure trade unions a measure of respectability, although, to be sure, there were always rough patches in the accord reached among employers, workers' organisations, and the state in the immediate post-World War II period. With fractious components of the Canadian workers' movement coming together in the Canadian Labour Congress in 1956, old divides separating craft and industrial unions were proclaimed to have been overcome, and there were signs that an awakening trade unionism in Quebec could well link arms with its counterparts across the country. Combined with the general climate of post-World War II affluence, in which employment possibilities were strong and employers' capacities to offer concessions seemingly expansive, the times seemed propitious for Canadian workers. The prospects for trade unions to continue their upward trajectory appeared good.

Few recognised the contradictions at the heart of labour's new found security. Older trade unionists and most labour leaders, for instance, knew well

---

[*] 'Wildcat Workers in the 1960s: The Unruly Face of Class Struggle', in *Labouring Canada: Class, Race, and Gender in Canadian Working-Class History*, edited by Bryan D. Palmer and Joan Sangster (Toronto: Oxford University Press, 2008), 373–94.

that it had taken a century to establish a state-monitored system of industrial relations that recognised workers' legal rights to join unions and bargain collectively with businesses and their management. Workers' leaders, then, were hardly in a position to guard against the ways in which the post-war settlement would move trade unions in increasingly legalistic directions, nor were they, understandably, all that concerned with problems that would be posed for workers and their organisations as the labour movement necessarily grew more and more bureaucratised. Basking in the warm glow of working-class accomplishment, barely a labour eyebrow was raised in recognition that what the state gave it could also, when pressures were brought to bear, take away. It would take decades before such concerns surfaced. They would not really be discernible until the fiscal crisis of the Canadian state manifested itself blatantly in the mid-1970s, and Pierre Elliott Trudeau's Liberals imposed wage and price controls, initiating a legislative assault on trade-union freedoms that would be picked up with a vengeance by Conservative, even New Democratic Party, governments in the 1980s and 1990s. Masking the cracks in the edifice of the post-war settlement were a host of 1960s developments. These included the expanding infrastructure of 'social safety net provisioning', which encompassed tremendous growth and stabilisation of health and education programmes and facilities; state commitment to principles of universality in family allowances and unemployment insurance; and a range of initiatives that took aim at the reduction of poverty or targeted youth as specific beneficiaries of state largesse, training, and aid.[1]

But the emergence of resentment and grievance in the arena of class struggle did nevertheless emerge in the 1960s.[2] In particular, it surfaced with a vengeance in 1964–6. This was at precisely the same point that protest was also emerging in other quarters. Radical nationalist agitation was developing in Quebec. Students were gravitating toward both countercultural alternative and the politics of challenge and dissent. Women were beginning to voice their discontents with a status quo that kept them confined to the constrained possibilities of a feminine sphere. Not surprisingly, as was the case elsewhere, the young led the way. Their vehicle of protest, driven by a rage and violence that was itself an expression of the frustrations of alienation and marginalisation

---

1   As an introduction to the unravelling of the post-war settlement and the contours of contemporary class struggle unfolding in its wake, see Panitch and Swartz 1993; Reshef and Rastin 2003; Palmer 2005, pp. 334–46; High 2003.

2   For a preface to the class confrontation of the decade see MacDowell 1971; Gindin 1995, pp. 139–66; Roberts 1990, pp. 91–104.

common to a wider generational revolt, was the single working-class act of rebellion that a major architect of the post-war settlement, Justice Ivan Rand, had been at pains to suppress. Rand's historic post-war packaging of trade unionism's rights and obligations in the era of 'industrial pluralism' had emerged out of his arbitration decision settling the tumultuous 1945 strike at Windsor's massive Ford plant. As the so-called Rand formula became the guiding light of Canada's modern industrial-relations system, unions were recognised as legitimate agents in the new order, but they were expected to enforce certain standards on their ranks, the most exalted of which was the sanctity of the collective agreement. The traditional weapon of workers, the withdrawal of their services in strike action, was thus never to be used until the collective agreement had run its course, bargaining efforts to reach new agreement had failed, and both labour and capital had exhausted all measures to keep the production that Rand thought pivotal to Canada's 'good life' going. Wildcat strikes, protests in which workers walked off the job in defiance of their contractual obligation not to disrupt the economics of peaceful class coexistence during the life of collective agreements, were the mid-1960s voice of an aggrieved, and youthful, layer of workers waging a most difficult war. For not only did this military-like campaign array itself against the traditional enemy, capital, it also found itself confronting two other powerful structures: the seemingly benevolent state and the embodiment of workers' mechanisms of defence, the trade union and its increasingly hierarchical officialdom.

The Demography of Dissent[3]

The Canadian labour force, like Canadian society in general, grew younger over the course of the 1960s. Whereas people between the ages of 15 and 24 accounted for 15.3 percent of the country's population in 1951, by the 1970s this figure was approaching nineteen percent.

In the pivotally important 1964–6 years, male youth were overwhelmingly concentrated in waged employment. If these young workers were the best schooled generation of working-class youth in Canadian history, they were nevertheless not yet beneficiaries of a mid-to-late 1960s education boom that saw

---

3   The following section draws directly on the evidence and argument in Palmer 1992, pp. 278–80. Much of the raw data is drawn from the 'Labour Force' tables in Leacy 1983. See, as well, Panitch and Swartz 1993, pp. 14–16; Jamieson 1968, pp. 480–3; and for a more general discussion of youth and its influence in the 1960s, Owram 1996.

a tremendous expansion of college and university facilities and the first serious possibility of lower-income youth taking advantage of what higher education had to offer. Only 11 percent of Canadians aged 18–24 were enrolled in university in 1965, with slightly less than fifteen percent of those aged 20–24 having any university experience at all.[4] Unlike young, working-class women, moreover, males in this age bracket were less likely to be reined in by family responsibilities, whether that involved care of the young or the old. The result was that in the mid-1960s, roughly eighty-eight percent of all males aged 20–24 were in the civilian labour force, compared to approximately fifty-four percent of women of the same age cohort. This gendered demographic explains much of the wildness of the wildcats, which were most emphatically male undertakings, marked by bravado and the macho posturing of youth in a pre-feminist working-class cultural moment. Understandably, as well, younger workers entered the workforce with less security than their older counterparts, and unemployment rates for the young in the mid-1960s indicated that their jobs were far more precarious than those in the 25–44 and 45–65 age groups. Young workers from 14–24 years of age faced unemployment rates of from 16.4 to 9.7 and 11.8 to 5.3 percent over the first half of the 1960s; comparable rates for older workers never reached much more than seven percent and sometimes bottomed out at just under three percent.[5]

Working-class youth, of course, were drawn into the same countercultural cauldron as their non-proletarian peers.[6] Many young workers lived at home, and resentment of adult – often patriarchal – authority fused domestic and workplace resentment in a populistic assault on 'the Establishment', an imprecise target that often seemed to lump together anyone over the age of 30 with the bastions of social and economic power. One 1968 study, addressing Canadian industrial relations, noted 'an undeniable tendency in this generation to question and challenge authority itself and those in a position to exercise it'.[7] As music, drugs, sex, fashion, and a generational tendency to refuse all authority

---

4   As evidence from Axelrod 1982, especially p. 41, suggests, while enrolment in and expenditure on higher education rose substantially from 1962–8, it would not be until the later years of this period that such trends would register in relevance for working-class youth. See as well Porter 1965, and for numerical data for the mid-1960s, Roussopoulos 1970, p. 136; Reid 1969, p. 7.

5   Aside from the quantitative data drawn from Leacy 1983, note Rinehart 1975, pp. 4, 57, 70; Humphries 1968, p. 610; Gil Levine, 'The Coming Youth Revolt in Labour', *Labour Gazette*, November 1971.

6   As introductions only see Kostash 1980, especially pp. 107–44; Westhues 1975, pp. 394–8.

7   Woods 1968, p. 99. Although from a slightly later period, note as well Gil Levine, 'The Coming Youth Revolt in Labour', *Labour Gazette*, November 1971.

congealed in an increasingly public and often consumer-paced popular culture of age differentiation,[8] a 'them vs. us' discontent coalesced among Canadian youth, who echoed the lyrics of the 1965 British rock anthem, 'My Generation'. Recorded by Peter Townshend and The Who, the song, presented with a patented stutter, was among the hardest-hitting statements of a newly-combative rock 'n' roll:

> People try to put us d-down, talking 'bout my
>   generation
> Just because we get around, talking 'bout my
>   generation
> Things they do look awful c-c-cold, talking
>   'bout my generation
> Hope I die before I get old, talking 'bout my
>   generation
> Why don't you all f-fade away, talkin' 'bout
>   my generation
> And don't try to dig what we all s-s-say, talkin'
>   'bout my generation
> I'm not trying to cause a big s-s-sensation,
>   talkin' 'bout my generation
> I'm just talking 'bout my g-g-g-generation,
>   talking 'bout my generation.
>   TOWNSHEND, 1965

Often perceived as a product of campus rebellion, this widening youth culture of discontent was, in actuality, far more widespread, and it affected the trade unions as well as the university classroom. 'Less cerebral, less able to articulate his discontent than the young student demonstrator', the youthful rebel within the mid-1960s trade union cause was nonetheless animated by the same spirit of discontent and alienation as his campus counterpart, according to senior labour commentator Ed Finn. As Finn's use of the masculine to identify discontent suggests, the wildcats were largely perceived as a male phenomenon.[9]

---

8   For a particularly virulent attack on the superficial aspects of youth revolt see Peter Desbarats, 'The Most Forgettable Generation: A Sad Glance at the Exhausted New Wave of Revolutionary Youth', *Saturday Night*, September 1969.

9   Ed Finn, 'The New Militancy of Canadian Labour', *Canadian Dimension*, November–December 1965. In the United States, a number of journalistic commentators focused on the growing

Eight years later, one union old-timer in Winnipeg's Transcona and Symington railway yards looked back on decades of labour-capital conflict, commenting on the rebelliousness of his younger co-workers. They were apparently seething with anger after union leaders forced the end of a job action and the provincial New Democratic Party government 'sold [striking workers] out for 4 cents an hour'. 'We've got three enemies', asserted the veteran militant, 'the company, the government and the union. We can't beat them all now, but we are starting something. It's the young guys that are responsible for this. They started it. If it weren't for them we wouldn't be here now. They're different. They're fearless. They don't give a damn for the company or the government or the union'. Memories of 1966 reverberated in this account. Young workers drew on this reservoir of a recent past to frame stories about how supervisors had to be kept in line; strike duty was thought to be 'more fun' if it was voluntary and spontaneous. The rebel workers insisted that they were no more likely to snap to attention if the boss shouting orders at them was from the union or the company. 'We're our own boss now'. The old-timer nodded in agreement. 'It's a new generation', he proclaimed.[10]

The revolt of the young within unions thus had a profound impact on class relations in the mid-1960s. It not only upped the level and nature of the conflict with employers, it also threatened the capacity of the state to contain struggles within respected boundaries of legalism and industrial pluralism, and it rocked the boat of trade unionism itself. Youthful rebels had none of the political baggage of their older labour-movement leaders. They had not experienced the anti-communist purges of the 1950s. Few had cultivated intense loyalties to a layer of social democratic trade union officials. And this younger generation had not, for the most part, known the difficult, insecure, and often violently vindictive times of the Great Depression and before, to which their fathers and mothers had a more organic connection through family or direct experience.[11] Younger workers took for granted much that their older predecessors and union leaders had struggled for, often at great cost and considerable sacrifice. As the

alienation of young workers in the late 1960s, and the consequent eruption of 'blue collar blues' and trade union rebelliousness. See Judson Gooding, 'Blue Collar Blues on the Assembly Line', *Fortune Magazine*, July 1970; 'Strike Fever ... And the Public Interest', *Life Magazine*, 26 August 1966; Weller n.d.; Watson 1971; Rothschild 1973. Serrin 1973, p. 39 notes that the number of official grievances at General Motors in the United States rose from 6,000 in 1960 to 256,000 in 1969.

10   'Trouble on the Line', *Canadian Dimension*, August–September 1973.

11   'Wildcat Strike Poses Question: Are Leaders Out of Touch with Members?', *Globe and Mail*, 19 November 1965.

post-war settlement delivered tangible benefits to unions, older leaders had grown cautious in their protections of the valued stabilities that had resulted. As Finn noted:

> Approximately 80 per cent of Canada's top labour leaders are between the ages of 50 and 70. Many of them have grown more conservative with the passing years, more wedded to the old ways and the old traditions. They fail to see the need for drastic changes in the structure and policies of the labour movement if it is to cope with automation, industrial and technological change, and other pressing challenges of the 1960s and 1970s. And while the leaders of most unions have aged, the turnover in their membership has brought in many thousands of young workers who are not tied to old union methods and traditions. Better educated, more aggressive, these younger workers have strong ideas about what they want and how to get it. They are taking over the leadership at the local level, and their radicalism often brings them into sharp conflict with the comparatively conservative leaders at the top.[12]

Writing in *Saturday Night*, Mungo James discussed the mid-1960s 'new ferment' in the unions, attributing it 'to the arrival, for the first time in any numbers, of the young, swinging, questioning generation'. In Quebec, one local labour activist noted that, '[i]t used to be that we waited for orders from the union representative, but that is not the way with the young people'. Murray Cottrell, a veteran unionist associated with the powerful United Steel Workers of America (USWA), summed up the problem of class relations as it appeared in the mid-1960s: 'These kids won't take it. They expect to be treated like human beings'.[13]

The Meaning of Wildcatting

One aspect of Cottrell's conclusion that youthful workers were refusing to 'take it' that was not easily understood or accepted by older unionists was that this

---

12   Ed Finn, 'The New Militancy of Canadian Labour', *Canadian Dimension*, November–December 1965.

13   Mungo James, 'Labour Lays it On the Line', *Saturday Night*, December 1966; Dumas 1974, p. 117. Note, also, Crispo and Arthurs 1968, pp. 237–64; Gil Levine, 'The Coming Youth Revolt in Labour', Labour Gazette, November 1971.

stand meant that the young were not only in revolt against employers and the state, but also against the union. An illegal railway striker in Montreal said, simply, that dissidents were 'fed up with excuses from their union leaders'.[14] The 1968 Task Force on Canadian Industrial Relations, headed by McGill University's H.D. Woods, pointed out that worker dissatisfaction in the mid-1960s was sometimes running 'as deeply against the union and collective bargaining as against management', producing a worrisome 'rebellion of union members against their leaders'.[15] Wildcat strikes were *the* most decisive articulation of this process, violating the legality of a contract, posing a threat to union security. Labour organisations found such rank-and-file rebellion threatening, for if they failed to uphold their legal responsibilities within the Canadian post-war settlement, trade unions could be subject to crippling financial penalties in the form of fines, often calculated as a daily sum per union member in defiance of the contract. Depending on the duration of the wildcat, such financial penalties might total hundreds of thousands, even millions, of dollars. As local and international treasuries were the material and symbolic measure of trade unionism's new-found security, this hit labour's developing bureaucracy where it truly hurt. Adding personal insult to the cash injury, these very same trade union tops who failed to stave off or muzzle wildcat strikes might well be jailed if they did not demonstrate sufficient zeal in getting their members back to work.

Wildcat strikes tend to combine informal organisation and exuberant spontaneity, marking them out from legal strikes. The latter are planned, coordinated, and announced by union officials well in advance. They have a timetable, which wildcats lack. Everyone involved in a legal strike knows that a collective agreement has run its course and management and labour have been unable to reach a consensus that a new contract will be signed. Wildcats are far less likely than legal strikes to be about wages, pensions, or what business unionists often see as the core issues of contract negotiations. If the legal strike is about securing a contract, the wildcat strike can either be about skirting the contract or, alternatively, it can present itself as a forceful statement from the shop floor that workers are tired of waiting for one. No labour *movement* has ever been built without the enthusiasm and mobilising potential of the illegal work stoppage, just as no *business* unionism, concerned overwhelmingly with narrow wage issues, has ever been comfortable with wildcats. As one observer told the *Canadian Forum*'s Louis Greenspan, 'The union leaders

14   Carrothers 1966, pp. 396–7.
15   Woods 1968, p. 98. See also Gindin 1995, p. 143.

have fought the old fights and won the old battles; they no longer negotiate ideas, they only negotiate money'.[16]

Often the concerns involved in wildcats are unclear to many of the workers who decide that they will make common cause with their fellow unionists in closing down the plant for an unspecified period. But there is an essential trust in the old trade-union maxim that 'an injury to one is an injury to all', and that some grievance of importance, or the build up of a series of resentments, necessitates direct action, outside of the usual slow, cumbersome, and officially mediated procedures of resolution. Wildcats are, implicitly, a blow against the hierarchy of state-monitored labour organisation. They are also an expression of discontent directed against the distance of an increasingly bureaucratised layer of officialdom from the actualities of waged working life; some wildcats can even be explicit protests against a contingent of trade-union tops judged inadequate in their response to rank-and-file needs and grievances. As John H. Crispo and Harry W. Arthurs reported in 1968, Canadian wildcats were an expression of 'rank-and-file restlessness' that was sometimes 'as much against the "union establishment" as against the "business establishment"'. One investigator found that a diffuse sense of 'participatory democracy' animated the 1965–6 Canadian wildcat wave, with workers demanding an expansion of their role in decision-making, especially on critically important issues such as technological innovation and automation. The intensity of commitment to a 'new version of Trade Unionism' surprised this commentator, who concluded that, 'just as the bureaucratised universities have created the militant student and faculty so have the bureaucratised plants created the new generation of union militants'. Talk of a 'new unionism' and 'the just society' spread in labour circles, prompting rebelliousness and a commitment to widening the effort to eradicate poverty and create more equitable income distribution.[17]

The wildcat strike, then, was the perfect vehicle (in both form and content) for the expression of youthful rebellion in the mid-1960s. It was often a spontaneous eruption of anger, alienation, and anxiety, ordered by workers themselves, rather than channelled through conservative union leaders and the procedural morass of the legally-ordered trade-union settlement. Like student protest meetings and demonstrations, wildcat strikes were 'happenings' rather than highly structured and routinely scripted events. They took place outside of

16   Louis Greenspan, 'Wages and Wildcats', *Canadian Forum*, February 1967.
17   Waisglass quoted in Mungo James, 'Labour Lays it On the Line', *Saturday Night*, December 1966; Louis Greenspan, 'Wages and Wildcats', *Canadian Forum*, February 1967; Jamieson 1976, p. 401.

the boundaries of what had come to be conventional class relations, and they struck blows against the peaceful co-existence that the post-war settlement was designed to secure for capital, labour, and the state.[18]

Class Struggle's Temperature Rising: Wildcat Fever and Youthful Labour Revolt

The mid-1960s seemed wild enough without the drama of illegal work stoppages being thrown into the mix. A *Globe and Mail* review of 'threatening labour disputes' suggested that Canadians needed to be jolted into awareness that they were being flooded with 'disastrous strikes'. Such upheavals, according to a statement by the Minister of Labour, John Nicholson, in the House of Commons, 'threaten[ed] the Canadian economy'. Nicholson was put off by 'a near epidemic of labour disputes and the hair trigger atmosphere that attends so many negotiations', and he feared a 'long summer of uncontrolled labour strife' that would 'exact its toll from every Canadian'.[19]

A precise count of the strikes and lockouts of these years is difficult to arrive at because the major government publication upon which such a tally would necessarily be based, 'The Strike and Lockout Reports' published annually in the Department of Labour's Economics and Research Branch *Strikes and Lockouts in Canada*, under-reported the level of conflict. Nevertheless, two separate calculations, one conducted by Stuart Marshall Jamieson, a Professor at the University of British Columbia's Institute of Industrial Relations in the 1960s, and another by Joy McBride, a PhD candidate at Queen's University in the late 1980s, confirm the unmistakable dimensions of an upturn in the class struggle. Jamieson, who ascertained the numbers of strikes and lockouts by surveying official statistics, records a total of 1,118 such conflicts in 1965–6, while McBride, studying the same period, but drawing on the aggregate data rather than reproducing the final published government statistics, suggests that 1,147 strikes occurred. Both scholars emphasise the dramatic rise in class conflict, with the workers involved, work days lost to strikes and lock-outs, and percentage of estimated working time sacrificed to such struggles soaring. The number of working days lost almost quadrupled over the course of 1963–5,

18   Standard statements on wildcat strikes can be found in Gouldner 1954; Glaberman 1980, pp. 35–61; Rinehart 1975, pp. 71–3; Flood 1972, pp. 603–15; 1968a, pp. 1–14; 1968b.

19   'A Plague of Strikes', *Globe and Mail*, 31 May 1966; 'The More Sensible Course', *Globe and Mail*, 2 June 1966.

climbing to 7.5 million in the two years of intense mid-1960s conflict. Estimated working time that evaporated in the heat of class struggle tripled to 33 percent, with almost 600,000 workers battling employers on picket lines in 1964–6.

Unemployment having been brought under control, contained at roughly four percent, inflation was the primary scourge of the organised working class. Its rising wage demands, which in the case of some sectors appeared outrageously excessive, peaked with a 1966 Canadian Union of Postal Workers announcement that the union would seek a mammoth 50 percent wage hike. When railway workers seemingly insisted on a 30 percent raise in 1966, politicians from Liberal Prime Minister Lester B. Pearson down to Ontario's Minister responsible for provincial highways cried foul, claiming that the government would be bankrupted. Contractors in Montreal were shocked when 10,000 building tradesmen and labourers associated with the Confederation of National Trade Unions (CNTU) brought $100 million worth of projects to a standstill, rejecting an agreement providing 'the largest and most rapid wage and fringe increases ever negotiated in Canada' for workers in the construction sector. Newspaper editorials and tavern talk turned against 'big unions' and their crippling inflationary wage demands.[20]

More telling (and more open to dispute in terms of differences in the numbers) is the tally of wildcat strikes in 1965–6. Certainly their importance is obvious, but Jamieson's reliance on official statistics alone probably understates significantly the number of wildcats in these years. He puts the figure at 359, while McBride's survey of illegal strikes approaches 575. What is undeniable is that such wildcat statistics, encompassing by 1965–6 anything from 20 to 50 percent of all strikes, highlight an earth shattering departure from the practices of the past. Even official statistics, such as those gathered for Ontario, conceded that 27 percent of the strikes in the province in 1966 were illegal, having been launched during the life of the collective agreement. And with this wave of wildcats, Canadian workers served notice that they were prepared to defy law and order, often resulting in violence. This was not so much new, since workers often had their backs placed against walls in ways that necessitated phys-

---

20   The above paragraphs draw on Palmer 1992, p. 280, summarising Jamieson's data; Jamieson 1968, pp. 371, 397; Joy McBride, 'The Wildcat Wave: Rank-and-File Rebellion in the Canadian Labour Movement, 1965–1966', unpublished paper, Queen's University, 17 August 1987, in the possession of the author. On inflation and wage demands see Mungo James, 'Labour Lays it on the Line', *Saturday Night*, December 1966; Louis Greenspan, 'Wages and Wildcats', *Canadian Forum*, February; Carrothers 1966, Volume 2, pp. 399–408, 586; 'Construction Workers End Montreal Strike', *Labour Gazette*, July 1966.

ical refusals and resistance, as it was a challenge to the post-war settlement's attempt to structure class relations in ways that effectively contained such turbulence and undermined the ability of militants in the union movement to re-enact the confrontational class struggles of the past. 'The peaceable kingdom', with its attachment to orderly understandings of British constitutional practices, was being assailed from within by an increasingly unruly, wildcatting working class.[21]

Many of these wildcat battles were epic confrontations that won workers considerable concessions from capital. Often strikers – legal and illegal – were forced to defy court injunctions ordering them to cease and desist from specific picket-line activities and return to their work. So blatant was the hostility to injunctions in mid-1960s labour circles that it threatened to shatter the hegemonic hold of the law. It was difficult to mask the extent to which injunctions prohibiting picket lines were not obvious tools relied on by capital to crush working-class resistance, exposing the class prejudices of the state and its infrastructure of 'justice'. Central Ontario became a particularly hot site of contestation as strikes of typographers at the *Oshawa Times* and poorly-paid female workers at the Tilco Plastics Company, both of which were slapped with restraining orders, culminated in a well-coordinated and province-wide Ontario Federation of Labour campaign against injunctions. Unionists declared that 'the war is on' and that they had 'no respect for the law'. When a sheriff in Oshawa tried to read an injunction to a huge crowd of union supporters he was pelted with snowballs and the offensive legal document was torn from his hands, shredded by its opponents. The New Democratic Party's Ontario leader, Donald C. MacDonald, told one group of defiant strikers that 'people who defy laws have in the past been at the centre of historic events'.[22]

---

21   Woods 1968, p. 131; Jamieson 1967, pp. 400–4; Joy McBride, 'The Wildcat Wave: Rank-and-File Rebellion in the Canadian Labour Movement, 1965–1966', unpublished paper, Queen's University, 17 August 1987, in the possession of the author; Gindin 1995, p. 145.

22   On the opposition to injunctions see Carrothers 1966, Volume 1; and the illuminating article by Sangster 2004, pp. 47–88. Carrothers 1966, Volume 2, contains reprints of *Globe and Mail* articles from September 1965 to September 1966 relating to the 1965–6 labour upsurge. This collation of material was prepared for Carrothers by M.T. Mollison and is an extremely valuable source. Specific items relating to the *Oshawa Times*, Tilco, and other injunction-related strikes and actions are found on pp. 313–56, 520–31. See also Donald C. MacDonald, 'Letter to the Editor', *Globe and Mail*, 2 August 1966; *Globe and Mail*, 12 February 1966; Ed Finn, 'The Lessons of Oshawa', *Canadian Dimension*, 3, January–February 1965; P. Kent, 'Ontario Unionists Defy Injunctions', *Workers Vanguard*, March 1966. On the British Columbia context see Isitt 2007, Chapter 10.

Labour spokesmen could barely stomach the crude way in which the proliferation of injunctions kneecapped striking workers. Paddy Neale, Secretary of
the Vancouver and District Labour Council, made no bones of his disdain for
a judiciary that would grant employers injunctions without even glancing at
sworn affidavits. 'The law is an ass', he railed. 'We must try to have it changed,
but if we can't, then we may have to ignore it ... If labour leaders and workers
are forced by law and injunctions into going to jail, let's go. But let's make an
issue out of it and keep the problem in the public eye'. Injunctions, by 1965,
were a particularly dirty word in British Columbia's militant-labour circles. 'We
used them to decorate the office as wallpaper', snorted one strike leader when
asked what he thought of the proliferating court orders. Young workers heard
such statements and no doubt considered them a license to flaunt the law in
general, especially as the class war gave every sign of heating up in the 1965–6
years.[23]

Typical of the complex levels of developing antagonism were strikes of
Hamilton and Sudbury steelworkers and miners and Montreal longshoremen
in 1966. Contract negotiations at the northern Ontario International Nickel
Company (Inco) plant were disrupted by a 16,000-member wildcat walkout
that union officials subdued only after three weeks. In spite of the leadership's
opposition to the job action, it helped win Sudbury's miners and metal pro-
cessors an impressive pay hike, making them, according to one newspaper
report, 'the highest paid group in the Steel Workers' Union'. When the contract
was eventually approved, however, only 57 percent of the union membership
thought it good enough and voted for ratification. To the south, in Hamilton,
discontent erupted in a violent wildcat at the Steel Company of Canada, where
workers fought police and union officials, destroyed property and won themselves a reputation for militancy and the highest steel-working wage in the
world. On the Montreal docks, the first illegal strike in years was fought by
longshoremen resisting the stevedoring companies' demands that new cargo-
handling machinery be used and that gangs be reduced in size accordingly.
Workers refused to recommend a settlement that contained lucrative wage
increases until a Royal Commission was established to inquire into the shipping firms' insistence that the size of work crews be pared down, cutting 600
jobs, and by this means the workers ensured that traditional long-shoring gangs
would be preserved for the duration of the contract, until 1968.

---

23   *Globe and Mail*, 21 June 1966. See also Carrothers 1966, Volume 2, p. 409; Roberts 1990,
     p. 100; Phillips 1967, p. 164; Ross Dowson, 'Urge General Strike as Judge Jails BC Leaders',
     Workers Vanguard, mid-September 1966 and mid-October 1966; and for background to the
     BC labour opposition to the injunction, Carrothers 1956.

Similar developments on the railways forced parliament to sanction 18 percent wage increases before it ordered strikers back to work after an October 1964 protest in which 2,800 Canadian National Railway employees booked off sick in an *en masse* protest. Meanwhile, 12,000 postal workers were poised to lead one of the largest nationwide wildcats in the 1965–6 upheaval, partly improving the depressed wage environment in which they had been incarcerated for some time. Their pay was markedly less ($2,000–$3,000 in some high wage locales such as Vancouver) than that of policemen and firemen of comparable seniority; unskilled municipal labourers might earn significantly more than Canadian Union of Postal Workers members. A *Globe and Mail* editorial worried over the spread of wildcat fever, seeing the postal conflict as a reflection 'of the loss of control by union leaders', noting the mail carriers' walkout 'spread like wildfire across the country despite efforts by the union leadership in Ottawa to douse it'.[24] Many strikes of this period, commentators were quick to point out, ended up headed by rebel leaderships and factions that 'refused to obey their national officers', as was evident among postal workers in 1965, the Stelco eruption of 1966, and in the rising militancy of Ontario's 8,500 teamsters.[25]

The demographics of youth figured centrally in these class battles. Time and time again, commentators underscored the origins of the wildcat movement in the impatience, intransigence, and volatility of workers 'new' to the game of stable, industrial relations, uninitiated in the procedural practices of post-war settlement unionism, layered as they were in bureaucratic legalism. The Secretary Treasurer of the CBRT noted in 1966 that three years earlier, during the most

---

24   The above paragraphs draw on standard accounts of such battles in Jamieson 1968, pp. 422–46, which contains the report on Inco's wage offer (p. 432); Flood 1968b; Freeman 1982, pp. 99–116; Freedman 1966, pp. 69–80; Peitchinis 1971; Ed Finn, 'Why Canadian Workers Are Kicking', *Canadian Dimension*, January–February 1967; Wace 1968; 'Longshoremen's Strike Ends – With Reservations', *Labour Gazette*, September 1966; Parrot 2005, pp. 5–20. For the comment on postal workers and union leadership see 'Wildcat Strike Poses Question: Are Leaders Out of Touch with Members?', *Globe and Mail*, 19 November 1965. Note as well Marvin Gandall, 'The Labour Movement: Two Decades Ago', *Canadian Dimension*, October–November 1984.

25   A sense of the Teamster strike's volatility can be gleaned from press reports culled from the *Globe and Mail* and gathered in Carrothers 1966, Volume 2, pp. 357–67, 383, 431. See, as well, Jamieson 1968, pp. 427–9; Arthur Kruger, 'Strike Wave–1966', *Canadian Forum*, July 1966; 'Brief Tucker Strike Sparked by Rebels', *London Free Press*, 4 October 1965; McKechnie 1968; P. Kent, 'Ontario Teamster Lockout Projects Battle Cry – No Contract, No Work!', *Workers Vanguard*, mid-January 1966; and 'Teamsters Solid, 40-hr. Week Now', *Workers Vanguard*, April 1966.

recent set of contract negotiations, half of his members had not been around at the time of the last strike in the industry, in 1950. 'It is doubtful whether many of these new members even know the names of the leaders, and they certainly have no personal identification, as was the case in the past'.[26]

Henri W. Joli, President of the Canadian Manufacturers' Association, feared that the escalating union demands of the mid-1960s imperilled the nation and its prosperity, fuelling inflation with strikes for 30 percent wage hikes and extravagant fringe benefits. 'Sparked by the younger members of the labour force', these job actions needed to be crushed, and Joli advocated the use of injunctions prohibiting pickets and other efforts to 'blockade' legitimate business. Recoiling in indignant horror at the 'growing militancy' and the 'picket line turmoil and violence' associated with many worker walkouts, Joli attributed the worsening climate of industrial relations to those young workers swelling the workforce, 'fresh from school who have no idea what the pre-war world was like and who always have got what they wanted. Many of them appear shocked when they find their demands are not going to be met automatically'.[27]

At Hamilton's Stelco plant, site of one of the more robust and ribald wildcats, it was young men in their twenties, according to various accounts, who precipitated the walkout. Some of these youthful workers had entered the Stelco workforce and the union through family connections, their fathers having long histories in the steel community. With contract negotiations having dragged on from May into August, stalling in a deadlock that stretched past the expiration date of the contract, resentments mounted in the massive steelworks. After a foreman taunted an evening shift that, 'You guys haven't got the guts to walk out', 20 young men marched to the plant gate and formed pickets. Two hundred others were quickly enlisted to circulate throughout the plant, calling workers out. Within a day the illegal walkout had spread throughout the sprawling Stelco works, leaving 16,000 workers idle. Among the 29 workers initially targeted as militants, arrested and charged with assault and various other picket-line criminal acts, and also suspected of sabotage, the average age was 28.6 years, the oldest being 42, the youngest 20. Of the arrested, one-third were 23 years old or less. When the reinstatement of these wildcatters became an issue of contention, management refusing to hire some of them back, one union leader responded to criticism with the comment, 'Look, Jesus Christ couldn't have got the jobs back of some of those guys. I know one. He was a

26 'Wildcat Strike Poses Question: Are Leaders Out of Touch with Members?', *Globe and Mail*, 19 November 1965.
27 Carrothers 1966, p. 452.

good kid, too. His father was a personal friend of mine. He'd only been working at Stelco for six months, but he got caught inside the plant cutting electrical cables and that sort of thing ... Now what are you gonna do about a case like that?'[28]

Even the upper echelons of labour leadership were not immune from what seemed to be the spreading mood of defiance in working-class ranks. At the head of the Canadian Labour Congress (CLC), for instance, a youthful Associate Research Director, Russell Irvine, moved with the times to embrace the position that labour organisations should not trap negotiations with employers in the cul-de-sac of a traditional *quid pro quo*. Capital's expectation had come to be that any increase in labour's remuneration must be met with rising productivity. Irvine refused such a profit-wage bargain, arguing that if workers accepted 'this line about being a responsible citizen and tying ... income to productivity, not only will [labour's] share not increase – it will get even smaller'. Tired of the assumption that unions had to act within the rules of a game that seemed to have been conceived and constructed by capital and the state, Irvine snorted, 'We're sick of being told to act responsibly. Let *them* act responsibly for a change'.[29] But if this was the rhetoric of militancy emanating from the upper echelons of the trade-union bureaucracy, as the wildcat wave peaked many a trade-union top exploded with frustrated antagonism toward young 'hot heads', who seemed to take labour spokesmen like Irvine at their word.

'Listen to the voice of reason', one Steelworker official pleaded, begging wildcatting workers to end their protest and allow the union to 'get back to the bargaining table'. As railway workers employed by the express-delivery wings of the Canadian National and Canada Pacific railways waged an illegal wildcat in the summer of 1966, a union official, prodded to get the workers back on the job, threw up his hands in despair: 'They said they weren't ready to go back, so what's the point of talking to them?' The strikers' words offered an insight into their antagonisms: 'This is a non-confidence vote (in the union executive), we are taking things into our own hands'. When USWA Local 1005 President John Morgan and Steelworkers' area supervisor Stewart Cooke implored wildcat pickets at Stelco's gates to open the lines and return to work they were shocked by the vehemence with which they were denounced. 'We're fed up with you,

---

28   On the role of youth in the Stelco wildcat see Freeman 1982, pp. 100–8; Flood 1968b, pp. 70–2; 'Vote to End Stelco Stirke', *Globe and Mail*, 8 August 1966, also in Carrothers 1966, Volume 2, p. 381.

29   Mungo James, 'Labour Lays it On the Line', *Saturday Night*, December 1966.

WILDCAT WORKERS IN THE 1960S: THE UNRULY FACE OF CLASS STRUGGLE 257

we don't want you', one picketer jeered in derision at his local union president. Morgan left in tears. One of his supporters reported, 'It was an ugly scene … They were shouting at us like some of them had gone mad. We were lucky to get out of there alive'.[30]

The Wildness of the Wildcat

This report of fear and loathing on the illegal picket-line trail conveys something of the unique wildness of the 1965–6 labour rebellion. If it did not manage to achieve the conscious radicalism or secure the decisive breakthroughs of previous strike waves in 1917–20, 1941–3, and 1946–7, it nevertheless marked a point of departure, suggestive of the limits that segments of labour were placing on their containment by the bureaucratic legalism of modern class relations. Writing a year after the wildcat wave, Ed Finn summarised the general importance of the new mood of labour militancy, drawing on his particular familiarity with railway workers:

> Impatient with the interminable delays, and with the seeming lack of assertiveness by their elected negotiators, they took measures into their own hands by staging several wildcat strikes. When they were ordered back to work by the strike-ending legislation, many thousands of them defied the government edict for several days before reluctantly submitting. Had they received the slightest encouragement from the leaders, Canada would have witnessed the spectacle of a mass defiance of Parliament by 120,000 citizens. These workers are now completely disillusioned with the whole railway labour-management system. Many are fed up with their own unions, or at least their present union leaders. The debacle that ended their strike last summer put the finishing touch to their disenchantment. The only thing that prevented them from engaging in further mass demonstrations of their displeasure was the size of the final wage settlement … more than double the 1964–5 wage increase.

Finn concluded that the bitterness engulfing Canadian labour ranks would unleash a new round of 'illegal work stoppages', and if it did not it 'certainly bodes ill for any peaceful settlement of the next round of negotiations'. More repression, he prophesied, would make the working-class upheavals of 1966

---

30   Carrothers 1966, pp. 373–5, 402; Flood 1968b, pp. 12–19; Freeman 1982, p. 103.

seem 'like a tea party by comparison'.[31] It is critical to appreciate the wildness of the strike wave, for it proved a forceful, if transitory, reminder that the much-heralded post-war settlement was less than universally welcomed by the first generation of workers tasting the actual fresh fruit, both bitter and sweet, of its offerings.

Not all of the wildness made front-page news and generated editorial attacks in the nation's mainstream press. Some of the illegal work stoppages were so mundane that they went unnoticed. But they were no less wild for being unheralded. It was not particularly surprising that young auto workers at Chrysler, Ford, and de Havilland plants routinely rebelled against the company imposing compulsory overtime. But when they wildcatted, and won, the right to be let off work early to attend a St. Thomas, Ontario hockey tournament in which their buddies were playing, it was a sign that the times were definitely changing.[32]

A general malaise at being subject to 'barnyard discipline', arbitrarily dispensed by junior executives, prompted a wildcat walk-out of Chrysler automobile assembly-plant workers. Peterborough's Firestone employees wildcatted in March 1966, fed up with managers treating them 'like imbeciles, like cattle'.[33] A walkout at a Canadian Westinghouse Limited plant involving 185 unionists developed when the Local's President refused to be time-studied. With both the company and the International union contending that the work stoppage was illegal, the wildcatters met with a representative of the union leadership, but 'voted overwhelmingly to remain out and tell the executive to go to hell'.[34]

Stevedores seemed particularly susceptible to wildcat fever, usually of the kind that many would dismiss as rather frivolous. They walked off the Montreal docks, 3,500 strong, on a spring day in April 1966, to voice their displeasure at police ticketing their cars parked adjacent to the waterfront. If any of their long-shoring brethren were disciplined for transgressions involving drinking, job action was often immediate. The Toronto docks were shut down in June 1966 when harbour police manhandled a longshoreman accused of having an

31   Ed Finn, 'The New Militancy of Canadian Labour', *Canadian Dimension*, November–December 1965.

32   Gindin 1995, p. 147.

33   Carrothers 1966, pp. 387, 437; 'Firestone Wildcat Ends as Workers Return', *Peterborough Examiner*, 7 March 1966.

34   Carrothers 1966, pp. 425, 433; Joy McBride, 'The Wildcat Wave: Rank-and-File Rebellion in the Canadian Labour Movement, 1965–1966', unpublished paper, Queen's University, 17 August 1987, in the possession of the author, p. 23.

open bottle of beer in a public place, slapping the unionist with a summons, and ignoring his protestations that he had not been drinking and had merely found the half-empty brew as he was unloading cargo. Hamilton's lakeside facilities were subjected to three wildcat walkouts over the course of ten days in November 1965. 'All three apparently were in protest against suspensions that followed liquor violations', the *Globe and Mail* reported soberly, noting that the job actions, unsupported by the union, were 'frustrating work at the docks at the peak of the busy end of the season'.[35]

Given what the post-war settlement was supposed to accomplish, and the order unions were expected to achieve in Canada's workplaces, this was all fairly wild. But the wildcats often got even wilder as pent-up frustrations exploded in violence. The largest wildcat in the 1965–6 upsurge, the illegal walkout of thousands of Inco workers, was a key case in point. As contract negotiations faltered in the summer of 1966, the wildcat spread from one operation to another and eventually, outside of all official union control, it took on the trappings of a 'wartime military machine', with illegal strikers using walkie-talkies to communicate, and threatening to disable a transport helicopter Inco was using to get supervisory personnel into company facilities. With provincial police appearing on the scene, the wildcatters armed themselves with lengths of pipe, baseball bats, steel bars, and ominous clubs. Roads were blockaded, hydro and telephone lines sabotaged, and a supply truck en route to the plant was stopped, overturned, and rolled down a hill. Shipments of nickel to the United States were stopped dead in their tracks. The *Toronto Telegram* reported that some pickets carried shotguns and were prepared 'to take on all comers'. Reports of firearms being discharged at Inco's Port Colborne refinery, where 1,800 employees soon joined their Sudbury counterparts, left a management team quaking in their air-lifted boots, incarcerated behind picket lines, awaiting supplies from the company helicopter. When a settlement was finally reached, and the dissident picket lines came down, worker discontent was barely assuaged by the company's wage concessions, which saw increases of almost 30 percent for skilled tradesmen, a bonus of five-week vacations on top of regular holiday time for all workers with half a decade of service under their belts, and greatly enhanced indemnity benefits for those unable to work because of sickness or accident. Some strikers refused to report for the midnight shift as the Inco rebellion ground to a halt in mid-September 1966. One steelworker official confessed his wonderment at the wildness, obviously relieved that it was winding down: 'I saw the Molotov

35   Carrothers 1966, pp. 539–40.

cocktails, the guns, and the dynamite. The union lost control of the situation. Eventually we took truckloads of arms of one kind or another away from the picket lines'.[36]

The situation was equally explosive in August 1966, as Hamilton's imposing Stelco operations were brought to a standstill by an illegal work stoppage. When USWA leaders invited picket captains at the Stelco gates to send a dozen representatives each to the Union Hall to meet with the Negotiating Committee, between 200–300 angry workers rushed the building. Panicked by what they interpreted as a growing 'mob psychology', union officials called the police, which merely made matters worse. 'Get the fuzz out of here. This is our hall. They have no right here!', screamed a militant striker. Union leaflets declaring that there was no authorised strike at Stelco; deploring 'leaderless, directionless, and futile' actions of 'irresponsible' elements; reminding the militants that there would be no strike relief or welfare for those engaging in the walkout; and insisting that all must return to work at their normal shifts, were torn from stewards' hands, crumpled, piled in the street, and burned. Then, according to one obviously less than progressive union official, the militants danced and howled around the pyre, 'just like a load of ... indians'. The USWA placed newspaper advertisements urging the wildcatters to terminate their illegal actions, took to radio airwaves to suppress the strike, and asked police to close down taverns in the vicinity of Stelco, thereby depriving the discontented workers of both venues to meet and places to bolster their bodies with food and drink. Eventually taking 12,500 production workers and 3,500 non-union office staff out of work, the Stelco strike, soon supported by wives of the wildcatters, erupted in a 'fist-swinging, gouging' battle between police and company guards, on the one hand, and a 'surging mob of 2,000 steelworkers' on the other. Arrests, assaults, and arson characterised the day, which also witnessed a mass sitdown of strikers that clogged a major Hamilton thoroughfare. Hanging over the USWA until 1 September 1966, the uprising at Stelco eventually cooled, but not until the company bumped up its contract offer considerably. Workers had an opportunity to turn down one union-endorsed potential agreement, and management promised it would at least review the cases of 51 workers fired or suspended for their role in the violent illegal job action in early August.[37]

---

36   On the Inco wildcat see especially Carrothers 1966, Volume 2, pp. 367–78; Jamieson 1968, pp. 429–32; Flood, 'The Wildcat Strike', p. 253, quoted in Joy McBride, 'The Wildcat Wave: Rank-and-File Rebellion in the Canadian Labour Movement, 1965–1966', unpublished paper, Queen's University, 17 August 1987, in the possession of the author, p. 43; and Palmer 1992, p. 317.

37   The most detailed account is in Flood 1968b, which forms the evidence base for the

These were not blips on the class-struggle radar screen. Labour violence in 1965–6 seemed endemic.[38] The wildness of the strike wave prompted the Ontario state to haul an 82-year-old justice Ivan Rand out of his judicial mothballs, setting him up to inquire into the increasingly tempestuous climate of industrial 'disputes'. Ostensibly instigated by the Peterborough Tilco strikers' violation of an injunction limiting them to 12 pickets, the Rand inquiry ranged broadly over a number of issues relating to strikes, lockouts, and the legal responsibilities of contending parties in the camps of labour and capital. Rand and his provincial royal-commission entourage traversed the province (and undertook some international junkets as well), accumulating testimony that totalled 5,000 pages. So masculinist were the assumptions of the inquiry, which undoubtedly pegged the problematic nature of class struggle on the picket line behaviour of combative males and the ascending *machismo* of union bargaining teams, as well as the stereotypical passivity and hen-pecking anti-unionism of women, that, as Joan Sangster tellingly notes, *not one woman* testified before the whole commission. Ironically enough, as the Rand Commission convened in Toronto, 100 distillery workers at Hiram Walker Limited wildcatted when their bosses refused three of their number an opportunity to attend the hearings.[39]

Rand was no longer the far-seeing progressive that he had been heralded as in 1946. Instead, his approach to the wildness of class battle as it had been enacted in 1965–6 was increasingly troubled. An advocate of responsible, freedom-loving unionism, Rand prided himself on his expertise in law and *orderly* labour relations, and had no time for the new breed of unionist who refused to see the courts and the police as esteemed protectors of basic rights. Haranguing one labour figure who failed to bow in deference to the majesty of the law, instead arguing that it dripped with class unfairness and collusion, Rand railed: 'I am astonished you have the opinion of the police and the courts that you do when they protect you from thugs, you talk as if they are utterly irresponsible. I know more about the courts than you do and I say there is nothing of the sort'. Rand recoiled from civil disobedience, mass picketing, and strike discipline that prevented scabs from entering workplaces – in short, the entire

---

discussion in Freeman 1982, pp. 99–114. See also Carrothers 1966, Volume 2, pp. 378–83; Jamieson 1968, pp. 433–5.

38 For official recognition of the problem of violence see Woods 1968, p. 133.

39 In this paragraph and below I draw on Joan Sangster's account of Rand 1968, in Sangster 2004. Sangster notes the Hiram Walker wildcat (Sangster 2004, p. 73), citing *Toronto Telegram*, 23 March 1967.

1945 edifice of militant tactics that Windsor's Ford workers had used to good effect in prompting his arbitration decision, which would stand for two decades as the cornerstone of the post-war settlement. In a stumbling statement, Rand reiterated the fundamental importance of law (and the necessity of legality in any strike action), retreating into a defence of beleaguered employers who now faced, in his view, a trade unionism that was more often than not an all-too-powerful adversary.[40]

The learned Justice was no fan of the wildness of wildcat workers. He claimed that history had not exactly absolved them. Small wonder, for Rand's survey of wildcat strikes showed that the law had been anything but a friend to the wild: in the approximately one hundred and ten Ontario strikes that Rand's data identified as having taken place during the life of collective agreements in the 1965–6 wildcat wave, almost seventy-five of these walkouts were slapped with some kind of disciplinary retribution. Fines were levied, arrests made, injunctions granted, employees dismissed, suspended, or reprimanded, and strikes declared illegal. Rand agreed with the notion that this kind of restraining rod should not be spared. Even granting that many union officials also took umbrage at the wildness of the wildcatters, few in the ranks of the workers' movement had much good to say about the final published Rand report. For the most part, it was regarded as 'a textbook for the promotion of conflict and turmoil in Ontario's industrial relations'.[41]

Politics and the Wildness of Working-Class Upheaval

Justice Ivan Rand saw little politics in the 1965–6 labour revolt, save for the bad manners of those who did not accept the boundaries of restraint in civil society. There was nevertheless no disguising the extent to which some of the wildness of the mid-1960s was related to a working class experiencing an often intense politicisation.

This was evident in Quebec, for instance, where some of the violence associated with working-class upheaval blurred into the class-ordered struggles of the rising independence movement. A shoe factory, for instance, was the site of ongoing picket-line violence pitting non-union workers against striking unionists. *Independantistes* associated with the Front de Libération du Québec (FLQ)

---

40   Rand 1968, pp. 6, 18, 29–30. See also, Sangster 2004, pp. 77–8.
41   My rough calculations from the tables in Rand 1968, pp. 232–49; Fisher and Crowe 1968;
       Ed Finn, 'Labour: The Rand Report', *Canadian Dimension*, September–October 1968.

stepped into the fray. Dragging on for the better part of a year, the 1965–6 battle culminated in a bomb explosion that killed a 64-year-old secretary and left eight others injured, closing the plant.[42] May 1965 saw a flurry of FLQ-associated bombings at various work sites and struck companies. In Drummondville, the Dominion Textile works were bombed, as 5,000 CNTU-affiliated workers walked picket lines, their job action having commenced in March. Twenty-four hours before 4,000 Montreal postal workers commenced wildcat strike action, a bomb was defused at the Peel Street Post Office. Job actions in a variety of economic sectors were marred by violence, dynamite, and Molotov cocktails. In an underground memo written in 1966, the FLQ's Pierre Vallières indicated that the organisation's 'military action is limited to sabotage, bombings, and organizing strikers' self defence', largely through detonating 'token explosions' during workers' walkouts.[43] Some Quebec strikes of these years were also joint efforts of unionists and members of the *Rassemblement pour l'indépendence nationale*. One such confrontation, involving the Dominion Ayers Company, a plywood concern in Lachute, began in the summer of 1966 and reached into early autumn. It culminated in a huge solidarity rally that was broken up by company guards on 'Tear Gas Sunday', as security forces battled workers and their supporters with batons, tossing tear gas canisters into the crowd. Molotov cocktails sailed back in reply. The next day a bomb was left near the Ayers plant. Even the company President's domestic residence did not go unscathed, rampaging strikers and their allies stoning the house and setting its grounds on fire.[44]

Paced by Montreal's Central Labour Council and its fiery President, Michel Chartrand, the CNTU unions moved aggressively to the left in the 1965–8 years, challenging imperialist war in Vietnam and issuing radical manifesto-like statements that widened the political parameters of trade unionism. Pressing for labour to struggle not only for the rights of organised workers, the CNTU embraced the causes of the unorganised, the unemployed, tenants, and consumers. This, in turn, paved the way for the tremendous explosion of class militancy in Quebec's Common Front mobilisations of 1970–2. Industrial workers and teachers, craft unions and radical supporters, marched arm-in-arm as French Canadian dissidents launched massive work stoppages and general

42   Carrothers 1966, p. 544; Black Rose Editorial Collective 1972, p. 21; Kostash 1980, pp. 216–7.

43   Fournier 1984, pp. 81, 97–9.

44   Fournier 1984, p. 109; Joy McBride, 'The Wildcat Wave: Rank-and-File Rebellion in the Canadian Labour Movement, 1965–1966', unpublished paper, Queen's University, 17 August 1987, in the possession of the author, p. 27.

strikes in March–April 1972. The rebelliousness was only tamed with back-to-work legislation, crippling fines levied by the courts against the unions, and selective imprisonment of labour leaders.[45]

None of this class conflict was unrelated to the emergence of a radical-nationalist movement that identified with the oppressed and exploited proletariat and found itself increasingly at odds with the centralised power of Canadian federalism. Montreal May Days in the 1960s became huge festivals of alternative thought and practice, the vessel of parade overflowing with working-class and radical-nationalist content. The CNTU embraced the cause of incarcerated Front de Libération du Québec members, demanding their release, and separatists such as Pierre Vallières steeled themselves in class-conflict defeats like the *La Presse* journalists' strike of 1964–5. Taxi drivers and students waged war at Montreal's airport, battling police in a 1968 show of force, protesting the monopoly held by the Anglo-Canadian firm, Murray Hill, over prime limousine and cab-service properties. An October 1969 demonstration of the Mouvement de Libération du Taxi, a violent encounter at the entryway to the Murray Hill Limousine Company, in which a Molotov cocktail was thrown, ended with a security guard firing a twelve-gauge shotgun into the crowd. A Quebec Provincial Police officer, rumoured to have been functioning as an undercover *agent provocateur* among the militant protesters, was mysteriously killed. Montreal mailtruck drivers formed their own cooperative company and eventually secured certification as a CNTU affiliate, managing, as well, to win the lucrative federal contract from Canada Post. This victory was soon undermined by the federal Liberal Party's decision, in February 1970, to divide the delivery of mail among four different companies. For two-and-a-half years *les gars de Lapalme*, as the drivers dubbed themselves, battled Ottawa and eventually their own union. They employed sabotage, intimidated drivers who took their jobs, and were not shy about the use of violence. In the short span of six months, the striking mail drivers damaged 1,200 postal boxes, attacked 662 postal trucks, vandalised 104 postal stations, and inflicted and suffered 75 reported injuries. Seven dynamite explosions were attributed to them, their ranks thinned by 102 arrests. Still, *les gars de Lapalme* turned out in force to give Pierre Elliott Trudeau the proverbial jeering raspberry on Parliament Hill. They were not pleased at Trudeau's shift in gears from his days as a 1950s advocate of Quebec's working class to the federal government's Minister of Justice

---

45   Black Rose Editorial Collective 1972; Drache 1972; Palmer 1992, pp. 312–13; Bryan D. Palmer, '40 Years of Class Struggle', *Canadian Dimension*, November–December 2003; McKay 2005, pp. 185–8.

and, eventually, Prime Minister of the country. Faced with their taunts, Trudeau snapped back in kind: 'Mangez de la merde!'[46] The post-war settlement was impolitely imploding.

In English Canada, youthful, militant working-class nationalism often took the mid-to-late 1960s form of antagonism to the old guard, international unions, headquartered in the United States.[47] Fully 1,125,000 workers, or almost seventy-two percent of the ranks of organised employees in Canada, belonged to 110 such American-affiliated unions, the largest of which were the USWA, the UAW, and the Brotherhoods of Carpenters & Joiners, Woodworkers, Electrical Workers, and Pulp & Paper Mill Workers. Only the rising public-sector unionists, concentrated in the 84,000-strong Canadian Union of Public Employees, as well as the 32,100 CBRT railway workers, cracked the top ten unions in Canada in terms of their memberships. By the mid-1970s, public-sector unionism in Canada, necessarily organised in national unions and thus different than the internationals of old, had expanded considerably and created a dramatic shift in the relations within the upper echelons of the labour movement. The percentage of organised workers belonging to international unions in 1975 had dropped to just over 51 percent, and CUPE and the Public Service Alliance of Canada, with their combined memberships of 250,000 in 1970, now rivalled steelworkers and autoworkers in terms of numerical significance. In the mid-1960s these developments were in the making, rather than already accomplished. Canadian workers often represented small minorities within their international unions: in the early 1960s, USWAers from Canada constituted just under eleven percent of the International's dues payers, while the comparable percentages for machinists, labourers in the auto sector, and packinghouse workers ranged from 4.5 to 6.7 to 21.9. Among Quebec workers, of course, nationally-organised unions were stronger, headed by the powerful CNTU, and the francophone state was even known to launch assaults on the American-based internationals.[48] But in English Canada there

---

46   Peter Allnutt and Robert Chodos, 'Quebec into the Streets', *Last Post*, December 1969; Nic auf der Maur, 'Montreal's Cabbies Fight City Hall', *Last Post*, April 1970; Nic auf der Mer, 'Les Gars de Lapalme', *Last Post*, October 1971; Vallières 1971, pp. 208–9; Kostash 1980, pp. 217–19; Morton 1980, p. 267; Fournier 1984.

47   For a brief, popular introductory statement see Stewart 1977, pp. 117–31.

48   'U.S. Unions Attacked by Lesage', *Montreal Star*, 16 June 1965. This kind of state attack on international unionism was rare in English Canada, although politicians seeking office could voice it in specific circumstances. See Crispo 1967, p. 294, citing 'Home Rule Asked for Labour Unions', *Globe and Mail*, 16 July 1964.

was no mistaking the weight of so-called international (in reality, bi-national) unionism.[49]

As the rebellious atmosphere of the 1960s permeated the unions, the American-based internationals were often, rightly or wrongly, subject to critique by dissident Canadians, who regarded them as ossified junior partners in a project of imperialist colonisation and class collaboration.[50] In the USWA the critique of American domination grew out of a highly politicised left-right factional split in the union that related to the longstanding feud between the ultimately victorious Steelworkers and their communist rivals, the Mine Mill and Smelter Workers Union. That battle was settled by the time of the wildcat wave of 1965–6, but advocates of Canadian unionism revived discontent with their calls for an autonomous labour movement. In Hamilton, the Stelco wildcat of 1966 was led by an Autonomy Group, described by Bill Freeman as 'a loosely organized collection of young inexperienced activists'. In spite of their rather lacklustre coherence, the autonomists effectively parlayed a fusion of popular nationalism, militancy, and anti-establishment bravado into loud attacks on 'sell-out' contracts and the complicity of the local and International leadership with management. During the illegal walkout there was much talk that the American leadership had cajoled Hamilton's USWA officials to force their dissident ranks back to work so that precious strike funds could be preserved in the event they were needed to support job actions in the United States.[51] If the Steelworkers were not necessarily guilty of bleeding Canadian unionists for dues (in the 1968–70 years Canadian USWA members contributed just over $4 million to the International's coffers, but drew out well over $12 million, in what amounted to a $55 subsidy for each Canadian member), other American-based unions could not make the same claim. In 1962–7 the Internationals collected a massive $166,322,000 in Canada, but returned less than $99,000,000 to union locals north of the border. American-based leaderships were not shy in using heavy-handed methods to coerce Canadians into compliance with their wishes. As the wildcat wave wound down, 26 Canadian union locals had been placed under trusteeship by their American headquarters.[52]

---

49   The standard account of international unionism in Canada in the mid-1960s is Crispo 1967. For the figure on international union members as a percentage of all Canadian unionists in 1975, see Stewart 1977, p. 131.

50   See, for period-type critiques, Howard and Scott 1972, pp. 68–87; Lipton 1972, pp. 102–19; Scott 1978.

51   Flood 1968b, pp. 68–9; Freeman 1982, p. 97.

52   Ed Finn, 'The Struggle for Canadian Labour Autonomy', Labour Gazette, November.

A series of breakaways and successions by Canadian union locals in the late 1960s and early 1970s wracked the International Brotherhood of Pulp, Sulphite, and Paper Mill Workers, International Union of Operating Engineers, the International Molders and Allied Workers Union, and the Retail, Wholesale and Department Store Union, as well as other labour organisations headquartered in the United States. This represented, in Finn's words, 'the first stirrings of the nationalist ferment now bubbling up within Canadian labour'. If stifled, Finn warned, the result would be that these 'incipient rumblings' would lead to a 'titanic – and ultimately successful – struggle for Canadian union emancipation'. The body of workers organised in truly independent English-speaking Canadian unions was small by the end of the 1960s, roughly 124 organisations with a membership of 60,000, but they were nevertheless a voice of discontent with the Internationals and their often staid leaderships. They had served vocal notice that they would not allow themselves to be easily subordinated to American leaders. Particularly among metal trades and smelter workers in British Columbia, there existed an ongoing challenge to the bureaucratised leaderships of the established Internationals, which included a successful raid of the nationalist Canadian Association of Smelter and Allied Workers (CASAW) against the USWA local at the Alcan Works in Kitimat. As a former President of the Traill Steelworkers local proclaimed in 1969, 'The younger workers, because of the environment they've been brought up under and seeing the fallacies of their society, these have a stronger feeling of anti-Americanism. It's there, let's not kid ourselves, not only in Canada but all over the world'. One Inco wildcatter had declared in 1966 that Canada was 'on the verge of a revolution ... when we see what is being taken out of this country by the Americans we are fed up. We want action'.[53]

Labour Walking a New Line

As young workers rampaged outside of plants closed by wildcats, as injunctions prohibiting picketing brought forth a deluge of denunciation in which the law was questioned if not repudiated, and as established unions and their conventional structures of collective bargaining, as well as their respectable leaderships, were chastised and jeered, labour seemed to be walking a newly

53   Ed Finn, 'Prospects for an Autonomous Labour Movement', *Canadian Dimension*, September–October 1968; Morris 1972, pp. 90–100; Knox and Resnick 1974; Resnick 1977a, pp. 178–89; Palmer 1988; 1992, pp. 318–20; King 1998.

unruly line in the mid-1960s. It threatened the post-war settlement. We are used to seeing this labour-capital accord undermined by capital and the state, a process that Leo Panitch and Donald Swartz have outlined rigorously in a detailed examination of post-1973 socioeconomic trends and government 'back-to-work' and other kinds of restrictive, anti-labour, legislation.[54] But the irony of the 1965–6 wildcat wave was that an initial blow at the system of so-called industrial pluralism was struck from within the House of Labour, albeit by workers who did not see themselves as owners of the respectable domicile. As this happened, long-established understandings of workers' place, in company and union, were challenged, and, in particular instances, came under violent assault.

Journalists referred to a 'new labour revolution, with all its threat of turmoil', suggesting that it had 'only just begun'.[55] They spoke with more insight than they knew. For the true possibility of revolution lay in politicising young and rebellious workers in the ideas and programmatic commitment to social trans-formation that grew out of workplace relations but that necessarily reached past the confining experiences of life on the assembly line or in the mine or mill. The task was to expand the political horizons of those trapped in the confines of industrial legality and unions, which were brokered at every point by their own containments. Around the corner of the wildcat wave of 1965–6 was a growing left challenge, one that, had it conjoined youth of the university and the unions, could well have reconfigured the nature of twentieth-century Canada. Class dif-ference is a difficult hurdle to leap, however, and as campus youth and women joined the unruly workers of the 1960s in an explosive embrace of militance and opposition, they did so, ultimately, divided from one another, in separate and unequal mobilisations.

---

54   Panitch and Swartz 1993.
55   Mungo James, 'Labour Lays it On the Line', *Saturday Night*, December 1966.

CHAPTER 7

British Columbia's Solidarity: Reformism and the Fight against the Right*

Since the end of the nineteenth century, the evolution of social democracy has been marked by a characteristic paradox. On the one hand, its rise has depended upon tumultuous mass working-class struggles, the same struggles which have provided the muscle to win major reforms and the basis for the emergence of far left political organizations and ideology. The expansion of working-class self-organization, power and political consciousness, dependent in turn upon working-class mass action, has provided *the* critical condition for the success of reformism as well as of the far Left. On the other hand, to the extent that social democracy has been able to consolidate itself organizationally, its core representatives – drawn from the ranks of trade union officials, parliamentary politicians, and the petty bourgeois leaderships of the mass organizations of the oppressed – have invariably sought to implement policies reflecting *their own* distinctive social positions and interests: positions which are *separate from* and interests which are, in fundamental ways, *opposed to* those of the working class. Specifically, they have sought to establish and maintain a secure place for themselves and their organizations within capitalist society. To achieve this security, the official representatives of social-democratic and reformist organizations have found themselves obliged to seek, at a minimum, the implicit toleration and, ideally, the explicit recognition of capital. As a result, they have been driven, systematically and universally, not only to relinquish socialism as a goal and revolution as a means, but beyond that to contain and at times actually to crush those upsurges of mass working-class action whose dynamics lead to broader forms of working-class organization and solidarity, to deepening attacks on capital and the capitalist state, to the constitution of working people as a self-conscious class, and, in some instances, to the adoption of socialist and revolutionary perspectives on a mass scale. They have done this des-

---

* 'Reformism and the Fight Against the Right: British Columbia's *Solidarity*', in *Reshaping the us Left: Popular Struggles in the 1980s*, edited by Mike Davis and Michael Sprinker (London: Verso, 1988), 229–54.

pite the fact that it is precisely these movements which have given them their birth and sustained their power, and which have been the only possible guarantee of their continued existence in class-divided, crisis-prone capitalism.

The paradoxical consequence has been that, to the extent that the official representatives of reformism in general and social democratic parties in particular have been freed to implement their characteristic worldviews, strategies, and tactics, they have systematically undermined the basis for their own continuing existence, paving the way for their own dissolution.

ROBERT BRENNER (1985)[1]

• •
•

Perhaps no contemporary slice of North American history corroborates so completely Brenner's assessment of the character and trajectory of reformism as the 1983 experience of Solidarity in Canada's west-coast province, British Columbia (BC).[2] Organised to oppose a legislative assault on workers, the poor and all sectors of the population who live daily with forms of special oppression (women, gays, racial and ethnic minorities, the disabled, and the elderly), Solidarity was the most important moment of class struggle in the Canadian far west since the organisational upheavals of the province's resource-sector workers in the 1940s. It drew hundreds of thousands of trade unionists, students, women, community activists, and previously uninvolved citizens into a politicised crucible of opposition to the state and the politics of socioeconomic retrenchment so championed by the New Right. As it ran its course, a perceived general strike seemed to be in the offing. For 130 days British Columbians were caught in a vice of class struggle from which there was no escape. 'Just how close the province came to spilling over the brink we need not speculate', editorialised the Vancouver *Sun* as the situation calmed in mid-November. Five months later, the Toronto *Globe and Mail* correspondent would write: 'Class warfare used to be a joke in this province. In the spring of 1984 no one is laughing'.[3]

---

1 Brenner 1985, pp. 36–7.
2 This article is based on the more extensive treatment in Palmer 1987b. Those wishing for access to fuller documentation and more detail should consult this study.
3 '130 Days', *Sun*, 14 November 1983; Ian Mulgrew, 'No one Laughs about Class War', *Globe and Mail*, 21 March 1984.

An examination of Solidarity supports Brenner's view of the trade-union bureaucrats and social-democratic leaders as inherently accommodationist and capitulationist. On one level, it also confirms his stress on the paradox of social democracy, for Solidarity's denouement – surely one of the most shameful instances of bureaucratic retreat before grassroots militancy in the recent North American past – undoubtedly bred the kind of cynicism and despair that weakens the hold of trade-union officialdom over its constituency and undermines social democracy's electoral pretences.

On another level, a critical and realistic appraisal of Solidarity and its aftermath emphasises the staying power of the trade-union leaders and their reformist project. This outcome was shored up by the infinite capacity of the 'labour Left' to dress itself in the garb of a 'progressive' counter to the macho-sectoralism of the crudest business unionists within the labour hierarchy, all the while expressing a ubiquitous faith in the spontaneity of the masses that left the complacent parliamentarianism of social-democratic wire-pullers in the mainstream electoral arena essentially unchallenged. However much class struggle threatened British Columbia's ordered capitalist relations in 1983, it is difficult not to assess the outcome of this momentous conflict and conclude that reformism has a long lease on the life of the workers' movement. Indeed, the tragedy of Solidarity is not simply that a mass upheaval of tremendous possibility was nullified by reformist commitments, but also that so few have been able to draw the conclusions necessary to re-forge and re-group the left against the very politics of moderation that crippled Solidarity.

Setting the Solidarity Stage I: The Political Economy of BC in the 1980s

In British Columbia, unlike other Canadian regions, the mainstream capitalist parties play little provincial role. Elections are fought out between Social Credit on the right and the social-democratic reformist New Democratic Party (NDP), rightly perceived as left-posturing 'liberals in a hurry'. The main contenders for federal power, the Liberals and Conservatives, have long since resigned themselves to roles of insignificance in provincial politics, or have liquidated their independence in the cause of defeating the so-called socialist threat posed by the NDP. In the May 1983 contest, the Social Credit Party, headed by Bill Bennett, a small-town merchant and son of the province's premier twentieth-century right-wing populist, 'Wacky' Bennett, won 35 of the 57 seats. Regarded as a stunning victory, the popular vote was in fact indecisive, with barely fifty percent of the participating electorate casting their lot with the

Social Credit machine. Bennett had been sold to the voters by a slick Tory pollster from Ontario, Patrick Kinsella: image was everything and the Socred programme of wage restraint and welfare cutting, destined to receive the praise of Milton Friedman, was but a subdued theme of the campaign.[4]

Obviously concerned with the depressed state of the regional economy and the impact of the new international division of labour, the Socreds looked around the province and found a recipe for economic revival. Mass plant shutdowns and staggering unemployment were the scourge that demanded redress. The large forestry-product multinationals had wound down their Pacific northwest operations to exploit the more lucrative potential of the open-shop American south or the low-wage under-developed Far East and Southern hemisphere.[5] Their revenues were no longer flowing into state coffers, and Bennett's Socreds needed to find ways of alleviating a growing fiscal crisis of the state. Finding no answers to the crisis of the 1980s in the experience of used-car dealerships, small-town stores and interior ranches which shaped their own business sense, Social Credit commodity-hucksters-turned-politicians looked elsewhere for advice. There were those who were willing to tell them what must be done. Consultations were soon arranged with Michael Walker and his colleagues in the BC-based right-wing think tank, the Fraser Institute, well known for its fulminations against unions, rent controls, state assistance to the unemployed and disadvantaged, and any and all fetters on initiative and the free movement of commodities and labour. The ideas of Walker and other Fraser Institute ideologues were soon being dispensed retail by Social Credit spokespersons.[6]

Bennett and the Socreds followed this capitalist teach-in with a 7 July 1983 budget, accompanied by 26 proposed bills which the governing party hailed as a much-needed programme of 'restraint'. This was to be the watchword of the new government. Some of the bills comprising the budget were of peripheral concern, but as a package the restraint legislation was awesome in its direct attack on labour, social rights and welfare-related services. Broadly defined, the crucial bills fell into three categories: those which undermined

4 See, for instance, Peter Cameron, 'The Kinsella Tapes', *New Directions*, June–July 1985; and, for comment on the marketing of the New Right, Davis 1986, especially pp. 157–80. On Bennett, see the populist journalistic account in Garr 1985.

5 For a brief introduction to the province's economic vulnerability in the context of world fluctuations in the price of forest resources, see Marchak 1984, pp. 22–40.

6 See Stainsby and Malcolmson 1983; Swankey 1983; Sid Tafler, 'Pushing the "Right" Ideas', *Globe and Mail*, 10 December 1983.

trade-union practices and the status of collective bargaining; those which abolished watchdog-type bodies and legislation, such as the Human Rights Commission/Code that aimed to protect those devoid of power; and those which cut services and centralised authority in the hands of the government, thereby curtailing the autonomy of specific groups. Particularly odious were the following:

> Bill 2: Public Service Labour Relations Amendment, which removed government employees' (organised in the British Columbia Government Employees Union, or BCGEU) rights to negotiate anything but wages.

> Bill 3: Public Sector Restraint Act, which enabled employers in the public sector to fire employees upon the expiration of a collective agreement. Originally the bill contained the provision that such firings could be undertaken 'without cause', but that wording was later removed. Broad termination conditions nevertheless remained.

> Bill 11: Compensation Stabilisation Amendment Act, which handled the wage issue by extending previously-established public-sector wage controls and limiting bargaining to the minus-5 percent to plus-5 percent range.

> Bill 5: Residential Tenancy Act, which abolished the Rentalsman's Office and rent controls (Vancouver has historically had one of the lowest vacancy rates in Canada and renters have long suffered at the hands of gouging landlords).

> Bill 27: Human Rights Act, which repealed the Human Rights Code, narrowed the definition of discrimination, limited the amount of compensation and abolished the Human Rights Commission.

A host of other bills supplemented these particulars.[7]

In one devastating blow Bennett and the Socreds sought to liberate capital from the fetters of past settlements with labour and the oppressed, striking out at public-sector unionism as the weak link in the chain of trade-union defences and abolishing state subsidies and protections for the poor, the disabled, and

---

7 On the bills see Marchak 1984, pp. 281–5; Operation Solidarity Leaflet, 'What Does the Legislation Mean to You?', Vancouver: Solidarity Coalition Files.

the underprivileged. An acute class foresight was at work, steeled by the New Right's intransigent opposition to softening such blows with obfuscation and petty concession. Reported unemployment in BC climbed from 12.1 to 15.6 percent between 1982 and 1984, a rate surpassed in North America only by Newfoundland and sections of Appalachia. The Socreds, knowing full well what lay ahead, demanded concessions from both the real and the social wage, givebacks which announced the advent of a new economic order in which both the high wage of unionised labour and the social minimum of the welfare state would no longer impede investment, accumulation and general economic restructuring.

Setting the Solidarity Stage II: Reformism and the Art of the Possible

Solidarity would be about resistance to this project. Resistance is necessarily related to organisation and leadership, at least if it is to be more than sporadic and inconsequential. Central to the history of Solidarity was the existence of a bureaucratised and thoroughly reformist layer of powerful labour leaders. The legalistic structuring of trade unionism in the direction of certification procedures rather than class struggle had been one consequence of the so-called 'post-war settlement' of the late 1940s. This, in turn, furthered the rise of a conservative, increasingly ossified trade-union officialdom in Canada. By the time of the 1983 budget, this contingent had been in unquestioned command of British Columbia's trade unionists for years. Moderate by inclination, the reformist bureaucracy that headed organised labour carved up the class struggle into its economic (trade union) and political (NDP electoralism) halves, in a manner not unlike that described by Rosa Luxemburg in *The Mass Strike, The Political Party and the Trade Union*. It imposed a bureaucratised and hierarchical form of authority within the labour movement and accommodated itself to the legalistic core of state policy via collective bargaining. Capable of wearing many different faces, the labour bureaucrats were nevertheless as one in their commitment to living within the capitalist order that secured the offices they held.[8]

Head of British Columbia's most powerful labour centre in 1983, the British Columbia Federation of Labour (BCFL/BC Fed), was Arthur Kube. Hailed as a

---

8   Note the discussions in Panitch and Swartz 1985; Bryan D. Palmer, 'Building the House of Labour', *Solidarity Times*, 30 November 1983. Profiles of the province's labour leaders appeared in *Sun* (Vancouver), 3 September 1983. Compare Luxemburg 1925, especially pp. 79, 88, 93.

moderate, Kube had a history as the consummate social democrat, the perfect bureaucrat. His early involvement in the trade-union movement included a role in the successful raiding of the communist-led Sudbury (northern Ontario) local of the Mine, Mill, and Smelter Workers' Union. 'Yeah', he relates, 'I was a Steel heavy. I did work on immigrants. There was the whole anti-communist thing. No question there was Red-baiting'. His loyalty to the union hierarchy tested and proven, Kube assumed a series of staff posts; for a time he organised white-collar workers and eventually he became Canadian Labour Congress (CLC) Director of Education in British Columbia.[9]

It was in this post that he first made a series of connections outside the labour movement, forging relationships with community activists and, more sordidly and less publicly, with the Royal Canadian Mounted Police. Behind the scenes at the BC Fed, Kube was the slatemaker, and to him goes the credit, in part, for the 1982 election by acclamation of the entire 32-member executive council. Running for the post of Secretary Treasurer of the Federation in 1976, Kube uttered some words of prophetic import: 'I think I'll have to go to Victoria one day to protest anti-labour legislation ... But I'm not going to be getting up each morning crying "general strike" ... Rather than hammering people, I'll talk to them about options'.[10] In the summer of 1985, when I interviewed Arthur Kube and was searching out a self-assessment of his political programme, he replied with a laugh: 'Someone once told me in jest, you're the Art of the Possible'. Social democracy, always eager to get what can be secured from the limitations of the moment, yet never seeking to transcend and change that moment, could not ask for a more fitting banner nor a more deserved epitaph.[11]

The Origins of Solidarity: 'Spontaneity', the CP, and the Road to Reformism

Opposition to the July budget was forthcoming almost immediately. Early organisation was mounted and sustained by the Vancouver and District Labour

---

9   Rod Mickleburgh, 'What You See is What you Get', *Province* (Vancouver), 29 January 1984.

10   'RCMP Labor Liaison with BC Federation of Labour Continues', *CLASP Bulletin*, August–September 1983; George Dobie, 'A New Shape for Labour', *Sun*, 3 November 1976.

11   Art Kube interview, Vancouver, 11 June 1985. On social democracy see Przeworski 1985. Przeworski's text, in my reading, is too sympathetic to social democracy, conceding that alternatives to capitalism are simply not realistic, and arguing that social-democratic struggles to improve capitalism are all we can now achieve. But his contention that social-democratic reformism is not socialism and cannot lead to socialism is incontestable.

Council, most particularly its Unemployment Committee, which converted a scheduled demonstration on Monday, 11 July into a meeting determined to create a coalition of groups and unions opposed to the legislation. Organiser George Hewison recalled that there wasn't enough room in the hall to hold the people. The next day hundreds attended a forum addressed by members of the about-to-be abolished Human Rights Commission. Twenty-four hours later Women Against the Budget (WAB) was created, a feminist body which soon drew hundreds of women to its regular and highly-charged meetings.

Out of all of this would come the Lower Mainland Budget Coalition and a six-point resolution calling for a demonstration and urging the BC Federation of Labour to initiate a province-wide protest. The demonstration was scheduled for 23 July.[12] Within two weeks an impressive mobilisation kicked off, with rallies in many of BC's communities, at least one workplace occupation by government employees, and coordinated protest whenever Social Credit cabinet ministers appeared in public. It all culminated in the 23 July protest rally, where almost 30,000 people gathered outside BC Place – a monument to the Socred penchant for megaprojects – to demand the withdrawal of the entire legislative package. An impressive movement of opposition was now off the ground.[13]

Art Kube, the rest of the labour hierarchy, and the NDP were conspicuous by their absence in this initial wave of protest, the implicit suggestions of Solidarity's official histories to the contrary.[14] Indeed, all evidence suggests that Kube tried to cool the protest. According to Kube himself, the 23 July action was premature, could not be successfully mobilised, and the early Budget Coalition was 'fairly narrow ... [composed of] advocacy groups ... What we had to bring in was the Uncle Tom groups we could make common cause with around human rights'. Behind Kube's high-sounding call to build a broader base lay a more calculating agenda: to rein in the growing mobilisation and contain it within a space capable of being controlled by the bureaucratised reformist leadership of the BC Fed, to drown the voices of the left in a popular-frontist sea of 'Uncle Toms'.[15]

12   George Hewison interview, Toronto, 8 August 1985; 'Coalition Against the Budget Launched', *Pacific Tribune*, 15 July 1983.

13   See 'Thousands Join Call to Battle Socred Budget', *Province*, 24 July 1983; 'Withdraw All the Legislation', *Pacific Tribune*, 29 July 1983; Ian Mulgrew, 'Thousands Protest Restraint in BC', *Globe and Mail*, 25 July 1983.

14   Note, for 'official' accounts of Solidarity's origins: Kube, Mickleburgh, and Brownstone 1984; and, more obviously, in the Operation Solidarity-sponsored video, 'Common Cause', 1984.

15   Evert Hoogers interview, 7 June 1985; Art Kube interview, 11 June 1985; Women Against

Those who had built the anti-budget coalition were indeed to the left of Kube and company. The mass base of the early protest was centred in the amorphous left, the activist rank-and-file militants of the unions and the women's movement, and community organisers among the poor, the oppressed, and the disabled. Perhaps the key player, however, was the Communist Party. Vancouver is the one city in Canada where the CP actually plays a significant role in the unions, local politics and mass movements. It was central in getting the anti-Socred mobilisation off the ground. Once that happened, however, the CP had no appetite to lead the fight-back, preferring, as it has historically since the 1920s, to form blocs with the more mainstream reformists in the labour hierarchy and social democracy, turning control of events over to them.

Claiming that 'we've refined the knowledge of how to operate in the labour movement to a fair science over 63 years and more', party leader and early anti-budget organiser George Hewison stressed that the party's perspective on the anti-Socred battle was that unity must prevail within the labour movement, regardless of the cost. In his words, the CP was there to 'play a constructive role ... keep unity ... aiming it at the Socreds and not the bureaucrats ... You can't have unity with those people and denounce them at the same time ... It's not possible ... in the middle of the struggle you don't kick shit out of your leaders'. When asked, 'How much thought do you give to the price you pay for doing that?', Hewison replied, 'You don't. You don't worry about the price; you worry about whether it is correct or not'. Determined to prod the Federation to act, Communist Party militants seized the initiative in July, but without the intention of continuing to carry the ball. They would hand it over willingly to the Fed brass, whom they hoped would not fumble it too badly, but whom they would in any case never criticise forcefully. The art of the possible was now very much on the agenda.[16]

---

the Budget interview (Jackie Larkin, Marion Pollack, Gail Meredith), 11 June 1985; Jean Swanson interview, 6 June 1985; Renate Shearer interview, 4 June 1985 (all Vancouver); and Hewison interview.

16 Hewison interview; Stan Persky, 'Seeing Reds', *This Magazine*, 19 June 1985; BC Municipal Affairs Committee, 'On Civic Parliamentary and Extra-Parliamentary Struggles', *Discussion Bulletin, Communist Party of Canada, 26th Convention*, 25 March 1985; George Hewison, 'Protesting Changing Political History', *Pacific Tribune*, 29 July 1983. See Angus 1981. Molyneux 1984, pp. 41–53, makes a series of generalised points about how Stalinist parties have functioned on the Left and within the workers' movement over the last 60 years, which bear remarkable resemblance to the situation discussed here.

Enter Solidarity

On the very day of the meeting that would end up creating the Lower Mainland Budget Coalition, Kube called a press conference to announce that the BCFL would be leading a major campaign of opposition to the budget. The Federation's public-sector committee was to kick off the drive midweek with a conference drawing together affiliated and non-affiliated public-sector unions representing some 240,000 members. At the end of the week Kube took the unprecedented action of convening representatives from all of the province's unions, including nationalist rivals from the Confederation of Canadian Unions (CCU). At that gathering the formation of a trade-union opposition to the budget was announced, and christened Operation Solidarity.

Masterminded by Kube, the plan of trade-union unity, drawing together labour bodies with a long history of ideological difference, raiding and acrimony, was opposed by some in the Federation, who jealously guarded their jurisdictional territories and affiliations with the American Federation of Labor and CLC. But generally the degree of labour unity was unprecedented. If the major labour figure in British Columbia, Jack Munro of the International Woodworkers of America (IWA), was subdued, others were willing to take up the slack. There were empty boasts that 'a general strike, possibly in October, is virtually a certainty'. Representatives of more than 500,000 organised workers (37 percent of the BC workforce) were now committed to opposing the Socred restraint program. Within three weeks over $1,500,000 had been raised for the fight-back, all but $200,000 generated in British Columbia.[17]

Operation Solidarity quickly got its feet wet with a demonstration on the lawns of the provincial legislature. Busloads of unionists, human-rights activists, tenants, feminists and unemployed workers, 25,000 strong, descended on Victoria on 27 July to call for the withdrawal of all of the offensive bills. An astounding success, the midweek rally convinced many of what could be gained by a coordinated, comprehensive campaign under the leadership of the Federation of Labour. The buses were barely back from Victoria when Operation Solidarity called for a broad province-wide coalition to beat back the threatening legislation.[18]

---

17   Bob Buzza to Kuehn et al. 'Operation Solidarity: BC Federation of Labour Meeting, 15 July 1983', 19 July 1983, in Larry Kuehn Papers, Box 5, File 9, Special Collections, University of British Columbia, Vancouver; *Globe and Mail*, 16 July 1983; *Pacific Tribune*, 15 July 1983.

18   Ian Mulgrew, '20,000 Join Protest Against BC Cuts', *Globe and Mail*, 28 July 1983; *Sun*, 28 July 1983; *Pacific Tribune*, 29 July 1983.

On Wednesday, 3 August, Operation Solidarity called together representatives from over 200 community-based organisations. From the chair, OpSol head Kube moved and secured acceptance of three co-chairs for a new coalition: himself; fired Human Rights Commissioner Renate Shearer; and a Langara College religious studies instructor, Father Jim Roberts, who had been a member of the steering committee of the original Budget Coalition. Money and organisers were promised by Kube and the old Budget Coalition looked amateurish in comparison with the high-profile, lucratively-funded project championed by the upper echelons of the BC Fed. Some protested that the old activists of the Budget Coalition were being bypassed without appropriate consultation, but resistance at this point seemed futile and the result a foregone conclusion.[19]

The success of Operation Solidarity initiatives and the new province-wide momentum silenced many critics. Over 50,000 people jammed into Vancouver's Empire Stadium on 10 August to see the city firefighters and bus drivers join other public-sector workers and Socred opponents in a massive and exhilarating show of force, tantamount to a one-day walkout of the metropolitan centre's public-sector workers. Rallies of one to six thousand were taking place in other communities and coalitions were springing up across the province. Unity was the cry of the hour, a call with understandable appeal to many, whether trade unionists or unaffiliated.[20]

Such unprecedented protests set the stage for the re-joining of the Lower Mainland Budget Coalition, which by mid-August had collapsed, into the new province-wide movement of budget resistance, re-named the Solidarity Coalition. When this body was formally launched in the immediate aftermath of the 10 August rally, there were voices of protest from various quarters. But the meeting had little time for dissent. 'Work was to be done', thundered Communist Party spokesperson George Hewison from the floor, and the liquidation of the original coalition was a *fait accompli*.

The new Solidarity Coalition was indeed wider than the old Lower Mainland Budget Coalition, and many on the broad left saw it as a step forward. In fact, it represented the consolidation of the organisational grip of the BC Fed bureaucracy over the burgeoning protest movement, a development evident in three features of the new coalition. First, in its structure the Solidarity Coalition was separate from Operation Solidarity, and both had their own distinct steering

---

19   Women Against the Budget interview, 11 June 1985.
20   'Fifty Thousand Jam Empire Stadium as Mass Budget Protests Sweep Province', *Pacific Tribune*, 19 August 1983; *Globe and Mail*, 10 August 1983; 11 August 1983; and 15 August 1983; *Province*, 11 August 1983; Hoogers interview; Denny Boyd, 'Lonely Voice Delivers a Message to Bill Bennett', *Sun*, 11 August 1983.

committees and assemblies. This institutionalised and legitimised the dichotomy of trade-union (economic) and social-service (human/political) issues.
Given who was paying the bills, such a separation inevitably reduced the Coalition to an adjunct of the more powerful OpSol trade-union leaders. Second,
the 'broad left' that had initiated the protest wave was now effectively marginalised, represented on the Solidarity Coalition steering committee and in its
assembly as the Lower Mainland Solidarity Coalition (LMSC), but effectively
swamped by the more than 150 provincial delegates who comprised the new
body, many of whom were, in one WAB activist's words, 'bureaucrats without
a rank-and-file'. Third, the leading figures in the Solidarity Coalition – its co-
chairs and organisers – were Kube's handpicked appointees. Lest anyone forget
where authority lay, Arthur Kube was the only direct link between Operation
Solidarity and the Solidarity Coalition, heading the former and appointing himself one of the three chairs of the latter. In their structures and interrelationship
the newly-created coalition and its labour movement parent were responses
to more than Bill Bennett. They were also answers to who would control the
mobilisation against the budget.

Reformism Shifts Gears

Surrounding the Empire Stadium protest was talk of the need for job actions.
With the government's dismissal of the significance of the large rallies that
had taken place between 23 July and 10 August there was discussion of the
need for a general strike. At the very least, some unionists favoured using
anonymously-mobilised flying pickets to close down particular work sites. But
Kube resisted, saying, 'A general strike is the last thing on my mind', and adding
that job actions would 'scare away a great number of groups'.[21]

The practitioners of the art of the possible concluded that mass demonstrations had served their purpose and were no longer likely to play a significant
role. At an OpSol think tank four days after the Empire Stadium rally it was
decided that phase one of the fight, in which mass protests had predominated,
was over. There was now a need to move towards a period of diversification in
which smaller protests would be staged and more educational work attempted. During late August and well into September, the labour bureaucracy thus
ordered the representatives in the Coalition to pursue two dubious tactics of
diversified mobilisation.

---

21   Mike Bocking, 'Rallying to the Cause Grows Difficult', *Sun*, 17 August 1983.

The first, initiated by Coalition-organiser Jean Swanson, was an eight-week consciousness-raising drive in which each specific social group attacked by the government would become the target of a week-long educational campaign. Closely coordinated with this was a petition drive, said to be organised through NDP constituency associations, which aimed to secure an overwhelming number of signatures to be tallied and presented to the government, thus revealing the hostility of the province to the budget legislation. Little came of either of these efforts, except that a great deal of money and time was expended. The petitions were never even presented to the Socreds.[22]

Both these gestures toward diversification were in fact attempts to demobilise the opposition and steer it back toward the parliamentary arena. By mid-September it was clear how much ground had been lost. In the words of a small leftist organisation, Socialist Challenge: 'Ever since the Empire Stadium rally, Operation Solidarity and the Solidarity Coalition have drifted, with no clear vision of what has to be done next. We have lost a lot of time, and a lot of momentum'.[23] When the amorphous left tried to reroute the opposition back on to the path of protest, coordinating an occupation of the Vancouver-based offices of the Social Credit cabinet and staging a 'stone soup luncheon' at the home of the Minister of Human Resources, it met with the cold shoulder of labour officialdom's displeasure, sneers from the NDP, and relatively small turnouts. That these events failed to accomplish their goals was in part due to the fact that they were initiated *without* any *public* critique of the Solidarity leadership's deliberate intention to take the steam out of the opposition protests. Indeed, more time was spent in attempts to curry favour with the bureaucracy and secure official endorsement than in any open challenge.

The role of the Communist Party, especially in the government offices sit-in, was pivotal in the making of this strategic orientation, but so too was the so-called independent left's willingness to conceive of itself as a pressure group committed to forcing the bureaucracy away from its undeclared demobilisation. This was a flawed approach for two reasons. First, given the strength of the labour hierarchy, now very much in control of Solidarity as a whole, such tentative and subdued opposition was too little, too late. Second, it tended to focus dissenting activity outside the trade-union movement. What was actu-

---

22   'Report on Operation Solidarity Think-Tank', Kuehn Papers, Box 5, File 9, Special Collections, University of British Columbia, Vancouver; Fred Wilson, 'Phase II: Pressure on Government must Escalate', *Pacific Tribune*, 19 August 1983.

23   Socialist Challenge Organization, 'Draft Program for Discussion within the Lower Mainland Solidarity Coalition', 17 October 1983; Kuehn Papers, Box 4, File 9, Special Collections, University of British Columbia, Vancouver.

ally required late in August and early in September was an attempt to galvanise some of the growing rank-and-file's uneasiness over the de-escalation of the struggle within the unions themselves, an attempt which would necessarily have had to penetrate both the public *and* private sectors. This kind of labour-centred activity, however, never materialised, and in its place the left substituted relatively ineffective media events.

The movement of opposition was now two-and-a-half months old, and no closer to the realisation of its goal of repeal of the repressive legislation. It was well known that the Social Credit Party's annual convention was scheduled to take place in mid-October at the Hotel Vancouver. As early as late August, the latter had been raised in Operation Solidarity circles, with the suggestion that a massive protest be organised to coincide with the gathering. But the labour leadership remained convinced that people could not yet again be enticed into the streets. One month away from the convention, nothing had been planned and, in the opinion of Vancouver Municipal and Regional Employees Union president David Cadman, who represented his union in Operation Solidarity, no action would have been taken had 'the Fed had its way'.[24]

It was in the Lower Mainland Solidarity Coalition that a spirited resolution was moved calling for all-out mobilisation of Solidarity forces for a 15 October Hotel Vancouver demonstration against the Socreds. Speaking against the motion was Jean Swanson, Kube's handpicked Coalition organiser. Stressing that work needed to be done on the petition campaign and fearful that a face-to-face confrontation with the Bennett people in downtown Vancouver would erupt in riotous tumult that would blacken the respectable image of Solidarity, Swanson urged the rejection of the proposed October action. But the day was carried decisively, and Swanson's was the only voice of opposition.

Faced with rank-and-file determination to proceed with the demonstration, Kube and company reluctantly orchestrated the mid-October protest. But they literally sabotaged the event, providing no media or billboard advertising, and structuring the march so that it culminated in an obscure cul-de-sac, well removed from the Socred convention: an enclave, in the words of one Coalition organiser, 'designed to camouflage a small crowd'. Kube actually commented to the press that 'feelings are starting to run so high among the rank-and-file that [I am] personally hoping the planned 15 October Solidarity march and rally doesn't get too large'.[25]

---

24   David Cadman interview, Vancouver, 13 June 1985.

25   Jean Swanson interview, 6 June 1985; Kube quote from an undated Vancouver *Sun* clipping, Solidarity coalition files.

Yet the groundswell from below overcame the timidity of the movement's leadership and the 15 October action was an unanticipated success, drawing between 60,000 and 80,000 militant anti-Socred oppositionists into the streets. They, and not the Solidarity helmsmen, put the flagging mobilisation back on its feet.

The Party of Social Democracy and Parliamentary Charades

If the union bureaucracy was hesitant and obstructionist, the political wing of reformism – the social-democratic NDP – was guilty of parliamentary cretinism at best and condescending abstentionism at worst.

The NDP in British Columbia, as elsewhere in Canada, epitomises the world-wide capitulation of social democracy to electoralism in the twentieth century. It has no sympathy for or conception of struggle outside parliamentary forums. Thus, while NDP activists were prominent in the Solidarity Coalition, and while Operation Solidarity leaders were staunch advocates of the social-democratic party, the NDP as an organisation and a caucus played no role in the events of the summer and autumn upheaval. To be sure, the party contained factions, and George Hewison confessed that in the Communist Party's quest for unity it often found itself trying to calm down hostile elements in the NDP and bring them closer to those social democrats who argued that the NDP must be involved in the anti-Socred fight.

The Solidarity crucible thus created an incongruous situation in which the CP was 'playing referee inside' the party of social democracy. But in spite of this reformist demonstration that their politics made strange bedfellows, the upper reaches of the NDP followed a path of abstentionism, withdrawing from overt involvement in the struggle and offering caustic and condescending comment to those involved in the movement. NDP leader Dave Barrett, known for his willingness to legislate strikers back to work when he held the reins of state power in the mid-1970s, offered Solidarity wise counsel at the first Victoria rally: 'You came in peace, now go in peace', adding as an afterthought, 'And please take your garbage'. Uninvited to the podium at the huge Empire Stadium rally, he characterised the event as a mere 'sprint'. The real race, he pontificated to reporters afterwards, was being run 'in the legislature'.[26]

---

26   Hewison interview; *Globe and Mail*, 11 August 1983; *Sun*, 11 August 1983; 'The NDP and Solidarity in BC', *Labour Focus*, January 1984. Background on the sorry record of social democracy in power is found in Resnick 1977b, pp. 3–20.

But by mid-September the legislature was little more than a parliamentary zoo. When the Socreds tried to ram their offensive legislation through the House the NDP filibustered and after a few days Bennett and his governing party declared war on debate and discussion. Closure, last used in BC in 1957, was invoked 20 times. All-night sittings, known as legislation by exhaustion, were common and in the three weeks after 19 September the House sat past midnight 11 times. In the midst of these fiascos, the leader of the opposition, Dave Barrett, was ejected from the legislature on two occasions, on the latter by physical removal, resulting in his banishment from the House until its next sitting. Having disposed of the parliamentary opposition, Bennett announced that the legislature would go into recess on 21 October, providing, in his terms, a 'much-needed cooling off' period. Seventeen acts had received royal assent, including four of the major anti-labour bills; nine others were left in limbo, including some of the most contentious legislation affecting human rights, tenants and health care. If Solidarity was preparing for phase three of the confrontation, so were the Socreds. They now had labour legislation to hold over the public-sector unionists, soon to enter into contract negotiations, and legislative chips, in the form of unpassed bills, with which to bargain with the social-service advocates.[27]

Barrett's social-democratic legislative race, run with a reformist blindness to the massive extra-parliamentary opposition in the streets, was thus halted as soon as the governing party decided it no longer cared for the niceties of parliamentary democracy. With the track closed down by the Socreds in mid-October, the course littered with closure, all-night sittings and a leaderless opposition, there was finally nowhere for the party of social democracy to run. It looked around, and ducked for cover. Little would be heard from the NDP in the time remaining to Solidarity. As Barrett would later comment: 'We are observers, and we observed'.[28]

That was the way the labour leadership wanted it. Well before mid-August, Operation Solidarity leaders and the NDP caucus had clandestine meetings. Protective of Solidarity's so-called non-partisanship, Operation Solidarity figureheads shoved the NDP rather far into the background, asking only that it try to stall the legislation. As events unfolded Kube would play up the extent to which the NDP was peripheral to the struggle: 'I presume the NDP caucus feels lonely in the legislature because the action is not in the legislature, it's out in

---

27   For a succinct account of legislative activity see Wilson 1984, pp. 114–30.

28   Sharon Yandle, 'The NDP in BC: Observing Their Friends on the Move', *Canadian Dimension*, March 1984.

the community'. He would later claim that the parliamentary opposition collapsed and 'Operation Solidarity and the Coalition had become the opposition'. But the extra-parliamentary leadership never severed the connection between the party and the unions; throughout the difficult days of September, Kube delegated trusted union officials to meet with the NDP caucus in Victoria.[29]

All of this saw the horses running true to form. For from the birth of Operation Solidarity it was always clear that in spite of the mobilisation of hundreds of thousands of British Columbians outside the arena of electoralism, the trade-union leadership always conceived of the anti-budget drive as leading to an election victory later in the decade. Trade-union leaders and NDP hacks were united in their view that the mass mobilisation had to be directed away from militant struggle and into the subdued politics of electoralism. By avoiding the contamination of its parliamentarianism with any association with militant forms of class struggle, the NDP sought a new lease on life as the 'political wing' of Solidarity, albeit one that could not, in the turmoil of September and October, be paraded before the public with much fanfare. Fearful of participating in the confrontation, the NDP was content to watch the 'economic' leaders of the class have their hour on the stage, waiting until the labour bureaucracy cooled militancy sufficiently to re-establish a role for the politicians.

The Bureaucrats Backtrack and Bluster

As calls for militancy swept through the Solidarity ranks in late October, it was apparent that the hour was fast approaching when action, not talk, was required. October 31 was the date set by the government for the firing of 1,600 civil servants (hundreds had already been sacked), part of the long-term Socred plan of 'downsizing', which projected some 11,000 job reductions in the state sector over a two-year period. The end of October also signalled the lapsing of the BCGEU contract, thus placing tens of thousands of government workers under the guillotine of the nefarious Bills 2 and 3, which threatened to wipe out collective-bargaining rights and any semblance of job security in the public sector.

Many wanted an all-out general strike. When delegates from Solidarity Coalitions across the province met in Vancouver on 22 and 23 October, they were

---

29   Kube interview; Mike Kramer interview, Vancouver, 10 June 1985; *Province*, 18 September 1983; 'Minutes of Expanded Public Sector Committee', 20 September 1983, Kuehn Papers, Box 5, File 17, Special Collections, University of British Columbia, Vancouver; Kube, Mickleburgh, and Brownstone 1984, p. 8.

unambiguous in endorsing such work-coordinated stoppages and a massive fight-back. Polls conducted in Vancouver indicated that only 45.7 percent of the *entire* population rejected outright the notion of an unlimited general strike to bring the government down. Even some labour spokespersons had rhetorically threatened such action throughout the summer and autumn mobilisation, as a last stand to force the repeal of the entire legislative assault.[30] Indeed, this was what Kube and company had always called for, and it was on this basis of striking down *all* the offensive bills that both Operation Solidarity and the Solidarity Coalition were launched. But as events moved to a head in mid-to-late October it began to be apparent that the labour hierarchy was willing to settle for a good deal less. The institutional separation of Operation Solidarity (trade union/economic) and the Solidarity Coalition (social/political issues) began to be reflected in the labour bureaucracy's subtle backing away from the human rights/social services side of the struggle, collapsing the fight into an opposition to the two bills which curbed collective bargaining in the public sector and which centred on the BCGEU contract negotiations.

If the trade-union hierarchy had simply stated that the struggle around the 'social' legislation was terminated, an upheaval in the ranks would have resulted. But they did not do this. They correctly perceived that if they placated the left-initiated call for a general strike and opportunistically concealed their own quite limited purposes, they might well ride out what appeared to be a potentially ugly storm. In leading with their left, they played it just right, and their radical critics got silenced and suckered in the process.

On 25 October the public-sector coordinating committee meeting of Operation Solidarity resolved to demand the withdrawal of all offensive legislation and, if that ultimatum was not complied with, 'to call for general public-sector

---

30   *Province*, 22 September 1983; *Sun*, 22 September 1983; Doug Ward, 'Coalition Tries to Sell a Shutdown', *Sun*, 28 September 1983; *Sun*, 6 October 1983; Kube interview; Alan Bayless, 'British Columbia Bracing for Labor Strife', *Wall Street Journal*, 21 August 1983; 'Resolution on Unity Adopted Unanimously by the LMSC Assembly', 17 October 1983, and 'Solidarity Coalition, Delegated Conference Resolutions from Local Coalitions/Groups', both in Kuehn Papers, Box 5, File 10, Special Collections, University of British Columbia, Vancouver; 'Coalition Promises Continued Struggle', *Pacific Tribune*, 26 October 1983; *Sun*, 19 October 1983. It is worth noting that the Communist Party adopted an ambiguous position toward the general strike. While their press often mentioned the general strike as a future possibility, the CP in practice aligned themselves with the labour bureaucracy in opposing calls to organise an unlimited general strike and in fact spoke against such proposals at numerous meetings. Some of this ambiguity is apparent in the Hewison interview.

political strike action'.[31] An escalating series of work stoppages was planned, beginning with government employees on 1 November, and followed by teachers, transport and health-care workers between 8 and 18 November, if the Socreds did not give ground. So great was the enthusiasm for militant strike action that there was little scrutiny of the questionable tactic of an 'escalating' strike which put teachers, a group with little history of work stoppages and union traditions, in the forefront of the struggle. (The state saved money when government clerks and teachers stayed off the job, while an added bonus was that it could condemn the 'irresponsibility' of those who would sacrifice the 'interests' of the public and school children in 'partisan' political protest). Nor was the crucial issue of what would settle the dispute resolved. 'Avoid use of the term "general strike"', noted one memo issued to Operation Solidarity spokespersons, 'Let others use it. You are not "making demands" but "securing" basic rights as your objective'. Blustering thus bought the bureaucracy a renewed mandate, and was taken as good coin by many on the 'broad left' who thought the planned escalation was the showdown they had been waiting for.[32]

November: The Thirteen Days

Thirty-five thousand government workers struck, as scheduled, on Halloween eve. Ten days of negotiations got nowhere. Right from the outset the conflict was depicted by the union leadership as a narrow struggle. An Operation Solidarity press release stated that, 'the negotiations currently underway can bring a general resolution to the conflict spawned by Bill 3'.

At a meeting of the Provincial Assembly of the Solidarity Coalition Kube argued: 'It's not the case that unions have forgotten human rights and other issues, but we don't know if we will be able to bargain for them'. With 200,000 workers committed to taking political action in the next weeks, however, Solidarity activists dedicated to striking down all of Bennett's bills failed to grasp the meaning of these words. Euphoria at a possible victory prevailed, rather than the hard-headed realisation that you are only as good as your leadership.[33]

---

31 'Public Sector Coordinating Meeting', 25 October 1983, Kuehn Papers, Box 5, File 9, Special Collections, University of British Columbia, Vancouver.

32 'Five Communication Principles', n.d., Kuehn Papers, Box 5, File 9, Special Collections, University of British Columbia, Vancouver.

33 *Sun*, 28 October 1983; 29 October 1983; 31 October 1983; 1 November 1983; Operation Solidarity Press Release, 3 November 1983, Kuehn Papers, Box 4, File 10, Special Collections, Uni-

In spite of this narrowing of the struggle to Bill 3 (which was done in such a way as to obscure the collapsing of the mobilisation into a single issue), the Socreds chose to hang tough rather than give even the most minor concessions to the BCGEU. They sensed, correctly, that they had the Solidarity leaders on the run. They also thought the teachers would never strike in sufficient numbers to pose any threat, and thus counted on a failed school walkout both to silence Solidarity and to reinforce their bargaining position with the BCGEU. Paradoxically, many within the union bureaucracy saw the situation similarly. They simply could not conceive of teachers striking effectively and saw the prospect of calming the Solidarity masses.[34] Week two of the escalation was thus pivotal: the government was willing to bet on the teachers disgracing themselves as unionists, while a failure of the education strikes was anticipated as a possible end of the conflict by some nervous reformists fearful of carrying the struggle further.

But the script was altered by unpredictable militancy at the base. The teachers took to the streets in unanticipated numbers and solidarity. Slandered by the state, facing a wave of injunctions to which the labour hierarchy cravenly capitulated, the teachers and their Solidarity supporters nevertheless sustained a momentous resistance. The success of the teacher's walkout meant that the ferry workers, who linked the Vancouver Island capital, Victoria, to the mainland, were scheduled to strike next. Bennett had decreed that if the ferry workers joined the protest he would legislate them back to work; the labour hierarchy had retaliated with the promise that any such action would be met with a full-scale general strike involving all organised workers in the private and public sectors. By mid-week things looked as if they were heading in just that direction, the empty rhetoric of tough-talking business unionists coming back to haunt them.

The eleventh hour had indeed arrived. Reformism wasted no time in acting. The ferry workers' walkout was quietly postponed until Monday. Kube appeared on national television and wept, then retired to his sickbed. Hardball negotiations at the Vancouver offices of the Labour Relations Board pitted government hired guns against Operation Solidarity figures Mike Kramer (sec-

---

versity of British Columbia, Vancouver; Provincial Assembly Meeting Minutes, 3 November 1983, Kuehn Papers, Box 5, File 10, Special Collections, University of British Columbia, Vancouver.

34   At a February 1984 debate at Simon Fraser University between secretary-treasurer of the BC Fed, Mike Kramer, and myself, Kramer confessed that many trade-union leaders thought 'the teachers would fold'. (My notes, but see as well, Doug Ward, 'Sell-out of Solidarity Debated', *Sun*, 3 February 1984).

retary treasurer of the BC Fed) and Jack Munro. Two days of haggling secured the government employees' union a three-year pact which 'won' the workers a grand total of 4 percent wage increases over the 36 months of the contract (0 percent the first year) and sacrificed union rights on hours and work-time flexibility. The union agreed to the 1,600 layoffs demanded by the government, as long as these were negotiated through the trade union rather than stipulated arbitrarily by the state, BCGEU negotiators apparently preferring to police the firings themselves than to be without a contract. Finally, the new contract exempted the BCGEU from the provisions of Bill 3, already passed in the legislature, an act which allowed the state to terminate public-sector employees upon the expiration of a collective agreement. (Since the Socreds had already secured the 1,600 lay-offs, the matter was somewhat academic). It was, according to BCGEU chief negotiator Cliff Andstein, a 'no concessions agreement', but that could not have fooled those who had been fired.

The government-BCGEU agreement was in fact the beginning of the end of Solidarity, but there was a need to secure something from the state to placate the activists who had sacrificed time, wages and in some cases jobs to back their brothers and sisters in the BCGEU and fight for the restoration of social services in British Columbia. Bill 2, applicable only to the BCGEU, threatened to eliminate collective-bargaining rights for the government clerks. It was killed, the Socreds recognising that its aims had been secured anyway in the union's give-back contract.

The other crucial piece of labour legislation, Bill 3, had been passed before Bennett closed down the House, but the provincial government now conceded that other public-sector unions had the dubious 'right' to follow in the BCGEU's footsteps and negotiate exemptions from the act. Advisory committees to hear submissions on human rights, tenants' legislation and proposed changes to the Labour Code were supposed to be established, and the money saved by the state on teacher/education-worker salaries during the protest was to remain in the educational system: promises which proved as empty as any thinking critic of the Socreds should have expected them to be. Far from the repeal of the entire legislative package, this was a bitter pill for the Solidarity ranks to swallow.[35]

None of this was public knowledge at the time. More galling than the paltry results for which Solidarity had been squandered was the form in which its

---

35   Conditions of the 'deal' were leaked to the press but there were no official confirmations and thus the terms of the settlement were essentially a matter for speculation. See 'Memo Lists Secret Labour Offer', *Sun*, 12 November 1983.

end was announced. As the corks were popping at the BCGEU hall on Sunday afternoon, in celebration of the 'victory' of the union figureheads, Jack Munro was on his way to the airport, flying to the Kelowna (a community in the interior of the province) home of Solidarity's nemesis, BC premier Bill Bennett. He was accompanied by none other than Bennett's chief negotiator, Norman Spector, fresh from his ego-boosting humiliation of the BCGEU. As the pact-makers took off, Spector reputedly turned to Munro and said, 'We've got you now. We are going to renege'. Instead of asking for a parachute Munro continued to Kelowna, posed for the television cameras shaking hands with Bennett, and announced that the Solidarity strikes were over.

There was no formal statement of what had been won, no concrete written agreement, no consultation with the Solidarity Coalition or the education-sector strikers, and no written agreement between the state and the Solidarity opposition. Much hailed in the weeks to come as the 'Kelowna Accord', Sunday evening's events were a shock to trade unionists, feminists and Solidarity activists, who were literally stunned that their movement had been shafted by an uncorroborated 'gentlemen's agreement', sealed with a handclasp in the enemy's den. The next night hundreds of angry militants congregated at a Vancouver union hall to rake some of the Solidarity mis-leaders over the coals. But it was too late: the movement was finished; Solidarity was now a dirty word.[36]

The Lessons of November

In the weeks to come Munro and Bennett and others involved in the settlement at the Labour Relations Board ended up disagreeing about what had been the conditions of the truce. It did not really matter. It was painfully obvious how much had been lost. Anger gave way to cynicism among the ranks as Solidarity withered. The movement's newspaper, the weekly *Solidarity Times*, was quietly folded up by the bureaucracy; it was now more of a liability than an asset given the hostile letters which began appearing. The living link that connected trade unionists, community activists, women's advocates and others who faced various kinds of special oppression was cut with the blunt knife of disillusionment and despair.

36   For the 'Kelowna Accord' see George Mason, 'Weekend in Kelowna', *Vancouver Magazine*, June 1984. For the meeting of denunciation, Terry Glavin, 'Kube Booed at Meeting', *Sun*, 15 November 1938; *Solidarity Times*, 16 November 1983.

Nothing is now clearer than that the paramount concern of the union leadership was to avoid a confrontation with Bennett. Key trade-union figures, far from leading the working class to do battle with right-wing ideologues, ended up playing the crucial role of demobilising and demoralising their own ranks. Ultimately the only way the bureaucracy could have been forced to fight was through the creation of a serious rank-and-file opposition. A key demand would have been for elected strike committees in every workplace, an organised working-class opposition that could have coordinated activity with non-union participants in the Coalition and formed labour-centred municipal, regional and province-wide strike committees. The formation of such a genuinely democratic committee structure would have substantially broadened the leadership of the movement, opening it out to the Coalition while retaining the economic muscle of the organised working class. Such a development would effectively have taken direction of the strike and Solidarity as a whole out of the hands of the labour bureaucrats. Moreover, these kinds of committees would have linked private- and public-sector workers, overcoming the forced separation of the House of Labour which contributed to defeat.

A serious oppositional current based on the politics of class struggle rather than tidy collaboration would have been obliged to utilise the unions as forums in which ruthless criticism of the labour hierarchy would have been posed at every step of the struggle. Even if this failed initially to break the hold of the professional labour statesmen over the massive groundswell of the rank-and-file and the many oppositional layers of British Columbian society, such a stance of hard resistance could have served as a pole of political attraction for the more advanced workers and left activists during the course of the fight-back. Instead of the demoralisation that followed in the wake of Solidarity's demise, some new beginnings might have been made. It is entirely possible that an opposition rooted in several key unions, but extending beyond them, would have considerably increased its base of support and, at the very least, compelled the bureaucracy to adopt a tougher bargaining stance. In the non-revolutionary situation of 1983 an organised, Marxist current in the unions, prepared to launch a political challenge to reformism and business unionism, might have opened the road to a real class battle to defeat the Socred offensive.

Why did nothing approaching this take place? First, ostensibly revolutionary groups such as the neo-Maoist In Struggle! and the Workers' Communist Party were in disarray, a consequence of internal crises and international confusions. The so-called Trotskyist left was hardly in better shape. In any case none of the groupings which constituted the 'far left' in British Columbia had any significant weight in the labour movement. More important, none of them had a staunch perspective of waging a political struggle against the bureaucrats of the BC Federation of Labour, generally opting instead to 'go with the flow' and attempting to pressure the labour leaders, pushing them to the left and hoping for the best.

Second, within the trade-union apparatus many of those who like to think of themselves as 'Marxists' or 'progressives' ended up being little more than the bureaucracy's aides: hired for their abilities and capacity for hard work, they were constantly engaged in an endless round of meetings and organisational activities. John L. Lewis, who fired many a communist in his early days only to hire the same kind of people back during the mass-production Congress of Industrial Organizations union drive of the mid-to-late 1930s, was fond of pointing out that there may be many differences between the hunter and the hunting dog, but the basic distinction eventually turns on 'who gets the bird'.[37] In British Columbia's Operation Solidarity/Solidarity Coalition there was no doubt who occupied hunter status and who, in contrast, functioned as bird dogs for the labour officialdom. Most paid members of staff, research directors and others retained by the labour movement, regardless of their subjective intent and endless hours on the job, were spending their time during that summer and autumn, getting birds for the bureaucracy.

Third, the whole tenor of left intervention turned on an essentially popular-frontist premise that emphasised 'collectivity' between labour and other social forces, including small business and professional elements. In the strict sense of the term, of course, Solidarity was not a popular front, because it was not a bloc across class lines for governmental power. But the labour bureaucracy deliberately sought to make Solidarity a 'broad' multi-class formation, playing especially on the movement's concern for the underprivileged outside the trade unions, a concern its 'settlement' shamefully tarnished. The appeal to petty capitalists and supposedly classless ethnic communities, the inclusion of police in demonstrations, the explicit efforts to draw in what the leadership itself referred to as 'Uncle Toms', and the bureaucracy's capitulationist slogan, 'Restraint does not mean repression', were all evidence of this.[38]

Recent attempts to whitewash the history of Solidarity and claim that the BC Federation of Labour has been transformed into a 'centre-left' entity (is there a vocabulary more appropriate to popular frontism?) ignore the devastation wrought within trade-union circles, skirt the fundamental losses experienced in the fields of human rights and social policy, and bypass the disillusionment

---

37   Lewis, as quoted in Brody 1980, p. 133.
38   On the popular front see Trotsky 1973a; 1973b; Klehr 1984; Isserman 1982.

which currently immobilises many whose first taste of politics and resistance soured in their once enthusiastic mouths.

Such a reading of Solidarity, moreover, is unashamedly cast within a political framework premised upon a bureaucratic and social-democratic reading of the possibilities of class struggle, focussing on 'who's where' in the Fed leadership and what the chances of NDP electoral success are. Much was always made of the NDP chances in the *next* election during the 1983 tumult, but when that next election did in fact roll around, in 1986, social democracy went down to yet another defeat.

On a building in East Vancouver a larger-than-life graffiti message jumps off the wall at passers-by, capturing the experience of Solidarity in six brief words: 'Rise up eat shit and die'. If these words, and the demoralising end they convey so bluntly, are not to be repeated, the vital question of working-class leadership and programme must be addressed. The real paradox of social democracy in Canada is that however much struggles like Solidarity reveal, in Brenner's terms, reformism's capacity to undermine itself, the seductive pull of social democracy and the labour bureaucracy, always capable of emerging from each self-inflicted catastrophe in a stance of timely renewal, remains a political force of considerable magnitude. As Gramsci commented in 1921, 'Illusion is the most tenacious weed in the collective consciousness. History teaches but it has no pupils'.[39]

---

39   Quoted in Williams 1975, p. 2.

Remapping the Landscape of Class Formation:
Comparisons and Conjunctures in Labour
History's Telescoped Longue Durée

∴

Introduction to Part 4

Social history, hegemonic within the wider discipline by the 1970s, reconfigured understandings of what constituted the proper terrain of historical investigation.[1] Labour movements and working-class culture were two areas of inquiry that received increasing attention, pioneering new approaches and generating theoretical insights. The study of the history of class society was now also necessarily done with due attention, in the aftermath of E.P. Thompson's *The Making of the English Working Class* (1963), to the agency of working people. Thompson explained his title in ways that charted orientations that would prove surprisingly innovative and influential:

> *Making* because it is a study in an active process, which owes as much to agency as to conditioning. The working class did not rise like the sun at any appointed time. It was present at its own making.[2]

This approach unleashed a plethora of analytic possibilities, extending well beyond class. As the Pandora's Box of subjectivity was pried open, the number of 'categories of historical analysis' that might be scrutinised in ways that revealed the wrestling of agency with conditioning multiplied and, in the process, often fragmented. Women's history morphed into the study of gender.[3] Addressing the history of families and their constitution and reconstitution in particular epochs blended into explorations of childhood and the import ance of demography in the development of capitalism.[4] Serious scrutiny of how sexuality had been forged through time necessarily prodded researchers to explore all manner of eroticised endeavours that related to the social construction of sexual minorities and identities that included not only the heterosexual, but the homosocial, the homosexual, the 'queer', and the transgendered.[5] As social history intersected fruitfully with economic history even the basic Marxist conception of modes of production was complicated, encompassing sophisticated exploration of transitional phases such as proto-industrialisation.[6]

---

1   For one statement among many see Eley 2005.
2   Thompson 1963, p. 9.
3   Scott 1988 is one indication of this trend.
4   For one insightful statement see Seccombe 1983.
5   In this development, so central to modern historiography, see Foucault 1976.
6   See Medick 1976 for an early statement of significance.

Inevitably, the rich canvas of diversity on which the new materialist social histories, born in the 1960s but coming to fruition in the 1970s and 1980s, were painted, began to be looked at differently. What had originally been regarded as a breakthrough into the inclusive detail of a much-needed democratisation of historical study came to be regarded as a retreat into specialised silos of containment, in which large and important dimensions of the past (once regarded as *the* proper terrain of historical study, but now apparently displaced) were seemingly hived off from narrow particularities. Different national contexts and specific vantage points from which critique might be waged posed the problem in distinct and often dramatically divergent ways. The analytic level of sophistication, and the nature of disagreement, were always contingent on the political standpoint of the critic, with commentary ranging from the usefully suggestive to red-baiting banality. There was a world of difference in the ways in which discontents with social history's practice were raised.

Criticisms of studies of class were indicative of the range of views. Some condemned the study of cultural aspects of working-class life because they were judged unimportant in the grand Whig march of labour's consolidating respectability and *entré* into the twentieth-century state's apparatus of accommodation. Others insisted that the study of almost anything relating to workers paled in importance before the need to return history to the examination of powerful men and significant events. More complicated yet was a growing malaise arising out of the fascination with the particular and the exotic, often posed in ways that called attention to the need for a radical-edged, hard-nosed assessment of who held power and how it was exercised. Agency, some suggested, had its limitations in the face of structured necessity and the ever-present, and often decisively important, counter-agencies of determination.

The basic point, all of these nuances aside, was difficult to miss. As studies of workers revealed, social history's project of inclusivity had focussed too much on what one mainstream Canadian historian in 1969 had called the 'limited identities' (which included class, ethnicity, and region)[7] of the country's past, to the exclusion of the 'big picture'. This needed to be brought back into focus. To do so meant ordering historical study more concertedly around large developments. Politics, the state, and economic structures established undeniable boundaries within which human behaviour unfolded, and it was the historian's task to explore this process of determination so that society's overall makeup was not shuffled to the sidelines.

---

7   Careless 1969.

The problem was of course international and the fragmenting outcomes of social history's endeavours were the cause of considerable complaint. Much was at stake in the confusing swirl of discussion and debate. As Peter Novick sums up the state of American historiography in these years, the outcome of social history's development was obvious. 'The founding fathers of the American historical discipline had grounded objectivity in a program of universalism versus particularism, nationalism versus localism', wrote Novick, but with 'every group its own historian', this foundational structure crumbled. 'By the 1980s all of the elements of this programme had become problematic'.[8]

Within the particular arena of working-class history as a crucial subset of social history, Marxists and other leftists weighed in on the issues. Tony Judt, then writing from a Marxist disillusionment with what he regarded as social history's promiscuous embrace of any-and-all subject matter, commenced his 1979 over-the-top polemical assault on the field with the words, 'This is a bad time to be a social historian'.[9] Geoff Eley and Keith Neld asked, more politely, 'Why Does Social History Ignore Politics'?[10] Elizabeth Fox-Genovese and Eugene D. Genovese bemoaned what they designated the political crisis of social history, suggesting that an undue focus on agency obscured who held power and how it was exercised.[11] Richard Johnson and his collaborators in the Centre for Contemporary Cultural Studies at the University of Birmingham unleashed a critical avalanche of commentary premised on the belief that certain key texts in social and labour history had taken a 'culturalist' turn and might be usefully subjected to 'structuralist' critique.[12] By the end of the 1980s, American labour historians were concerned that their own area of study lacked 'synthesis',[13] and it was not long before there was a growing chorus of complaint that the overall transnational field was 'in crisis'.[14]

There is no denying, retrospectively, that social history's rise and undoubted prominence in the aftermath of the 1960s enriched our understanding of the past. It also tended, over time, to fragment and focus historical analysis in ways that were troubling to those who took seriously Marxism's injunction to utilise theory and interpretation to change the world, a project that necessarily

---

8   Novick 1988, p. 521.
9   Judt 1979.
10   Eley and Nield 1980; and for a later update Eley and Nield 2007.
11   Fox-Genovese and Genovese 1976.
12   Johnson 1978; Clarke, Critcher, Johnson 1979.
13   Moody and Kessler-Harris 1989.
14   See, for instance, Berlanstein 1993.

involved broadening understanding of totalities rather than narrowing concerns to the particular. Marxism and historical practice were thus, by the 1980s, locked into a complicated tension in which the realisation of social history's promise seemed to be advancing on some tracks, at the same time as it was following others along paths that were not always so promising. But just how these routes were charted, and identifying why they were either extending the interpretive reach of important projects or proceeding into analytic and political cul-de-sacs, proved increasingly difficult to explore, let alone expose. It was possible, from a Marxist vantage point, to agree with what J.A. (Jack) Hexter, a conservative historian, had written in 1971. Hexter ventured two dramatically opposed but not mutually exclusive propositions as a comment on the state of historiography:

1) Never in the past has the writing of history been so fatuous as it is today; never has it yielded so enormous and suffocating a mass of stultifying trivia, the product of small minds engaged in the congenial occupation of writing badly about insignificant matters to which they have given little or no thought and for which they feel small concern.
2) Never in the past have historians written so competently, vigorously, and thoughtfully as they do today, penetrating into domains hitherto neglected or in an obscurantist way shunned, bringing effectively to bear on the record of the past disciplines wholly inaccessible to their predecessors, treating the problems they confront with a catholicity and a rigor and sophistication of method hitherto without precedent among practitioners of the historical craft.[15]

That this historiographic development was unfolding at the same time as the Cold War world of *realpolitik* was winding down and moving towards the implosion of 'actually existing socialism' in the Stalinist denouement of 1989 dealt Marxism, as an analytic framework animating social history, a series of unwarranted and cruel ideological blows. This, in turn, had an undeniable impact in fostering the intellectual shift away from a materialist social history towards a postmodernist-inflected cultural history, a trajectory that will be addressed in the essays that lead off Volume II of *Marxism and Historical Practice*.

In Canada the 1980–90s debate over social history was overdetermined by an especially crude set of ideological polemics. Attacks on the study of working-

---

15   Hexter 1971, p. 136.

class culture proceeded from empiricist and atheoretical assumptions. Repudiations and dismissals of Marxism were cavalier in their scapegoating conventionalities. There were, to be sure, criticisms from other quarters, including particular kinds of structuralist Marxism and postmodern-influenced gender historians, but on the whole these more complicating rejoinders either failed to register clearly or were posed in idiosyncratic and incomplete ways.[16]

A curmudgeonly empiricist and ardent advocate of civic education as nation-building, J.L. Granatstein, seized centre stage with a no-holds-barred attack on Canadian historiographic trends. He assailed social historians for the sin of capturing academic power and using it to narrow specialisations and turn the study of history into a catalogue of oppressions, depicting the nation as little more than the site of power's ugliness. This tirade, which had been gathering momentum with a number of essays attacking new histories of labour and everyday life over the course of the 1980s and 1990s, culminated in Granatstein's 1998 *enragé* text, a slight, popularly-pitched provocation entitled *Who Killed Canadian History?*, which contained a chapter titled 'Professing Trivia: The Academic Historians'. According to Granatstein, social historians 'freely denounced the political historians as second rate, teaching unimportant subjects and publishing shoddy work'. Lacking an interest in elites, social historians were concerned only to 'denounce the representatives of Canadian governments and business'. Fixated on blame, social historians presented Canada as 'guilty of genocide against the Indians, the bombing of Germany, the ecological rape of the landscape ...' The purpose of this social history was to use history 'to cure white males of their sense of superiority'. All of this began, according to Granatstein, 'in labour history', a small field which quickly became the site of vicious confrontations between Marxists and non-Marxists. '[N]o one can compete with Marxists in vituperation', Granatstein asserted knowingly. Soon the Marxists 'had complete control of the labour history field, including the journals and the students'. Even though Marxism was discredited 'everywhere in the world', Canadian universities offered them shelter and protection. Women followed suit, and so too did historians of ethnicity and region. The result was that history was written, according to Granatstein, in petty, partisan, and parochial ways: 'It was far more important to study how the workers resisted industrialization, the Marxist historians claimed; to investigate how birth control was practiced before the Pill, feminist historians maintained; or to document gay

---

16   This context, and citations of the relevant writings, is explored in Chapter 3 of Volume II of *Marxism and Historical Practice*, in my essay entitled 'Writing About Canadian Workers: An Historiographic Overview'.

men's experiences in Toronto's bath houses, than to study the boring lives of prime ministers, the efforts of the Canadian Corps in the Great War, or the Quiet Revolution in Quebec'.[17]

Much of what Granatstein wrote was, of course, ideological nonsense. Sources were not cited; evidence rarely offered. But Granatstein did capture, however wrongly he posed matters, a drift away from mainstream political history, and a tendency of social historians to make more and more about less and less. There was a fragmenting dynamic at work in the study of Canadian social history over the course of the 1980s and 1990s, and it only intensified with the drift from the study of the social to the cultural that was ongoing in these same years, and that has continued to this day. Granatstein and others thus posed their historiographic criticisms in ways that were rightly taken to reflect an antediluvian privileging of privilege that truncated historical practice in postures hostile not only to theory but also to a healthy inquisitiveness. Unfortunately, this meant that the need to address the narrowing limitations of social and cultural histories never materialised. Instead, social historians banded together in self-congratulatory denial, rightly refusing what was wrong in Granatstein's critique, but wrongly avoiding some rather obvious issues. Precisely because Granatstein's rant tended towards reductionist banalities, this defensiveness could be mounted with confident moral certitude: a comforting solidarity united those outraged at the 'political incorrectness' of a displaced Old Guard.[18]

My response was different. I questioned a popular front that was now an increasingly mainstream cohort of social-cum-cultural historians bent upon constructing a unity of all – regardless of the clear politics of interpretive difference that separated some – against the retrograde enemy. It was too easy, and it short-circuited discussion of the relationship between historical practice and Marxism, which I saw as increasingly divided, while many of the insights of historical materialism appeared either lost or, worse, repudiated.[19] In my view it was critically important to take the gains of established materialist social histories of particular, discrete experiences and begin to assemble them in commentaries that were more totalising. We had to draw the fragments of the past, studied with such richness, into a more comprehensive whole. This meant extending the project of inclusiveness back into discussions of those institutions, structures, and determining agencies that had thwarted the realisation of

---

17   Granatstein 1998, pp. 58–64.
18   For the fullest statement see McKillop 1999.
19   Palmer 1994; Palmer 1999.

democratic initiatives and resistance to oppression and exploitation. Entailed in such a project was the utilisation of the particular in order to address the general.

This was necessary in all fields of study. But it was decisive within working-class history itself. It was understandable, in Canada especially, that social historians struggling to create a new kind of understanding of class formation, transcending the acute limitations of studies of the past, which had focussed narrowly on the formation of trade unions and the electoral politics of workers, would turn to community studies and the exploration of local developments. But once research of this kind had been undertaken, there was also the need to use it to create a new set of sensibilities about institutions, politics, and states, and their relationships to the social and the cultural; to draw together histories of families and of workplaces; to connect the dots that invariably linked cultures, conflicts, and change over time. This kind of history could not be written out of the pages of one place, or usefully presented through analysis of limited chronologies. It demanded a broader brush than was usually being employed by social historians. On this much, Granatstein and I could agree. We needed, in my view, more writing that was less dissertation-like in its full probing of specificity. Instead of continuing to narrow historical research concerns, we needed venturesome and broader reflections that reached towards larger, often speculative, statements that would stimulate and provoke.

For much of the 1980s and 1990s I argued for the need to publish this kind of work in the pages of *Labour/le Travail*, a journal with which I had been affiliated since its founding in 1976 and to which I would be appointed editor in 1997. But there were few takers. Most of the articles we published tended to be focussed examinations of quite particular developments, the kinds of chapters in doctoral studies that can be converted to an article suitable for the pages of a scholarly journal. Even more senior scholars were prone to send us meticulously-researched statements on subjects that, however important, were set within well-defined boundaries of subject, time and place. And there were, of course, inhibitions that worked against broad-ranging, more speculative attempts to address the past in ways that reached deliberately towards more totalising understandings. When, for instance, I submitted an article to the *Canadian Historical Review* on the history of mutual benefit societies in Canada from the 1830s into the 1950s, suggesting the ways in which the fraternal tradition had intersected with the making and unmaking of class, the piece was rejected. It was all too apparent that some peer reviewers and editors simply could not wrap their heads around the notion of writing on a subject in which the author was comfortable suggesting that he or she had not exhausted each and every possible archival source relevant to the topic – an impossible feat when the subject studied was being examined over centuries rather than years. Authors who consciously drew on considerable published and unpublished scholarship as well as accessible and relevant primary sources, suggesting a possible framework for future research, posing a set of analytic considerations of importance, and dealing with change through time rather than a particular event in time, were not likely to receive a welcome reception from scholarly journals in the Canadian historical profession.[20]

It was largely in this context, over a number of years, that the essays in this concluding section were written. All were also affected by particular intellectual and political contexts.

In the case of the first statement, 'Social Formation and Class Formation in North America, 1800–1900', two developments were of crucial importance. One related to the nature of social history's narrowing agendas and publication strictures, another to a specific conjuncture. The animating intellectual-political context, as I recall the early 1980s in which the piece was conceived and written, was the fruitful dialogue between feminist historians and the so-called 'new' labour historians that had, at least in Canada, been ongoing for a decade. This interaction, which took place in professional committees of historians and on editorial boards of journals such as *Labour/Le Travail*, meant that women's history and working-class history developed together. There were, of course, distinct orientations and writings, but there were also undeniable overlapping concerns that defined a mutually supportive project. This was before a late 1980s movement in the direction of gender history, structured around theoretical imperatives less Marxist and materialist than they were postmodern and discourse-driven, that drove something of a generational wedge into the feminist/working-class history encounter in Canada.[21]

---

20   Palmer 1996, which had originally been prepared for and presented to a conference on the subject of organised mutuality at the International Institute of Social History in Amsterdam. Ironically, Canadian social historians would so avoid generalisation that when Ian McKay tapped into the vacuum of interpretive reach created by the fragmenting impulse of contemporary historiography with his article 'The Liberal Order Framework' (McKay 2000), it became a panacea for those thirsting for a new overarching framework for understanding Canadian history. Like all panaceas, McKay's framework has tended to limit creative vision rather than extend it. The uncritical embrace of 'the liberal order framework', which has been mechanically grafted onto almost any and all subject matter studied by Canadian social and cultural historians, is thus confirmation of resistance to theorising rather than engagement with broad conceptualization of a Marxists kind. Both 'the liberal order framework' and its reception cries out for a Marxist critique. For brief critical comment on McKay's approach see Palmer 2009.

21   See Sangster 2000.

'Social Formation and Class Formation' developed at this interface, in order to bring together concerns that animated historians influenced by socialist-feminism *and* Marxist working-class history. It was the conjuncture of class formation, on the one hand, and, on the other, the changing materialities of production and reproduction, that constituted the substance of the essay. The opportunity to explore this subject matter came about because of the difficulties in disseminating pieces that might try to transcend the limitations on publishing in the social history field, where discrete studies were more likely to find themselves in print than broader, more generalised, discussions. I had been invited to produce a lengthy, speculative overview of a broad historical terrain by David Levine. Levine had concluded that scholarly journals were not prone to publish the kinds of statements that he thought might benefit historians of family and class, and he thus engineered a collection of original essays that were specifically conceived as being longer, more far-reaching in their interpretive grasp, and deliberately more speculative and suggestive than most articles that appeared in conventional journals governed by somewhat constipated 'standards' and peer review practices.

Similarly, but somewhat differently, the final essay in this section, a periodisation of Canadian class struggle spanning the nineteenth and twentieth centuries, set against the backdrop of the legal frameworks within which workers were enmeshed, was solicited by Judy Fudge. It was written for a conference at Osgoode Law School, relating to civil disobedience, civil resistance, and civil rights. Precisely because this overview was presented to an audience of legal scholars and activists, it again steps outside of the framework of the usual academic article, written for publication in an historical journal. Instead, it scaffolds an overtly political understanding of the necessity for class struggle that challenges law, in order to address the legacy of a trade-union movement that, after decades of legitimation, has tended to take on the trappings of bureaucratised timidity. Challenges to the state are curbed; law is obeyed; militancy is dampened. This conditions a convenient lapse in historical memory. The nature of class struggle in the past, which often pushed the boundaries of juridical constraint to the point of stretching and then breaking various laws, is forgotten. This suppresses awareness of the extent to which, in its origins, the workers' movement progressed by taking bold actions that often succeeded by flaunting convention, respectability, and propriety, rather than adhering to them slavishly.

Finally, the article on capitalist crisis and Toronto's dispossessed, originally written with Gaetan Heroux, whom I encountered in my support of the rebellious activities of the Ontario Coalition Against Poverty, was produced for a conference on workers and economic crisis held in Washington, D.C. in 2011. In the aftermath of the economic crisis of 2008, with its devastating aftershocks, which reverberate to this day, the impetus behind the writing of this article is obvious. So, too, to some extent is the collaboration of a Marxist working-class historian and an anti-poverty activist. This happened, moreover, at the point that the Occupy Movement was attempting to reconfigure political activism in ways that stretched understanding of oppression and exploitation under capitalism in new and inclusive ways. The article that Heroux and I wrote jointly is an attempt to take labour history beyond the study of waged work, circumventing the arguable limitations of an exploration of class formation that takes place on the basis of an examination of employed workers. As Heroux and I argue, it is critical to see proletarianisation as a process involving unpaid work as well as paid labour. Labour historians have generally studied workers who are employed, and this is entirely understandable. But if we are to truly grasp the ways in which capitalism has affected adversely all of the dispossessed, social histories of class formation must also pay attention to those who have been locked out of remunerative employment, forced to rely on a range of non-waged survival strategies. Heroux and I thus place our interpretive focus on the ways in which class has been made through a long history of capitalist crisis, which has contributed immensely to what constitutes the bedrock of proletarianisation, expropriation. Our purpose is to reconsider the process of class formation in ways that join the experience of the skilled unionised worker and the poor impoverished domestic worker; the labourer who faces seasonal layoffs, times of unemployment, and long periods without being able to secure any paid work and the man or woman who manages to secure more ready access to the wage. Such workers all face the upheaval and insecurity that result from economic crisis, which, as we suggest, is endemic to capitalist society.

Taken together, these last three essays are an attempt to present a history of workers viewed through the prism of the *longue durée*. They are part of an effort to write the history of the working class in a more holistic manner, situating it at the intersections of specific conjunctures, acknowledging the ways in which class changes through time. This kind of history is difficult to write and, perhaps, is even impossible to realise; but this wider interpretive reach is mandatory. Broad overviews of working-class experience, always developed out of the study of the particular, are an explicit attempt to advance labour history by both situating it within the theoretical framework of Marxism and placing it more consciously alongside the historical development of economy and society. This entails contextualising class formation and struggle in ways that include the state and its institutional and ideological initiatives, just as it demands of us that we situate class within material relations and their determinations, lived out not only at the point of production but also in families and other forums. It is this remapping of the landscape of class formation that brings together Marxism, as a set of conceptual guidelines, and historical research as an empirical project of reconsideration.

CHAPTER 8

Social Formation and Class Formation in North America, 1800–1900*

Conceiving Labour and Capital in Past Times

The positing of the individual as a *worker*, in this nakedness, is itself a product of *history*.

MARX, *Grundrisse* (1857–8)

The process of proletarianisation in the New World commenced in the late fifteenth century. It was premised not on demographic growth but on demographic destruction. In the words of C.L.R. James:

Christopher Columbus landed first in the New World at the Island of San Salvador, and after praising God enquired urgently for gold. The natives, Red Indians, were peaceable and friendly and directed him to Haiti ... The Spaniards, the most advanced Europeans of their day, annexed the island, called it Hispaniola, and took the backward natives under their protection. They introduced Christianity, forced labour in the mines, murder, rape, bloodhounds, strange diseases, and artificial famine (by the destruction of cultivation to starve the rebellious). These and other requirements of the higher civilization reduced the native population from an estimated half-a-million, perhaps a million, to 60,000 in 15 years.[1]

For Marx, this original accumulation was the outcome of economic power, of that brutish midwife, sheer force, cast in new, internationalist dress:

The discovery of gold and silver in America, the extirpation, enslavement and entombment in the mines of the aboriginal population, the beginning of the conquest and looting of the East Indies, the turning of Africa into a warren for the commercial hunting of black skins, signalised the

---

* 'Social Formation and Class Formation in Nineteenth-Century North America', in *Proletarianization and Family History*, edited by David Levine (New York: Academic Press, 1984), 229–308.
1 James 1963, pp. 3–4. See also Williams 1966.

rosy dawn of the era of capitalist production. These idyllic proceedings are the chief momenta of primitive accumulation.[2]

By the early eighteenth century, the historical consciousness of the stages of these developments noted by James and Marx was sufficiently rooted to find expression in popular fiction. *Robinson Crusoe*, among other things, can be seen as an allegorical depiction of the origins of the rising bourgeoisie:

> My island was now peopled, and I thought myself very rich in subjects; and it was a merry reflection which I frequently made, how like a king I looked. First of all, the whole country was my own property, so that I had undoubted right of dominion. Secondly, my people were perfectly subjected. I was absolute lord and lawgiver; they all owed their lives to me, and were ready to lay down their lives, if there had been occasion of it for me. It was remarkable, too, we had but three subjects, and they were of three different religions. My man Friday was a Protestant, his father was a pagan and a cannibal, and the Spaniard was a Papist. However, I allowed liberty of conscience throughout my dominions.[3]

Crusoe's self-satisfied assessment introduces us to themes of relevance in the history of class formation. We are immediately confronted with a series of relationships: population and property, subordination and superordination, and hegemony and segmentation. But this complacent and controlled caricature of class formation is ahistorical. As Stephen Hymer suggests, we also need 'the story of Friday's grandchildren'.[4] And we need to recognise, as well, that no society, let alone one as vast and complex as that of North America, is an island as simple as Crusoe's domain.

Capitalism in North America was premised on an initial expropriation of aboriginal peoples. The diversity of paths to this end ran the gamut from the genocidal assault on Newfoundland's Beothuks[5] to the less overt, but massively brutal, clearances of Andrew Jackson's southern 'campaigns' (1814–24).[6] Equally traumatic were the superficially more benign disruptions associated with the range of European interventions – cultural, religious, physiological, social,

---

2 Marx 1967, vol. 1, p. 751.
3 Hymer 1971, pp. 14–15.
4 Hymer 1971, pp. 14–15; Hill 1980; Fliegelman 1982, pp. 67–82.
5 Upton 1977, pp. 133–53.
6 Rogin 1975.

and economic – in the ecosystems of the tribes of the coasts and woodlots. The universal aim was the appropriation of profit from a commerce in luxury commodities harvested through native people's skills, knowledge, and proximity to the fur-bearing animal world.[7] This was not an unmediated process of Indian acquiescence and subjugation.[8] As studies of Indian women and the fur trade have shown, it did not always leave the white population in firm and settled control of the land. The production of furs was, on occasion, inseparable from the reproduction of a mixed-blood population that would prove a thorn in the side of capitalist development in the Canadian West, well into the 1880s.[9] Despite all the complexities, the paths of appropriation and expropriation converged, by the 1880s, in a hegemony that merged class and racial interests.[10]

Seldom has this history received its due, and rare are the attempts to tie together the processes of expropriation, accumulation, and racial authority in the early history of American capital. It was this initial development, however, that established the preconditions for much of the march of economic and social differentiation in North America. Andrew Jackson was perhaps understating the importance of this historical process in a curt line on Indian-white relations in his message to Congress (1829): 'Our conduct toward these people is deeply interesting to our national character'.[11] But he was nevertheless aware of its continuity. His programme of Indian removal had precedents in the northeast and could unite plantation slaveholder, independent yeoman, merchant trader, manufacturer, and the waged plebeian masses in often unattainable agreement. Where the 'Indian question' was settled first and most decisively, the economic, social, and political separation of labour and capital proceeded to quick consolidation. In the cities of the eastern seaboard, well before 1800, essential inequalities were a recognisable part of the social order[12] and as early

7   See, among many sources, Bailey 1969; Jaenen 1976a; Trigger 1976; Ray 1974; Martin 1974, pp. 3–26; Schlesier 1976, pp. 129–45.
8   Rich 1960, pp. 35–53; Martin 1978; Fisher 1977. For a critique of Martin, see Krech 1981.
9   Van Kirk 1980; Brown 1980. Note the suggestive argument in Pannekoek 1976, pp. 83–95.
10   For an assessment of this process in the peculiar context of British Columbia, see Knight 1978.
11   See especially Rogin 1975, pp. 165–205, the Jackson quotation being on p. 3. Drinnon 1980, extends Rogin's analysis.
12   The literature is now extensive. An early synthetic statement was provided by Henretta 1973. Among the best of the many specialised studies of the last two decades are Henretta 1965, pp. 75–92; Kulikoff 1971, pp. 375–412; Nash 1976, pp. 545–84; 1979; Smith 1981, pp. 163–202; Salinger 1983, pp. 62–84.

as the 1760s had solidified sufficiently to manifest explicit cultural and political expression.[13]

At the risk of leaving many of the essential interpretive and empirical knots unravelled, this essay aims to present a view of social and class formation in nineteenth-century North America. It seeks to explore the material contexts of a changing series of social formations, establishing the boundaries within which a working class was formed. To be sure, Canada and the United States were never entirely collapsible into a single unit; indeed, within each large geographic entity, regional peculiarities readily separated themselves out from the political economy as a whole, as the processes of combined and uneven development ran their course. But there were, nevertheless, general patterns and parallels of striking similarity. It is these that are thrown into relief in the pages that follow.

To address the relation of social and class formation in nineteenth-century North America, it is necessary, first, to conceptualise a periodisation of capitalist development and, second, to root that process in the concrete context of a particularly cluttered and ever-changing social formation. It is striking how little of this basic kind of rethinking of the nineteenth-century experience has been done. The so-called new social history, in spite of the advances it has made, generally neglects this kind of analysis.[14] For all the flaws in the older John R. Commons literature, it at least never abandoned so readily the *longue durée* for a substitutionist immersion in the particular.[15] An older set of reifications – the market and the union – has been replaced with a newer, more fashionable and formidable fetishisation of method and discrete subjects.[16] We in North America are dangerously close to 'a historical practice, which, however far removed from traditional canons, confines itself to specialist areas, partial problems, and tentative technical innovations, and thereby remains loyal in

---

13   Consider, for instance, Foner 1976; Shaw 1981; Hoerder 1976, pp. 233–71, in Young 1976. Young's work is itself the most exciting expression of this writing. See Young 1973; and 1981, pp. 561–623.

14   One early attempt was Gutman 1973b, pp. 531–88. Katz, Doucet, and Stern 1982 present a rather cavalier, if tantalising, periodisation (pp. 18–19, 364–5). More recently, we have seen efforts from the left to address this imbalance: Aglietta 1976, a generally abstract and economistic overview; and Davis 1980, pp. 3–46, a work of powerful synthesis premised on a highly selective reading of the history and the historiography.

15   See Dawley 1976, especially pp. 180–4, for a critique of Commons; but for the strengths of this earlier tradition, note, in particular, Commons 1909, pp. 39–84.

16   See Hershberg 1981. For critiques of social history, see Judt 1979, pp. 66–94; Fox-Genovese and Genovese 1976, pp. 205–21.

fact to the least creative kind of empiricism'. As Pierre Vilar continues, '"Real" Marxist history, by contrast, must be ambitious in order to advance'.[17]

My ambitions here are threefold. First, I want to introduce some essential Marxist notions regarding the stages of capitalist development into the discourse on North American class formation. To do so, of course, is to generalise broadly and to select, across the span of a century, chunks of historical time that bear some resemblance to one another. (I have further simplified the complexities by taking the century as my chosen field and the decades as my rough points of division. As will be apparent, any exact dating of various moments of historical transition within a geographic and socioeconomic entity as cumbersome and unwieldy as North America will prove contentious, but it is the larger patterns of development I am concerned with here).[18] Second, if it is essential to return to Marxist categories, it is also my aim to suggest some possible ways of rethinking these analytic premises. It should be clear that Marx's analytic categories, derived from the 'classical' case of English proletarianisation, may well require some 'groping' through if they are to stand the test of the American experience. And that, the testing of a Marxist sense of periodisation against the class formations and struggles of a set of North American social formations, is my third and final aim.

Marx, writing before the advent of monopoly capital, posited three stages in capitalist development: so-called primitive accumulation, the period of manufacture proper, and the culmination of capitalism's protracted development in modern industry. In the period of primitive accumulation, the preconditions necessary for the realisation of capitalist accumulation were established, giving rise to forms of production and discrete social formations favourable to the future accumulation of capital at the same time that they were, internally, inhibited in their capacity to generate development along purely capitalist lines. With the creation of a wage-labour force, the commodification of labour power, and the concentration of capital, the process of primitive accumulation precipitated a crisis in the social order. Out of this restructuring emerged the period of manufacture proper. Its defining characteristic was the subordination of productive and property forms to the generalised hegemony of industrial capital, which in turn was marked by the cooperative employment of labour and the emergence of a rudimentary division of labour in handicraft

---

17   Vilar 1973, p. 101; 1982, pp. 47–78.
18   See Gordon, Edwards, and Reich 1982. Though attentive to certain Marxist concerns and though focusing on the long-term transformation of class relations, this book is nevertheless cast as a neoclassical repudiation of Marx's conception of capitalist development.

production. Productive life, though turning on the cooperative employment of labour, retained its reliance on human beings and the 'subjection of labour was only a formal result of the fact that the labourer, instead of working for himself, works for and consequently under the capitalist'.[19] With the division of labour, upon which manufacture rested, arose a refinement of the instruments of labour. This refinement, in turn, transformed the tool into the machine, and with the development of machinery there occurred a fundamental change in the historical development of the productive process: the breakthrough into modern industry. Technical change and the pulse of mechanisation, according to Marx, precipitated the productive process into the final stages of capitalist development.[20]

As far as this goes, it is a significant conceptual formulation providing the essential ground on which a Marxist historiography of the transition from feudalism to capitalism has come to rest.[21] But some silences, ambiguities, and ambivalences intrude. First, Marx and subsequent Marxists, as Wally Seccombe stresses, have reduced the field of production to the goods, instruments, and site of waged labour. Production has been divorced from the complex range of socioeconomic activities – gestation and generation of the species, domestic socialisation, and a range of productions associated with use-, as opposed to exchange-, values – that have come to be associated with the reproductive realm. Yet these productions are, in fact, historically central to the creation and continuity of specific social formations.[22] Second, Marx's stages of capitalist development, conceived as the apparent zenith of a single mode of production, convey too easily an impression of stasis, in which one stage supersedes another, restructuring the social order with a decisiveness and finality that much recent historical investigation calls into question.[23] Third, as

---

19   See, for instance, Marx 1967, vol. 1, pp. 713–74; 1973b, p. 502.

20   Sweezy 1968, pp. 107–26; Levine 1973, pp. 119–81, 248–87.

21   Dobb 1973; Hilton 1976.

22   See Seccombe 1980a, pp. 25–99; 1980b, pp. 217–66; and, most pointedly, 1983, pp. 28–9. Note the discussion in Barrett 1980, especially pp. 19–29.

23   Hence, Raphael Samuel's 'Workshop of the World: Steam Power and Hand Technology in Mid-Victorian Britain' (Samuel 1977, pp. 6–72) establishes the coexistence of earlier modes of production within the period of modern industry, just as Gutman 1973b suggests that one part of the process of primitive accumulation – the recruitment and disciplining of the wage-labour force – was not simply accomplished but was reproduced over time. In this context Gordon, Edwards, and Reich, whose *Segmented Work, Divided Workers* (1982) emphasises the constant process of restructuring the character and mode of social accumulation, might be read as an attempt to speak to capitalism's vitality as a consequence

Michael Lebowitz suggests, Marx's oeuvre, and necessarily his stages of capitalist development, were one-sided: concentrating on capital, his analysis 'overdetermined' his argument away from concerns with the multifarious agencies of class experience.[24] Class formation was both structured necessity and active self-creation.[25]

Let us turn to the stages of North American capitalist development, exploring the complexity of specific social formations in the discrete periods suggested by Marx's own periodisation. But let us also extend the argument on those lines originally suggested by Robinson Crusoe. The reductionist, static, and one-sided analysis of capitalist development (and consequently of class formation) over time can be avoided by bearing in mind those very relationships that Crusoe called attention to: population and property, subordination and superordination, and hegemony and segmentation.

To do this, however, presupposes a rejection of the stress, in much Marxist literature, upon mode(s) of production. And here, though not in many other analytic realms, it is possible to reach agreement with Hindess and Hirst, who argue:

> At most the concept of determinate social formation specifies the structure of an 'economy' (forms of production and distribution, forms of trade, conditions and reproduction of these forms), forms of state and politics and forms of culture and ideology and their relation to that economy, economic classes and their relations, and the conditions for transformation of certain of these forms.[26]

Thus, the movement away from the mode of production as a conceptual core of interpreting class formation is an attempt to supersede 'the unjustifiable reduction of analysis to an extremely limited range of economic class relations in which there is one category of possessing agent and one of non-possessing agent and the consequent neglect of ... more complex forms of class relations'. Refocusing our attention on the social formation promises to liberate Marxist analysis from 'a false narrowing of the field of the socio-economic', overcoming

---

       of the persistence of forms of primitive accumulation past the epoch of manufacture into
       the ages of modern industry and monopoly capital.

24   Lebowitz 1992; 1983. This, as well, is central to Thompson 1978b, pp. 247–62; and Clarke
       1979, pp. 145–50.

25   Consider Thompson 1967, pp. 55–97; and Saville 1969, pp. 247–71.

26   Hindess and Hirst 1977, pp. 27, 62.

almost a century of 'failure to conceptualize adequately the integration of the socio-economic with politico-legal relations of state and the cultural formation of groups and classes'.[27]

The Social Formation, 1800–50

The Hegemony of Merchant Capital

Especially during the rise and expansion of capitalism, merchant capital displayed a particular ability to organize various, and even competing forms of labour; to centralize the profits from disparate economic activities and even economic systems; to coexist with a wide range of political institutions, ideologies, and regimes; to link different economic systems through the manipulation of their respective surpluses; to promote economic growth and yet to freeze it within a particular set of social relations of production; and, in short, to act as an agent of economic and social change within narrow limits and as an agent of political stability and *status quo* outside those limits.

> FOX-GENOVESE AND GENOVESE, 'The Janus Face of Merchant Capital' (1983),
> pp. 5–6

Merchant capital – as the Genoveses have recently reminded us and as Dobb, following Marx, long ago argued – is neither a mode of production nor a stage in economic development.[28] Rather, it is an intermediary, always prone to parasitism and political compromise, quick to assert the primacy of an economism of commercial exchange over the more substantive transformation of the social relations of production.[29]

A merchant in Defoe's *The Compleat English Gentleman*, when confronted with a squire's dismissal that he was no gentleman, reached into the very substance of his class position to reply: 'No sir, but I can buy a gentleman'. Historical destiny, however, cannot be purchased. The merchants, ever dependent on the

---

27   The phrases are Seccombe's (1983), although his 'Reworking the Mode of Production Concept' is in fact an unacknowledged jettisoning of that concept in favour of analysing the social formation.

28   Fox-Genovese and Genovese 1983, pp. 3–25. Dobb 1973, pp. 120–2.

29   For a particularly strident and one-sided view of merchant capital's backward role in Canadian development, see Naylor 1972, pp. 1–42.

allies they aimed to subordinate to their commercial ends, could never dispense with these other social groups. As a class, the merchants 'nowhere turn up on their own: here we find merchants plus planters, there, merchants plus the representatives of the state'. To see merchant capital in this way is not to minimise its importance or to dismiss its historical impact:

> The fruits of merchant capital included the primitive accumulation of capital that proved indispensable to the flowering of the capitalist mode of production; organised and far-reaching markets with extensive dealing not only in luxuries but increasingly in the staples that would lay the basis for a mass world market; systems of law and procedures of accounting appropriate to the rational conduct of business; territorial enclaves of bourgeois social relations in still fundamentally precapitalist societies; and the gruesome resurrection of such ancient forms of business and labour as the slave trade and chattel slavery.[30]

In an epoch of late primitive accumulation, in which a market system was in place, but a market society, rooted in the impersonality of productive relations, was not yet consolidated, merchant capital looked always to the past while the movement of socioeconomic life twisted its head in the direction of the future.

Across the length and breadth of the pre-1850 North American social formation, merchant capital was hegemonic: in the South a planter ruling class embedded in the slave relations of production was nevertheless structured to depend on the world market and its bourgeois relations; in much of the manufacturing Northeast, commercial capital orchestrated sweatshop labour and craft forms of production; and among the many farms of British North America and the free states, subsistence was supplemented by mercantile credit and staples production. Merchant capital restructured the social order at the same time that it sought to solidify tried and true modes of accumulation. Ever attentive to the movement of goods, it created a transportation infrastructure to facilitate exchange. Such projects necessarily called into being a wage-labour force, altered relations of town and country, and demanded stark self-examinations on the part of promoters, politicians, and planters. All of this

---

30   The quotations are from Dobb 1973, p. 121, and Fox-Genovese and Genovese 1983, pp. 6 and 7, but I am here laying greater stress on the limits of merchant capital than the latter's *Fruits of Merchant Capital* (especially in 'The Slave Economies in Political Perspective', p. 36) allows.

took place, moreover, against any conscious attempt to revamp the nature of the political economy. But the consequences were anything but a preservative for the status quo. A home market was in the making, and its rise signalled the emergence of a social order bent towards commodity production. Trade had created the pre-conditions eroding its own hegemony as the movement of staples came to be overshadowed by the output of goods.[31]

Merchant capital, its face turned to the past, had brought such relationships into being, though at the same time it knew little of what their impact would be in the future. Bargains were struck between contending factors but were structured along lines determined by merchant capital's hegemony. Jeffersonian agrarians and Hamiltonian commercialists reached the ultimate compromise, reflective of merchant capital's capacity to conciliate seemingly competitive economies, political institutions, ideologies, and forms of extraction of labour surplus. Bowden's *Industrial History of the United States* offers a cogent description of this process:

> To the Jeffersonians the propertied classes most worthy of power were the landed classes. To them the moneyed classes cherished by Hamiltonian policy were at first anathema. But ... the Jeffersonian party came to terms with men of money property. There was a reconciliation of the business men with the agrarian government on the basis of their acquiescence in 'the reformed order of things' – which meant not a whole loaf as under Hamilton but a goodly portion.[32]

This metaphor of 'not a whole loaf ... but a goodly portion' captures the character of social relations in an epoch of primitive accumulation and the hegemony of merchant capital. The preconditions of capitalist accumulation were everywhere being established and forcing merchant capital against its conservative grain in the direction of a truly revolutionary role.

---

31   See, for instance, McMichael 1977, pp. 497–512; Fox-Genovese and Genovese 1983, pp. 24–5. This paragraph and the next draw on an as yet still to be appreciated synthesis: Hacker 1940, especially part 2. For the Canadas, see Tulchinsky 1977; Myers 1972; Pentland 1981; Macdonald 1975, pp. 263–81.

32   Bowden 1930, pp. 231–2.

The Momenta of Primitive Accumulation: Reaching towards the Crisis of Mid-Century

The specific economic form in which unpaid surplus-labour is pumped out of direct producers, determines the relationship of rulers and ruled, as it grows directly out of production itself and, in turn, reacts upon it as a determining element. Upon this, however, is founded the entire formation of the economic community which grows up out of productive relations themselves, thereby simultaneously its specific political form. It is always the direct relationship of the owners of the conditions of production to the direct producers – a relation always naturally corresponding to a definite stage in the development of the methods of labour and thereby its social productivity – which reveals the innermost secret, the hidden basis of the entire social structure, and with it the political form of the relation of sovereignty and dependence, in short, the corresponding specific form of the state.

MARX, *Capital*, vol. 3 (1894)

A hegemonic merchant capital served as broker for at least three distinct economic forms of appropriating surplus in the social formation of the pre-1850s years: plantation slavery; agrarian petty capital rooted in the productive household; and early, if inhibited, manufacturing.[33] As Brenner has stressed, though, in the case of European development, town and country – divorced from one another in our arbitrary classifications and empirical inquiries – were in fact caught up in similar processes of large-scale transformation.[34] What proves decisive in the North American case is the extent to which each of these specific economic forms gave rise to internal contradictions that, by the mid-century, demanded resolution. Out of the dissolution of these momenta of primitive accumulation came the transition to industrial capitalism.

Plantation Slavery and the South

Slavery was neither peculiar to the South nor numerically predominant in the slave states. It existed for two centuries in the Canadas but eventually lapsed as a form of labour organisation, although other types of bound labour prevailed there, as in other regions of early America.[35] Nearly three-quarters of

---

33   These forms, often conceived differently, are discussed in Post 1982, pp. 30–51.

34   See Brenner 1976, pp. 30–75; and 1982, pp. 16–113. I have offered some brief and overly general comments on this problem in its Canadian context in Palmer 1983a, pp. 131–9.

35   See Pentland 1981, pp. 1–23; and Morris 1965, pp. 310–512.

all free southerners owned no slaves, nor were they connected with slavery in any direct sense. In 1860, 358,000 southern slave owners, 72 percent of whom owned fewer than 10 slaves, were dwarfed by the well over one million non-slaveholding free families. Slaves themselves, though expanding in numbers from 1,538,022 in 1820 to 3,953,760 in 1860 (a reproductive capacity that surpassed all other Western slave economies), made up less than one-third of the population of the South.[36] Yet slavery was absolutely fundamental in 'supplying the dominant propertied classes with their surplus', because 'slavery provided the foundation on which the South rose and grew ... The hegemony of slaveholders, presupposing the social and economic preponderance of great slave plantations, determined the character of the South ... They imparted to Southern life a special social, economic, political, ideological, and psychological content'.[37]

A long and distinguished line of analysts of the slave South, stretching from Gray and Hacker to Fogel and Engerman, have detailed the economics of slavery and, despite many disagreements, they posit slavery as a planter capitalism.[38] Yet detailed criticism, directed most frontally at *Time on the Cross*, has now made this position untenable. It is apparent that the slave South, though at times exhibiting capitalist tendencies, was profoundly un-capitalistic.[39] The social relations of production, the extraction of surplus, and the organisation of the labour process under slavery were consistently determined and structured by the master-slave relation in ways that defied capitalism's capacity to restructure the mode of accumulation by rationalising a diversity of ways in which labour power could be orchestrated and appropriated. When the labourer was owned outright with direct and unmediated claims to his or her body, such a range of potentials did not present itself. To look at the slave South between 1800 and 1850 is to see a rigidly limited mode of extracting surplus caught in the vice of crisis.

Alone in sustaining the slave South was the region's domination of the world market for raw cotton. Southern cotton production, stimulated by both soaring demand and technological innovations, rose from 150,000 bales in 1815 to 2.25 million bales in 1849 (doubling, as well, between 1849 and 1859). Cotton comprised between twenty-two and twenty-seven percent of all American

---

36   Stampp 1956, pp. 29–30; Degler 1959, pp. 271–7; United States Bureau of the Census 1961 p. 9; Hacker 1940, pp. 287–9.

37   De St. Croix 1981, p. 55. The quotation is from Genovese 1965, p. 13; but see as well Genovese 1971; 1972; 1974; and Fox-Genovese and Genovese 1983, pp. 249–64.

38   Gray 1933; Hacker 1940, pp. 280–320; Fogel and Engerman 1974, especially pp. 67–78.

39   Fox-Genovese and Genovese 1983, pp. 136–72; Gutman 1975; David et al. 1976.

exports between 1810 and 1860. Prices, however, moved downward from 1802, bottoming out in 1844 and recovering modestly throughout the late 1840s and 1850s. As long as productivity soared, this deflation proved no great catastrophe to the masters, and the 1850s were years of escalating profit for the planters.[40]

But the weak link in this chain of slavery's development was its continuity and potential for expansion, a potential that had to be met if the slave South was to survive as an economic, political, and sociocultural entity. The slaveholders were dependent on a form of economic extraction of surplus that allowed few options. Gang labour and the absolute appropriation of surplus dictated the necessity of simple instruments of production[41] and restricted the possibility of driving labour to expanded production. The initial costs of securing slave labour were sufficiently prohibitive to restrict the possibility of intensifying labour through increasing the numbers of slaves working a particular acreage, especially for the smaller slaveholders who comprised the bulk of farming producers in the South. According to Ulrich B. Phillips, slave prices rose dramatically between 1812 and 1819, 1830 and 1837, and 1845 and 1860. In New Orleans, the ratio of cents of cotton per pound to hundreds of dollars for the average slave dropped from 5 to 1 in 1805 to 0.6 to 1 in 1860, indicating that the price of slaves after 1845 was outstripping the returns of cotton production, giving rise to the 'fire-eaters' agitation to reopen the slave trade.[42] Taken in conjunction with soil exhaustion, slavery's tendency to retard economic diversification and to stifle wage labour, mounting marketing costs, and the post-1845 threat to reverse the Missouri Compromise of 1820, the slaveholding planters of the South and their many advocates saw clearly the imperative of the hour. In this context (1) the price of labour had to be reduced, preferably by reviving the African trade; (2) free trade had to be secured to lessen southern dependency on the North and open the market to preferable English goods; (3) the hegemony of the northern mercantile and banking interests over shipping, brokerage, insurance, and credit had to be broken; (4) obstacles needed to be erected against the emerging alliance of north-eastern capital and western enterprise, including resistance to the north-western railways, homesteading, and immigration; and (5) movement into western lands had to be checked to curb the consolidation and expansion of political power in the free states.[43]

---

40   Fogel and Engerman 1974, vol. 1, pp. 59–63; Hacker 1940, pp. 284–6.
41   See Garrett 1978, chapter 4.
42   Phillips 1963, pp. 48, 93, 173–87, 246; Hacker 1940, pp. 302–4; Genovese 1965, p. 264.
43   Hacker 1940, pp. 299–301.

Throughout the 1850s, merchant capital balanced the strategic interests of its various productive forms, one against the other, producing here a decision of one camp, there a judgement for another, and yet again another compromise. This was the history of the years stretching from Clay's Compromise of 1850 through the Kansas-Nebraska Act of 1854 to the Dred Scott decision of 1857. This strategy of conciliation had served merchant capital well for over a century. But by the 1850s its time had passed, for other economic forms of appropriation were also maturing to the point that their co-existence in a social formation characterised by competing and contradictory modes of accumulation, however mediated by merchant capital, proved increasingly difficult and contentious.[44]

One measure of this development and a telling indication of the obvious symbiosis of production and reproduction under slavery was the extent to which a slave South caught in this vice of crisis responded with 'slave breeding'. Though Robert Fogel and Stanley Engerman dismiss such 'breeding' as mere myth, Richard Sutch has presented conclusive empirical evidence demonstrating that those slaves states of the border and Atlantic coast, where soils were poor and more depleted, were providing the newer slave plantations of Texas, Arkansas, Florida, Mississippi, and Louisiana with a labour force.[45] In the 'breeding' states of slavery's productive demise, the reproduction of labour power essential to the slave order as a whole was proceeding apace: slave women in these states exhibited higher fertility than did those of the importing Southwest, and sex ratios saw inordinate surpluses of women.[46] Small wonder that the slave family, so central to the plantation's capacity to produce profit and reproduce itself – an agent of organisation, socialisation, and discipline – became the locus of class struggle in the slave South.[47]

Agrarian Petty Capital and the Productive Household

Beyond slavery, production and reproduction also meshed in the many households of agrarian America. For a time these households coexisted with slavery, content to subsist and market a minimal portion of their product. But by the 1840s and 1850s, household economies had been largely structured into commodity relations, deepening the North American social division of labour and

---

44   Note the lucid statement in Post 1982, pp. 37–8.
45   Fogel and Engerman 1974, vol. 1, pp. 78–86; Sutch 1975, pp. 173–210.
46   Gutman and Sutch 1976, p. 155.
47   At the risk of pairing the incompatible, see Gutman 1976a, part 1; and Genovese 1974, pp. 70–5, 443–584.

extending the home market. As Michel Aglietta argues[48] for the United States and as John McCallum contends for Upper Canada/Ontario (which lagged a decade or more behind developments to the south), agrarian petty capital stimulated the emergence of farm implements industries, processing plants, and urban expansion.[49] In the process, agrarian petty capital was both subordinated to industrial capital and pitted against slavery, which, if allowed to expand, promised to smother the emerging social formation of manufacture and stifle its politics of growth.

Slavery, of course, was regionally based. Indeed, it had to be if it was not to overtake other productive forms and subjugate merchant capital itself. Agrarian petty capital, by contrast, was pervasive. Some have seen it as an independent mode of production, bounded by patriarchal authority: a brake on capitalist development governed by the logic of subsistence.[50] In the seventeenth-century world of 'New England peasants', in which the importance of land, patrilineage, and the stem family outweighed the incursions of market and merchant, this may have been the case.[51] But in seventeenth-century French Canada, ironically, where one would have expected traditional social relations to consolidate on the legal bedrock of seigneurialism, the *menu peuple* of the land exhibited an irksome individualism and valued their independence.[52]

The *habitants'* refusal to accommodate themselves placidly to a 'natural economy' hinted at the degree to which merchant capital and the market mediated the social relations of a patriarchal landed society. To be sure, on the frontier of agrarian production where farms and families marched hand in hand, such forces were far from pervasive even as late as the 1820s. Work was arranged along familial lines, and cash was not a universal equivalent but only one of many useful products. Authority was vested not in wealth but in legal control over land, an age- and gender-bound process of social differentiation.[53] Mary Ryan's study of the family in Oneida County, New York, moreover, suggests that between 1790 and 1820 the household was the principal, if not the solitary, place of both production and social reproduction. Parents conceived children as their flesh and blood at the same time that they conceived of their offspring

---

48   Aglietta 1978, pp. 19–21.

49   McCallum 1980, especially pp. 54–70, 83–92.

50   Lenin 1974, pp. 175–90; Luxemburg 1968, pp. 396–411; O'Connor 1975; Merrill 1977, pp. 42–71; Henretta 1978, pp. 3–32; Johnson 1981, pp. 93–112.

51   Waters 1976, pp. 3–22; Henretta 1971, pp. 379–98.

52   Diamond 1961, pp. 3–34; Macdonald 1971, pp. 121–43.

53   Henretta 1978, p. 21; Merrill 1977, pp. 57–9; Gagan 1981, pp. 50–3.

as labour power, owing them time. In such a context, large families were a sign of the 'prosperous farmer'. Family loyalty was an economic calculation resting on the expectation of compensation in the single most valued commodity of productive life: land.[54]

Petty capital in the household economy of the agrarian milieu, like slavery, was thus premised on expansion. It managed, with the movement of the farmers to the West, to stave off its ultimate reckoning for a time, but this postponement of its own demise was secured by the disintegration of the household economy and the rise of a commercialised agriculture, centred in the West, that was subordinate to merchant capital. Indeed, through land policy, speculation, and internal improvements, the latter fostered a climate of technical invocation and rising productivity on the newly established farms of the 1840s and 1850s, raising the costs of farming and striking the decisive and final blow against whatever autonomy and subsistence-character the household economy had once possessed.[55]

Even before this process had run its course, petty capital was traumatised by the demographic and sociocultural realities of a disintegrating rural milieu. Across rural North America fertility plummeted, access to the land tightened considerably, a generalised crisis introduced aged landholders to insecurity and the inability to provide for their offspring, and the young were forced to migrate or become proletarians. In discrete rural cultures, the paths to this end took different twists and turns. The ultimate consequences were not, however, dissimilar.

Old Quebec experienced the most severe dislocations. Hardly reducible to agrarian petty capital, the seigneurial system of Lower Canada nevertheless illuminated the tendency toward the disintegration of the rurally-rooted productive household. Precisely because seigneurialism was a long-standing, if juridically archaic, social organisation of landed relations, it brings into relief the process of rural decay in the pre-1850 social formation. Rural prosperity, increasing marriage and birth rates, and the declining mortality of French Canada in the years of seigneurial revival (1792–1802) gave way to a widespread malaise. Falling prices and yields were exacerbated by crop failures, the devastating impact of the wheat fly epidemics of 1836 and 1837, soil exhaustion, overpopulation, and a system of perfectly partible inheritance among the

---

54   Ryan 1981, pp. 21–43; Parr 1980, p. 83.

55   See Post 1982, p. 43; Gates 1964, pp. 182–96; Shannon 1945, pp. 31–7; Danhof 1941, pp. 317–59; Parket and Klein 1973; Pomfret 1976, pp. 399–415. An important historical theoretical argument is made in Sherry 1976, pp. 52–8.

habitants. The internal market constricted; the size of individual farms shrank; and in older parishes fertility declined, many of them recording an absolute loss of population after 1822. The landless labourers proliferated: thousands were forced off the land and some to outright rebellion in 1837–8. The crisis of French Canadian society began to resolve itself in the settling of accounts with an emerging industrial capital in the 1840s and 1850s. Seigneurialism was abolished in 1853–4. Over 500,000 *canadiens* migrated to the mill towns and woodlots of New England and Michigan, as countless others ventured into the urban centres of Montreal and Quebec or trekked to the northern shield. Not until a second agricultural revolution and concentration on commodity production for the dairy industry tipped the rural scales in the direction of agribusiness in the 1880s, did the Quebec countryside exhibit any semblance of even the most modest recovery.[56]

On the Upper Canadian frontier, a crisis on the land did not develop until well after 1840, but early speculators held much of the best land, and church and state each took one-seventh of the province's acreage. Free land grants, originally designed to attract settlers, were turned back in 1826, replaced by sale through public auctions that were exploited by large land companies and unscrupulous colonising agents. Assisted emigration efforts were curtailed, and prospective landowners now had to pay for their passages and purchase their lots. Small freeholders, who had gained a foothold before and during the 1820s, found the going rather rough in later decades. Even large families could not insure their prosperity, and prior to 1840 only two to five percent of all rural producers in Upper Canada had over 100 acres in cultivation. Although a distinct minority could afford to hire labour for the initial land clearance, few new arrivals in Upper Canada were willing to work for wages. As Lord Goderich, the colonial secretary, explained in 1831: 'Without some division of labour, without a class of persons willing to work for wages, how can society be prevented from falling into a state of almost primitive rudeness, and how are the comforts and refinements of civilized life to be procured?'[57]

By the mid-1830s, land policy, speculative endeavours and hoarding, and the penetration of the market and social differentiation in town and country were

---

56 Harris 1966; Pentland 1981, pp. 63–78; Parker 1969, pp. 209–18; Ouellet 1980; Bernier 1980, pp. 71–83. For a critical assessment of the literature on the agricultural crisis, see McInnis 1982, pp. 9–49.

57 Goderich is quoted in Johnson 1973, p. 66. See also Johnson 1971, pp. 41–60; Wynn 1979, pp. 51–2; Russell 1982, pp. 138–44; Parr 1983; Teeple 1972, pp. 43–55.

lending considerable force to Goderich's insistence that 'there should be in every society a class of labourers as well as a class of Capitalists or Landowners' (presaging Edward Gibbon Wakefield's later enunciation, in 1833, of his theory of 'systematic colonization').[58] An irate Kingston mechanic complained in the midst of the severe depression of the late 1830s that 'country mechanics, like birds of passage, this summer are pouring into undertakers, working late and early for *twelve dollars a month* subject to be hired out again like slaves, to others at advanced wages – a degradation that the meanest bushwacker swaying an axe, who neither spent years nor months in practice or study of his calling seldom submits to'. By 1851, in the rural areas of the Home District to the east of Toronto, some 10,172 out of 14,994 labouring-age males (67.8 percent) were landless, and wage rates had plummeted across the Canadas.[59]

The demographic dimensions of the mid-century crisis in Canadian rural life have been explored by Gagan in a study of Peel County. His research confirms the alienation of land in the 1830s, the place of speculation and land policy in the creation of early fortunes, and the privileges and economic stability accruing to those present at the outset of Peel's settlement. In the ensuing years, families devised new inheritance strategies that attempted to offset the more debilitating consequences of the wheat boom in the 1840s and 1850s when land prices soared. But the depression of 1857 burst this bubble, and by the 1860s rural society had collapsed. Its fall was secured by the historical drift into over-specialisation in a commodity that could no longer reap an economic bonanza. As wheat production declined markedly between 1860 and 1870 by approximately sixty percent, the uncertainties of a hopeful generation were confirmed in their worst possible light. Indeed, over time, farm families had been adapting to the structural collapse of the household economy. They grew smaller and more persistently simple (signifying the disappearance of relatives, visitors, boarders, and hired help), at the same time that the birth rate dropped and marriage was delayed until later ages. These were the demographic contours of a society of constricting opportunity and deteriorating potential, the reproductive reflection of productive disorder: the historical development of forces pushing people into wage labour and closing the door on the independent household economy. The expansion and contraction of the wheat monoculture thus provided the agricultural surplus that stimulated economic growth and set the stage for rising land prices that moved the newly arrived into the labour market. Finally, it forced the 'surplus' offspring of petty producers in the

---

58 Quoted in Johnson 1973, p. 68.
59 Quotation from Palmer 1980, p. 19. On the Home District, see Johnson 1971, pp. 57–9.

same direction as the promise of rural Canadian life faded in the face of pressures it could not absorb and had to deflect.[60]

Elsewhere, too, merchant capital fostered reliance on staples that stifled economic diversification and conditioned particular forms of proletarianisation and specific modes of social reproduction. This process had vast ramifications in the interconnected productive and reproductive spheres. The subversion of the household economy revamped social structure and may well have had far-reaching cultural consequences. In the timber colony of New Brunswick this could give rise to a derogatory mythology of the lumber workers' demoralisation,[61] while in the Newfoundland family fishery, it might be reflected in a uniquely ritualistic reorganisation of the social relations of working life during the Christmas and New Year's festive mumming.[62] And in the farming communities of the north-eastern United States, where the emergence of urban markets and a transportation system capable of reaching them engendered commercialised agriculture after 1820, declining fertility signalled the end of the patriarchal household. With this came the recognition that economic considerations based on the limited availability of land now overrode customary inheritance practices and the primacy of family preservation.[63] In Oneida County, for instance, an 'undulating wave of evangelical fervor' in the pre-1840 years expressed 'a more decidedly privatised and feminised form of religious and social reproduction'.[64] Coupled with the increasing penetration of commercial specialisation, this development challenged the patriarchal household and proclaimed the arrival of a more differentiated social order, leaning noticeably towards acquisitive individualism.[65]

In its capacity to transform its very substance, the productive household of agrarian petty capital was able, unlike slavery, to subordinate itself to commodity relations and the voracious demands of merchant capital. It paid the price that slavery never could, relinquishing its particular form of accumulation, ideology, and culture, privatising the family, and ultimately subjecting itself to a revolutionary economic rationality. Movement west was thus a striving for independence and a rejection of the familial restrictions of past productive life

60   Gagan 1981; 1978, pp. 293–318. I have presented some brief critical comments on Gagan's demographic determinism in Palmer 1983a.
61   Wynn 1981, especially pp. 137, 149; 1980, pp. 168–87.
62   Sider 1977, pp. 23–8.
63   Blumin 1977, especially p. 105.
64   Ryan 1981, pp. 52–104; Cross 1950.
65   Fliegelman 1982, p. 267; Rogin 1975, p. 37.

in the household.[66] In this 'levelling spirit' of expansion, however, merchant capital remained hegemonic. A transplanted and commercialised agrarian capital adapted to, rather than challenged, its dominance.[67] Early manufacturing, for a time, followed a similar course, as yet another momentum of primitive accumulation could be expected to do. But unlike slavery and the rural household, it was destined to do more than mark time while waiting for another economic form to swamp it in its wake.

Early Manufacturing

In 1794 Tench Coxe described American manufacturers as 'farmer craftsmen'. By 1825 Zachariah Allen had characterised them as 'village artificers'. On the eve of the Civil War James M. Williams's *An American Town* viewed such manufacturers as 'city operatives'.[68] These evolving perceptions capture the drift from household production to mill town to the factory system. But at any given time, textile production could take place in the homespun manufactures of New England villages, the declining putting-out system of New York, or the mechanised mills of Pennsylvania's Rockdale.[69] Cotton manufacturing outpaced all other production, employing 33,150 males and 59,136 females by mid-century, with over 1,000 establishments scattered across 24 of the 31 states, turning out goods valued at more than $43 million.[70] The diversity, volume, and geographic distribution of early manufacturing was remarkable. Competitive shoe manufacturers were found in Lynn (Massachusetts), Montreal, and Toronto;[71] rural iron works early located in St. Maurice, Lower Canada, Marmora and Potter's Creek, Upper Canada, Pennsylvania, and the slave states of Georgia and South Carolina;[72] metal manufactures gravitated toward the large cities.[73] Specific products, both luxury specialities and the essentials specific to an age of merchant capital, were associated with particular locales: Dan-

---

66   Hacker 1940, pp. 199–226.

67   Clark 1949, volume 1, p. 463.

68   Clark 1949, vol. 1, pp. 438–9.

69   Stansell 1982, pp. 79–80; Wallace 1978.

70   Rosenberg 1969, p. 209. Note the excellent documentary collection, Kulik, Parks, and Penn 1982; Dublin 1979, pp. 14–22; Prude 1982, pp. 1–36.

71   Dawley 1976, especially pp. 11–41, 73–96; Faler 1981, pp. 58–76; Kealey 1973a, pp. 137–58; Burgess 1977, pp. 187–210.

72   Pentland 1981, pp. 34–48; Clark 1949, p. 446; Walker 1974; Commons et al. 1958, vol. 2, pp. 304–13.

73   Rosenberg 1969, pp. 264–80; Clark 1949, vol. 1, pp. 412–21; Gutman 1976b, pp. 211–33; Palmer 1979a, p. 10; Kealey 1980, pp. 20–1; Tulchinsky 1972, especially pp. 130–1.

bury (Connecticut) with hat making, Waterbury (Connecticut) with cutlery, and shipbuilding with Quebec City.[74] By the late 1840s, paced by Jerome I. Chase and Cyrus McCormick, the agricultural implements industry had consolidated in the Midwest and gave indications of its future centrality in the capitalist transformation of the third quarter of the century, when it would comprise one-quarter of all machine production.[75] Dwarfed by agriculture, manufacturing employed roughly 1.26 million in mid-nineteenth-century North America, a bare five percent of a population of approximately 25.5 million.[76]

Although manufacturing was concentrated in both town and country, the former locale was the most visible. Indeed, town and country divisions were increasingly broken down, the two productive sites being linked by the port cities of the eastern seaboard and the Great Lakes. It was here, in the commercial *entrepôts* of merchant capital, that 'metropolitan industrialisation' developed most unambiguously, a process capturing Toronto, Montreal, New York, Philadelphia, and a host of other North American cities between 1820 and 1850.[77]

Bruce Laurie has delineated the diversity of the structural contexts of work settings in this metropolitan industrialisation. In Philadelphia no less than five 'discrete but overlapping' labouring milieus existed, 'distinguished by scale and mechanization as the first order of differentiation and market orientation as the second'.[78] Factories powered by steam or water were concentrated in iron and textile production. They were largely unrestrained by traditional craft organisation, employing relatively large workforces, averaging over 35 workers. Manufactories lacked the power sources to drive mechanised processes but employed more than 25 workers per site. Such enterprises, displacing small shops and the putting-out system, were bound by handicraft organisation. They were common to printing, saddle or harness-making, hatting, cabinet or

---

74 Clark 1949, vol. 1, p. 464; Cole 1968, p. 19; Rosenberg 1969, p. 262; Rice 1977, pp. 168–98.
75 Clark 1949, vol. 1, p. 464; Post 1982, pp. 48–9; and for Canada, note McCallum 1980.
76 My calculations, all too problematic, are from the Occupational Census for 1851 of the colonies of Upper Canada, Lower Canada, New Brunswick, and Nova Scotia and from data on industrial distribution of gainful workers (1820–40) in the United States. In the former I equated manufacturing with the category *industrial*, and in the latter I utilised the classification of *manufacturing and hand trades*. See Canada Department of Agriculture 1876, vol. 4; United States Bureau of the Census 1961, pp. 7, 74.
77 The term is employed in Wilentz 1982, especially pp. 40–3; but see as well, Montgomery 1968, pp. 3–22; Rock 1979, pp. 235–319; Taylor 1951, pp. 215–20, 250–2; Hirsch 1978, pp. 15–52; Tulchinsky 1977, 203–31; Goheen 1970, pp. 44–57.
78 Laurie 1980, pp. 3–30.

clothing production. Beneath factory and manufactory was the sweatshop, a vehicle for capital-starved journeymen to make the leap to employer status. Hiring cheap, rushing in season, devastated during dull times, trimming costs at every opportunity, and toiling among their workers (who numbered between six and twenty-five per shop) – such garret capitalists dominated the tobacco trades. They were also a significant force in furniture, hat and cap, and boot and shoe output. Butchers, blacksmiths, and bakers often laboured in a fourth type of establishment, the ubiquitous small artisan neighbourhood shop, in which fewer than six workers produced for an immediate market. An absolute majority of Philadelphia's employers as late as 1850, such master craftsmen purchased only a minor, and declining, share of the city's labour power (12.8 percent of the work force). The lowliest of all producers, many of them women, were hired by manufacturers or merchant capitalists as outworkers, whose weaving, tailoring, or shoemaking could be done in the home, for wages that could not 'decently support life'.[79]

Such a range of labour-process organisation suggests why early manufacturing cannot be considered the establishment or the consolidation of accumulation on unambiguously capitalist grounds. Rather, like slavery and petty capital in agrarian production, it was yet another moment in primitive accumulation, establishing the preconditions for capital's ultimate seizure of the social formation. Unlike slavery and the household economy of rural production, however, manufacturing was the beneficiary of the epoch of primitive accumulation. But this was a post-1850 phenomenon, and at least five factors contributed to early manufacturing's limits.

First, even at the very centre of metropolitan industrialisation, the factory system was never more than a harbinger of what, in the future, could develop. In the advanced city of Philadelphia, for instance, factories employed only marginally more than one-quarter of all workers as late as 1850 and comprised less than five percent of all firms. The pervasive segmentation of the local labour markets meant that mechanisation was not an immediate imperative. Tradesmen could exploit the advantages of skill, access to credit, and a generation of stability to advance up a few rungs of the social ladder. Continued reliance on artisanal forms of production and the commercial city's demand for luxury goods simply exacerbated the basic inhibitions to a generalised proliferation of factory conditions.[80] By mid-century, 60 percent of all New York City clothing workers may have been outworkers or sweated labour.

---

79   Stansell 1982, p. 78.
80   Laurie 1980, pp. 17, 26; Wilentz 1982, pp. 42–3, 70.

In the less developed economic context of the Canadas, similar developments unfolded. Hamilton boasted a mere 53 machinists in 1851, and less than a quarter of the labour force worked in establishments with 10 or more employees. In Toronto in the late 1840s almost 50 shoemaking shops coexisted with two factories. Across the populated southern parts of Canada West only the foundries averaged more than 10 workers in 1851 (14.6), and the usual productive concern employed only 3.3 workers.[81] As Wilentz argues, such limitations cannot be conceived only as stasis, for changes in work, marketing, and social differentiation had revamped the very nature of craft production: 'The shell of the old artisan system remained; within that shell, the system disintegrated, creating new social tensions between large groups of masters and employees'.[82]

Such limitations on the organisation of production led to a second confinement: manufacturing was restricted for much of the early nineteenth century by the relative scarcity of labour.[83] Labour recruitment necessitated specific concessions. In the textile industry New England employers adopted one of two methods to secure labour power: the Waltham-Lowell system of hiring single women, housing them in dormitories, and substituting an industrial paternalism for the disintegrating patriarchy of the family farm; or the Rhode Island option, in which patriarchy's form was preserved in the face of its economic nullification by acquiring whole families to labour in the mills.[84] And where the factory system was less developed, as in the Canadas, labour scarcity induced employers to practise a pervasive paternalism.[85] The social relations of impersonality, in which nothing but the wage stood between capital and labour, had not yet arrived. This provided the ideological and material foundation on which craft workers laboured for a 'price', battled to secure a 'competency', and 'United to support – not combined to Injure'.[86] It circumscribed their struggles, as we shall see, but it also confined capital, which was often forced to toast its respectable co-producers or sit down among them to a dinner of cabbage and goose.[87]

---

81   Palmer 1979a, p. 16; Katz, Doucet, and Stern 1982, p. 35; Kealey 1980, p. 21; Spelt 1972, p. 74.
82   Wilentz 1982, p. 43.
83   Note the argument, however flawed, in Habakkuk 1967.
84   Dublin 1979; Gitelman 1967, pp. 227–53; Kulik, Parks, and Penn 1982, pp. 373–480; Sorge 1977, pp. 60–5.
85   The essential and pioneering statement is Pentland 1981, pp. 24–60. I have elaborated upon this theme in Palmer 1983b, pp. 7–59.
86   See Wilentz 1981, pp. 1–22.
87   Langdon 1975, p. 6; Armstrong 1967, pp. 187–8; Langer 1981, pp. 317–32.

The labour shortages that necessitated such class compromises were not overcome until the massive waves of immigration of the 1840s and 1850s, the need for which indicated a third, related limitation of early manufactures. Although substantial in the 1820s (128,502) and 1830s (538,381), immigration to the United States transformed the social structure in the 1840s, particularly in the five years from 1846 to 1850, when 1,282,915 new Americans flooded into the urban labour markets and formed 'nomadic armies' of canal and railway navvies. Almost half of these were Irish (593,700), many of them adherents of the Church of Rome, and between 1840 and 1860 the number of American Catholics soared from 663,000 to over 3 million. To the north, the famine-induced migrations of Irish to British North America were no less phenomenal, totalling approximately 230,000 (or 12.5 percent of the 1851 population of Ontario-Quebec) in the same half-decade. Sheer numbers of this order helped in the creation of a capitalistic labour market.[88]

It was the very hegemony of merchant capital, a fourth curb on manufacturing, that facilitated such massive demographic inputs into the social formation of the 1840s and 1850s. Between 1843 and 1856, merchant capital experienced its years of 'last hurrah'. Mechanised consumer-goods industries in New England, the colonisation of the Pacific Slope and the Southwest, and the wildly fluctuating returns of King Cotton filled its coffers. These years saw the completion of the North American canal system and the expansion of railway mileage from 4,185 to almost 24,000 miles. Merchants stood directly behind such expansion. As Glenn Porter and Harold Livesay have revealed, they marketed the wares of early manufactures and financed the production of both consumer goods and the heavy needs of the railway supply industry. Their control was as pervasive as it was problematic.[89] Along with land policy and the chaos of early banking, which both 'settled' new territories and structured recently arrived immigrants in specific, eventually class, directions,[90] immigration provided the labour force so essential to merchant capital's transportation revolution.

A fifth and final brake on capital accumulation lay in the realm of policy. Merchant capital dictated, in its erratic and fluctuating quest to balance off the particular needs of specific forms of appropriation with the dictates of exchange, the economic programme of the state. This was most evident in the

---

88   United States Bureau of the Census 1961, p. 57; Davis 1980, pp. 16, 20; Akenson 1982, pp. 111, 204–56; Pentland 1981, pp. 96–129.

89   United States Bureau of the Census 1961, p. 427; Young 1981, especially pp. 53–85; Myers 1972, pp. 168–217; Bleasdale 1981, pp. 9–39; Porter and Livesay 1971.

90   See, for instance, Hammond 1948, pp. 1–25; Le Duc 1966, pp. 299–314.

wide-ranging debate over tariff protection, a central political issue in the realm of economic policy. In the United States a protective tariff of 1832 was immediately succeeded by the classic compromise, as merchant capital bowed to the demands of Calhoun's slaveocracy in 1833. Future tariff acts offered manufactures only the most modest protections, and not until the Civil War years were duties revised significantly upward. In 1850 Phillips could write that 'the income of capital, that is, the advantage annually accruing to every man, rich, or of ever so small possessions, in land, tools, or industrial materials or means of whatever description' was depressed by the curtailment of employment resulting from the neglect of protection, 'a wicked, calamitous, and ruinous' aspect of state legislation.[91] Running through the history of the evolution of Canadian 'national policy' – from the debates of the 1840s through to the writings of Robert Baldwin Sullivan, Isaac Buchanan, and William Weir, into the agitation of the Association for the Promotion of Canadian Industry, culminating in the Galt-Cayley tariff of 1858, Confederation (1867), and the beefing up of protection in 1879 – was the same refrain.[92] Not until merchant capital had been reduced to a compliant background was state policy turned to capital's ends.

By 1850, then, in various and different ways, the momenta of primitive accumulation had run their respective courses. Competing forms of appropriation had either reached their limits or were perched on the edge of an historical ledge separating them from their future potential. Through its own contradictory complex of inertia, dynamism, and class compromise, merchant capital brought North America to the brink of an economic transformation that would have far-reaching social and political ramifications, not the least of which would be the nature of the emerging working class.

Class Formation, 1800–50

Does not the true character of each epoch come alive in the nature of its children?

MARX, *Grundrisse* (1857–8)

Labour was the child of the pre-1850 social formation, and, like its parentage, it was both complex and limited. Historical demographers have paid far too

---

91   Taussig 1930, pp. 109–54; Phillips 1850, pp. 18–19. See Siracusa 1979.
92   Note Kealey 1980, pp. 3–17.

little attention to the reproduction of labour power in North America. Rising from just over 4 million in 1790 to approximately 25.5 million by mid-century, population growth was clearly one component of economic development and specialisation.[93]

Little, however, has been done to address the class component of this demographic explosion, reducing much of what little work exists to what Marx dismissed as 'an abstraction ... a chaotic conception of the whole'.[94] Moreover, historical demographers have been far too inattentive to the property structures and forms of appropriation within which demographic change took place and which must have conditioned particular reproductive strategies.[95] At the very same moment of historical crisis – the 1840s and 1850s – within merchant capital's epoch of primitive accumulation, slave fertility in sections of the South was rising, farm family fertility was declining, and whole communities were being created out of people displaced from the Old World to the New.

All such demographic developments were conditioned by the limits of particular forms of appropriation, and all led toward increasing social differentiation. About one in six working Americans in 1800 was engaged in non-agricultural labour; by 1850 the proportion had more than doubled to over one-third. The numbers gainfully employed in non-agricultural pursuits rose from 812,000 in 1820 to 2,795,000 in 1850, and the number of those working on the land climbed from 2,069,000 to 4,902,000, the rate of increase in non-farm labour exceeding that of agricultural work by a ratio of almost three to two. Whereas the general population grew 2.4 times in these three decades, the numbers working in non-agricultural labour expanded 3.4 times. In the four mainland colonies of the Canadas, the workforce was more difficult to categorise but may have been even less tilted toward the land, with 276,000 labouring in non-agricultural realms, 215,000 in agriculture, and 159,000 in unclassifiable settings.[96]

Numbers such as these, situated in the schematically outlined contexts of labouring life presented above, are a part of the process of class formation. To

---

93   See, for instance, Medick 1976, pp. 295–315; Rutman 1977, pp. 16–37; Lockridge 1968, pp. 62–80; Henretta 1971, pp. 379–98; Easterlin 1976, pp. 600–14. Figures taken from United Statues Bureau of the Census 1961, p. 7; Pentland 1981, p. 61.

94   Marx 1973b, p. 100.

95   For an even more forceful rejoinder to neo-Malthusianism, see Brenner 1976, p. 31; 1977, pp. 25–92; 1982, pp. 16–17. Note in Seccombe's 'Marxism and Demography' the call for a softening of Brenner's suppression of demographic imperatives (Seccombe 1983, pp. 23–4).

96   Pessen 1976, p. 57; United States Bureau of the Census 1961, pp. 7, 57; Canada Department of Agriculture 1876, vol. 4.

see the 1800–50 social formation as a hybrid of forms of appropriation presided over by merchant capital is to comprehend the essential complexity of class formation in these years. Concerned principally with exchange and only secondarily with production, merchant capital was incapacitated in its ability to effect a revolutionary and universal transformation in the social relations of production. In its fixation on the short term and on the movement of goods through trade, it was willing to co-exist peaceably with various productive modes, adapting to them and reconciling their interests as long as its own hegemony remained unchanged. The result was that a segmented working class was recruited and structured into an emerging home market. In such societies, in which capital has not yet usurped the right to rule, class struggle is both a central component of the class's own contribution to its making and a broad process extending past collective acts of resistance into the very substance of the everyday relations of exploitation. This was what Marx and Engels meant when they wrote, 'The history of all hitherto existing society *is* the history of class struggles'.[97] That such struggles unfold outside any explicit awareness of class, behind the back of a direct political consciousness of common class grievance or programme, has been argued forcefully by E.P. Thompson and G.E.M. de Ste. Croix. The confrontations of class experience were therefore exceedingly complex and unfolded in obscure realms, including the patterns and pace of reproduction itself. 'In the period of its formation, before the Industrial Revolution', Seccombe concludes, 'the working class evidently "made itself" in more ways than one'.[98]

Much of the class struggle of the epoch of primitive accumulation, for instance, is intelligible as resistance to proletarianisation. Such resistance, however, took various forms rooted in the specific contexts of appropriation prevailing under the patriarchal agrarian household, slavery, or the manufactories of town and country. It coloured the social relations of families and the politics of the age.

Class struggles on the land, for instance, took place predominantly within families. Those driven to landlessness, hiring themselves out to a patriarchal

---

97   Marx and Engels 1968, p. 35.

98   De Ste. Croix 1981, pp. 42–69; Thompson 1978a, pp. 133–65; Seccombe 1983, p. 47. I am here ignoring Raymond Williams's insistence that there is a sharp division between class conflict and class struggle, with the latter representative of more conscious levels of class antagonism. It seems, however, that struggle conveys, semantically, a sense of pervasive, rather than episodic activity, however strong or weak. I thus use the term *class struggle* throughout the remainder of this chapter to denote a wide range of both conscious and unconscious developments within class formation. See Williams 1979.

head, proved a troublesome lot. Moodie saw them as an abusive, insulting, and independent contingent, likely to reply to a stern rebuke with hostile dismissal of their 'place' and a curt reminder that 'they are as good as you; that they can get twenty better places by the morrow, and that they don't care a snap for your anger'.[99] More problematic were the traumas associated with the easing of one's own kin into proletarianisation. Sons whose access to the land was blocked and who lacked alternatives to farming found their lives of labour stressful in the extreme. One such disgruntled 25-year-old reported in 1834: 'I take no peace when at my labor. My father and elder brother are scolding me everytime they come into my presence. Everything I do is all wrong. It is impossible to please them and I get nothing for my labor scarcely at all'.[100] Daughters fared even worse and, until they were able to establish their own households, suffered through years of dependency. Those mill women of New England 'liberated' from such forms of patriarchal domination, however, found little to their liking in the new regime of waged labour. For some, a few days at the machines cured their 'mill fever' forever, and according to Norman Ware, turnover was extensive. To stave off this stark confrontation with proletarianisation, many families modified inheritance and devised adaptive 'strategies of heirship'. Cash began to replace land as fathers struggled both to settle their offspring and to leave customary man-land ratios intact. When parents rocked the fragile social order with rash acts of 'unnatural' second marriage, threatening the interests of the children of the first bed, a charivari might result.[101]

The pervasive unease at potential proletarianisation even seeped into the political arena, defining much of the ferment associated with discontented Upper Canadian yeomen attracted to Mackenzie or the exotic range of ideological energies associated with the Age of Jackson (Skidmoreite agrarianism, Owenite perfectionism, anti-bankism, Mormonism, revivalism).[102] For Seth Luther the crisis of proletarianisation was the disintegration of the household economy and of 'name':

---

99   Moodie 1962, pp. 140–2.

100   Ryan 1981, pp. 57–8.

101   Gagan 1981, pp. 53–60; Henretta 1978; Dublin 1979, pp. 58–74; Luther 1832, especially pp. 17–23; Ware 1964a, p. 149; Goody 1976, pp. 86–117; Thompson 1976, pp. 328–60; Palmer 1978, pp. 5–63.

102   Note the suggestive comments in Merrill 1977, pp. 65–6; Gates 1959, pp. 185–209; Rea 1968, pp. 223–35; Landon 1937a, pp. 79–91; Creighton 1937b, pp. 322–34; Reid 1982; Pessen 1967.

Where shall we bury our shame?
Where in that desolate place,
Hide the last wreck of a name,
Thus broken and stained by disgrace?

A debased patriarchy threw down the gauntlet of challenge to inequality and the emerging 'American system': 'But if you want to improve your minds, take care of your families, and educate your children, you are called *"Disturbers of the peace"*, "Agitators", "An unholy alliance", Disorganizers, a "Dangerous Comination" against the *higher* ORDERS'.[103] Class struggle on the land, at the shared point of reproduction and production, reached out of the family into the very fabric of the social formation.[104]

For slaves the process of resistance was both more subtle and, on rare occasions, more bloodily explicit. This was as it had to be in a system of absolute appropriation of labour power and direct brutalising ownership. Notable slave revolts – Prosser's Virginia plot (1800), the St. John Parish, Louisiana, uprising (1811), Vesey's Charleston conspiracy (1822), and the Nat Turner rebellion (1831) – were but the visible tip of a veritable iceberg of discontent.[105] In a society so pervasively patriarchal, the family was an agent of class oppression and exploitation at one level and an essential force in the defence of a humanity undercut daily, on another.[106] Family ties sustained Afro-Americans through their enslavement, building bridges to their future freedom, republicanism, and difficult entry into the working class. 'White folks', testified one ex-slave in the 1930s, 'do as they please, and the darkies do as they can'.[107] With the nature of choice severely limited under slavery, the class struggle assumed forms familiar to all, encompassing efforts less dramatic than open revolt, nurtured in 'quarters which produced a collective spiritual life'.[108]

At the classic point of production, the class struggle assumed more easily recognisable forms, although much of the best recent work in social history underscores the need to see past the work site into the evangelical fervour, pleasurable recalcitrance, street festivals, and attachments to raucous, respectable, or republican behaviour that themselves coloured so much conflict in the

103 The verse and quotation are taken from Luther 1832, p. 25.
104 For a sampling of reform thought, see the early entries in Stein and Taft 1969.
105 The literature is extensive. It commences, however, with Aptheker 1943 and has been extended in Genovese 1974, pp. 587–96; Genovese 1979.
106 On patriarchy and the slave South, see Wyatt-Brown 1982.
107 Gutman 1976a, p. 99.
108 Genovese 1974, p. 598; Morgan 1982, pp. 563–99; O'Brien 1975; Rachleff 1979.

cultural, political, and ideological realms.[109] By the 1830s, especially in the commercial cities of metropolitan industrialisation, craft workers were cognisant of the exploitation and invasion of their 'dearest rights' following in the wake of a social differentiation that was:

> Rigid, unequal, and unjust
> That monster ground us to the dust, –
> And rolled us in the gutter.

The formation of unions, labour parties, benevolent associations, and a general trades assembly that marched through Philadelphia's streets under the banner 'We Are All Day Laborers' attested to the skilled workers' emerging challenge. For the first time, moreover, the trades, as indicated in verse from the port city of Saint John, New Brunswick, were reaching toward an unprecedented solidarity of labour:

> And more of old Jack's Kin
> Would flock to our banners;
> We do not mean Merchants, Priests,
> Doctors, or Lawyers,
> But Founders and Fishermen
> Hewers and Sawyers,
> With Sad'lers, Sailmakers, and
> Coopers and Barbers,
> And pondmen and others who
> work round our harbours,
> You may guess we have still a
> vast host left behind,
> And to show you still more of
> the public mind,
> Zoby Zog signs for scores who
> go on barefoot or hobnail,
> Buck-sawyers and rabble and
> rag-tag and bob tail[110]

---

109   See Laurie 1980, pp. 33–84, although Laurie's ideal typology of worker cultures is neither convincing nor unproblematic (see Palmer 1981–2, pp. 160–2); Wilentz 1982, pp. 37–77; Gutman 1973b, pp. 533–88; Faler 1979, pp. 121–48; Dawley and Faler 1979, pp. 61–76. For Canada, note Forsey 1982, pp. 9–31; and my own attempt at a survey in Palmer 1983b.

110   Verses quoted in Scott 1974, p. 29.

But for all the promise of collectivity, the early workingmen's movement was not an expression of the unified class front that it strove to present.[111]

If the working women of the New England mills succeeded in integrating their struggle for the 10-hour day in the 1840s with craftmen's demands, the cohesion of these years was fragile at best and about to wither as the mill women were replaced by incoming Irish and French-Canadian labour.[112] Among the women domestics and sweated toilers of home 'industry', however, few possessed ties to labour in an organised sense. They were outside such developments, just as they remained inside the isolation of work ecologies walled in by the kitchen or the attic.[113] Equally outside were the timber workers of the Ottawa Valley, whose Shiners' wars of the 1830s defied incorporation in anything resembling a labour movement, or the rough canalers who, if not isolated from one another, lived in worlds apart from the printers, building tradesmen, shoemakers, stone masons, and shipwrights of the urban trades.[114] Segmented labour markets differentiated by gender, level of skill, ethnicity, region, and organisation of production, fostered divisions and tensions that coexisted uneasily with developing forms of protest.[115]

These were the reflection of the many fragmentations conditioned by merchant capital's hegemony and the nature of an epoch of primitive accumulation. At the level of the state, such limitations were incorporated in a range of barriers erected against the freedoms and impersonalities of market relations. Certain tradesmen – butchers, cartmen, porters, and coachmen – were licensed by authority, but others were confined by the legal conception of conspiracy. This was defined by English criminal law and the Combination Acts of 1799–1800, to which, ironically, both revolutionary Americans and loyalist Canadian colonists looked.[116] As this class struggle in the legal arena was fought out between 1806 and 1842, it threatened to stifle more visible forms of collective action. Yet it was never entirely successful in muffling the voice of labour.

---

111 See, for instance, Commons et al. 1966, vol. 1, especially pp. 169–334; Bernstein 1950, pp. 322–39; Laurie 1980, pp. 85–106; Palmer 1980, pp. 7–32; Whitman 1943; Hugins 1966.

112 Dublin 1979, especially pp. 86–164; Ware 1964a, pp. 125–53; Gitelman 1967, pp. 227–53; Wallace 1978, pp. 291–2.

113 Stansell 1982, pp. 78–103; Groneman 1977, pp. 33–46.

114 Cross 1973, pp. 1–25; Bleasdale 1981, pp. 9–39; Pentland 1948, pp. 255–77; Wynn 1980, pp. 168–87.

115 Note Montgomery 1972, pp. 411–46; Hirsh 1978, pp. 37–132; Ross 1980.

116 Morris 1965, especially pp. 92–207; Rock 1979, pp. 205–34; Commons et al. 1958, vols. 3–4; Armstrong 1967, pp. 187–96.

In British North America in the first 50 years of the nineteenth century, at least 45 local unions were formed, and 60 or more strikes were waged. As the legal assault on early unionism peaked in the mid-1830s, 173 strikes were waged in Jacksonian America (1833–7), and at least 26,250 were enrolled in the ranks of trade unions.[117] To fully comprehend class struggle and collective resistance, however, it is necessary to supplement our meagre knowledge of strikes with an appreciation of the riot as an expression of class grievance in both the economic and ethnocultural-sociopolitical realms. Over 400 such riots have been identified in the Canadas prior to 1855, and they occurred in equal numbers in the states to the south.[118]

Class formation, then, both structurally and as an active process of self-making, was a fitful process. It proceeded outside of any conscious collectivity or commonality among diverse segments of the producing poor. The forms of struggle engendered were unique to particular forms of appropriation. Strategies of resistance were dramatically divergent. Even within a generalised context, such as wage labour, the range of possibilities was striking. An epoch of primitive accumulation had produced a social formation in which the preconditions for capital accumulation were, by 1850, finally established. The development of class was similarly circumscribed, and the years prior to mid-century saw workers' expanding numbers, rudimentary organisation, and acts of resistance reveal the potential of class formation. Yet a child, labour would grow to adolescence and eventual adulthood in the future social formations of late nineteenth-century North America.

The Social Formation, 1850–80

In the United States of America every independent movement of the workers was paralysed so long as slavery disfigured a part of the Republic. Labour cannot emancipate itself in the white skin where in the black it is branded.

MARX, *Capital*, vol. 1 (1867)

---

117 Canadian figures are from unpublished research I have conducted, forthcoming as a plate, 'The Changing Character of Working-Class Organization and Protest, 1820–1890', in *Historical Atlas of Canada*, vol. 2. The American figures are from Commons et al. 1966, vol. 1, pp. 391, 424. Because of Commons's problematic use of early statistics on labour organisation, I have utilised only the most cautious data. See Neufeld 1982, pp. 599–607.

118 See Cross and Kealey 1982, p. 139; Feldberg 1975.

Marx's assessment of the limitations of class formation in the United States has often, quite rightly, been taken as a statement on the ways in which slavery and racism inhibited class consciousness and class struggle. Yet it could equally stand as an evaluation of the social formation, for slavery's persistence attested to the coexistence of various and competing forms of the appropriation of labour power. Merchant capital thrived on such coexistence, even though the social relations of production were consequently crippled. In many spheres of production, then, the revolutionary rupture of the various shackles on the 'free' disposal of labour power was postponed until slavery was vanquished, agrarian petty capital sufficiently rooted to expand capital's growing home market (a development slavery's expansionism thwarted), and state policies conducive to capital accumulation on a large scale implemented.[119] Then and only then could labour realise – in both senses of the word – its freedom, comprising the right to sell its power to a 'vampire [that would] not lose its hold ... so long as there [was] a muscle, a nerve, a drop of blood to be exploited'.[120]

'I know, as you know', declared William H. Seward, an expansionist Republican and future secretary of state, in 1858, 'that a revolution has begun. I know, and all the world knows, that revolutions never go backward'.[121] In the same year, in language more cautiously Canadian, the lieutenant governor of New Brunswick warned the colonial office: 'All British North America is fermenting'.[122] What began as a pervasive set of socioeconomic changes in the 1850s gathered momentum over the course of the next two decades, sweeping aside entrenched social relations of production and restructuring the balance of class forces in North America.

Between 1854 and 1877 the American industrial bourgeoisie triumphed, forged a party to pilot it through the perils of policy formation, seized the reins of state, militarily defended that federal government against an armed secession, consolidated regional support in the West and neutralised the border states, and finally and reluctantly cut the visible chains of chattel slavery.[123] The Canadas had no confrontation with slavery, but the railway promoters who conceived the union of the provinces and engineered the process of state

119   This is the reason for much of the ideological battle of the 1850s and 1860s. Note Foner 1970; Marx 1967, vol. 1, p. 302.
120   Marx 1967, vol. 1, p. 302.
121   Foner 1970, p. 315.
122   Ryerson 1973, p. 325.
123   A voluminous literature might be cited, but see Montgomery 1980, pp. 202–3; Woodward 1956; Dubois 1964, p. 56.

formation, culminating in Confederation in 1867, were not unlike their counterparts south of the 49th parallel. They, too, were moved by fears of incursions upon their terrain, especially of the free soil American expansion into Rupert's Land and the Pacific Northwest, where a bellicose Americanism had reared its head in the Oregon movement. George Brown, the voice of capitalistically inclined agrarianism, articulated the coming of national and class aspirations:

> The opening up of the country belongs not to Great Britain, but to those who will benefit by it, to Canada ... It is an empire we have in view, and its whole export and import trade will be concentrated in the hands of Canadian merchants and manufacturers if we strike for it now ... If we let the west go to the United States, if the rest of the continent outside Canada and the Atlantic provinces acknowledges the sway of the Republic, we should be unable to contend with her. Our ultimate absorption would be inevitable.

Nor were propertied interests unaware of the economic returns to be reaped from integrating a home market. In the Confederation debates, Alexander Galt voiced this promoter's perspective:

> One of the greatest ... benefits to be derived from the union (of the province) will spring up from the breaking down of these barriers, and the opening up of the markets of all provinces to the different industries of each. In this manner we may hope to supply Newfoundland and the great fishing districts of the Gulf with agricultural production of western Canada, we may hope to obtain from Nova Scotia our supply of coal; and the manufacturing industry of Lower Canada may hope to find more extensive outlets in supplying many of these articles which are now purchased in foreign markets.[124]

If such class forces did not have to address a regional identity defined by slavery, their compromise would nevertheless unite class factions by discarding the historical and democratic rights of such 'national' minorities (which were, of course, effective majorities in meaningful locales) as Quebecois and Métis.[125]

---

124 Quotes in Ryerson 1973, pp. 320–1.
125 See Myers 1972, pp. 168–263; Young 1981, especially pp. 53–136.

If the freedmen, francophones, and mixed bloods of North America came up short in this bargaining away of their needs and values, merchant capital was also overtaken. The severe depressions of the late 1850s and 1873–9 not only proletarianised masses of producers; they also dealt a series of harsh blows to those who found their mercantile houses resting on foundations of shifting sand.[126] Overextension of credit to failed handicraftsmen and the vicissitudes of unpredictable markets undermined precarious enterprises.[127] At the same time, industrial capital was securing its own long-term interests. As depression drove the weakest to the wall, concentration resulted. The failure rate among US businesses nearly doubled between 1870 and 1878, climbing from 83 to 158 per 10,000 establishments, but the average number of workers per concern increased by 24 percent. In the industrial heartland of the Dominion of Canada, the depression of the 1870s consolidated capital: over the course of the decade, the number of agricultural implements works decreased by 32, but the hands engaged increased by over 1,000; 100 fewer sawmills employed 3,000 more mill hands; and six more factories turned out railway carriages and locomotives, but their labour force had increased thirty-fold.[128] Especially during the period from the Civil War into the depression of 1873–8, capital utilised such crises to extract concessions from the state, most visible in favourable tariff schedules secured in the United States in 1864 and in Canada in 1878 and 1879.[129]

If a servile state did not fall easily into line, capital intervened with that most effective persuader: cash. The railway scandals of 1872, around Credit Mobilier and the Canadian Pacific line, were but the public revelations of what Friedrich Sorge dubbed 'a true witches' sabbath of corruption ... in official, business, and financial circles in all bourgeois enterprises'.[130] An Ohio spokesman described the House of Representatives in 1873 as 'an auction room where more valuable considerations were disposed of under the speaker's hammer than in any other place on earth'.[131] He apparently had not been to Parliament Hill in Ottawa. After more than two decades of scandal, bribery, and blatant theft of public lands and resources, the *Saturday Review* could declare that Canada

126   Katz 1975a, pp. 1–29.
127   McCalla 1972; 1973, pp. 247–54.
128   My calculations, United States Bureau of the Census 1961, pp. 409, 570; Wells 1982, pp. 5–6; Ross 1980, pp. 121–4.
129   House of Commons 1876; Montgomery 1967, pp. 24, 46.
130   Sorge 1977, p. 123.
131   Josephson 1938, p. 118; Cochran and Miller 1966, pp. 4–6.

could 'modestly challenge comparison' with the United States. Although 'her opportunities and means are not so great as those wielded by the lobbyists and log-rollers of Washington, or the bosses and wire-pullers of New York ... the most has been made of them'.[132]

These actions, legal as well as illicit, fed into industrial capital's emerging hegemony. That hegemony grew out of the developments of the 1850s and 1860s as railway mania and the proliferation of banks and rationalisation of currency allowed industrial capital to liquidate debts and break the financial hold that merchant capital exercised over it. Wartime 'profit' inflation, most directly in the United States but also in Canada, gave a decisive push to the modest beginnings of such developments that were present in the 1850s. The 1860s, then, as Toronto's *People's Journal* announced, was a decade that 'set a going an industrial revolution'.[133]

That industrial revolution was unfolding because the old limitations of an age of primitive accumulation were in the process of being displaced. With slavery replaced by sharecropping, the cotton South no longer posed, through its imperialistic designs on free soil, a threat to western farming. Liberalised immigration laws, land acts, and tariff policies all attested to both the state's pliancy in industrial capital's hands and the subordination of mercantile interests. In the realm of manufacturing, Marx's 'really revolutionary' path to capitalist production was being followed by many North American direct producers. In 1869 the *New York Times* reported that small manufacturers were being swallowed up by 'the greater establishments, whose larger purses, labor-saving machines, etc., refused to allow the small manufactures a separate existence'.[134] By 1872 industry could now be regarded as hegemonic, a product of historical and political, as well as economic advance:

> In the study of our industry, and its effects upon the growth of civilization, and also of the effects produced upon industry by political and other causes, the United States offer a most important and suggestive field. In the first place our history is complete; the beginning of the nation dates from a definite historical period, and the foundation of its industry is not lost in the obscuring mists of tradition. Then, again, the political constitution of the country, its social equality, and the necessities of the

---

132   Myers 1972, p. 337.
133   Porter and Livesay 1971, pp. 116–30; Montgomery 1967, pp. 340–56, 425–47; Langdon 1975, p. 3; Pentland 1950, pp. 457–74; Vatter 1976, pp. 45–59; Coman 1920, pp. 269–312.
134   Cited in Montgomery 1967, p. 25.

new conditions of its settlement, all conspired to make more evident the
fact that productive industry is of necessity the foundation of progress of
civilization.[135]

Certainly there were signs of industrial capital's vitality. Canadian cities like
Hamilton, Toronto, and Montreal boasted significant industrial populations
by 1870. Between 50 and 60 percent of such workforces, moreover, laboured
in factory-like settings employing 50 or more workers, a dramatic shift away
from the character of work organisation at mid-century. By 1880, as Laurie and
Schmitz have shown, Philadelphia's factory production expanded markedly,
encompassing 90 percent of the workers in textiles, 75 percent in printing, and
45 percent in food processing – rates of distribution that had almost doubled
since 1850. Across the United States the percentage of the total labour force
engaged in non-agricultural production increased from 41 to 47 percent during
the 1860s. Technological change, accelerating in the post-1850 years with the
introduction of the McKay stitcher and a range of specialised machine tools,
lent force to such developments. So, too, did the adaptation of the well over
2 million immigrants, largely German and Irish, who came to North America
between 1846 and 1857. They and their offspring were the cannon fodder of
industrial battle, confined to the lowliest, most poorly paid jobs. Social forces
such as these lay behind the rising productivity in the pivotal industrial sections
of iron, coal, and railway lines, as well as in the sweated trades of the metropolitan centres. Manufacturing output increased substantially in the depression-
ridden decade between 1869 and 1879, outpacing both the 1850s and 1860s.
North American capitalism had apparently arrived.[136]

   In fact, it had not, although the vast changes of three brief decades convinced most contemporaries that something was afoot. But just what to call
it was never precisely defined, and Americans referred to their particular political economy not as *capitalism* but as the *free labour system*. Real producers
saw their interests as manufacturers or mechanics in reciprocal rather than
antagonistic terms.[137] Although technology had diluted skills in shoemaking
and tailoring and was about to debase cigar-making and coopering, there were
a vast array of trades that were not yet subordinated to capital. Even where

---

135   Greeley et al. 1872, pp. 25–6. See Gutman 1976b, pp. 211–33; Post 1982, pp. 46–9.
136   McCallum 1980, pp. 83–114; Kealey 1980, pp. 18–34; Laurie and Schmitz 1981, pp. 43–92;
        Montgomery 1967, pp. 3–44; Vatter 1975, p. 134; Ward 1971, pp. 11–84; Young 1875, especially
        pp. 175–95; Burn 1970, pp. 77–98; Rosenberg 1963, pp. 414–46; Pernicone 1973.
137   Montgomery 1967, pp. 25–44; Palmer 1979a, pp. 97–122; Kealey 1980, pp. 154–71.

significant specialisation had developed, as in hatting or the building trades, an element of workmanship and considerable pride remained in the workplace lives of the skilled. Especially among some crucially placed and thoroughly industrial sectors, such as iron working (molders, rollers, and puddlers), control mechanisms were consolidated in early union legislation. In the perhaps overstated words of David Montgomery, 'all the boss did was ... buy the equipment and raw materials and sell the finished product'.[138]

Capital itself rarely revolutionised the social relations of production. Instead, it adhered to traditional guidelines and practices and saw production as a quantitative problem reduced to 'so many hands, so many dollars'. It concentrated on producing more rather than rationalising the work process or the market. Not until the later 1870s, when the debilitating consequences of the resulting crisis of overproduction, falling rate of profit, deflation, and business disorder revealed themselves in the catastrophic collapse of economic life, did capital turn away from the competitive anarchy of entrepreneurial capitalism and the limitations of the patriarchal firm to embrace combinations, pools, and trusts. Before this, however, throughout much of the period between 1850 and 1880, capital strove relentlessly to reduce rather than reform its labour costs, holding stubbornly to the entrenched if archaic methods of wage cuts, script payment, fines, and month-long pay periods that were the peculiar privilege of an atavistic industrial paternalism straddling both town and country.[139]

Industrial capital's march to hegemony thus commenced in this period of manufacture, from 1850 to 1880, but it was not completed. Capital subordinated other productive forms to its dictates and consolidated a capitalist labour market. But its pace of growth and expansion was slowed by internal incapacities, and it was locked into the limitations of a social formation bounded by the productive relations of an age of manufacture. Much industrial activity remained concentrated in the country, and nearly sixty percent of Canadian manufacturing as late as 1880 was located in communities of less than 10,000 people; scarcely one-quarter of the American population lived in settings of 2,500 or more inhabitants. Between 1860 and 1870, US manufacturing employment in the three largest cities increased by 53 percent, but in those smaller enclaves, ranked 21st to 50th in population, the increase was almost 80 percent. Although the conquest of the country by the town, so essential to capitalist

---

138   Kealey 1980, pp. 37–97; Palmer 1979a, pp. 71–96; Bensman 1977; Barnett 1909, pp. 182–208; Blum 1908, pp. 295–319. The quotation is from Montgomery 1979, pp. 9–31, especially p. 12.

139   Montgomery 1980a, p. 203; Laurie and Schmitz 1981, pp. 87–8; Dawley 1976, p. 74; Levine 1979b, pp. 38–43; and on price deflation, Vatter 1975, especially pp. 243–51.

transformation, was thus under way, it had not yet proceeded to the point that it had 'ruralised' the country, curbing proto-industrialisation and reducing the agrarian economy to an adjunct of industry: agriculture. Nor had manufacture's expansion of productivity subordinated labour to capital in other than formal ways.[140]

In fact, it was reproduction rather than production that was crucially responsible for rising output. Gallman argued that the increased supply of labour between 1839 and 1899 accounted for two-thirds of the growth in commodity production. It was not until the 1880s that the output per worker increased significantly (it had stagnated over the 1860s and risen marginally in the 1870s).[141] In this context of limitation and the relatively high social cost of appropriating surplus, the real subjection of labour to capital awaited another epoch. Class formation bore the contradictory marks of this protracted moment of transition.

Class Formation, 1850–80

> It is not what is done for the people, but what people do for themselves, that acts upon their character and condition.
>
> WILLIAM H. SYLVIS, 'Speech to the Iron Molders International Union' (1865)

Between 1867 and 1880 the population of the United States and Canada increased by roughly twenty-six percent, from 40,839,000 to 54,517,000. Immigration provided much of this growth, with almost 4,500,000 largely British, Irish, and German newcomers moving into North American cities and counties. They and their second generation offspring became, in many urban enclaves, the American working class. In 1880, more than 70 of every 100 persons in San Francisco, St. Louis, Cleveland, New York, Detroit, Milwaukee, and Chicago were immigrants or the sons and daughters of the foreign-born. As Herbert G. Gutman has demonstrated, it was the second generation that was pivotal in reconstituting the demographic contours of the working class. Aggregate data indicating that immigrants constituted only one-third of the nation's industrial workers mask the numbers of second-generation ethnic labourers in the more

---

140   Acheson 1972, p. 162; Montgomery 1967, pp. 26–7; Merrington 1976, pp. 171, 189–90; Gordon, Edwards, and Reich 1982, p. 88. Note the local discussions in Cordulack 1975; Ross 1980, p. 126.

141   Gallman 1960, p. 34; Woytinsky 1953, p. 29; Vatter 1975, p. 68; Gordon, Edwards, and Reich 1982, pp. 81–90.

than 3.3 million non-farm wage earners who were classified as native-born Americans. Thus, between 1848 and 1881, the percentage of Toronto's population born in Canada rose from 35 to 60, but the census figures hide the extent to which the majority must have come from immigrant stock. In some locales, like New York, the immigrant workers' significance could not be understated, with 12 of every 13 common labourers coming from their ranks. Among miners, cigar makers, bakers, and stonecutters, the foreign-born and their offspring were highly visible. 'Not every workingman is a foreigner', noticed one clergyman, 'but in the cities, at least, it may almost be said that every foreigner is a workingman'.[142]

Class formation was thus deeply affected by the movement of European peoples into the North American social formation. It was also transformed by the aftermath of slavery, which saw African-Americans become acclimatised to wage labour and new forms of dependency. Although this process would not run its course until well after Reconstruction, indeed not until the great migrations of the early twentieth-century war years, its origins lay in this period. As W.E.B. Dubois and Leon Litwack have shown, ex-slaves tasted the first exhilarating breath of freedom in this period, joined the restless movement that a whole series of mobility studies have confirmed was central to white labour, and then found themselves the class losers in a 'counterrevolution of property'.[143] This was a process encompassing continuity and change, degradation and delight. One part was articulated in the advice of a white reverend from Louisville, Kentucky to African-American Episcopalians:

> You know it is better to work for Mr. Cash than Mr. Lash. A black man looks better now to the white than he used to do. He looks taller, brighter, and more like a man. The more money you make, the lighter your skin will be. The more land and houses you get, the straighter your hair will be.

---

142 Urquhart and Buckley in Leacy 1983, pp. 14–15, 23; United States Bureau of the Census 1961, pp. 7, 57; Montgomery 1967, pp. 35–40; Gutman 1976b, p. 40; Kealey 1980, p. 100; Ross 1980, pp. 85–8; Levine 1979b, pp. 73, 78. Gutman's argument about the centrality of the second generation forms the core of a series of unpublished papers delivered across North America over the last three years. I heard the argument stated most thoroughly in Gutman 1982.

143 Almost forty-five years separate the publication of two magisterial treatments, Dubois 1964, and Litwack 1980. On mobility of white labour, the pioneering work was Thernstrom 1964; and in a less interpretive mode, Knights 1971. For a Canada-United States comparison, see Katz, Doucet, and Stern 1982, pp. 102–30. On southern migrations northward, see Coles 1972; Tuttle, 1969, pp. 408–32; Spero and Harris 1968.

A black preacher, however, saw the options and possibilities as more open-ended, urging his peers in Florida: 'you mus' move clar away from de ole places what you knows, ter de ne places what you don't know, whey you kin raise up yore head douten no fear o' Marse dis un Marse Tudder'. Like the freedman's song he saw freedom as leaving behind the oppressions of racial inequality associated with place and one people's power over another: 'Bye, bye, don't grieve arter me,/ 'Cause you be here an' I'll gone'.[144]

Many lacked the ex-slaves' compulsion to move and were apt to explore other avenues of seizing the new potentials of a social formation given over to manufacture. The quantitative expansion of the means of production, coupled with the levelling of skills attendant upon the limited use of machines, opened corners of the labour market to women and children. With the introduction of the cigar mould in the 1860s, the number of women cigar makers in the United States soared from 731 to 21,409 in a brief 10 years. 70 percent of all women in US manufacturing in 1870 laboured in the needle trades, boots and shoe production, and the textile industry in which, with children, they supplied between 50 and 67 percent of the workforce. Some sectors, such as iron making, flour milling, the building trades, and furniture construction, employed males almost exclusively, leading some historians to minimise the vital place of female-child labour in these years. Yet were we to have looked to Toronto in 1871, we would have noted that 74.6 percent of all employees in the clothing industry were female or under the age of 16. In printing, tobacco, and even furniture production, between one and five workers in 10 were women or children. American cities like Chicago, New York, and Cincinnati were known as hives of female and child labour. In Montreal, women and the young were pivotal in production, as they were in mill towns like Cornwall, where three factories in 1881 employed 133 men, 227 women, 186 boys and 190 girls, a woman-child to man ratio of about 4.6 to 1. Indeed, whole segments of the North American working class depended on the collective wages of all members of the family for survival. Children totalled 13 to 29 percent of the labour force in the cotton mills of Massachusetts, Pennsylvania, and South Carolina. In the face of dire need and expanding employment opportunities for women and the young, families struck reproductive strategies resonating with the new possibilities of productive labour.[145]

---

144   Quotations from Litwack 1980, pp. 387, 292.

145   Gordon, Edwards, and Reich 1982, pp. 93–4; Katz, Doucet, and Stern 1982, p. 395; Kealey 1980, pp. 310–15; Kealey and Palmer 1982, pp. 43–4; Bradbury 1979, pp. 71–96; Montgomery 1967, pp. 33–4; Ross 1980, pp. 129–30; Pernicone 1973, p. 171. On poverty, see Walkowitz 1978, pp. 145–54.

Whereas the birth rate per thousand native whites in the United States and industrial Ontario declined between 1850 and 1880 and continued to fall in the following years, recent studies have indicated that this precipitous drop in fertility was not shared by all classes. Professionals, agents, clerks, merchants, manufacturers, and employing craftsmen lowered their fertility rates in order to appropriate rationally the optimum in material goods and social benefits for their family units. In contrast, skilled workers increased their fertility over the same period, and labourers, especially from the poorer immigrant groups, raised even more dramatically the number of children they were having. In cities like Montreal, in which one in every four boys aged 11–15 was engaged in wage labour, children were an economic asset to working-class families. Those social classes most constrained by economic necessity responded positively to the opportunities of an expanding teenage labour market, which could be exploited to help provide sustenance for the family. A social formation guided by manufacture's stress on expanding the workforce and cutting the absolute unit costs of labour welcomed the influx of cheaply employable women and children, at least in some spheres. Production and reproduction were two halves of the same economic coin, part of the currency of class formation. 'Why did you dismiss my daughters?' asked one irate mother of a cotton boss; 'I have need of their assistance to live'.[146]

To be sure, as capitalism moved out of manufacture and into the age of modern industry, there were signs that 'the mature proletarian household' was emerging. This was, as Seccombe has argued, a family formation character-ised by dependency on the male wage, rather than on the collective wages of family members. Premised on the 'family wage', or the right of the male bread-winner to remuneration capable of sustaining fathers, mothers, and children in respectable status, the mature proletarian household was characterised by declining fertility, by the termination of the practiced use of children as eco-nomic assets. Its locale was the fully industrial capitalist setting of the mine, heavy industry, or the technologically advanced factory; its children were in school; and its wives were working at unpaid domestic labour.[147] Never an option for the immigrant masses or the unskilled, such an 'ideal type' of family structure was perched precariously, even for the trades, on the harsh and dis-ruptive realities of depression, seasonality, unemployment, short time, and the

---

146   United States Bureau of the Census 1961, p. 23; Bradbury 1979, pp. 71–96; Katz, Doucet, and Stern 1982, pp. 336–42; Henripin 1972; Katz 1981, pp. 579–606; Kessler-Harris 1982, pp. 109–10.

147   Seccombe 1983, pp. 38, 44–7.

blacklist. Michael Katz and Mark Stern, in a study of Buffalo and Erie County, New York, saw the 'overproduction' of children grinding to a halt between 1855 and 1900 among just those kinds of workers likely to raise the banner of the family wage. Fertility ratios, giving the number of children under age five per 1,000 married women aged 20 to 49, establish a labourers' increase of 13.5 percent and a skilled workers' decrease of almost 18 percent. Similarly, in Hamilton, labourers and the 'dishonourable' trades devastated by machines saw rising fertility ratios between 1851 and 1871, compared with stable or declining ratios for more prosperous crafts.[148] What this underscores, and what much demographic inquiry bypasses, is the reciprocity of reproduction and resistance, of class formation in the structural sphere, and of class struggle in the social relations of production.

The family wage was not simply a revival of patriarchy in the working class. It was also the locus of class struggle, of a pervasive demand on the part of skilled workers not yet fully subordinated to capital, for wages sufficient to compensate them for their labour power and provide for its replenishment on a day-to-day basis. If the wage was all that was involved in this struggle, matters might have been settled easily. But there were inevitably other issues: demeanour, dignity, and the limits that the class placed on the development of dependency.[149]

From 1850 to 1880 North America's first labour movement emerged. Led by skilled workers embedded in local communities and associational networks of fraternal orders, sporting associations, clubs, and benevolent societies, it consolidated on a bedrock of emerging class antagonism and conflict.[150] In Canada and the United States, these three decades were marked by the emergence of class struggle and parallel organisational ferment. 'An insurrection of labor', in the words of contemporary newspapers, swept across the industrial heartland of the Canadas from Hamilton to Montreal, driving tradesmen into 62 strikes between 1851 and 1855, an unprecedented agitation followed by 11 often riotous confrontations between the unskilled and their employers in the deteriorating

---

148 Katz and Stern 1981, especially pp. 75–8; Katz, Doucet, and Stern 1982, p. 342. For the implications of the persistence in rural areas of what Seccombe (1983, pp. 38, 43–5) terms the 'early proletarian household', where the fertility was higher, see Gaffield 1979, pp. 48–70; Brookes 1982, pp. 93–108.

149 Note Barrett 1980, pp. 194, 204, 218–19; Humphries 1977a; 1977b.

150 Palmer 1979a, pp. 35–70; Palmer 1983b, pp. 60–95; Kealey 1980, pp. 98–123; Van Tine 1973, especially pp. 1–18, 33–40; Walkowitz 1978, pp. 110–42, 156–70; Greenberg 1980, pp. 65–113, 163–86.

economic climate of the later 1850s. This early wages movement of the skilled peaked in 1853–4, the same years that witnessed a remarkably comparable upsurge in strike activity in the United States. 400 labour-capital confrontations were fought in the more populous American states (a rough strike-to-population ratio in the United States would be 1:14.6 compared with 1:14.1 for the Canadas). Alongside this escalating conflict, the trade unions developed. The 1850s were marked by the proliferation of local bodies and the faint beginnings of international organisation among the shoemakers, engineers, and moulders. Characterised by a high degree of mortality and localism, unions were almost entirely restricted to the skilled, and of the 30 or more active in the Canadas in the decade, only two were not founded on craftsmanship. Inhibited by nativism and Know-Nothingism, still disfigured in the South by slavery, and later devastated by the 1857–9 collapse, this initial moment of class resolve foundered.[151]

The pieces were picked up in the 1860s and early 1870s as class conflict challenged the social formation; localism gave way to efforts at national organisation; and labour reform consolidated a leadership and an ideological presence. Guided by a 'producer ideology' that championed labour's respectability and 'independence', the reform cause was premised on moulders leader William Sylvis's words that people themselves could alter their 'character and condition'. '*They* cut down our PRICES!' thundered Ira Steward, 'We *shall cut down* THEIR HOURS!'[152] It was an argument and an orientation peculiarly suited to those skilled workers not yet brought to their collective knees by capital. Out of their growing discontent they created Eight-Hour Leagues, the National Labor Union, cooperatives, workingmen's institutes, the Knights of St. Crispin, protective associations, secret assemblies such as the Knights of Labor, brotherhoods of railway workers, and a host of craft unions that convened, over the course of the 1860s and 1870s, in city, state, national, and bi-national assemblies representing well over 300,000 workers. Across the industrial United States the hours of labour became the focal point of conflict, erupting in the eight-hour campaigns that rocked Massachusetts, Connecticut, Wisconsin, Missouri, Illinois, California, and New York. In Canada the nine-hour movement thrust the 'labour question' to the forefront in Hamilton, Toronto, and Montreal,

---

151   Bryan D. Palmer, 'The Changing Character of Working-Class Organization and Protest, 1820–1890', in *Historical Atlas of Canada*, vol. 2, forthcoming; Forsey 1982, pp. 31–6; Commons et al. 1966, vol. 1, pp. 601–20; Ware 1964a, pp. 227–40; Shugg 1972, pp. 76–156; Ross 1980, pp. 342–7; Shaw 1973, pp. 48–84.

152   Silvis and Steward quoted in Montgomery 1967, pp. 229, 257.

resulting in the legalisation of labour organisation in the Tory Trades Union
Bill of 1872 and the formation of the first centralised labour body in 1873, the
Canadian Labor Union.[153]

The shorter-hours struggles of these decades were but the episodic pinnacle
of daily agitations culminating in the founding of 40 new national trade unions
in the United States between 1860 and 1879; 16 similar bodies were established
in Canada, embracing more than 81 locals, by 1873.[154] Organisation led directly
into conflict, with the number of strikes in Canada almost tripling over the
course of the 1860s and 1870s, rising from 72 to 276. No such data, however
rudimentary, exist for the United States, but it does seem that the pattern of
conflict shifted subtly over these decades. During the 1860s and early-to-mid
1870s, as the great moulders' confrontations unfolded in Hamilton and Troy,
strikes were fought over national issues of moment, but they were waged
within local communities. By 1876 and 1877, however, with the insurrectionary
railway strikes of December and July, national conflicts, fought out in local
areas, were sweeping together the communities of North America, just as the
lines themselves integrated larger home markets. The resulting threat to social
order necessitated, on a level previously unanticipated, the intervention of a
state power guarding capital's rights of property. As one contemporary noted,
'the spontaneity of the movement show[ed] the existence of a widespread
discontent, a disposition to subvert the existing social order, to modify or
overturn the political institutions ... Never before in this country – perhaps in
no other country in the world – have so vast a number of men taken part in
riots and strikes for increased wages'.[155]

By the time of the railway strikes, however, a new social formation was
hammering the last nails into the coffin of the age of manufacture. The spontaneity of the first truly mass strikes in the history of North American labour
merely awaited harnessing before the ambiguities of class formation partially
resolved themselves in the Great Upheaval. Everywhere the old radicalism of
the 1860s and 1870s was eclipsed by the failure to cultivate a politics of opposition uncompromised by the 'free labour' ideology of Republicanism, the 'pro-

---

153 Ware 1964b, pp. 1–54; Commons et al. 1958, vol. 10; Battye 1980, pp. 25–56; Ross 1980,
       pp. 368–458.
154 Commons et al. 1958, vol. 10, p. vii; Forsey 1982, p. 61.
155 Bryan D. Palmer, 'The Changing Character of Working-Class Organization and Protest,
       1820–1890', in *Historical Atlas of Canada*, vol. 2, forthcoming; Palmer 1979a, pp. 78–82;
       Walkowitz 1978, pp. 95–8, 183–218; Montgomery 1980a, p. 203; 1980b, pp. 81–104; Morton
       1977, pp. 6–34; Debouzy 1983, pp. 61–77; Brecher 1972, pp. 1–24. The quotation is from Dacus
       1877, pp. 16–17. On military intervention, see Cooper 1980, pp. 43–98.

ducer ideology' of the manufacturer-mechanic alliance, or the paternalism of astute Tories. In the work place, resistance was weakened by the tendency of those skilled advocates of the family wage to regard those who could not wrestle such concessions from capital as marginal to labour reform. But to the working women, common labourers, and immigrants relegated to the periphery, it was the labour reform ideology itself that was marginal. What were they to make of a Boston labour paper's statement that 'it is the high and holy mission of labor reform to show to men an object worthier than wealth?'[156] As industrial capitalism's relentless accumulation and concentration of wealth eroded the credibility of this free labour doctrine, materially lessening the distance among segments of the working class, new forms of collectivity emerged.[157]

The Social Formation, 1880–1900

On the one hand the enormous and continuing stream of humanity, year after year driven to America, leaves behind stagnant sediments in the east of the United States, while the wave of immigration from Europe throws men on the labour market there more rapidly than the wave of immigration to the west can wash them away. On the other hand, the American Civil War brought in its train a colossal national debt, and with it, pressure of taxes, the growth of the vilest financial aristocracy, the relinquishment of a huge portion of the public lands to speculative companies ... the most rapid centralization of capital. Thus the great republic has ceased to be the Promised Land for emigrating workers. Capitalist production there advances with giant strides ...

> MARX, *Capital*, Volume I (1867)

Great change coexisted with considerable continuity in the transformation of American economic life between 1800 and 1880. The factory often remained, in Nelson's words, 'a congress of craftsmen's shops rather than an integrated plant'.[158] But in the last two decades of the nineteenth century the dramatic shift to modern industry transformed the social relations of production. In the United States the number of wage earners in manufacturing soared from 2.7 million to 4.5 million. Factories employing more than 500 workers, of which

---

156   The quotation is from Montgomery 1980a, p. 120.

157   Montgomery 1967, pp. 335–86; Palmer 1979a, pp. 97–152; Kealey 1980, pp. 124–53.

158   Nelson 1975, pp. 3–10.

there were but a handful in 1870, now became commonplace and by 1900 numbered over 1,500. The average number of wage earners per establishment increased sharply, growing from 65 to 333 in iron and steel, eight to 65 in agricultural implements, and 31 to 214 in carpets and rugs between 1860 and 1900. Technological change – the precursor of the assembly line in meat packing, Cyrus McCorrnick's moulding machine at International Harvester, the Bessemer process in steel – extended the factory system as, with the rise of mechanised and often interchangeable machine parts, processes used in one industry became transferable to another. The expansion of installed horsepower per wage earner increased dramatically from 13 percent in the 1880s to 36 percent in the 1890s. When the first steel slabs from which nails could be cut rolled out of Pennsylvania's Wheeling's Crescent Iron Works, they were the signs of a managerial assault on labour. A disgruntled puddler responded to such technological innovation by chalking the steel with the words PUDDLERS' TOMBSTONES. But skilled workers were not the only dying breed. All of these developments sounded the death knell of competitive and patriarchal capitalism, moving the United States decisively in the direction of monopoly capital. By 1894 American industrial production ranked first in the world, and the country turned out one-third of the world's manufactured goods. Output per worker, by decade, rose significantly during both the 1880s and 1890s. Experimentation with new corporate forms and new relations with the state, in conjunction with the first attempts to restructure work itself, signalled the 'turning point of capital accumulation'. Small firms succumbed to the oligopolistic tendencies of the market and the devastating impact of price deflation and depression (1893–6). The rate of business failures per 10,000 listed enterprises exceeded 100 in 13 of the 16 years from 1883 to 1898, a rate in excess of that of the Great Depression of the 1930s. In popular parlance, capitalism had arrived, and the 'robber barons' were in control. As Marx noted in 1858, 'when the inevitable transition to the factory system takes place in [the United States], the ensuing concentration will, compared with Europe and even England, advance in seven league boots'.[159]

The Canadian social formation was outpaced by this hectic expansion to the south. But between 1870 and 1890 it too tasted the fruits, both bitter and sweet, of economic transformation. Canadian establishments capitalised at $50,000 and over increased by about fifty percent; employment in manufacturing rose by 76 percent and output in constant dollar terms by 138 percent;

---

159   Gordon, Edwards, and Reich 1982, pp. 84, 94–106; Steindl 1976, p. 191; Foner 1962, p. 58, where Marx is quoted; Kolko 1965; Vatter 1975, pp. 132–40; Bennett 1977, pp. 34–5.

railway mileage increased from 3,000 in 1873 to over 16,000 in 1896; manufacturing's place, in terms of value added, rose from 19 percent of the Gross National Product in 1870 to 23.5 percent in 1890; the real rate of manufacturing output increased over the course of the 1880s; and many industries consolidated during the cresting fortunes of the National Policy (1880–4). Between 1880 and 1890, for instance, the value of cotton cloth output rose by 125 percent. Even this dramatic increase understated the gains of the decade's first five years: the number of mills, spindles, looms, and capital investment in cotton cloth tripled in that short period.[160]

To be sure, capital still had some hurdles to overcome before it would reign hegemonic over politicians and regional interest groups, its own internal competitiveness, and its major adversary, labour. On balance, however, it was between 1880 and 1900 that decisive steps were taken in just the directions demanded if capital accumulation was to proceed unchallenged. In Canada the 1880s and 1890s saw the final suppression of the Métis inhabitants of the western interior, central Canada's penetration of the eastern coal fields, and the colonisation of west coast resources and the integration of British Columbia into the Dominion via the completion of the Canadian Pacific Railway. Although Canadian society was far from urbanised (not until the 1920s would the urban population exceed that of rural areas), the subordination of the country to the town was nevertheless a recognised feature of social relations, drawing out the organised resentments of farmers. From 1874, with the rise of the Dominion Grange of Patrons of Husbandry, through the 1880s and into the revolt of the Patrons of Industry in the 1890s, rural Canada challenged the social formation with cooperative panaceas and eventual opposition in the political arena. The rise of the 'new South' and the curbing of independence on the frontier farm, both instigating massive mobilisations of 'the people' in the populist revolt of the West and the Southwest, were parallel developments in the United States. Out of them all would proceed the very uneven growth and structured underdevelopment so central to capitalist accumulation.[161]

Such momentous accomplishments were not achieved without the formalisation of the increasingly prominent ties between capital and the state. Federal governments became regulatory bodies, shielding capital from cut-throat competition and price deflation, strike-breakers and agents of repression facing down unruly workers and anarcho-communist dissidents, and bagmen arran-

---

160   Drawn from more extensive data/sources cited in Kealey and Palmer 1982, pp. 29–35.
161   Howard 1965; Frank 1977, pp. 3–34; Robin 1972, pp. 49–86; Woodward 1951; Vatter 1975, pp. 87–130; Pollack 1968; Goodwyn 1976; Hicks 1931; Hann 1975; Wood 1975, pp. 9–146.

356

ging land deals, schemes, and promotions. In an age ideologically captivated by laissez-faire and acquisitive individualism, the social formation, through the words of one of its products, John D. Rockefeller, was proclaiming that 'the age of individualism is gone, never to return!'[162] For labour advocate Phillips Thompson, schooled in the class struggles of Boston and Toronto, the lessons were all too clear. 'Capitalism is king', he declared and added his assessment of the prostitution of politics on the bed of powerful interests: 'The real rulers are not the puppet princes and jumping-jack statesmen who strut their little hour upon the world's stage, but the money kings, railroad presidents and great international speculators and adventurers who control the money-market and highways of commerce'.[163]

Thompson's words spoke of labour resistance and, implicitly, of capital's need to crush recalcitrant workers. There are indications that these years, which predated Taylorism, the rationalisation of the labour process and much of the restructuring of work associated with Fordism and twentieth-century deskilling, saw labour hold considerable ground in its battles with capital. The social cost of labour may well have remained relatively high as wage rates stabilised in a context of falling consumer prices.[164] Craft unions and Knights of Labor local assemblies surged forward during the Great Upheaval, culminating in the continent-wide agitations of 1886. Employers reacted with intensive applications of capital, brute force, and early drives to displace workers with machines.[165] An age of opulence and sham individualism spawned a collectivity and awareness among the working class, which came to perceive its declining status and true place in the relations of exploitation. A decidedly capitalistic social formation conditioned a class formation rooted in a mass movement of opposition and challenge.

Class Formation, 1880–1900

The Knights of Labor are the first national organization created by the American working class as a whole; whatever be their origin and history, whatever their shortcomings and little absurdities, whatever their

162 Kolko 1965; Bain 1964, p. 623; Vatter 1975, pp. 168–212; Cooper 1980; Myers 1972, pp. 301–37.
163 Thompson 1887, p. 93.
164 Kealey and Palmer 1982, pp. 30–2; Montgomery 1980a, p. 113.
165 Clark 1949, vol. 2, pp. 79, 106; Ozanne 1967, pp. 22–6; Gordon, Edwards, and Reich 1982, pp. 115–16; Bennett 1977, pp. 10–39.

platform and constitution, here they are, the work of practically the whole class of American wage earners, the only national bond that holds them together, that makes their strength felt to themselves not less than to their enemies, and that fills them with the proud hope of future victories.

FRIEDRICH ENGELS, *The Condition of the Working Class in England* (1885)

Population boomed in the last two decades of the nineteenth century. Canada and the United States grew in size by 33 percent, from 54.5 million in 1880 to approximately 81.4 million by 1900. Those gainfully employed in non-agricultural pursuits, however, increased their numbers by more than fifty percent, to almost 18.5 million, or 23 percent of the total population. Modern industry literally created new proletarian populations: a mere 55,000 American machinists in 1870 expanded 415 percent to 283,000 by 1900, whereas iron and steel workers saw their ranks expand by 1,200 percent between 1870 and 1910. The complex of oil, chemical, and rubber industries experienced a 1,900 percent growth in employment over the same years. In this latter realm, two-thirds of the labour force was immigrant. Many of them came in the post-1886 (in Canada, post-1896) wave of eastern and southern Europeans that would 'remake' the working class demographically in the opening years of the twentieth century. Between 1880 and 1900 the annual numbers of Italians immigrating to North America jumped from 12,500 to 105,000; of central Europeans (Germans, Poles, Czechs, Austro-Hungarians, and so on), from 41,000 to 144,000. These figures soared even more dramatically in the pre-war years as the corporate octopus of monopoly capital wound its tentacles around an increasingly differentiated work force.[166]

Many distractions prevailed within this growing working class in spite of a general drift toward the homogenisation of labour.[167] New industries created new skills, and in other spheres organisation insulated some crafts from the degradations of deskilling. Regions, as well, experienced this levelling process unevenly: the large industrial cities of the East and the Midwest witnessed a marked convergence of wage rates. Wages, however, remained the badge of respectability, so that higher rates of remuneration were the tangible material expression of privilege and status.

---

166   United States Bureau of the Census 1961, pp. 7, 56–7; Urquhart and Buckley in Leacy 1983, pp. 12, 27–8, 59; Montgomery 1980a, pp. 109, 111; 1979, p. 35; Avery 1979; Neufeld 1982, p. 606.

167   The term is employed and the process is outlined in Gordon, Edwards, and Reich 1982, pp. 106–32. Note the discussion of wage convergence in the Northeast in Bennett and Earle 1982, pp. 383–405.

One loose assessment[168] suggests that approximately forty percent of all working-class families hovered at or near the poverty line, many of them thrust into the depths of destitution by unemployment, disease, or the departure of the male breadwinner. Immigrants, labourers, and the unorganised most often faced such poverty directly. By overcrowding, under-consuming, and scavenging for food and fuel, they could stay alive from one year to the next, but it was often child labour that kept their economic heads above water. An 1882 New York state inquiry into child labour heard this testimony in Cohoes, a cotton mill town:

Q. How many children have you in the mills?
A. For now – three girls and the old man [her husband].
Q. Could you support your family without the help of the children?
A. No, it would be too hard to support them all.
Q. How many have you?
A. Just eleven ...
Q. Are you able to save any of the earnings?
A. No, sir, not and keep clothes on them.[169]

Such words could have been heard across industrial North America between 1880 and 1900, when families unable to scrape together the $400 to $600 needed to provide the basic necessities relied on the earnings of their young.[170]

Among the more skilled trades – moulding, mining, carpentry – in which as much as 45 percent of the working class could be located, incomes were sufficiently high, in good times, to ensure adequate food, clothing, and shelter, with the possibility for some small expenditure for recreation or luxury items. A Toronto moulder's wife wrote to a Hamilton orphanage in 1889, depositing funds on her adopted daughter's account and revealing the imposed limits and cultivated resiliency of working-class family life:

Dear Madam,
I am sending you $4.00 on my little daughter's account – would like to have sent more but could not on account of my Husband being sick for 2 weeks which leaves us rather short of funds however I hope to get it

---

168   The following general description of working-class family incomes comes from Mont-
        gomery 1980a, pp. 117–18. But see, as well, the particular study of family life in three groups
        (carpenters, teamsters, and day labourers) in Tygiel 1977, pp. 179–227.
169   Walkowitz 1978, p. 150.
170   Kessler-Harris 1982, p. 121; Cole 1963, p. 118; Kealey 1982, pp. 177–80.

settled as soon as possible then on the new year pay in advance ... We are paying for a $300 piano for Edna and giving her a good education so that if anything should happen to her papa or I she will be able to earn a living for herself and be independent of the world ...[171]

Sustained by their respectable self-conception, the wage of the skilled male, the arduous domestic labour of wives, and frugal budgeting, families such as this woman's weathered the storms of a precarious life in industrial America. Their circumstances shifted with the fluctuations in the business cycle and the state of their personal good or bad fortune.[172]

Finally, among those blessed with jobs that were likely to be secure as well as skilled – locomotive engineers or glass blowers, for instance – annual income in the late nineteenth century might exceed $800, running to $1,100. Perhaps as many as fifteen percent of working-class families were headed by craftsmen like these: proud, independent, and experienced in labour that could not be displaced. Here the wage was male terrain, the well-kept home the responsibility of the woman.

These gradations in family life had obvious ramifications in the productive and reproductive realms, with those more stable elements of the working class likely to be 'protected' by unionisation and smaller families, the others 'dependent' on children and casual employment. Union affiliation and the family wage were thus generally paired, and one part of class formation was the divide separating those who embraced this dyad from those who could not afford it, let alone the luxury of fewer children.

On the eve of the 1880s, after pulling through the depression of the 1870s, most workers belonged to the latter category. Only 18 national or bi-national unions were then operative in Canada and the United States, a core group that formed the Federation of Organized Trades and Labor Unions of the United States and Canada (1881) and later the American Federation of Labor (1886). With a total membership in 1886 of no more than 350,000, the trade unions were overwhelmingly composed of male skilled craftsmen. They represented only a small minority of the North American working class, certainly no more than three percent of the non-agricultural workforce. This, of course, understates the range of organisational reach, because the large national unions were also supplemented by local unions, in which the unskilled might find

---

171   Record of Orphan's Apprenticeships, Hamilton Orphan Asylum, April 1881–1905, Hamilton Collection, Hamilton Public Library.

172   Kleinberg 1976, p. 61.

more of a voice. Throughout the 1880s in Canada, for instance, purely local unions still outnumbered the locals of the internationals by two to one, with over 220 surviving into the age of modern industry. American manufacturing centres, like Cincinnati, had 35 unions, local and international, joined in the trades and labour assemblies that surfaced in so many cities between 1879 and 1883.[173]

If this upsurge of largely male and skilled workers had encompassed the entirety of labour's response to modern industry, the qualitative transformation of the social formation would have been unmatched in the realm of class formation: women workers would have remained marginal to the process of class struggle; the unskilled and immigrant masses would have been locked into the isolation of previous decades; and the family wage, won in sharp class conflicts over the 1860s and 1870s, would have spawned only patriarchal chauvinism and a condescending dismissal of those who could not win it for themselves. But this was not what happened. Over the course of the 1880s, women, the unskilled, and immigrants fought their way into the North American working-class movement, where they joined a skilled leadership contingent.[174] Together, these working-class elements forged an alliance that burst onto the North American industrial scene in the Great Upheaval, a moment of class formation guided by the Knights of Labor.

Formed in 1869, the Knights of Labor was initially confined by the contexts of its origins, restricted by its attachment to secrecy. Although committed to a broad conception of labour reform characteristic of the ideological ferment of the 1860s and 1870s, when manufacture's limitations cultivated belief in the possibilities of imminent change, the Noble and Holy Order officially refused admittance to women until 1879. In 1881, its ranks hidden behind a façade of secrecy and still bound by gender, the Knights of Labor's North American membership was less than 20,000. Later in that year, partly as a concession to the Catholic Church, the Knights abandoned the religious content of their secrecy by going public. A woman shoeworker in Philadelphia, Mary Stirling, defiantly challenged both the Knights of Labor and the largest shoe manufacturer in the city. Leading her co-workers out on strike, she organised a local assembly and successfully petitioned the Cincinnati General Assembly for admission to the Order. Victorious in both confrontations, Stirling's successes and the

---

173   Neufeld 1982, p. 606; Beard 1931, pp. 86–9; Foner 1962, pp. 497–524; Bryan D. Palmer, 'The Changing Character of Working-Class Organization and Protest, 1820–1890', in *Historical Atlas of Canada*, vol. 2, forthcoming; Ross 1980, p. 396; Forsey 1982, pp. 169–290.

174   See Fink 1977, pp. 389–409.

public presence of the Knights of Labor signalled the arrival of a new vitality in working-class circles. The next five years saw a veritable transformation in class relations, culminating in the Great Upheaval, bred of at least four vital shifts in the nature of class struggle in the 1880s.[175]

Crossing the Quantitative Threshold
Organisation

Organisationally, the Knights drew workers into their ranks through a relatively simple procedure and institutional apparatus. Individual members joined locals (LAS), either in mixed (diverse occupational affiliations) or trade (adhering more rigidly to specific craft categories) assemblies. Normally those who were part of a specific trade assembly followed a particular skilled calling, but occasionally the trade assembly was merely an organisation of the workers employed in the same plant, shop, or factory. For an LA to be organised formally, a minimum of 10 members was required and, once established, LAS were known to swell in membership to over 1,000. Initiation fees were set by the local, but the minimum fee was $1 for men and 50¢ for women. Local dues, again, were controlled by individual assemblies, but they were to be no less than 10¢ per month. When a specific geographical region, or occasionally even a trade, contained five or more assemblies, a district assembly (DA) could be formed. Each LA then sent delegates to the DA, based on each 100 members, which in turn elected delegates to the annual general assembly, at which the national officers and the general executive board were elected.

There were approximately 15,000 LAS organised across the United States in these years and slightly fewer than 400 in Canada (which should be considered alongside the 35 lodges of the Nova Scotia-based Provincial Workmen's Association, a competing body that was nevertheless strikingly similar to the Order in its ideology, rituals, and organisational form). As many as 3.5 million workers may have passed through such local assemblies over time, and at the peak of their strength, in 1886, the Knights were said to have enrolled between 700,000 and one million members. Some of these new recruits to labour's cause were skilled craftsmen, whose own union affiliations apparently posed no barrier to their entry into the order. But many were previously unorganised workers, often unskilled, and one advocate in 10 was a woman.[176]

---

175   Kessler-Harris 1982, p. 86; Ware 1964b, p. 93; Montgomery 1980a, p. 107.

176   On the general organisational contours, see Garlock 1974; Kealey and Palmer 1982, pp. 57–91; Forsey 1982, pp. 138–66; Palmer 1983b, chapter 3; Bryan D. Palmer, 'The Changing Character of Working-Class Organization and Protest, 1820–1890', in *Historical Atlas of Canada*,

Such an influx of unskilled men and women into the workers' movement must have at least tripled the percentage of the organised non-agricultural work force. Among those located in that pivotal urban-based manufacturing sector, the expansion of organised labour's ranks was truly phenomenal. However cautiously the problematic figures are interpreted, it appears that, at the zenith of the Great Upheaval in 1886, at least eight percent of the workforce was organised by Knights and unionists, a figure dwarfing previous nineteenth-century levels of union affiliation and one not to be matched until the pre-1907 recession growth or the 1916–22 upheaval.[177]

In local communities, the impact of the order was unmistakable. In New York City, 400 LAS contained at least 30,000 workers, and Boston and Cincinnati each boasted nearly one hundred assemblies and 17,000 members. Detroit's 70 LAS contained roughly the same number of workers, 8,000 (the city also claimed 5,000 craft unionists), as did the combined membership of Toronto's and Hamilton's 88 assemblies. In Montreal, both French and English flocked to the Order, with approximately sixty assemblies drawing more than 3,000 men and women to the workers' cause. Oestreicher estimates that 20.5 percent of Detroit's manufacturing workforce was organised by the combined Knights of Labor craft-union forces in 1886, compared with a mere 3.8 percent in 1880 and 6.2 percent in 1901. In Ontario, between twenty and thirty percent of the manufacturing workforce was organised by the Knights of Labor and trade unions in a host of metropolitan centres, railway towns, and industrial communities of the hinterland.[178]

Nor were the Knights confined to the well-trod regional paths of trade unionism's previous North American journeys. They opened up new territories to organised labour, such as the Canadian prairie and coastal West, where 21 local assemblies were formed among railway labourers, miners, and urban craftsmen. In the American South the mixed assembly proved a boon in the organisation of textile workers and landless labourers. The beginning of black-white

---

vol. 2, forthcoming. On women, see Kessler-Harris 1982, p. 86; Kealey and Palmer 1982, pp. 316–26. For an assessment of one critical uprising, note Cassity 1979, pp. 41–61.

177   Problems of realistically defining the workforce, of estimating the size of organised labour's ranks, and of dealing with the volatility of labour's episodic organisational history intrude on efforts to gauge the impact of bodies such as the Knights of Labor. See Neufeld 1982, p. 606; and the debate flowing from our preliminary statement in Kealey and Palmer 1981, pp. 369–411, outlined in Piva 1983, pp. 169–74; and Kealey and Palmer 1983, pp. 175–89.

178   See Kealey and Palmer 1982, pp. 63–4; Ross 1979; Oestreicher 1979, pp. 228, 492–5; Martin 1965.

unity was fostered in cities like New Orleans, where an 1892 general strike was fought by workers who had rallied to the nearly one hundred labour bodies formed between 1880 and 1893, or Richmond, Virginia, where the 35 LAS were organised in two mutually supportive but socially separate district assemblies in which blacks outnumbered whites four to three. The woodlots of Michigan and Ontario were first penetrated by labour organisers in these years, as were a plethora of manufacturing hamlets in which the mixed assembly could survive where the craft union could not. The Knights of Labor had accomplished a part of what Terence V. Powderly, the Order's Grand Master Workman, perceived as their purpose when he proclaimed, in Providence, Rhode Island: 'Something must be done to bring these people together, so that they may know that a blow struck at labor in one place affects those in another, that the evil is felt everywhere men live, from the rising to the setting of the sun'.[179]

Indeed, the Great Upheaval had done much to popularise the need for solidarity, to force recognition that capital necessitated a powerful and united front of opposition. 'Each for himself is the bosses plea/Union for all will make you free', was, in 1880, a coopers' banner.[180] By 1885 to 1886 it was an ideal and a practice held high by North American labour as a whole. Engels remarked on the Knights of Labor in just this context. He described the order as 'an immense association spread across an immense amount of country ... held together ... by the instinctive feeling that the very fact of their clubbing together for their common aspiration makes them a great power in the country'. As an impressive showing of 'potential energy evolving slowly but surely into actual force',[181] the Knights of Labor were inevitably drawn into larger arenas of conflict. Just as the organisation of the working class crossed a quantitative threshold in the 1880s, so too did class struggle.

Conflict

'The year 1886 was prolific in events that stirred the world from end to end', reminisced One Big Unionist Richard Kerrigan in 1927, 'and particularly affected' – he continued with a revolutionary's capacity to understate – 'the social and political tranquility of the American continent'.[182] Led by the Knights of

---

179   Powderly 1886, pp. 19–20; Palmer 1983b, chapter 3; McLaurin 1978; Fink 1978, pp. 324–49; Rachleff 1979; Kann 1977, pp. 49–70; Kealey and Palmer 1982, pp. 359–61; Bennetts 1972, especially pp. 313–92.

180   Oestreicher 1979, p. 122.

181   Engels 1958, pp. 356–7.

182   Richard J. Kerrigan, 'The Dynamic Year of 1886', *One Big Union Monthly*, 23 September 1927.

Labor in Milwaukee, Chicago, and New York, nearly 340,000 American workers demanded an eight-hour day. As its militancy crested, the Order found itself at the very centre of an unprecedented explosion of class militancy, despite its leadership's pious utterances on the desirability of arbitration and the futility of strikes. Strike activity in both Canada and the United States leapt upward in the 1880s and 1890s: in Canada roughly 430 strikes were fought in the 1880s, perhaps as many as 500 over the course of the 1890s, or more in each decade than had been mounted in the entire preceding 80 years. More than three times as many strikes were fought in the United States in 1886 than in any single year between 1881 and 1884. Of the 1,432 strikes launched in that climax to the Great Upheaval, 900 were for wages and 286 for the eight-hour day. Moreover, although the number of workers involved in strikes did not exceed the 407,000 of 1886 again until 1894 (and thereafter not until 1902), the numbers of strikes fought continued to climb, totalling 7,340 between 1881 and 1889 and 12,474 over the 1890s. Many of these strikes, as Jon Amsden and Stephen Brier have argued in the case of coal mining, were part of a process of transformation, in which workers groped through the limitations of the past and struggled to create permanent institutions of self-defence, establishing productive relations at the workplace that were less exploitative and more egalitarian. As the century came to a close, increasing numbers of strikes, including such momentous clashes as the Pullman Boycott and the bituminous coal strike, were planned and highly organised affairs, called and led by disciplined unionists.[183]

Many of the Knights of Labor-led battles of the 1880s and early 1890s were stepping-stones in this schoolroom of class experience, galvanising whole communities to action. Toronto's street-railway strike, Ottawa-Hull's 1891 Chaudière strike, or the battles at Cornwall's cotton mills were just such Canadian confrontations. Across North America the Order waged countless small struggles buttressing skilled workers' attempts to secure or consolidate workplace controls or acceptable wage levels. The Knights also provided the mechanism through which previously unorganised workers gained some small measure of industrial citizenship. But it was the mass strike that left its exhilarating mark so emphatically on the epoch. 'One go, all go', was a Polish worker's cry in the turmoil of Detroit's eight-hour strikes of 1886. An earlier epic struggle, the 1883

183   Bryan D. Palmer, 'The Changing Character of Working-Class Organization and Protest, 1820–1890', in *Historical Atlas of Canada*, vol. 2, forthcoming; research notes for *Historical Atlas of Canada*, vol. 3, courtesy of G.S. Kealey and Doug Cruikshank; Montgomery 1980b, pp. 92–100; Van Tine 1973, p. 59; Amsden and Brier 1977, pp. 583–616. See Edwards 1981; Bennett and Earle 1982, pp. 383–405.

telegraph operatives' unsuccessful challenge to Jay Gould's monopoly, bound
North American labour into an oppositional mass:

> We're bound to fight,
> Our cause is right,
> Monopoly is sore.
> We have left our keys
> To take our ease,
> Let Jay Gould walk the floor.[184]

The massive struggles on southwestern railway lines, in Chicago's packing
houses, and around sympathetic support for New York City's freight hand-
lers, all ordered by Knights of Labor officials, were equally influential in cultivating solidarity. 'All I knew then of the principles of the Knights of Labor',
remembered union pioneer Abraham Bisno, 'was that the motto ... was One
for All, and All for One'.[185]

Workingmen's Democracy
Labour's quantitative gains in organisation and concerted opposition to capital
had, by 1886, transformed themselves into qualitative shifts in class experience.
No less dramatic was the evolution of political practice, as workingmen turned
increasingly to:

> The ballot-box, the ballot box!
> There comrades, you will find the rocks
> To hurl against the Giant's head;
> Nor iron, dynamite or lead
> Can match the ever potent knocks
> Shot from our Yankee ballot box.[186]

Between 1883 and 1889, coalitions of Knights and unionists entered local politics, and after May 1886 there are references to labour tickets in 189 towns
and cities in 34 of the 38 states, as well as considerable political ferment in
Ontario's industrial heartland, Montreal, and New Westminster-Vancouver-

---

184   Kealey and Palmer 1982, pp. 116–26, 330–75, verse on p. 147; Oestreicher 1979, p. 335; Forsey
       1971, pp. 245–59; McKenna 1972, pp. 186–211.
185   Bisno 1967.
186   Fink 1977, pp. 10–11.

Victoria, where a problematic assault on Chinese workers drew British Columbia white labour into the political arena. Running on Union Labor, United Labor, Knights of Labor, Workingman, Labor Political Association, Independent Labor Party, or Independent tickets, workers achieved considerable success, especially in municipal campaigns. There they elected representatives to authoritative posts as aldermen, mayors, councillors, and school board officials. Although national lobbying efforts on the part of the Knights of Labor have received the most attention, it was at these lower levels of government that workers were more effective in securing civic improvement, curtailing political corruption, defending workplace interests by establishing minimum wage bylaws or outlawing subcontracting, and propagandising for a national political movement. When not demanding political independence for labour, many working-class candidates wrung concessions from the established parties. In largely rural constituencies, such tactics, although compromised, could secure victories that otherwise would have been squandered.[187] But politics was, even when weakest, most visible in the metropolitan centres. There were two sides to this urban presence.

One side was the tremendous support galvanised by United Labor Party [ULP] candidates, despite their losses: Henry George received 68,000 votes in the 1886 New York mayoralty campaign, or 31.2 percent of the vote; the United Labor ticket won more than one-quarter of the 92,000 votes cast in Chicago's 1886 election, securing seats for five judges and several pro-labour assemblymen; in Cincinnati the ULP candidate, bricklayer William Stevenson, was narrowly defeated by 600 votes, losing to a Republican but gaining the support of 7,000 voters.

Beyond these impressive showings lay the second side of the working class's political impact, reform and patronage. The Knights of Labor literally stampeded the ruling parties in both Canada and the United States into concessions, changing the very character of political life. Sir John A. Macdonald, Tory leader in Canada, claimed that the Knights of Labor were one of four reefs threatening the Conservative Party ship in the 1880s, and he established a Royal Commission in 1887 to investigate the conditions of labour and capital in Canada. Liberal opposition leader Edward Blake largely adopted the Knights of Labor platform in his 1887 campaign. Factory acts, suffrage extension, bureaus of labour statistics, arbitration measures, employers' liability acts, a recognised Labour Day, and other concessions were thrown into the ring of class struggle. Tammany Hall played a similar game in the United States, wooing labour men to the

187   Palmer 1983b, chapter 3; Kealey and Palmer 1982, pp. 204–76; Fink 1982, pp. 104–22.

Democratic Party. Patronage became the key carrot in this process, with politicians promising and delivering much in their quest to quiet dissident workers. There were more than 400 Knights of Labor on the municipal payroll of Chicago in the 1880s. In Detroit John Devlin, a Powderly loyalist and general executive board member, was put in charge of the American consulate in Windsor. He promptly filled the customs house with Knights of Labor appointees, 23 in all.[188]

Politics, as patronage revealed, was often a soiled pursuit. The Knights, many of whom rolled in the mud of this process, especially in the Order's post-1887 decline, had always known this. T.W. Brosnan, the district master workman of Minnesota's DA 79, noted perceptively: 'As we grow older and stronger the politicians will use their most strenuous efforts to get control of the organization'. Wherever the Knights were a presence, similar words were spoken. Actions were taken, in Richard Trevellick's phrase, to rise above 'the poverty and slavery to the masses that toil'[189] that partisan political behaviour produced. By creating a movement culture, a practice of solidarity and collectivity pitted against the acquisitive individualism and amorality of the age, the Knights of Labor struggled to educate men and women in the principles of labour reform.

A Movement Culture
As the Boston *Labor Leader* reflected in February 1887, one of the essential contributions of the Knights of Labor lay 'in the fact that the whole life of the community is drawn into it, that people of all kinds are together ... and that all get directly the sense of each others needs'.[190] Albert Cross of Hamilton, Ontario's LA 2481, came to the same conclusion four months later, explaining that individual Knights 'were taught that in [the] home of labour there would be no distinctions ... because all were of the Earth and with equal rights ... and we solemnly resolved that we would do all in our power to strengthen the bonds of unity between the workers of the world ...'[191] Within the particular struggles and wants of specific families, ethnic groups, genders, and skill levels, North American workers were becoming united by the common realisation that their separate strategies, however divergent, were all pitted against bourgeois ethics

---

188   Sorge 1977, pp. 218–29; Oestreicher 1979, pp. 374, 483; Ross 1979; Montgomery 1980a, p. 14; Kealey and Palmer 1981, pp. 397–401, 410–11.
189   Quotations from Kealey and Palmer 1982, p. 203.
190   *Labor Leader*, 5 February 1887, cited in Fink 1975, pp. 56–74.
191   Cross is quoted in Kealey and Palmer 1982, p. 312.

and material deprivations. For the first time in the history of class formation, divisions among workers were being overcome by the essential class division between bourgeois and proletarian. Workers, as George McNeill noted in 1887, were becoming cognisant of their place in the transformed and increasingly rigid social relations of appropriation. When at work they saw themselves belonging to those 'lower orders ... continually under surveillance'. When out of work, however, the wage earner was reduced to the position of 'an outlaw, a tramp ... the pariah of society'.[192] Resignation could have been one response to this process of degradation. But out of their consciousness of their social place, in conjunction with an assessment of all that was noble in the past (the Knights extolled the chivalry of medieval times, the republican virtues of revolutionary America, and the Civil War's assault on slavery), the Noble and Holy Order of the Knights of Labor conditioned a climate of romantic rebellion against an 'age of shoddy'. The result was a renewed faith in the possibilities of the future:

> But while we dream of the chivalry of yore
> And wish for knighthood to redress all wrong.
> We know our time has braver deeds in store.[193]

The Knights of Labor prepared the way for the working class's capacity to embrace such 'braver deeds' by cultivating collectivity, mutuality, and unity across the range of North American communities where they were a public presence. In local assembly halls the symbolism and ritual of the order reverberated with the dignity of labour and the necessity of sustaining the 'Circle of Universal Brotherhood' through mutual assistance.[194] Funerals, parades, 'monster picnics' and demonstrations proclaimed to all that:

> For well we know if sons of toil
> Will all go hand in hand
> There's none can us asunder break
> If all united stand.[195]

Soirees and balls brought families and youth together in displays of self-organised leisure activities, liberated from both the degradations of the saloon[196]

---

192   McNeill et al. 1887, p. 455, cited in Montgomery 1980a, p. 205.

193   McNeill 1902, pp. 111–12.

194   See the argument in Kealey and Palmer 1982, pp. 227–329.

195   *Trade Union Advocate*, 20 July 1882.

196   On saloons, see de Lottinville 1981–2, pp. 9–40; Brundage 1979.

and the confinements of commercialism or paternalism. Victory Drury of New York's Home Club commented on one such gathering:

> I have heard from the lips of those who are here that this meeting is called by an organisation known as the Knights of Labor. It is claimed by some that the working classes are ignorant, that they are brutes and imbeciles, and are, in fact, the dregs of society. And yet what do I find? I believe that I see before me an audience of working men and women, and the first thing I heard when I came in this hall was the excellent piano of two ladies ... honest people who earn their bread by the sweat of their brow and rob not any man.[197]

Here, in a moment of recreation, leadership, radicalism, and respectability coexisted easily and without trauma.

An emerging intellectual contingent that came to be known as 'brain workers' had in fact surfaced in almost every Knight of Labor locale.[198] This group edited countless labour newspapers, travelled through regions to give rousing speeches, and headed up local assemblies, in which, as 'schoolrooms of instruction', tracts of political economy and lines of verse were read and debated:

> And hosts of artisans are fired
> In their industrial hives
> With the same spirit that inspired
> The 'Farmer of St. Ives';
> Which has brought forth a great power,
> Without the gun and sabre,
> Before which tyrannies shall cower.
> Hail to the Knights of Labor.[199]

Among the radical immigrant quarters in the United States, labour's more militant leadership might align itself with bodies such as the International Working Peoples Association. But the Knights of Labor were, as a mass movement, seldom isolated from such developments.[200] In Detroit, debates on the place of

---

197   *Palladium of Labor*, 24 April 1886.
198   See Hann 1976, pp. 35–57.
199   *Canadian Labor Reformer*, 22 May 1886.
200   Fink 1977, pp. 399, 335–41; *National Labor Tribune*, 1 August 1885; Roy 1970, p. 262; Montgomery 1980a, pp. 207–8.

dynamite in the politics of class struggle (the resolution in favour of such 'direct action' was defeated, but only by a vote of 100 to 95) received coverage in the Knights of Labor journal, the *Labor Leaf*, an organ not incapable of editorialising on armed struggle:

> When there are robbers about it is a good thing to have a rifle handy. When you have a gun and know how to use it, you are not so likely to have trouble ... should trouble come, the capitalists will use the regular army and militia to shoot down those who are not satisfied. It won't be so if the people are equally ready, like their forefathers of 1776.

Such a stand was possible because the movement culture of labour reform had reached well past the economism of labour's battles over the wage, into a very way of life. As Oestreicher concludes in his study of Detroit, 'by 1886 the movement included a weekly labor press, in both English and German, a workers' militia, the Detroit Rifles, regular debates in the Dialectical Union, a theatre group, singing societies, and almost nightly social or educational events'.[201] It was precisely this mixture of the seemingly mundane and the startlingly militant that struck fear in the bosom of bourgeois America.

That fear lay behind the harsh repression of May and June 1886. The police 'shot to kill' and used the courts to jail and execute immigrant radicals and native-born American anarchists and socialists in Chicago and Milwaukee. Although the targets were individuals (Albert Parsons – himself a Knight of Labor – August Spies and others), the aim was a wider suppression. In the hanging of the Haymarket martyrs, as Montgomery suggests, the ruling class found its 'psychic revenge for ... insubordination'.[202] It also found a handy club to wield against the movement culture, which was thrown into a state of retreat. The pleas of Knights of Labor militants for solidarity with the Haymarket martyrs fell on too many deaf ears. The cautious leaders of the Order, especially Powderly, condemned the victims to suffer their consequences at the hand of capitalist justice.[203] This abdication of solidarity was all the more tragic because the movement culture of the Knights of Labor was premised on a concern for all workers and an unprecedented entry into the entire range of working-class experience. Among women, the immigrant community, and the

---

201   Oestreicher 1979, pp. 258, 280; Commons et al. 1966, vol. 2, pp. 386–94.
202   Montgomery 1980b, pp. 98–9.
203   Ware 1964b, pp. 299–319; Sorge 1977, pp. 209–18.

unskilled, the movement culture had addressed needs seldom confronted by previous unions or earlier notions of labour reform.[204]

Refusing to close the door of 'brotherhood' on women workers and the confinements of a domesticity that they themselves often embraced as an ideal, the Knights of Labor entered simultaneously into the realms of production and reproduction. They provided the organisational focus for a series of women's mass strikes in Cohoes (1882), Fall River (1885), Louisville (1887), and Cornwall (1887–9) at the same time that they demanded political rights for women. Campaigning for equal pay for equal work across North America, the Knights were also capable of establishing socialistic day nurseries in mill towns like Olneyville, Rhode Island. To be sure, male Knights did not universally step outside the consensual norms of Victorian gender relations. Many remained inhibited by their conventional views of femininity, adhering to a chauvinistic sentimentality and a nostalgic conception of women's role. In St. Louis, male contractors affiliated with the Order's tailors' assembly were not above telling the parents of seamstresses that 'no dissent girl belong to an assembly'.[205] Still, there were signs of significant advance, with women organisers like Leonora M. Barry demanding 'complete emancipation from political and industrial bondage'.[206] A Montreal labourer recognised unpaid domestic labour as 'just as essential to the well being of the workingman as the fair's day's wage itself'.[207] Most dramatic was the Knights of Labor's imaginative blending of the class struggle's demand for solidarity with the social relations of domestic life. In New York City, 'whenever the Knights of Labor girls went to a picnic or ball they were to tell all the brother Knights that none of the latter were to walk with a non-union girl in the opening promenade so long as a union girl was without a partner. Should any male Knight violate this rule, all the girl Knights are to step out of the promenade and boycott the entire crowd'.[208] Many decades before contemporary feminists coined the phrase 'the personal is political', women in the Noble and Holy Order demonstrated an awareness of the need to infuse everyday life with the practices of both equality and solidarity. 'Not man's dependant will she be', declared one woman Knight from Richmond, Virginia,

---

204 Kealey and Palmer 1982, pp. 19–20.
205 Quoted in Montgomery 1979, p. 21; Foner 1976, p. 206; Dye 1979; Buhle 1978, p. 58; Walkowitz 1978, p. 299.
206 Kealey and Palmer 1982, p. 317.
207 *Palladium of Labor*, 25 April 1885.
208 Montgomery 1980a, pp. 204–5.

'But his co-worker, equal free'.[209] The Knights, as John Swinton long ago noted, recognised 'the rights and principles of womanhood'.[210]

Among immigrants and various ethnic groups, the Knights opened up similar possibilities. Irish workers, long divided internally by religious affiliation and isolated from English and native-born North American labour, were drawn into the movement culture of the 1880s. The institutional expression of this historical process was the Irish National Land League, a body that effectively wedded the North American Irish masses to the reform tradition. Upon the particular oppression of Ireland was constructed a passionate critique of power, privilege, and authority willingly embraced by the predominately working-class Irish of North America. As Powderly noted, this swelling of Irish nationalism fed directly into the Knights of Labor. 'When the public, or Land League, meeting would be over', he recalled, a 'secret meeting of the Knights of Labor would follow'.[211] Thus, as Eric Foner has argued, the Knights of Labor quietly intersected with the more radical strains of Irish nationalism, providing 'a social ethic that challenged the individualism of the middle class and the cautious social reformism'[212] of the established political culture and the church. Other immigrant groups experienced a similar process of integration. In Milwaukee, for instance, the Great Upheaval of 1885–6 eroded the established skilled German workers' reluctance to rub shoulders with the newly arrived and relatively unskilled Poles, as 1,000 Polish workers entered the Polonia Assembly in one fell swoop.[213]

Both women and the immigrant masses were part of a larger contingent, the unskilled, that the movement culture also attracted. Selig Perlman, who saw the Knights of Labor as tragically flawed in their emphasis on this segment, nevertheless captured a part of what the Great Upheaval really was:

> All the peculiar characteristics of the dramatic events of 1886 and 1887, the highly feverish pace at which organisation grew, the nation-wide wave of strikes, particularly sympathetic strikes, the wide use of the boycott, the obliteration, apparently complete, of all times that divided the labouring class, whether geographic or trade, the violence and turbulence which accompanied the movement – all of these were the signs of a great move-

---

209   Quoted in Kealey and Palmer 1982, p. 320.
210   The essential source on women and the Knights of Labor is Levine 1979b, where Swinton is quoted on p. 133.
211   Powderly 1940, p. 179.
212   Kealey and Palmer 1982, pp. 313–16; Bennett 1979; Foner 1978, pp. 6–55, especially p. 46.
213   Fink 1977, pp. 308–88.

ment by the class of the unskilled, which had finally risen in rebellion ... The movement bore in every way the aspect of a social war. A frenzied hatred of labour for capital was shown in every important strike.[214]

In spite of the Order's backtracking between 1887 and 1894, efforts to revive the Knights of Labor in 1894 remained premised on the exhortation that 'they must stand or fall with the unskilled workers'.[215]

The movement culture that so transformed the social relations of productive life and that pushed class formation in new and exhilarating directions in the 1880s nevertheless stumbled and fell in the 1890s. Let us conclude this discussion of social formation and class formation in nineteenth-century North America with an attempt to understand just why this demise took place.

Conclusions

In the United States, things go damned slowly.
          MARX to ENGELS (1863)

During the nineteenth century, North American social and class formations experienced two decades of profound transformation and dissolution, the 1850s and the 1890s. Commenting on the speculation and expansion of the productive forces in 1851, Marx asked, 'Is this not approaching a crisis? The revolution may come sooner than we wish'. Thirty years later he saw communist tendencies spreading among the masses, the assault on 'all forms of associated capital' paving the way for a vast social transformation.[216] Indeed, these were years of great moment in the history of North American capital, and if communism did not come in the 1880s, the next decade saw the social formation restructured in the direction of monopoly capitalism. Both the 1850s and the 1890s were thus vital turning points that displayed striking similarities, including the prominence of major depressions that shifted the character of productive relations and forced working-class activists to retreat in the face of the harsh realities of the business cycle. It was in the period between these two points of crisis that the late nineteenth-century North American labour movement came of age.

---

214 Commons et al. 1966, vol. 2, pp. 350–4.
215 Joseph R. Buchanan to Powderly, 7 December 1983, Powderly Papers, Catholic University, Washington, D.C.; Buchanan 1971, p. 439.
216 Quoted in Padover 1972, pp. 38, 46.

Industrial capitalism took the final unhesitating steps toward establishing its economic supremacy in North America in the 1850s, ushering in a late nineteenth-century context of ruthless competition among entrepreneurs. In these years as well, the labour market was transformed, as waves of immigrants inundated North American shores, famine-Irish finding their way to port cities in Canada and the United States, and German Forty-Eighters establishing themselves in a number of American industrial cities. Such economic and demographic change conditioned a virulent nativism that may well have helped undercut the early beginnings of working-class organisation and solidarity, a process of disintegration facilitated by the onslaught of economic crisis in 1857.

The 1890s, set against the earlier background of the 1850s, appears remarkably similar. A new stage of capitalist development appeared in the increasingly close connections of finance and industrial capital, which stimulated a series of vitally important mergers, pushing the economy toward monopoly and oligopoly. Although this merger movement had attained some maturity in the United States by the 1890s, it appeared only tentatively in Canada, with significant consolidations in the textile industry, agricultural machinery production, and in the faint beginnings of the steel industry. American branch plants, especially those in nascent industries such as rubber, chemicals, and electrical products, began to invade Canadian territory, quick to reap the benefits of markets, materials, and labour. As this shift in the character of capitalism proceeded, it was strengthened by new supplies of labour, as immigration from eastern and southern Europe restructured the internal composition of the North American labour force between 1880 and 1910. Bolstered by the acquisition of plentiful supplies of unskilled labour and consolidated through the depression's impact on the small shop and the family firm, the North American political economy entered the twentieth century in its monopoly phase. Once more, this process of transformation was accompanied by a nativist reaction, centred in the American Protective Association in the United States and in its Canadian counterpart, the Protestant Protective Association. This had dramatic and debilitating consequences in former Knights of Labor strongholds like Detroit, where the retreating movement culture was challenged by nativist rhetoric threatening to 'chase the Dagos back to Italy'. Anti-Catholicism in Canada was further strengthened by a series of French-English disputes, beginning with the Jesuits' Estates Act and culminating in the Manitoba Schools Question in the 1890s. In this period of ethnocentrism the workers' movement suffered tangible setbacks. By the end of the 1890s jingoism was also prominent in both countries, as America's popular war with Spain and Canada's patriotic response to the Boer War undercut class solidarities and emphasised national aspirations. Although not all workers were enthralled with such militaristic adventures around the world and although a number of working-class recruits to the cause of imperialism were undoubtedly attracted by economic need and the soldier's stipend, these campaigns nevertheless enjoyed considerable support, especially among British immigrant and native-born American and Canadian workers.[217]

Equally significant developments in the political sphere paralleled these vast changes in the economy and society of late nineteenth-century North America. Between 1860 and 1890, the national prominence of the state was emerging, overshadowing previously dominant concerns of particular regions and specific locales. In the United States, the state developed as a vital force in the aftermath of the Civil War, as the victory of the Republicans and the forging of national parties in the throes of conflict ushered in a new age. Similarly, north of the border, the Canadian state was forged in 1867, with the 1870s and 1880s the first decades of national party activity in the newly created Dominion.

These large structural changes of the late nineteenth century are vital to an understanding of both the accomplishment and failure of the Noble and Holy Order of the Knights of Labor. The 1880s represented the culmination of an age of competitive capitalism and localism as well as the first faint beginnings of monopoly. The Knights of Labor developed within this context and embodied a working-class challenge that had been building strength for three decades. A series of perceptive studies, many of them as yet unpublished, demonstrates conclusively that in the United States, the Knights of Labor were able to unite a working class long fragmented, bridging the divisions between workers that had been the historical legacy of the 1850s and drawing them out of the cross-class alliances that had developed during the contest against slavery. In the resulting 'moral universality' of the Gilded Age labour movement, as Montgomery has suggested, the Knights of Labor represented a 'crusade' to 'impose economic order' on a ruthlessly individualistic capitalism. A large part of the attraction of this orientation lay in its repudiation of the acquisitive egotism that the system spawned and acclaimed. This movement culture peaked,

---

217   On the rise of nativist groups like the American Protective Association and the Canadian variant, the Protestant Protective Association, both products of the 1890s and not without impact in working-class circles, see Kinzer 1964; Higham 1963, pp. 81–2; Davis 1980, p. 34; Oestreicher 1979, pp. 56–61; Watt 1967b, pp. 57–67; 1967a, pp. 45–58. On the Jesuits' Estate Act, see Dalton 1968; Miller 1974, pp. 36–50. On the Manitoba Schools Question, see Crunican 1976. Jingoism deserves further study, but note Montgomery 1980a, p. 210; Miller 1975, pp. 219–37.

however, at precisely that moment – the 1880s – when the economic, social, political, and cultural forces that had ushered it into being were on the brink of suppression by an eminently monopolistic social formation.

The Knights of Labor thus emerged in the context of an anarchic, laissez-faire capitalism. Though the movement shook its fist at monopoly, political corruption, and the drift toward centralised control of everyday life, it found itself facing changing conditions and staunch opposition as employers united to oppose its members and the omniscient state began an open intervention in the social relations of productive life. Although the state's role in suppressing the insurrectionary railroad strikes of 1877 must have appeared as something of an aberration, by the 1890s, worker militants came to see government repression as the norm. Haymarket, Homestead, and Pullman imprinted this lesson on their consciousness. An eclectic radical critique, capable of uniting the working class around the perceived threat of an economic and political oligarchy tyrannising labour saw its worst fears confirmed in the 1880s and 1890s. This new situation was further complicated by immigration and severe depression, both of which weakened the bonds of unity. As the crisis deepened, the whole process of forging a collective response had to be begun anew. What had been adequate in the 1870s and early 1880s was now seen to be inadequate, and as a consequence, the 'moral universality' that the Knights of Labor had done so much to create began to disintegrate.[218]

Splits between socialists and Knights, eclectic radicals and unionists, and factions within the Order, such as the New York-based 'Home Club', highlighted division not unity. Moments of repression such as Haymarket pitted conservative and cautious labour reformers against those willing to stand up against the state and its orchestrated 'red scare'. Business unionism, revolutionary syndicalism, DeLeonite socialism, and ethnic politics vied for the allegiance of North American workers. Although the depression of the 1890s, the nationalisation of politics, the increasing prominence of ethnic allegiances, and the crisis of leadership unfolding in the upper echelons of the Knights of Labor all played a part in ensuring the ultimate defeat of the Noble and Holy Order, the demise of the Knights and the victory of the American Federation of Labor (AFL) was anything but a settled issue in the 1880s. Major leaders, later identified with the rise of the AFL and the ideological primacy of craft unionism within the American labour movement, were themselves uncertain in these years of turmoil in the 1880s. P.J. McGuire of the Carpenters' Union, for instance, was known to

---

218   See Ross 1980, p. 596; Oestreicher 1979, p. 193; Levine 1979b; Bensman 1977; Gordon 1977; Horner 1978; Montgomery 1980a, p. 204; Davis 1980, pp. 26–30; Fink 1977.

advocate the liquidation of the trade unions into the Knights of Labor well past the crisis of 1886; yet he is often seen as the ideological ancestor of business unionist carpenters's spokesman, 'Big Bill' Hutcheson. Other labour leaders of the 1880s – Samuel Gompers, Thomas Morgan, Joseph Buchanan, Jo Labadie, and Frank Foster – were riding the wave of class militancy and consensus without a forceful sense of organisational direction or ideological clarity. All had been shaped in a radical milieu that contained Marxist, Lasallean, Anarchist, Greenback, Georgite, Freethinking, and Irish Nationalist influences.

Canada's labour leadership was more subdued ideologically, perhaps because capital's consolidation had not proceeded as fast north of the border. The Canadian state was therefore not compelled to utilise repression to the same extent, and finally, the demographic structure of the Canadian working class – predominantly English speaking outside Quebec – did not give rise to immigrant radicalism. Few were the Marxist or anarchist influences that swirled in the debates of the 1880s in Ontario: it was Gladstonian liberalism, Irish nationalism, and Tory paternalism that more often than not formed the backdrop against which working-class militants argued out their differing perspectives on labour activities. But the situation was also complicated by attachments to the single tax, currency reform, Bellamyite nationalism, and other reform panaceas associated with Canada's particular variant of the producer ideology. Those who want to adopt the perspective of Gerald Grob and his predecessors, arguing that business unionism in Canada was inevitable, will have difficulty explaining how the so-called father of the Canadian labour movement, Irish Dan O'Donoghue, defended and supported the Knights of Labor until its last twentieth-century days.

In short, though hindsight may facilitate North American historians' efforts to sift through the labour controversies of the 1880s, sorting out various positions and structuring them into supposedly coherent philosophical orientations, the participants themselves – Canadian and American – were far from being intellectually surefooted. In the late 1880s and 1890s they were propelled in a number of different directions, especially in the United States where a more advanced economy and a radical working-class immigrant community gave rise to more precise strategies for labour in the emerging age of monopoly capital. The Canadian labour movement retreated into an effort to survive the hard years of the 1890s downturn and re-emerged in the economic upswing and craft union boom of the 1898–1904 years.[219]

---

219   Grob's *Workers and Utopia* is challenged by a range of other work, aside from sources cited

The structural transformations of the late nineteenth century and the attempt to come to grips with them ideologically and organisationally thus underlay the demise of the Knights of Labor across North America. Working themselves out evenly and in part coloured by local conditions and developments, these transformations and responses wrote *finis* to the movement culture of the 1880s. Class formation was thus constantly shifting, no less so in the 1880s and 1890s than in the 1830s and 1840s, as the social formation underwent vast change. The velocity of this change in late nineteenth-century America, the quickening pace of accumulation and the rapid growth of monopoly, restructured productive relations at an unprecedented rate, literally decade by decade. As Marx predicted but could not theorise, America's rate of concentration outstripped all previous European experience, advancing 'in seven league boots'. With the social formation undergoing such change, class formation was characterised by just the kind of episodic struggles and chaotic disruptions that fed into labour's apparent defeats. To put it differently: things moved so damned slowly in America because they also moved so damned quickly; America was exceptional.

But slow or fast, the historical impact of the 1880s was not lost on North American workers. They looked back to that past as years in which advances had been registered.[220] This collective memory brings us back to an assessment of class formation. Always situated in a particular context and a specific social setting, class formation is one part structured necessity (what the social formation determines) and one part active creation (what the particular components of the working class do within the limits imposed upon them). Struggles in the productive arena are by no means the sum total of this latter realm. The working class, while being made, has also made itself in diverse ways, many of them markedly distanced from the workplace if not uninfluenced by it.[221] Nor have these conscious, if limited, choices been insignificant in their impact on the social formation itself, which they have often pushed in new directions.

Social formation and class formation are thus reciprocal developments, bound up in their own mutuality. If the former is decisive in setting the limits within which the latter unfolds, those limits are constantly changing and adapting to further accommodate and hedge in the latter. The consequences

---

frequently throughout this chapter: Lyon 1972, especially p. 271; Scharnau 1969; Marlatt 1975; Cotkin 1978; Kaufman 1973.

220   Dubofsky 1974, p. 383; Dubofsky and Van Tine 1976, p. 12; Brooks 1978, pp. ix, 17–18; *Citizen and Country*, 4 May 1900; Bernstein 1960, p. 34.

221   See, for example, Hareven 1982.

for our understanding of the historical process within which both unfold is perhaps decisive in moving us away from the tendencies in Marxist theory to situate too rigidly both social formation and class formation. Marx wrote before monopoly capitalism had emerged as an unambiguous social formation, and his periodisation of primitive accumulation, manufacture proper, and modern industry implies termination and ultimate stasis. Yet the history of twentieth-century capital, of its specific modes of accumulation and of its changing social and class formations, is a history of dramatic ruptures and restructuring of the modes of appropriation. Primitive accumulation, as a process establishing the preconditions for capital accumulation, initiated the first stirrings of class formation. In an age of monopoly capital, with the constant reordering of accumulation, the process would begin anew: the original was renewed. What are we to see in twentieth-century developments such as Taylorism, the open shop drive, Fordism, neo-colonialism, new waves of immigration, runaway shops, the dismantling of the welfare state, the institutionalisation of labour market segmentation and job ghettos, the expansion of the reserve army of labour, and the war economy other than primitive accumulation? As new preconditions for both social and class formation are established, however, we can expect the resulting consequences to be as different as those that emerged over the course of the nineteenth century. We have only to look to the past to know how fundamentally different our future will look and how desperately necessary it is to challenge the many debasements and degradations that are now flowing in the wake of capital's project. Like the late 1840s in France and the 1880s in North America, the 1980s is one of those historical moments 'which make all turning back impossible and the conditions themselves cry out: Hic Rhodus, hic salta'.[222] How and where the working class leaps will be of no small moment in determining whether it lands on Friday's feet or Crusoe's.

---

222   Marx 1968, p. 100.

'Cracking the Stone': The Long History of Capitalist Crisis and Toronto's Dispossessed, 1830–1930[*]

Capitalism as Crisis

His eyes are staring, his mouth is open, his wings are spread. This is how one pictures the angel of history. His face is turned toward the past. Where we perceive a chain of events, he sees one single catastrophe which keeps piling wreckage and hurls it in front of his feet. The angel would like to stay, awaken the dead, and make whole what has been smashed. But a storm is blowing in from Paradise; it has got caught in his wings with such a violence that the angel can no longer close them. The storm irresistibly propels him into the future to which his back is turned, while the pile of debris before him grows skyward.

WALTER BENJAMIN, 'Theses on the Philosophy of History' (1940)

Writing amidst fascism and war, but with capitalism coming out of the economic collapse of the 1930s, Benjamin's storm was 'what we call progress'. Today, with Paradise increasingly difficult to envision, that storm might well be called crisis.[1]

It is difficult, as many economic histories have suggested, to scrutinise the century reaching from the 1830s to the 1930s and not discern a series of long

---

[*] '"Cracking the Stone": The Long History of Capitalist Crisis and Toronto's Dispossessed', *Labour/Le Travail*, 69 (Spring 2012), 9–62, co-authored by Gaetan Heroux.

[1] For a mid-twentieth-century view of History as Progress see Carr 1975, pp. 109–32. On contemporary, post-1970 capitalist crisis see Mandel 1978; Brenner 2006; Albo, Gindin, and Panitch 2010. Our purpose in this paper is *not* to define crisis or difference among different kinds of capitalist crisis. This requires a separate, and lengthy, study. Rather, we stress the more general interpretive point that crisis is inherent in the capitalist mode of production and, in particular, that this has consequences for class formation in terms of how to understand the reciprocal and interrelated nature of waged labour and wagelessness. On the nature of capitalism, which necessarily generates crisis, see Smith 2010. Finally, if capitalism is inherently crisis-ridden, this is *not* to suggest that capitalism, *per se*, is *in crisis*, and its existence threatened. For that to be the case, a class conscious opposition, on a mass basis, must exist, with the potential to create an alternative socioeconomic order.

economic downturns, punctuated by relatively short periods of prosperity. At the very least, in much of the developing capitalist world in this era, we must recognise the continuity of crisis: economic dislocation and troubling political turmoil in the 1830s; the 'Hungry Forties'; major depressions lasting for years, the initial outbreaks of which took place in 1857, 1873, and 1893; a generalised malaise that blanketed much of the 1880s, and the pre-World War I years; the recessionary dip in the business cycle associated with 1919–22, which marked a part of the 1920s with the label 'lean'; and, finally, the great collapse of 1929, which lifted, again, only with that modern solvent of capitalist crisis, war. Good times were rare times in capitalist development.[2] This insight framed Marx's *oeuvre*, with the 1873 afterword to the second German edition of *Capital: A Critical Analysis of Capitalist Production*, declaring:

> The contradictions inherent in the movement of capitalist society impress themselves upon the practical bourgeois most strikingly in the changes of the periodic cycle, through which modern industry runs, and whose crowning point is the universal crisis. That crisis is once again approaching, although as yet but in its preliminary stage; and by the universality of its theatre and the intensity of its action it will drum dialectics even into the heads of the mushroom upstarts ...[3]

One critical component of Marx's vision was thus his fundamental grasp of the inner dynamic of capitalism. More clearly than any other thinker of his time, Marx understood that capitalism's logic was premised on an internal reciprocity, in which progress was dependant on destructiveness. 'The growing incompatibility between the productive development of society and its hitherto existing relations of production expresses itself in bitter contradictions, crises, spasms', Marx wrote in the *Grundrisse*, concluding that, 'The violent destruction of capital not by relations external to it, but rather as a condition of its self-preservation, is the most striking form in which advice is given it to be gone and to give room to a higher state of social production'. It was precisely because capitalism was a socioeconomic order in which positive gains could only be registered with the negatives of loss that Marx saw the necessity of socialism. Production for profit, the rate of which was bound over time to fall, led invariably to new, intensified, and aggressive acts of capitalist exploitation, oppression, and despoliation. Replacing this systemic destruction with

---

2   See, as one economic history example, Vatter 1976.
3   Marx n.d., Volume I, p. 20.

production for use was the only way in which human society could survive and progress. Marx looked forward to the day 'When a great social revolution shall have mastered the results of the bourgeois epoch, the market of the world and the modern powers of production, and subjected them to the common control of the most advanced peoples'. This and only this would provide answers to humanity's needs, so debased by 'the supreme rule of capital' whose 'destructive influence' was felt in a metaphorical 'trade in the murder and prostitution perpetrated in the temple of Juggernaut' by men of 'Property, Order, Family, and Religion'.[4]

The Analytics of Nomenclature

> Not man or men but the struggling, oppressed class itself is the depository of historical knowledge.
>
> WALTER BENJAMIN, 'Theses on the Philosophy of History' (1940)

When capitalism is understood as a political economy of development, progress, advance, *and* destruction, as well as a social order, not just of contradictory impulses and episodic clashes of counterposed interests, but of fundamental *crisis*, even the meaning of labour must be partially rethought. Michael Denning has recently suggested the necessity of radically reconceptualising life under capitalism in ways that 'decentre wage labour' and replace a 'fetishism of the wage' and the 'employment contract' with attention to 'dispossession and expropriation'. Marx, after all, did not invent the term 'proletarian', but adapted it from its common usage in antiquity, when, within the Roman Empire, the word designated the uncertain social stratum, divorced from property and without regular access to wages, reproducing 'recklessly'. J.C.L. Simonde de Sismondi drew on this understanding in an 1819 work of political economy that chronicled the 'threat to public order' posed by a 'miserable and suffering population', dependent as it was on public charity. '[T]hose who had no property', Sismondi wrote, 'were called to have children: *ad prolem generandum*'. Max Weber commented similarly: 'As early as the sixteenth century the proletarianising of the rural population created such an army of unemployed that England had to deal with the problem of poor relief'. Three centuries later, across the Atlantic, transient common labourers were being described in a discourse seemingly impervious to change: 'a dangerous class, inadequately

---

4   Marx 1973b, pp. 749–50; Marx 1973a, pp. 324–5.

fed, clothed, and housed, they threaten the health of the community'. Denning concludes that:

> Rather than seeing the bread-winning factory worker as the product-ive base on which a reproductive superstructure is erected, imagine the dispossessed proletarian household as a wageless base of subsistence labour – the 'women's work' of cooking, cleaning and caring – which sup-ports a superstructure of migrant wage seekers who are ambassadors, or perhaps hostages, to the wage economy ... Unemployment precedes employment, and the informal economy precedes the formal, both his-torically and conceptually. We must insist that 'proletarian' is not a syn-onym for 'wage labourer' but for dispossession, expropriation and radical dependence on the market.

'You don't need a job to be a proletarian', Denning insists, with a bluntness that is both insightful and myopic; 'wageless life, not wage labour, is the starting point in understanding the free market'.[5]

For all that Denning captures the fundamental importance of wagelessness, all the more so within a context of capitalism *as crisis*, his dichotomisation of wageless life and waged labour is myopic. It near-sightedly clarifies the import-ance of dispossession while obscuring the extent to which proletarianisation is meaningless outside of the existence of the (often distant) wage as both an enduring if universally unpleasant end and a decisive means of survival within capitalist political economy. David Montgomery captures the connec-tedness of being waged and unwaged in his rich discussion of common labour-ers: 'Whether they were working flat out, sleeping behind a furnace or inside a boxcar, getting "quitting mad", enjoying the conviviality of the saloon, or being thrown back into the ranks of the unemployed ... one thing was clear: For com-mon laborers, work was the biblical curse. It was unavoidable, undependable, and unrewarding. But they had urgent need for money'. Similar reciprocities characterised the lives of North American canallers in the period 1780–1860 studied by Peter Way, and these also frame Andrea Graziosi's discussion of unskilled labour in the United States of 1880–1915.[6] Wagelessness and waged employment are not oppositions, then, but gradations on a spectrum traversing

---

5   Denning 2010, pp. 79–81; Sismondi 1819, vol. 2, pp. 262, 305, and vol. 1, p. 146, quoted in Jones 2004, p. 151; Weber 1961, quoted in De Ste. Croix 1981, p. 262; Abbott 1905, p. 324; and Lis and Soly 1984, pp. 163–228.

6   Montgomery 1987, p. 91; Way 1993; Graziosi 1981, pp. 512–44.

desire and necessity that encompasses many different outcomes for the proletarianised masses. Between these 'ideal types' exist other shared structures
of the social relations of material life, which include seasonal employment, a
range of reproductive labours,[7] gendered and racialised constructions of 'work',
and subsistence economising that is based on exchange relations of all kinds,
including debt peonage, sexualised barter, and criminalised commerce.[8]

As Marx noted in *Capital*, 'Every combination of employed and unemployed
disturbs' the harmonious and sacred laws of bourgeois order, articulated most
rigorously in the market freedom of the laws of supply and demand, the necessity of capital governing and disciplining a labour force for whom work defines
being.[9] Such major destabilising combinations of the waged and the wageless
were a part of the eruptions of class struggle in Canada and the United States
that repeatedly disturbed social order in 1877, 1886, 1894, 1919, and throughout
the 1930s. They were often associated with insurrection-like uprisings of railroad and mill workers, campaigns for the shorter workday, and, in the case of
the post-World War I revolt, with growing anxiety over working-class interna-
tionalism, increasingly expressed in variants of revolutionary syndicalism and
Bolshevism that exploded in the General Strike. The mailed fist of military
suppression, the psychic satisfactions of bringing anarcho-communists to the
gallows in 1887, and the brute force of the deportations and jailings that flowed
in the wake of the state trials of the Red Scare era of 1917–19 no doubt eased
bourgeois minds ridden with anxiety.[10]

What all of this suggests is the necessity of seeing the waged and the wageless as part of a dispossessed class whole, one in which the obscured forms of
resistance that have historically developed among the jobless demand consideration. Capitalism as an economic system has conjoined the order of manufacture and accumulation with the disorder of destructive crisis. The social
relations of production have been constituted in a like symbiosis, in which

---

7   Most stimulating have been the early publications of Wally Seccombe. See, for instance,
    Seccombe 1983, pp. 28–9.
8   Consider, for instance, the discussion in Palmer 2000.
9   Marx n.d., vol. 1, p. 640.
10 On this well-known history see, among many possible sources, Brecher 1972; Montgomery
    1980b, pp. 81–104; Stromquist 1987; Morton 1977, pp. 5–34; Dacus 1877; Kealey 1984, pp. 11–
    45; Peterson 1984, pp. 115–32; Kramer and Mitchell 2010; and McCallum 2004, a much
    revised and conceptually reconfigured version of which is about to appear with Athabasca
    University Press under the tentative title *Hobohemia and the Crucifixion Machine: Rival
    Images of a New World in 1930s Vancouver*. See as well McCallum 2005, pp. 51–88; 2007,
    pp. 43–68; and for Toronto in particular the important work of Klee 1998; 2000, pp. 123–52.

labouring life, for much of the nineteenth and twentieth centuries, has oscillated between wagelessness and waged work. Yet these apparent opposites are
but components of a complex totality. Their connectedness is premised on a
fundamental dispossession, the defining feature of proletarianisation. That dispossession, in as much as it marks out human beings as destitute of ownership
of the means of their production, exists *regardless of whether one happens to
be working for wages or not*. It continues to define and constitute the worker,
no matter the level of security achieved, or unrealised, in employment. Marx
noted this when he suggested that capitalist enrichment was premised on, 'The
condemnation of one part of the working class to enforced idleness by the
over-work of the other part', accelerating 'the production of the reserve army
on a scale corresponding with the advance of social accumulation'. Every proletarian can thus be categorised, not so much according to their waged work,
but to the possible forms of surplus population, which Marx labelled 'the floating, the latent, and the stagnant'. This is why the accumulation of capital is also
the accumulation of labour, but the Malthusian multiplication of the proletariat does not necessarily mean the working class will, in its entirety, be waged.
Marx writes:

> The lowest sediment of the relative surplus-population, finally dwells in
> the sphere of pauperism ... the quantity of paupers increases with every
> crisis ... Pauperism is the hospital of the active labour-army and the dead
> weight of the industrial reserve army. Its production is included in that
> of the relative surplus population, its necessity in theirs; along with the
> surplus population, pauperism forms a condition of capitalist production,
> and of the capitalist development of wealth. It enters into the *faux frais*
> of capitalist production.[11]

As John Bellamy Foster, Robert W. McChesney, and R. Jamil Jonna suggest in a
recent issue of *Monthly Review*, Marx's way of seeing class formation was much
ahead of his time. He anticipated how modern imperialism and the relentless
march of capital accumulation on a world scale would result in the quantitative
expansion and qualitative transformation of the global reserve army of labour.
This massive reserve, from which capital draws much sustenance for its accu-
mulative appetite, now amounts to billions. As it has grown, so has the misery
of the dispossessed expanded: 'Accumulation of wealth at one pole, is therefore, at the same time accumulation of misery, agony of toil, slavery, ignorance,

---

11   Marx n.d., I, pp. 641, 643–4.

rituality, mental degradation, at the opposite pole, i.e., on the side of the class that produces its own product in the form of capital'.

The International Labor Organisation has recently estimated that what might be called the global reserve army of labour is now larger than the approximately 1.4 billion workers who are totally reliant on wage labour. This reserve now extends well beyond the roughly 218 million unemployed, an astronomical 1.7 billion workers being designated the 'vulnerably employed'. A significant portion of this reserve is undoubtedly wageless, composed of members of marginal domestic economies who eke out material being through unpaid labours, scavenging, and other 'Dickensian' endeavours of the kind associated with life in the favelas, barrios, and shanty towns of the global South. Characterised by the fundamental precariousness of its everyday life, this sector knows little of the securities of the wage, which is usually unavailable or accessed intermittently, in sporadic, but always finite, clusters of paid employment. Often this segment of the dispossessed, reliant on scratching its day-to-day remunerations out of an *informal* economy where the struggle for subsistence relies as much on the trappings of petty entrepreneurialism of the self-exploiting penny capitalist kind, is as wageless as it is waged. All of this prompts recognition of the historical importance of considering class formation not only in terms of wage labour, but as an ongoing process of dispossession, encompassing a spectrum of possibilities that include classic waged employment relations defined by hourly rates as well as a number of other scenarios that combine types of labour that evolve outside the wage form. Mike Davis insists that what he calls the 'global informal working class', a socioeconomic stratum that he sees 'overlapping with but non-identical to the slum population', now surpasses one billion in number, 'making it the fastest growing, and most unprecedented, social class on earth'.[12]

Study of the dispossessed, then, must begin with an understanding that working-class life is not defined by either the wage or wagelessness, but is bounded by both. Proletarianisation, to be sure, has conventionally been studied by labour historians fixated on waged employment, and the modern field of working-class history has been highly influenced, even structured, by discussions that have tended to reify the waged dimension of labouring lives. The animating notions of the 'labour process' literature that grew out of Harry Braverman's influential study of the degradation of work in the twentieth century could be cited as but one example of many equivalent developments.[13]

---

12   Foster, McChesney, and Jonna 2011; Marx n.d., vol. 1, pp. 644–5; Davis 2006, p. 178.
13   Braverman 1974a.

There is no need to cast the insights of past scholarship aside in a quest for new and singular models of what constitutes the essence of proletarianisation. There is a little of this at work in the analytics of nomenclature structuring recent scholarly trends, as our critical welcoming of the contributions of Denning suggests. But we offer a slightly different orientation. Against the refusals of what are presented as orthodox Marxism, which we suggest contain as much easy caricature as critical dissection, we offer a more open-ended understanding of how to approach the diversities of proletarianisation and, in particular, the study of the wageless. If Denning finds terms like the reserve army of labour and the lumpenproletariat inadequate, just as the declaration of lack that is present in more mainstream designations of the *un*employed inevitably forces consideration in directions of the determinative influence of the wage relation, we find in all of these categories something of value. For along the continuum of proletarianisation encompassing waged work and wagelessness, free labour and outlawed outcast, lie many way stations in which the dispossessed, as an historical collectivity, find that they must pause, in varying ways at different times, to sustain and reproduce themselves, to adapt and to resist. This, as much as the arrival of the factory system, is the stuff of class formation. The dispossessed, to adopt a phrase from E.P. Thompson, constituted a proletarianised stratum 'present at its own making'.[14]

Moments in an Obscure History of Crisis and the Dispossessed: Toronto, 1830–1925

> The past can be seized only as an image which flashes up at the instant when it can be recognized and is never seen again ... For every image of the past that is not recognized by the present as one of its own concerns threatens to disappear irretrievably.
>
> WALTER BENJAMIN, 'Theses on the Philosophy of History' (1940)

Origins of the House of Industry

In Canada, proletarianisation as an act of dispossession reaches into the early nineteenth century. This historical context is not easily assimilated to the formalised labour markets, state initiatives, and class mobilisations of later periods. The history of this original accumulation of capitalist dispossession is untidy as it blurs lines of distinction that we have come to see as natural and inev-

---

14   Thompson 1963.

itable: urban/rural; waged-employment/public charity; paternalism/freedom; petition/conflict. Those experiencing dispossession did so in varied ways that yielded nothing approximating a collective, working-class solidarity. As native-born rural producers, immigrant newcomers,[15] or British mechanics, their separation from the land, their subordination to contractors and militias ruthless in enforcing the roughest of labouring environments on the early public works of canal and railroad construction, or their sense of artisan, apprenticed skills being debased, conditioned no community of common class interests. Nonetheless, these distinct streams of proletarianisation were tributaries destined to feed a common process, one in which dependency on the wage was always rendered precarious by the harsh and recurring realities of wagelessness.

On the Upper Canadian frontier, in which Old Toronto, or Muddy York, was a metropolitan outpost destined for post-Confederation provincial dominance, the revolution in social relations that would follow in the wake of capitalist industrialisation explored by Gregory S. Kealey may well seem obscure.[16] Toronto in 1834 had a population of a mere 9,000. Its productive apparatus, dominated by the often paternalistic master-journeymen reciprocities of the artisan manufactory and the ostensible *noblesse oblige* of the Tory oligarchy, hardly crystallised unambiguous class antagonisms. Yet as Albert Shrauwers has recently shown, the 1830s was a turning point in Toronto's evolution. The bitter fruits of dispossession were increasingly visible in the transition from a landed order in which the authority of the gentlemanly elite held sway to a more socially revolutionised and commodified market economy, in which the agricultural, commercial, financial, and industrial components of Toronto's economy were all subordinated to capitalist disciplines.[17]

Although a crisis in the countryside did not, in general, precipitate mass rural migration to the towns or to less concentrated farming settlements in the west until the 1840s and 1850s, Upper Canadian landed relations were anything but tranquil.[18] The gentlemanly capitalists that Schrauwers identifies with the traditional Family Compact held much of the best farm plots, either working them through hired hands or holding such acreage in speculation. The estab-

---

15   For a recent discussion of managing the migrants that accents the role of the developing layers of the state over the course of the nineteenth century, see Chilton 2011, pp. 231–62.

16   Industrial-capitalist Toronto in the late nineteenth century is the subject of Kealey's pioneering account of workers confronting the disciplines of the new order: Kealey 1980.

17   Schrauwers 2010, pp. 9–46.

18   See Gagan 1978, pp. 293–318; 1981; Wood 2000; and for the experience of workers on the land, Crowley 1995, pp. 17–41.

lished church and nascent state with which this elite was intimately connected each took one-seventh of the colony's available land. Free land grants, originally designed to attract settlers, were turned back in 1826, replaced by sale through public auctions that were exploited by large land companies, unscrupulous colonising agents, and primitive banking institutions, all of which were, again, never far removed from the influence and the interests of powerful circles of Compact alignments. Assisted emigration efforts were curtailed, and prospective landowners now had to pay for their passages and purchase their lots on credit. As one contemporary wrote in 1835, 'The system of selling land on credit, and contracting debt at stores, hath proved ruinous of later years to settlers without capital, who have no other means of extricating themselves than selling their properties'. Even large families could not ensure their prosperity, and prior to 1840, only two to five percent of all rural producers in Upper Canada had over 100 acres in cultivation. A distinct minority, to be sure, could afford to hire labour for the initial land clearance, but demand for such proletarians exceeded supply. Lord Goderich, the colonial secretary, explained in 1831 the dilemma faced by patrician, polite society: 'Without some division of labour, without a class of persons willing to work for wages, how can society be prevented from falling into a state of almost primitive rudeness, and how are the comforts and refinements of civilised life to be procured'.[19] Consolidating capitalism faced a decisive imperative: dispossession or ruin. It drove relentlessly in the direction of the former.

By the mid-1830s, land policy, speculative endeavours and hoarding, and the penetration of the market and its solvent of social differentiation in town and country were lending considerable force to Goderich's insistence that 'there should be in every society a class of labourers as well as a class of Capitalists or Landowners'. This presaged Edward Gibbon Wakefield's later enunciation, in 1833, of a theory of 'systematic colonisation', which Marx integrated into his discussion of capitalist primitive accumulation.[20] In the rural areas of the Home District, within which Toronto was located, some 10,172 out of 14,994 labouring-age males (68 percent) were landless by mid-century, and wage rates had plummeted across the Canadian colonial landscape.[21] With some 230,000 Irish immigrants crashing the Ontario-Quebec labour market in their flight

---

19   Teeple 1972, pp. 43–55; Wynn 1979, pp. 51–2; Russell 1982, pp. 138–44; Shirreff 1835, pp. 363–5, quoted in Schrauwers 2010, pp. 27, 29–30; 2011, pp. 1–30; Clarke 2001, especially pp. 266–72; Johnson 1971, pp. 41–60; with Goderich quoted in Johnson 1973, p. 66.

20   Johnson 1973, p. 68; Marx n.d., vol. 1, pp. 766–73.

21   Johnson 1971, pp. 57–9.

from Old World famine in the later 1840s, the dispossession of this transatlantic proletarian contingent translated into a rural reserve army of labour, some of which inevitably found its way to Ontario's cities.[22]

Toronto inevitably confronted the fallout from this process of dispossession. Over the course of the winter of 1836–7 an economic crisis exacerbated the problem: commerce stagnated; houses stood empty for want of rent; the Bank of Upper Canada pressured its debtors to settle accounts, including an ironworks that was forced to close, its 80 employees thrown out of work; a Mechanics' Association was formed to lobby for the protection of the interests of tradesmen; and printers and tailors struck their masters. William Lyon Mackenzie, a newspaper editor and proprietor whose notoriety as a relentless critic of the aristocratic governing Tories and outspoken leader of the Reform element was well known, railed that his typographers should spend their evenings 'studying the true principles of economy which govern the rule of wages'. Meanwhile, the flood of pauper emigrants passing through Toronto, estimated in the 1830s to be in the tens of thousands annually, continued, with fears of recent cholera epidemics associated with the immigrant ships fresh in the minds of many.[23] A wageless, diseased population, increasingly visible on city streets and challenging its ruling order's sense of public propriety and paternal responsibility necessitated a response. This was especially the case if firebrands like William Lyon Mackenzie were not to make ideological capital out of their constant harangues that social development and harmonious relations were threatened by a pernicious oligarchy, which was daily fomenting a 'universal agitation'. Mackenzie's obnoxious claims that 'privilege and equal rights' were at loggerheads in Upper Canada in 1837, forcing a terrible contest, were but one reflection of dispossession's distressing consequences.[24]

At the centre of this history of dispossession was the 1830s creation of a set of carceral institutions which, as Albert Schrauwers has argued, criminalised the poor.[25] Pivotal in this development, which extended beyond the

---

22   Palmer 1984, p. 247; Akenson 1981, pp. 111, 204–356; Pentland 1981, pp. 96–129, especially p. 109; Speisman 1973, p. 37; Duncan 1974, pp. 140–63; Bleasdale 1981, pp. 9–40; Weaver 1986, p. 186; Matthews 1985, pp. 41–5.

23   Schrauwers 2009, p. 189; Forsey 1982, p. 20; Armstrong 1967, pp. 187–96; Romney 1990, pp. 205–6; Bilson 1980, p. 63. Discussion of the economic crisis of 1836–7 appears in Read and Stagg 1985, pp. xxix–xxx, with a number of relevant documents following. Note as well Creighton 1937a, pp. 288–320.

24   W.L. Mackenzie, *The Constitution*, 26 July 1837, quoted in Schrauwers 2010, p. 10.

25   See Schrauwers 2009, especially pp. 56–65, and for a useful more general statement, Katz 1978, pp. 6–23. Note as well Weaver 1995.

Kingston Penitentiary and local and debtors' gaols, was Toronto's House of Industry. As conflicting historiographic interpretations of the meaning of the House of Industry suggest, it was, like almost everything in the city in 1837, contested terrain, pitting Tories against Reformers. The clash of oppositional forces around the establishment of the Toronto House of Industry played out in Radical Reformers, such as Mackenzie and James Lesslie, opposing the establishment of what they perceived to be an arm of the old-style English Poor Law discipline, long rejected in Upper Canada,[26] at the same time as they embraced the need to extend relief of the poor. The practice of the Toronto House of Industry ironically ended up bringing some reformers and some members of the Family Compact together, bound as they were as men of property to a broad agency of class discipline. Impaled on the horns of class formation's incomplete development in 1836–7, both the clash of views around the House of Industry and the fate of the insurrectionary impulse of the Rebellion itself reflected a politics that was compromised and incompletely differentiated into oppositional interests. As Stanley Ryerson long ago noted, the proletariat, waged *and* wageless, was 'not yet in a position to act in [its] own name or give independent leadership to the struggle'.[27]

Something less punitive than was perhaps envisioned by crusading former English Poor Law Commissioner and recently-ensconced Lieutenant-Governor of Upper Canada, Sir Francis Bond Head, the Toronto House of Industry was nonetheless a decisive expression of the view that new initiatives had to be undertaken to address the poverty, disease, and wagelessness that engulfed Toronto.[28] The Bond Head-endorsed 1837 statute, authorising Houses of Industry to be erected across Upper Canada, produced little immediately. No such establishments, which at first were to be funded entirely by voluntary subscriptions, were set up outside of Toronto until the late 1840s. Nonetheless, the criminalisation and institutionalisation of the wageless reflected both the growing unease among the patrician and propertied, as well as their panicked recourse to disciplining the unruly:

> That the persons who shall be liable to be sent into, employed and governed in the said House, to be erected in pursuance of this Act, are all Poor and Indigent Persons, who are incapable of supporting themselves; all persons able of body to work and without any means of maintaining

---

26   Smandych 1995, pp. 99–129.
27   See Romney 1990, pp. 192–216; Palmer 2008, pp. 403–39; Ryerson 1968, p. 132.
28   Contrast Baehre 1981, pp. 57–80 and Smandych 1991, pp. 81–6.

themselves, who refuse or neglect so to do; all persons living a lewd dis-
solute vagrant life, or exercising no ordinary calling, or lawful business,
sufficient to gain or procure an honest living; all such as spend their time
and property in Public Houses, to the neglect of lawful calling ...

... That all and every person committed to such House, if fit and able,
shall be kept diligently employed in labour, during his or her continuance
there; and in case the person so committed or continued shall be idle
and not perform such reasonable task or labour as shall be assigned,
or shall be stubborn, disobedient or disorderly, he, she or they, shall be
punished according to the Rules and Regulations made or be made, for
ruling, governing and punishing persons there committed.[29]

'The chief objects' of Toronto's House of Industry, wrote one commentator
supporting its creation in 1836, were 'the total abolition of street begging,
the putting down of wandering vagrants, and securing an asylum at the least
possible expense for the industrious and distressed poor'.[30] Toronto's Poor
House, as it was colloquially known, fittingly took over an old, abandoned
building that had previously served as York's Court House. At first the House
was used primarily by widows, deserted women, and their children, and few
receiving so-called indoor relief as inmates were actually male. Outdoor relief,
or the dispensing of food and fuel to needy families, constituted most of the
House of Industry's work in providing for the poor. The first annual report of
the House of Industry indicated that 46 persons received indoor relief, while
the corresponding figure for recipients of outdoor relief was 857. In its earliest
years, two-thirds of those seeking aid from the new institution were Irish,
demonstrating how poverty, criminalisation, and ethnicity came together.[31]

    In 1848 the House of Industry acquired a substantial new building. By the
early 1850s, the refuge began taking in small numbers of homeless men, on
average three a night, providing 'an asylum to the indigent poor'. According
to antiquarian histories, 'many a homeless waif' received 'a night's lodging,
with supper and breakfast, to invigorate him for the coming day's search for
work', which was to be undertaken after male 'lodgers' chopped some wood for

---

29   *The Statutes of the Province of Upper Canada* (Toronto 1837), pp. 80–2, reprinted in Clark
      1942, pp. 232–3.
30   Quoted in Baehre 1981, p. 74.
31   These early figures and the House of Industry's First Annual Report are cited in House of
      Industry 1897, pp. 5–6. See also Duncan 1974; and Speisman 1973, p. 37.

the institution. These innovations and expanded assistance were implemented as temporary expedients, judged necessary as 'the surest means of doing away with street begging'. It was understood that the 'casual homeless' would have one night of shelter and then be on their way. From 1837 to 1854, Toronto's refuge accommodated 2,620 indigents, but its outdoor relief remained especially important.[32] As Richard B. Splane suggested decades ago, the Toronto House was, in its beginnings, both a house of refuge and a house of correction, a hybrid that could appeal to conservatives and liberals alike.[33]

James Buchanan's *Project for the Formation of a Depot in Upper Canada, with a View to Receive the Whole Pauper Population of England* (1834) envisioned a Foucauldian institution of inspection, monitoring, and training in religion, work discipline, and, for children, the rudiments of an education. This kind of response might be associated with high Toryism, congruent with its author's claimed 'hatred of Democracy', but Buchanan had kinship connections with the leading family of moderate Reform, the Baldwins. Indeed, Dr. William Baldwin was to take up management of the Toronto House of Industry when it was established in March 1837. Thus the House of Industry proved a meeting ground of Tory and Reform on the eve of the Rebellion of 1837, foreshadowing the extent to which the political antagonists of this era might well share a common unease as the threatening portents of the dispossessed were increasingly obvious.[34] Toronto's wageless would exist in the shadow of the House of Industry for decades.

In the Era of Confederation: State Formation and the Poor

The Reform insurrection of 1837, however anti-climactic, dealt a series of death-blows to the *ancien régime*. In the subsequent era of state formation, culminating in Confederation in 1867, new senses of public responsibility and political culture consolidated, beginning in the 1840s.[35] Mechanics and tradesmen petitioned legislatures in ways that would have been unimaginable in decades past, while local government was fundamentally reconfigured.[36] Toronto's 1846 Act of Incorporation was amended, widening the possible reach of control and

---

32   Scadding 1966, p. 214; Mulvany et al. 1885, p. 325; Speisman 1973, pp. 38–9; House of Industry 1852, p. 8.

33   Splane 1965, p. 71; Careless 1984, p. 100.

34   Buchanan 1834, quoted in Baehre 1981, p. 70; and for documents relating to Buchanan, Sanderson 1943, vol. 1, pp. 16–17, 229–31; Schrauwers 2009, p. 192.

35   An important older statement is Ryerson 1968, while newer analytic sensibilities and perspectives emerge in many of the essays in Greer and Radforth 1992.

36   See McNairn 2000; Wilton 2000.

coercion that could be deployed against the wageless. The establishment of an industrial farm complemented the already existing House of Industry, which drew, from 1839 onwards, not only on private donations but on annual provincial grants. Over the course of the 1850s a spate of municipal legislation addressed the growing need to attend to the destitute and the workless; by 1866 the Municipal Institutions Act mandated that all townships in the province of Ontario with a population of over 20,000 provision houses of industry or refuge. Between 1840–60, moreover, Toronto's House of Industry competed with eight other local private charitable institutions receiving government grants for the relief of the poor.[37] One crucial piece of legislation that followed on the heels of Confederation was the 1867 Prison and Asylum Inspection Act. It defined provincial responsibilities for social welfare and, of course, deepened the process whereby criminalisation, incarceration, and relief of the indigent were not just associated as part of a common response to proletarianisation, but were now bureaucratically congealed in legislative statute. Responsibility for these spheres of 'correctional intervention' was assigned to a single inspector, John Woodward Langmuir.[38]

Small wonder that the oscillating reciprocities of waged and wageless life instilled in those undergoing proletarianisation a recurrent sense of grievance. A carpenter questioned the state of affairs in 1852: 'He asks that it be fair, that for five months in the year able and willing mechanics, are compelled to accept the alternative of walking the streets or working for wages which do not afford ample remuneration for the labour performed'. Finally, 'after submitting to all this, with apparent resignation – after enriching their employers by the sweat of their brow, on terms which barely keep the thread of life from snapping – they are told with barefaced effrontery that they were employed in charity'. Seasonal labour markets, with their harsh material ritual of winter's idleness and paternalistic alms, were by mid-century being challenged by the dispossessed.[39]

37 Aitchison 1953, especially pp. 656–7; Splane 1965, pp. 40, 72–9; Matthews 1986, especially pp. 306–78, which deals with the consequence of the 1856 commercial collapse.

38 Splane 1965, pp. 43–51. There is much on Langmuir in McCoy 2011. Chilton 2011, pp. 252–6, has useful information on emigration agents and the subsidisation of transportation costs for immigrants making their way to Toronto in these years.

39 The carpenter is quoted in Fingard 1974, pp. 74–5, but the entire article is now a classic statement on poverty, early Canadian unemployment, and charitable relief of the poor. In the period that Fingard addresses, nascent capitalist developments jostled uneasily with older social and productive relations rooted in pre-capitalist economic forma-

Economic crisis was the necessity that proved the mother of this new inventive stage in the developing responses to wagelessness, emanating not only from capital and the state, but from the proletarianised as well. The massive social dislocation occasioned by the arrival of tens of thousands of ill and impoverished famine Irish immigrants in the post-1847 years was one part of this process, helping to swell Toronto's population to 45,000 by 1860–1. At that point Toronto contained more people who were Irish by birth than it did people born in England, and the 12,441 Irish-born trailed only the 19,202 Canadian-born, many of whom likely had Irish parentage.[40] So, too, with the emergence of the railroad and the advancing stages of industrial-capitalist production in urban centres was class differentiation, organisation, and conflict becoming more visible. The number of strikes in Canada soared in the 1850s, when 73 such work stoppages represented 50 percent of all labour-capital conflicts taking place in the entire 1815–59 period. No other decade saw more than 30 strikes.[41] For the workless, however, it was the commercial collapse of 1857 that registered discontent most decisively.

The cruel impact of the economic downturn occasioned perhaps the first mass protests of the obviously organised unemployed in the Canadian colonies. Upwards of 3,000 Quebec City out-of-work labourers, many of them shipwrights and other workers employed in the building of vessels, convened St. Roch protest meetings, marched through the streets of Lower Town, and demanded work, not alms. Recognising that their wageless plight was 'the effect of "the crisis" upon the shipbuilding interest', the demonstrations of the workless, however moderate and often contradictory (though rejecting alms, they could also plead for bread and charitable relief from sources of government or private citizens), generated a mixed response on the part of the powerful. Newspapers could side with the demands of the workless, urging the colonial government to provide significant relief for the labouring poor, but as protests

---

tions. In some ways the seasonality of winter and the employment crises that came with its onslaught would be exacerbated by intensified capitalist crises in the latter half of the nineteenth century.

40   Goheen 1970, pp. 75–6.

41   Kealey 1980, pp. 3–34, suggests the importance of the 1840s and 1850s as pivotal decades in the transition to industrial capitalism. On the Irish, the views of Pentland 1981 and Akenson 1982 provide perspectives that probably need to be blended into one another rather than counterposed polemically. For class struggle in this period an older, unpublished work still repays examination: Appleton 1974. For an introduction to the nature and dimensions of working-class activity see Palmer 1987a, pp. 61–84. Inequality and class differentiation is addressed substantively in Katz 1975b.

continued, reporting took on a more critical tone, with headlines such as 'More Mob Demonstrations'.[42]

The crash of 1857 had a devastating effect on Toronto. Nineteenth-century commentators recorded the extent of the crisis, seizing the opportunity to moralise, conveying well the extent to which wagelessness was now associated with incorrigibility and criminality. 'There was much suffering and want among the labouring classes, with a corresponding amount of drunkenness, vice, and crime', declared one source. Police records indicate that in 1857 alone, one in nine Toronto residents faced arrest, finding themselves before the police magistrate. This state of affairs necessarily heightened class tensions. Jesse Edgar Middleton's 1923 multi-volume official history of Toronto declared cryptically, 'Much disorder was caused by railway construction laborers between 1852 and 1860'. Newspapers from the local Toronto *Colonist* to the distant New York *Herald* noted the profusion of beggars: 'They dodge you round corners, they follow you into shops, they are found at the church steps, they are at the door of the theatre, they infest the entrance to every bank, they crouch in the lobby of the post office, they assail you in every street, knock at your private residence, walk into your place of business ...' Asserting that 'begging has assumed the dignity of a craft', the *Colonist* complained that, 'Whole families sally forth, and have their appointed rounds; children are taught to dissemble, to tell a lying tale of misery and woe, and to beg or steal as occasion offers'. Correspondents bemoaned that Toronto's 'streets swarmed with mendicants' and that it was impossible to go into public thoroughfares without annoyance from them.[43]

Over the course of the 1850s the House of Industry reported that the number of people seeking relief doubled. The municipality upped its grant to the refuge by 100 percent. Immigration agents attended to the newly arrived, providing bread, temporary shelter, passage money, and information relevant to settlement and employment. A House of Providence soon outstripped the Toronto House of Industry in terms of those it sheltered, with the annual collective days stay of the poor in the former totalling 45,722 compared to 27,863 for the latter in 1872. An Orphan's Home, Boys and Girls Homes, and a Female Aid Society supplemented the charitable role of the House of Industry by the 1860s. But Toronto's Poor House still received the largest provincial grant of any such institution in Ontario, its annual subsidy of $2,900 amounting to 10.5 cents for each inmate's daily stay. With small towns and villages in Toronto's hinterland

42   Cooper 1949, pp. 338–9; Fingard 1974, pp. 74–5, 89; Baskerville and Sager 1998, pp. 23–4.
43   Scadding and Dent 1884, pp. 212–13; Strachan to Hutcheson, Toronto City Council Papers, quoted in Masters 1947, p. 80; Middleton 1923, p. 264.

urging their poor to seek relief at the House of Industry, it served an increasingly mobile contingent of the dispossessed, some of whom came, not only from across Ontario, but also from Europe and the United States. Bishop Strachan suggested, in 1857, that Toronto, with its 'central position has become a sort of reservoir, and a place of refuge to the indigent from all parts of the Province'.

There was growing discontent among the small and concentrated bureau-cratised, managerial officialdom that monitored the funding and activities of houses of industry and providence. Langmuir, for instance, disapproved of Toronto's refuge even being called a 'House of Industry'. No industry, he claimed, took place within its walls. The poor, Langmuir argued, should indeed be made to labour for their bed and breakfast. Toronto's House of Industry and other such institutions were misnamed: they were 'Poor-houses and nothing but that'. Langmuir also suggested that absolute reliance on provincial funding was misplaced, since he believed it was well established that 'every Municipal-ity shall take care of its own poor'. He further regretted that a generalised per-missiveness undermined the good that an institutionalised response to poverty and wagelessness might accomplish, bemoaning the lack of more compulsory measures. Largely responsible for the Ontario Charity Aid Act of 1874, Lang-muir elaborated a political economy of poor relief rooted in the belief that, 'unless we desire to see local Poor Houses *mainly* supported by Government but *entirely* controlled by municipalities or private boards, the principle that fur-ther Government aid to such establishments should depend upon the amount they obtain from the general public, cannot be yielded'.[44]

In the aftermath of the destabilising consequences of the 1840s and 1850s, especially the crisis unleashed with the commercial crash of 1857, state forma-tion in Canada culminated in what Langmuir would later describe as 'one of the most complete charitable and correctional systems on the continent'. This was part and parcel of what Michael B. Katz, Michael J. Doucet, and Mark J. Stern have called 'the social organisation of early industrial capitalism'.[45] The long

---

44   The above paragraphs rely on House of Industry 1852, p. 8; 1854, p. 9; Speisman 1973, pp. 39–49, as well as Splane 1965, pp. 47–51, 79–84, which draws on, among other sources, Langmuir's annual reports in Ontario's *Sessional Papers*. See as well Careless 1984, p. 100; Mulvany 1884, pp. 63–9.

45   Ontario, *Sessional Papers* (1881), Number 8, 15, quoted in Splane 1965, p. 49; Katz, Doucet, and Stern 1982. A recent study documenting the extent to which the old connections of master and man remained embedded in craft production understates the extent to which the long and complex process of proletarianisation had indeed affected the social relations of production and the social organisation of early industrial capitalism. See Kristofferson 2007. Contrast it with the perspectives outlined in Katz 1975b and the later

recessionary downturn of 1873–96, punctuated by acute crises in the 1870s and 1890s, however, taxed this system. As the wageless proliferated, those afflicted by poverty and joblessness organised and resisted both their condition and its criminalisation. Their consciousness and activism challenged both the increasingly oppressive conditions imposed upon them by economic depression and the pressures towards compulsion that were inevitably at work in a relief order that could not accommodate the expanding numbers of indigent families and out-of-work labourers.

The Underside of the Great Upheaval, 1873–96

The 1873–96 years witnessed the culmination of Toronto's nineteenth-century industrial-capitalist revolution. In tandem, the city also experienced the unmistakable growth of workers' organisations, political mobilisations, and protests, including strikes, with 122 of a national total of 425 fought over the course of the 1880s being waged in Toronto. Labour newspapers like the *Ontario Workman* and the *Palladium of Labor* anchored themselves in Toronto, just as the Nine-Hour League and the Canadian Labour Union in the 1870s and the Knights of Labor and the Trades and Labor Congress of Canada played significant roles in the now bustling manufacturing metropolis, which boasted a population approaching 200,000 by the end of the nineteenth century. This was the unmistakable expression of a working-class presence that, however much it was accommodated to the logic of capitalist class relations and the disciplines of the wage, did indeed challenge employers and their often servile state.[46]

Since waged life was never entirely separable from wageless life, the articulation of proletarian interests through organisations of labour, demands for improved conditions in workplaces, and the withdrawal of waged services, it follows that further expressions of working-class protest would also surface, not at the point of production, but against the coercions of non-production. In this latter struggle, the entrenched ideologies of British Poor Law discourse figured forcefully. The 'undeserving poor' were to be subject to the laws of 'less eligibility'. This ideology stipulated that relief would only be made available to those among the wageless who *would* work for their aid, which could only be doled out in ways that made it even less attractive than what could be secured by the worst-paid unskilled labour. Toronto's *Globe* made all of this abundantly clear in an 1877 manifesto-like declaration on the wageless:

study of Katz, Doucet, and Stern 1982, as well as Palmer 1979a, especially the discussion of the producer ideology, pp. 97–123.

46   Kealey 1980; Palmer 1987a, p. 73; Kealey and Palmer 1982.

We do not advocate a system which could leave them to starve, but we do say that if they are ever to be taught economical and saving habits, they must understand that the public have no idea of making them entirely comfortable in the midst of their improvidence and dissipation. If they wish to secure that they must work for it and save and plan. Such comfort is not to be had by loafing around the tavern door, or fleeing to charity at every pinch.

Three years earlier, with the 1873 depression as its backdrop, the same newspaper denounced any 'poor law as a legislative machine for the manufacture of pauperism. It is true mercy to say that it would be better that a few individuals should die of starvation than a pauper class should be raised up with thousands devoted to crime and the victims of misery'.[47]
Over the course of the long downturn of the late nineteenth century, evidence of the precariousness of working-class life was unambiguous. The rhetorical assault on the wageless went into overdrive. A floating mass of workless males generated intensified panic as the depression of 1873 deepened into 1877–8. Masses of migrant labourers, ostensibly travelling to secure illusive waged employment, became the scourge of small towns and large cities alike. Welcomed with the lock-up and public derision in the press, tramps were criminalised and vilified, socially constructed as thieves and denigrated as 'pests', 'voracious monsters', 'outrageously impertinent', an 'irrepressible stampede' deserving of 'a well-aimed dose of buckshot rubbed in well with salt-petre' and other forms of vigilante, lynch law. In Lindsay, Ontario, roughly ninety miles from Toronto and studied by Richard Anderson, the local newspaper (the *Canadian Post*) carried over a hundred news items relating to tramps in the 1874–8 years. Their tone was almost universally derogatory, and tramps were in general depicted as an outcast stratum rarely interested in finding employment, poor because they were 'work-shy and degenerate'. Many, riding the rails, were en route to Toronto, where police stations, in 1877 and 1878, reported sheltering over 1,200 'waifs' annually.[48]

---

47   *Globe*, 26 January 1877, as cited in Cross 1974, p. 196 and in Struthers 1983, p. 7; *Globe*, 27 February 1874, as cited in Splane 1965, p. 16.

48   Anderson 1992, pp. 33–56. This period saw repeated concern expressed by trustees of the House of Industry that other Ontario municipalities were dumping their poor on Toronto, especially in the depths of winter. See House of Industry 1879, p. 6. The late nineteenth-century war on the tramp can be informed by a range of commentary, including Marx's discussion of 'The Nomad Population', in Marx n.d., vol. 1, pp. 663–7; Higbie 2003; Phillips 1990, pp. 128–62; Montgomery 1993, pp. 87–8; and Kelly 1908.

If the 1880s saw the economy struggle out of its 1870s doldrums, the recovery was anything but robust. The migratory wageless continued to unsettle respectable society, as established in a study by James Pitsula. Toronto's newspapers competed against one another, pushing the denunciations of the 'loafing aristocracy' to new extremes, calling for the expulsion of tramps from the city, judicious use of the lash against those for whom work was 'aversion', and vigilant police monitoring of peripatetic vagrants given to 'murders, burglaries, incendiaries, and highway robberies'. A little 'hard labour', suggested the *Globe*, would do this 'dissipated' and 'shiftless' element good, since the Poor House had become increasingly lax in enforcing earlier expectations that those seeking accommodations for the night would chop wood for their food and lodging. Toronto's Associated Charities pressed new forms of 'labour tests' in 1881–5 as a prerequisite for relief, requiring tramps to break stone. Many left the yard rather than undergo the rigours of the 'labour test'. At the House of Industry, the Associated Charities crusade to force the refuge to adopt similar unwaged work requirements proved futile, even though the House had in the past required manual work from all of those who availed themselves of indoor relief. Instead the refuge concentrated on establishing an expanded wayfarer's lodge in 1884–5, where large numbers of indigent men could be put up for the night in a casual ward. Their bodies were to be soaked in a hot bath, their heads doused in vermin-killing liquid solution, and their clothes fumigated, 'cleansed and classified', in the vernacular of poor relief officialdom. Prior to this renovation, the cramped House of Industry had drawn complaints of the lodging's 'sickening smell'. Residents of the overcrowded Poor House 'apartments' had been described as 'thickly packed as herrings in a barrel', the atmosphere likened to 'a carload of hogs in transit'.[49]

The growing number of habitual tramps furnished with temporary board and lodging by the House of Industry in the mid-1880s necessitated yet another adoption of a modified 'labour test', if only to deter the ostensibly shiftless and physically weak from staying in the expanded casual ward too long. Making inmates saw a quarter-cord of wood, a job that took the able-bodied and reasonably dexterous approximately three hours before they were allowed to lunch on a watery bowl of soup and a hunk of bread (managers insisted that it was not their responsibility to provide the workless with 'sumptuous fare'), had its effect. Those checking into the wayfarer's lodge declined from totals of 730 in 1886 to 548 in 1889. The worsening economic climate of the depressed 1890s

49   Pitsula 1980, pp. 116–32; 'The Support of the Poor', *The Canadian Presbyterian*, 7 January 1881; 'Tramps and Waifs', *Globe*, 22 March 1887.

saw an expanded need for relief, however, and the casual ward was opened for the summer as well as winter months. The numbers of casuals staying at the House thus soared, climbing to highs of 1,700 in 1891 and 1,500 in 1895 and 1897, rarely falling below 1,200. The average contingent sleeping at the House per night never dipped below 60 between 1890 and 1897, when a high of 100 was reached (a comparable figure for the 1880–5 years had been roughly 26). In 1891, 832 casuals stayed in the wayfarer's lodge of Toronto's House of Industry for two or three nights, while 415 lodged in the Poor House for more than three days; 24 hard-core recidivists spent more than 100 nights in the refuge.[50]

The economies of this crisis of wagelessness drove the ideology and practice of poor relief in more disciplinary directions. Reverend Arthur H. Baldwin, rector of Toronto's All Saints Church and one of the House of Industry's most outspoken trustees, gave evidence at the Toronto sessions of the Royal Commission on Prisons and Reformatory Systems in November 1890. Baldwin provided advance notice that Toronto's premier institution of poor relief was not interested in coddling 'the loafing system that is now going on', stressing that a more rigorous 'work test' than that of cutting wood was needed if the encouragement of pauperism was to be avoided. 'It seems a great pity', he pontificated, 'that these people should be allowed to go in and dwell [in the casual ward] and do nothing but cut a little wood, as we insist upon their doing'.[51] A new labour regime was clearly in the offing.

It was in this context that the House of Industry shifted what was expected of casuals lodging with it from wood-cutting to the more onerous stone-breaking. 'Until the vagrant is offered some alternative that even he will recognize as more unpleasant and disagreeable than work', claimed the Board of the House of Industry in 1891–2, 'the tramp trouble will never be cured'. Cutting wood wasn't cutting it: relatively few refused this 'labour test'. Between 1891 and 1895, according to Pitsula's calculations from the *Annual Reports of the House of Industry*, 29,652 requests of the indigent to cut wood were complied with, while a bare 432 refusals were registered. In 1896, when the stone-breaking regime was implemented, the situation altered dramatically: only 792 completed the

50 Pitsula 1980, pp. 116–32; 'Tramps and Waifs', *Globe*, 22 March 1887. One part of the inner history of wood cutting as a 'labour test' involved the Board of the House of Industry subcontracting the delivery of cord wood and the transportation of cut wood sold to clients to the Rogers Coal Company. The owner of this enterprise, Elias Rogers, was involved in a price-fixing ring in the coal industry in the late 1880s. See Careless 1984, p. 143.
51 Ontario Prison Reform Commission 1891, pp. 682–5. See also the comments on 'work tests' in *All Saints Church Parish Magazine*, December 1895.

task of stone-breaking, compared to 1,202 who refused to undertake the 'labour test'. As indicated by the vagrancy convictions of John Curry and Thomas Wilson in January 1896, those who refused stone-breaking assignments were soon subject to confinement. Magistrate Denison sentenced this duo, who said they preferred jail to the new 'labour test', to a three-month term in the refuge of their choice. One month later, upping the ante, City Alderman Jolliffe introduced a motion making it mandatory for all able-bodied applicants for relief in Toronto seeking outdoor assistance to break a yard of stone in return for their coal subsidy, doubling the amount of work required to receive winter fuel. 'The stonepile', as Pitsula concludes, had become 'an emblem for the work ethic'. And those who demonstrated insufficient commitment to the regime of labour discipline were to be criminalised. When Reverend Brown was asked at the hearings into prisons and reformatory systems in Ontario in 1890 whether or not it would be a good idea to turn the House of Industry into a correctional facility, he replied authoritatively: 'I think it would be a great advantage to the city'.[52]

A war against the tramps was clearly being waged in the name of morality and the disciplining power of relief. The Toronto *Evening Star* fired on the poor in an editorial volley:

> 'If ye work not, neither shall ye eat', has, as dictum the sanction of the Holy Writ. Nothing can be more demoralizing than giving alms to men who are quite able to work, but very unwilling. At the instance of Ald. Jolliffe, the management of the House of Industry, one of the most costly and important of the Toronto charities, obtained from the City Council a large quantity of stone, with the intention of having it broken by the 'casuals', who resort thither for out-door or indoor relief. The complaint of these people generally is that they can find no work to do, and are, therefore, forced to beg. The truth, as tested experiment is that very few of them are willing to work, while all are willing to depend on charity for their living. The discouraging result of the labor test in the House of Industry, so far from causing abandonment of the experiment, ought to impress on the City Council the absolute and urgent necessity of making a more general application of it ... While we have nothing but words of praise for the many excellent men and women who do so much to relieve distress,

52   House of Industry 1892, p. 9; Pitsula 1980, pp. 131–2; 'Talking of the Law', Toronto *Evening Star*, 10 January 1896; 'House of Industry Still in a Bad Way Financially', Toronto *Evening Star*, 19 February 1896; Ontario Prison Reform Commission 1891, p. 684.

we have no toleration for that good natured, shiftlessness which prompts soft-hearted and soft-headed people to add to the demoralization of those who are already paupers in spirit. The best tonic for them is a strong daily dose of hard, manual labor, with a threat of starvation on the one hand, and the inducement of decent living on the other.[53]

Thomas Conant voiced all-too-common prejudices in his *Upper Canada Sketches*, asking bluntly 'whether the hard-working and the thrifty ought to be taxed to provide for the lazy and the thriftless. Or again, is it wise to foster the growth of a class of persons whose filth and foul diseases are the result of laziness and their own vices'.[54]

This class war was not waged one-sidedly. Not only was stone-breaking unpopular, but the refusal to comply with the more stringent 'labour test' occasioned organised protests by the poor. The rush of refusals in 1896 could not have happened without discussions and deliberations on the part of the wageless. Consequences of their recalcitrance were quite severe. Refusal to break stone left the single unemployed indigent men without visible means of support and sustenance, subject to incarceration for vagrancy. Family men seeking outdoor relief in the form of food and fuel put themselves, their wives, and children at risk with their refusals. Yet not only was stone-breaking rejected, the poor gathered outside of City Hall to protest Jolliffe's motion. An unidentified spokesman, described as 'a strong hulk fellow', spoke for his wageless counterparts: 'And they calls that charity, do they? Got to crack a heap o' stones for what yer get. Ain't no charity in that es' I can see'.[55]

The rebellion of stone-breaking refusal in the 1890s was, to be sure, a minor event, but it signalled a shift in the activities of the workless, which took a more organised and collective turn in the depression of 1873–7 and its immediate aftermath. With industrialists acknowledging that, 'fifty percent of the manufacturing population of the country are out of work', and fledgling newspapers of the organised working class addressing unemployment and its evils, it was but a short step to deputations of the jobless marching in demand of some kind of redress.[56] Ottawa became a centre of this 1870s agitation, a natural enough

---

53   'The Labor Test', Toronto *Evening Star*, 16 May 1896.

54   Conant 1898, p. 195.

55   'Around a Stove. Daily Gathering of Queer People at City Hall. Men out of Employment and Those Seeking Charity. How They View Officials and How Officials View Them', Toronto *Evening Star*, 22 February 1896. See also 'Stone Test Scares Them. Tramps Object to Work for Food and Lodging', Toronto *Evening Star*, 21 December 1897.

56   B. Rosamund, *House of Commons Journals* (1876), App. 3, p. 200, quoted in Langdon 1973,

development given parliament's proximity and the possibility of federal politicians voting funds for expanded public works.[57] Over the course of the winter of 1879–80, Ottawa newspapers bristled with accounts of petitions, marches, torch-lit processions, and other gatherings of hundreds of 'unemployed workingmen'. Editorials chastened those who were described as looking 'needy and seemed determined to get work or fight', claiming that the government could not be expected to provide for them. Canada was not a land of 'State Socialism'.[58]

To be sure, the unemployed protests of 1873–80 were seldom unambiguous stands of unity expressing a solidarity of the waged and the wageless. Much of the respectable labour discourse of dissent in these years still clung to an ideology of the deserving versus undeserving poor. Too much was conceded to the antiquated and class-compromised assumptions of earlier Poor Law perspectives. And in this era labour racism was never far from the resentments against mainstream politicians who, while glorying in the nation-building exploits of the Canadian Pacific Railroad, seemed to care little for the plight of the workingman. The unemployed of 1880 protested the fairness of suggesting that mechanics in Canada's capital 'leave the city' of Ottawa when they had contributed so much to 'building it up'. They buttressed this legitimate argument with angry statements far less salutary: 'It was nonsense to ask residents of the city to go away west and live with Indians and half-breeds, and to work upon the railway in British Columbia, competing with Chinese cheap labour'.[59]

Nonetheless, the trajectory of labouring experience in the 1880s was *towards* a more inclusive sense of the collectivity of class experience, the common interests of skilled and unskilled, and, as a consequence, the importance of addressing not only the struggles of the waged, but also the plight of the wageless. This demanded organisation, and the Knights of Labor promoted an understanding of the importance of 'one big union' of all workers. Labour reform intellectuals of the 1880s, such as Toronto's Phillips Thompson, were acutely aware of the ongoing nature of capitalist crisis, of the economic system's

Part II, p. 21. For relevant discussions in the Toronto-based *Ontario Workman*, see 'Number and Condition of the Unemployed', 18 December 1873; 'The Unemployed', 5 February 1874.

57   Wells 1982. Much of the discussion of unemployed demonstrations in this thesis is summarised in Baskerville and Sager 1998, pp. 30–3. For political context see as well Ostry 1960, pp. 93–127.

58   See, for instance, Ottawa *Herald*, 23 February 1880; Ottawa *Daily Free Press*, 23 February 1880, among dozens of other newspaper accounts that might be cited.

59   Quoted in Wells 1982, p. 98, and cited in Baskerville and Sager 1998, p. 33. For a general discussion see Goutor 2007.

insatiable appetite for accumulation, and of how this acquisitive individualism could only be fed on the contributions of labour and the despoliation of the working class:

> The wheels of industry and commerce revolve at high pressure, and short-sighted politicians and publicists are loud in their congratulations on the prosperity of the country, ignoring entirely the fact that all this crowding on of sail and expenditure of surplus productive energy is simply preparing the way for the inevitable return of hard times. The inflation period is generally of short duration. Present demands are soon supplied, and goods again begin to accumulate in the factories and warehouses. The competition between producers is no longer as to which shall turn out goods most rapidly and in greatest volume, but which shall sell the cheapest. Production slackens, wages fall, employés are discharged. Enforced economy diminishes the purchasing power and causes further stringency and greater distress among workers, and so the vicious circle is completed. Those who, reluctantly in some cases and willingly in others, crowded two days work into one, now think themselves fortunate to obtain one day's work in two.

'Capitalism has created a monster which threatens to destroy the classes, if not the system, that gave it life', Thompson wrote. 'The number of men and women who cannot get work on any terms implies a far larger class whose pay has become a mere pittance ...' Thompson's *The Politics of Labor* (1886) sought to break down the separations of the skilled and unskilled, and eradicate, to some degree, the barriers to working-class solidarity erected by gendered and racialised prejudice, not to mention craft exclusion. Against the constant appeals of capitalist competition, Thompson posed the possibilities of true working-class cooperation. 'Where is the advantage of cheapness of production to the army of the unemployed and half-employed, or to those whose labor has been so cheapened by competition that their purchasing power is correspondingly lessened?' he asked. The question was an acknowledgement of how proletarians necessarily shared the fruits, bitter and sweet, of always confronting the possibility of being waged and being wageless. The half-employed, the cheapeningly employed, and the unemployed – for Thompson this was the army that would march against capital. It was, arguably, the beginning of a union of the dispossessed.[60]

---

60   Thompson 1887, pp. 186–8; Baskerville and Sager 1998, pp. 171–2; Hann 1976, pp. 35–57. The

As this union struggled, against all odds, to realise itself in the 1880s, evidence of how the lives of the waged and the wageless shaded into one another surfaced in many quarters. Toronto workers surveyed by the Bureau of Industries at the end of the decade averaged only 44 weeks of employment a year, if they happened to find work six days a week. This was in the best of times. For many workers, as Eric Sager and Peter Baskerville have pointed out, being out of work for a goodly part of every year was the norm. By the end of the century at least one out of five urban Canadian workers found themselves wageless at some point in the year, regardless of whether the times were lean or fat. Testimony before the Royal Commission on the Relations of Labor and Capital in the late 1880s, from both employers and workers, made it abundantly clear that few industrial establishments, building projects, and transportation endeavours paid workers for more than eight to ten months of any given year. The Toronto House of Industry accommodated tramps, to be sure, but to the extent that the migratory wageless who depended on its shelter and subsistence fare can be classified occupationally, skilled workers were not far behind unskilled labourers in lining up for relief. Toronto printers claimed that 30 percent of their number were without work in the 1890s. 'I am not alone in my trouble', declared one Toronto unemployed father of six in 1891, 'There are two hundred members of the union to which I belong in the same position as myself'. If the organisation of the wageless was not dramatic in this period, it had nonetheless surfaced and made particular kinds of statements. At one of the 1880 Ottawa demonstrations of the unemployed, a black flag was unfurled. As a fitting symbol, the anarchist banner signified for the angry workers who marched under it the possibility of death. This was the wages of the war on the dispossessed. But if those out of work understood that their own demise by starvation might well be imminent, they shook their defiant fists in the face of authority and vowed 'death to the government' that they claimed was responsible for their destitution. Carrying such a provocative symbol, some who hoisted the black flag thought they 'would be clubbed by the Police and shot down like dogs'.[61]

In February 1891 two Toronto procession protests of the wageless also carried a black flag, emblazoned with the words 'Work or Bread'. Taking place on a Wednesday and a Thursday, the marches drew from 300–1,000 unemployed workers.

Knights of Labor stimulated many approaches to the problem of unemployment. See, for instance, DeBernardi 1888.

61 Bradbury 1995, p. 417, citing *Bureau of Industries*, 1888, p. 42; Kealey 1973b, for a small sampling of the testimony; Lipton 1973, p. 90; Ottawa *Free Press*, 27 February 1880; Wells 1982, p. 95; Baskerville and Sager 1998, pp. 33 and 40, quoting *Globe*, 21 February 1891.

Some of the out-of-work were reluctant to admit that they had appealed 'to the charities' for the first time in their lives, but the crowd was also an angry one. It grew progressively more agitated as Mayor Clarke, who at first seemed sympathetic and promised that the City would look into finding work for the jobless, later shifted ground, telling the protesters that there were no more public works projects that could be funded. Clarke's remarks, from the steps of City Hall, drew angry heckling. Threatening disorder, one man shouted, 'Necessity knows no law', and that his need was for immediate work to feed a 'dependant family'. To be sure, these protests did not bridge all of the significant gaps separating those who felt themselves deserving because of their longstanding waged status and those who, as habitués of the House of Industry, might often be perceived as more acclimatised to their wagelessness. One reflection of this was discontent that family men were not being privileged over the single unemployed in the granting of work on some City sewer construction jobs. Such a 'breadwinner' argument pitted the 'casuals' and tramps of the House of Industry against the out-of-work building tradesmen, transportation workers, printers, and others who made up the bulk of the February 1891 protesters.[62] Yet a new page had been turned in the late nineteenth century. Workers began to address the experience of dispossession as one in which the discontents of the waged and wageless congealed. This hinted at the decisive role that a left politics would play in future mobilisations of what had now come to be referred to as 'the unemployed'.

The black flag that flew at demonstrations of the wageless in the late nineteenth century proclaimed the presence of the left among the unemployed. Memories of this haunted Toronto's community of relief workers for some time. In 1908, Superintendent Arthur Laughlen of Toronto's House of Industry explained how it had come to pass that the 'labour test' of breaking stone, so exemplary in its disciplining capacities, had been charitably reduced from two yards to half a yard, which still constituted a crate weighing over 600 pounds:

> Our work test is a splendid thing and tends to keep down the number of applicants for help to a minimum. Well, you see, we were the victims of considerable imposition during the depression about 14 years ago,

---

62   The *Globe*'s 19 February 1891 image of a black flag, 'Work or Bread', demonstration adorns the cover of Baskerville and Sager 1998, where the event of 11 February 1891 is discussed, pp. 39–40, citing and quoting 'Work or Bread', *Globe*, 12 February 1891; *Globe*, 13 February 1891; *Labor Advocate*, 20 February 1891; 27 February 1891. See also Lipton 1973, p. 90; Hann, G.S. Kealey, L. Kealey, and Warrian 1973, pp. 9–10.

when the unemployed were carrying the black flag ... We then decided to
establish a stone-yard, and before we would give relief each able-bodied
man had to break two yards of stone. This innovation was pronounced a
success, and the applications for relief began to fall off at a rapid rate, until
we had very few families to talk of. We found, however, that two yards of
stone was too much for a man to break, and at my suggestion the Board
reduced it to one yard. It was afterwards reduced to half, and today they
only have to break a quarter of a yard.

'The labour test' of 'cracking the stone', it turns out, was both born and somewhat beaten back under the black flag.[63]

The Left and the Toronto Wageless before the Great Depression, 1900–25

To be sure, the left would fly other flags, including those of 'deepest red' that
were associated with the arrival of socialism and communism in the 1890–1925
years. And among some in this often fissiparous and differentiated left, antagonism to the wageless as little more than capitalism's refuse would surface
in denunciations of the poor as parasites. John Rivers, a writer in the socialist
newspaper the *Western Clarion*, lumped hoboes, transients, the unemployed
and the poor with others 'at the bottom of the social pit' who were 'unable
to help themselves or assist others'. The best thing for a socialist to do was to
'ignore them'. In Lindsay, Ontario, echoes of the earlier 1870s tramp panic could
be heard in a Socialist Party of Canada publication, *Gems of Socialism* (1916),
which declared confidently that, 'The tramp and the millionaire are brothers under the skin. They both live without labor, or rather, live on the labor
of others'. 'Revolts of the unemployed' erupted across Canada in the opening

---

63   'Need Not Hunger If They'll Work. Superintendent Laughlen of House of Industry Willingly
     Feeds the Industrious. He Has a Work Test – It's Work ... Soup, Fuel and Grocery Orders
     Result', Toronto *Daily Star*, 28 January 1908. On the amount of stone that had to be broken
     and its weight see Guest 1980, p. 37. Black flags and anarchism would have been associated
     in this period with Chicago's Haymarket events of 1886–7. See Avrich 1986; Green 2007.
     The unemployed who carried the black flag in Toronto's 1891 protest did so a mere four
     years after the execution of the Haymarket anarchists. Toronto radical Phillips Thompson
     recorded his sense of the climate surrounding this first North American Red Scare at the
     time: 'the entire press gave rise to a furious insensate howl for blood and vengeance ...
     The case was prejudiced against men on trial for their lives'. He condemned 'the hideous
     brutality which found in the death sentence of the ... convicted Anarchists a subject for
     ghoulish rejoicing and heartless jests ...' Thompson 1887, p. 167.

decades of the twentieth century, fuelled as often as not by the crisis-prone nature of capitalism. With the revolutionary left's involvement in and support of these uprisings, a more expansive understanding of the complex reciprocity that joined the waged and the wageless under capitalism emerged.[64]

Toronto had helped nurture the Canadian socialist left in the 1880s and 1890s, becoming a haven for bohemian radicalism and dissident thought. It was a centre of the Canadian Socialist League, the first indigenous and popularly-based socialist organisation in the country, founded in 1899. The long capitalist crisis of 1873–96 had convinced many Toronto radicals, nascent socialists, and developing Marxists that chronic unemployment, among other afflictions plaguing the working class, could only be resolved by a root-and-branch alteration of the entire capitalist system. Many such critics were Christian socialists, and they found themselves locking horns with more conservative, church voices in the eclectic Social Problems Conferences that often addressed issues of poverty in the 1890s. As early as 1889 such radical types had clashed in the Toronto Labour Council with one of Canada's leading public intellectuals, Goldwin Smith, who had a penchant for denouncing William Morris, John Ruskin, the British Fabians and other 'poverty destroyers'. As this broad left coalesced, it articulated increasingly radical views on how capitalism, recurring economic crises, mechanisation of industry, and concentration of wealth and ownership of the productive forces were widening the domain of wagelessness.[65]

During the period 1900–25, Toronto was transformed. The largest manufacturing centre in Ontario, the heartland of Canada's regionalised industrial-capitalist development, the city grew by leaps and bounds. Fed by a massive influx of immigrants from the British Isles, the United States, the 'white Dominions' of Australia, New Zealand, South Africa, other parts of Canada such as Newfoundland, and non-English speaking Europe, Toronto's population soared, increasing 75 percent between 1901–11, when it surpassed 375,000. Annexation gobbled up new physical territory, which was needed for developing industries and working-class suburbs. Capital invested in manufacturing increased by 618 percent between 1900 and 1921, while the gross value of production, indexed at 100 in 1900, climbed to 148 in 1905, 255 in 1910, and 847 in 1919.

---

64   For discussion of socialists and 'the degenerate and dangerous class', where quotes such as those in the above paragraph appear, see McKay 2008, pp. 208–11.

65   See the important statement on Toronto radicalism in the 1890s in Homel 1980, pp. 7–32. For one accessible collection of writings by a Canadian socialist of this era that commented on unemployment and capitalist crisis, see McKay 1996, especially pp. 34–9, 47–52.

Changes in the lives of working-class people living in Toronto abounded. White-collar jobs expanded as the offices and financial institutions needed in the invigorated new economic environment grew. Work opportunities for women, who now had employment alternatives to domestic service and sweated work in the garment trades, increased significantly. But for all the change experienced by Toronto's expanding working class, the continuity in capitalism-as-crisis was perhaps most evident. Boom years were never long enough. Bust inevitably followed. Panics and acute depressions occurred in 1907–8, 1911–15, and again in the post-war climate of 1919–21. Wagelessness, for a time, became the lot of 'all but a relatively small number of wage earners'.[66]

The left perspective on capitalism, crisis, and unemployment may not have resonated that well in Toronto's boom years of expansion that followed on the heels of the final ending of the long, late nineteenth-century economic malaise. Samuel Gompers, patriarch of the conservative craft unions affiliated with the American Federation of Labor, received a rousing ovation from Toronto organised labour at an open-air rally in May 1900. His Hamilton delegate, John Flett, was quite successful in expanding the number of chartered locals of international unions in Canada, condemned by some employers as an 'invasion'. Claims were made that the Trades and Labor Congress of Canada had grown from a membership of 8,000 in 1900 to 100,000 in 1914, and much of this affiliation would have been in Gompers's international craft unions. These bodies, numbering only 16 in Toronto in the 1880s, totalled 106 in 1902. No other city came even close to rivalling this AFL presence. When the voice of the unemployed was heard early in the century it often spoke in the idiom of the rights of the skilled to be protected from competition in the labour market.[67]

In December of 1903 a 'meeting of the unemployed of the city of Toronto', undoubtedly spurred to action by the prospects of winter's oncoming layoffs, adopted a resolution deploring the misrepresentation of industrial conditions in Canada and the resulting 'encouragement of indiscriminate immigration'. By 1907–8, however, with the economy slowed to a snail's pace and the ranks of the out-of-work reaching crisis proportions, Toronto was forced to open a Civic Bureau to register the names of those in need of work in January 1908. Three thousand promptly signed up, with 300 fortunate enough to secure paid toil at snow removal. They received $2.00 daily for a maximum three day stint.

---

66   For an introduction to Toronto's economic transformation in these years and the condition of the working class, see Piva 1979. See as well Marsh 1933, pp. 134–5; and for women workers Marsh 1940, pp. 273–9.

67   Babcock 1974, pp. 44, 53; Palmer 1987a, p. 82; Goutor 2007.

The next December, winter again threatening, another Free Employment Bureau was opened. Within three months 5,500 jobless workers had registered. Working-class suburbs on the outskirts of Toronto, where labourers had purchased small plots and thrown up shacks, were said to be suffering for want of employment. As the usual means of offering relief to city residents was not available, the *Globe* started a subscription campaign to alleviate the distress of 'this class'. City of Toronto disbursements for the House of Industry's usual outdoor relief jumped from an average of around $10,000 annually in 1904–7 to over $26,000 in these depressed years of 1908–9. The carrot of relief, however, was never far distant from the stick. Coercions included the awful conditions prevailing in the House of Industry, the rigours of the 'labour test', and the threat of legal confinement if the poor refused to abide by the disciplinary rules. At the height of the 1908 economic crisis, 240 so-called tramps were being sheltered in Toronto's House of Industry, with 90 of them forced to sleep on concrete floors for lack of beds. Those who refused to 'crack the stone' for such accommodations faced the increased possibility of criminal charges and incarceration. Vagrancy arrests, never above 975 in any two-year period between 1901–6, ballooned to over 800 annually in 1908–10. In this climate, when the wageless were driven to destitution and marked out for a variety of coercions, the left critique of capitalist crisis undoubtedly registered more forcefully with Toronto's dispossessed.[68]

Organised protests reflected this. March 1908 saw 1,000 unemployed converge on Toronto's City Hall, demanding work. Rebuffed by the Mayor, who stated clearly that temporary employment would never be provided solely as a means of relief, the wageless retreated. Nine months later they were back in force, a contingent of socialists at their head. The Toronto wageless rebellion of January 1909 was led by well-known socialist agitators, Ernest Drury and Wilfred Gribble. More militant than their 1908 predecessors, 1,000 unemployed surrounded City Hall and spilled over into an adjacent street, blocking the road. Drury had barely begun to address the crowd when the police intervened, forcing the unemployed protest to reassemble in Bayside Park, a kilometre distant from the downtown core. Ankle-deep in mud, the wageless listened to a parade of revolutionaries, whose speeches scaled the heights of political denunciation of capitalism as well as addressing more immediate prosaic demands. There was talk of the forcible seizure of property to provide for the poor. But there

---

68   Robin 1968, p. 177; Piva 1979, pp. 69, 71–4; *Labour Gazette*, July 1903–June 1904; July 1907–
      June 1908; 'Toronto Free Employment Bureau', *Labour Gazette*, July 1908–June 1909; 'Need
      Not Hunger if They'll Work', Toronto *Daily Star*, 28 January 1908.

was also interest in building a sustained movement of the jobless. Whatever the subject, the politics of class grievance animated every word. Socialist Party of Canada soap-boxer Wilfred Gribble told the assembled that, 'It goes hard with me to have to stand here in three or four inches of mud when we want to hold a meeting. You men built these great buildings ... you built these railways, you built the big halls in this city, but when you want to meet you can't have one of them'. A petition was soon placed with the City's Board of Control, demanding a hall at which the unemployed could assemble.[69]

A few days later, the wageless again convened at City Hall, their mood described as 'dangerous'. Albert Hill climbed atop a wagon to address the large throng, which had once more spilled over into streets, prompting the police to disperse the gathering. He pointed out, as had Gribble earlier, that while the 'big guns and important people' were received warmly by civic officials, the unemployed could not find a place to meet. Making their way to Bayside Park, the body promptly appointed a committee of twelve to return to City Hall and demand access to St. Andrew's Hall as a place where the out-of-work could gather. Five hundred demonstrators trailed the delegation and, upon arrival at the seat of municipal power, swarmed the front and side entrances, seeking out the top-floor meeting rooms of the Board of Control. Told to depart by the police, the unemployed offered no resistance, but determined to return.[70]

As several hundreds of the unemployed milled about City Hall the next day, their movements watched closely by the police, Drury led a delegation into the building, where the Board of Control was addressed. It was beseeched to let out St. Andrew's Hall for regular meetings of the unemployed and to urge upon civic officials the necessity of providing the unemployed with work. The delegation was treated to gratuitous insults. Mayor Oliver remarked that Drury had led 'every unemployed deputation' that had crossed his threshold over the course of the last year and a half. As Drury detailed the great suffering experienced by the wageless, he was told by the Mayor that the House of Industry was always available to the destitute. One of the delegation heckled the city's chief civic official, referring to the beds in the refuge as 'bug traps'. Controller Geary demanded to know how many of the small delegation were socialists. Three of the contingent acknowledged that they were indeed advocates of a

---

69   *Globe*, 17 March 1908, cited in Piva 1979, p. 74; 'Hot Talk in Muddy Park. Orators of the Soap-Box Order Harangue a Crowd on the Waterfront. And Talk of Taking Forcible Possession of Contents of Warehouse', Toronto *Daily Star*, 5 January 1909.

70   'Ugly Temper of Idle Men. The Unemployed Gathered Swiftly this Morning into Army at City Hall. Blocked Street but Had to Move On', Toronto *Daily Star*, 13 January 1909.

radical overhaul of capitalist institutions. This unleashed a flurry of concern that St. Andrew's Hall would be used to 'preach a doctrine of discontent'. No doubt sensing that the municipal authorities cared less about the plight of the poor than they did about policing the politics of the wageless, Drury and his comrades withdrew. Accompanied by 30 watchful police, a large crowd of the unemployed made its way back to Bayside Park, now a traditional gathering place.[71]

Over the next few days the nascent unemployed movement enlisted the support of sympathetic reverends, preeminent among them Dr. G.S. Eby of the College Street People's Church, a.k.a., The Church of the Revolution. The travails of the outdoor relief system were now being complained about by religious figures, who questioned the long delays experienced by destitute families applying for emergency aid from the House of Industry. This, in turn, elicited criticisms from a Toronto alderman. Meanwhile, an organised group of 85 refused the 'labour test' at the Poor House two days running, in what was obviously a direct action protest, albeit one that left the single unemployed 'casuals' homeless in the dead of winter.[72] Having wrested from the Board of Control the right to meet at St. Andrew's Hall, over 1,000 unemployed gathered there on 21 January 1909 to hear a rousing social gospel address from the Reverend Dr. Eby. 'The day has come when men are tired of talking of hell and heaven', Eby thundered. 'There are multitudes of people in the churches who want to bring heaven to earth'. Drury proved more provocative in his speech. Urging the wageless to refuse both the symbolism and the substance of the discipline of 'cracking the stone', he railed against the quality of the House of Industry's provisions: 'I advise you men to go there', he told the wageless, 'not with the intention of breaking stone but of stealing a loaf of bread. I wouldn't give a pig the provisions I got there'.[73]

Out of this initial St. Andrew's Hall meeting came an extraordinary set of recommendations, quite unlike anything previously articulated by those seeking relief. Given what we know of the practices of the House of Industry, the

---

71   'To Get Work for Idle Men. Heard Deputation Today. The Speaker Dropped the Violent Tone When They Entered City Hall. A Large Force of Police on Hand to Guard Against Any Disturbance', Toronto *Daily Star*, 14 January 1909.

72   'Stuck a Pin in Ald. J.J. Graham', Toronto *Daily Star*, 18 January 1909.

73   'A Preacher to the Unemployed. Rev. Dr. Eby Roused the Crowd to Very High Pitch of Enthusiasm. Then Speaker Got Hot and Proceeded to Abuse the Civic Authorities in Angry Terms', Toronto *Daily Star*, 21 January 1909. On the social gospel see Allen 1973. McKay 2008, p. 472, refers to Eby's 1909 Church of the Revolution, noting its connection to the Social Democratic Party and the encouragement of early socialist feminism.

list of six demands generated out of the unemployed mobilisation of January 1909 stood as an unambiguous indictment of decades of Toronto's treatment of the dispossessed, governed as it was by routines of 'labour tests' and procedures of 'cleansing and classifying'. They also united the interests of the 'casual' single unemployed men who stayed overnight in the House of Industry, recipients of indoor relief, and those families who drew on the outdoor dispensations of the Poor House. The wageless, whatever their station, wanted the abolition of the civic relief department; the establishment of 'running baths' for workmen; daily fare composed of more than eleven-cent-a-day servings of adulterated soup and stale bread; provision of adequate and warmer clothing in winter; investigation of the bread depots so that there was monitoring of their activities and assurances that distressed families would not suffer; and, finally, and most strikingly, to take control of the distribution of charity out of the hands of the Associated Charities of Toronto and to vest it in the committee of the unemployed. Not yet ready to demand the abolition of 'cracking the stone', the socialist-led wageless had, in 1909, nonetheless mobilised their ranks, broadened their struggle, and crystallised a fundamental challenge to their dispossession.[74]

This rebellion of the dispossessed generated a predictable opposition, one that undoubtedly stifled the stirrings of the unemployed. Mayor Oliver made threatening noises to the effect that trouble-makers would be deported. A letter to the editor of the Toronto *Star* bemoaned the 'Brutal Treatment of the Unemployed', hinting at the way in which resistance to 'cracking the stone' had unleashed an ideological counterassault of property and propriety:

> Though this city claims to be so very religious, you have a savage way of treating poor fellows that have nowhere to go. The statement that some of the men refused to work has appeared in the whole Canadian press from the Atlantic to the Pacific. But nobody ever asked why such a large percentage of men refused to work. No, they are simply put down as lazy. Now, when a man goes to a place like the House of Industry, it is plain that he is half starved already. There he gets bread and some warm water called tea, at night, and in the morning. Most likely he will not get a bed the first three nights, but will sleep on a floor, with hardly any room to turn. When he gets up in the morning, after what little sleep he had been able to get, he is required to break a lot of stones. The quantity of stones to be broken will take a man used to it three hours, but a man not used

74   'A Preacher to the Unemployed', Toronto *Daily Star*, 15 February 1909.

to that kind of work will take from four to six hours. Six hours hard work for a bit of dry bread and a rest on the floor. And we sing 'Britons Never Shall be Slaves'. Let the people of Toronto reflect a little on the conditions in this city and cease casting slurs upon those who are for the time being in bad circumstances.

The letter, signed simply 'Out of Work', was a reflection of what the dispossessed were up against in their daily struggle to survive, as well as in their organised effort to resist.[75]

A year later, in February 1910, seven members of the non-stone-breaking brotherhood refused the House of Industry 'labour test' and found themselves before Magistrate Ellis, charged with vagrancy. Amidst growing speculative animosity to the workless flooding into Toronto from parts unknown, turning the city into an 'Eldorado of the tramp fraternity', the men became scapegoats in an age-old ideological assault on the 'undeserving poor'. The Superintendent of the House of Industry chastised the group refusing to 'crack the stone' as merely 'playing with the whole thing [labour test]', feigning indifference to 'even go in the yard to look at the pile of stone'. He saw in this workless crew proof that many 'casuals' seeking lodging at his institution 'spend their money in outside towns and then come back to Toronto in droves and expect to be kept'. Disgusted that one of the men, Alfred Lawson, 'wouldn't break eight ounces of stone in eight hours', the Poor House official urged the court to get tough on those who defied the 'labour test'. The Magistrate, unimpressed with the lot before him, decided to teach those indigents who opted for recalcitrance a lesson: he sentenced them to jail terms lasting from 30 days to three months, promising them 'a chance to do real work'. Meanwhile, the House of Industry, pleading economies, doubled the quantity of stone it required from all 'casuals' receiving bread, water, and a place to lay their heads.[76]

The criminalisation of the dispossessed proceeding apace, the crisis of worklessness deepened in 1911–12 and plummeted even further in a severe depression in 1913–14. By this latter date, the federal government estimated the ranks

75   'Brutal Treatment of the Unemployed', Toronto *Daily Star*, 15 February 1909.
76   'Vagrants Sent Where They'll Have to Work. House of Industry Too Easy for them and They go to Prison – Early', Toronto *Daily Star*, 8 February 1910; 'More Stone Breaking. Casuals at House of Industry Must Crack Double Quantity', Toronto *Daily Star*, 25 January 1910; 'Toronto a Mecca of Tired Tramps. Tramps Flock Here, and the Associated Charities Want Steps Taken to Keep them Working. Also Asks that Province Make a Grant to the House of Industry', Toronto *Daily Star*, 21 December 1910.

of the unemployed had swelled to 100,000 nationally. Toronto claimed 15,000 out-of-work in January of 1914 and 20,000 unemployed over the course of October 1914 to May 1915. The municipality's relief system sagged under the pressures of more and more applications for aid, with Superintendent Laughlen complaining that he 'had never before seen anything like it'. In the winter of 1914–15 more than 5,000 families, representing in excess of 25,000 people, were applying for relief to the beleaguered House of Industry. Long queues of men, 'two and three deep, lined up outside the ... building waiting for shelter for the night'. The usual recourse to a series of start-up/close-down Civic Employment Bureaus did little to ease the situation. Maladministered and overwhelmed by applications, such *ad hoc* agencies competed with corrupt private employment enterprises and managed, for the most part, only to secure temporary work, in limited amounts, for the growing army of the unemployed. Throughout the crisis, which one historian has termed a 'Canadian unemployed revolt' led by the Industrial Workers of the World in the west and the Social Democratic Party in Ontario, calls for 'able-bodied vagrants' to be 'made to work for their living until they have acquired the habit of self-support' continued to be heard. Ontario's Commission on Unemployment singled out Toronto as an example of the worst abuses:

> The vagrant thrives on Soup Kitchens, Houses of Industry, Salvation Army Shelters and similar institutions maintained for the purpose of rendering temporary assistance to a worthier class. The experience of Toronto in this respect is conclusive ... Men are coming into Toronto from the mining camps and smaller places, spending their money in drink, and complaining of not being able to get work. A lot of them don't want it and wouldn't take it if they had a chance. This class of men augment the already too numerous criminal class.

Decimating the trade unions, whose memberships in Ontario dropped 25 percent, and straining the disciplinary order of relief to breaking point, the crisis of 1913–14 left the waged and the wageless in the same sinking boat of capitalist crisis. In September 1914, 600 delegates to the Toronto Trades and Labour Council gathered in an effort to compile information on the unemployment crisis. They set up a committee system with captains appointed for each ward, tasked to assemble complete statistical returns on the dimensions of joblessness in the city. A labour-movement-funded Trades Industrial Toy Association was set up to give work to unemployed mechanics in the manufacture of children's playthings. Joseph T. Marks, his *Industrial Banner* something of a beachhead of Toronto trade-union labourite radicalism, spearheaded a 'Provincial Publicity Campaign on Unemployment', but his efforts apparently led to little. The situation for working women was particularly dire, and the Women's Patriotic League urged 'girls, whether office clerks or factory hands, or in whatever position held previously, to accept what can be secured for them to tide themselves over this period'. A single advertisement for a stenographer elicited 500 applications. For the first time in living memory, the demand for domestic servants exceeded the supply, and many women were driven to accept 'situations in the country, glad to be able to rely thereby upon board and lodging at least'. Contemporary claims were made that the unemployment crisis of 1913–14 was the most severe in the history of the Dominion of Canada, with routine reports in the *Labour Gazette* detailing the worsening conditions in Toronto.[77]

Toronto's wageless thus faced an uphill battle in the crisis of 1911–15. Many refused the labour discipline of 'cracking the stone', expressing preference that they be jailed rather than subjected to the 'labour test'. When William Brothers, an elderly homeless man, was brought before Magistrate Denison on vagrancy charges in December 1912 and admonished to go to the House of Industry, he replied with conviction that, 'I'd lay down on the street and die' before checking himself into the Poor House. 'The jail's the place for me'. The Magistrate accommodated his wish, sentencing Brothers to four months. In February 1915 'casuals' spending nights in the wayfarer's lodge ward of the House of Industry were again refusing to break stone for their keep. George Bust and Nick Melasel were charged with vagrancy for their insubordinate behaviour. Courtroom dialogue reveals a defiance bred in the realisation of the unemployed that the inequalities of the class system produced counterposed interests in the midst of capitalist crisis, a sensibility that was being promoted among the wageless by socialist soap-boxers and organisers.

Constable McBurney stated in prosecution that Bust had been getting his meals free at the House of Industry and had refused to work for them – that is, crack stone.

'That's correct', said Bust with defiant air.
'Oh, I see, you are one of those who has come to the conclusion that
    somebody has to support you', said Squire Ellis.

---

77 Piva 1979, pp. 75–86 presents a good summary of the Toronto situation, and provides the quote from Ontario Commission on Unemployment 1916, pp. 77–8, 201–2. Note as well McKay 2008, p. 209; Naylor 1991, pp. 18–19, 80; Baskerville and Sager 1998, pp. 176–84; *Labour Gazette*, July 1914 to June 1915; House of Industry 1921, pp. 7, 10; Abella and Millar 1978, pp. 73–6; Struthers 1983, pp. 12–16; Stewart 1923, pp. 286–93.

'Oh yes', said Bust, who had a sullen expression on his face.
'Did you refuse to crack stone for your meals'?
'Yes, and there's lots like me'.
'And do you sleep at the police stations'?
'Yes, with a hundred others', replied Bust.
'Have you hunted for work'?
'I certainly have'.
'Yet you refused to work for your food'? continued the Squire.
'That's one way of looking at it – your way' said Bust.

Stands of combativeness before constituted authority had a way of being repaid in kind. 'Well, I think you need looking after', concluded his Worship Squire Ellis, 'it'll be $20 and costs or 90 days'. Other shelters, too, faced similar resistance to the 'labour test'. At the Fred Victor Mission, which housed upwards of seventy homeless people a night, the unemployed organised a protest against what they considered 'unfair practice'. The Mission was of the view that the agitation was the work of socialists.[78]

World War I ended the particular 1911–15 capitalist crisis. Wartime production eased wagelessness. This happened, for the most part, in the aftermath of military enlistment, be it coerced or voluntary. Roughly 600,000 served in the Canadian Expeditionary Force, with 250,000 joining between June 1915 and May 1916. The pressures put on the relief order both by the sheer numbers of unemployed requiring assistance and the increasing and challenging activism of resistance to 'cracking the stone', often orchestrated by left agitators, lessened. One measure of this is revealed in the statistics of the poor's utilisation of police jail cells as lodging. In 1915, the Toronto reports indicated that over 10,500 people had been sheltered at various police stations across the city. One year later, in 1916, with the war drive and its recruitment campaigns in full swing, less than 375 had availed themselves of jail beds. The Canadian Patriotic Fund, privately financed and administered, provided the families of unemployed men who enlisted a 'reasonable standard of comfort', and tens of thousands of single men joined the armed forces to extricate themselves from wagelessness. Around 60,000 families benefited from the Patriotic Fund's

---

78   'Preferred the Jail to Any Other Place. Aged Vagrant Insisted on Being Sent Across the Don, and He was Obliged', Toronto *Daily Star*, 18 December 1912; 'Refused to Work, But Took Meals – Jailed. George Bust was Defiant in Police Court – Received a Lesson. Couldn't Find Work. Wouldn't Crack Stone at the House of Industry for His Breakfast', Toronto *Daily Star*, 5 February 1915; Fagan 1993, p. 62.

largesse, which totalled almost $40 million in the 1914–19 years. The unemployed had been vanquished, as it were, as capitalism found something of a resolution to its economic and political crises in the breakout of hostilities in Europe. Defiant resistance was difficult to mount in these circumstances, especially as inducements to patriotic duty were everywhere and often overrode understandings of the class solidarities of the waged and the wageless. In a January 1915 fundraising entertainment at Massey Hall, organised by the Toronto District Labor Council on behalf of the unemployed, the message of the necessity of fighting against wagelessness was drowned out in dutiful renditions of 'The Death of Nelson' and 'We'll Never Let the Old Flag Down', the evening being capped off by a recitation of 'The Empire Flag', the address delivered by a speaker wrapped in the Union Jack.[79] No black flags flew at this unemployed rally.

War mobilised the state to harness the productive enterprise and energy of the nation, refining a new apparatus of the regulatory state, and in doing so it galvanised initiatives in monitoring and addressing unemployment. By the war's end, amidst the winding down of specialised industrial pursuits and the return of jobless veterans, it was feared that unemployment would swell to 250,000 in 1918 alone. Labour, having tasted the possibilities of full employment during wartime, providing waged and wageless to the battlefront lines, both domestically and in the European theatre, was in a combative mood. Tensions were exacerbated by a growing left-wing presence in the unions and among the unorganised and unwaged working class, where talk of the Revolution in Soviet Russia and ideas of production for use not for profit were common. Coalition government leader, Sir Robert Borden, was warned by one high-ranking advisor in 1918: 'People are not ... in a normal condition. There is less respect for law and authority than we probably have ever had in the country. If ... Canada faces acute conditions of unemployment without any adequate programme to meet the situation, no one can foresee just what might happen'. Setting up the Employment Service of Canada, a national network of labour exchanges funded and run by the joint efforts of provincial and federal governments, was one component of the state response. Unemployment insurance systems were studied, and drew a surprisingly strong consensus of favourable opinion among government officials, mainstream trade-union leaders, and progressive employers. But the political will to implement such a system evaporated in the Red Scare climate of 1919. Clamping down on working-class militancy,

---

79   *Toronto Police Report, 1915*, p. 20; *Toronto Police Report, 1916*, p. 20; Morris n.d., pp. 23, 271,
     cited in Struthers 1983, p. 14; Morton and Wright 1987, pp. ix, 24; Naylor 1991, p. 23.

suppressing a 1919 General Strike wave, deporting 'alien' radicals, and using state trials of socialist agitators to establish decisively that the red flag, Soviets, and workers' control of production would not become part of the Canadian way of life trumped a forceful state programme that would decisively address unemployment in new ways.[80]

Toronto contributed more recruits to the war effort than any other city. It would see the return of more soldiers, all of them looking for work, as well. No city, however, had been harder hit than Toronto in the closure of the wartime munitions industries. Amidst the labour revolt of 1919, there was a push, not only for sympathetic and general strikes, but for a cash bonus to be paid to World War I veterans. One commentator described the proposed $2,000 gratuity as 'one grand solution for virtually all the troubles due to unrest, unemployment, discontent and Bolshevism'. Many Toronto veterans agreed, and rallied at Queen's Park where they were treated to a rabble-rousing speech from J. Harry Flynn, an opportunistic demagogue who quickly established himself as a leading voice of the returned soldiers. 'Let us put a peaceful demand', shouted Flynn about the bonus, 'and if it is not answered, I say let us take it by force'. There was, however, to be no bonus granted, or seized, in 1919. Instead, out-of-work veterans were advised to head to the hinterland. A 'Back to the Land' movement, said many employers and not a few farmers, would allow rural producers to 'get labour more cheaply'. At this the Toronto Great War Veteran's Association took considerable umbrage, arguing that those who had served overseas for four years had not been separated from loved ones and served their country only to be told they could 'take employment mucking in the bush', far from the family hearth.[81] Toronto-headquartered Frontier College put a novel spin on the idea that movement to the country could alleviate unemployment, suggesting that municipalities purchase homesteads and employ the jobless in clearing 160 acres and building a house and barn on each improved lot, which could then be sold for a profit.[82]

The crisis of wagelessness that afflicted veterans and non-soldiers alike deepened until, in the autumn of 1920, the economy took another turn for the worse, plunging into depression. Toronto employers reduced working time

---

80   Struthers 1983, pp. 14–27; Ontario Commission on Unemployment 1916; Sauter 1980, pp. 89–112; Morton and Wright 1987, p. 108. On the climate of this era see Kealey 1984, pp. 11–44; McKay 2008, pp. 417–530; Kramer and Mitchell 2010; and Heron 1998.

81   Morton and Wright 1987, pp. 124–9; Struthers 1983, p. 28.

82   'Work of the Frontier College: Proposal for Reduction of Unemployment', *Labour Gazette*, 1921.

in order not to have to effect mass layoffs, but such band-aid solutions only covered the wound of wagelessness incompletely and for limited periods of time. Veterans who had managed to secure work now lost their jobs, with estimates being that one in five able-bodied ex-soldiers were forced into wagelessness with the new depression. As national unemployment rates climbed to over ten percent, encompassing 214,000 jobless individuals, the situation in Toronto taxed the public employment bureaus to the breaking point. Over the winter of 1919–20 these bodies, which favoured the returned soldier, managed to secure employment for 70 percent of all applicants, but in 1920–1 that figure dropped to 58 percent. More than 3,000 of those registered with the Bureaus were 'unplaced' and at the height of the crisis that number skyrocketed to 15,000. Federal payments to the municipality of Toronto for the emergency relief of the unemployed over the course of December 1920 to April 1921 totalled $134,128, or almost forty percent of the total distributed across the country. Toronto police cells, a home to so many destitute in 1915, but largely empty of these patrons in 1916, began to fill again. By 1925, a record 16,500 people were housed in city jails, many of them ex-servicemen who had joined the army of the unemployed.[83]

At the Toronto House of Industry the litany of complaints and registers of inadequacy rose. The poor and unemployed insisted that the outdoor relief doled out to the destitute was woefully insufficient. Social workers claimed that families dependent on assistance were slowly starving. Civic support to the Poor House was challenged as too meagre to begin to address the nature of the unemployment crisis. A nurse who regularly visited homes of the Toronto indigent saw children going hungry. She concluded that it was 'impossible for human beings to live at all on what the city supplies'. The plight of the workless, claimed these critics, was reminiscent of the 'Dark Ages'.[84] Such charges and allegations were met with the usual arsenal of denial. Officially constituted and often church-affiliated Neighbourhood Workers' Associations and the superintendent at the House of Industry continued age-old claims that, 'Everyone should know that no man needs to sleep in the parks or walk the streets in Toronto. There is shelter for him. When we encourage begging on

83   G.D. Robertson to Walter Rollo, 15 December 1921, in *Labour Gazette*, 1921; Morton and Wright 1987, p. 142; Struthers 1983, p. 29; Piva 1979, pp. 83–4; 'Emergency Relief for Unemployed in Canada', *Labour Gazette*, 1921; *Toronto Police Report, 1925*, p. 24; Marsh 1940, pp. 257–70.

84   'Can't Keep Wolf From Door with Does from City. Families Would Starve If They Had to Depend on Civic Help Alone. Tales of Sufferers. Work of Other Institutions Hampered by Parsimony of the City', Toronto *Daily Star*, 27 August 1921.

the street – which is against the law in the first place – you are encouraging something at the same time that is most deadly for the man'.[85]

When frustrated jobless veterans sought relief in paying overdue rent, they found themselves 'chasing around from one place to another ... for ... three weeks', unable to find any agency to lend them a hand. Fearing evictions and seeking only loans which they committed to pay back, the ex-servicemen formed a delegation and went to City Hall to seek out Mayor Maguire. Finance Commissioner Ross curtly dismissed the group. 'Anybody who thinks that we are going to liquidate his arrears of rent is in error'. The former soldiers who decided to organise a Toronto-to-Ottawa trek in protest against inaction on unemployment fared no better. They hoofed it 220 miles to the nation's capital, only to be sent back empty-handed on the train.[86] Liberal reformers like Bryce Stewart looked disdainfully on the tendencies of those in power to pass the buck of unemployment to the next generation. 'If we wait long enough', he wrote in 1921, 'the bread lines and out-of-work doles will cease, unemployment will be gone, men and women will rise out of dull inaction and find joy again in the work of head and hands'. Then, all would be forgotten: 'The present time will be referred to as the "hard times of 1920–1921" an unfortunate experience to be forgotten if possible'. But Bryce had seen it all before, having written on the 1913–15 crisis, and he was convinced that 'the divine right of unpreparedness' was not going to stave off the next, inevitable downturn: 'Men will pursue their usual ways and in 1925, or 26 or 27 or some other year, the dark ogre of unemployment will again thrust his long arm into the factories and mines and shops and offices, tear the workers from their tasks, bank the fires, hang out the "No Help Wanted" signs and shut the doors against them'.[87]

Even as the economy resuscitated somewhat in the years after 1921, the 1920s hardly saw unemployment extinguished. Between 1922 and 1929, the annual average unemployment rate was 11 percent, and 30 percent of all workers found themselves wageless at some point in the year, usually for around eighteen weeks.[88] Ex-servicemen remained central to the ongoing crisis of the Toronto

85   'No Man Needs to Beg on Streets Though Destitute in Toronto. Your Response to Appeal of Furtive Individuals is Likely to be Tribute to Professional "Pan-Handler"', Toronto *Daily Star*, 14 January 1922.

86   'Where to Get Relief. Many Still in Doubt', Toronto *Daily Star*, 7 February 1922; *Report of the Commissioner of the Ontario Provincial Police, 1922* in *Ontario Sessional Papers*, 84 (1923), pp. 29–31, cited in Morton and Wright 1987, p. 142.

87   Bryce Stewart, 'The Problem of Unemployment', *Social Welfare*, March 1921 quoted in Struthers 1983, p. 43.

88   Struthers 1983, p. 4.

dispossessed well into the mid-1920s. By 1925 the presence of beggars on city streets and the ongoing influx of the wageless into Toronto from other municipalities precipitated yet another round of ideological and material attacks on the poor. Toronto's chief-medical-officer, Dr. Charles Hastings, campaigned to rid the city of beggars, whom he considered a variant of the age-old 'undeserving poor'. Known as an aggressive advocate of improved public health and an enemy of slum conditions, Hastings was also capable of sounding the tocsin of vigilance against the vagrants. He suggested that Toronto civic officials publicise 'through the local papers and the Canadian press generally' their intention next winter to terminate 'relief to non-residents, or anyone unable to prove their residence, and that, in addition to this, citizens of Toronto be urged not to give promiscuously to men soliciting help at private houses, or to those accosting individuals on the streets, but that they be asked to refer all such persons to the House of Industry, where their case can be properly investigated and where those deserving will receive the necessary food and shelter'. Hastings's harangue occurred at a time when one George Hamilton, of a government employment bureau, noted that every day between 1,500 and 2,500 men were applying for jobs of any kind. For every 100 of them there was work for one of their number. Malnutrition and exposure incapacitated many of those seeking labour, 75 percent of whom, according to one representative of the unemployed, Frank Fleming, were veterans.

Moderate in his views, Fleming still stressed that for all its efforts to relieve the poor, the House of Industry was not able to keep up with the rising pressures on its resources. Hundreds of the unemployed spent their nights huddled in 'cold box cars and [on] cement floors', experiencing anything but the pampered existence of the indulged indigent. If there was indeed unrest among these poor folk, Fleming suggested, it was the work of 'Reds' and 'Communists', who were prodding the army of the unemployed to vocalise its discontents and mobilise its ranks.[89]

The red flag had apparently been unfurled among the wageless. The Workers Party of Canada, born amidst the post-World War I downturn, had from its inception been active in forming what James Naylor refers to as 'large and militant' Unemployed Associations in Toronto and Hamilton. Capitalism was assailed as the cause of the crisis of wagelessness, and among these advocates

---

89   On Hastings, see Piva's repeated accounts of his aggressiveness as a public health official in Piva 1979; 'Is Appointed to Study Single Man's Problem. Dr. Hastings Also Warns Non-Residents Not to Expect Aid During Winter', Toronto *Daily Star*, 17 September 1925; 'Women Pledge to Help Unemployed Men', Toronto *Daily Star*, 3 February 1925.

of a Soviet Canada the demand among the jobless was for 'work or full maintenance'. Communists considered unemployment central to the class struggle,
on a par with wage reductions and the open shop as an issue around which
revolutionaries organised and cultivated resistance. 'Moscow Jack' MacDonald, a Toronto patternmaker who would emerge in the 1920s as one of Canadian communism's mass leaders, toured the country in the hard winter of 1921,
speaking to fellow militants on the scourge of unemployment. Nonetheless, the
communist presence in Canadian working-class circles, be they of the waged or
wageless kind, was weak. It was always subject to the red-baiting of the mainstream press as well as employers, not to mention a contingent of died-in-the-
wool reactionaries ensconced in the most conservative echelons of trade-union
officialdom. Since 1919, this layer of the labour bureaucracy had taken direct
aim at revolutionaries in the workers' movement.

Two Toronto District Labor Council figures, W.J. Hevey and Arthur O'Leary,
launched the *Labor Leader* as the Winnipeg General Strike was winding to a
close. The paper, cuddling up to employers and screaming from its masthead
fierce opposition to IWWism, One Big Unionism, and Bolshevism, was a strident
voice of anti-communism and a proponent of the most entrepreneurial wing
of business unionism. The wageless found little in the way of support within
its pages. Repudiated by organised labour because of its ideas and its paymas-
ters, large corporations who footed the bill for its publication, the *Labor Leader*
nonetheless survived into the mid-1920s. It denounced Toronto's communists
as servants of Moscow masters, suggesting that Russian Reds were not above
threatening good and godly churchgoers with death. As the economic downturn of the early 1920s sapped the strength of the waged and threw more and
more of the wageless into the trough of material despondency, conservative
tendencies could be discerned within the Toronto dispossessed. Tim Buck, a
Toronto machinist and perennial communist candidate for the presidency of
the Trades and Labor Congress of Canada, polled 25 percent of the delegates at
the 1923–4 annual convention. Thereafter it was downhill, and as the capitalist
crisis of the early 1920s passed into the complacency of 1925–6, the workless,
their numbers declining, had a brief reprieve. The red flag, flying listlessly over
the thinning ranks of the unemployed, readied itself for the next downturn. It
would not be long in coming. In the next offensive of the outcasts, the reception
of this red flag, prepared in the 1900–25 years, was unprecedented.[90]

---

90   Naylor 1991, pp. 118–21, 248; Rodney 1968, pp. 47–8; Palmer 1992, p. 227. On early Canadian
      communism see Angus 2004.

Conclusion: The Outcasts' Offensive

The tradition of the oppressed teaches us that the 'state of emergency' in
which we live is not the exception but the rule.

WALTER BENJAMIN, 'Theses on the Philosophy of History' (1940)

As we enter the 1930s, the obscure history of the wageless and resistance that
we have outlined above becomes more familiar. Study of the crisis of unemployment in Canada in the Great Depression is a staple of modern historiography.
There are excellent, deeply researched monographic accounts and proliferating journal articles on the state and provisioning for the jobless, work camps
and their discontents, and the organisation of the unemployed, including much
discussion on major events such as the On-To-Ottawa trek, a protest march that
culminated in a police attack on wageless demonstrators in Regina in 1933.[91]
Document collections on the 'dirty thirties' provide powerful and provocative
evidence of the depth of resentment and anger that engulfed the jobless in
the precipitous economic collapse of 1929–35.[92] Popular historians like William
Gray, Barry Broadfoot and Pierre Berton have written widely-read accounts that
explore the Great Depression as a crisis of unemployment.[93] Novelist Irene
Baird captured something of the west coast plight of single unemployed men,
but did so with the traditional sense that their oppression bore no relation to
the comfortable privileges of the waged.[94] And recent unpublished work by
scholars such as Todd McCallum and Marcus Klee builds on this past research
and writing to craft imaginative perspectives on the working and the workless that place in a new light the always evolving relations and reciprocities
of waged and wageless life.[95]

The wageless, then, get some of their due in treatments of the single decade
in Canadian history that is most readily associated with an undeniable crisis

---

91   Struthers 1983; Lefresne 1962; Howard 1973; Liversedge 1973; Brown 1987; Waiser 2003.

92   Horn 1972; Grayson and Bliss 1971.

93   Gray 1966; Broadfoot 1975; Berton 1990.

94   Baird 1974.

95   McCallum 2004, and other works cited above; Klee 1998; 2000. Klee's work is notable in
      focusing on Toronto, which has received surprisingly little attention. Note that in Horn
      1972, the representation of the Depression follows a classic contour – dating it from the
      stock market crash of October 1929 – and accents the significance of Canadian staple
      resource production in the west. This necessarily leaves important centres of manufac-
      turing and urban concentrations of the working class marginalised in the study of the
      economic collapse and its human dimensions.

of capitalism and its human costs in terms of unemployment. It is not hard to understand why. By February 1930 the numbers of unemployed in Canada were estimated to be 323,000, with the rate of joblessness at 12.5 percent and climbing. Sixteen months later, in June 1931, 435,000 of Canada's 2.5 million wage earners were unemployed, or roughly seventeen percent. That rate soared to 25 percent by February 1932, and then crossed the incredible 30 percent threshold in 1933. Dominion Bureau of Statistics estimates were that between 600,000 and 700,000 Canadians were unemployed in 1932, and a year later that number had grown to 876,000. The percentage of the unemployed among trade unionists rose each year from 1929–32, more than tripling to 22 percent. Almost a million-and-a-half people were on relief. There was no denying the dimensions of the crisis.[96]

The problems posed by wagelessness were neither obscure nor unrecognised. H.M. Cassidy and the Unemployment Relief Committee of Ontario summarised what many mainstream commentators considered to be the contours of a deteriorating socioeconomic order:

> Unemployment has also interfered with the normal mode of life of the unemployed in a dozen and one other ways. It has made for fewer marriages and fewer births, and probably for a greater proportion of illegitimate births; for a greater number of suicides; for wives working and husbands staying at home; for discontent, unrest, and the development of bad habits among boys and girls of the school-leaving age; for overcrowding in the home; for family friction and disagreement; and for an increased number of deportations and the consequent disruption of the plans and aspirations of immigrant groups. It has induced attitudes of discontent, unrest and suspicion of established institutions in many people. The fact of drawing relief over long periods bids fair to develop in many an attitude of dependency. The effects of unemployment upon the unemployed and their families must be to make of them poorer citizens and poorer workers. Our most precious asset, the good quality of our population, is threatened with serious deterioration if unemployment continues.[97]

---

96 Struthers 1983, pp. 12–103 presents an excellent summary of the dimensions of the unemployment crisis in the early 1930s, but for a usefully concentrated contemporary account, on which we also draw, see Whiteley 1934, pp. 110–26. Note as well the excellent discussion and compilation of data in Cassidy 1932; and the national overview in Marsh 1940.

97 Cassidy 1932, p. 274. For an explicitly anti-socialist discussion of unemployment that continued to stress the importance of ex-servicemen, see Gilman and Sinclair 1935.

Yet, as federal, provincial, and municipal governments toyed with reforms and new initiatives in their ostensible efforts to address the catastrophic impact of rampant worklessness, little was accomplished. Liberal Prime Minister William Lyon Mackenzie King, who recognised in 1919 that 'the fear of unemployment' lay at the root of much of the discontent among working people, reduced the plight of the out of work to infighting among politicians in 1929. He considered municipal and provincial pleas for federal aid to buttress their relief efforts as little more than a Tory raid on the Liberal government's budget surplus, which the incumbent Prime Minister wanted to use to good effect in the forthcoming election. When it came to giving any sitting Conservative government funds 'for these alleged unemployment purposes', King told the House of Commons in April 1930, 'I would not give them a five-cent piece'.[98] King's replacement as leader of the country, the Tory R.B. Bennett, assumed the office of Prime Minister in 1930. He acknowledged that the economy had bottomed out, but deplored, in 1931, that 'people are not bearing their share of the load'. The unemployed, Bennett complained, would not 'work their way out of their difficulties'. Rather, they chose to 'look to a government to take care of them'. Himself a rich man, Bennett espoused an ideology of individualistic self-help: 'the fibre of some of our people has grown softer and they are not willing to turn in and save themselves. They now complain because they have no money'.[99] Eventually prodded to do more than King in terms of alleviating distress and destitution, Bennett's main concern seemed to be to thwart the communists, who powerful correspondents across the country advised him were an imminent threat. British Columbia's premier, S.F. Tolmie, warned Bennett's Minister of Labour, Gideon Robertson, in 1931 that, 'The unemployment situation is becoming daily more acute and with communistic agitation it is a much more serious question ... The Reds in Vancouver are already talking about revolution'. Indeed the Communist Party of Canada and its Workers Unity League were organising a nationwide campaign for a non-contributory unemployment insurance programme, which would fund a minimum level of relief for all Canadians by appropriating funds from defence spending and upping taxation on all incomes over $5,000 a year. Following a national day of protest against unemployment, Bennett received a petition signed by almost 100,000 Canadians.[100]

---

98   Quoted in Struthers 1983, p. 42.

99   Bennett correspondence quoted in Grayson and Bliss 1971, p. xx.

100   Struthers 1983, p. 52; and for similar warnings see Horn 1972, pp. 320–2. For Communists and the unemployed see as well Manley 1998, pp. 466–91.

This was the background to a memorable suggestion, made in an address at Toronto's tony Royal York Hotel, earning the millionaire Tory Prime Minister his scornful nickname, 'Iron Heel' Bennett:

> What do they offer you in exchange for the present order? Socialism, Communism, dictatorship. They are sowing the seeds of unrest everywhere. Right in this city such propaganda is being carried on and in the little out of the way places as well. And we know that throughout Canada this propaganda is being put forward by organizations from foreign lands that seek to destroy our institutions. And we ask every man and woman in this country to put the iron heel of ruthlessness against a thing of that kind.[101]

Bennett, however, was behind the times. Toronto civic authority, especially Police Chief Draper's 'Red Squad', had been practising what Bennett preached for some time.

The ostensible prosperity of the late 1920s masked the extent to which unemployment returned each winter with a vengeance. Thus, over the course of January–April 1929, well before the stock market crash that for many signalled the arrival of the Great Depression, the out-of-work numbered between 263,000 and 290,000. These official figures of joblessness plummeted in summer months, to as low as 39,000, before rising again in the autumn. By 1930, however, seasonal abatements in unemployment had lessened considerably, and by 1932 the numbers of jobless simply increased month-by-month regardless of the weather. There were approximately 50,000 more Canadians unemployed in June 1932 than there had been the previous January.[102]

Toronto followed these trends. In June 1931, of 242,000 wage earners in the city, fully 40,500 were not working. From August to November of 1931, 36,550 unemployed men registered with the Toronto Central Bureau of Employment Relief, 16,664 of them single and 19,886 of them married with dependents. A large number of these men were returned soldiers, 60 percent could be classified as unskilled or semi-skilled, and one-third of the wageless were natives of Canada. Among the significant number of immigrants who were without work, roughly half had been in the country less than five years, and were thus liable to be deported should they become recipients of public relief. Virtually none of the workless had any tangible property, such as real estate or automo-

---

101   Toronto *Mail and Empire*, 10 November 1932, quoted in Penner 1988, p. 117.
102   Cassidy 1932, pp. 17–51 presents a wealth of figures on the dimensions of unemployment and dependency.

biles, and only 4.4 percent could claim to have a bank account. Many were of course forced to turn to institutions of relief, such as the House of Industry, which saw the number of Toronto families drawing from its resources increase from 3,470 in 1929 to over 20,000 in 1932. The 63,000 Torontonians drawing relief in January 1932 constituted roughly ten percent of the population of 631,207. In specific working-class suburbs, like East York, the crisis of unemployment hit even harder, with residents on assistance surpassing 45 percent in February 1935. Toronto, with roughly eight percent of the nation's population, accounted for almost one-fifth of the country's relief bill.[103]

The Communist Party of Canada stepped into this capitalist crisis with a vengeance, and was met, almost immediately, with ruthless repression. Well before the economic downturn was recognised, communist open air meetings were precipitously attacked by the police, and leaders like Jack MacDonald brutally beaten. Part of the reason the civic 'Red Squad' moved with such viciousness to crush communist 'free speech' rallies was the fear that the wageless would be drawn to the politics of the red flag. 'In Toronto, the capital of the province, [the communists] are endeavouring in every way to spread their evil doctrines', declared Police Commissioner Judge Coatsworth in defence of the actions of the cops in savagely dispersing a 13 August 1929 evening gathering of 5,000 at Queen's Park, in which the crowd was anticipating speeches from known Communist Party of Canada members. With even local newspapers suggesting that the police had acted with unnecessary and illegal violence, and the Mayor of Toronto calling for charges to be laid against the offending officers, Coatsworth explained that the revolutionary element needed to be kept in check because 'at a time of unemployment they become dangerous'.[104]

Indeed, in the years to come, communists, as well as a range of other revolutionaries and radicals, among them Trotskyists, social democrats affiliated with the newly-established Co-operative Commonwealth Federation, socialists and labourites of various stripes, and anarchists, would agitate among the unemployed.[105] Organisations would be formed, demands posed, demonstrations

---

103   Cassidy 1932, especially pp. 35–44; Lemon 1985, p. 62; Schulz 1975, especially pp. 5–8.
104   'Chief Draper's Stand in Quelling Reds Here is Upheld by Mayor. Insists, However, Policemen Responsible for Brutality Must be Disciplined', Toronto *Daily Star*, 14 August 1929; 'Mayor Insists Police Must be Disciplined. Toronto Police Use Fists, Feet and Batons to Clear Queen's Park', Toronto *Daily Star*, 14 August 1929; 'Bolshevism Must Go Asserts Coatsworth in Supporting Draper', Toronto *Daily Star*, 15 August 1929.
105   For only a sampling of evidence see Workers Educational League, *Unemployment – wage reductions – the open shop* (Toronto 1930), 2pp broadside; and for unstudied Trotskyist

and marches planned and carried out, evictions resisted, and police battled. A new militancy breathed life and vibrancy into the often enervating experience of dispossession. A Toronto demonstration of several thousand jobless in March 1930 foreshadowed developments of the next decade. Gathering a few blocks from the House of Industry, the group carried banners and were headed by Communist Party of Canada secretary, Tom McEwen. Marching to City Hall, the unemployed protest was monitored by police forces; the gendarmes quickly moved in when McEwen climbed up the municipal building's steps to address the protesters. Before he could get more than a few words out of his mouth, McEwen was arrested and the police, some on horseback and some on foot, began dispersing the crowd. Many of the wageless resisted. Fights between the unemployed and the cops broke out as the demonstrators were pushed away from City Hall and herded down Bay Street. One woman and ten men were eventually taken into police custody. In the days to come the demands of the wageless surfaced as delegations of the unemployed, subjected to heavy police surveillance and intimidation, waited on the Toronto Board of Control. The out-of-work demanded jobs at trade-union wages; relief paid in cash rather than dispensed in charitable 'gifts' of food and fuel; the abolition of all work tests; a reduction in the hours of the waged; and unemployed representatives on all relief committees in the city. A new day in the history of the wageless, their sense of themselves, and their understanding of what they needed and deserved, had dawned.[106]

There were of course those who wanted to preserve the old days of charitable relief, dispensed only grudgingly to those who could establish their deservedness. Communists and other radicals were the new 'undeserving'. One of the unemployed delegation presenting the demands of the wageless at Toronto's City Hall was Harvey Jackson, a 25-year-old member of the Communist Party. Jackson, whom a poverty inspector working with the police had previously singled out with a benign offer of waged employment, had not reported for his labour assignation. He was promptly arrested and charged with vagrancy after

---

agitation among the unemployed, 'Unemployment Crisis Does not Slacken', *The Vanguard*, November–December 1932; 'Unemployed Organize!', *The Vanguard*, December 1934; 'R.B. Bennett's New Deal to Dupe the Masses', *The Vanguard*, February 1935; 'Figures Show Plight of Canadian Workers: Employed and Jobless Suffer Alike', *The Vanguard*, 17 December 1935; 'Unemployed Strike in Toronto's Suburb', *The Vanguard*, July 1936; Schulz 1975.

106   '"Red Thursday" in Toronto Proves a Fiasco. Police Disperse Mob as "Red" Agitators Obey Moscow Order. Communists Whisked into City Hall After Leaders Attempt to Spout Doctrines – Kicking Shins Chief Method of Attack. Eleven Arrested At Disturbance', Toronto *Daily Star*, 7 March 1930.

the Board of Control meeting. A popular organiser with the National Unemployed Workers' Association, Jackson 'frequented labour bureaus, missions, and flop-houses looking for recruits', flying the red flag in his wageless labours among the jobless. To the Toronto police, however, Jackson was simply 'one of those ungrateful people who lived off the church mission charity and then complained that they did not get proper food'. Jackson found himself sentenced to 60 days 'hard labour'. To add insult to injury, he got a dressing down from the magistrate, who declared Jackson 'just the type who should go to Burwash', an Industrial Farm/Correctional Prison south of Sudbury in northern Ontario where inmates were given a taste of work discipline. The judge was anything but impressed with Jackson: 'Looking for work and praying he does not find it. Just a lazy loafer of the worst kind. The police treated this man with every consideration – even got him a job – and then he fails to come back to get it. Then the next day the police find him as one of the agitators right here in City Hall'. Jackson's work for the wageless was put on hold.[107]

The sheer numbers of the unemployed, obviously present at their own making in ways that were finally registering in the political, social, and economic spheres of civic society, opens a new chapter in the history of wagelessness in Canada. As the 1930s unfolded, and more and more Canadians found themselves jobless, it became difficult to sustain the ideological typecasting that had long relied on social constructions like 'the undeserving poor'. There is of course no doubt that the particularities and depth of the capitalist crisis of the Great Depression had much to do with this. Nevertheless the new, and extreme, circumstances of the 1930s did indeed unfold against the backdrop of a century of developments associated with wagelessness, including the long history of the dispossessed, which encompassed dissident ideas symbolised by flags of black and red, and acts of refusal both individual and collective. Toronto figured forcefully in this development, as a rich history of wageless activism and agency reveals.[108]

Before this outcasts' offensive, however, lay decades of a developing history of the Toronto dispossessed, inseparable from the equally long history of capitalist crises. 'Cracking the stone' seems an appropriate title for an account of this

---

107 'Say City's Relief Scale is Totally Inadequate. Unemployed Ask for Increased Allowance, Declaring they are Undernourished. Police Stand on Guard', Toronto *Daily Star*, 12 March 1930; Betcherman 1982, pp. 109–10.

108 For all the excellent work that has been done on communists, the left, and the unemployed in Canada in the 1930s (see Manley 1998 as but one important example), the particularities of the Toronto campaigns of the workless remain to be explored. We are engaged in that project, which represents a continuation of this paper.

exploration into wagelessness in Toronto in the 1830–1930 years. First, it conveys well both the significance of and resistance to the longstanding belief that the wageless needed to prove their deservingness through labour. This is the empirical substance of our narrative of the House of Industry and its disciplines and the poor's refusals to be brought entirely under the sway of these kinds of rigours. Second, there is in the symbolism of 'cracking the stone' an appropriate representation of wider struggles against capital and the state. Such resistance has historically challenged a hard and intractable capitalism that inevitably produces not just the aberration of crises, in the plural, but the constant of crisis as a singular, defining feature of the relations of exploitation, a breeding ground of inequality and oppression. Third, the imagery of 'cracking the stone' speaks as well to the rigidities of conceptualisations of class formation that separate waged and wageless into static, abstract categories of differentiation within working-class experience. We reject this stone-like ossification, and indeed want to crack it apart, by insisting that 'labour' always encompasses under capitalism the reciprocities of waged and wageless life. With these principles as our point of departure, we follow Benjamin's maxim that 'the sequence of events' in the chronicle of the dispossessed must not be told 'like the beads of a rosary'. Instead, we have tried to grasp these moments of a long past so that they can illuminate 'the constellation which [our] own order has formed with a definite earlier one'.[109] This confirms us in our conviction that capitalist crisis is the rule rather than the exception, that class struggle is necessarily composed of a variety of parts, the totality of which brings waged and wageless together rather than separating them in the judgemental ideology of the Poor Law. If we have less faith than Benjamin in the ultimate capacity of the angel of history to contain the storm of progress, its inherent crises growing both more intense and following more and more closely on the heels of one another, we nonetheless appreciate, as did Benjamin, that there is no turning back.

Capitalism *as* crisis makes such a retreat impossible. We take hope in the almost inexhaustible resources of the wageless, who have shown, time and time again, the capacity to confound the condescension of critics in their challenge to crises not of their own making, but in which their being is inevitably entwined. Finally, we grasp that the history of the dispossessed is always about movement, possibility, and change, much of which happens in ways that are difficult not only to interpret, but even to see.

---

109   This and all previous quotations from Walter Benjamin's 'Theses on the Philosophy of History' (1940) come from Benjamin 1968, pp. 253–64. An older study, outlining an understanding of the relationship of history and social analysis, still repays reading: see Mills 1959, pp. 143–64.

As the economy lay in shambles in the winter of 1931, a thousand men a day were eating their February meals in a Toronto soup kitchen located in St. Lawrence Hall. They filed into the auditorium as volunteers punched their tickets, authorising a feed of beans, stew, and coffee. 'By keeping stomachs filled', wrote one journalist, Toronto was preventing 'riots, perhaps bloodshed'. There appeared no life in the wageless dining at St. Lawrence Hall: no collectivity, no communication, no combativeness. Few signs apparently existed that the *un*employed could possibly generate protest. Those reduced to this status were apparently devoid of a great deal. 'They are men without emotions', declared an account in the Toronto *Star*. 'They ate in complete silence. No one spoke to their neighbour'.[110] Two police officers were present to see that it was so. In the years that followed, squads of gendarmes would be needed to keep the peace, and Toronto's wageless would mobilise by the tens of thousands, turning Queen's Park, Allan Gardens, Earlscourt Park, Trinity Park and other public spaces into spirited forums for the unemployed and their spokesmen. 'Labour tests' of all kinds would be opposed vigorously, and the out-of-work built new associations, councils, and organisations throughout Toronto's wards and working-class suburbs, all of them questioning and challenging relief practices and demanding better treatment of the indigent. Defiant in the face of a relentlessly condescending authority, the wageless marched and assembled without official approval and without the demanded permits. They were adamant that they would gather as they saw fit, until 'the iron heelism of Chief Draper is stamped out'.[111] Often led by communists, social democrats, and others on the left, the wageless expanded their challenge to the relief order, calling for, among other things, non-contributory unemployment insurance; cash relief for the unemployed; an end to the evictions, seizures, and foreclosures of the homes and other property of the wageless; free medical and health service for the unemployed and their dependents; uninhibited access to public buildings and parks used for meetings of the jobless; no deportations; and unity of the employed and unemployed. This movement, growing out of the realities of dispossession, was nonetheless grounded in something more than the kinds of essential *absence* that so often characterises – in the past as well as in the present – the representation of those in need of waged work.[112]

---

110 'Apathetic Acceptance Marks Club Dinners. No Anger or Resentment Shown as 500 Jobless Eat in Dead Silence', Toronto *Daily Star*, 23 February 1931.

111 'Charge Police Refused Aid to Girl Trampled by Horse. Protest Alleged Neglect as Allan Gardens Meeting Broken Up', Toronto *Daily Star*, 30 August 1933.

112 These demands constituted planks in the programme of the Communist Party-led Unem-

Indeed, it is one chapter in the long text of struggles, reaching back centuries, according to Christopher Hill, in which the social construction of the dispossessed relied explicitly on structures of incarceration and ideologies of criminalisation, generating refusals and resistance of many kinds. The decades of defiance and dissent that followed the English Revolution of 1640, for instance, saw radical pamphleteers argue that 'houses of correction, so far from curing begging, were more likely to make honest men vagabonds and beggars by destroying their reputation and self-respect'.[113] This moment of the Diggers, Levellers, and Ranters was certainly an early instance of the modern *historical* project of reclaiming the *commonwealth* that Peter Linebaugh chronicles in the *Magna Carta Manifesto*. What Hill and Linebaugh document in their recovery of the quest for 'liberties and commons for all' has been effectively articulated in the Occupy Wall Street (and similar) mobilisations of 2011–12:

> In 1649
> To St. George's Hill,
> A ragged band they called the Diggers
> Came to show the people's will
> They defied the landlords
> They defied the laws
> They were the dispossessed reclaiming what was theirs
>
> We come in peace they said
> To dig and sow
> We come to work the lands in common
> And to make the waste ground grow
> This earth divided
> We will make whole
> So it will be
> A common treasury for all
>
> From the men of property
> The orders came
> They sent the hired men and troopers
> To wipe out the Diggers' claim

---

ployed Councils movement. See National Committee of Unemployed Councils, *Building a New Unemployed Movement* (Toronto 1933).

113   Hill 1972, p. 33; Linebaugh 2008.

Tear down their cottages
Destroy their corn
They were dispersed
But still the vision lingers on[114]

Toronto's workless carried this vision from the nineteenth century into the twentieth, from which it would live on into our own times. In determining not to 'crack stone', a seemingly mundane refusal to oblige authority's demands that the poor comply with a regime of forced labour to receive food, lodging, and other necessities, the indigent of Toronto did their part in breaking many larger metaphorical boulders, which weighed so heavily on labour's collective experience. In the process, blows were struck, and fissures forced, in the harsh disciplines of capitalist crisis and its relentless assault on the working class, be it waged or wageless. This was and remains one part of the project of emancipation in which class figures so centrally. Such human liberation, encompassing workers but reaching beyond them as well, depends, in part, on working-class self-activity confronting the perpetual crises of capitalism in such a way that capitalism itself is forced into a final, transformative crisis. Out of this cauldron will necessarily emerge a different socioeconomic order, one premised on human concerns and needs rather than the ledgers of production's profitability. Benjamin's 'angel of history' will then be able to see beyond the accumulated debris of the past, and human progress will finally 'cease to resemble that hideous pagan idol, who would not drink the nectar but from the skulls of the slain'.[115]

---

114   For one of the many insightful commentaries on the Occupy Movement see Mike Davis, 'No More Bubble Gum', *Los Angeles Review of Books*, 21 October 2011. The lyrics are from Billy Bragg's *'The World Turned Upside Down'*.

115   Marx 1973a, p. 325.

What's Law Got To Do With It? Historical Considerations on Class Struggle, Boundaries of Constraint, and Capitalist Authority*

1   Law, Subordination, and Social Change

How do subordinate groups register their presence and their protest? Bounded by various constraints, struggling to have their voices heard as walls of silence are everywhere erected around them, battling often merely to be seen as they are made invisible by a political economy that measures their materiality as inconsequential, such peoples face a range of obstacles in their efforts to function with the rights of citizenship. How might they conceive of law, and how might we understand law's relationship to them, especially in terms of acts that are oppositional and dissident, that carry the designation of civil disobedience, and that are construed, in specific quarters, as *illegal*? These are some of the larger questions that frame my comments on class and other struggles as they relate to law over the course of the nineteenth and twentieth centuries. For law, while it is undoubtedly many things, is also a constraint, both imposed and internalised; it is a wall of silence and an articulation of political economy's material and hierarchical ordering of society around its concepts of property and propriety, an expression of cultures that have, from antiquity to the present day, valued rank and hierarchy whatever the evolving rhetorics of equality. And law has always erected boundaries within which protest, resistance, and collective organisation have been meant to exist.

But law is also a malleable construct, a changing set of understandings that demands historical appreciation. As the history of chattel slavery, patriarchal rights to physical punishment of wives and children, and master and servant legislation all confirm, yesterday's law is today's crime. This is reflected in the way the illegalities of decades past are today's conventional behaviours, as the history of the condom would suggest. Without the disobedient – those

---

*   'What's Law Got To Do With It? Historical Considerations on Class Struggle, Boundaries of Constraint, and Capitalist Authority', *Osgoode Hall Law Journal*, 41 (Summer/Fall 2003), 466–90.

willing to challenge law in everyday acts of irreverence and defiance as well as in organised mobilisations of protest – we would be living in a very different world.

2   Theorising Law and Civil Disobedience

Contemporary theory of law has addressed this complexity in an array of useful discussions, none of which, however, has entirely resolved a sequence of contradictions.

At the heart of these is law's instrumentality, its relation to structure and agency (a persistent and wide-ranging dilemma that relates to a range of structures conceptualised beyond the narrowly defined 'economic'), and the problematics of humanist or structuralist readings of resistance. Maureen Cain and Alan Hunt, for instance, compiled a fairly exhaustive account of the ways in which Karl Marx and Frederick Engels wrote in relation to law. Stimulated by Althusserian appreciations of determination's complexities, the articulation of levels of structural domination beyond the merely economic, and of a consequent opposition to humanist explanation that commences with reified 'man', Cain and Hunt provide a starting point for the radical interrogation of law as it relates to economic relations, ideology, the state, and politics. Beyond the reductionist view of law as 'an instrument in the hands of a ruling class', suggest Cain and Hunt, lies the need to theorise law in ways that accord a primacy to structures, situating law within ensembles of capitalist social relations, but that also restore 'to people their dignity by acknowledging that they are capable of changing their world'.[1]

Just how this self-acknowledged Althusserian approach springs us out of an ostensible humanist trap is not entirely clear, and this should have been evident to Cain and Hunt in so much as they cited and admired the discussion of law in E.P. Thompson's *Whigs and Hunters*, an account as resolutely humanist as it is perhaps possible to imagine.[2]

Hunt and Wickham's later elaboration of a sociology of law as governance, keying now not on Marx and Engels, but on Michel Foucault, continues in this tentative vein; Foucault is situated in relation to law in ways that accent interpretive possibility, which Hunt and Wickham designate as 'ground clearing,

---

1   Cain and Hunt 1979, pp. xi, xiii.
2   Cain and Hunt 1979, p. 68, n. 3.

surveying, and mapping.[3] Indeed, as a recent debate in *Social & Legal Studies* suggests, Foucault scholars can differ markedly on how they situate Foucault in terms of law and the analytics of governmentality.[4] And, as Hunt and Wickham stress, at the point that resistance to structures of domination appears in civil disobedience, Foucault's relevance is immediately compromised. For Foucault, whatever his suggestive insights vis-à-vis the power/resistance coupling, attended to resistance weakly at best.[5]

The governmentality theorists have, of late, chosen to valorise this Foucauldian shortcoming in a way that Foucault might well have been uncomfortable with. For if Foucault did not place resistance at the centre of his own research agenda, his entire *oeuvre* can hardly be read as diminishing the significance of opposition; it simply was not what he, for the most part, studied. And it should never be assumed that because a scholar has chosen to highlight one dimension of the past's many layers, he or she therefore derides the significance of other unstudied realms. Mariana Valverde, in an admittedly all-too-cavalier article, expresses scepticism concerning 'resistance'. A more intellectually rigorous discussion in Nikolas Rose's *Powers of Freedom* contains a curious backing away from the political meaning of resistance,[6] especially its collective organised variants, which are central to the history of what we might designate civil disobedience.

More fruitful, I would suggest, for an appreciation of law's historical meaning, particularly as it relates to civil disobedience, is an understanding of law's materialised discourse as well as of acts of law-breaking that either changed law or contributed to the development of new law. This relationship of articulation/contestation constructed and reconfigured boundaries within which social relations unfolded, those relations simultaneously influenced by law and pushing law's development in new directions. To be sure, actors in this contested theatre were not always entirely conscious of what law's actual codes entailed, understandably so in specific periods and contexts, such as early Canada, when knowledge of law was weak at best. Nor, alternatively, were such agents of change acutely aware of how tilting their human sails against law's winds reconfigured the legal climate. But outside of such consciousness, the law changed, and with it a part of the environment of social relations, and thus, again, the social relations themselves. 'Men make their own history, but they

---

3   Hunt and Wickham 1994, p. 132.

4   Rose and Valverde 1998, p. 541; Pearce and Tombs 1998, p. 567.

5   Hunt and Wickham 1994, p. 17.

6   Valverde 2000, pp. 59–77; Rose 1999, pp. 279–80.

WHAT'S LAW GOT TO DO WITH IT?

do not make it just as they please'. Law, one aspect of those many 'traditions' of 'dead generations' that weigh 'like a nightmare on the brain of the living', is thus not so much historically separable and above various conflicts, as it is forged and reformed within them.[7]

Such ways of conceptualising law and civil disobedience resonate theoretically with Habermas's conceptually detailed, if often dense and difficult, grasp of law's location within what he calls the place of social mediation situated between facts and norms.[8] Eric Tucker's account of how nineteenth-century workers contested the social and legal zones of toleration within which their collective endeavours were situated also animates one of the more interesting discussions of the history of early Canadian labour law.[9] In many ways this kind of perspective on law allows us to reconsider some of E.P. Thompson's reflections on the Rule of Law, which form something of an endnote to his account of the foresters' struggles in eighteenth-century England:

> What was often at issue was not property, supported by law, against no-property; it was alternative definitions of property-rights: ... for official-dom, 'preserved grounds' for the deer; for the foresters, the right to take turfs. For as long as it remained possible, the ruled – if they could find a purse and a lawyer – would actually fight for their rights by means of law; occasionally the copyholders, resting upon the precedents of sixteenth-century law, could actually win a case. When it ceased to be possible to continue the fight at law, men still felt a sense of legal wrong: the proper-tied had obtained their power by illegitimate means.[10]

Thompson may well go too far in his argument that class relations were actually expressed 'through the forms of law'; he reaches past the point where analysis needs to go, in an effort to carry on a specific war of intellectual position that he had been waging with the editors of the *New Left Review* since the early 1960s. It is nevertheless the case that Thompson's close attention to the field of force that law ordered reminds us of the constant historical play between resistance and incorporation, in which law as written and as lived figured prominently.[11]

---

7   Marx 1968, p. 97.

8   Habermas 1996.

9   Tucker 1991, pp. 15–54.

10   Thompson 1975, cited in Cain and Hunt 1979, p. 261.

11   Thompson 1975, cited in Cain and Hunt 1979, p. 262. For background on Thompson's intellectual-political differences with the *New Left Review* of Perry Anderson, Tom Nairn,

This is not unrelated to Marx's original 1842 discussion on 'Debates of the Law on Thefts of Wood'.[12] But it takes us in entirely different directions than the conventional, if somewhat counterposed, Marxist discussions of legal norms, modes of production, and evolving abstractions of bourgeois individuality expressed in the pre-Althusser writings of Karl Renner and E.B. Pashukanis.[13] Moreover, as Leon Trotsky suggested in one of his more contentious pieces of polemical writing, *Their Morals and Ours*, it is imperative never to lose sight of the elasticity of law as it relates to ethics and moral governance, especially in terms of the ways in which fundamental reversals can take place in extraordinary situations. This alerts us to how zones of tolerance can find themselves inverted, not only for societies, but also for collectivities, *if* extreme contexts condition acute shifts in subjective rationales of particular acts and behaviours:

> Under 'normal' conditions a 'normal' person observes the command-ment: 'Thou shalt not kill'. But if one kills under exceptional conditions for self-defense, the jury acquits that person. If one falls victim to a murderer, the court will kill the murderer. The necessity of courts, as well as that of self-defense, flows from antagonistic interests. In so far as the state is con-cerned, in peaceful times it limits itself to legalized killings of individuals so that in time of war it may transform the 'obligatory' commandment, 'Thou shalt not kill!' into its opposite. The most 'humane' governments, which in peaceful times 'detest' war, proclaim during war that the highest duty of their armies is the extermination of the greatest possible number of people.[14]

As Trotsky then went on to suggest, situations develop, albeit rarely, in which the usual categorical imperatives of law for society's members are weakened substantially, and '[t]he solidarity of workers, especially of strikers or barricade fighters, is incomparably more "categoric" than human solidarity in general'.[15] In such moments it is not the case that law is dispensed with so much as that law is redefined. Such redefinition can be transitory and open to reversal or, in

and Robin Blackburn, in which understandings of law and its relation to capitalist repres-sion certainly figure prominently, see, among many other sources, Kenny 1995.

12   Marx 1975a, pp. 224–63. See also Sherover-Marcuse 1986, pp. 17–44.

13   Renner 1976; Pashukanis 1978; and the discussion in Bottomore et al. 1983, 'law'.

14   Trotsky, Dewey, and Novack 1973, p. 22.

15   Trotsky, Dewey, and Novack 1973, p. 22.

rare circumstances of either revolution or readjustment, law can be remade. But this never happens entirely outside of civil disobedience. My purpose here is to provide a broad overview containing some guidelines for an understanding of how law and civil disobedience are related in Canadian history, especially in terms of the class contests that have unfolded over time, and that have often pushed the parameters of zones of toleration, reconfiguring legislation and the boundaries of law's constraints. I am not suggesting so much law's irrelevance – 'what's law got to do with it?' – as insisting on law's malleability; I claim not so much law's refusal of civil disobedience as, in its actual evolution, its reciprocities with resistance; and I accentuate less law's codes and concepts and continuities, important as these are, as its ruptures and reformations. Finally, what I try to negotiate is a middle ground in which the tendency to present modern law as merely bourgeois confinement and class constraint is refused, for no social movement of resistance and civil disobedience will flourish and succeed if it lacks a moral grounding in precepts of behaviour. Equally objectionable is the all-too-common tendency on the part of entrenched bureaucracies to reify law as given as somehow irreversible and unchallengeable, an accepted articulation of the fundamental order necessary to society's governance and the continuity of rarefied rights.

3   Early Canada: Uncertain Legal Class Relations and Physical Force
       Law

Let me begin in early nineteenth-century Canada when the law of labour and the response to civil disobedience, as H. Clare Pentland once pointed out, were rather arbitrary. For there was little in the way of authoritative and established law, generalised in its prescriptions. Instead, in this period, much was up for interpretive legal grabs. Neither the law of labour, largely centred in master and servant relations, nor appreciations of the law of combinations and conspiracies in restraint of trade, through which nascent trade unions were seemingly regulated, were well understood. Neither jurists (yet to cohere as a professional body) nor the general public in its plebeian and patrician components, had a sure grasp of what law did and did not address in these fields. Furthermore, the legal response to civil disobedience – often understood as riots suppressed by troops, police, and local militias – was most often framed by the decidedly limited knowledge and personalities of individual employers and magistrates. It did not so much matter what the law actually was, and where it came from, or whether it was applicable in the colonial context – the questions legal historians have most often asked – although these are not uninteresting and inconsequential issues. Rather, law was a lived application that was uneven and uncertain in its translation into social relations. More important than 'abstract right', as Pentland suggests, was which side could mobilise force more successfully:

> Attempts to resume operations during a strike nearly always provoked violence, and the various questions of right dropped into the background as questions of physical attack came to the fore. The final arbiter of most of the disputes was not abstract right but physical force: the power of the massed labourers to do violence against the similar power of the troops that employers were able to call to their assistance.[16]

The boundaries of constraint, in these formative years, were thus not so much legal as they were physical: who might twist whose arm the hardest. And the outcome was by no means certain, except over the long haul.

In that extended period, from the 1820s into the 1850s, the Canadian state was taking its first steps toward formation. A not inconsiderable component of its birth pangs involved the police forces that came into being on early public works projects as a consequence of the need to suppress civil disobedience on the largest worksites of pre-Confederation Canada, the railways and canals that intersected the old and the new mercantile-industrial order.[17] In this sense, the beginnings of the Canadian state were indeed, in Marx's words, heavily invested in establishing 'the intermediary between man and man's freedom'. As Engels was later to put it more bluntly, the state was 'force in its organized form'.[18]

To grasp law's meaning in this period of Canadian history, it is critical to see, not some hegemonic force, but a sticky filament that was necessary to brush against in specific circumstances in order to secure wages due, employments owed, or conventions to be observed. In the absence of deep structures of class and state formations, yet to be anchored in early Canadian socioeconomic relations, the law was a presence, but one always to be negotiated, by both the propertied and the property-less. This was evident in one contemporary's description of Peter Aylen, an ethnic leader of the rough Irish timber-worker Shiners of the Ottawa Valley, and something of a *lumpenbourgeoisie*: 'The laws are like cobwebs to him'.[19] Pentland, too, appreciates this character of early law,

---

16   Pentland 1981, p. 190.
17   Pentland 1981, pp. 189–97. See also a number of essays in Greer and Radforth 1992; and especially Greer 1992, pp. 17–49.
18   Marx 1975b, p. 152; Engels 1983, p. 163.
19   Cited in Cross 1971, pp. 177–82.

noting that unlike in Ireland, it was not, even for the most rowdy of canallers, 'altogether regarded as an alien oppression'.[20]

Thus, among the most disobedient demographic and occupational sectors of early Canadian society, the unskilled Irish immigrant labourers, Pentland saw this group's emergence as a class force as related to its coming to grips with the boundaries of class constraint. One part of these limitations related directly to law and civil disobedience. For the Irish labourer developed an appreciation of the necessity of constraining the use of violence in defiance of law, but of keeping it in judicious reserve. Physical force and civil disobedience were marshalled so that they would be most effective. Although the situation was markedly different among the smaller collectivities of skilled tradesmen who faced early conspiracy charges for their proto-unionisation efforts in the 1830s and 1840s, such craft workers also brushed their way uncertainly against law's constraints. At times they secured legal vindication for their rights of association, at other times they faced defeat in the courts.[21]

4   Preliminary Codification: Class Contests and the 1872 Trades Union Act

Mobilisations of Canadian workers that reached beyond specific public-works sites, large factories and mills, or small craft shops were rare between 1840–70. When organised labour stoppages happened, such events were almost always called acts of civil disobedience; an 1853–4 strike wave was dubbed 'an insurrection of labour'[22] by the Canada West newspapers. Such defiance of conventional relations of labour and capital challenged understandings of uncertain laws of conspiracy. The boundaries of legal restraint containing workers' collective actions in this period were legislatively real. That said, for all practical intents and purposes it was other limitations established in the material relations of production and the small spaces of worker-employer contestation that were the more critical determinants of whether tradesmen and labourers organised or whether they could be successful in their petitioning of employers over wage and job condition issues.[23] The law was cobweb-like, to be sure, in its sticky traversing of the boundaries of class relations, but it was indefinite

20   Pentland 1981, p. 196.
21   For the most useful discussion of this matter see Tucker 1991, pp. 8–41.
22   Appleton 1974.
23   See, for instance, Palmer 1992, pp. 81–91; 1987a, pp. 67–76.

enough to never quite be a final deciding arbiter. Yet it necessarily influenced significantly working-class self-activity in terms of class mobilisation for political or economic reasons, defining such activity as civil disobedience.

On the surface it would appear that 1872, and the passage of the Trades Union Act, changed all of this, ending years of legal uncertainty about unions' legal status. Yet as scholars have shown, the 1872 legislation, which was after all a direct outgrowth of civil disobedience in the form of demands for the nine-hour day that encompassed mobilisations of skilled workers in most major Ontario cities, a planned general strike called for 15 May 1872, and the Toronto printers' conspiracy trial of April of that year, was indeed quite ambiguous in the legal sense. It granted unions legal status only if they followed certain legal guidelines. None did. The class conflict and initial legal clarifications of what constituted legitimate acts on the part of trade unions in 1872 were thus quickly followed by other pieces of legislation that hemmed in what workers could do in strike situations. In reality, the 1872 Trades Union Act and subsequent follow-up legislation refused to easily concede the legal right of freedom of association and collective bargaining. The consequence was that almost the entire history of class relations and working-class self-activity in the 1870–1945 period was placed in legal limbo. This was a long, drawn-out interregnum, but it was one in which, interestingly, the zones of toleration and the boundaries of legal constraint that had limited trade-union possibilities in the past were expanded greatly, at the same time that they were also hedged in more effectively vis-à-vis legal statutes. Whatever the legalistic obfuscation that flowed from the aftermath of 1872, Canadian workers took it as their legal right to organise and negotiate with employers, however difficult those projects were going to be. But law also now had a more precise, if discretionary, power to prosecute. In this sense, the law of 1872 was a product of class organisation, civil disobedience, and a legal regime that refused to concede the obvious. The arm of the law had, in effect, been twisted by labour. In this twisting, it gave certain necessary ground, acknowledging that the everyday practices of the Canadian working class would no longer routinely be cast as criminal, but could, if necessary, be subject to legal proceedings.[24]

It is in this context that the labour upheavals of 1886, 1919, 1937, and 1946 must be understood. To be sure, each of these major moments of working-class mobilisation differed markedly: their times, places, and characters were distinguished by particularity, not commonality. But they were all in their way brushing up against the law, pushing against its cobweb-like confinements to expand,

---

24   Tucker 1991, pp. 51–4; Palmer 1992, pp. 106–16.

stretch, and even break the boundaries of constraint that were an integral feature of capitalist authority.

5 Labour Upheavals and the Origins of Law in Civil Disobedience

5.1 *1886: The Knights of Labor*

Much of the ritualism, attachment to secrecy and symbolism, and clandestine character of the Knights of Labor, for instance, was not unrelated to the sure grasp that working-class agitators in the 1880s had of the necessity of organising in ways that skirted the power of employers. In so doing they were challenging tangible hangovers from the pre-1872 legal regime of toleration that narrowed labour's possibilities. The Knights of Labor courts were concrete articulations of attachment to political and ethical strictures, to a notion of law as 'right' that nevertheless openly confronted other legal constraints. In their everyday engagements with local bylaws, employer boycotts, early-closing legislation, lobbying for factory acts, various protective laws for women and children (whose meaning was always criss-crossed with gender and class content), strikes, and suffrage extensions, members of the Order were constantly both on the cusp of civil disobedience and working to reconstruct the law and legitimise it in the eyes of a working population more and more aware of the ravages of monopolistic power.[25]

> It is now axiomatically manifest that this country will soon be in a condition where its entire wealth is represented by interest-bearing securities, that can be locked up in safety deposit vaults by their plutocratic owners. When this time comes, and it is almost at hand, the whole body of the toiling producers will be the mere serfs of capitalistic drones. The wages allowed them will only be sufficient to enable them to do their tasks, and reproduce themselves, while the great bulk of the wealth created in their hands will go to swell the enormous hoards of the already monstrously rich. A system under which this devastation of humanity can go on, as it is going on today, is not civilized, nor semi-civilized, nor barbaric, nor savage; it is simply infernal, and unless extirpated root and branch will surely bring the nation that tolerates it to merited destruction.[26]

---

25   See Kealey and Palmer 1987.

26   Hubbard 1891, pp. 459–60. A copy of this book in my possession belonged to the Toronto Knights of Labor figure, A.W. Wright.

Such language, read from the twentieth-century vantage point of revolutionary programme or social-democratic reform, seems antiquated, easily tarred
with the brush of populism. But it was no less a language of recalcitrance and
resistance for all that. And it was often directed against the 'dead hand' of
law that had drawn the boundaries of constraint in narrowly circumscribed,
anti-democratic ways. In the words of one of the leading 'brainworkers' of the
Knights of Labor, Phillips Thompson:

> All the weight of tradition and precedent arising out of altogether dif-
> ferent conditions than those which now confront us is thrown against
> Labor Reform. The battle will be more than half won when we emancip-
> ate ourselves from this thraldom to the ghosts and shadows of the past.
> Why should new questions be judged by old precedents? Why should we
> on this continent and in this bustling industrial age be ruled by the judi-
> cial interpretations, the legislative maxims, or the social and economic
> formulas originated by the idlers and parasites of society at a time when
> the world was supposed to have been created for the benefit of the rulers
> and the rich – and the people to have no rights whatever but that of sweat-
> ing and fighting for their benefits? How strange that inherited traditions
> and ideas should have such a hold that men who are themselves workers,
> themselves sufferers from caste oppression, should be largely guided in
> their conduct by the public sentiment and code of principles inculcating
> respect for birth, money, position, vested rights, etc., created by the dead,
> and no doubt damned, old despots and sycophants of the middle ages.[27]

Less lyrical was the letter one semi-literate Knight of Labor from the small
enclave of Alvinston, Ontario, wrote to the Order's figurehead, Terence V. Powderly, in 1886: 'To look after and in speaking of the strikes of the Labouring of
those railroads now unsettled as yet I regret that their should been any necesity
to resort to fier arms as that nearly always results bad. But it is necesary sometimes to fight for your rights'.[28]

5.2   1919: General and Other Strikes

If we move forward in time two decades and more to the post-World War I
labour revolt, much has changed. The Knights of Labor expanded the boundaries of constraint and challenged the legal and other dimensions of capitalist

---

27   Thompson 1887, p. 146.
28   Letter from Howard Rickard to T.V. Powderly (12 April 1886) in Kealey & Palmer 1987, p. 375.

authority out of the widened zone of toleration that flowed in the wake of 1872 and the Trades Union Act. In some senses the Order's legitimacy was a reflection of the newness of massive working-class upheaval. The Knights challenged conventional class relations, to be sure, but they often did so with an understandable uncertainty. This necessarily meant that the traditions that labour reformers like Phillips Thompson saw as weighing the movement down were also in some senses drawn upon. Nor were the class antagonists of the workers' movement always all that more sure-footed.

By 1919, new traditions, especially those associated with Marxism and its language of production for use, not profit, were being absorbed into the more revolutionary variants of class struggle. Internationally, the actuality of world war and the threat of Bolshevism and revolution was very much in the air.[29] This hardened the stance of authority ideologically. Equally critically, employers were now a more coherently organised force and the state was at this point a far more developed entity, especially on the playing field of labour relations, which had emerged as pivotal in the aftermath of the depression of the 1890s. Canada's political economy was revamped: the flooding of the labour market by a massive influx of immigrants, a huge jump in productive capacity associated with Canada's second industrial revolution, the expansion of workplace size, numbers of corporate mergers, technologies and managerial rigour, the consolidation of a Department of Labour, and the role of William Lyon Mackenzie King in mediating class tensions in the pre-World War I years, reconstituting understandings of how the legal system could intervene in class relations, all figured forcefully.[30]

When the inevitable clash of class forces occurred in 1917–25 (with the last gasp occurring in the Cape Breton Coal fields),[31] the zone of legal toleration of class self-activity had in fact been tightened and compressed. State trials in the aftermath of the Winnipeg General Strike were but the most visible component of a changed climate. The winds of powerful state and class opposition to civil disobedience now flew directly in the face of so-called enemy alien radicals who were to be deported; Bolsheviks, anarchists, and all 'One Big Unionists' who were to be suppressed; and returned war vets who opted for dissidence, and who were therefore to be silenced.

---

29   This forms a central theme in an older radical historiography, exemplified by Kealey 1984, p. 11; and Peterson 1984, p. 115. It is challenged and complicated somewhat by the more moderate, social-democratic cast of some presentations in Heron 1998.

30   Among many sources see, for instance, Craven 1980; Russell 1990, pp. 57–126.

31   On the Cape Breton experience see Frank 1999.

The stakes in legally constraining all class challenges now appeared much higher than they had been in 1886, and the vehemence of constituted authority was consequently much greater. Repression unfolded in the courts, and was articulated daily in the press. The capacity to suppress radicalism and working-class resistance was strengthened immeasurably in the consolidation of a national police force, constituted in good part on the claimed need for mechanisms of counter-subversion. The law of labour and the law of sedition blurred. Dissidents such as R.B. Russell and J.B. McLachlan, working-class leaders of revolts in the Canadian west and in the Maritime coal towns, tasted the bitter fruit of this new regime of heighted repression. They and other jailed victims of the 1919–25 clamp-down on proletarian insurgency experienced first-hand how the zone of toleration vis-à-vis class organisation was, for a time, pressured into realms, not of conspiracy in restraint of trade, but of treason to the nation and its now increasingly combative state. Section 98 of the Canadian Criminal Code, which gave the state considerable leeway in prosecuting treasonous activity, was adopted in 1919 and was but one expression of how the law sought to put the lid on class struggle, which had widened immeasurably in this period. Battles over collective bargaining rights among Winnipeg building tradesmen and metalworkers leapfrogged into the country's most illustrious general strike, while sympathetic strikes erupted across the land, from Amherst, Nova Scotia, to Victoria, British Columbia, as workers used the withdrawal of their economic power not to enhance their wages and lighten the burdens of the daily tasks, but to support their fellows, as a matter of principle.

Not surprisingly, when One Big Union proponent and Winnipeg General Strike advocate W.A. Pritchard came to address the jury in the aftermath of his trial for seditious conspiracy and common nuisance in 1919–20, he spoke in great detail about the law and its meanings. He drew on the experience of various sectors of the peripatetic bindle-stiff workforce of the Canadian west. It had struggled to organise, and in the process confronted the ways in which the law as codified inevitably came to be stretched and challenged by the working class, precisely because such law had been stretched and challenged in other ways by capitalist employers:

> And suppose, gentlemen, that in addition to the development of the machine I have shown you, the workers were confronted with other conditions; supposing that Laws on the Statute Book respecting health and sanitation, the time of payment of wages, etc., etc., set down in the Provincial Laws, are just a picture book; suppose the conditions in the places in which you work are not at all like what they should be if the

Laws on the Statute Book were enforced. Suppose, gentlemen, that there be a Law which tells the Employer in the camp that he must put on the water supply in such and such a fashion; that he can only build bunks in the bunk house of such and such a character; that they must not be tier bunks, one bunk above another; that two men shall not sleep together in what lumber-jacks call double-barreled bunks; that they shall not be built so that you crawl in head first or foot first – what lumber-jacks call muzzle-loading; supposing it says that reports shall be turned in respecting those bunk houses and despite the Law, suppose this: these mattresses are made of a decomposed substance that might at one time have been hay, and suppose all these things are done, and put upon the Statute Book, what are you going to do about it as workers? Would you organize as best you could and force your demands right there upon these chaps where you work, and see if you could not, 'by virtue of your industrial strength, make such demands as such workers may at any time consider necessary to their maintenance and well being?' Would you not, gentlemen of the jury, consider it good policy on the part of these workers if they could by their efforts build up an organization which would save themselves to some extent?[32]

Pritchard continued on in this vein, and virtually no side of his 200-page statement was without reference to this process of how workers struggled for law against law, of how law was abused and resisted, in matters large and small. Pritchard insisted that there was 'no more peaceful or Law abiding section of the community under the sun than the industrial worker', yet he acknowledged 'there is no man or set of men who have been more goaded by their conditions than these same men'.[33] And it was that process of commitment to law in conjunction with law's failure that translated into the making of revolutionaries such as Pritchard.

The nature of a mattress was a springboard into support for the insurgent revolutionary working class of St. Petersburg's metal shops. The absurdity of censorship laws that dictated that ownership of a volume of Marx's *Capital* published in London was within the law, but that the same book published by Charles H. Kerr of Chicago was banned, moved Pritchard to a denunciation of censorship and an articulation of large issues of freedom: to read, to associate, to act. From the smallest of issues flowed the largest and most expansive of

---

32   Pritchard 1920, pp. 100–1.
33   Pritchard 1920, p. 102.

concerns. Out of the struggle to fight for collective bargaining rights in one city, Winnipeg, came the commitment to the organisation of the international working class, to world revolution:

> No more industrial rivalries – this is what I am honestly striving for, gentlemen ... Reason, wisdom, intelligence, forces of the minds and heart, whom I have always devoutly invoked, come to me, aid me, sustain my feeble voice, carry it, if that may be, to all the peoples of the world and diffuse it everywhere where there are men of good-will to hear the beneficent truth. A new order of things is born, the powers of evil die poisoned by their crime. The greedy and the cruel, the devourers of people, are bursting with an indigestion of blood. However sorely stricken by the sins of their blind or corrupt masters, mutilated, decimated, the proletarians remain erect; they will unite to form one universal proletariat and we shall see fulfilled the great Socialist prophecy: 'The union of the workers will be the peace of the world'.[34]

In one sense, the voices of the bourgeois Committee of 1000, the Canadian Manufacturers' Association, and leading conservative politicians like Robert Borden and Arthur Meighen were not wrong: labour's revolt *was* an uprising of the seditious, if not legally then potentially. Winnipeg's General Strike, which traditionalist labour historiography understands as little more than a mundane struggle for collective bargaining rights that was defeated by a powerful and all-too-paranoid state, was indeed an act of civil disobedience that threatened treason, in as much as the possibility of revolutionary upsurge was buried, albeit deeply, in the conflictual relations of capital and labour. The class struggle always contained within itself this possibility of shattering boundaries of capitalist authority and erasing law's ultimate constraints.[35] One of those extraordinarily rare moments in our past when this was brought out into the open occurred during 1919.

No doubt there were those among the poor for whom the meaning of this uprising was confused. In prison in 1926, for instance, the fiery communist coal miner leader, J.B. McLachlan, was asked by one inmate why he was behind bars. '"Sedition" said Jim. The prisoner drew back in amazement and awe. "Is that something to do with women?" he whispered! "Sometimes", said Jim. "How

---

34   Pritchard 1920, p. 102.
35   Pritchard 1920. For the traditional labour history perspective see Bercuson 1974.

many times did you do it?" "Dozens", said Jim'.[36] But anecdotes of misinterpretation and close-lipped, ironically-poised stoicism aside, the terms of trade vis-à-vis law, class struggle, boundaries of constraint, and capitalist authority shifted in the 1920s. Judy Fudge and Eric Tucker show this well in their Canadian study of the regulation of workers' collective action in the first half of the twentieth century.[37]

5.3   1936: Depression and Dissent

Another peak in class struggle climaxed in the industrial union sit-down strikes and Congress of Industrial Organizations (CIO) agitations of 1936–7. This mobilisation saw plant occupations and militant outbursts throughout southern Ontario, culminating in the organisation of Oshawa auto workers.[38] Years of obsolete craft unionism, on the one hand, and of depression and state inaction around the basic provisioning of relief, on the other, had reconditioned the meaning of both accommodation and resistance. In the 'dirty thirties', labour law was moving toward an eventual narrowing of boundaries and reification of capitalist authority in contract law, collective bargaining being premised on management rights clauses and the union being, in part, responsible for policing its members. This was to be a decade in the making, but as the career of perhaps the most significant labour lawyer of the period, J.L. Cohen, reveals, it was in the mid-1930s that irreversible strides were taken in this direction. Industrial unionism, if weak and wobbly, was nevertheless assured a future stand in Canadian class relations because of events that transpired in the late 1930s.[39]

The point that I want to stress here is that labour law, narrowly conceived, was constricting the boundaries of class struggle through entrenching, codifying, professionalising, and integrating the worker into a state-orchestrated system that tended towards the production of labour-capital rapprochement. But the actual legal spaces where class was now operative were in fact expanding. Their boundaries were pushed by those human sectors blocked from industrial employment, the high wage, and collective bargaining rights by the economic collapse of the Great Depression that threw millions of Canadians out of work and that made the breadwinner wage less and less the touchstone of conflictual class relations; the relief system and its relation to the structure of the wage regime became a pivotal factor in everyday life. To be sure, the state continued

---

36   Frank 1999, p. 340.
37   See Fudge and Tucker 2001, pp. 104–52.
38   See, for a preliminary analysis, Abella 1973, pp. 1–40; Abella 1974, pp. 93–128.
39   MacDowell 2001, pp. 13–108; and, for another vantage point, Gonick 2001, pp. 72–123.

to use its repressive capacity to construct almost all unionism as a treasonous act and any militancy as seditious conspiracy, especially in terms of the early 1930s. From 1930–4, the Communist Party of Canada engaged in a Third Period battle for the streets that resulted in a replay of coercive state trials and arrests of dissidents. Well into the late 1930s, especially in Duplessis's Quebec, legislation like the infamous Padlock Law was trained on communists and industrial unionists in a blatant curtailment of civil liberties.[40]

But the ways that law was actually challenged most directly in the 1930s were most evident in the class-related but union-separated struggles of the jobless, the homeless, and the relief-dependent poor. Such victims of the capitalist marketplace's vicissitudes sustained a creative arsenal of resistance and opposition that flaunted the laws of the land in the same way that the laws of the market had bluntly bypassed their needs. Large grocery stores were subject to mass looting; power and hydro accessibility, cut off by powerful local utilities for non-payment, was reconnected by unemployed electricians and plumbers; tenants facing eviction blockaded themselves in their buildings in defiance of landlord efforts to put them on the street; and tin-panners and relief protesters routinely marched down the city thoroughfares in defiance of police and authorities, parading without permits and clashing violently with police. Far more than the tramp and vagabond masses of nineteenth-century depressions – who had elicited fear, loathing, and the passage of restrictive local ordinances – these uprisings of the Depression's destitute were well nestled into neighbourhood relations and represented familial continuities, gender conventions, identities of nation and empire, and cross-generational connections that ran through schools, workplaces, and families. These battles struck to the core of law's confinements. They constantly raised high the banner of universal laws of right and entitlement, which none could deny had taken a beating in the material downturn of the 1930s.[41]

---

40 Consider the discussion in Fudge and Tucker 2001, pp. 153–227; Palmer 1992, pp. 226–67; Betcherman 1982.

41 I have benefited greatly from discussions with two PhD students, whose research on Vancouver and Toronto has addressed the relief system and the unemployed and underemployed of the 1930s. Todd McCallum's forthcoming PhD thesis, '"Still Raining, Market Still Rotten": The Early Years of the Great Depression in Vancouver', has brought me to an acute awareness of the struggles and subjective mindset of the unemployed. Klee 1998 and Klee 2000, p. 13 are suggestive forays into the relations of the paid and underpaid, the labour market, and the relief order. See, as well, for the struggles of the unemployed and tenants resisting eviction: Schulz 1975; Palmer 1988, pp. 28–56. For background on the state's

Thus, the battle around labour law in 1936–7 was not just restricted to the freedom of association of the Oshawa sit-downers, however much that was a critical fight and whatever the ease with which we can conceptualise that struggle in terms of traditional understandings of industrial legality. Equally pivotal was the context in which 400,000 Ontario residents were on relief in that year. Work payment on municipal relief projects was slashed from 15 to 50 percent. A morally-ordered, regulatory apparatus of state surveillance intruded, often in explicitly gendered ways, into the everyday lives of those designated dependent, particularly women and children. Angry relief strikers fought pitched battles with police, physically restrained municipal welfare staffers until they rescinded wage cuts, and successfully secured the reinstatement of those chopped from the dole.[42]

To grasp the spaces that opened up for labour in the 1930s, then, we need to appreciate not only the CIO and mass production unionism, but also the many federations of the unemployed and their relief-dependent families that mushroomed in a growth that spread from coast to coast, and that contextualised class relations in almost every city in the land. Too often telescoped into the highly visible, and violently rebuffed, On-To-Ottawa Trek, this unemployed-relief agitation was by necessity constantly engaged in civil disobedience. And in so doing it framed the union campaigns of this and later periods, their successful outcomes determined somewhat by the actions of the rowdy crowds that made the high-waged industrial organisations of the employed more palpable to capital and the state. The debt owed to this tradition, of course, has yet to be paid by the unions, which managed, in their increasing respectability, to distance themselves from their early relationship to illegality.

5.4   1946: The Coming of Industrial Legality

One reason for this distance was the changed context and complexly ironic outcomes of the next episode of labour upheavals associated with the post-World War II mass strikes that rocked Canada's manufacturing and resource industries. To begin with, this large-scale national mobilisation of workers, fuelled by union membership roughly tripling over the course of a decade, culminated in a 1946–7 strike wave involving 220,000 workers in logging, mining, meatpacking, shipping, auto, rubber, steel, textiles, and electrical products. Over seven million days of pay and production were lost. This working-class mobilisation took

---

legislative response to unemployment see Struthers 1983. The classic account of the unemployed is Liversedge 1973.

42   MacDowell 2001, pp. 55–6; Little 1998, pp. 76–106.

place in years of prosperity and its concurrent optimisms, the rough protests of the unemployed, the evicted, and the relief-dependent having faded far from view. The labour protest of this period thus framed understandings of the zones of social and legal toleration in highly traditional ways. The organised male worker, conceived as stable, employed, and a family breadwinner, was understood as the archetypal unionist.

More critically, this late 1940s upheaval was something of an endnote to a half century of labour organisation, protest, and overt class struggle. It sealed a post-war settlement that consolidated a corporate relationship between capital and labour, mediated by a mature state. This was truly the birth of industrial legality, which now hardened, and ironically narrowed, the zone of legal toleration to a space conceived as a seemingly broad, but in actuality quite constricted, industrial pluralism. That this pluralism was politically secured through an unwritten pact, involving an emerging and increasingly conservative tradeunion hierarchy, an evolving body of law and a judicial and state 'community' of personnel dedicated to its enforcement, and a cohort of capital far-seeing enough to appreciate that stabilising class relations was indeed the need of the hour, was crucial to industrial legality's meaning. Just as it was pressured into being via channels of explicit class struggle, so too was it premised on driving the very communists who had often pushed that process of contestation from the labour organisations that they had played pivotal roles in building. This purge was presented as a necessary pill to swallow if labour was to be accepted into the corporatist club alongside capital and the state; if some gagged in the process, workers and their collective bargaining agents largely took their Cold War, anti-communist medicine willingly. This inevitably produced a somewhat domesticated trade-union movement. The late 1940s was thus marked by some of the most momentous class confrontations of the twentieth century at the same time that it harnessed those confrontations.[43]

Civil disobedience was never far from the turbulent strikes of the times, and never were acts of civil disobedience more creative and audacious than in the famous, and legally critical, strike at the Windsor Ford plant. Illegal strikers, or wildcatters, blockaded the auto factory with its own product on a cold November morning. They stalled their cars, seizing the vehicles of unwary commuters, occupying the streets by comandeering nine Greyhound buses,

---

43   For a recent sophisticated statement on the 1940s see McInnis 2002. An older treatment, still invaluable, is Abella 1973; my own broad overview is in Palmer 1992, pp. 268, 305; Panitch and Swartz 1988 is suggestive of the corporatist contours of what has come to be called 'the post-war settlement'. For a dissenting view see MacDowell 2001, p. 39.

either parked strategically by sympathetic drivers or taken forcefully by the union's Flying Picket Squad. Automobile owners stranded in the street were left to scratch their heads in bewilderment. 'I've never seen anything like it', said one puzzled car owner. Amidst frenzied City Council meetings, in which discordant discussion of public safety boiled over into acrimonious taking of sides, pro- and anti-union, the *Windsor Star* labelled the events 'an insurrection'.[44]

In Ottawa, the Congress of Canadian Labour was inundated with telephone calls on the part of irate workers demanding a General Strike. Four hundred union delegates from a range of unions called on Ontario's Conservative Premier, George Drew. No friend of labour, he was reportedly 'out to lunch'. But the response among the trade-union tops was of a different kind. Among the more cautious of labour leaders there was wide-ranging criticism of what was labelled a dangerous assault on democracy, law, and order. D.N. Secord of the Canadian Brotherhood of Railway Employees pontificated in the language of paternalism: 'We must recognize some of our faults and if the mob is ruling here we are wrong ... You can't deprive women and children of bread and milk'. The words could have come out of the mouths of the Winnipeg General Strike's Citizen's Committee of One Thousand.[45]

Government arbitrator and Supreme Court Justice, Ivan Rand, worked labour and capital through their impasse, drafting a statement of binding arbitration that was incorporated into the eventual collective agreement signed by the union and the company in February 1946. Rand's 'formula' became the basis of the relations of labour-capital-state for 30 years. It did for the legal zone of toleration in 1946 what the Trades Union Act of 1872 had done in a much different era: it legitimised unions at the same time that it constrained them, drawing them into the accommodationist magnetic pull of state mediation and the hegemonic ideas of bourgeois order and its seeming safeguard, democracy. When endorsed by a majority of workers, unions secured the automatic check-off of dues by employers, the right to bargain collectively for workers, grieve for them, and, within defined boundaries, strike. But to keep these rights unions had to behave 'responsibly', which meant lawfully. To do this, unions were expected to police their members, to end wildcat walkouts, threats to property, and violent picket line behaviour. If they did not, they faced fines from the courts and jailings of their leaders. By the end of the 1940s, as Ford-like battles

---

44   Quoted in Colling 1995, p. 89.
45   See Moulton 1974, pp. 129–61; Colling 1995, especially pp. 85–114.

in other parts of the country, such as the Asbestos strike of 1949,[46] re-enacted similar class-struggle theatrics, the wisdom of Rand's compromise began to be grasped more and more within the structures of the state. It was increasingly embraced by employers once given to recalcitrance in their dealings with organised labour.

This rapprochement was also being played out in collective agreements, as studies by Peter Warrian and David Matheson have shown.[47] Matheson notes a generational difference between the pre-1939 agreement, the transitional collective bargaining documents of 1940–5, and the mature labour-capital contracts of the post-World War II years. Short and to-the-point, union-employer agreements of the 1930s might be five or six pages in length. By 1949, however, similar documents could contain as many as 70 provisions, 60 or more sub-provisions, hundreds of pages, and increasingly complicated legal language. Management rights clauses, almost unheard of in 1939, were the norm ten years later, usually ending agreements by conceding to capital anything not codified explicitly in the collective agreement. As Ian McKay concludes, before the reign of Rand, workers and their unions had asked themselves simple questions before tussling with a boss: 'Are we stronger than our employers? How long can we hold out'? In the aftermath of industrial legality, with the separation of rank-and-file unionists from shop stewards and other layers of leadership, with the collective agreement an increasingly distant and incomprehensible, yet determinative, document, new concerns were more and more evident: 'Does this conflict with the collective agreement? When does this go before the conciliation board? How can we sell this politically?'[48]

6   Legacies of Industrial Pluralism

Class conflict, relations of labour and capital, and the role of the state and its initiatives in the post-1946 years existed very much in the shadow of this post-war compromise. Affluence helped grease the wheels of accommodation, although

---

46   See Trudeau 1974.
47   Warrian 1986; Matheson 1989.
48   McKay 1985, p. 82. McKay actually extends the coming of industrial legality in the Halifax building trades back into the 1930s, even the 1920s, citing legislation such as the Industrial Standards Act as pivotal breakthroughs. Whatever the fine points of historical dating and argument, Rand codified industrial legality in the late 1940s in ways that marked something of a turning point in class relations and state involvement in them. See also the argument in Fudge and Tucker 2001, pp. 263–315.

there were signs of skidding, even derailment, throughout the 1950s and into the 1960s. An overt challenge to the so-called post-war settlement was raised explicitly in 1965–6. Some 369 wildcat strikes pitted Canadian rank-and-file workers against a triumvirate of employers, union bosses, and state official-doms at the same time that a militant war against injunctions raged in labour movement circles, rocking the legal regime of class incorporation to its core. Union bureaucracies weathered this storm. The twin process of the trade-union tops beating down youthful labour dissidents and courts and judges defending the sanctity of injunctions and the class Rule of Law, as they did in 1966, jailing a number of union protesters in Peterborough's infamous Tilco strike, helped to tame the relations of labour and capital. Justice Ivan Rand was called upon to play a different role than he had in 1946, and the 1966 Royal Commission investigating industrial disputes and injunctions placed the lid firmly on class conflict in ways that would have been impossible in 1946.[49]

Yet a decade after the Tilco strikers fought a recalcitrant employer and uni-onists rallied to their cause to face prison cells for their refusal to concede that the courts had the right to curtail labour protest, the terms of class trade had shifted very much in favour of capital and the state. Global uncertainties asso-ciated with the 1973 oil crisis, and growing state deficits and capital flight in the advanced capitalist economies of the West, spelled the end of the boom cycle of what has come to be known as the Fordist regime of accumulation. This boom had always been the plush context in which the post-war settle-ment's legal negotiations of class struggle had been successfully bartered. This reversal of economic fortunes effectively ended capital and the state's willing-ness to abide by the old terms of industrial pluralism, but labour, its interests now defined as those of trade-union officials and associated with bureaucratic structures, remained a captive of its contractual commitments. Even as the premises and practices of the post-war settlement came to be overridden in a different climate in the 1970s,[50] the ideology of industrial legality/pluralism permeated the spontaneous, popular consciousness of class relations within which organised workers often found their thought suspended. This same trun-cated, increasingly mythological, foundational perspective was adhered to by a more and more entrenched layer of labour officialdom that owed its mater-ial being and privileges as well as its broad political allegiance to the legalistic pluralism of the post-World War II industrial order. Precisely because the left in the unions had been vanquished in the Cold War decade of the 1950s, and

---

49   Jamieson 1968, pp. 431–3; Palmer 1992, pp. 315–16; Sangster 2004, pp. 47–88.
50   This is the fundamental argument of Panitch and Swartz 1988.

isolated from and marginalised within the unions in the New Left upheavals
of the 1960s, organised labour's trajectory in these decades was right-leaning
within its general social-democratic field of force. The trade-union bureaucracy was anti-communist in the 1950s and early 1960s. It was less than warmly
received as the Co-operative Commonwealth Federation adapted to liberalism in the making of the New Democratic Party (NDP). With some exceptions,
most prominent in the Canadian affiliates of the United Automobile Workers,
where a 1965 Canada-United States Automotive Products Agreement constructed union politics differently, trade-union officialdoms were highly dubious of
the New Left and its influence in the social-democratic milieu in the late 1960s
and early 1970s. During this time, for instance, most mainstream elements in
the leadership of the labour movement were unmistakably hostile to developments like the left-nationalist dissident mobilisation inside the NDP, known as
the Waffle. Instead, this conservative layer of trade-union officialdom curried
closer and closer favour with the rightward inclinations of the NDP establishment.[51]

As the small revolutionary left of the 1920s and 1930s virtually passed into
non-existence and the ephemeral leftism of the 1960s imploded in programmatic confusion in the 1970s, the trade unions atrophied politically. The final
decades of the twentieth century represented a time when the trade-union bureaucracy, now stronger than it had ever been and supported by a network of
law, faced almost no critique from the left. The result was that while labour
leadership was capable of sustaining left positions and encouraging militancy
and combativeness within the ranks of the organised workers, more common
was a public face of the trade-union hierarchy that oscillated between a kind of
episodic confrontationalism and a more continuous accommodation. Specific
leaders such as Jean-Claude Parrot, nurtured in enclaves of left and working-
class militancy like the Canadian Union of Postal Workers and Montreal's Common Front unionists, were willing to struggle to expand the zone of legal toleration by defying injunctions, refusing to curtail wildcat strikes, and organising
massive protests across the spectrum of organised labour.[52]

But for the most part, labour's leadership was either ossified and cautious
or cynically performative, turning the tap of class struggle on when pressured
from the base, but snapping it back off when mobilisation threatened to actually overreach the inadequacies of a tepid leadership. By the late 1970s, with
former United Automobile Workers' President, Dennis McDermott, heading

---

51   A curiously skewed presentation of this period appears in Gindin 1995, pp. 139–62.
52   Gindin 1995, pp. 162–5; Drache 1972.

the Canadian Labour Congress, this oscillation between militancy and qui-escence had come to characterise labour's leadership. It would produce an eerily anti-climactic denouement to one of the most widespread politicised mobilisations of Canadian workers in the 1980s, British Columbia's 1983 Solidarity uprising against the New Right Social Credit government. This four-and-a-half-month battle threatened an all-out general strike, featured patently-illegal teacher walk outs and other state-defiant work stoppages, and gave rise to wide-spread coalition-building, left-union educational efforts, and massive public protests involving hundreds of thousands of increasingly militant citizens and workers. But to the extent that such upheavals were led by the labour bureau-cracy they were also, in the end, terminated by them. This was demonstrated again in the 1990s when Ontario workers battled the Conservative-orchestrated 'Common Sense Revolution' of Mike Harris's Tory government, bent as it was on downsizing the public sector and curbing the power of the unions. Milit-ant, politicised and illegal strikes of Ontario teachers in the autumn of 1998 were wound down. The Ontario Federation of Labour-orchestrated Days of Action campaign against Harris's reactionary agenda promised much in its left-militant potential and impressive labour-led protests (which included rotating general strikes and political rallies). But the Days of Action, which threatened to culminate in a province-wide general strike, collapsed like the teacher walkouts when the trade-union leaders, fearful of the mass protests moving beyond their control, called off the campaign.[53]

7   The Heritage of Civil Disobedience

In this context, civil disobedience has been handcuffed on the Labour left. Its capacity to extract concessions, secure victories, and expand the zones of legal and social toleration seems decidedly limited. Indeed, Canada of late has seemed dominated not by the civil disobedience of labour and other social movements, but rather by state and employer illegality. The wilful breaking of agreements, the defiance of established law, and the dictating of exceptions to past rules of conduct, seem to be the prerogatives of capital and the state.

As economic recession curbed possibilities, and as moments of ideological construction such as 11 September 2001 (9/11) pressured the political climate to

---

53   See Palmer 1987b; 'Halloween in Harrisland: Teachers, Bureaucrats, and Betrayal', *Cana-dian Dimension*, September/October 1998; 'Where Ya At, General Strike?!', *Canadian Di-mension*, September/October 1998. A more positive view of this later 1990s period appears in Rapaport 1999.

the right, the labour bureaucracy adapted by truncating class struggle, retreating into the legalisms of collective bargaining, and abandoning commitments to wide-ranging struggles and protests that demand more than organised workers treading water in pursuit of wage and work-condition benefits. Few unions at this point engage in civil disobedience, and the militant core of Canadian trade unionism and labour leadership in the 1980s, such as the Canadian Automobile Workers (CAW) and its head, Basil 'Buzz' Hargrove, had, by the 1990s, gravitated more and more to the mainstream. Hargrove treated the combative Flying Squadrons of the CAW a little like a personal armed guard, dismantling them when they threatened to use their muscle on behalf of forces he questioned and struggles he backed away from, but turning them loose when a union cause, such as striking workers in south-western Ontario, rationalised their revival. A measure of Hargrove's retreat was registered in 2002 with his cutting of the modest annual CAW contribution to the Ontario Coalition Against Poverty (OCAP), ostensibly on the grounds that OCAP was guilty of engaging in unnecessarily violent acts of civil disobedience. Speaking increasingly in the language of law and order, Hargrove was sidling up to the NDP, a political force he had recently criticised as spent in its possibilities through its incorporation into the logic of the liberal democratic order. When anti-globalisation activists challenged the symbol of transnational, imperialist power at the Quebec City Summit protests in April 2001, it was the labour hierarchy that led its union masses away from the struggle and refused to march up the hill to confront the fence and the state violence that defended it with police, tear gas, rubber bullets, and chemical sprays.[54]

Unless thwarted, this acquiescence will prove the death of the unions and the Left. For no successful struggle against capital and the state on our home ground, let alone internationally, can be successful when the working class is inhibited by a leadership fearful to lead and antagonistic to the one force that has historically insured humanity's advance: civil disobedience. To be sure, civil disobedience does indeed require deft development and a leadership that can negotiate law's limits and convey a sense of people's need for new law – law that sustains justice rather than refusing to recognise the need for justice. Even the rough Irish canallers of the pre-Confederation era understood this well, prefacing an 1843 strike with the statement that, 'notwithstanding the hopes entertained by our enemies, we are fully determined to steer clear of any infraction of the law'.[55] Of course, in their actions the canal labourers stretched

54   MacKay 2002, p. 21.
55   Cited in Palmer 1992, p. 61.

this statement of intent beyond its legal limits. The zones of legal and social toleration bequeathed to labour and the left, the people, and our environment, by a century of bourgeois order demands further stretching and redefinition, just as, in 1872, 1886, 1919, 1937, 1946, and 1965–6, the law of labour was in need of new codes, legislation, and freedoms. To the extent that change happened, it came about because of civil disobedience. Those afraid to protest in ways that challenge law will never remake the law. They will never be a part of the creation of law that all can live with profitably, rather than law that the few profit from richly. And, finally, without civil disobedience we can never even imagine that a society in which law, like the state itself, withers away, is indeed possible. For society's ultimate advance will only be realised when law's coercive presence is no longer necessary to constrain human beings who can, in circumstances barely imaginable in our times, be truly free. To repudiate or abandon that utopian longing for a society finally liberated from law is to give up the vision of human perfection without which living is reduced to the most base, self-centred propositions. Succumbing to that would be the ultimate act of an unfortunately blinkered, constrainingly individualistic and acquiescently subdued, *civil* disobedience.

References

AA.VV. 1861, *Journal of the Board of Arts and Manufactures for Upper Canada*, 1.

———— 1863, *Journal of the Board of Arts and Manufactures for Upper Canada*, 3.

———— 1864, *Journal of the Board of Arts and Manufactures for Upper Canada*, 4.

———— 1887, *Mandements: lettres pastorales et circulaires des évêques de Québec*, Volume 1, publiés par H. Têtu et C.-O. Gagnon, Québec: Imprimerie générale A. Coté et Cie.

———— 1889, *Appletons' Annual Cyclopaedia and Register of Important Events of the Year 1888*, New Series, Volume 12, New York: D. Appleton and Company.

———— 1911, *The Americana: A Universal Reference Library*, Volume 17, edited by Frederick Converse Beach and George Edwin Rimes, New York: Scientific American Compiling Department.

Abbott, Edith 1905, 'The Wages of Unskilled Labor in the United States', *Journal of Political Economy*, 13, June: 324.

Abella, Irving Martin 1973, *Nationalism, Communism, and Canadian Labour*, Toronto: University of Toronto Press.

———— (ed.) 1974, *On Strike: Six Key Labour Struggles in Canada, 1919–1949*, Toronto: James Lorimer & Company.

———— and David Millar (eds.) 1978, *The Canadian Worker in the Twentieth Century*, Toronto: Oxford University Press.

Abelove, Henry, et al. (ed.) 1983, *Visions of History: Interviews with E.P. Thompson ...*, New York: Pantheon.

Acheson, T.W. 1972, 'The Social Origins of the Canadian Industrial Elite, 1880–1885' in *Canadian Business History: Selected Studies, 1947–1971*, edited by David S. Macmillan, Toronto: McClelland and Stewart.

Adamic, Louis 1931, *Dynamite: The Story of Class Violence in America*, New York: Viking.

———— 1938, *My America, 1928–1938*, New York: Harper Brothers.

Adams, George R. 1972, 'The Carolina Regulators: A Note on Changing Interpretations', *North Carolina Historical Review*, 49, 4: 345–52.

Adams, Graham, Jr. 1966, *Age of Industrial Violence, 1910–1915*, New York: Columbia University Press.

Aglietta, Michel 1976, *A Theory of Capitalist Regulation: The U.S. Economic Experience*, London: NLB.

———— 1978, 'Phases of U.S. Capitalist Expansion', *New Left Review*, 110, July–August: 19–21.

Aitchison, J.H. 1953, 'The Development of Local Government in Upper Canada', PhD dissertation, University of Toronto.

Aitken, H.G.J. 1960, *Taylorism at Watertown Arsenal: Scientific Management in Action, 1908–1915*, Cambridge, MA: Harvard University Press.

———— 1975, 'The Family Compact and the Welland Canal Company' in *Historical Essays on Upper Canada*, edited by J.K. Johnson, Toronto: McClelland and Stewart.

Akenson, Donald H. 1982, 'Ontario: Whatever Happened to the Irish?' in *Canadian Papers in Rural History*, Volume 3, edited by Donald H. Akenson, Gananoque, ON: Langdale Press.

———— 1984, *The Irish in Ontario: A Study in Rural History*, Kingston, ON: McGill-Queen's University Press.

Albo, Greg, Sam Gindin, and Leo Panitch 2010, *In and Out of Crisis: The Global Financial Meltdown and Left Alternatives*, Oakland, CA: PM Press.

Alford, L.P. 1918, 'An Industrial Achievement of the War', *Industrial Management*, 55, February: 97–100.

Alford, Violet 1959, 'Rough Music or Charivari', *Folklore*, 70, 4: 505–18.

Alinksy, Saul 1970, *John L. Lewis*, New York: Vintage.

Allan, D.G.C. 1952–3, 'The Rising in the West, 1682–31', *Economic History Review*, 2nd ser., 5: 76–85.

Allen, Richard 1973, *The Social Passion: Religion and Social Reform in Canada, 1914–28*, Toronto: University of Toronto Press.

Amsden, Jon and Stephen Brier 1977, 'Coal Miners on Strike: The Transformation of Strike Demands and the Formation of a National Union', *Journal of Interdisciplinary History*, 9: 583–616.

Ancient Order of United Workmen n.d., *Ritual*, n.p.

Anderson, Richard 1992, ' "The Irrepressible Stampede": Tramps in Ontario, 1870–1880', *Ontario History*, 84, 1: 33–56.

Angus, Ian 1981, *Canadian Bolsheviks: The Early Years of the Communist Party of Canada*, Montreal: Vanguard.

———— 2004, *Canadian Bolsheviks: The Early Years of the Communist Party of Canada*, Victoria: Trafford Publishing.

Appleton, Paul Campbell 1974, 'The Sunshine and the Shade: Labour Activism in Central Canada, 1850–1860', MA thesis, University of Calgary.

Aptheker, Herbert 1943, *American Negro Slave Revolts*, New York: International Publishers.

Armstrong, Frederick H. 1962, 'The Carfrae Family: A Study in Early Toronto Toryism', *Ontario History*, 54, 3: 161–81.

———— 1967, 'The Reformer as Capitalist: William Lyon Mackenzie and the Printers' Strike of 1836', *Ontario History*, 59, 3: 187–96.

———— 1971, 'William Lyon Mackenzie: Persistent Hero', *Journal of Canadian Studies*, 6, 3: 21–35.

———— 1989, 'The Oligarchy of the Western District of Upper Canada, 1788–1841' in *Historical Essays on Upper Canada: New Perspectives*, edited by J.K. Johnson and Bruce G. Wilson, Ottawa: Carleton University Press.

Aronowitz, Stanley 1973, *False Promises: The Shaping of American Working Class Consciousness*, New York: McGraw Hill.

Atwood, E. Bagby 1964, 'Shivarees and Charivaris: Variations on a Theme' in *A Good Tale and a Bonnie Time*, edited by Mody C. Boatright, Wilson M. Hudson, and Allen Maxwell, Dallas: Southern Methodist University Press.

Atwood, Margaret 1970, *The Journals of Susanna Moodie: Poems*, Toronto: Oxford University Press.

Aufhauser, P. Keith 1973, 'Slavery and Scientific Method', *Journal of Economic History*, 33, December: 811–24.

Avrich, Paul 1986, *The Haymarket Tragedy*, Princeton: Princeton University Press.

Axelrod, Paul 1982, *Scholars and Dollars: Politics, Economics, and the Universities of Ontario, 1945–1980*, Toronto: University of Toronto Press.

Avery, Donald 1979, *'Dangerous Foreigners': European Immigrant Workers and Labour Radicalism in Canada, 1896–1932*, Toronto: McClelland and Stewart.

Avis, Walter et al. (eds.) 1967, *A Dictionary of Canadianisms on Historical Principles: Dictionary of Canadian English*, Toronto: W.J. Gage.

Babcock, Robert H. 1974, *Gompers in Canada: A Study in American Continentalism Before the First World War*, Toronto: University of Toronto Press.

Baehre, Rainer 1981, 'Paupers and Poor Relief in Upper Canada', Canadian Historical Association, *Historical Papers*: 57–80.

Bailey, A.G. 1969, *The Conflict of European and Eastern Algonkian Cultures, 1504–1700*, Toronto: University of Toronto Press.

Bain, Joe S. 1964, 'Industrial Concentration and Anti-Trust Policy' in *Growth of the American Economy*, edited by Harold Williamson, Englewood Cliffs, NJ: Prentice-Hall.

Baird, Irene 1974 [1939], *Waste Heritage*, Toronto: Macmillan.

Bamford, Samuel 1905, *Bamford's Passages in the Life of a Radical in Two Volumes*, London: Fisher Unwin.

Bancroft, Hubert Howe 1887, *The Works of Hubert Howe Bancroft, Volumes XXXVI–VII: Popular Tribunals*, San Francisco: History Company Publishers.

Barde, Alexandre 1861, *Histoire des comités de vigilance aux Attakapas*, Sainte-Jeane-Baptiste: Imprimerie du Meschacébé et de l' Avant-Coureur.

Barnett, George 1909, 'The Printers: A Study in American Trade Unionism', *American Economic Association Quarterly*, 10: 182–208.

Barrett, Michèle 1980, *Women's Oppression Today: Problems in Marxist-Feminist Analysis*, London: New Left Books.

Bartlett, John Russell 1877, *Dictionary of Americanisms: A Glossary of Words and Phrases Usually Regarded as Peculiar to the United States*, Boston: Little, Brown, and Company.

Baskerville, Peter A. and Eric W. Sager 1998, *Unwilling Idlers: The Urban Unemployed and Their Families in Late Victorian Canada*, Toronto: University of Toronto Press.

Bassinet, Eloi-Christophe 1833, *Histoire morale, civile, politique et littéraire du charivari: depuis son origine, vers le IVe siècle*, Paris: Delaunay.

Battye, John 1980, 'The Nine-Hour Pioneers: Genesis of the Canadian Labour Movement', *Labour/Le Travailleur*, 4: 25–56.

Bauman, Zygmunt 1968, 'Marxism and the Contemporary Theory of Culture', *Co-Existence*, 5, July: 161–73.

Beard, Mary Ritter 1931, *The American Labor Movement*, New York: Macmillan.

Beattie, John 1977, *Attitudes towards Crime and Punishment in Upper Canada, 1830–1850: A Documentary Study*, Toronto: University of Toronto Centre of Criminology.

Belden, H. & Co. 1878, *Illustrated Historical Atlas of the Counties of Hastings and Prince Edward, Ont.*, Toronto: H. Belden & Co.

Bell, Daniel 1970, *Work and Its Discontents: The Cult of Efficiency in America*, New York: LID.

Bendix, Reinhard 1956, *Work and Authority in Industry: Ideologies of Management in the Course of Industrialization*, New York: Wiley.

Benjamin, Walter 1968, *Illuminations*, edited and with an introduction by Hannah Arendt, New York: Harcourt, Brace and World.

Bennett, John William 1977, 'Iron Workers in Woods Run Johnstown: The Union Era, 1865–1901', PhD dissertation, University of Pittsburgh.

——— 1979, 'The Knights of Labor and the Clan-Na-Gael', paper presented to the Knights of Labor Centennial Conference, Newberry Library, Chicago, 17–19 May.

Bennett, Sari J. and Carville V. Earle 1982, 'Labour Power and Locality in the Gilded Age: The Northeastern United States, 1881–1894', *Histoire Sociale/Social History*, 15, November: 383–405.

Bennetts, David Paul 1972, 'Black and White Workers: New Orleans, 1880–1900', PhD dissertation, University of Illinois at Urbana-Champaign.

Bensman, David Harlan 1977, 'Artisan Culture, Business Union: American Hat Finishers in the Nineteenth Century', PhD dissertation, Columbia University.

Bercé, Yves-Marie 1976, *Fête et révolte: Des mentalités populaires du XVIe au XVIIIe siècle*, Paris: Hachette.

Bercuson, David Jay 1974, *Confrontation at Winnipeg: Labour, Industrial Relations, and the General Strike*, Montreal: McGill-Queen's University Press.

——— 1978, *Fools and Wise Men: The Rise and Fall of the One Big Union*, Toronto: McGraw-Hill Ryerson.

Berlanstein, Leonard 1993 (ed.), *Rethinking Labor History: Essays on Discourse and Class Analysis*, Urbana and Champaign: University of Illinois Press.

Bernier, Bernard 1980, 'The Penetration of Capitalism in Quebec Agriculture' in *Class, State, Ideology and Change: Marxist Perspectives on Canada*, edited by J. Paul Grayson, Toronto: Holt, Rinehart & Winston.

Bernstein, Irving 1960, *The Lean Years: A History of the American Worker, 1920–1933*, Boston: Houghton Mifflin.

Bernstein, Leonard 1950, 'The Working People of Philadelphia from Colonial Times to the Central Strike of 1835', *Pennsylvania Magazine of History and Biography*, 74: 322–39;

Berton, Pierre 1990, *The Great Depression, 1929–1939*, Toronto: McClelland & Stewart.

Bertram, Gordon W. 1964, 'Historical Statistics on Growth and Structure of Manufacturing in Canada, 1870–1957' in *C.P.S.A. Conference on Statistics, 1962 and 1963*, edited by J. Henripin and A. Asimakopulos, Toronto: University of Toronto Press.

Betcherman, Lita-Rose 1982, *The Little Band: The Clashes between the Communists and the Political and Legal Establishment in Canada, 1928–1932*, Ottawa: Deneau.

Bigsby, John Jeremiah 1850, *The Shoe and the Canoe; or Pictures of Travel in the Canadas*, London: Chapman and Hall.

Bilson, Geoffrey 1980, *A Darkened House: Cholera in Nineteeth-Century Canada*, Toronto: University of Toronto Press.

Bimba, Anthony 1927, *The History of the American Working Class*, New York: International.

Bing, Alexander 1921, *Wartime Strikes and Their Adjustment*, New York: E.P. Dutton.

Bisno, Abraham 1967, *Abraham Bisno, Union Pioneer*, Madison: University of Wisconsin Press.

Black Rose Editorial Collective 1972, *Quebec Labour: The Confederation of National Trade Unions Yesterday and Today*, Montreal: Black Rose.

Bland, Warren 1974, 'The Location of Manufacturing in Southern Ontario in 1881', *Ontario Geography*, 8: 8–39.

Bleasdale, Ruth 1981, 'Class Conflict and the Canals of Upper Canada in the 1840s', *Labour/Le Travailleur*, 7, Spring: 9–40.

Bliss, Michael 1974, *A Living Profit: Studies in the Social History of Canadian Business, 1883–1911*, Toronto: McClelland and Stewart.

Blum, Solomon 1907, 'Trade Union Rules in the Building Trades' in *Studies in American Trade Unionism*, edited by Jacob H. Hollander and George C. Barnett, New York: Henry Holt.

Blumin, Stuart M. 1977, 'Rip Van Winkle's Grandchildren: Family and Household in the Hudson Valley, 1800–1860' in *Family and Kin in Urban Communities, 1700–1930*, edited by Tamara K. Hareven, New York: New Viewpoints.

Board of Arts and Manufactures for Upper Canada 1867, *The Journal of the Board of Arts and Manufactures for Upper Canada*, 7.

Bode, Patrick 1984, *Sir John Beverley Robinson: Bone and Sinew of the Compact*, Toronto: University of Toronto Press.

Boller, Paul F., Jr. 1969, *American Thought in Transition: The Impact of Evolutionary Naturalism, 1865–1900*, Chicago: Rand McNally.

Bonnain-Moerdyk, Rolande et Donald Moerdyk 1977, 'A propos du charivari: discours bourgeois et coutumes populaires', *Annales: E.S.C.*, 32: 381–98.

Bonthius, Andrew 2003, 'The Patriot War of 1837–1838: Locofocoism with a Gun?' *Labour/Le Travail*, 52, Fall: 9–44.

Bottomore, Tom et al. (eds.) 1983, *A Dictionary of Marxist Thought*, Cambridge, MA: Harvard University Press.

Bowden, Witt 1930, *Industrial History of the United States*, New York: Adelphi.

Bradbury, Bettina 1979, 'The Family Economy and Work in an Industrializing City: Montreal in the 1870s', Canadian Historical Association, *Papers*: 71–96.

———— 1995, 'The Home as Workplace', in *Labouring Lives: Work & Workers in Nineteenth-Century Ontario*, edited by Paul Craven, Toronto: University of Toronto Press.

Brandeis, Louis 1911, 'The New Conception of Industrial Efficiency', *Journal of Accountancy*, 12, May: 35–43.

———— 1919, 'Scientific Management' in *Selected Articles on Modern Industrial Movements*, edited by Daniel Bloomfield, New York: H.W. Wilson.

Braverman, Harry 1974a, *Labor and Monopoly Capital: The Degradation of Work in the Twentieth Century*, New York: Monthly Review.

———— 1974b, 'Labor and Monopoly Capital: The Degradation of Work in the Twentieth Century', *Monthly Review*, 26, July–August: 1–134.

Brecher, Jeremy 1972, *Strike!*, San Francisco: Straight Arrow Books.

Brenner, Robert 1976, 'Agrarian Class Structure and Economic Development in Pre-Industrial Europe', *Past and Present*, 70, February: 30–75.

———— 1977, 'The Origins of Capitalist Development: A Critique of Neo-Smithian Marxism', *New Left Review*, 104, July–August: 25–92.

———— 1982, 'The Agrarian Roots of European Capitalism', *Past and Present*, 97, November: 16–113.

———— 1985, 'The Paradox of Social Democracy: The American Case' in *The Year Left 1985: An American Socialist Yearbook*, edited by Mike Davis, Fred Pfeil, and Michael Sprinker, London: Verso.

———— 2006, *The Economics of Global Turbulence: The Advanced Capitalist Economies from Long Boom to Long Downturn, 1945–2005*, New York: Verso.

Brewer, John 1976, *Party Ideology and Popular Politics at the Accession of George III*, London: Cambridge University Press.

Bridenbaugh, Carl 1955, *Cities in Revolt: Urban Life in America, 1743–1776*, New York: Knopf.

Brissenden, Paul 1922, *Labor Turn-over in Industry*, New York: Macmillan.

Broadfoot, Barry 1973, *Ten Lost Years, 1929–1939: Memories of Canadians Who Survived the Depression*, Toronto: Doubleday Canada.

Brody, David 1960, *Steelworkers in America: The Nonunion Era*, New York: Harper.

———— 1968, 'The Rise and Decline of Welfare Capitalism' in *Change and Continuity in Twentieth Century America: The 1920's*, Akron, OH: Ohio State University Press.

———— 1980, *Workers in Industrial America: Essays on the Twentieth-Century Struggle*, New York: Oxford University Press.

Broeker, Galen 1970, *Rural Disorder and Police Reform in Ireland, 1812–36*, Toronto: University of Toronto Press.

Brookes, Alan A. 1982, 'Family, Youth, and Leaving Home in Late Nineteenth-Century Rural Nova Scotia: Canning and the Exodus, 1868–1893' in *Childhood and Family in Canadian History*, edited by Joy Parr, Toronto: McClelland and Stewart.

Brooks, Thomas R. 1978, *Clint: A Biography of a Labor Intellectual – Clinton S. Golden*, New York: Atheneum.

Brown, Jennifer 1980, *Strangers in Blood: Fur Trade Company Families in Indian Country*, Vancouver: University of British Columbia Press.

Brown, Lorne 1987, *When Freedom Was Lost: The Unemployed, the Agitator, and the State*, Montreal: Black Rose Books.

Brown, Richard Maxwell 1963, *The South Carolina Regulators*, Cambridge, MA: Belknap Press of Harvard University Press.

———— 1973, 'Violence and the American Revolution' in *Essays on the American Revolution*, edited by Stephen G. Kurtz and James H. Hutson, Chapel Hill, NC: Published for the Institute of Early American History and Culture, Williamsburg, VA, by the University of North Carolina Press.

Brown, Theo 1952, 'The Stag hunt in Devon', *Folklore*, 63, 2: 104–9.

Bruchey, Stuart 1965, *The Roots of American Economic Growth, 1607–1861*, New York: Harper.

Brundage, David 1979, 'The Producing Classes and the Saloon: Denver in the 1880s', paper presented for the Knights of Labor Centennial Conference, Newberry Library, Chicago, 17–19 May.

Buchanan, Isaac 1857, 'Election Fly-sheet' in *The Hamilton Charivari: An Election Fly-Sheet, Edited on This Occasion Only, by Canadian Sepoys! Dulce et Decorum est Pro Hamiltonia Vivere, Vitat! Regina!*, Hamilton: C.W.

Buchanan, James 1832, *Project for the Formation of a Depot in Upper Canada, with a View to Receive the Whole Pauper Population of England*, New York: William A. Mercein.

Buchanan, Joseph 1970, *The Story of a Labor Agitator*, Westport: Greenwood Press.

———— 1971, *The Story of a Labor Agitator*, Freeport, NY: Books for Libraries Press.

Buckler, Ernest 1952, *The Mountain and the Valley*, New York: Holt.

Budish, J.M. and George Soule 1966 [1920], *The New Unionism in the Clothing Industry*, New York: Russell & Russell.

Buhle, Paul 1978, 'The Knights of Labor in Rhode Island', *Radical History Review*, 18, Spring: 39–73.

Burgess, Joanne 1977, 'L'industrie de la chaussure à Montréal, 1840–1870: Le passage de l'artisant à la fabrique', *Revue d'histoire de l'Amerique français*, 31: 187–210.

Burlingame, Roger 1938, *March of the Iron Men: A Social History of Union Through Invention*, New York: Scribners.

Burn, D.L. 1970, 'The Genesis of American Engineering Competition, 1850–1870' in *Technological Change: The United States and Britain in the Nineteenth Century*, edited by S.B. Saul, London: Methuen.

Cable, George W. 1883, *Old Creole Days*, New York: Charles Scribner's Sons.

——— 1890, *Old Creole Days*, with an etching by Percy Moran, New York: Charles Scribner's Sons.

Cadigan, Sean T. 1987, 'Paternalism in Upper Canada, 1800–1841', MA thesis, Queen's University.

——— 1991, 'Paternalism and Politics: Sir Francis Bond Head, the Orange Order, and the Election of 1836', *Canadian Historical Review*, 72, September: 319–47.

Cain, Maureen and Alan Hunt 1979, *Marx and Engels on Law*, New York: Academic Press.

Calhoun, Arthur W. 1917, *A Social History of the American Family from Colonial Times to the Present, Volume 1: Colonial Period*, Cleveland, OH: The Arthur H. Clark Company.

Callahan, Raymond E. 1962, *Education and the Cult of Efficiency: A Study of the Social Forces that Have Shaped the Administration of the Public Schools*, Chicago: University of Chicago Press.

Calvert, Monte A. 1967, *The Mechanical Engineer in America, 1830–1910*, Baltimore, MD: John Hopkins Press.

Campbell, Marjorie Freeman 1966, *A Mountain and a City: The Story of Hamilton*, Toronto: McClelland and Stewart.

Canada Department of Agriculture 1876, *Census of Canada, 1665 to 1871: Statistics of Canada*, Ottawa: I.B. Taylor.

Canniff, Wm. 1869, *History of the Settlement of Upper Canada, (Ontario,) with Special Reference to the Bay Quinte*, Toronto: Dudley & Burns, Printers.

Capp, Bernard 1977, 'English Youth Groups and *The Pinder of Wakefield*', *Past & Present*, 76, August: 127–33.

Cardullo, Forrest E. 1914, 'Industrial Administration and Scientific Management' in *Scientific Management*, edited by C.B. Thompson, Cambridge, MA: Harvard University Press.

Careless, J.M.S. 1969, 'Limited Identities in Canada', *Canadian Historical Review*, 50, March: 1–10.

——— 1984, *Toronto to 1918: An Illustrated History*, Toronto: J. Lorimer & Co.

Carlton, Frank T. 1914, 'Scientific Management and the Wage Earner' in *Scientific Management*, edited by C.B. Thompson, Cambridge, MA: Harvard University Press.

Carlton, Robert 1843, *The New Purchase: or, Seven and a Half Years in the Far West*, New York: D. Appleton & Co.

Carr, E.H. 1975 [1961], *What is History?*, Harmondsworth: Penguin Books.

Carrothers, A.W.R. 1956, *The Labour Injunction in British Columbia, 1946–1955: With Particular Reference to the Law of Picketing*, Toronto: CCH Canadian, Limited.

——— 1966, *Report of a Study on the Labour Injunction in Ontario*, Toronto: n.p.

Cassidy, H.M. 1932, *Unemployment and Relief in Ontario, 1929–1932: A Survey and Report*, Toronto: Dent.

Cassity, Michael J. 1979, 'Modernization and Social Crisis: The Knights of Labor and a Midwest Community, 1885–1886', *Journal of American History*, 66, June: 41–61.

Caston, Nicole de 1971, 'La criminalité familiale dans le ressort du Parlement de Toulouse, 1690–1730' in *Crimes et criminalité en France sous l'Ancien Regime: 17e–18e siècles*, edited by A. Abbiatecci et al., Paris: A. Colin.

Caughey, John W. (ed.) 1960, *Their Majesties The Mob*, Chicago: University of Chicago Press.

Cayton, Horace R. and George S. Mitchell 1939, *Black Workers and the New Unions*, Chapel Hill, NC: The University of North Carolina Press.

Chambers, Edward and Gordon Bertram 1966, 'Urbanization and Manufacturing in Central Canada' in *C.P.S.A. Conference on Statistics, 1966*, edited by Sylvia Ostry, Toronto: University of Toronto Press.

Chambers, Robert 1864, *The Book of Days: A Miscellany of Popular Antiquities in Connection with the Calendar, Including Anecdote, Biography & History, Curiosities of Literature and Oddities of Human Life and Character*, Edinburgh: W. & R. Chambers.

Chan, Oscar 1949, 'The Canadian Knights of Labor with special reference to the 1880s', MA thesis, McGill University.

Chandler, Alfred D. 1959, 'The Beginnings of "Big Business" in American Industry', *Business History Review*, 32, Spring: 1–31.

The Charivari: or Canadian Poetics: A Tale after the Manner of Beppo 1824, Montreal: Printed for the publisher.

Chevalier, Louis 1973, *Laboring Classes and Dangerous Classes in Paris During the First Half of the Nineteenth Century*, New York: Howard Fertig.

Chilton, Lisa 2011, 'Managing Migrants: Toronto, 1820–1880', *Canadian Historical Review*, 92, June: 231–62.

Chisamore, Dale et al. 1975, *Brockville: A Social History*, Brockville, ON: Waterway Press.

Church, A. Henry 1900, 'The Meaning of Commercial Organization', *Engineering Magazine*, 20, December: 391–8.

City of Hamilton 1902, *Hamilton City Directory*, Hamilton.

City of Kingston 1907, *By-Laws of the City of Kingston From the Date of Its Incorporation as a City in 1846 to December 1906*, Kingston.

Clapin, Sylvia n.d., *A New Dictionary of Americanisms*, New York: Louis Weiss & Co., Publishers.

———— 1897a, *New Dictionary of Americanisms*, Volume 1, New York: Century Dictionary.

———— 1897b, *New Dictionary of Americanisms* Volume 8, New York: Century Dictionary.

Clark, Evans 1920, 'The Industry is Ours', *Socialist Review*, 9, July: 59.

Clark, Kenneth Lloyd 1976, 'Social Relations and Urban Change in a Late Nineteenth Century Southwestern Ontario Railroad City: St Thomas, 1868–1890', MA thesis, York University.

Clark, S.D. 1942, *The Social Development of Canada: An Introductory Study with Select Documents*, Toronto: The University of Toronto Press.

―――― 1959, *Movements of Political Protest in Canada, 1640–1840*, Toronto: University of Toronto Press.

Clark, Victor S. 1949 [1929], *History of Manufactures in the United States*, New York: Peter Smith.

Clarke, John, Chas Critcher, and Richard Johnson (eds.) 1979, *Working-Class Culture: Studies in History and Theory*, London: Hutchinson.

Clarke, John 2011, *Land, Power, and Economics on the Frontier of Upper Canada*, Montreal: McGill-Queen's University Press.

Cluer, Andrew 1974, *Plymouth and Plymouthians: Photographs & Memories*, Plymouth: Lantern Books.

Cochran, Thomas C. and William Miller 1966, 'The Business of Politics' in *Views of American Economic Growth: The Industrial Era*, edited by Thomas C. Cochran and W. Brewer, New York: McGraw-Hill.

Cole, Arthur H. (ed.) 1968, *Industrial and Commercial Correspondence of Alexander Hamilton*, New York: Kelley.

Cole, Donald 1963, *Immigrant City: Lawrence, Massachusetts, 1845–1921*, Chapel Hill, NC: University of North Carolina Press.

Coles, Robert 1972, *South Goes North*, Boston: Little, Brown.

Colling, Herb 1995, *Ninety-Nine Days: The Ford Strike in Windsor, 1945*, Toronto: NC Press.

Collins, J.E. 1883, *Life and Times of the Right Honourable Sir John A. Macdonald, Premier of the Dominion of Canada*, Toronto: Rose Publishing Company.

Colls Robert 1977, *The Collier's Rant: Song and Culture in the Industrial Village*, London: Croom Helm.

Coman, Katharine 1920, *The Industrial History of the United States*, New York: Macmillan.

Commons, John R. 1909, 'American Shoemakers, 1648–1895: A Sketch of Industrial Evolution', *Quarterly Journal of Economics* 24, November: 39–84.

―――― 1911, 'Organized Labor's Attitude Towards Industrial Efficiency', *American Economic Review*, I, September: 463–72.

Commons, John R. et al. (ed.) 1958, *A Documentary History of American Industrial Society*, New York: Russell & Russell.

―――― 1966, *History of Labor in the United States*, New York: Kelley.

Conant, Thomas 1898, *Upper Canada Sketches*, Toronto: W. Briggs.

Conner, James McCarthur 1923, 'Trade Unions in Toronto' in *The Municipality of Toron-*

to: A History, Volume 1, edited by Jesse Edgar Middleton, Toronto: Dominion Publishing.

Conway, Sean Gerard 1977, 'Upper Canadian Orangeism in the Nineteenth Century: Aspects of a Pattern of Disruption', MA thesis, Queen's University.

Cook, Ezra (ed.) 1886, *Knights of Labor Illustrated: Adelphon Kruptos: The Full Illustrated Ritual Including the 'Unwritten Work' and an Historical Sketch of the Order*, Chicago: Ezra A. Cook.

Cook, Terry 1975, 'John Beverley Robinson and the Conservative Blueprint for the Upper Canadian Community' in *Historical Essays on Upper Canada*, edited by J.K. Johnson, Toronto: McClelland and Stewart.

Cooke, Morris, Samuel Gompers, and Fred J. Miller (eds.) 1920, 'Labor, Management and Productivity', *Annals of the American Academy of Political and Social Science*, 91, September.

Cooper, J.I. 1949, 'The Quebec Ship Labourers' Benevolent Society', *Canadian Historical Review*, 30, December: 338–9.

Cooper, Jerry M. 1980, *The Army and Civil Disorder: Federal Military Intervention in Labor Disputes, 1877–1900*, Westport, CT: Greenwood Press.

Cooper, Leonard 1959, *Radical Jack: The Life of John George Lambton*, London: Cresset Press.

Cope, William Henry 1883, *A Glossary of Hampshire Words and Phrases*, London: Trübner & Co.

Copley, Frank B. 1923, *Frederick W. Taylor: Father of Scientific Management*, New York: Harpur.

Copp, Terry 1974, *The Anatomy of Poverty: The Condition of the Working Class in Montreal, 1897–1929*, Toronto: McClelland and Stewart.

Cordulack, John Herbert 1975, 'The Artisan Confronts the Machine Age: Bureau County, Illinois, 1850–1880', PhD dissertation, University of Illinois at Urbana-Champaign.

Cosentino, Frank 1975, 'A History of the Concept of Professionalism in Canadian Sport', *Canadian Journal of Sport and Physical Education*, 6, December: 75–81.

Cotkin, George 1978, 'Working Class Intellectuals and Evolutionary Thought in America, 1870–1915', PhD dissertation, Ohio State University.

Cour, Lykke de la, Cecilia Morgan, and Mariana Valverde 1992, 'Gender Regulation and State Formation in Nineteenth-Century Canada' in *Colonial Leviathan: State Formation in Mid-Nineteenth-Century Canada*, edited by Allan Greer and Ian Radforth, Toronto: University of Toronto Press.

Cowherd, Thomas 1884, *The Emigrant Mechanic and other tales in verse, together with numerous songs upon Canadian subjects ... by the Brantford tinsmith rhymer*, Brantford: published by author.

Coyne, James H. (ed.) 1909, *The Talbot Papers*, Ottawa: Transactions of the Royal Society of Canada.

Craig, Gerald M. 1963, *Upper Canada: The Formative Years, 1784–1841*, Toronto: McClelland and Stewart.

Craigie, William A. and James R. Hurlbert (eds.) 1938, *A Dictionary of American English on Historical Principles*, Volume 1, Chicago: University of Chicago Press.

Craven, Paul 1980, *'An Impartial Umpire': Industrial Relations and the Canadian State 1900–1911*, Toronto: University of Toronto Press.

———— (ed.) 1995, *Labouring Lives: Work & Workers in Nineteenth-Century Ontario*, Toronto: University of Toronto Press.

Creighton, Donald 1937a, *The Commercial Empire of the St. Lawrence, 1760–1850*, Toronto: The Ryerson Press.

———— 1937b, 'The Economic Background of the Rebellions', *Canadian Journal of Economics and Political Science*, 3: 322–34.

Crispo, John 1967, *International Unionism: A Study in Canadian-American Relations*, Toronto: McGraw-Hill.

Crispo, J.H.G. and H.W. Arthurs 1968, 'Industrial Unrest in Canada: A Diagnosis of Recent Experience', *Relations Industrielles/Industrial Relations*, 23, April: 237–64.

Cross, Michael S. 1971, 'Stony Monday, 1849: The Rebellion Loses Riots in Bytown', *Ontario History*, 63, 3: 177–90.

———— 1973, 'The Shiners' Wars: Social Violence in the Ottawa Valley in the 1830s', *Canadian Historical Review*, 54, March: 1–26.

Cross, Michael S. (ed.) 1974, *The Workingman in the Nineteenth Century*, Toronto: Oxford University Press.

———— and Gregory S. Kealey (eds.) 1982, *Pre-Industrial Canada, 1760–1849: Readings in Canadian Social History* Volume 11, Toronto: McClelland and Stewart.

———— and Robert L. Fraser 1983, '"The Waste that Lies before Me": The Public and Private Worlds of Robert Baldwin', Canadian Historical Association, *Historical Papers*: 164–83.

———— and Robert L. Fraser 1985, 'Robert Baldwin' in *Dictionary of Canadian Biography*, Volume 18 (1851–60), edited by Frances G. Halpenny and Jean Hamelin, Toronto: University of Toronto Press.

Cross, Whitney 1950, *The Burned-Over District: The Social and Intellectual History of Enthusiastic Religion in Western New York*, Ithaca: Cornell University Press.

Crowley, Terry 1995, 'Rural Labour' in *Labouring Lives: Work and Workers in Nineteenth-Century Ontario*, edited by Paul Craven, Toronto: University of Toronto Press.

Crozier, E.W. 1899, *The White-Caps: A History of the Organization in Sevier County*, Knoxville: Bean, Warters & Gaut.

Crunican, Paul 1976, *Priests and Politics: Manitoba Schools and the Election of 1896*, Toronto: University of Toronto Press.

Cumbler, John T. 1974, 'Labor, Capital and Community: The Struggle for Power', *Labor History*, 15, 3: 395–415.

Cunningham, B.H. 1930, 'A Skimmington in 1618', *Folklore*, 41, 3: 287–98.

Cutler, James Elbert 1969 [1905], *Lynch-Law: An Investigation into the History of Lynching in the United States*, Montclair: Patterson Smith.

Dacus, J.A. 1877, *Annals of the Great Strikes in the United States: A Reliable History and Graphic Description of the Causes and Thrilling events of the Labor Strikes and Riots of 1877*, Chicago: C.B. Beach.

Dale, Ernest 1954, 'Union Management Co-operation' in *Industrial Conflict*, edited by Arthur Kornhauser et al., New York: McGraw-Hill.

Dalton, Roy 1968, *The Jesuits' Estates Question, 1760–1888: A Study of the Background for the Agitation of 1889*, Toronto: University of Toronto Press.

Danhof, Clarence 1941, 'Farm-Making Costs and the "Safety Valve": 1850–1860', *Journal of Political Economy*, 49, June: 317–59.

Daunay, J. 1966, 'Carnavals au bois', *Revue du folklore de l'Aube*, 9: 1–19.

Davey, Ian E. 1975, 'Educational Reform and the Working Class: School Attendance in Hamilton, Ontario, 1851–1891', PhD dissertation, University of Toronto.

David, Paul A. et al. 1976, *Reckoning with Slavery: A Critical Study in the Quantitative History of American Negro Slavery*, New York: Oxford University Press.

Davies, Ralph C. 1959, 'Frederick Taylor and the American Philosophy of Management', *Advanced Management*, 24, December: 4–7.

Davin, Nicholas Flood 1877, *The Irishman in Canada*, Toronto: Maclear and Company.

Davis, Alva L. and Raven I. McDavid, Jr. 1949, '"Shivaree": An Example of Cultural Diffusion', *American Speech*, 25, December: 251.

Davis, Mike 1975, 'The Stop Watch and the Wooden Shoe: Scientific Management and the Industrial Workers of the World', *Radical America*, 8, January–February: 69–95.

———— 1980, 'Why the u.s. Working Class Is Different', *New Left Review*, I/123: 3–46.

———— 1986, *Prisoners of the American Dream*, London: Verso.

———— 2006, *Planet of Slums*, London: Verso.

Davis, Natalie Zemon 1975, *Society and Culture in Early Modern France*, Stanford: Stanford University Press.

Dawley, Alan 1976, *Class and Community: The Industrial Revolution in Lynn*, Cambridge, MA: Harvard University Press.

Dawley, Alan and Paul Faler 1976, 'Working-Class Culture and Politics in the Industrial Revolution: Sources of Loyalism and Rebellion', *Journal of Social History*, 9, 4: 466–80.

———— 1979, 'Working-Class Culture and Politics in the Industrial Revolution: Sources of Loyalism and Rebellion' in *American Working-Class Culture: Explorations in American Labor and Social History*, edited by Milton Cantor, Westport, CT: Greenwood Press.

Day, Ernest and Charles Melay 1962, 'Hamilton McFarland Barksdale and the DuPont

Contributions to Systematic Management', *Business History Review*, 36, Summer: 127–52.

De Lottinville, Peter 1979, 'The St. Croix Manufacturing Company and its influence on the St. Croix Community, 1880–1892', MA thesis, Dalhousie University.

——— 1981–2, 'Joe Beef of Montreal: Working-Class Culture and the Tavern, 1869–1889', *Labour/Le Travailleur*, 8–9: 9–40.

De Ste. Croix, G.E.M. 1981, *The Class Struggle in the Ancient Greek World: From the Archaic Age to the Arab Conquests*, London: Duckworth.

Dean, W.G. (ed.) 1969, *Economic Atlas of Ontario*, Toronto: University of Toronto Press.

DeBernardi, G.B. 1888, *The Equitable Industrial Association of America: A Beneficient Co-operative Association for the Employment of Idle Labor through Mutual Exchange*, Sedalia, MO: Stereo. Works of J.C. Parmerlee.

Debouzy, Marianne 1983, 'Workers' Self-Organization and Resistance in the 1877 Strikes' in *American Labor and Immigration History, 1877–1920: Recent European Research*, edited by Dirk Hoerder, Urbana, IL: University of Illinois Press.

DeCosta, B.F. 1887, *The White Cross: Its Origins and Progress*, Chicago: Sanitary Publishing Co.

Dechêne, Louise 1971, 'L'evolution du régime seigneurial au Canada: le cas de Montréal aux XVIIe et XVIIIe siècles', *Recherches sociographiques*, 12, 2: 143–83.

Degler, Carl N. 1959, 'Starr and Slavery', *Journal of Economic History*, 19: 271–7.

Denning, Michael 2010, 'Wageless Life', *New Left Review*, II/66, November–December: 79–81.

Dent, John Charles 1881, *The Last Forty Years: Canada since the Union of 1841*, 2 Volumes, Toronto: George Virtue.

——— 1885, *The Story of the Upper Canadian Rebellion*, 2 Volumes, Toronto: Blackett Robinson.

Derber, Milton 1966, 'The Idea of Industrial Democracy in America, 1898–1915', *Labor History*, 7, Fall: 259–86.

——— 1967, 'The Idea of Industrial Democracy in America, 1915–1935', *Labor History*, 8, Winter: 3–29.

Diamond, Sigmund 1961, 'An Experiment in Feudalism: French Canada in the Seventeenth Century', *William and Mary Quarterly*, 18, 1: 3–34.

Diamond, Stanley 1974, *In Search of the Primitive: A Critique of Civilization*, New Brunswick, NJ: Transaction Books.

Dimsdale, Thomas J. 1953 [1866], *The Vigilantes of Montana: or Popular Justice in the Rocky Mountains*, Norman, OK: University of Oklahoma Press.

Dobb, Maurice 1973, *Studies in the Development of Capitalism*, New York: International Publishers.

Doctorow, E.L. 1975, *Ragtime*, New York: Bantam.

Dodge, James 1914, 'A History of the Introduction of Shop Management' in *Scientific Management*, edited by C.B. Thompson, Cambridge, MA: Harvard University Press.

Donnelly, F.K. 1987, 'The British Background of William Lyon Mackenzie', *British Journal of Canadian Studies*, 2, 1: 61–73.

Douglas, R. Alan 1980, *John Prince: A Collection of Documents*, Toronto: Champlain Society.

Drache, Daniel (ed.) 1972, *Quebec – Only the Beginning: The Manifestoes of the Common Front*, Toronto: New Press.

Drinnon, Richard 1980, *Facing West: The Metaphysics of Indian-Hating and Empire-Building*, Minneapolis: University of Minnesota Press.

Drury, Horace B. 1922, *Scientific Management: A History and Criticism*, New York: Columbia University Press.

Dublin, Thomas 1979, *Women at Work: The Transformation of Work and Community in Lowell, Massachusetts, 1820–1860*, New York: Columbia University Press.

Dubofsky, Melvyn 1969, *We Shall Be All: A History of the Industrial Workers of the World*, Chicago: Quadrangle Books.

———— 1974, 'The Origins of Western Working Class Radicalism, 1890–1905' in *Workers in the Industrial Revolution: Recent Studies of Labor in the United States and Europe*, edited by Peter N. Stearns and Daniel J. Walkowitz, New Brunswick: Transaction.

———— 1975, *Industrialism and the American Worker, 1865–1920*, New York: Crowell.

Dubofsky, Melvyn and Warren Van Tine 1976, *John L. Lewis: A Biography*, Chicago: Quadrangle.

———— 1977, *John L. Lewis: A Biography*, New York: Quadrangle/New York Times Book Co.

Dubois, W.E.B. 1964, *Black Reconstruction in America, 1860–1880*, Cleveland: Meridan.

Duchez, Louis 1911, 'Scientific Business Management – What Is It? What Effect Will It Have On the Revolutionary Movement?', *International Socialist Review*, 11, April: 628–31.

Dumas, Evelyn 1974, 'The New Labour Left in Quebec' in *Quebec and Radical Social Change*, edited by Dimitrios I. Roussopoulos, Montreal: Black Rose.

Dunayevska, Raya 1958, *Marxism and Freedom: From 1776 Until Today*, New York: Bookman.

Duncan, Kenneth 1974, 'Irish Famine Immigration and the Social Structure of Canada West' in *Studies in Canadian Social History*, edited by Michiel Horn and Ronald Sabourin, Toronto: McClelland and Stewart.

Dunham, Aileen 1927, *Political Unrest in Upper Canada, 1815–1836*, London: Longmans, Green.

Dye, Nancy 1979, 'Louisville Woolen Mill Operatives and the Knights of Labor', paper presented for the Knights of Labor Centennial Conference, Newberry Library, Chicago, 17–19 May.

Easterlin, Richard A. 1976, 'Factors in the Decline of Farm Fertility in the United States: Some Preliminary Research Findings', *Journal of American History*, 63: 600–14.

Edwards, J.R. 1912, 'The Fetishism of Scientific Management', *Journal of the American Society of Naval Engineers*, 24, May: 355.

Edwards, P.K. 1981, *Strikes in the United States, 1881–1974*, New York: St. Martin's Press.

Eggleston, Edward 1872, *The End of the World: A Love Story*, New York: Orange Judd and Company.

Eley, Geoff 2007, *A Crooked Line: From Cultural History to the History of Society*, Ann Arbor: University of Michigan Press.

Eley, Geoff and Keith Nield 1980, 'Why Does Social History Ignore Politics?' *Social History*, 5, 2: 249–72.

——— 2007, *The Future of Class in History: What's Left of the Social?* Ann Arbor, MI: University of Michigan Press.

Eliot, T.S. 1971, *The Complete Poems and Plays, 1909–1950*, New York: Harcourt, Brace & World.

Emerson, Harrington 1911, 'The Fundamental Truth of Scientific Management', *Journal of Accountancy*, 12, May: 17–25.

——— 1912, *The Twelve Principles of Efficiency*, New York: Engineering Company.

Engels, Frederick 1983, 'Materialien Anti-Duhring' in *Marx and Engels: A Conceptual Concordance*, edited by Gérard Bekerman, translated by Terrell Carver, Oxford: Blackwell.

——— 1958, 'Preface to the American Edition of 1887' in *The Condition of the Working Class in England*, edited by W.O. Henderson and W.H. Chaloner, Oxford: Allen & Unwin.

Epstein, James 1994, *Radical Expression: Political Language, Ritual, and Symbol in England, 1790–1850*, New York: Oxford University Press.

Ermatinger, C.O. 1994. *The Talbot Regime, or, the First Half Century of the Talbot Settlement*, St. Thomas, ON: Municipal World.

Errington, Elizabeth Jane 1987, *The Lion, the Eagle, and Upper Canada: A Developing Canadian Ideology*, Kingston, ON: McGill-Queen's University Press.

——— 1995, *Wives and Mothers, School Mistresses and Scullery Maids: Working Women in Upper Canada, 1790–1840*, Kingston, ON: McGill-Queen's University Press.

Evans, Ivor H. (ed.) 1970, *Brewer's Dictionary of Phrase and Fable*, London: Cassell.

Evans, Margaret 1967, 'Oliver Mowat and Ontario: a Study in Political Success', PhD dissertation, University of Toronto.

Evans, Samuel L. 1960, 'Texas Agriculture, 1880–1930', PhD dissertation, University of Texas.

Extracts from General Orders for the Guidance of Troops in Affording Aid to the Civil Power 1868, Quebec: G. Stanley.

Fagan, Cary 1993, *The Fred Victor Mission Story: From Charity to Social Justice*, Winfield, BC: Wood Lake Books.

Fairley, Margaret 1946, *The Spirit of Canadian Democracy: A Collection of Canadian Writings from the Beginnings to the Present Day*, Toronto: Progress Books.

——— 1960, *Selected Writings of William Lyon Mackenzie*, Toronto: Oxford University Press.

Faler, Paul 1974, 'Cultural Aspects of the Industrial Revolution: Lynn, Massachusetts, Shoemakers and Industrial Morality, 1826–1860', *Labor History*, 15, 3: 367–94.

——— 1979, 'Cultural Aspects of the Industrial Revolution: Lynn, Massachusetts, Shoemakers and Industrial Morality, 1826–1860' in *American Working-Class Culture: Explorations in American Labor and Social History*, edited by Milton Cantor, Westport, CT: Greenwood Press.

——— 1981, *Mechanics and Manufacturers in the Early Industrial Revolution: Lynn, Massachusetts, 1780–1860*, Albany, NY: State University of New York Press.

Farmer, John S. 1889, *Americanisms – Old and New*, London: Privately printed by Thomas Poulter & Sons.

Farnham, Dwight D. 1919, 'Brief for Scientific Management' in *Selected Articles on Modern Industrial Movements*, edited by Daniel Bloomfield, New York: H.W. Wilson.

Feldberg, Michael 1975, *The Philadelphia Riots of 1844: A Study of Ethnic Conflict*, Westport, CT: Greenwood Press.

Ferland, Jacques 1980, 'The Problem of Change in the Rate of Surplus Value Studied Through the Evolution of the "Social Cost of Labour" in Canada, 1870–1910', unpublished MA thesis research paper, McGill University.

Ferns, Henry and Bernard Ostry 1976, *The Age of Mackenzie King*, Toronto: J. Lorimer.

Fielding, William J. 1942, *Strange Customs of Courtship and Marriage*, New York: The New Home Library.

Fine, Sidney 1967, *Laissez Faire and the General Welfare State: A Study of Conflict in American Thought, 1865–1901*, Ann Arbor, MI: University of Michigan Press.

——— 1969, *Sit-Down: The General Motors Strike of 1936–37*, Ann Arbor, MI: University of Michigan Press.

Fingard, Judith 1974, 'The Winter's Tale: The Seasonal Contours of Pre-Industrial Poverty in British North America, 1815–1860', Canadian Historical Association, *Historical Papers*: 74–5.

Fink, Leon 1975, 'Class Conflict in the Gilded Age: The Figure and the Phantom', *Radical History Review*, 3, 1–2: 56–73.

——— 1977, 'Workingmen's Democracy: The Knights of Labor in Local Politics, 1886–1896', PhD dissertation, University of Rochester.

——— 1978, 'Irrespective of Party, Color, or Standing: The Knights of Labor and Oppositional Politics in Richmond, Virginia', *Labor History*, 19: 324–49.

——— 1979, 'The Uses of Political Power: Towards a Theory of the Labor Movement in the Era of the Knights of Labor', paper presented to the Knights of Labor Centennial Symposium, Chicago, 17–19 May.

———— 1982, 'The Uses of Political Power: Toward a Theory of the Labor Movement in the Era of the Knights of Labor' in *Working-Class America: Essays on Labor, Community, and American Society*, edited by Michael H. Frisch and Daniel J. Walkowitz, Urbana: University of Illinois Press.

Fireman's Benefit Fund 1920, *History of the Hamilton Fire Department*, Hamilton: n.p.

Firth, Edith G. 1962, *The Town of York, 1793–1815: A Collection of Documents of Early Toronto*, Toronto: The Champlain Society for the Government of Ontario.

Fisher, Douglas and Harry Crowe 1968, *What Do You Know about the Rand Report?*, Don Mills: Ontario Federation of Labour.

Fisher, Robin 1977, *Contact and Conflict: Indian-European Relations in British Columbia, 1774–1890*, Vancouver: University of British Columbia Press.

Fitch, John 1924, *The Causes of Industrial Unrest*, New York: Harper Brothers.

———— 1969, *The Steel Workers*, New York: Arno Reprint.

Flaten, Nils 1900, 'Notes on American-Norwegian with a Vocabulary', *Dialect Notes*, 2: 115–26.

Fliegelman, Jay 1982, *Prodigals & Pilgrims: The American Revolution Against Patriarchal Authority, 1750–1800*, New York: Cambridge University Press.

Flom, George T. 1926, 'English Loanwords in American Norwegian, as Spoken in the Koshkonong Settlement (Dane County, Wisconsin)', *American Speech*, 1, July: 541–8.

Flood, Maxwell 1968a, 'Some Reflections on Wildcat Strikes', *Summation*, 1, June: 1–14.

———— 1968b, *Wildcat Strike in Lake City*, Ottawa: Queen's Printer.

———— 1972, 'The Growth of the Non-Institutional Response in the Canadian Industrial Sector', *Relations Industrielles/Industrial Relations*, 27: 603–15.

Fogel, Robert William and Stanley L. Engerman 1974, *Time on the Cross: The Economics of American Negro Slavery*, Volume 1, Boston: Little, Brown.

Foner, Eric 1970, *Free Soil, Free Labor, Free Men: The Ideology of the Republican Party Before the Civil War*, New York: Oxford University Press.

———— 1976, *Tom Paine and Revolutionary America*, New York: Oxford University Press.

———— 1978, 'Class, Ethnicity, and Radicalism in the Gilded Age: The Land League and Irish America', *Marxist Perspectives*, 1, 2: 6–55.

Foner, Philip S. 1962, *History of the Labor Movement in the United States*, Volume 1, New York: International Publishers.

———— 1976, *Women and the American Labor Movement: From Colonial Times to the Present*, New York: International University Press.

Forsey, Eugene 1971, 'The Telegraphers' Strike of 1883', *Transactions of the Royal Society of Canada*, 4th ser., Volume 9: 245–59.

———— 1982, *Trade Unions in Canada, 1812–1902*, Toronto: University of Toronto Press.

Fortier-Beaulieu, P. 1940a, 'Le charivari dans le Roman de Fauvel', *Revue de folklore français et Folklore colonial*, 11: 1–16.

———— 1940b, 'Le veuvage et le remarriage', *Revue de folklore français et folklore colonial*, 11: 67–9.

Foster, John 1974, *Class Struggle and the Industrial Revolution: Early Industrial Capitalism in Three English Towns*, London: Weidenfeld and Nicholson.

Foster, John Bellamy, Robert W. McChesney, and R. Jamil Jonna 2011, 'The Global Reserve Army of Labor and the New Imperialism', *Monthly Review*, 63, November: www .monthlyreview.org, 21 November.

Foster, William Z. 1939, *Pages from a Worker's Life*, New York: International.

Foucault, Michel (ed.) 1975, *I, Pierre Rivière, having slaughtered my mother, my sister, and my brother …: A Case of Parricide in the 19th Century*, New York: Pantheon Books.

———— 1976 *The History of Sexuality, Volume 1: An Introduction*, London: Allen Lane.

Fountain, Clayton W. 1949, *Union Guy*, New York: Viking.

Fournier, Louis 1984, *FLQ: The Anatomy of an Underground Movement*, Toronto: NC Press.

Fox-Genovese, Elizabeth and Eugene D. Genovese 1976, 'The Political Crisis of Social History: A Marxian Perspective', *Journal of Social History*, 10, 2: 205–21.

———— 1983, *Fruits of Merchant Capital: Slavery and Bourgeois Property in the Rise and Expansion of Capitalism*, New York: Oxford University Press.

Frank, David 1977, 'The Cape Breton Coal Industry and the Rise and Fall of the British Empire Steel Corporaton', *Acadiensis*, 7, 1: 3–34.

———— 1999, *J.B. McLachlan: A Biography*, Toronto: James Lorimer & Company.

Franklin, Benjamin A. 1915, *Experiences in Efficiency*, New York: Engineering Company.

Freedman, Mr Justice Samuel 1966, *Report of Industrial Inquiry Commission on Canadian National Railways 'Run-Throughs'*, Ottawa: Queen's Printer.

Freeman, Bill 1982, *1005: Political Life in a Union Local*, Toronto: James Lorimer.

Frey, John 1913 'The Relation of Scientific Management to Labor', *Journal of Political Economy*, May: 400–11.

Friedmann, Georges 1955, *Industrial Society: The Emergence of the Human Problems of Automation*, Glencoe, IL: Free Press.

Fudge, Judy and Eric Tucker 2001, *Labour Before the Law: The Regulation of Workers' Collective Action in Canada, 1900–1948*, Toronto: Oxford University Press.

Gaffield, Chad M. 1979, 'Canadian Families in Cultural Context: Hypotheses from Mid-Century', Canadian Historical Association, *Papers*: 48–70.

Gagan, David 1978, 'Land, Population, and Social Change: The "Critical Years" in Rural Canada West', *Canadian Historical Review*, 59, 3: 293–318.

———— 1981, *Hopeful Travellers: Families, Land, and Social Change in Mid-Victorian Peel County, Canada West*, Toronto: University of Toronto Press.

Galambos, Louis 1970, 'The Emerging Organizational Synthesis in Modern American History', *Business History Review*, 44, 3: 282–4.

Gallman, Robert 1960, 'Commodity Output, 1839–1899' in *Trends in the American Economy in the Nineteenth Century: A Report of the National Bureau of Economic Research, New York*, edited by Conference on Research in Incoem and Wealth, Princeton: Princeton University Press.

Gardner, H.F. 1923, 'When the "Plain Speaker's" Type was Pied', Ontario Historical Society, *Papers & Records*, 20: 84–9.

Garlock, Jonathan 1973a, *Knights of Labor Data Bank*, Ann Arbor, MI: Inter University Consortium.

—— 1973b, 'The Knights of Labor Data Bank', *Historical Methods Newsletter*, 6: 149–60.

—— 1974, 'A Structural Analysis of the Knights of Labor: A Prolegomenon to the History of the Producing Classes', PhD dissertation, University of Rochester.

Garr, Allen 1985, *Tough Guy: Bill Bennett and the Taking of British Columbia*, Toronto: Key Porter Books.

Garrett, Richard D. 1978, 'Primitive Accumulation in the Antebellum Cotton South', PhD dissertation, New School for Social Research.

Gates, Lillian 1959, 'The Decided Policy of William Lyon Mackenzie', *Canadian Historical Review*, 40, September: 185–208.

Gates, Paul W. 1964, 'The Role of the Land Speculator in Western Development' in *Issues in American Economic History*, edited by G.D. Nash, Boston: Little Brown.

Gauvard, Claude and Alan Gokalp 1974, 'Les conduits de bruit et leur signification à la fin du Moyen Age: le charivari', *Annales: E.S.C.*, 29: 693–704.

Gavin, Martin 1959, 'The Jubilee Riots in Toronto', Canadian Historical Association, *Annual Report*: 93–107.

Geertz, Clifford 1973, *The Interpretation of Cultures*, New York: Basic Books.

Genovese, Eugene D. 1965, *The Political Economy of Slavery: Studies in the Economy and Society of the Slave South*, New York: Vintage Books.

—— 1971, *The World the Slaveholders Made: Two Essays in Interpretation*, New York: Vintage Books.

—— 1972, *In Red and Black: Marxian Explorations in Southern and Afro-American History*, New York: Vintage Books.

—— 1974, *Roll Jordan, Roll: The World the Slaves Made*, New York: Pantheon Books.

—— 1979, *From Rebellion to Revolution: Afro-American Slave Revolts in the Making of the Modern World*, Baton Rouge, LA: Louisiana University Press.

Gibbons, Floyd 1914, 'A Fight to the Finish', *International Socialist Review*, 15, August: 72–8.

Gillis, Peter 1975, 'E.H. Bronson and Corporate Capitalism', MA thesis, Queen's University.

Gilman, C.P. and H.M. Sinclair 1935, *Unemployment: Canada's Problem*, Ottawa: The Army and Navy Veterans in Canada.

Gindin, Sam 1995, *The Canadian Auto Workers: The Birth and Transformation of a Union*, Toronto: James Lorimer.

Gitelman, Howard M. 1967, 'The Waltham System and the Coming of the Irish', *Labor History*, 8: 227–53.

Glaberman, Martin 1980, *Wartime Strikes: The Struggle Against the No-Strike Pledge in the UAW during World War II*, Detroit: bewick/ed.

Glazebrook, G.P. de T. 1964, *A History of Transportation in Canada* 2 Volumes, Toronto: McClelland and Stewart.

Glazer, Walter S. 1972, 'Participation and Power: Voluntary Associations and the Functional Organization of Cincinnati in 1840', *Historical Methods Newsletter*, 5, September: 151–68.

Goheen, Peter G. 1970, *Victorian Toronto, 1850–1900: Pattern and Process of Growth*, Chicago: University of Chicago, Dept. of Geography.

Goldfield, Michael 1987, *The Decline of Organized Labor in the United States*, Chicago: University of Chicago Press.

Gonick, Cy 2001, *A Very Red Life: The Story of Bill Walsh*, St. John's: CCLH.

Goodwyn, Lawrence 1976, *Democratic Promise: The Populist Movement in America*, New York: Oxford University Press.

Goody, Jack 1976, *Production and Reproduction: A Comparative Study of the Domestic Domain*, Cambridge: Cambridge University Press.

Gordon, David M., Richard Edwards, and Michael Reich 1982, *Segmented Work, Divided Workers: The Historical Transformation of Labor in the States*, New York: Cambridge University Press.

Gordon, Michael 1977, 'Studies in Irish and Irish-American Thought and Behaviour in Gilded Age New York City', PhD dissertation, University of Rochester.

Gosh, Rev. A.B. 1869, *The Odd Fellows Improved Pocket Manual*, Philadelphia: Odd Fellows.

Gouldner, Alvin W. 1954, *Wildcat Strike*, Yellow Springs, OH: Antioch Press.

Goulet, Robert 1961a, *Le Charivari*, Paris: Albin Michel.

———— 1961b, *The Violent Season*, New York: G. Braziller.

Gourlay, Robert 1822, *Statistical Account of Upper Canada: Compiled with a View to a Grand System of Emigration*, Volume I, London: Simpkin & Marshall.

Goutor, David 2007, *Guarding the Gates: The Canadian Labour Movement and Immigration, 1872–1934*, Vancouver: UBC Press.

Graff, Harvey J. 1976, 'Respected and Profitable Labor: Jobs, Literacy and the Working Class' in *Essays in Canadian Working Class History*, edited by Gregory S. Kealey and Peter Warrian, Toronto: McClelland and Stewart.

Graham, C.M. 1967, 'Have You Ever Heard of the White Caps?' *New Mexico Genealogist*, 6, December: 3–8.

Graham, Hugh Davis and Ted Robert Gurr (eds.) 1969, *Violence in America: Historical and Comparative Perspectives*, Washington: U.S. Government Print Office.

Gramsci, Antonio 1971, *Selections from the Prison Notebooks*, New York: International.

Granatstein, J.L. 1998, *Who Killed Canadian History?* Toronto: Harper Collins.

Grand Lodge of Ancient Free and Accepted Masons of Canada 1866, *The Book of Constitution of the Grand Lodge of Ancient Free and Accepted Masons, of Canada*, Hamilton, ON: Thomas Bird Harris.

Gray, James Henry 1966, *The Winter Years: The Depression on the Prairies*, Toronto: Macmillan.

Gray, Lewis C. 1933, *History of Agriculture in the Southern States to 1860*, 2 Volumes, Washington, D.C.: Carnegie Institute.

Gray, R.Q. 1973, 'Styles of Life, The "Labour Aristocracy" and Class Relations in Later Nineteenth Century Edinburgh', *International Review of Social History*, 18: 428–52.

Grayson, L.M. and Michael Bliss (eds.) 1971, *The Wretched of Canada: Letters to R.B. Bennett, 1930–1935*, Toronto: University of Toronto Press.

Graziosi, Andrea 1981, 'Common Laborers, Unskilled Workers, 1880–1915', *Labor History*, 22, Fall: 512–44.

Greeley, Horace et al. 1872, *The Great Industries of the United States: Being an Historical Summary of the Origin, Growth, and Perfection of the Chief Industrial Arts of This Country*, Hartford, CT: J.B. Burr & Hyde.

Green, James 2007, *Death in the Haymarket: A Story of Chicago, the First Labor Movement, and the Bombing that Divided Gilded Age America*, New York: Pantheon Books.

Greenberg, Brian 1980, 'Worker and Community: The Social Structure of a Nineteenth-Century American City, Albany, New York, 1850–1884', PhD dissertation, Princeton University.

Greenhill, Pauline 2010, *Make the Night Hideous: Four English-Canadian Charivaris, 1881–1940*, Toronto: University of Toronto Press.

Greer, Allan 1990, 'From folklore to revolution: charivaris and the Lower Canadian rebellion of 1837', *Social History*, 15, 1: 25–43.

———— 1992, 'The Birth of the Police in Canada' in *Colonial Leviathan: State Formation in Mid-Nineteenth-Century Canada*, edited by Allan Greer and Ian Radforth, Toronto: University of Toronto Press.

———— 1995, '1837–1838: Rebellion Reconsidered', *Canadian Historical Review*, 76, 1: 1–18.

Greer, Allan and Ian Radforth (eds.) 1992, *Colonial Leviathan: State Formation in Mid-Nineteenth-Century Canada*, Toronto: University of Toronto Press.

Grimwood, Carrol J. 1934, 'The Cigar Manufacturing Industry in London, Ontario', MA thesis, University of Western Ontario.

Grob, Gerald N. 1961, *Workers and Utopia: A Study of Ideological Conflict in the American Labor Movement, 1865–1900*, Chicago: Quadrangle.

Groneman, Carol 1977, '"She Earns As a Child – She Pays As a Man": Women Workers in a Mid-Nineteenth Century New York Community' in *Immigrants in Industrial America, 1850–1920*, edited by Richard L. Ehrlich, Charlottesville, VA: University of Virginia Press.

Grose, Francis 1785, *A Classical Dictionary of the Vulgar Tongue*, London: S. Hooper.

Grove, F.P. 1967, *The Master of the Mill*, Toronto: McClelland & Stewart.

Guest, Dennis 1980, *The Emergence of Social Security in Canada*, Vancouver: University of British Columbia Press.

Guillet, Edwin C. 1933, *Early Life in Upper Canada*, Toronto: Ontario Publishing Co.

————— 1938, *The Lives and Times of the Patriots: An Account of the Rebellion in Upper Canada, 1837–1838 and of the Patriot Agitation in the United States, 1837–1842*, Toronto: Thomas Nelson and Sons.

————— 1968, *The Lives and Times of the Patriots: An Account of the Rebellion in Upper Canada 1837–1837, and of the Patriot Agitation in the United States, 1837–1842*, Toronto: University of Toronto Press.

Gundy, H.P. 1964, 'Who Was Carl Fechter', *Historic Kingston*, 12, January: 11–18.

Gutch, Eliza. 1912, *County Folk-lore Volume VI – Examples of Printed Folk-lore Concerning the East Riding of Yorkshire*, London: Nutt for the Folk-Lore Society.

Gutman, Herbert G. 1968a, 'Class, Status and Community Power in Nineteenth Century Industrial Cities – Paterson, New Jersey: A Case Study' in *The Age of Industrialism in America*, edited by Frederic Cope Jaher, New York: Macmillan.

————— 1968b, 'Protestantism and the American Labor Movement' in *Dissent: Explorations in the History of American Radicalism*, edited by Alfred F. Young, DeKalb, IL: Northern Illinois University Press.

————— 1970, 'The Workers Search for Power' in *The Gilded Age*, edited by H. Wayne Morgan, Syracuse, NY: Syracuse University Press.

————— 1973a, 'Class, Status, and the Gilded Age Radical: A Reconsideration' in *Many Pasts: Readings in American Social History*, edited by Herbert G. Gutman and Gregory S. Kealey, Englewood Cliffs, NJ: Prentice Hall.

————— 1973b, 'Work, Culture, and Society in Industrializing America, 1815–1919', *American Historical Review*, 78, 3: 531–88.

————— 1975, *Slavery and the Numbers Game: A Critique of Time on the Cross*, Urbana, IL: University of Illinois Press.

————— 1976a, *The Black Family in Slavery and Freedom, 1750–1925*, New York: Pantheon Books.

————— 1976b, *Work, Culture, and Society in Industrializing America: Essays in American Working-Class and Social History*, New York: Knopf.

————— 1982, 'Class Formation and Class Development in 19th Century America', paper delivered at Simon Fraser University, Burnaby, British Columbia, 14 October.

Gutman, Herbert G. and Richard Sutch, 'Victorians All? The Sexual Mores and Conduct of Slaves and Their Masters' in *Reckoning with Slavery: A Critical Study in the Quant-*

itative History of American Negro Slavery, by Paul A. David et al., New York: Oxford University Press.

Haber, Samuel 1964, *Efficiency and Uplift: Scientific Management in the Progressive Era*, Chicago: University of Chicago Press.

Habermas, Jürgen 1996, *Between Facts and Norms: Contributions to a Discourse Theory of Law and Democracy*, translated by William Rehg, Cambridge, MA: MIT Press.

Hacker, Louis M. 1940, *The Triumph of American Capitalism*, New York: Columbia University Press.

Haight, Canniff 1885, *Country Life in Canada Fifty Years Ago: Personal Recollections and Reminiscences of a Sexagenarian*, Toronto: Hunter, Rose & Co.

Hall, James 1835, *Tales of the Border*, Philadelphia: Harrison Hall.

Hamil, Fred Coyne 1955, *Lake Erie Baron: The Story of Thomas Talbot*, Toronto: Macmillan.

Hamilton Board of Police 1842, *Minutes, 1841–1842*, 22 March.

Hamilton and Gore Mechanics' Institute 1867, *Act of Incorporation, Rules and Regulations*, Hamilton, ON: Lawson.

Hamilton Mechanics' Institute 1965, *Exhibition of Fine Arts, Manufactures, Machines, Natural History, Curiosities, Etc.*, Hamilton, ON: Spectator.

Hamilton Mercantile Library Association and General News Room 1845, *Constitution and By-Laws of the Hamilton Mercantile Association and General News Room, 1845*, Hamilton, ON: Journal and Express.

Hamilton St. George's Benevolent Society 1844, *Constitution of the Hamilton St. George's Benevolent Society*, Hamilton, ON: J. Robertson.

Hammond, Bray 1948, 'Banking in the Early West: Monopoly, Prohibition and Laissez-Faire', *Journal of Economic History*, 8, May: 1–25.

Hanley, Miles L. 1933, 'Charivaria II: "Serenade" in New England', *American Speech*, 8, April: 24–6.

Hann, Russell 1975, *Farmers Confront Industrialism: Some Historical Perspectives on Ontario Agrarian Movements*, Toronto: Hogtown.

———— 1976, 'Brainworkers and the Knights of Labor: E.E. Sheppard, Phillips Thompson, and the Toronto *News*, 1883–1887' in *Essays in Canadian Working Class History*, edited by Gregory S. Kealey and Peter Warrian, Toronto: McClelland and Stewart.

Hann, Russell, Gregory S. Kealey, Linda Kealey, and Peter Warrian, *Primary Sources in Canadian Working Class History*, Kitchener, ON: Dumont Press.

Hardy, Jack 1935, *The Clothing Workers: A Study of Conditions and Struggles in the Needle Trades*, New York: International.

Hardy, Thomas 1920, *The Mayor of Casterbridge*, London: Macmillan.

Hareven, Tamara 1982, *Family Time and Industrial Time: The Relationship Between the Family and Work in a New England Industrial Community*, Cambridge: Cambridge University Press.

Harris, Abram L. and Sterling D. Spero 1968 [1931], *The Black Worker: The Negro and the Labor Movement*, New York: Atheneum.

Harris, Howell John 1982, *The Right to Manage: Industrial Relations Policies of American Business in the 1940s*, Madison, WI: University of Wisconsin Press.

Harris, R.C. 1966, *The Seigneurial System in Early Canada: A Geographical Study*, Madison, WI: University of Wisconsin Press.

Harrison, Brian 1973, 'For Church, Queen and Family: The Girl's Friendly Society, 1874–1920', *Past & Present*, 61, November: 107–38.

Hart, Jerome Alfred 1910, *A Vigilante Girl*, Chicago: A.C. McClurg & Co.

Harvey, Fernand 1978, *Révolution industrielle et travailleurs: une enquête sur les rapports entre le capital et le travail au Québec à la fin du 19e siècle*, Montreal: Boréal Express.

Hastings, David 1905, *Historical Sketch of Acacia Lodge, No. 61, G.R.C., Ancient, Free and Accepted Masons*, Hamilton, ON: Spectator.

Haswell, A.H. 1923–4, 'The Story of the Bald Knobbers', *The Missouri Historical Review*, 18, October–July: 30–1.

Hay, Douglas 1975, 'Property, Authority, and the Criminal Law' in *Albion's Fatal Tree: Crime and Society in Eighteenth-Century England*, edited by Douglas Hay et al., New York: Pantheon Books.

Hazlitt, W. Carew 1905, *Brand's Popular Antiquities of Great Britain. Faiths and Folklore*, Volume 2, New York: Charles Scribner's Sons.

Head, Francis Bond 1839, *A Narrative*, London: John Murray.

Headlight Assembly No. 4069, K. of L. 1885, *Statistics as Collected by Headlight Assembly No. 4069, K. of L., for Its Exclusive Use*, St Thomas.

Henderson, William 1967, *Notes on the Folk-lore of the Northern Counties of England and the Borders*, Nendeln/Liechtenstein: Kraus Reprint.

Hennock, E.P. 1973, *Fit and Proper Persons: Ideal and Reality in Nineteenth Century Urban Government*, Montreal: McGill-Queen's University Press.

Henretta, James 1965, 'Economic Development and Social Structure in Colonial Boston', *William and Mary Quarterly*, 22: 75–92.

——— 1971, 'The Morphology of New England Society in the Colonial Period', *Journal of Interdisciplinary History*, 2, 2: 379–98.

——— 1973, *The Evolution of American Society, 1700–1850: An Interdisciplinary Analysis*, Lexington, KT: Heath.

——— 1978, 'Families and Farms: *Mentalité* in Pre-Industrial America', *William and Mary Quarterly*, 35, 1: 3–32.

Henripin, Jacques 1972, *Trends and Factors of Fertility in Canada*, Ottawa: Government Publications.

Herity, Owen 1931, 'Journalism in Belleville', Ontario Historical Society, *Papers & Records*, 27: 400.

Heron, Craig (ed.) 1998, *The Workers' Revolt in Canada, 1917–1925*, Toronto: University of Toronto Press.

Herrick, James B. 1949, *Memories of Eighty Years*, Chicago: University of Chicago Press.

Hersey, Frank W.C. 1937–42, 'Tar and Feathers: The Adventures of Captain John Malcolm', Colonial Society of Massachusetts Publications, *Transactions*, 34: 429–73.

Hershberg, Theodore (ed.) 1981, *Philadelphia: Work, Space, Family, and Group Experience in the 19th Century – Essays Toward and Interdisciplinary History of the City*, New York: Oxford University Press.

Hexter, J.H. 1971, *Doing History*, Bloomington, IN: Indiana University Press.

Hicks, J.D. 1931, *The Populist Revolt*, Minneapolis: University of Minnesota Press.

Higbie, Frank Tobias 2003, *Indispensable Outcasts: Hobo Workers and Community in the American Midwest, 1880–1930*, Urbana, IL: University of Illinois Press.

Higgins, W.H. 1887, *The Life and Times of Joseph Gould: Reminiscences of Sixty Years of Active Political and Municipal Life*, Toronto: C. Blackett Robinson.

High, Steven 2003, *Industrial Sunset: The Making of North America's Rust Belt, 1969–1984*, Toronto: University of Toronto Press.

Higham, John 1963, *Strangers in the Land: Patterns of American Nativism, 1860–1925*, New York: Vintage Books.

Hill, Christopher 1972, *The World Turned Upside Down: Radical Ideas During the English Revolution*, New York: Viking Press.

———— 1980, 'Robinson Crusoe', *History Workshop Journal*, 10, Autumn: 17–24.

Hill, George Handel 1836, *Hill's Yankee Story Teller's Own Book; and Reciter's Pocket Companion*, New York: Turner & Fisher.

Hill, J.D. 1932, 'The Early Mining Camp in American Life', *Pacific Historical Review*, 1: 303–6.

Hilton, Rodney (ed.) 1976, *The Transition from Feudalism to Capitalism*, London: New Left Books.

Hindess, Barry and Paul Hirst 1977, *Mode of Production and Social Formation: An Auto-Critique of Pre-Capitalist Modes of Production*, London: Macmillan.

Hirsch, Susan E. 1978, *Roots of the American Working Class: The Industrialization of Crafts in Newark, 1800–1860*, Philadelphia: University of Pennsylvania Press.

Hobsbawm, E.J. 1971, *Primitive Rebels: Studies in Archaic Forms of Social Movement in the 19th and 20th Centuries*, Manchester: Manchester University Press.

———— 1971a, 'From Social History to the History of Society', *Daedalus*, 100, 1: 20–45.

Hoerder, Dirk 1976, 'Boston Leaders and Boston Crowds, 1765–1776' in *The American Revolution: Explorations in the History of American Radicalism*, edited by Alfred F. Young, Dekalb, IL: University of Northern Illinois Press.

Hoffman, Charles 1956, 'The Depression of the Nineties', *Journal of Economic History*, 16, June: 137–64.

Hoffpauir, Roy V. 1968, 'Acadian Marriage Customs', *Attakapas Gazette*, 3, December: 3–19.

Hole, Christina 1940, *English Folklore*, London: B.T. Batsford.

Holmes, William F. 1969, 'Whitecapping: Agrarian Violence in Mississippi, 1902–1906', *Journal of Southern History*, 35, 2, May: 165–85.

Homel, Gene 1980, '"Fading Beams of the Nineteenth Century": Radicalism and Early Socialism in Canada's 1890s', *Labour/Le Travailleur*, 5, Spring: 7–32.

Hopkins, Ellice 1883, *The White Cross Army*, London: Hatchards.

Horn, Michiel (ed.) 1972, *The Dirty Thirties: Canadians in the Great Depression*, Toronto: Copp Clark Pub. Co.

Horner, Clare Dahberger 1978, 'Producers' Co-operatives in the United States, 1865–1890', PhD dissertation, University of Pittsburgh.

Horwood, Harold 1966, *Tomorrow Will Be Sunday*, Garden City: Doubleday.

House of Commons 1876, 'Report of the Select Committee on the Causes of the Present Depression of the Manufacturing, Mining, Commercial, Shipping, Lumber and Fishing Interests' in *Journals*, Volume 10, Ottawa: McLean, Roger, and Company.

House of Commons Select Committee on the Administration, Operation, and Effects of the Contagious Diseases Acts of 1866–1869 1882, 'Report of the House of Commons Select Committee on the Administration, Operation, and Effects of the Contagious Diseases Acts of 1866–1869', *Parliamentary Papers, 1882*, Volume 9.

House of Industry 1852, *Report of the Trustees of the House of Industry, City of Toronto, 1852*, Toronto: The House.

——— 1854, *Report of the Trustees of the House of Industry, City of Toronto, 1854*, Toronto: The House.

——— 1879, *Report of the Trustees of the House of Industry, City of Toronto, 1879*, Toronto: The House.

——— 1892, *Eighty-Fourth Annual Report of the House of Industry, City of Toronto, 1891–1892*, Toronto: The House.

——— 1897, *Sixtieth Annual Report of the House of Industry, City of Toronto, 1920–1921*, Toronto: The House.

——— 1921, *Sixtieth Annual Report of the House of Industry, City of Toronto, 1896–1897*, Toronto: The House.

Howard, Joseph Kinsey 1965, *The Strange Empire of Louis Riel*, Toronto: Swan.

Howard, Roger and Jack Scott 1972, 'International Unions and the Ideology of Class Collaboration' in *Capitalism and the National Question in Canada*, edited by Gary Teeple, Toronto: University of Toronto Press.

Howard, Victor 1970, *The On to Ottawa Trek*, Vancouver: Copp Clark.

Howe, Irving 1976, *World of Our Fathers: The Journey of East European Jews to America and the Life They Found and Made*, New York: Harcourt, Brace, Jovanovitch.

Howell, Nancy and Max L. Howell 1969, *Sport and Games in Canadian Life: 1700 to the Present*, Toronto: Macmillan of Canada.

Howison, John 1821, *Sketches of Upper Canada: Domestic, Local, and Characteristic*, Edinburgh: Oliver and Boyd.

Hoxie, Robert Franklin 1916, 'Scientific Management and Labor Welfare', *The Journal of Political Economy*, 24, November: 833–54.

——— 1966 [1915], *Scientific Management and Labor*, New York: Kelley.

Hubbard, Lester C. 1891, *The Coming Climax in the Destinies of America*, Chicago: Charles H. Kerr.

Huggett, Frank E. 1972, *A Day in the Life of A Victorian Farm Worker*, London: Allen and Unwin.

Hugins, Walter 1966, *Jacksonian Democracy and the Working Class: A Study of the New York Workingmen's Movement*, Palo Alto: Stanford University Press.

Humphries, Jane 1977a, 'Class Struggle and the Persistence of the Working-Class Family', *Cambridge Journal of Economics*, 1, 3: 241–58.

——— 1977b, 'The Working Class Family, Women's Liberation, and Class Struggle: The Case of Nineteenth Century British History', *Review of Radical Political Economics*, 9, 3: 25–41.

Humphries, Michael 1968, 'The Insensitivity of the Union Movement to the Real Need of Union Members', *Relations Industrielles/Industrial Relations*, 23, October: 610.

Hunt, Alan and Gary Wickham 1994, *Foucault and Law: Towards a Sociology of Law as Governance*, London: Pluto Press.

Hyatt, Harry Middleton 1965, *Folk-Lore from Adams County, Illinois*, Hannibal, MO: Western Print. And Lithographing.

Hymer, Stephen 1971, 'Robinson Crusoe and the Secret of Primitive Accumulation', *Monthly Review*, 23, September: 11–36.

Independent Order of Oddfellows, Manchester Unity Friendly Society 1879, *Rules of the Independent Order of Oddfellows, Manchester Unity Friendly Society*, Chorltonn-upon-Medlock, England: n.p.

Isitt, Benjamin 2007, 'Working Class Agency, the Cold War, and the Rise of a New Left: Political Change in British Columbia, 1948–1972', preliminary draft of PhD dissertation, presented to University of New Brunswick.

Isserman, Maurice 1982, *Which Side Were You On? The American Communist Party During the Second World War*, Middletown, CT: Wesleyan University Press.

Jackman, Sydney 1958, *Galloping Head: The Life of the Right Honourable Sir Francis Bond Head, Bart., P.C., 1793–1875, Late Lieutenant-Governor of Upper Canada*, London: Phoenix House.

Jaenen, Cornelius J. 1976a, *Friend and Foe: Aspects of French-Amerindian Cultural Contact in the Sixteenth and Seventeenth Centuries*, Toronto: McClelland and Stewart.

——— 1976b, *The Role of the Church in New France*, Toronto: McGraw-Hill Ryerson.

James, C.L.R. 1963, *The Black Jacobins: Toussaint L'Ouverture and the San Domingo Revolution*, New York: Vintage Books.

Jameson, Fredric 1981, *The Political Unconscious: Narrative as a Socially Symbolic Act*, Ithaca, NY: Cornell University Press.

Jamieson, Stuart Marshall 1968, *Times of Trouble: Labour Unrest and Industrial Conflict in Canada 1900–1966*, Ottawa: Queen's Printer.

——— 1976, *Times of Trouble: Labour Unrest and Industrial Conflict in Canada, 1900–66*, Ottawa: Task Force on Labour Relations.

Jehan, D.A. n.d., *A Century of Service: Hamilton Fire Department, 1867–1967*, Hamilton, ON: Spectator.

Jenks, Leland 1960, 'Early Phases of the Management Movement', *Administrative Science Quarterly*, 5, December: 421–47.

John M. Gresham & Company 1889, *Biographical and Historical Souvenir for the Counties of Clark, Crawford, Harrison, Floyd, Jefferson, Jennings, Scott and Washington. Indiana*, Chicago: Chicago Printing Company.

Johnson, C.M. 1958, *The Head of the Lake: A History of Wentworth County*, Hamilton, ON: Wentworth County.

Johnson, J.K. 1989, *Becoming Prominent: Regional Leadership in Upper Canada, 1791–1841*, Kingston, ON: McGill-Queen's University Press.

Johnson, Leo A. 1971, 'Land Policy, Population Growth, and Social Structure in the Home District, 1793–1851', *Ontario History*, 63, March: 41–60.

——— 1973, *History of the County of Ontario, 1615–1875*, Whitby, ON: Corporation of the County of Ontario.

——— 1975, 'Land Policy, Population Growth and Social Structure in the Home District, 1793–1851' in *Historical Essays on Upper Canada*, edited by J.K. Johnson, Toronto: McClelland and Stewart.

——— 1977, *A History of Guelph, 1827–1927*, Guelph, ON: Commissioned and published by the Guelph Historical Society.

——— 1981, 'Independent Commodity Production: Mode of Production or Capitalist Class Formation', *Studies in Political Economy*, 6, Autumn: 93–112.

Johnson, Richard 1978, 'Edward Thompson, Eugene Genovese, and Socialist-Humanist History', *History Workshop Journal*, 6, Autumn: 79–100.

Jones, E.D. 1925, *The Administration of Industrial Enterprise*, New York: Longman, Green & Co.

Jones, Gareth Stedman 1974, 'Working-Class Culture and Working-Class Politics in London, 1870–1900: Notes on the Remaking of a Working Class', *Journal of Social History*, 7, 4: 460–508.

——— 2001, 'History and Theory: an English Story', *Historeian: A Review of the Past and other Stories*, 3: 103–24.

——— 2004, *An End to Poverty? A Historical Debate*, London: Profile Books.

Joseph, F.J. 1889, *The Municipal Manual: Containing the Municipal, Assessment, Liquor License, and Other Acts Relating to Municipal Corporations. Together with the Amending Acts of 1888 and 1889*, Toronto: Roswell & Hutchison.

Josephson, Matthew 1938, *The Politicos, 1865–1896*, New York: Harcourt Brace.

Judt, Tony 1979, 'A Clown in Regal Purple', *History Workshop Journal*, 7, Spring: 66–94.

Kakar, Sudher 1970, *Frederick Taylor: A Study in Personality and Innovation*, Cambridge, MA: MIT Press.

Kann, Kenneth 1977, 'The Knights of Labor and the Southern Black Worker', *Labor History*, 18: 49–70.

Kaplan, Sidney 1956, 'Social Engineers as Saviors: The Effects of World War I on Some American Liberals', *Journal of the History of Ideas*, June: 354–5.

Kaplow, Jeffry 1972, *The Names of Kings: The Parisian Laboring Poor in the Eighteenth Century*, New York Basic Books.

Katz, Michael B. 1972, 'Occupational Classification in History', *Journal of Interdisciplinary History*, 3, 1: 63–88.

———— 1975a, 'The Entrepreneurial Class in a Canadian City: The Mid-Nineteenth Century', *Journal of Social History*, 8, 2: 1–29.

———— 1975b, *The People of Hamilton, Canada West: Family and Class in a Mid-Nineteenth Century City*, Cambridge, MA: Harvard University Press.

———— 1978, 'The Origins of the Institutional State', *Marxist Perspectives*, 4, 1: 6–23.

———— 1981, 'Social Class in North American Urban History', *Journal of Interdisciplinary History*, 11, Spring: 579–606.

Katz, Michael B. and Mark J. Stern 1981, 'Fertility, Class, and Industrial Capitalism: Erie County, New York, 1855–1915', *American Quarterly*, 33, 1: 63–92.

Katz, Michael B., Michael J. Doucet, and Mark J. Stern 1978, 'Migration and the Social Order in Erie County, New York: 1855', *Journal of Interdisciplinary History*, 8, 4: 669–701.

———— 1982, *The Social Organization of Early Industrial Capitalism*, Cambridge, MA: Harvard University Press.

Kaufman, Burton 1972, 'The Organizational Dimension of United States Foreign Policy', *Business History Review*, 46, 1: 17–44.

———— 1973, *Samuel Gompers and the Origins of the American Federation of Labor, 1848–1896*, Westport, CT: Greenwood Press.

Kealey, Gregory S. 1973a, 'Artisans Respond to Industrialism: Shoemakers, Shoe Factories, and the Knights of St. Crispin in Toronto', Canadian Historical Association, *Historical Papers*: 137–58.

———— (ed.) 1973b, *Canada Investigates Industrialism: The Royal Commission on the Relations of Labor and Capital 1889*, Toronto: University of Toronto Press.

———— 1976a, '"The Honest Workingman" and Workers' Control: The Experience of Toronto Skilled Workers, 1860–1892', *Labour/Le Travailleur*, 1: 32–68.

———— 1976b, 'The Orange Order in Toronto: Religious Riot and the Working Class' in *Essays in Canadian Working Class History*, edited by Gregory S. Kealey and Peter Warrian, Toronto: McClelland and Stewart.

———— 1980, *Toronto Workers Respond to Industrial Capitalism, 1867–1892*, Toronto: University of Toronto Press.

———— 1982, 'Hogtown: Working Class Toronto at the Turn of the Century' in *Readings in Canadian History: Post-Confederation*, edited by R. Douglas Francis and Donald B. Smith, Toronto: Holt, Rinehart & Winston.

———— 1984, '1919: The Canadian Labour Revolt', *Labour/Le Travail*, 13, Spring: 11–45.

Kealey, Gregory S. and Bryan D. Palmer 1981, 'The Bonds of Unity: The Knights of Labor in Ontario, 1880–1900', *Histoire Sociale/Social History*, 14, 28: 369–411.

———— 1982, *Dreaming of What Might Be: The Knights of Labor in Ontario, 1880–1900*, Cambridge: Cambridge University Press.

———— 1983, 'The Bonds of Unity: Some Further Reflections', *Histoire Sociale/Social History*, 16, 31: 175–89.

———— 1987, *Dreaming of What Might Be: The Knights of Labor in Ontario, 1880–1900*, Toronto: New Hogtown Press.

Keane, Patrick 1975, 'A Study in Problems and Policies in Adult Education: The Halifax Mechanics' Institute', *Histoire Sociale/Social History*, 8, 16: 255–74.

Kelly, Edmond 1908, *The Elimination of the Tramp by the Introduction into America of the Labour Colony System Already Proved Effective in Holland, Belgium, and Switzerland, with the Modifications Thereof Necessary to Adapt This System to American Conditions*, New York: G.P. Putnam's Sons.

Kennedy, Douglas 1956, *The Knights of Labor in Canada*, London: University of Western Ontario.

Kenny, Michael 1995, *The First New Left: British Intellectuals After Stalin*, London: Lawrence & Wishart.

Kerr, Clark 1949, 'Employer Policies in Industrial Relations' in *Labor in Postwar America*, edited by Colston E. Warne, Brooklyn: Remsen Press.

Kessler-Harris, Alice 1982, *Out to Work: A History of Wage-Earning Women in the United States*, New York: Oxford University Press.

Kilbourn, William 1977, *The Firebrand: William Lyon Mackenzie and the Rebellion in Upper Canada*, Toronto: Clarke, Irwin.

King, Al with Kate Braid 1998, *Red Bait! Struggles of a Mine Mill Local*, Vancouver: Kingbird.

King, John S. 1891, *Early History of the Sons of England Benevolent Society*, Toronto: Thomas Moore.

Kingsford, R.E. 1878, *Collection of Such of the Revised Statues of Ontario, and of the Acts of the Legislature of that Province Passed in the Session 41 Victoria, 1878 as Relate to Municipal Matters*, Toronto: Hunter, Rose & Co.

Kinzer, Donald C. 1964, *An Episode in Anti-Catholicism: The American Protective Association*, Seattle: University of Washington Press.

Klee, Marcus 1998, 'Between the Scylla and Charybdis of Anarchy and Despotism: The

State, Capital, and the Working Class in the Great Depression, Toronto, 1929–1940', PhD dissertation, Queen's University.

———— 2000, 'Fighting the Sweatshop in Depression Ontario: Capital, Labour, and the Industrial Standards Act', *Labour/Le Travail*, 45, Spring: 123–52.

Klehr, Harvey 1984, *The Heyday of American Communism: The Depression Decade*, New York: Basic Books.

Kleinberg, Susan J. 1976, 'Technology and Women's Work: Lives of Working-Class Women in Pittsburg, 1870–1900', *Labor History*, 17, 1: 58–72.

Klinck, Carl F. (ed.) 1976, *Literary History of Canada: Canadian Literature in English*, Toronto: University of Toronto Press.

Knight, Rolf 1978, *Indians at Work: An Informal History of Native Indian Labour in British Columbia, 1858–1930*, Vancouver: New Star.

Knights of Labour, General Assembly 1884, *Proceedings*.

Knights of St. Crispin, London Lodge, No. 242 1872, *Constitution, By-Laws, and Rules of Order of London Lodge, No. 242, K.O.S.C.*, London, ON: Free Press Steam Printing Company.

Knights, Peter R. 1971, *The Plain People of Boston, 1830–1860: A Study of City Growth*, New York: Oxford University Press.

Knox, Paul and Philip Resnick (eds.) 1974, *Essays in BC Political Economy*, Vancouver: New Star Books.

Kolker, Kenneth H. 1948, 'The Changing Status of the Foreman', *Business History Review*, 22, June: 84–105.

Kolko, Gabriel 1965, *Railroads and Regulations, 1877–1916*, Princeton: Princeton University Press.

Korman, Gerd 1967, *Industrialization, Immigrants and Americanizers: The View From Milwaukee, 1866–1921*, Madison, ON: State Historical Society.

Kostash, Myrna 1980, *Long Way from Home: The Story of the Sixties Generation in Canada*, Toronto: Lorimer.

Kramer, Reinhold and Tom Mitchell 2010, *When the State Trembled: How A.J. Andrews and the Citizens' Committee Broke the Winnipeg General Strike*, Toronto: University of Toronto Press.

Kraus, Henry 1947, *The Many and the Few*, Los Angeles: Platin.

Krech, Shepard, III (ed.) 1981, *Indians, Animals, and the Fur Trade*, Athens, GA: University of Georgia Press.

Kristofferson, Robert 2007, *Craft Capitalism: Craftworkers and Early Industrialization in Hamilton, Ontario, 1840–1872*, Toronto: University of Toronto Press.

Kube, Art, Rod Mickleburgh, and Meyer Brownstone 1984, *British Columbia's Operation Solidarity: What Can We Learn?*, Ottawa: Centre for Policy Alternatives.

Kulik, Gary, Roger Parks, and Theodore Penn (eds.) 1982, *The New England Mill Village, 1790–1860*, Cambridge, MA: MIT Press.

Kulikoff, Allan 1971, 'The Progress of Inequality in Revolutionary Boston', *William and Mary Quarterly*, 28, 3: 375–412.

Kurath, Hans 1949, *A Word Geography of the Eastern United States*, Ann Arbor, MI: University of Michigan Press.

Labour News 1914, *Labor News, Labor Day, 1914, Annual Review*, Hamilton: Labor News.

Landon, Fred 1931, 'The Duncombe Uprising and Some of Its Consequences' in *Proceedings and Transactions of the Royal Society of Canada*, 25, Section II.

———— 1937a, 'The Common Man in the Era of the Rebellion in Upper Canada', Canadian Historical Association, *Report*: 79–91.

———— 1937b, 'The Knights of Labor: predecessors of the CIO', *Quarterly Review of Commerce*, 1, Autumn: 1–7.

———— (ed.) 1960, *An Exile from Canada to Van Diemen's Land: Being the Story of Elijah Woodman Transported Overseas for Participation in the Upper Canadian Troubles of 1837–1838*, Toronto: Longmans, Green.

———— 1966, *Western Ontario and the American Frontier*, Toronto: McClelland and Stewart.

———— 1974, 'The Common Man in the Era of the Rebellion in Upper Canada' in *Aspects of Nineteenth-Century Ontario: Essays Presented to James J. Tallman*, edited by F.H. Armstrong et al., Toronto: University of Toronto Press.

Langdon, Steven 1973, 'The Emergence of the Canadian Working-Class Movement, 1845–1875', *Journal of Canadian Studies*, 8, 2: 21.

———— 1975, *The Emergence of the Canadian Working-Class Movement*, Toronto: New Hogtown Press.

Langer, Friedrich 1981, 'Class, Culture and Class Consciousness in Ante-Bellum Lynn: A Critique of Alan Dawley and Paul Faler', *Social History*, 6: 317–32.

Larson, Robert W. 1975, 'The White Caps of New Mexico: A Study of Ethnic Militancy in the Southwest', *Pacific Historical Review*, 44, May: 171–85.

Laurie, Bruce 1973, 'Fire Companies and Gangs in Southwark: The 1840s' in *The Peoples of Philadelphia: A History of Ethnic Groups and Lower-Class Life, 1790–1940*, edited by Allen F. Davis and Mark H. Haller, Philadelphia: Temple University Press.

———— 1974, '"Nothing on Compulsion": Life Styles of Philadelphia Artisans, 1820–1850', *Labor History*, 15, 3: 337–66.

———— 1980, *Working People of Philadelphia, 1800–1850*, Philadelphia: Temple University Press.

———— and Mark Schmitz 1981, 'Manufacture and Productivity: The Making of an Industrial Base, Philadelphia, 1850–1880' in *Philadelphia: Work, Space, Family, and Group Experience in the Nineteenth Century: Essays toward and Interdisciplinary History of the City*, edited by Theodore Hershberg, New York: Oxford University Press.

Le Duc, Thomas 1966, 'History and Appraisal of the U.S. Land policy to 1862' in *Views of American Economic Growth: The Agricultural Era*, edited by Thomas C. Cochran, New York: McGraw-Hill.

Leacy, F.H. (ed.) 1983, *Historical Statistics of Canada*, second edition, Ottawa: Statistics Canada.

Lebowitz, Michael 1983, 'One-Sided Marxism', paper presented to Conference on Marxism: The Next Two Decades, Winnipeg, 12–15 March.

———— 1992, 'The One-Sidedness of *Capital*', *Review of Radical Political Economy* 14, 4: 40–51.

Lefebvre, Henri 1971, *Everyday Life in the Modern World*, New York: Harper.

Lefresne, G.M. 1962, 'The Royal Twenty Centers: The Department of National Defense and Federal Unemployment Relief, 1932–1936', History thesis, Royal Military College.

Leiserson, William 1921, *Adjusting Immigrant and Industry*, New York: Harper.

Lemon, James 1985, *Toronto Since 1918: An Illustrated History*, Toronto: J. Lorimer.

Lenin, V.I. 1964, *The Development of Capitalism in Russia*, Moscow: Progress.

———— 1974, *The Development of Capitalism in Russia*, Moscow: Progress.

Lévi-Strauss, Claude 1969, *Introduction to a Science of Mythology: The Raw and the Cooked*, New York: Harper & Row.

Levine, David 1973, 'Accumulation and Technical Change in Marxian Economics', PhD dissertation, Yale University.

———— 1974, 'Marx on Technical Change', unpublished manuscript, Yale University.

Levine, Susan 1978, 'The Best Men in the Order: Women in the Knights of Labor', unpublished paper presented to the Canadian Historical Association, London, ON.

———— 1979a, 'The Knights of Labor and Romantic Ideology', paper presented to the Knights of Labor Centennial Symposium, Chicago, 17–19 May.

———— 1979b, 'Their Own Sphere: Women's Work, the Knights of Labor, and the Transformation of the Carpet Trade, 1870–1890', PhD dissertation, City University of New York.

Lewis, Sinclair 1961, *Main Street*, New York: Signet Classic.

Lewis, Wilfred 1914, 'An Object Lesson in Efficiency' in *Scientific Management*, edited by C.B. Thompson, Cambridge, MA: Harvard University Press.

Lindsay, Almont 1942, *The Pullman Strike: The Story of a Unique Experiment and a Great Labor Upheaval*, Chicago: University of Chicago Press.

Lindsey, Charles 1862, *The Life and Times of William Lyon Mackenzie, with an Account of the Rebellion of 1837–1838 and the Subsequent Frontier Disturbances, Chiefly from Unpublished Documents*, 2 Volumes, Toronto: P.R. Randall.

Linebaugh, Peter 2008, *The Magna Carta Manifesto: Liberties and Commons for All*, Berkeley, CA: University of California Press.

Lipton, Charles 1972, 'Canadian Unionism' in *Capitalism and the National Question in Canada*, edited by Gary Teeple, Toronto: University of Toronto Press.

———— 1973, *The Trade Union Movement of Canada, 1827–1959*, Toronto: NC Press.

Lis, Catharina and Hugo Soly 1984, 'Policing the Early Modern Proletariat, 1450–1850' in *Proletarianization and Family History*, edited by David Levine, Orlando, FL: Academic Press.

Litterer, Joseph A. 1961, 'Systematic Management: The Search for Order and Integration', *Business History Review*, 25, Winter: 461–76.

———— 1963, 'Systematic Management: Design for Organizational Recoupling in American Manufacturing Firms', *Business History Review*, 37, Winter: 369–91.

Little, Margaret Jane Hillyard 1998, *'No Car, No Radio, No Liquor Permit': The Moral Regulation of Single Mothers in Ontario, 1920–1997*, Toronto: Oxford University Press.

Litwack, Leon F. 1980, *Been in the Storm So Long: The Aftermath of Slavery*, New York: Vintage Books.

Liversedge, Ronald 1973, *Recollections of the On to Ottawa Trek*, Toronto: McClelland and Stewart.

Lizars, Robina and Kathleen M. 1897, *Humours of '37: Grave, Gay, and Grim – Rebellion Times in the Canadas*, Toronto: William Briggs.

Lockridge, Kenneth 1968, 'Land, Population, and the Evolution of New England, 1630–1790', *Past and Present*, 39: 62–80.

Long, John 1922, *Voyages and Travels in the Years 1768–1788*, edited with historical introduction and notes by Milo Milton Quaife, Chicago: The Lakeside Press.

Longley, R.S. 1933, 'Mob Activities in Revolutionary Massachusetts', *New England Quarterly*, 6, March: 112–14.

Longmore, George 1977, *The Charivari; or Canadian Poetics*, edited and introduced by Mary Lu Macdonald, Ottawa: The Golden Dog Press.

Luther, Seth 1832, *An Address to the Workingmen of New England, on the State of Education, and on the Condition of the Producing Classes in Europe and America*, Boston: S. Luther.

Luxemburg, Rosa 1925, *The Mass Strike, the Political Party and the Trade Union*, Detroit: Marxian Educational Society.

———— 1968, *The Accumulation of Capital*, New York: Monthly Review Press.

Lynd, Robert S. & Helen Merrell Lynd 1956, *Middletown: A Study in Modern American Culture*, New York: Harcourt, Brace & World.

Lyon, David 1972, 'The World of P.J. McGuire: A Study of the American Labor Movement, 1870–1890', PhD dissertation, University of Minnesota.

Macdonald, L.R. 1971, 'France and New France: The Internal Contradictions', *Canadian Historical Review*, 52, 2: 379–98.

———— 1975, 'Merchants Against Industry: An Idea and Its Origins', *Canadian Historical Review*, 56, 3: 263–81.

MacDonald, Norman 1945, *The Barton Lodge, A.F. & A.M., No. 6, G.R.C., 1795–1945*, Toronto: Ryerson.

MacDowell. G.F. 1971, *The Brandon Packers Strike: A Tragedy of Errors*, Toronto: McClelland and Stewart.

MacDowell, Laurel Sefton 2001, *Renegade Lawyer: The Life of J.L. Cohen*, Toronto: University of Toronto Press.

MacKay, Kevin 2002, 'Solidarity and Symbolic Protest: Lessons for Labour from the Quebec City Summit of the Americas', *Labour/Le Travail*, 50: 21–72.

MacTaggart, John 1829, *Three Years in Canada: An Account of the Actual State of the Country in 1826-7-8*, Volume 1, London: Henry Colburn.

Malcolmson, Robert W. 1973, *Popular Recreations in English Society, 1700–1850*, London: Cambridge University Press.

Mandel, Ernest 1978, *The Second Slump: A Marxist Analysis of Recession in the Seventies*, London: NLB.

Manley, John 1998, '"Starve, Be Damned!" Communists and Canada's Urban Unemployed, 1929–1939', *Canadian Historical Review*, 79, 3: 466–91.

Marchak, Patricia 1984, 'The New Economic Reality: Substance and Rhetoric' in *The New Reality: The Politics of Restraint in British Columbia*, edited by Warren Magnusson et al., Vancouver: New Star.

Marglin, Stephen 1971, 'What Do Bosses Do? The Origins and Function of Hierarchy in Capitalist Production', unpublished manuscript, Harvard University, August.

——— 1974, 'What Do Bosses Do?: The Origins and Functions of Hierarchy in Capitalist Production', *Review of Radical Political Economics*, 6, 2: 60–112.

——— 1975, 'What Do Bosses Do? Part II', *Review of Radical Political Economics*, 7, 1: 20–37.

Marlatt, Gene 1975, 'Joseph Buchanan: Spokesman for Labor During the Populist and Progressive Eras', PhD dissertation, University of Colorado.

Marsh, Leonard C. 1933, 'The Problem of Seasonal Unemployment: A Quantitative and Comparative Survey of Seasonal Fluctuations in Canadian Employment', MA thesis, McGill University.

——— 1940, *Canadians In and Out of Work: A Survey of Economic Classes and Their Relation to the Labour Market*, Toronto: Published for McGill University by the Oxford University Press.

Martin, Calvin 1974, 'The European Impact on the Culture of a Northeastern Algonquian Tribe: An Ecological Interpretation', *William and Mary Quarterly*, 31, 1: 3–26.

——— 1978, *Keepers of the Game: Indian-Animal Relationships and the Fur Trade*, Berkeley, CA: University of California Press.

Martin, Jacques 1965, 'Les chevaliers du travail et le syndicalisme international a Montréal', MA thesis, Université de Montréal.

Marx, Karl n.d., *Capital: A Critical Analysis of Capitalist Production*, Moscow: Foreign Languages Pub. House.

——— 1934, *Capital*, Volume 1, Berlin.

———— 1967, *Capital*, New York: International Publishers.

———— 1968, 'The Eighteenth Brumaire of Louis Bonaparte' in *Marx and Engels: Selected Works*, Moscow: Progress Publishers.

———— 1973a, 'The Future Results of the British Rule in India' in *Surveys from Exile: Political Writings*, edited and introduced by David Fernbach, Harmondsworth: Penguin.

———— 1973b, *Grundrisse: Foundations of the Critique of Political Economy* (*Rough Draft*), Harmondsworth: Penguin.

———— 1975a, 'Debates on the Law on Thefts of Woods' in *Karl Marx, Frederick Engels: Collected Works*, Volume 1, Moscow: Progress.

———— 1975b, 'On the Jewish Question' in *Karl Marx, Frederick Engels: Collected Works*, Volume 3, Moscow: Progress.

Marx, Karl and Friedrich Engels 1968, 'Manifesto of the Communist Party' in *Marx and Engels: Selected Works*, Moscow: Progress Publishers.

Massicotte, E.Z. 1926a, 'Un charivari à Québec en 1683', *Bulletin des recherches historique*, 32.

———— 1926b, 'Le charivari au Canada', *Bulletin des recherches historiques*, 32, November: 717–25.

Masters, D.C. 1947, *The Rise of Toronto: 1850–1890*, Toronto: University of Toronto Press.

Matheson, David W.T. 1989, 'The Canadian Working Class and Industrial Legality, 1939–1949', MA thesis, Queen's University.

Mathews, Mitford M. (ed.) 1951a, *A Dictionary of Americanisms on Historical Principles*, Volume I, Chicago: University of Chicago Press.

———— (ed.) 1951b, *A Dictionary of Americanisms: On Historical Principles*, Volume II, Chicago: University of Chicago Press.

Matthews, William Thomas 1985, 'By and For the Large Propertied Interests: The Dynamics of Local Government in Six Upper Canadian Towns During the Era of Commercial Capitalism, 1832–1860', PhD dissertation, McMaster University.

Mayhew, Henry 1864, *German Life and Manners as Seen in Saxony at the Present Day*, Volume I, London: Wm H. Allen & Co.

McCalla, P. Douglas 1973, 'The Buchannan Businesses, 1834–1872', PhD dissertation, Oxford University.

———— 1974, 'The Decline of Hamilton as a Wholesale Centre', *Ontario History*, 65, 4: 247–54.

McCallum, John 1980, *Unequal Beginnings: Agriculture and Economic Development in Quebec and Ontario Until 1870*, Toronto: University of Toronto Press.

McCallum, Todd 2004, '"Still Raining, Market Still Rotten": Homeless Men and the Early Years of the Great Depression', PhD dissertation, Queen's University.

———— 2005, 'The Reverend and the Tramp, Vancouver, 1931: Andrew Roddan's "God in the Jungles"', *BC Studies*, 147, Autumn: 51–88.

———— 2007, 'Vancouver Through the Eyes of a Hobo: Experience, Identity, and Value in the Writing of Canada's Depression-Era Tramps', *Labour/Le Travail*, 59, Spring: 43–68.

McClung, Nellie L. 1910, *The Second Chance*, Toronto: Ryerson Press.

McCormack, A. Ross 1977, *Reformers, Rebels, and Revolutionaries: The Western Canadian Radical Movement, 1899–1919*, Toronto: University of Toronto Press.

McCoy, Edward 2011, 'The Rise of the Modern Canadian Penitentiary, 1835–1900', PhD dissertation, Trent University.

McInnis, Peter S. 2002, *Harnessing Labour Confrontation: Shaping the Postwar Settlement in Canada, 1943–1950*, Toronto: University of Toronto Press.

———— 2012, '"Hothead Troubles": Sixties-Era Wildcat Strikes in Canada', in *Debating Dissent: Canada and the Sixties*, edited by Dominique Clément, Lara A. Campbell, and Gregory S. Kealey, Toronto: University of Toronto Press.

McInnis, R.M. 1982, 'A Reconsideration of the State of Agriculture in Lower Canada in the First Half of the Nineteenth Century' in *Canadian Papers in Rural History*, Volume 3, edited by Donald H. Akenson, Gananoque, ON: Langdale Press.

McKay, Colin 1996, *For a Working-Class Culture in Canada: A Selection of Colin McKay's Writings on Sociology and Political Economy, 1897–1939*, edited and annotated by Ian McKay, St. John's, NL: Canadian Committee on Labour History.

McKay, Ian 2000, 'The Liberal Order Framework: A Prospectus for a Reconnaissance of Canadian History', *Canadian Historical Review*, 81, 4: 617–645.

———— 2005, *Rebels, Reds, Radicals: Rethinking Canada's Left History*, Toronto: Between the Lines.

———— 2008, *Reasoning Otherwise: Leftists and the People's Enlightenment in Canada, 1890–1920*, Toronto: Between the Lines.

McKechnie, Graeme 1968, *The Trucking Industry*, Ottawa: Queen's Printer.

McKelvey, Jean T. 1952, *AFL Attitudes Toward Production, 1900–1932*, Ithaca, NY: ILR.

McKenna, Barbara A. 1978, 'The Decline of the Liberal Party in Elgin County', unpublished paper presented to the Canadian Historical Association, London, ON.

McKenna, Edward 1972, 'Unorganized Labour versus Management: The Strike at the Chaudière Lumber Mills, 1891', *Histoire Sociale/Social History*, 5, November: 186–211.

McKenna, Katherine 1994, *A Life of Propriety: Anne Murray Powell and Her Family, 1755–1849*, Kingston, ON: McGill-Queen's University Press.

McKenney, Ruth 1939, *Industrial Valley*, New York: Harcourt & Brace.

McKillop, A.B. 1999, 'Who Killed Canadian History: A View from the Trenches', *Canadian Historical Review*, 80, 2: 269–99.

McLaurin, Melton 1978, *The Knights of Labor in the South*, Westport, CT: Greenwood Press.

McMichael, Philip 1977, 'The Concept of Primitive Accumulation: Lenin's Contribution', *Journal of Contemporary Asia*, 7, 4: 497–512.

McNab, John 1865, *The Magistrates' Manual: Being a Compilation of the Law Relating to the Duties of Justices of the Peace in Upper Canada*, Toronto: W.C. Chewett & Co.

McNairn, Jeffrey L. 2000, *The Capacity to Judge: Public Opinion and Deliberative Democracy in Upper Canada, 1791–1854*, Toronto: University of Toronto Press.

McNeill, George Edwin 1903, *Unfrequented Paths: Songs of Nature, Labor, and Men*, Boston: James H. West.

——— et al. 1887, *The Labor Movement: The Problem of To-Day* ..., New York: A.M. Bridgman & Co.

Medick, Hans 1976, 'The Proto-Industrial Family Economy: The Structural Function of Household and Family During the Transition from Peasant Society to Industrial Capitalism', *Social History*, 3, October: 295–315.

Mellinkoff, Ruth 1973, 'Riding Backwards: Theme of Humiliation and Symbol of Evil', *Viator: Medieval and Renaissance Studies*, 4: 153–77.

Meredith, Marnie 1933, 'Charivari I: "Belling the Bridal Couple" in Pioneer Days', *American Speech*, 7, April: 22–4.

Merrill, Michael 1977, 'Cash Is Good to Eat: Self-Sufficiency and Exchange in the Rural Economy of the United States', *Radical History Review*, 13, Winter: 42–71.

Merrington, John 1976, 'Town and Country in the Transition to Capitalism' in *The Transition from Feudalism to Capitalism*, edited by Rodney Hilton, London: New Left Books.

Metcalfe, Henry 1886, 'The Shop-Order System of Accounts', *Transactions of the American Society of Mechanical Engineers*, 7: 440–88.

Meuli, Karl 1953, 'Charivari' in *Festschrift Franz Dornseiff*, edited by Horst Kusch, Leipzig: VEB Bibliographisches Institut.

Meyers, G.J. 1914, 'The Science of Management' in *Scientific Management*, edited by C.B. Thompson, Cambridge, MA: Harvard University Press.

Middleton, Jesse Edgar 1923, *The Municipality of Toronto: A History*, Toronto: Dominion Pub. Co.

Millar, David 1980, 'A Study of Real Wages: The Construction, Use and Accuracy Check of a Constant-Dollar Plotter', unpublished research paper, University of Winnipeg.

Miller, Carmen 1975, 'A Preliminary Analysis of the Socio-Economic Composition of Canada's South African War Contingents', *Histoire Sociale/Social History*, 8, November: 219–37.

Miller, J.R. 1974, 'The Jesuits' Estates Act Crisis', *Journal of Canadian Studies*, 9, 3: 36–50.

Miller, Orlo 1949, *A Century of Western Ontario: The Story of London, The 'Free Press', and Western Ontario*, Toronto: Ryerson.

Mills, C. Wright 1959, *The Sociological Imagination*, London: Oxford University Press.

Mills, David 1988, *The Idea of Loyalty in Upper Canada, 1784–1850*, Kingston, ON: McGill-Queen's University Press.

Mintz, Sidney W. 1975, 'History and Anthropology: A Brief Reprise' in *Race and Slavery in the Western Hemisphere: Quantitative Studies*, edited by Stanley L. Engerman and Eugene D. Genovese, Princeton: Princeton University Press.

Molyneux, John 1985, *What is the Real Marxist Tradition*, London: Bookmarks.

Montgomery, David 1967, *Beyond Equality: Labor and the Radical Republicans, 1862–1872*, New York: Knopf.

———— 1968, 'The Working Classes of the Pre-Industrial City, 1780–1830', *Labor History*, 9: 3–22.

———— 1972, 'The Shuttle and the Cross: Weavers and Artisans in the Kensington Riots of 1844', *Journal of Social History*, 5, 4: 411–46.

———— 1974, 'The "New Unionism" and the Transformation in Workers' Consciousness', *Journal of Social History*, 7, 4: 509–29.

———— 1979, *Workers' Control in America*, New York: Cambridge University Press.

———— 1980a, 'Labor and the Republic in Industrial America, 1860–1920', *Mouvement social*, 111, April–June: 202–3.

———— 1980b, 'Strikes in Nineteenth-Century America', *Social Science History*, 4, February: 81–104.

———— 1987, *The Fall of the House of Labor: The Workplace, the State, and American Labor Activism, 1865–1925*, New York: Cambridge University Press.

———— 1993, *Citizen Worker: The Experience of Workers in the United States with Democracy and the Free Market During the Nineteenth Century*, New York: Cambridge University Press.

Moodie, Susanna 1913, *Roughing It in the Bush, or, Forest Life in Canada*, Toronto: Bell and Cockburn.

———— 1962, *Roughing It in the Bush*, Toronto: McClelland and Stewart.

Moody, J. Carroll and Alice Kessler-Harris 1989, *Perspectives in American Labor History: The Problems of Synthesis*, DeKalb, IL: Northern Illinois University Press.

Morgan, Cecilia 1996, *Public Men and Virtuous Women: The Gendered Language of Religion and Politics in Upper Canada, 1791–1850*, Toronto: University of Toronto Press.

Morgan, E.C. 1965, 'Pioneer Recreation and Social Life', *Saskatchewan History*, 18, Winter: 41–54.

Morgan, Philip D. 1982, 'Work and Culture: The Task System and the World of Lowcountry Blacks, 1700–1880', *William and Mary Quarterly*, 39, 4: 563–99.

Morgan, Captain William n.d., *The Mysteries of Free Masonry*, New York: Wilson and Company.

Morris, Bruce 1949, 'Industrial Relations in the Auto Industry' in *Labor in Postwar America*, edited by Colston E. Warne, Brooklyn: Remsen Press.

Morris, Lucille 1939, *Bald Knobbers*, Caldwell, ID: The Caxton Printers Ltd.

Morris, Phillip H. (ed.) n.d., *The Canadian Patriotic Fund: A Record of Its Activities from 1914 to 1919*, no place, no publisher.

Morris, R.B. 1972, 'The Reverter Clause and Break-Aways in Canada' in *Capitalism and the National Question in Canada*, edited by Gary Teeple, Toronto: University of Toronto Press.

Morris, Richard B. 1965, *Government and Labor in Early America*, New York: Octagon Books.

Morrison, Monica 1974, 'Wedding Night Pranks in Western New Brunswick', *Southern Folklore Quarterly*, 38, December: 285–97.

Mortimer, Wyndham 1971, *Organize! My Life as a Union Man*, Boston: Beacon Press.

Morton, Desmond 1977, 'Taking on the Grand Trunk: The Locomotive Engineers Strike of 1876–1877', *Labour/Le Travailleur*, 2: 5–34.

———— 1980, *Working People: An Illustrated History of Canadian Labour*, Ottawa: Deneau and Greenberg.

Morton, Desmond and Glenn Wright 1987, *Winning the Second Battle: Canadian Veterans and the Return to Civilian Life, 1915–1930*, Toronto: University of Toronto Press.

Moulton, David 1974, 'Ford Windsor 1945' in *On Strike: Six Key Labour Struggles in Canada, 1919–1949*, edited by Irving Abella, Toronto: James Lorimer & Company.

Mulvany, Charles Pelham 1884, *Toronto, Past and Present: A Handbook of the City*, Toronto: W.E. Caiger.

———— et al. 1885, *History of Toronto and County of York, Ontario ... Volume I*, Toronto: C. Blackett Robinson.

Myers, Gustavus 1972, *A History of Canadian Wealth*, Toronto: James Lorimer.

Nadworny, Milton J. 1953, 'The Society for the Promotion of Scientific Management', *Explorations in Entrepreneurial History*, 5, May 15: 244–7.

———— 1955, *Scientific Management and the Unions, 1900–3?· A Historical Analysis*, Cambridge, MA: Harvard University Press.

———— 1957, 'Frederick W. Taylor and Frank Gilbreth: Competition in Scientific Management', *Business History Review*, 31, Spring: 23–42.

Nash, Gary B. 1976, 'Urban Wealth and Poverty in Pre-Revolutionary America', *Journal of Interdisciplinary History*, 6, 4: 545–84.

———— 1979, *The Urban Crucible: Social Change, Political Consciousness, and the Origins of the American Revolution*, Cambridge, MA: Harvard University Press.

Naylor, James 1991, *The New Democracy: Challenging the Social Order in Industrial Ontario, 1914–1925*, Toronto: University of Toronto Press.

Naylor, R.T. 1972, 'The Rise and Fall of the Third Commercial Empire of the St. Lawrence' in *Capitalism and the National Question in Canada*, edited by Gary Teeple, Toronto: University of Toronto Press.

Neary, P.F. 1973, '"Traditional" and "Modern" Elements in the Social and Economic History of Bell Island and Conception Bay', Canadian Historical Association, *Papers*: 105–36.

Neilly, Andrew 1959, 'The Violent Volunteers: A History of the Volunteer Fire Department of Philadelphia, 1736–1871', PhD dissertation, University of Pennsylvania.

Nelles, H.V. 1966, 'Loyalism and Local Power: The District of Niagara, 1797–1837', *Ontario History*, 58, June: 99–114.

———— 1974, *The Politics of Development: Forest, Mines & Hydro-Electric Power in Ontario, 1849–1941*, Toronto: Macmillan.

Nelson, Daniel 1975, *Managers and Workers: Origins of the New Factory System in the United States*, Madison, WI: University of Wisconsin Press.

———— and Stuart Campbell 1972, 'Taylorism Versus Welfare Work in American Industry', *Business History Review*, 46, Spring: 1–16.

Neufeld, Maurice 1969, 'Realms of Thought and Organized Labour in the Age of Jackson', *Labor History*, 10, Winter: 5–43.

———— 1982, 'The Size of the Jacksonian Labor Movement: A Cautionary Account', *Labor History*, 23, 4: 599–607.

Nicholson, Meredith 1915, *The Hoosiers*, New York: Macmillan.

Noble, Madelein M. 1973, 'The White Caps of Harrison and Crawford Counties, Indiana: A Study in the Violent Enforcement of Morality', PhD dissertation, University of Michigan.

North, Douglas C. 1966, *Growth and Welfare in the American Past*, Englewood Cliffs, NJ: Prentice Hall.

Northall, G.F. 1892, *English Folk-Rhymes: A Collection of Traditional Verses Relating to Places and Persons, Customs, Superstitions, etc.*, London: K. Paul, Trench, Trübner.

Novick, Peter 1988, *That Noble Dream: The 'Objectivity Question' and the American Historical Profession*, Cambridge: Cambridge University Press.

O'Brien, John 1975, 'From Bondage to Citizenship: The Richmond Black Community, 1865–1867', PhD dissertation, University of Rochester.

O'Connor, James 1975, 'The Twisted Dream', *Monthly Review*, 26, March: 41–54.

O'Dea, Mark 1922, *Red Bud Women: Four Dramatic Episodes*, Cincinnati: Stewart Kidd Company.

Onslow, John 1962, *Bowler-Hatted Cowboy*, Edinburgh: Blackwood.

Ontario Bureau of Industry 1887, *Annual Report*, Toronto.

———— 1888, *Annual Report of the Bureau of Industries for the Province of Ontario, 1888*, Toronto: The Bureau.

———— 1889, *Annual Report of the Bureau of Industries for the Province of Ontario, 1889*, Toronto: The Bureau.

Ontario Commission on Unemployment 1916, *Report of the Ontario Commission on Unemployment*, Toronto: A.T. Wilgress.

Ontario Prison Reform Commission 1891, *Report of the Commissioners Appointed to Enquire into the Prison and Reformatory System of Ontario*, Toronto: Warwick & Sons.

Oestreicher, Richard J. 1979, 'Solidarity and Fragmentation: Working People and Class Consciousness in Detroit, 1877–1895', PhD dissertation, Michigan State University.

Orange Association of British America 1892, *Constitution and Laws of the Orange Association of British America*, Toronto: Sentinel.

Ostry, Bernard 1960, 'Conservatives, Liberals, and Labour in the 1870s', *Canadian Historical Review*, 61, June: 93–127.

———— 1961, 'Conservatives, Liberals, and Labour in the 1880s', *Canadian Journal of Economics and Political Science*, 27, May: 141–61.

Ouellet, Fernand 1980, *Economic and Social History of Quebec, 1760–1850*, Toronto: Gage.

Owram, Doug 1996, *Born at the Right Time: A History of the Baby Boom Generation*, Toronto: University of Toronto Press.

Ozanne, Robert 1967, *A Century of Labor-Management Relations at McCormick and International Harvester*, Madison: University of Wisconsin Press.

Padover, Saul K. (ed.) 1972, *Karl Marx on America and the Civil War*, New York: McGraw-Hill.

Palmer, Bryan D. 1976a, '"Give us the road and we will run it": The Social and Cultural Matrix of an Emerging Labour Movement' in *Essays in Canadian Working Class History*, edited by Gregory S. Kealey and Peter Warrian, Toronto: McClelland and Stewart.

———— 1976b, 'Most Uncommon Common Men: Craft and Culture in Historical Perspective', *Labour/Le Travailleur*, 1: 5–32.

———— 1977, 'Most Uncommon Common Men: Craft, Culture, and Conflict in a Canadian Community, 1860–1914', PhD dissertation, State University of New York at Binghamton.

———— 1978, 'Discordant Music: Charivaris and Whitecapping in Nineteenth-Century North America', *Labour/Le Travailleur*, 3: 5–63.

———— 1979a, *A Culture in Conflict: Skilled Workers and Industrial Capitalism in Hamilton, Ontario, 1860–1914*, Montreal: McGill-Queen's University Press.

———— 1979b, review of *Worker City, Company Town: Iron and Cotton-Worker Protest in Troy and Cohoes, New York, 1855–84* by Daniel J. Walkowitz, *Labour/Le Travilleur*, 4: 261–7.

———— 1980, 'Kingston Mechanics and the Rise of the Penitentiary, 1833–1836', *Histoire Sociale/Social History*, 13, May: 7–32.

———— 1981–2, 'Classifying Culture', *Labour/Le Travailleur*, 8/9: 160–2.

———— 1983a, 'Town, Port and Country: Speculations on the Capitalist Transformation of Mid-Nineteenth Century Canada', *Acadiensis*, 12, 2: 131–9.

———— 1983b, *Working-Class Experience: The Rise and Reconstitution of Canadian Labour, 1800–1980*, Toronto: Butterworth's.

———— 1984, 'Social Formation and Class Formation in North America, 1800–1900' in *Proletarianization and Family History*, edited by David Levine, Orlando: Academic Press.

——— 1987a, 'Labour Protest and Organization in Nineteenth-Century Canada, 1820–1890', *Labour/Le Travail*, 20, Fall: 61–84.

——— 1987b, *Solidarity: The Rise and Fall of an Opposition in British Columbia*, Vancouver: New Star.

——— (ed.) 1988, *A Communist Life: Jack Scott and the Canadian Workers Movement, 1927–1985*, St. John's, NL: Committee on Canadian Labour History.

——— 1992, *Working-Class Experience: Rethinking the History of Canadian Labour, 1800–1991*, Toronto: McClelland and Stewart.

——— 1994, 'Canadian Controversies', *History Today*, 44, 11: 44–49.

——— 1996, 'Mutuality and the Masking/Making of Difference: Mutual Benefit Societies in Canada, 1830–1950' in *Social Security Mutualism: The Comparative History of Mutual Benefit Societies*, edited by Marcel van der Linden, Bern: Peter Lang.

——— 1999, 'Of Silences and Trenches: A Dissident's View of Granatstein's Meaning', *Canadian Historical Review*, 80, 4: 676–686.

——— 2000, *Cultures of Darkness: Night Travels in the Histories of Transgression*, New York: Monthly Review Press.

——— 2003, 'What's Law Got To Do With It? Historical Considerations on Class Struggle, Boundaries of Constraint, and Capitalist Authority', *Osgoode Hall Law Journal*, 41, 2: 465–90.

——— 2005, 'System Failure: The Breakdown of the Post-War Settlement and the Politics of Labour in our Time', *Labour/Le Travail*, 55, Spring: 334–46.

——— 2005a, 'The Personal Dimension: Becoming a Left Oppositionist', *Canadian Dimension*, 39, September – October: 56–63.

——— 2008, 'Popular Radicalism and the Theatrics of Rebellion: The Hybrid Discourse of Dissent in Upper Canada' in *Transatlantic Subjects: Ideas, Institutions, and Social Experience in Post-Revolutionary British North America*, edited by Nancy Christie, Montreal: McGill-Queen's University Press.

——— 2009, 'Radical Reasoning', *Underhill Review: A Forum of History, Ideas, and Culture*, Fall: online journal accessible at http://www.carleton.ca/underhillreview/09/fall/index.htn

Panitch, Leo and Donald Swartz 1986, *From Consent to Coercion*, Toronto: Garamond.

——— 1988, *The Assault on Trade Union Freedoms: From Consent to Coercion Revisited*. Toronto: Garamond.

——— 1993, *Assault on Trade Union Freedoms: From Wage Controls to Social Contract*, Aurora, ON: Garamond Press.

Pannekoek, Frits 1976, 'A Probe into the Demographic Structure of Nineteenth-Century Red River' in *Essays on Western History: In Honour of Lewis Gwynne Thomas*, edited by Lewis H. Thomas, Edmonton, AB: University of Alberta Press.

Parker, W.H. 1969, 'A New Look at Unrest in Lower Canada, 1833–1838', *Canadian Historical Review*, 40: 209–18.

Parket, W.N. and J.L. Klein 1973, 'Productivity Growth in Grain Production in the United States, 1840–1860 and 1900–1910' in *The New Economic History*, edited by Peter Temin, Harmondsworth: Penguin.

Parr, Joy 1980, *Labouring Children: British Immigrant Apprentices to Canada*, Montreal: McGill-Queen's University Press.

———— 1983, 'Hired Men: Ontario Agricultural Wage Workers in Historical Perspective', paper presented to the Ontario Museum's Conference, Toronto, January.

Parrot, Jean-Claude 2005, *My Union, My Life: Jean-Claude Parrot and the Canadian Union of Postal Workers*, Halifax, NS: Fernwood.

Parton, Mary Field (ed.) 1972, *The Autobiography of Mother Jones*, Chicago: Charles H. Kerr & Company.

Pashukanis, Evgeny B. 1978, *Law and Marxism: A General Theory*, edited by Chris Arthur, translated by Barbara Einhorn, London: Ink Links.

Patterson, Graeme 1970, 'Studies in Elections and Public Opinion in Upper Canada', PhD dissertation, University of Toronto.

———— 1989, 'An Enduring Canadian Myth: Government and Family Compact' in *Historical Essays on Upper Canada: New Perspectives*, edited by J.K. Johnson and Bruce G. Wilson, Ottawa: Carleton University Press.

Pearce, Frank and Steve Tombs 1998, 'Foucault, Governmentality, Marxism', *Social & Legal Studies*, 7, 4: 567.

Peitchinis, Stephen G. 1971, *Labour-Management Relations in the Railway Industry*, Ottawa: Queen's Printer.

Pelham, Nettie H. 1891, *The White Cups*, Chicago: T.S. Denison.

Penner, Norman 1988, *Canadian Communism: The Stalin Years and Beyond*, Toronto: Methuen Publications.

Pentland, H.C. 1948, 'The Lachine Canal Strike of 1843', *Canadian Historical Review*, 29: 255–77.

———— 1950, 'The Role of Capital in Canadian Economic Development Before 1875', *Canadian Journal of Economics and Political Science*, 4, November: 457–74.

———— 1959, 'The Development of a Capitalistic Labour Market in Canada', *Canadian Journal of Economics and Political Science*, 25, November: 450–61.

———— 1960, 'Labor and the Development of Industrial Capitalism in Canada', PhD dissertation, University of Toronto.

———— 1968, 'A Study of the Changing Social, Economic, and Political Background of the Canadian System of Industrial Relations', draft study for the Task Force on Labour Relations, Ottawa.

———— 1981, *Labour and Capital in Canada, 1650–1860*, edited by Paul Phillips, Toronto: J. Lorimer.

Pernicone, Carole Groneman 1973, '"The Bloody Auld Sixth": A Social Analysis of a New York City Working Class Community in the Mid-Nineteenth Century', PhD dissertation, University of Rochester.

Perrot, Michelle 1974, *Les ouvriers en grève: France 1871–1890*, Volume 2, Paris: Mouton.

Person, Carl E. 1918, *The Lizard's Trial: A Story of the Illinois Central and Harriman Lines Strike of 1911 to 1915 Inclusive*, Chicago: Lake Publishing.

Pessen, Edward 1967, *Most Uncommon Jacksonians: Radical Leaders of the Early Labor Movement*, Albany, NY: State University of New York Press.

———— 1969, *Jacksonian America: Society, Personality and Politics*, Homewood, IL: Dorsey Press.

———— 1976, 'Building the Young Republic' in *The U.S. Department of Labor History of the American Worker*, edited by Richard B. Morris, Washington, D.C.: Government History Office.

Peterson, Larry 1984, 'Revolutionary Socialism and Industrial Unrest in the Era of the Winnipeg General Strike: The Origins of Communist Labour Unionism in Europe and North America', *Labour/Le Travail*, 13, Spring: 115–32.

Phelan, Josephine 1976, 'The Tar and Feather Case, 1827', *Ontario History*, 68, March: 17–23.

Phillips, David Graham 1908, *Old Wives for New: A Novel*, New York: Grosset & Dunlap.

Phillips, George 1860, 'Ueber den Ursprung der Katzen-musiken' in *Vermischte Schriften*, Volume III, Vienna: W. Braumüller.

Phillips, Jim 1990, 'Poverty, Unemployment, and the Administration of the Criminal Law: Vagrancy Laws in Halifax, 1864–1890' in *Essays in the History of Canadian Law: Nova Scotia*, Volume 3, edited by Philip Girard and Jim Phillips, Toronto: Published for the Osgoode Society by University of Toronto Press.

Phillips, Paul 1967, *No Power Greater: A Century of Labour in B.C.*, Vancouver: BC Federation of Labour.

Phillips, U.B. 1963, *Life and Labor in the Old South*, Boston: Little, Brown.

Phillips, Willard 1850, *Propositions Concerning Protection and Free Trade*, Boston: Little, Brown.

Pinon, Roger 1969, 'Qu'est-ce q'un charivari? Essai en vue d'une definition opératorie' in *Kontakete und Grenzen. Probleme der Volks-, Kultur- und Sozialforschung*, Gottingen.

Pitsula, James M. 1980, 'The Treatment of Tramps in Late Nineteenth-Century Toronto', Canadian Historical Association, *Historical Papers*: 116–32.

Pitt-Rivers, J.A. 1954, *The People of the Sierra*, New York: Criterion Books.

Piva, Michael J. 1979, *The Condition of the Working Class in Toronto, 1900–1921*, Ottawa: University of Ottawa Press.

———— 1983, '"The Bonds of Unity": A Comment', *Histoire Sociale/Social History*, 31, May: 169–74.

Pollack, Norman 1966, *The Populist Response to Industrial America*, New York: Norton.

———— 1967, *The Populist Mind*, New York: Bobbs Merrill.

———— 1968, *The Populist Response to Industrial America*, New York: Norton.

Pomfret, R. 1976, 'The Mechanization of Reaping in Nineteenth-Century Ontario: A Case Study of the Pace and Causes of Diffusion of Embodied Technical Change', *Journal of Economic History*, 36, 2: 399–415.

Pope, Sir Joseph (ed.) 1921, *The Correspondence of Sir John A. Macdonald*, Toronto: Oxford University Press.

Porter, Enid 1969, *Cambridgeshire Customs and Folklore*, London: Routledge & K. Paul.

——— 1974, *The Folklore of East Anglia*, Totowa: Rowman and Littlefield.

Porter, Glenn and Harold C. Livesay 1971, *Merchants and Manufacturers: Studies in the Changing Structure of Nineteenth-Century Marketing*, Baltimore: Johns Hopkins University Press.

Porter, John 1965, *The Vertical Mosaic: An Analysis of Social Class and Power in Canada*, Toronto: University of Toronto Press.

Post, Charles 1982, 'The American Road to Capitalism', *New Left Review*, 1/133, May–June: 30–51.

Potter, Janice 1989, 'Patriarchy and Paternalism: The Case of Eastern Ontario Loyalist Women', *Ontario History*, 81, 1: 3–24.

Powderly, Terence V. 1940, *The Path I Trod: The Autobiography of Terence V. Powderly*, New York: Columbia University Press.

Preston, William B. 1971, 'Shall This Be All? U.S. Historians Versus William D. Haywood et al.', *Labor History*, 12, Spring: 435–71.

Pritchard, W.A. 1920, *Address to the Jury in The Crown vs. Armstrong, Bray, Ivens, Johns, Pritchard, and Queen (R.B. Russell was tried previously) Indicted for Seditious Conspiracy and Common Nuisance, Fall Assizes, Winnipeg, Manitoba, Canada 1919–1920*, Winnipeg: Wallingford Press.

Prude, Jonathan 1982, 'The Social System of Early New England Mills: A Case Study, 1812–1840' in *Working-Class America: Essays on Labor, Community, and American Society*, edited by Michael H. Frisch and Daniel J. Walkowitz, Urbana, IL: University of Illinois Press.

Przeworski, Adam 1985, *Capitalism and Social Democracy*, New York: Cambridge University Press.

Queen's University 1903, 'The Canadian Locomotive Company Limited: History of the Works at Kingston', *Queen's Quarterly*, 10, April: 455–65.

Rachleff, Peter 1979, 'Black Richmond and the Knights of Labor', paper presented to the Knights of Labor Centennial Conference, Newberry Library, Chicago, May 17–19.

Radin, Paul 1953, *The World of Primitive Man*, New York: Schuman.

Radosh, Ronald 1966, 'The Corporate Ideology of American Labor Leaders from Gompers to Hillman', *Studies on the Left*, 6, November–December: 66–88.

——— 1969, *American Labor and U.S. Foreign Policy*, New York: Vintage.

Raible, Chris 1992, *Muddy York: Scandal and Scurrility in Upper Canada*, Creemore, ON: Curiosity House.

Rand, Ivan 1968, *Report of the Royal Commission Inquiry into Labour Disputes*, Toronto: Queen's Printer.

Rapaport, David 1999, *No Justice, No Peace: The 1996 OPSEU Strike Against the Harris Government in Ontario*, Montreal: McGill-Queen's University Press.

Ray, Arthur J. 1974, *Indians in the Fur Trade: Their Role as Hunters, Trappers, and Middlemen in the Lands Southwest of Hudson Bay, 1660–1870*, Toronto: University of Toronto Press.

Rea, J.E. 1968, 'William Lyon Mackenzie – Jacksonian?', *Mid-America*, 60: 223–35.

Read, Colin 1982, *The Rising in Western Upper Canada, 1837–1838: The Duncombe Revolt and After*, Toronto: University of Toronto Press.

———— and Ronald J. Stagg (eds.) 1985, *The Rebellion of 1837 in Upper Canada: A Collection of Documents*, Toronto: Champlain Society in cooperation with the Ontario Heritage Foundation.

Read, D.B. 1896, *The Canadian Rebellion of 1837*, Toronto: Blackett Robinson.

'Red-Ink' 1890, *'Pi': A Compilation of Odds and Ends Relating to Workers in Sanctum and Newsroom, Culled from the Scrap-Book of a Compositor*, Hamilton, ON: Griffin & Kidner.

Reid, Colin 1982, *The Rising in Western Upper Canada: 1837–1838*, Toronto: University of Toronto Press.

Reid, Julyan 1969, 'Some Canadian Issues' in *Student Power and the Canadian Campus*, edited by Tim Reid, Toronto: Peter Martin.

Renner, Karl 1976, *The Institutions of Private Law and their Social Functions*, London: Routledge and Kegan Paul.

Reshef, Yonatan and Sandra Rastin 2003, *Unions in the Time of Revolution: Government Restructuring in Alberta and Ontario*, Toronto: University of Toronto Press.

Resnick, Philip 1977a, *The Land of Cain: Class and Nationalism in English Canada, 1945–1975*, Vancouver: New Star Books.

———— 1977b, 'Social Democracy in Power: The Case of British Columbia', *BC Studies*, 34, Summer: 3–20.

Rice, Richard 1977, 'Shipbuilding in British America, 1787–1890', PhD dissertation, University of Liverpool.

Rich, E.E. 1960, 'Trade Habits and Economic Motivation Among the Indians of North America', *Canadian Journal of Economics and Political Science*, 26, February: 35–53.

Riddell, Hon. Wm. R. 1922, 'An Old Provincial Newspaper', Ontario Historical Society, *Papers & Records*, 19: 139.

Riddell, William Renwick 1931, 'The "Shivaree" and the Original', Ontario Historical Society, *Papers & Records*, 27, Toronto: 522–4.

Ridgely 1867, *The Odd Fellows Pocket Companion: A Correct Guide to All Matters Relating to Odd-Fellowship*, Cincinnati: Odd Fellows.

Rinehart, James W. 1975, *The Tyranny of Work*, Don Mills: Academic Press.

Ripley, George and Charles A. Dana (eds.) 1864, *The New American Cyclopaedia: A Popular Dictionary of General Knowledge*, Volume 4, New York: D. Appleton and Company.

Robert, Jean-Claude 1977, 'Montréal 1821–1871: aspects de l'urbanisation', Volume 1, Thesis de doctorat, Université de Paris.

Roberts, George 1856, *The Social History of the People of the Southern Counties of England in Past Centuries*, London: Longman, Brown, Green, Longmans & Roberts.

Roberts, Wayne 1976, 'The Last Artisans: Toronto Printers, 1896–1914' in *Essays in Canadian Working Class History*, edited by Gregory S. Kealey and Peter Warrian, Toronto: McClelland and Stewart.

———— 1978, 'Studies in the Toronto Labour Movement, 1896–1914', PhD dissertation, University of Toronto.

———— 1990, *Cracking the Canadian Formula: The Making of the Energy and Chemical Workers Union*, Toronto: Between the Lines.

Robin, Martin 1968, *Radical Politics and Canadian Labour, 1880–1930*, Kingston, ON: Industrial Relations Centre, Queen's University.

———— 1972, *The Rush for Spoils: The Company Province, 1871–1933*, Toronto: McClelland and Stewart.

———— 1976, *The Bad and the Lonely: Seven Stories of the Best and Worst Canadian Outlaws*, Toronto: J. Lorimer.

Robinson, John Beverley 1957, 'A Defence on Constitutional Grounds' in *The Family Compact: Aristocracy or Oligarchy*, edited by David W. Earl, Toronto: Copp Clark.

Robinson, Sarah 1913, *The Soldier's Friend: A Pioneer's Record*, London: R. Fisher Unwin.

Rock, Howard B. 1979, *Artisans of the New Republic: The Tradesmen of New York City in the Age of Jefferson*, New York: New York University Press.

Rodney, William 1968, *Soldiers of the International: A History of the Communist Party of Canada, 1919–1929*, Toronto: University of Toronto Press.

Rogin, Michael 1975, *Fathers and Children: Andrew Jackson and the Subjugation of the American Indian*, New York: Vintage Books.

Romney, Paul 1990, 'On the Eve of the Rebellion: Nationality, Religion and Class in the Toronto Election of 1835' in *Old Ontario: Essays in Honour of J.M.S. Careless*, edited by David Keane and Colin Read, Toronto: Dundurn Press.

Rose, Nikolas 1999, *Powers of Freedom: Reframing Political Thought*, Cambridge: Cambridge University Press.

Rose, Nikolas and Mariana Valverde 1998, 'Governed by Law?', *Social & Legal Studies*, 7, 4: 541.

Rosenberg, Nathan (ed.) 1969, *The American System of Manufactures: The Report of the Committee on the Machinery of the United States (1855) and the Special Report of George Wallis and Joseph Whitworth (1854)*, Edinburgh: University Press.

——— 1963, 'Technological Change in the Machine Tool Industry, 1840–1910', *Journal of Economic History*, 23, 4: 414–46.

Ross, Steven H. 1979, 'Strikes, Knights, and Political Fights: The May Day Strikes, the Knights of Labor, and the Rise of the United Labor Party in Nineteenth-Century Cincinnati', paper presented to the Knights of Labor Centennial Conference, Newberry Library, Chicago, 17–19 May.

Ross, Steven Joseph 1980, 'Workers on the Edge: Work, Leisure, and Politics in Industrializing Cincinnati, 1830–1890', PhD dissertation, Princeton University.

Rostow, W.W. 1965, *The Stages of Economic Growth: A Non-Communist Manifesto*, Cambridge: University Press.

Rothschild, Emma 1973, *Paradise Lost: The Decline of the Auto-Industrial Age*, New York: Random House.

Roussopoulos, Dimitrios I. 1970, 'Towards a Revolutionary Youth Movement and an Extraparliamentary Opposition in Canada' in *The New Left in Canada*, edited by Dimitrios I. Roussopoulos, Montreal: Our Generation Press.

Rowse, A.L. 1947, *A Cornish Childhood: Autobiography of a Cornishman*, New York: Macmillan.

Roy, Andrew 1970, *A History of the Coal Mines of the United States*, Westport, CT: Greenwood Press.

Roy, Donald 1969, 'Making Out: A Counter System of Workers' Control of Work Situations and Relations' in *Industrial Man*, edited by Tomm Burns, Baltimore: Penguin.

Roy, Pierre-Georges (ed.) 1930, *La ville de Québec sous le régime français*, Quebec: Publié pas le service des Archives du government de la province de Québec.

Royal Commission on the Relations of Labor and Capital in Canada 1889, *Report of the Royal Commission on the Relations of Labor and Capital in Canada*, 'Ontario Evidence', Volume 2, Ottawa: Queen's Printer.

Royce, Josiah 1886, *California from the Conquest in 1846 to the Second Vigilance Committee in San Francisco: A Study of American Character*, Boston: Houghton, Mifflin and Company.

Royle, E. 1971, 'Mechanics' Institutes and the Working Classes, 1840–1860', *The Historical Journal*, 14: 305–21.

Russell, Bob 1990, *Back to Work? Labour, State, and Industrial Relations in Canada*, Scarborough, ON: Nelson.

Russell, Peter A. 1982, 'Upper Canada: A Poor Man's Country? Some Statistical Evidence' in *Canadian Papers in Rural History*, Volume 3, edited by Donald H. Akenson, Gananoque, ON: Langdale Press.

Rutman, Darret B. 1977, 'People in Process: The New Hampshire Towns of the Eighteenth Century' in *Family and Kin in Urban Communities, 1700–1930*, edited by Tamara K. Hareven, New York: New Viewpoints.

Ryan, Mary P. 1981, *Cradle of the Middle Class: The Family of Oneida County, New York, 1780–1865*, New York: Cambridge University Press.

Ryerson, Stanley B. 1937, *1837: The Birth of Canadian Democracy*, Toronto: Francis White.

———— 1968, *Unequal Union: Confederation and the Roots of Conflict in the Canadas, 1815–1873*, Toronto: Progress Books.

———— 1973, *Unequal Union: The Roots of Crisis in the Canadas, 1815–1873*, Toronto: Progress Books.

Saintyves, P. 1935, 'Le charivari de l'adultère et les courses à corps nus', *L'ethnographie*, 31, new ser.: 7–36.

Salinger, Sharon V. 1983, 'Artisans, Journeymen, and the Transformation of Labor in Late Eighteenth-Century Philadelphia', *William and Mary Quarterly*, 40, 1: 62–84.

Samuel, Raphael 1977, 'Workshop of the World: Steam Power and Hand Technology in Mid-Victorian Britain', *History Workshop Journal*, 3, Spring: 6–72.

Sanderson, Charles R. (ed.) 1943, *The Arthur Papers: Being the Papers Mainly Confidential, Private, and Demi-Official of Sir George Arthur*, Toronto: Toronto Public Libraries.

———— (ed.) 1957, *The Arthur Papers; Being the Canadian Papers Mainly Confidential, Private, and Demi-Official of Sir George Arthur, K.C.H. Last Lieutenant-Governor of Upper Canada*, Toronto: University of Toronto Press.

Sangster, Joan 2000, 'Feminism and the Making of Canadian Working-Class History: Exploring the Past, Present and Future', *Labour/Le Travail*, 46, Fall: 127–166.

———— 2004, '"We No Longer Respect the Law": The Tilco Strike, Labour Injunctions, and the State', *Labour/Le Travail*, 53, Spring: 47–88.

Saunders, Robert E. 1975, 'What Was the Family Compact?' in *Historical Essays on Upper Canada*, edited by J.K. Johnson, Toronto: McClelland and Stewart.

Saville, John 1969, 'Primitive Accumulation and Early Industrialization in Britain' in *Socialist Register*, edited by John Saville and Ralph Miliband, London: Merlin.

Scadding, Henry 1966, *Toronto of Old*, edited by Frederick H. Armstrong, Toronto: Oxford University Press.

———— and John Charles Dent 1884, *Toronto: Past and Present, Historical and Descriptive: A Memorial Volume for the Semi-Centennial of 1884*, Toronto: Hunter, Rose.

Scharnau, Ralph W. 1969, 'Thomas J. Morgan and the Chicago Socialist Movement, 1876–1901', PhD dissertation, University of Northern Illinois.

Schele de Vere, M. 1872, *Americanisms; The English of the New World*, New York: Charles Scribner & Company.

Scherck, Michael Gonder [A 'Canuck'] 1905, *Pen Pictures of Early Pioneer Life in Upper Canada*, Toronto: William Briggs.

Schlesier, Karl H. 1976, 'Epidemics and Indian Middlemen: Rethinking the Wars of the Iroquois, 1609–1653', *Ethnohistory*, 23: 129–45.

Schlesinger, Andrew Bancroft 1971, 'Las Gorras Blancas, 1889–1891', *Journal of Mexican-American History*, 1, Spring: 87–143.

School, Amos Tuck 1911, *Conference on Scientific Management*, New York: Harpur.

Schrauwers, Albert 2009, *'Union is Strength': W.L. Mackenzie, the Children of Peace, and the Emergence of Joint Stock Democracy in Upper Canada*, Toronto: University of Toronto Press.

———— 2010, 'The Gentlemanly Order & the Politics of Production in the Transition to Capitalism in Upper Canada', *Labour/Le Travail*, 65, Spring: 9–46.

———— 2011, '"Money Bound You – Money Shall Loose You": Micro-Credit, Social Capital, and the Meaning of Money in Upper Canada', *Comparative Studies in Society and History*, 53, 2: 1–30.

Schulz, Patricia V. 1975, *The East York Workers' Association: A Response to the Great Depression*, Toronto: New Hogtown Press.

Schwartz, Joel 1974, 'Morissania's Volunteer Firemen, 1848–1874: The Limits of Local Institutions in a Metropolitan Age', *New York History*, April: 159–78.

Scott, Benjamin S. 1930, 'The Economic and Industrial History of the City of London, Canada from the Building of the First Railway, 1855 to the Present, 1930', MA thesis, University of Western Ontario.

Scott, Jack 1974, *Sweat and Struggle: Working Class Struggles in Canada, 1780–1899*, Vancouver: New Star.

———— 1978, *Canadian Workers, American Unions*, Vancouver: New Star.

Scott, Joan 1988, *Gender and the Politics of History*, New York: Columbia University Press.

Seccombe, Wally 1980a, 'Domestic Labour and the Working-Class Household' in *Hidden in the Household: Women's Domestic Labour Under Capitalism*, edited by Bonnie Fox, Toronto: Women's Press.

———— 1980b, 'The Expanded Reproduction Cycle of Labour Power in Twentieth-Century Capitalism' in *Hidden in the Household: Women's Domestic Labour Under Capitalism*, edited by Bonnie Fox, Toronto: Women's Press.

———— 1983, 'Marxism and Demography', *New Left Review*, 1/137, January–February: 22–47.

Séguin, Robert-Lionel 1968, *Les divertissements en Nouvelle-France*, Ottawa: Imprimeur de la reine.

———— 1970, 'La raillerie des cornes en Nouvelle-France' in *Les Cahiers Des Dix*, 35.

Seidman, Joel 1942, *The Needle Trades*, New York: Farrar and Rinehart.

Select Committee on the Causes of the Present Depression of the Manufacturing, Mining, Commercial, Shipping and Fishing Interests 1876, *Report of the Select Committee on the Causes of the Present Depression of the Manufacturing, Mining, Commercial, Shipping, Lumber and Fishing Industries*, Ottawa.

Senior, Hereward 1972a, *Orangeism: The Canadian Phase*, Toronto: McGraw-Hill.

———— 1972b, 'Orangeism in Ontario Politics' in *Oliver Mowat's Ontario*, edited by Donald Swainson, Toronto: Macmillan.

Serrin, William 1973, *The Company and the Union*, New York: Knopf.

Shannon, Fred 1945, 'A Post-Mortem on the Labor-Supply Safety-Valve Theory', *Agricultural History*, 19, January: 31–7.

Shaw, A.W. 1914, 'Scientific Management in Business' in *Scientific Management*, edited by C.B. Thompson, Cambridge, MA: Harvard University Press.

Shaw, Douglas Vincent 1973, 'The Making of an Immigrant City: Ethnic and Cultural Conflict in Jersey City, New Jersey, 1850–1877', PhD dissertation, University of Rochester.

Shaw, Peter 1981, *American Patriots and the Rituals of Revolution*, Cambridge, MA: Harvard University Press.

Sherover-Marcuse, Erica 1986, *Emancipation and Consciousness: Dogmatic and Dialectical Perspectives in the Early Marx*, Oxford: Blackwell.

Sherry, Robert 1976, 'Comments on O'Connor's Review of *The Twisted Dream*', *Monthly Review*, 28, May: 52–8.

Shipley, Stan 1972, *Club Life and Socialism in Mid-Victorian London*, Oxford: History Workshop.

Shirreff, Patrick 1835, *A Tour Through North America: Together with a Comprehensive View of the Canadas and the United States, as Adapted for Agricultural Emigration*, Edinburgh: Oliver and Boyd.

Shorter, Edward 1975, *The Making of the Modern Family*, New York: Basic Books.

Shugg, Roger W. 1972, *The Origins of Class Struggle in Louisiana: A Social History of White Farmers and Laborers During Slavery and After, 1840–1875*, Baton Rouge, LA: Louisiana State University Press.

Sider, Gerald M. 1976, 'Christmas Mumming and the New Year in Outport Newfoundland', *Past & Present*, 71, May: 102–25.

———— 1977, *Christmas Mumming in Outport Newfoundland*, Toronto: New Hogstown.

Siracusa, Carl 1979, *A Mechanical People: Perceptions of the Industrial Order in Massachusetts, 1815–1880*, Middletown, CT: Wesleyan University Press.

Siringo, Charles A. 1912, *Cow-Boy Detective: A True Story of Twenty-Two Years with a World Famous Detective Agency*, New York: W.B. Conkey Company.

Sismondi, J.C.L. Simonde de 1819, *Nouveaux principes d'économie politique, ou, De la richesse dans ses rapports avec la population* 2 Volumes, Paris: Delaunay.

Smandych, Russell 1991, 'Rethinking "The Master Principle of Administering Relief" in Upper Canada: A Response to Allan Irving', *Canadian Review of Social Policy*, 27: 81–6.

———— 1995, 'William Osgoode, John Graves Simcoe, and the Exclusion of the English Poor Law from Upper Canada' in *Law, Society, and the State: Essays in Modern Legal History*, edited by Louis A. Knafla and Susan W.S. Binnie, Toronto:

Smith, Billy G. 1981, 'The Material Lives of Laboring Philadelphians, 1750 to 1800', *William and Mary Quarterly*, 38, 2: 163–202.

Smith, Henry T. n.d., *Introduction of Royal Arch Masonry Into Toronto*, n.p.

Smith, J.H. 1903, *The Central School Jubilee Reunion, August 1903: A Historical Sketch*, Hamilton, ON: Spectator.

Smith, Murray E.G. 2010, *Global Capitalism in Crisis: Karl Marx and the Decay of the Profit System*, Black Point, NS: Fernwood Pub.

Smith, Thomas 1975, 'Reconstructing Occupational Structures: The Case of the Ambiguous Artisans', *Historical Methods Newsletter*, 8, June: 134–46.

Smucker, J. 1980, *Industrialization in Canada*, Scarborough, ON: Prentice Hall.

Sorge, Frederich A. 1977, *Labor Movement in the United States: A History of the American Working Class from Colonial Times to 1890*, Westport, CT: Greenwood Press.

Speisman, Stephen A. 1973, 'Munificent Parsons and Municipal Parsimony: Voluntary vs. Public Poor Relief in Nineteenth-Century Toronto', *Ontario History*, 65, March: 32–49.

Spelt, Jacob 1972, *Urban Development in South-Central Ontario*, Toronto: McClelland and Stewart.

Spero, Sterling D. and Abram L. Harris 1968, *The Black Worker: The Negro and the Labor Movement*, New York: Atheneum.

Splane, Richard B. 1965, *Social Welfare in Ontario, 1791–1893: A Study of Public Welfare Administration*, Toronto: University of Toronto Press.

St. Andrew's Benevolent Society of Hamilton 1860, *Constitution of the St. Andrew's Benevolent Society of Hamilton*, Hamilton, ON: Gillespy and Robertson.

——— 1882, *Constitution of the St. Andrew's Benevolent Society of Hamilton, Ontario, with a List of Office Bearers*, Hamilton, ON: Lawson.

St. Clair, Sheila 1971, *Folklore of the Ulster People*, Cork: Mercier Press.

Stainsby, Cliff and John Malcolmson 1983, *The Fraser Institute, the Government, and a Corporate Free Lunch*, Vancouver: Solidarity Coalition.

Stampp, Kenneth 1956, *The Peculiar Institution: Slavery in the Ante-Bellum South*, New York: Vintage Books.

Stansell, Christine 1982, 'The Origins of the Sweatshop: Women and Early Industrialization in New York City' in *Working-Class America: Essays on Labor, Community, and American Society*, edited by Michael H. Frisch and Daniel J. Walkowitz, Urbana, IL: University of Illinois Press.

Stefanson, V. 1903, 'English Loan-Nouns used in the Icelandic Colony of North Dakota', *Dialect Notes*, 2: 354–62.

Stein, Leon and Philip Taft (eds.) 1969, *Religion, Reform and Revolution: Labor Panaceas in the Nineteenth Century*, New York: Arno.

Steindl, Joseph 1976, *Maturity and Stagnation in American Capitalism*, New York: Monthly Review Press.

Stephens, Nan Bagby 1929, 'Charivari' in *Plays of American Life and Fantasy*, edited by Edith J.R. Isaacs, New York: Coward, McCann Inc.

Stevenson, John L. 1914, 'Labor and Capital', *Popular Science Monthly*, 84, May: 459–70.

Stewart, Bryce 1923, 'Unemployment and Organization of the Labour Market', American Academy of Political and Social Science, 'Social and Economic Conditions in the Dominion of Canada', *The Annals*, 107, May: 286–93.

Stewart, Walter 1977, *Strike!*, Toronto: McClelland and Stewart.

Stock, Brian 1973, 'English Canada: The Visible and Invisible Cultures', *Canadian Forum*, 52, March: 29–33.

Stone, Katherine 1973, 'The Origins of Job Structures in the Steel Industry', *Radical America*, 7, 6: 19–66.

——— 1974, 'The Origins of Job Structures in the Steel Industry', *Review of Radical Political Economics*, 6, 2: 113–73.

Stone, Lawrence 1977, *The Family, Sex and Marriage in England, 1500–1800*. New York: Harper and Row.

Stromquist, Shelton 1987, *A Generation of Boomers: The Pattern of Railroad Labor Conflict in Nineteenth-Century America*, Urbana, IL: University of Illinois Press.

Struthers, James 1983, *No Fault of Their Own: Unemployment and the Canadian Welfare State, 1914–1941*, Toronto: University of Toronto Press.

Stuart, Jesse 1938, *Beyond Dark Hills: A Personal Story*, New York: E.P. Dutton.

——— 1941, *Men of the Mountains*, New York: E.P. Dutton & Co.

Stunden, Nancy 1974, 'Oshawa Knights of Labor Demonstration Medal', *Canadian Labour History, Newsletter of the Committee on Canadian Labour History*, 4: 1–2.

Súilleabháin, Seán Ó 1963, *A Handbook of Irish Folklore*, London: H. Jenkins.

Sumner, William Graham 1906, *Folkways: A Study of the Sociological Importance of Usages, Manners, Customs, Mores, and Morals*, New York: Ginn and Company.

Sutch, Richard 1975, 'The Breeding of Slaves for Sale and the Westward Expansion of Slavery, 1850–1860' in *Race and Slavery in the Western Hemisphere: Quantitative Studies*, edited by Stanley L. Engerman and Eugene D. Genovese, Princeton: Princeton University Press.

Swainson, Donald 1968, 'The Personnel of Politics: A Study of the Ontario Members of the Second Federal Parliament', PhD dissertation, University of Toronto.

——— 1974, 'Sir Henry Smith and the Politics of Union', *Ontario History*, 66, September: 161–79.

Swankey, Ben 1983, *The Fraser Institute: A Socialist Analysis of the Corporate Drive to the Right*, Vancouver: Socialist Education Centre.

Sward, Keith 1972, *The Legend of Henry Ford*, New York: Atheneum.

Sweezy, Paul 1968, 'Karl Marx and the Industrial Revolution in England' in *Events, Ideology, and Economic Theory*, edited by R. Eagly, Detroit: Wayne State University Press.

The System Company 1911, *How Scientific Management Is Applied*, New York: The System Company.

Talbot, Edward Allen 1824, *Five Years' Residence in the Canadas: Including a Tour*

Through Part of the United States of America in the Year 1823, London: Printed for Longman, Hurst, Rees, Orme, Brown and Green.

Tannenbaum, Frank 1921, *The Labor Movement: Its Conservative Functions and Social Consequences*, New York: Putnam.

Tarkington, Booth 1899, *The Gentleman From Indiana*, New York: Doubleday & McClure Co.

Taussig, F.W. 1930, *The Tariff History of the United States*, New York: Putman's.

Taylor, Frederick Winslow 1869, 'Workmen and Their Management', unpublished manuscript, Harvard.

———— 1895, 'A Piece Rate System: Being a Partial Solution of the Labor Problem', *Transactions of the American Society of Mechanical Engineers*, 17: 856–903.

———— 1914a, 'On the Art of Cutting Metals' in *Scientific Management*, edited by C.B. Thompson, Cambridge, MA: Harvard University Press.

———— 1914b, 'A Piece Rate System' in *Scientific Management*, edited by C.B. Thompson, Cambridge, MA: Harvard University Press.

———— 1914c, 'The Principles of Scientific Management' in *Scientific Management*, edited by C.B. Thompson, Cambridge, MA: Harvard University Press.

———— 1947, *Scientific Management; Comprising* Shop Management, The Principles of Scientific Management, *and* Testimony Before the Special House Committee, New York: Harper.

Taylor, George R. 1964, 'American Economic Growth Before 1840: An Exploratory Essay', *Journal of Economic History*, 24, December: 427–44.

———— 1965, 'The National Economy Before and After the Civil War' in *Economic Change in the Civil War Era: Proceedings*, edited by David T. Gilchrist & W. David Lewis, Greenville, SC: Eleutherian Mills-Hagley Foundation.

———— 1951, *The Transportation Revolution, 1815–1860*, New York: Harper.

Taylor, John 1971, *From Self-Help to Glamour: The Working Man's Club, 1860–1972*, Oxford: History Workshop.

Teeple, Gary 1972, 'Land, Labour and Capital in Pre-Confederation Canada' in *Capitalism and the National Question in Canada*, edited by Gary Teeple, Toronto: University of Toronto Press.

Thale, Mary (ed.) 1972, *The Autobiography of Francis Place, 1771–1854*, London: Cambridge University Press.

Thernstrom, Stephen 1964, *Poverty and Progress: Social Mobility in a Nineteenth-Century City*, Cambridge, MA: Harvard University Press.

Thompson, C.B. 1913, 'The Relations of Scientific Management to the Wage Problem', *Journal of Political Economy*, 21, July: 631.

———— 1914a, 'The Case for Scientific Management', *The Sociological Review*, 7, October: 315–27.

———— 1914b, 'The Literature of Scientific Management' in *Scientific Management*, edited by C.B. Thompson, Cambridge, MA: Harvard University Press.

————— (ed.) 1914c, *Scientific Management*, edited by C.B. Thompson, Cambridge, MA: Harvard University Press.

————— 1914d, 'Wages and Wage Systems as Incentives' in *Scientific Management*, edited by C.B. Thompson, Cambridge, MA: Harvard University Press.

————— 1915, 'Scientific Management in Practice', *Quarterly Journal of Economics*, 19, February: 262–307.

Thompson, E.P. 1963, *The Making of the English Working Class*, New York: Pantheon.

————— 1965, 'The Peculiarities of the English', *The Socialist Register*, London: The Merlin Press.

————— 1967, 'Time, Work-Discipline, and Industrial Capitalism', *Past and Present*, 38: 55–97.

————— 1972a, 'A Special Case', *New Society*, 24, February: 402–4.

————— 1972b, 'Rough Music: Le charivari anglais', *Annales: E.S.C.*, 27: 285–312.

————— 1974, 'Patrician Society, Plebeian Culture', *Journal of Social History*, 7, 4: 382–405.

————— 1975, *Whigs and Hunters: The Origin of the Black Act*, New York: Pantheon Books.

————— 1976, 'The Grid of Inheritance: A Comment' in *Family and Inheritance: Rural Society in Western Europe, 1200–1800*, edited by Jack Goody, Joan Thirsk, and E.P. Thompson, London: Oxford University Press.

————— 1976a *William Morris: Romantic to Revolutionary*, New York: Pantheon.

————— 1978a, 'Eighteenth-Century English Society: Class Struggle Without Class?', *Social History*, 3, 2: 133–65.

————— 1978b, *The Poverty of Theory and Other Essays*, London: Merlin Press.

————— 1994, 'Hunting the Jacobin Fox', *Past & Present*, 142, February: 94–140.

Thompson, T. Phillips 1887, *The Politics of Labor*, New York: Belford, Clarke & Co.

Thurman, Robert S. 1969, '"Twas Only a Joke', *Tennessee Folklore Society Bulletin*, 35, September: 86–94.

Tolman, William 1909, *Social Engineering*, New York: McGraw Hill.

Tomlins, Christopher 1985, *The State and the Unions: Labor Relations, Law, and the Organized Labor Movement in America, 1880–1960*, New York: Cambridge University Press.

Towne, H.R. 1886, 'The Engineer as Economist', *Transactions of the American Society of Mechanical Engineers*, 7: 425.

Trades and Labor Council of Hamilton 1897, *Official Programme and Souvenir of the Labor Day Demonstration Held at Dundurn Park Hamilton, Ont. 1897 September 6th under the Auspices of the Trades and Labor Council*, Hamilton, ON: Spectator Printing Company.

Trigger, Bruce G. 1976, *The Children of the Aataentsic: A History of the Huron People to 1660*, 2 Volumes, Montreal: McGill-Queen's University Press.

Trotsky, Leon 1973a, *The Spanish Revolution (1931–1939)*, New York: Pathfinder.

────── 1973b, *Writings of Leon Trotsky, 1939–1940*, New York: Pathfinder.

Trotsky, Leon, John Dewey, and George Novack 1973, *Their Morals and Ours: Marxist versus Liberal Views on Morality*, New York: Pathfinder.

Trudeau, Pierre Elliott (ed.) 1974, *The Asbestos Strike*, translated by James Boake, Toronto: James, Lewis & Samuel.

Trumper, Richard A. 1937, 'The History of E. Leonard & Sons, Boilermakers and Ironfounders, London, Ontario', MA thesis, University of Western Ontario.

Tuck, Clyde Edwin 1910, *The Bald Knobbers: A Romantic and Historical Novel*, Indianapolis: B.F. Bowen & Company.

Tucker, Eric 1991, '"That Indefinite Area of Toleration": Criminal Conspiracy and Trade Unions in Ontario', *Labour/Le Travail*, 27, Spring: 15–54.

Tulchinsky, Gerald 1972, 'The Montreal Business Community, 1837–53' in *Canadian Business History: Selected Studies, 1497–1971*, edited by David S. Macmillan, Toronto: McClelland and Stewart.

────── 1977, *The River Barons: Montreal Businessmen and the Growth of Industry and Transportation, 1837–1853*, Toronto: University of Toronto Press.

Tuttle, William M., Jr. 1969, 'Labor Conflict and Racial Violence: The Black Worker in Chicago, 1894–1919', *Labor History*, 10, 3: 408–32.

Turner, Frederick Jackson 1920, *The Frontier in American History*, New York: Henry Holt and Company.

Tygiel, Jules Everett 1977, 'Workingmen in San Francisco, 1880–1901', PhD dissertation, University of California at Los Angeles.

U.S. Congress 1911, House Committee on Labor, *Investigation of the Taylor System of Shop Management*, 62nd Congress, 1st Session, House Resolution #90, Washington: Government Printing Office.

────── 1916, *Final Report and Testimony Submitted to Congress by the Commission on Industrial Relations*, 64th Congress, 1st Session, Document #415, Volume 1, Washington: Government Printing Office.

United Green Glass Workers' Association of the United States and Canada 1893, *Proceedings of the U.G.G. Workers' Association of the United States and Canada ... 1893*, Lockport, NY: James Murphy.

United States Bureau of the Census 1961, *Historical Statistics of the United States, Colonial Times to 1957: A Statistical Abstract Supplement*, Washington, DC.: U.S. Bureau of the Census.

Upton, L.F.S. 1977, 'The Extermination of the Beothuks of Newfoundland', *Canadian Historical Review*, 48, June: 133–53.

Urwick, Lyndall F. 1958, 'The Integrity of Frederick Winslow Taylor', *Advanced Management*, 23, March: 5–8.

Valentine, Robert G. 1916, 'Co-operation in Industrial Research', *The Survey*, 36, September: 586–8.

———— and Ordway Tead 1917, 'Work and Pay: A Suggestion for Representative Government and Industry', *Quarterly Journal of Economics*, 31, February: 241–58.

Vallières, Pierre 1971, *White Niggers of America: The Precocious Autobiography of a Quebec 'Terrorist'*, New York: Monthly Review Press.

Valverde, Mariana 2000, 'Some Remarks on the Rise and Fall of Discourse Analysis', *Histoire Sociale/Social History*, 65: 59–77.

van Gennep, Arnold 1943, *Manuel de folklore français contemporain*, Paris: Picard.

———— 1946, *Le folklore des Hautes-Alpes*, Paris: G.P. Maisonneuve.

Van Kirk, Sylvia 1980, *'Many Tender Ties': Women in Fur Trade Society, 1670–1870*, Winnipeg: Watson & Dwyer.

Van Tine, Warren 1973, *The Making of the Labour Bureaucrat: Union Leadership in the United States, 1870–1920*, Amherst, MA: University of Massachusetts Press.

Vance, Catherine 1965, '1837: Labour and the Democratic Tradition', *Marxist Quarterly*, 12, Winter: 29–42.

Vatter, Harold G. 1975, *The Drive to Industrial Maturity: The U.S. Economy, 1860–1914*, Westport, CT: Greenwood Press.

Vernon, Foster 1969, 'The Development of Adult Education in Ontario, 1790–1900', PhD dissertation, University of Toronto.

Vilar, Pierre 1973, 'Marxist History, A History in the Making: Towards a Dialogue with Althusser', *New Left Review*, I/80: 64–106.

———— 1982, 'Marx and the Concept of History' in *The History of Marxism: Marxism in Marx's Day*, Volume 1, edited by E.J. Hobsbawm, Bloomington, IN: Indiana University Press.

Wace, Stephen T. 1968, *The Longshoring Industry: Strikes and Their Impact*, Ottawa: Queen's Printer.

Wagner, Leopold 1894, *Manners, Customs, Observances: Their Origin and Signification*, London: William Heinemann.

Waiser, Bill 2003, *All Hell Can't Stop Us: The On to Ottawa Trek and the Regina Riot*, Calgary, AB: Fifth House.

Wait, Benjamin 1843, *Letters from Van Dieman's Land written during Four Years Imprisonment for Political Offences committed in Upper Canada*, Buffalo: A.W. Wilgus.

———— 1976, *The Wait Letters*, introduction by Mary Brown and afterword by Michael Cross, Erin, ON: Press Porcepic.

Walker, Joseph E. 1974, *Hopewell Village: The Dynamics of a Nineteenth-Century Iron-Making Community*, Philadelphia: University of Pennsylvania Press.

Walkowitz, Daniel J. 1975, 'Working Class Political Culture', *Newsletter on European Labor and Working Class History*, 7, May: 13–18.

———— 1978, *Worker City, Company Town: Iron and Cotton-Worker Protest in Troy and Cohoes, New York, 1855–84*, Urbana, IL: University of Illinois Press.

Wallace, Anthony E.C. 1978, *Rockdale: The Growth of an American Village in the Early Revolution*, New York: Knopf.

Wallot, J.P. 1971, 'Religion and French Canadian Mores in the Early Nineteenth Century', *Canadian Historical Review*, 52, March.

Walsh, William S. 1893, *Handy-Book of Literary Curiosities*, Philadelphia: J.B. Lippincott Company.

—— 1898, *Curiosities of Popular Customs and of Rites, Ceremonies, Observances, and Miscellaneous Antiquities*, Philadelphia: J.B. Lippincott Co.

Ward, David 1971, *Cities and Immigrants: A Geography of Change in Nineteenth-Century North America*, New York: Oxford University Press.

Ware, Norman 1964a, *The Industrial Worker, 1840–1860*, Chicago: Quadrangle.

—— 1964b, *The Labor Movement in the United States, 1860–1890: A Study in Democracy*, New York: Vintage Books.

—— 1968, *Labor in Modern Industrial Society*, New York: Russell and Russell.

Warrian, Peter 1971, 'The Challenge of the One Big Union Movement in Canada, 1919–1921', MA thesis, University of Waterloo.

—— 1986, 'Labour is not a Commodity: A Study of the Rights of Labour in the Canadian Postwar Economy', PhD dissertation, University of Waterloo.

Waters, John J. 1976, 'The Traditional World of the New England Peasants: A View from Seventeenth-Century Barnstable', *New England Historical and Genealogical Register*, 130, January: 3–22.

Watson, Bill 1971, *Counter-planning on the Shop Floor*, Somerville, MA: New England Free Press.

Watson, John F. 1843, 'Notilia of Incidents at New Orleans in 1804 and 1805' *American Pioneer*, 2: 229.

Watt, F.W. 1959, 'The National Policy, the Workingman and Proletarian Ideas in Victorian Canada', *Canadian Historical Review*, 40, March: 1–26.

Watt, James T. 1967a, 'Anti-Catholic Nativism in Canada: The Protestant Protective Association', *Canadian Historical Review*, 48: 45–58.

—— 1967b, 'Anti-Catholicism in Ontario Politics: The Role of the Protestant Association in the 1894 Election', *Ontario History*, 59: 57–67.

Watts-Dunton, Theodore 1902, 'Bret Harte', *Athenaeum*, 24 May.

Way, Peter 1993, *Common Labour: Workers and the Digging of North American Canals, 1780–1860*, Cambridge: Cambridge University Press.

Weaver, John C. 1986, 'Crime, Public Order, and Repression: The Gore District in Upheaval, 1832–1851', *Ontario History*, 78, September: 175–207.

—— 1995, *Crimes, Constables, and Courts: Order and Transgression in a Canadian City, 1816–1870*, Montreal: McGill-Queen's University Press.

Weaver, John C. and Peter de Lottinville 1978, 'The Conflagration and the City: Disaster and Progress in British North America During the Nineteenth Century', paper presented at the Canadian Historical Association meetings, London, Ontario.

Webb, Sidney and Beatrice Webb 1920, *The History of Trade Unionism*, New York: Longmans, Green and Co.

Weber, Eugene 1976, *Peasants into Frenchmen: The Modernization of Rural France, 1870–1914*, Stanford: Stanford University Press.

Weber, Max 1961, *General Economic History*, translated by Frank H. Knight, New York: Collier.

Weinstein, James 1968, *The Corporate Ideal in the Liberal State*, Boston: Beacon Press.

Weller, Ken n.d. [circa 1970], *The Lordstown Struggle and the Real Crisis in Production*, London: Solidarity.

Wells, Debi 1982, ' "The Hardest Lines of the Sternest School": Working-Class Ottawa in the Depression of the 1870s', MA thesis, Carleton University.

Wentworth, Harold (ed.) 1944, *American Dialect Dictionary*, New York: Thomas Y. Crowell.

Westhues, Kenneth 1975, 'Inter-Generational Conflict in the Sixties' in *Prophecy and Protest: Social Movements in Twentieth-Century Canada*, edited by Samuel D. Clark, J. Paul Grayson, and Linda M. Grayson, Toronto: Gage.

Whiteley, A.S. 1934, 'Workers During the Depression' in *The Canadian Economy and Its Problems*, edited by H.A. Innis and A.F.W. Plumptre, Toronto: Canadian Institute of International Affairs.

Whitman, Alden 1943, *Labor Parties, 1827–1834: Initial Steps Independent Political Action ...*, New York: International Publishers.

Whittenburg, James P. 1977, 'Planters, Merchants, and Lawyers: Social Change and the Origins of the North Carolina Regulation', *William and Mary Quarterly*, 34, 2: 215–38.

Wiebe, Robert 1967, *The Search for Order, 1877–1920*, New York: Hill & Wang.

Wilentz, Sean 1981, 'Artisan Origins of the American Working Class', *International Labor and Working-Class History*, 19, Spring: 1–22.

——— 1982, 'Artisan Republican Festivals and the Rise of Class Conflict in New York City, 1788–1837' in *Working-Class America: Essays on Labor, Community, and American Society*, edited by Michael H. Frisch and Daniel J. Walkowitz, Urbana, IL: University of Illinois Press.

Williams, C.B. 1964, 'Canadian-American Trade Union Relations: A Case Study of the Development of Bi-National Unionism', PhD dissertation, Cornell University.

Williams, David 1955, *The Rebecca Riots: A Study in Agrarian Discontent*, Cardiff, NSW: University of New Wales Press.

Williams, Edward 1897, 'Labor Day' in *Official Programme and Souvenir of the Labor Day Demonstration Held at Dundurn Park Hamilton, Ont. 1897 September 6th under the Auspices of the Trades and Labor Council*, edited by the Trades and Labor Council of Hamilton, Hamilton, ON: Spectator Printing Company.

Williams, Eric 1966, *Capitalism & Slavery*, New York: Capricorn.

Williams, Gwyn A. 1975, *Proletarian Order: Antonio Gramsci, Factory Councils, and the Origins of Communism in Italy, 1911–1921*, London: Pluto Press.

Williams, Mary Floyd 1969 [1921], *History of the San Francisco Committee of Vigilance of 1851: A Study of Social Control on the California Frontier in the Days of the Gold Rush*, New York: Da Capo Press.

Williams, Raymond 1973, 'Base and Superstructure in Marxist Cultural Theory', *New Left Review*, I/82, November–December: 1–16.

——— 1977, *Marxism and Literature*, London: Oxford University Press.

——— 1979, *Politics and Letters: Interviews with New Left Review*, London: New Left Books.

Williams, Whiting 1921, *What's on the Workers Mind: By One Who Put on Overalls to Find Out*, New York: Scribners.

Wilson, J. Donald 1973, 'Adult Education in Upper Canada Before 1850', *The Journal of Education*, 19: 43–54.

Wilson, Jeremy 1984, 'The Legislature Under Siege' in *The New Reality: The Politics of Restraint in British Columbia*, edited by Warren Magnusson et al., Vancouver: New Star.

Wilton, Carol 2000, *Popular Politics and Political Culture in Upper Canada, 1800–1850*, Montreal: McGill-Queen's University Press.

Wingfield, Alex H. 1873, *Poems and Songs in Scotch and English*, Hamilton: Times.

Winner, Julia Hull 1964, 'A Skimeton', *New York Folklore Quarterly*, 20, June: 134–6.

Wintemberg, W.J. 1918, 'Folklore Collected in the Counties of Oxford and Waterloo, Ontario', *Journal of American Folklore*, 31, April–June: 137–8.

Wise, S.F. 1974, 'Sport and Class Values in Old Ontario and Quebec' in *His Own Man: Essays in Honour of Arthur Reginald Marsden Lower*, edited by W.H. Heick and Roger Graham, Montreal: McGill-Queen's University Press

——— 1993, *God's Peculiar Peoples: Essays on Political Culture in Nineteenth Century Canada*, edited and introduced by A.B. McKillop and Paul Romney, Ottawa: Carleton University Press.

Wood, Gordon R. 1971, *Vocabulary Change: A Study of Variation in Regional Words in Eight of the Southern States*, Carbondale, IL: Southern Illinois University Press.

Wood, J. David 2000, *Making Ontario: Agricultural Colonization and Landscape Re-Creation Before the Railway*, Montreal: McGill-Queen's University Press.

Wood, Louis Aubrey 1975, *A History of Farmers' Movements in Canada: The Origins and Development of Agrarian Protest, 1872–1924*, Toronto: University of Toronto Press.

Wood, Thomas W. 1941, 'The Contribution of Frederick W. Taylor to Scientific Management', PhD thesis, University of North Carolina.

Woodress, James 1955, *Booth Tarkington: Gentleman from Indiana*, New York: Greenwood Press.

——— 1967, 'Popular Taste in 1899: Booth Tarkington's First Novel' in *Essays in American and English Literature Presented to Bruce Robert McElderry, Jr.*, edited by Max F. Schulz, Athens, OH: Ohio University Press.

Woods, H.D. 1968, *Canadian Industrial Relations: The Report of the Task Force on Labour Relations*, Ottawa: Privy Council Office.

Woodward, C. Vann 1951, *Origins of the New South*, Baton Rouge, LA: Louisiana State University Press.

———— 1956, *Reunion and Reaction: The Compromise of 1877 and the End of Reconstruction*, Garden City, KS: Doubleday.

Woodward, C. Vann 1966, *The Strange Career of Jim Crow*, New York: Oxford University Press.

Woytinsky, W.S. 1953, *Employment and Wages in the United States*, New York: Twentieth Century Fund.

Wright, Carrol D. 1887, 'An Historical Sketch of the Knights of Labor', *Quarterly Journal of Economics*, 1, January: 142–3.

Wright, Elizabeth Mary 1914, *Rustic Speech and Folk-lore*, London: Humphrey Milford; Oxford University Press.

Wright, Joseph (ed.) 1905, *The English Dialect Dictionary* Volume 5, New York: G.P. Putnam's Sons.

Wright, Thomas 1867, *Some Habits and Customs of the Working Classes*, London: Tinsley Brothers.

Wyatt-Brown, Bertram 1982, *Southern Honour: Ethics & Behaviour in the Old South*, New York: Oxford University Press.

Wynn, Graeme 1979, 'Notes on Society and Environment in Old Ontario', *Journal of Social History*, 13, 1: 51–2.

———— 1980, 'Deplorably Dark and Demoralized Lumberers: Rhetoric and Reality in Early Nineteenth-Century New Brunswick', *Journal of Forest History*, 24: 168–87.

———— 1981, *Timber Colony: A Historical Geography of Early Nineteenth Century New Brunswick*, Toronto: University of Toronto Press.

Young, Alfred F. 1973, 'Pope's Day, Tar and Feathers, and Cornet Joyce, Jun.: From Ritual to Rebellion in Boston, 1745–1775', unpublished manuscript prepared for the Anglo-American Conference of Labor Historians, Rutgers University, April.

———— (ed.) 1976, *The American Revolution: Explorations in the History of American Radicalism*, Dekalb, IL: University of Northern Illinois Press.

———— 1981, 'George Robert Twelves Hewes (1742–1840): A Boston Shoemaker and the Memory of the American Revolution', *William and Mary Quarterly*, 38, 4: 561–623.

———— 1984, 'English Plebeian Culture and Eighteenth-Century American Radicalism', in *The Origins of Anglo-American Radicalism*, edited by Margaret C. Jacob and James R. Jacob, London: Allen and Unwin.

Young, Brian 1981, *George-Etienne Cartier: Montreal Bourgeois*, Montreal: McGill-Queen's University Press.

Young, Edward 1875, *Labor in Europe and America: A Special Report on the Rate of Wages, the Cost of Subsistence in Great Britain, France, Belgium, Germany, and Other Countries of Europe, Also in the United States and British North America*, Philadelphia: S.A. George and Company.

Index